Handbook of

FACILITY MANAGEMENT

TOOLS AND TECHNIQUES, FORMULAS AND TABLES

JAMES E. PIPER

PRENTICE HALL
Englewood Cliffs, New Jersey 07632

Prentice-Hall International, Inc., *London*
Prentice-Hall of Australia Pty., Ltd., *Sydney*
Prentice-Hall Canada, Inc., *Toronto*
Prentice-Hall Hispanoamericana, S.A., *Mexico*
Prentice-Hall of India Private Ltd., *New Delhi*
Prentice-Hall of Japan, Inc., *Tokyo*
Prentice-Hall of Southeast Asia Pte., Ltd., *Singapore*
Editora Prentice-Hall do Brasil, Ltda., *Rio de Janeiro*

© 1995 by

PRENTICE-HALL
Englewood Cliffs, NJ

10   9   8   7   6   5   4   3   2   1

Library of Congress Cataloging-in-Publication Data

Piper, James E.
    Handbook of facility management : tools and techniques, formulas
and tables / James E. Piper.
        p.   cm.
    Includes Index.
    ISBN 0–13–554296–0
    1. Facility management—Handbooks, manuals, etc.   I. Title.
TS155.P487   1994
658.2—dc20   94–33199
                                                                        CIP

ISBN 0-13-554296-0

PRENTICE HALL
Career & Personal Development
Englewood Cliffs, NJ 07632

A Simon & Schuster Company

PRINTED IN THE UNITED STATES OF AMERICA

This book is dedicated to the memory of
Robert L. Hafer.

ABOUT THE AUTHOR

James E. Piper is an engineer who has been active in the field of facilities management for more than twenty years. As a licensed engineer, he has worked in all phases of facility management, from the installation and maintenance of mechanical and electrical systems to the overall management of the facility management organization. He currently works for the Department of Physical Plant at the University of Maryland at College Park.

The author received a Bachelor's degree and a Master of Science degree in Mechanical Engineering from the University of Akron, and a Ph.D. in Educational Administration from the University of Maryland. Dr. Piper has written more than 100 articles for a wide range of facility management publications including *Building Operating Management, Plant Engineering, American School and University, Plant Facilities, Hospital Progress,* and *Office Administration and Automation.*

WHAT THIS BOOK WILL DO FOR YOU

The *Handbook of Facility Management: Tools and Techniques, Formulas and Tables* offers a wide range of practical data and procedures that you can use to evaluate and improve your maintenance operation. Every day you are faced with having to provide quick answers to complex maintenance problems. While you can use detailed calculation techniques, studies, or consultants to provide the answers, often there isn't enough time. In maintenance operations, decisions must be made quickly and accurately.

This book is written for the maintenance manager. It is designed to serve as a source for quick answers to maintenance questions. It provides simple, straightforward methods for solving maintenance problems in all areas of facilities management. Since the methods presented are independent of the type of facility, they may be used to reduce operating costs and increase the efficiency of any maintenance operation.

This *Handbook* is organized into four parts: mechanical maintenance, electrical maintenance, buildings and grounds maintenance, and energy use. Each part presents practical data and procedures to evaluate your operation and get the best return for the investment of the maintenance dollar. Step-by-step instructions are given for using the tables, charts, graphs, and worksheets.

Here are just a few of the benefits you will get from this book:

- ➤ a method for comparing heating fuel costs (Chapter 1)
- ➤ the key elements in preventive maintenance programs for heating and air conditioning systems (Chapter 3)
- ➤ a method for increasing your system's efficiency and reducing operating costs by correcting your system's power factor (Chapter 12)
- ➤ the steps required to establish a preventive maintenance program for mechanical and electrical equipment (Chapters 1, 2, 3, 7, and 8)
- ➤ the requirements for a complete roofing maintenance program (Chapter 17)
- ➤ the elements of a housekeeping inspection program (Chapter 18)
- ➤ how to establish a grounds preventive maintenance program (Chapter 19)
- ➤ easy-to-use methods for calculating the annual energy costs for walls, windows, and roofs (Chapter 21)

A portion of the material presented in this *Handbook* is in the form of figures and worksheets, which are found at the end of each chapter. Detailed step-by-step instructions are provided for using each figure and worksheet.

Some of the figures have been selected from authoritative sources in the field, including equipment manufacturers and trade associations. Other figures are new and cannot be found in any other source. Some of the worksheets follow accepted industry calculation or estimation practices. Others are the result of computer simulation. All of the worksheets are original.

In all, this book will help you solve any maintenance problem, and increase the efficiency of your operation.

CONTENTS

CHAPTER 2

HOW TO OPERATE AND MAINTAIN CENTRAL CHILLED WATER EQUIPMENT AND DISTRIBUTION SYSTEMS—51

CHAPTER 5

SELECTING AND OPERATING MISCELLANEOUS MECHANICAL EQUIPMENT—174

PART II
ELECTRICAL MAINTENANCE

CHAPTER 6
DETERMINING CABLES AND WIRE FACTORS FOR A SAFE AND EFFICIENT DISTRIBUTION SYSTEM—191

CHAPTER 7
HOW TO SELECT AND OPERATE ELECTRIC MOTORS TO SAVE ENERGY—215

CHAPTER 8
SELECTING, OPERATING, AND MAINTAINING TRANSFORMERS FOR MAXIMUM PERFORMANCE—240

CHAPTER 10
HOW TO SELECT A LIGHTING SYSTEM THAT MEETS YOUR NEEDS AND MINIMIZES ENERGY USE—285

CHAPTER 11

USING UNINTERRUPTIBLE POWER SUPPLIES TO PROTECT COMPUTERS AND ELECTRONIC EQUIPMENT—340

CHAPTER 12

HOW TO INCREASE CAPACITY AND SAVE MONEY BY CORRECTING YOUR FACILITY'S POWER FACTOR—363

CHAPTER 13

HOW TO USE STANDBY GENERATORS TO IMPROVE THE RELIABILITY OF YOUR ELECTRICAL SYSTEM—381

CHAPTER 14

UNDERSTANDING THE ELEMENTS OF YOUR POWER BILL TO HELP CONTROL OPERATING COSTS—395

PART III
BUILDINGS AND GROUNDS MAINTENANCE

CHAPTER 15
USING PAINT AND PROTECTIVE COATINGS TO REDUCE MAINTENANCE COSTS—411

CHAPTER 16
HOW TO SELECT FLOOR COVERINGS FOR LONG LIFE AND LOW MAINTENANCE—430

CHAPTER 19

PROMOTING THE APPEARANCE OF YOUR FACILITY THROUGH A GROUNDS MAINTENANCE PROGRAM—507

PART IV

FACILITY ENERGY USE

CHAPTER 20

WEATHER AND CLIMATE FACTORS AND THEIR IMPACT ON ENERGY USE IN YOUR FACILITY—527

CHAPTER 21

HOW TO ESTIMATE THE ENERGY SAVINGS OF MODIFICATIONS
TO THE BUILDING ENVELOPE—569

INDEX—669

Part I

MECHANICAL MAINTENANCE

## CHAPTER 1

HOW TO OPERATE CENTRAL COMBUSTION AND DISTRIBUTION EQUIPMENT FOR LONG EQUIPMENT LIFE AND LOW OPERATING COSTS

This chapter examines central combustion and distribution equipment typically found in facility central heating systems. Material presented in this chapter can be used to estimate solutions to problems ranging from improving boiler operation to sizing steam mains and traps.

FOUR COMMON BOILER TYPES AND HOW THEY OPERATE

Boilers can be classified by a number of different parameters. The most common classifications are working pressure, fuel used, type of construction, and class of steam generated.

Working Pressure

Boilers and steam or water distribution systems can be classified on the basis of their operating pressures. There are two general classes; low and high. **Low-pressure** boilers and distribution systems include those steam systems with a maximum working pressure of 15 psi and hot water systems with a maximum operating pressure of 160 psi. Low-pressure hot water systems are further limited to operating temperatures of 250°F or less. **High-pressure** boilers and distribution systems include those steam systems that operate at pressures greater than 15 psi and hot water systems that operate at pressures greater than 160 psi or temperatures greater than 250°F.

Fuel Type

When classifying boilers by fuel type, the classification given to a particular boiler depends on the fuel that the boiler was initially designed to burn, even though the boiler may have been converted to a different fuel after installation. Primary fuel classifications include coal, wood, several grades of oil, various types of gas, and electric. An additional classification, **multi-fuel,** includes those boilers that were originally designed to burn multiple fuels, such as natural gas and #6 oil.

Construction

Two of the major classifications of boilers based on their construction are firetube and watertube. Both make use of a heat exchanger that is a series of tubes. A **firetube** boiler is one where the flue gases are passed through the tubes and the fluid being heated surrounds the tubes. A **watertube** boiler is the opposite. The fluid being heated passes through the tubes while the flue gases surround the tubes.

Class of Steam Generated

Another classification used to describe boilers and steam systems relates to the properties of the steam being generated or distributed. The temperature at which water boils varies with the pressure in the system and is known as the **saturation temperature.** Steam generated and distributed at this temperature and pressure is called **saturated steam.** As heat is added, the temperature of the steam is increased beyond the saturation temperature, and the steam becomes **superheated.** Steam systems, depending on the requirement of the particular application, will operate as saturated or superheated systems.

THE ENERGY CONTENT OF FUEL

The most common means of measuring the energy content of a fuel is its **heating value.** Expressed in Btu per gallon, Btu per 1,000 cubic feet, or Btu per pound, the heating value is the gross energy content of the fuel. Under normal operating conditions, the actual usable energy content will be somewhat less.

Figure 1.1* lists typical heating values for common fuels. The heating value for a particular type of fuel varies in some cases with where the fuel is produced or with the moisture content of the fuel. The values listed in the figure can be used to determine a facility's energy use in Btu. If more than one type of fuel is used for heating a facility, the total heating energy use can be determined by first converting each fuel use to Btu, then adding the values.

A QUICK METHOD FOR COMPARING FUEL COSTS

One of the most important economic considerations when laying out a new boiler plant is the type of fuel that will be used. Plant operators who have the ability to burn

---

* Figures are located at the end of respective chapters and are organized in numerical order.

more than one type of fuel also must examine which fuel is the most economical to burn. Other factors, such as fuel availability and environmental controls, must be taken into consideration. Use Worksheet 1.1** to provide a quick estimation of the economics of different fuel types.

Step 1. Determine the fuel average unit cost (dollars per gallon, pound, or cubic feet) and enter the value in section #1 of the worksheet. The average unit cost should include all delivery, demand, and other related charges.

Step 2. For the type of fuel selected, determine the heating value (Btu per unit of fuel) using Figure 1.1. If the fuel supplier can give you the average heating value specific for the fuel being supplied, use that value as the values given in the figure are averages. Enter the value in section #1 of the worksheet.

Step 3. The fuel efficiency factor is used to correct the gross heating value of the fuel to its net value. The difference is primarily the result of moisture or other non-combustible materials in the fuel. Select the fuel efficiency factor from the table at the bottom of the worksheet for the type of fuel being burned. Enter the value in section #1 of the worksheet.

Step 4. If the combustion efficiency of the boiler is known from manufacturer's data or from tests performed on the boiler, enter the value in section #1 of the worksheet. If the combustion efficiency is not known, use the table at the bottom of the worksheet to determine the approximate combustion efficiency. Enter the value in section #1 of the worksheet.

Step 5. Multiply the fuel unit cost by the heating value, fuel efficiency factor, and the combustion efficiency. Divide by 1,000 to determine the fuel cost in dollars per thousand Btu. Enter the value in section #1 of the worksheet.

Step 6. Repeat steps #1 through 5 for additional fuel options.

Once the fuel costs have been calculated on a Btu basis for a variety of fuels, the facility manager will know the economics of each fuel source. Other factors, such as availability and storage requirements will have to be considered in making the decision to use one fuel over another.

ENERGY AND STEAM

The amount of energy that can be extracted from steam at a given temperature and pressure is the **enthalpy** or heat content of the steam. Expressed in Btu per pound of

---

** Worksheets are located at the end of respective chapters, are organized in numerical order, and begin after the five last figures listed.

steam, enthalpy figures are available for a wide range of steam temperatures and pressures in steam tables published by various sources. Figure 1.2 lists properties of saturated steam for pressures up to 600 psig. Figure 1.3 lists the properties of superheated steam for pressures up to 4,000 psia. Both figures are condensed from steam tables produced by the American Society of Mechanical Engineers.

Figures 1.2 and 1.3 can be used in a wide range of steam calculations including those that determine the energy content of steam at specific operating temperatures and pressures.

BOILER EFFICIENCY

There are a number of different ways of measuring boiler efficiency. Three of the most common are combustion, overall, and production efficiency.

Combustion efficiency is defined as follows:

$$\text{Combustion Efficiency} = \frac{\text{(Energy Input) - (Stack Loss)}}{\text{(Energy Input)}}$$

where the energy input is the heat content of the fuel measured in Btu and the stack losses are also measured in BTU. Combustion efficiency can be measured under any load conditions by metering the fuel input to the boiler and measuring the temperature of and percentage of O_2 or CO_2 in the flue gases.

Combustion efficiencies for conventional boilers typically range between 75 and 85 percent. For condensing boilers, combustion efficiencies can range as high as 95 percent.

Overall efficiency is defined as the gross energy output of the boiler divided by the energy input. Since overall efficiency calculations include additional losses, a boiler's overall efficiency rating is always lower than its combustion efficiency. It is almost impossible to calculate the overall efficiency rating for an installed boiler as the calculations require precise measurement of factors that are difficult to measure in the field. Overall efficiency ratings, however, give one the ability to compare the performance of one boiler to another under similar operating conditions.

Production or net efficiency is the ratio of the net useful energy output of the boiler to its gross energy input. While production efficiency varies with the load on the boiler, it is one of the most meaningful measures of the energy costs of steam production and therefore should be used when estimating the cost of steam either at the boiler plant output or at the point of use.

Worksheet 1.2 can be used to estimate the production efficiency of a boiler for a specific load condition. The calculation would have to be completed for other loads to determine the efficiency profile for a given boiler. Completion of the efficiency estimate requires the use of accurate instrumentation to meter the steam generated, steam temperature and pressure, fuel use, and the temperature of the feedwater supplied to the boiler.

Use Worksheet 1.2 as follows:

Step 1.   Monitor the boiler's operation for a set period of time, such as a several hour interval or a day. Factors such as steam temperature, steam pressure, and feedwater temperature should remain fairly constant during this interval. Enter the average steam temperature, steam pressure, and feedwater temperature in section #1 of the worksheet.

Step 2.   Divide the total steam production during the test interval by the number of hours the test lasted to determine the average steam generation rate. Divide the total fuel use during the test interval by the number of hours the test lasted to determine the average fuel use rate. Enter the values in section #1 of the worksheet.

Step 3.   Since the heating value of fuels varies fairly widely, contact the fuel supplier to determine the heating value for the type of fuel that you are burning. If the supplier cannot provide you with an accurate value, Figure 1.1 can be used to estimate the heating value for various fuels. Enter the value in section #1 of the worksheet.

Step 4.   Enter the values from section #1 for the steam generation rate in pounds per hour; the fuel use rate in pounds, gallons, or cubic feet per hour; and the fuel heating value in pounds, gallons, or cubic feet per hour in section #2.

Step 5.   Divide the steam generation rate by the fuel use rate and the fuel heating value to determine the steam-fuel ratio. Enter the value in section #2 of the worksheet.

Step 6.   Enter the steam-fuel ratio from section #2 of the worksheet in section #3.

Step 7.   Determine the enthalpy of the feedwater (h_f) using Figure 1.2. For the temperature of the feedwater, determine from the figure the enthalpy for the feedwater and enter the value in section #3 of the worksheet.

Step 8.   If superheated steam is generated, skip to step #9. For saturated steam, the heat content of the steam is the enthalpy of the steam vapor (h_g). Using Figure 1.2 determine the enthalpy of the vapor for the pressure of the steam generated. Enter the value in section #3 of the worksheet. Skip to step #10.

Step 9.   For superheated steam, use Figure 1.3 to determine the enthalpy of the steam. For the temperature and the pressure of the steam generated, determine the enthalpy of the steam. Enter the value in section #3 of the worksheet.

Step 10.   Subtract the enthalpy of the feedwater from the enthalpy of the steam. Multiply the difference by the steam-fuel ratio to determine the production efficiency of the steam boiler. Enter the value in section #3 of the worksheet.

The efficiency value calculated by using the worksheet will help the facility manager in making decisions about upgrading or replacing the central steam generation equipment.

Estimating the Impact of Intermittent Firing on Boiler Efficiency

All efficiency calculations for boilers assume that the boiler operates continuously. However, if the boiler is oversized or the load is low and the boiler cannot be throttled back to match the load, the boiler will have to be operated intermittently. Such intermittent operation decreases the operating efficiency as energy must be used to reheat the boiler after periods when it has been cycled off.

Figure 1.4 can be used to estimate the impact that intermittent firing will have on boiler efficiency. To estimate the impact, determine the approximate percentage of time that the boiler's burner will be on. From the figure, determine the efficiency multiplication factor for that percentage of "on time." Multiply this factor by the rated efficiency of the boiler to determine the efficiency under intermittent firing conditions.

It can be seen from the figure that the efficiency of a burner decreases significantly as the time that the boiler remains on decreases. To decrease intermittent firing, boilers should be properly sized to match the load. Oversizing only increases the number of intermittent firings. Multiple boilers or multistage burners are two ways of more closely matching boiler capacity to varying loads.

How to Improve Boiler Efficiency and Estimate Fuel Savings

One of the most effective ways of improving boiler efficiency is through the reduction of the amount of excess combustion air that is supplied to a boiler.

Excess combustion air is the quantity of air supplied to a boiler that is above and beyond the minimum needed for complete combustion of the fuel. The higher the volume of excess combustion air, the lower the efficiency of the boiler as a portion of the heat generated from burning the fuel is absorbed by the excess volume of air passing through the boiler and is exhausted through the stack. Although excess combustion air robs the boiler of efficiency, it is used in nearly every boiler to insure complete combustion of the fuel, for too little air causes even greater decreases in boiler efficiency.

Estimating Excess Combustion Air

The excess combustion air being supplied to a boiler can be estimated by sampling the flue gases exhausted from the boiler. Figure 1.5 can be used to estimate the percent excess combustion air when the percentage of O_2 in the exhaust gas is known. The figure produces reasonable results for natural gas, #2 oil, and #6 oil. Figure 1.6 can be used to estimate the percent excess combustion air when the percentage of CO_2 in the exhaust gas is known. Separate curves are provided for natural gas, #2 oil, and #6 oil.

Data from both figures can be used to evaluate the burner adjustment in combustion equipment.

Estimating Fuel Savings

Figure 1.7 can be used to estimate the savings in fuel that would result by reducing the amount of excess combustion air. The figure presents the savings that would result if the amount of excess combustion air were reduced to zero percent. If the volume of excess combustion air is to be reduced to a minimum (zero percent), the fuel savings can be read directly from the figure. However, most boiler controls are not capable of operating effectively at zero percent excess air and therefore are set at some minimum value, such as five percent. The figure can be used to estimate the savings in fuel for these applications as follows:

Step 1   For the percentage of excess combustion air measured in the system and for the measured flue gas temperature, determine the percent fuel saved that would result by reducing the excess combustion air to zero.

Step 2.   Although the flue gas temperature will change with a decrease in excess combustion air, for estimation purposes it can be assumed to remain the same. For the percentage excess combustion air at which the boiler will be operated at reduced excess combustion air and for the flue gas temperature measured in step #1, determine the percent fuel saved.

Step 3.   The estimated savings produced by reducing the amount of excess combustion air will be the difference between the two values calculated for percent fuel saved in steps #1 and #2 above.

The savings produced by proper adjustment of excess combustion air can be significant. For residential-sized units, the rule of thumb is to adjust the burners once per year. For larger commercial units, it is cost effective to routinely adjust the combustion air controls daily, weekly, or monthly based on the size of the unit. In large, central steam plants, automatic controls are routinely used to adjust combustion air.

Estimating Required Boiler Blowdown to Control Solids Buildup

Water entering a boiler system contains dissolved solids of various types and concentrations. The steam leaving the boiler carries away very few of these solids. Thus with time, the concentration of solids in the boiler water increases. Without corrective action, this increased concentration of solids will result in scaling and corrosion of interior surfaces of the boiler, valves, piping, turbines, and other components of the steam system.

The level of solids buildup can be controlled through a process called blowdown. **Blowdown** essentially is the process of bleeding off a portion of the boiler water containing a high concentration of solids and replacing it with fresh, makeup water. Since the concentration of solids in the makeup water is low relative to the boiler water, the overall concentration level of solids is reduced.

The American Society of Mechanical Engineers has established recommended maximum concentration of solids in boilers based on the operating pressure of the boiler. Ideally the boiler should be operated close to this recommended maximum value. Concentrations higher than these values result in damage to the boiler and steam system components. Introducing additional blowdown water to lower the concentration below these values wastes water and energy. Too much blowdown also results in a decrease in the concentration of water treatment chemicals used to prevent or remove deposit forming contaminants.

Boiler blowdown can be regulated manually or automatically to keep the concentration level of solids in the acceptable range without wasting water, energy, or water treatment chemicals. How much blowdown is required depends on the load placed on the boiler, how much of the condensate is returned to the boiler, and the characteristics of the makeup water.

Use Worksheet 1.3 to estimate the quantity of boiler blowdown required to meet the above operating conditions. Use the worksheet as follows:

Step 1. If the rate at which makeup water is added to the system is known, enter the value (in pounds per hour) in section #1 and skip to step #4. If the makeup water addition rate is not known, determine the load on the boiler in pounds per hour and enter the value in section #1 of the worksheet.

Step 2. From metered data, determine the return rate for condensate in pounds per hour. Enter the value in section #1 of the worksheet.

Step 3. Subtract the condensate return rate from the steam production rate to determine the rate at which makeup water must be added to the system. Enter the value in section #1 of the worksheet.

Step 4. If equipment is available that can determine the concentration of solids in the makeup water in parts per million (ppm), use the measured value. If the solids concentration cannot be measured directly, contact the local water company to get an estimate, or have samples analyzed. Enter the value in two areas of section #2 on the worksheet.

Step 5. Enter in section #2 the rate at which makeup water is added to the system as determined in section #1.

Step 6. The table at the bottom of the worksheet lists the ASME recommended limits for solids in boiler water. For the operating pressure of the boiler, determine the ASME solids limit. Enter the value in section #2.

Step 7. Multiply the concentration of solids in the makeup water by the makeup water addition rate, and divide by the difference between the ASME recommended solids limit and the concentration of solids in the makeup water to determine the required boiler blowdown rate. Enter the value in section #2 of the worksheet.

Compare the blowdown rate calculated by the worksheet with the boiler manufacturer's recommended rates to determine if too high or too low a blowdown rate is in effect.

How to Convert Boiler Capacity Ratings

The capacity ratings for a boiler are generally given in pounds of steam per hour or boiler horsepower. The **pounds per hour** rating is the steam generation capacity of the boiler operating with feedwater at 212°F and producing steam at 212°F and zero psig. One boiler **horsepower** is equal to 34.5 pounds of steam per hour of steam at 212°F generated from feedwater supplied at 212°F and zero psig.

Caution: both capacity ratings can be misleading as almost all systems use feedwater at temperatures less than 212°F and generate steam at pressures greater than zero psig. When considering a boiler for a particular application, consult the manufacturer for the boiler's actual capacity given the system feedwater temperature and steam operating temperature and pressure.

Use Worksheet 1.4 to convert between boiler horsepower and pounds per hour ratings. Use the worksheet as follows:

Step 1.	Enter (depending on which value is known) the boiler rated horsepower or the rated capacity in pounds per hour in section #1 of the worksheet.
Step 2.	Enter the average feedwater temperature and the steam pressure of the system in section #1 of the worksheet. If the system generates superheated steam, also enter the temperature of the superheated steam.
Step 3.	If you are converting from pounds per hour to horsepower, skip to line #8. Enter the boiler horsepower in section #2 of the worksheet.
Step 4.	From Figure 1.2, determine the enthalpy (h_f) of the feedwater based on its temperature. Enter the value in section #2 of the worksheet.
Step 5.	If the steam generated by the boiler is superheated, skip to line #6. For saturated steam, determine the enthalpy (h_g) of the steam from Figure 1.2. Enter the value in section #2 of the worksheet. Skip to line #7.
Step 6.	For superheated steam, determine the enthalpy of the steam from Figure 1.3. Enter the value in section #2 of the worksheet.
Step 7.	Multiply the boiler horsepower by 33,475 and divide by the difference between the enthalpy of the steam and feedwater to determine the capacity of the boiler in pounds per hour. Enter the value in section #2 of the worksheet.
Step 8.	From Figure 1.2, determine the enthalpy (h_f) of the feedwater based on its temperature. Enter the value in section #3 of the worksheet.
Step 9.	If the steam generated by the boiler is superheated, skip to line #10. For saturated steam, determine the enthalpy (h_g) of the steam from Figure 1.2. Enter the value in section #3 of the worksheet. Skip to line #11.

Step 10.   For superheated steam, determine the enthalpy of the steam from Figure 1.3. Enter the value in section #3 of the worksheet.

Step 11.   Enter the rated capacity of the boiler in pounds per hour in section #3 of the worksheet.

Step 12.   Multiply the rated capacity by the difference between the enthalpy for the feedwater and steam, and divide by the number 33,475 to determine the boiler horsepower. Enter the value in section #3 of the worksheet.

HOW TO ESTIMATE THE COST OF STEAM

Two of the most widely used measures for the cost of steam are its generation cost and its point of use cost.

Steam generation cost is a measure of what it costs to produce the steam at the boiler. It includes energy, labor, water, chemical, and plant maintenance costs. It is used primarily in gauging the overall generation efficiency of the plant.

Steam point of use costs is a measure of what it costs to generate and supply steam to a particular load. It includes the same expenses associated with steam generation cost, but includes additional factors for in-plant steam requirements and distribution losses. Therefore, point of use cost will always be greater than generation cost. It is also the basis for setting billing rates for steam charges.

Worksheet 1.5 can be used to estimate both steam generation cost and steam point of use cost. Costs can be estimated on any time interval, the most commonly used ones being monthly, quarterly, or annually. All figures entered into the worksheet must be based on the time interval selected. For example, if the generation cost is being estimated on a quarterly basis, all expenses should be the total costs for that quarter. Similarly, the steam generated should be the total figure for the quarter. Use the worksheet as follows:

Step 1.   The total fuel cost for operating the boiler includes both the fuel used by the boiler and the electricity used by the auxiliary equipment associated with it during the calculation period. Enter the value in section #1 of the worksheet.

Step 2.   The labor cost includes all salaries associated with the operation and maintenance of the boiler and its auxiliary equipment during the calculation period. Depending on how your particular organization operates, labor costs may include the cost of benefits for those employees. Enter the value in section #1 of the worksheet.

Step 3.   Enter the total cost for the water supplied to the boiler for steam generation and blowdown during the calculation period in section #1 of the worksheet.

Step 4.   Enter the costs of the chemicals used in the boiler's water treatment program during the calculation period in section #1 of the worksheet.

Step 5. Maintenance costs are difficult to define. At a minimum, they should include the cost of all maintenance contracts associated with the operation of the boiler and the cost of materials during the calculation period. If depreciation is to be figured into the cost of steam, add it to the maintenance cost figure. Enter the value in section #1 of the worksheet.

Step 6. Enter the amount of steam generated during the calculation period in thousands of pounds in section #1 of the worksheet.

Step 7. Sum the fuel, labor, water, chemical, and maintenance costs and divide by the amount of steam that was generated during the calculation period to determine the generation cost for steam. Enter the value in section #1 of the worksheet.

Step 8. Enter in section #2 the steam generation cost calculated in section #1 of the worksheet.

Step 9. The in-plant use factor corrects for steam that is used by boiler plant auxiliary equipment; turbines, deaireators, etc. If meters are installed on auxiliary equipment that uses steam, calculate the factor by dividing the total steam used by that equipment by the total steam generated during the calculation period. If no meter data is available, then the in-plant use factor will have to be estimated based on how much steam using auxiliary equipment is associated with the boiler. For most applications, the in-plant use factor will be between 0.85 and 0.95. Enter the value in section #2 of the worksheet.

Step 10. The distribution factor takes into account losses in the system between the boiler and the point where the steam is used. For small systems where the distribution system is in good operating condition and the steam traps are maintained on a regular basis, the distribution factor is typically around 0.95. For large systems, it can range from as high as 0.90 to as low as 0.50 depending on the condition of the piping and insulation in the distribution system and how well the steam traps are maintained. Select a value based on the conditions in that particular application and enter it in section #3 of the worksheet.

Step 11. Divide the generation cost by the in-plant use factor and the distribution factor to determine the point of use cost for steam. Enter the value in section #3 of the worksheet.

The cost of steam both at the generation point and at the point of use for that steam will help the facility manager to make decisions concerning alternative heat sources and where to place those sources. Additionally, both costs will help to define the cost of distributing steam, particularly in large central systems that operate year round.

14
14 CHAPTER 1

ESTIMATING THE COST OF STEAM LEAKS

Steam leaks can represent a significant expense to the operators of a steam system. Even small leaks can be expensive. For example, a one-eighth inch diameter leak in a system operating at 100 psig loses more than 462,000 pounds of steam in one year. Chances are that the losses would be even greater as the erosion action of the steam passing through the hole would tend to increase the size of the hole with time, resulting in the loss of even more steam.

Figure 1.8 was developed to estimate the steam loss through failed steam traps but can also be applied to steam leaks. It will estimate the leakage rate for holes ranging in diameter from $1/32''$ up to $1/2''$, and for pressures from 2 psig to 300 psig.

You can estimate the cost of a steam leak by using Worksheet 1.6. The worksheet will determine the cost on a daily, weekly, monthly, or yearly basis. Use the worksheet as follows:

Step 1.   Estimate the physical size of the leak. For the operating pressure of the system and the leak size, use Figure 1.8 to determine the rate at which steam is leaking. Enter the value in section #1 of the worksheet.

Step 2.   Use the point of use steam cost calculated in section #2 of Worksheet 1.5. Enter the value in section #1 of the worksheet.

Step 3.   Determine how many hours per day the steam system operates. Using the table at the bottom of the worksheet, determine the hours factor for the time interval selected and the hours per day that the system is operated. Enter the value in section #1 of the worksheet.

Step 4.   Multiply the leak rate by the point of use steam cost and the hours factor, and divide by 1,000 to determine the cost of the leak. Enter the value in section #1 of the worksheet.

The cost of a steam leak is surprisingly high to most facility managers. In large central steam plants with extended distribution systems, it is common to find a crew dedicated to the task of identifying and correcting leaks.

GUIDELINES FOR AN EFFECTIVE BOILER MAINTENANCE PROGRAM

Proper boiler maintenance is essential to insure reliable operation of the boiler and its auxiliary equipment, maximum possible equipment life, maximum operating efficiency, and safety. In spite of its importance to the safe and economical operation of a facility, facilities report millions of dollars in annual losses as the result of boiler accidents. Records kept by the Hartford Steam Boiler Inspection and Insurance Company indicate that the leading causes of these accidents are overheating, corrosion, and operator error.

While you can reduce the chances of operator error through a thorough training program, the other two leading causes of boiler accidents and failures are the direct result of inadequate maintenance programs. Boiler overheating results primarily from problems in feedwater equipment and controls, or from scale formation on the boiler's heat transfer surfaces. A thorough maintenance, testing, and inspection program can reduce the chances of problems with feedwater equipment and controls. You can control scale formation through a well designed water treatment program. You can also control corrosion of piping and heat transfer surfaces through proper treatment of the feedwater. In other words, a good maintenance program can reduce two of the three leading causes for boiler accidents and failures.

Figure 1.9 lists typical boiler maintenance activities and the intervals at which they should be performed.

Caution: These maintenance activities are generic in nature and represent the basis for a maintenance program. They are not intended to be complete or directly applicable to all boilers in all applications. Contact the manufacturer of the boiler for a more complete listing of maintenance requirements and intervals.

ESTIMATING STEAM LINE SIZES

In order to economically meet the load requirements placed on a steam system, all piping runs must be carefully sized. Undersized piping results in excessive pressure drop. Oversized piping increases installation costs. Properly sized piping will provide adequate steam flow under all load conditions without experiencing unacceptable pressure losses in the line.

Pressure Drop Method

The pressure drop method is a commonly used technique for sizing steam lines. The method assumes a maximum acceptable pressure drop per hundred feet of steam line, then sets the pipe diameter based on the estimated steam flow through the line. Use Figures 1.10 and 1.11 to estimate steam pipe diameter. Figure 1.10 is for schedule 40 pipe. Figure 1.11 is for schedule 80 pipe. Both figures are for steam at 100 psig, but correction factors are provided for pressures ranging from zero to 600 psig.

Step 1. The allowable pressure drop in a system is determined by the length of the line, the steam pressure at the source, and the steam pressure required at the connected load. There is no set value for all applications. Typical values range from 0.5 to 1.0 psi per 100 ft. Higher pressure drops are common in short lines, while longer lines typically are designed for lower pressure drops. Determine the maximum acceptable pressure drop per 100 feet of main for the application.

Step 2. Since the figures are set up for 100 psig saturated steam, the allowable pressure drop determined in step #1 must be multiplied by a correction factor before the figures can be used. Using the table on the right side of the figure, determine the correction factor for the operating pressure of the system. Multiply the correction factor by the acceptable pressure drop from step #1 to determine the pressure drop to be used in the figure.

Step 3. Starting at the corrected pressure drop value, move across the figure until you reach the estimated steam flow for the line. Select the next line size to the right of the intersection of the corrected pressure drop and the estimated steam flow.

The pressure drop method for sizing steam mains will give a reasonable estimate of the required pipe size for steam load. If the system is anticipated to undergo any growth in the future, don't forget to include the anticipated additional loads in estimating the steam line size.

WHY THE CORRECT STEAM TRAPS ARE ESSENTIAL FOR SAFETY AND EFFICIENCY

One of the most important elements in a steam system in terms of performance and safety is the steam trap. A steam trap is essentially a self-actuated valve that is used to remove condensate and noncondensible gases from a steam system. When operating properly, the trap will open in the presence of condensate, regardless of temperature, and allow the condensate to pass out of the system, but close before steam escapes.

The proper operation of steam traps is essential to the safe and efficient operation of the steam system. Applications that use steam require that the steam be free of moisture. Wet steam (steam that contains moisture condensed from the steam) reduces the heat capacity of the line and equipment connected to it as the condensed moisture heat content is much less than that of the same mass of steam.

Wet steam can also be destructive. Steam velocities, particularly in large systems, can range as high as 6,000 feet per minute. If the steam is wet, the moisture tends to settle in the bottom of the steam line where it is pushed along by the rapidly moving steam. The action of the steam passing over the condensed moisture results in the formation of ripples in the condensate. These ripples grow, forming waves. Given enough condensate and a long enough steam line, these waves can combine to form a slug of condensate that completely fills the steam line. Moving at the same velocity as the steam, the slug of condensate can have enough momentum to damage obstructions, such as valves, joints, or even turns in the steam pipe.

In order to prevent the buildup of condensate within the steam system, steam traps are added to provide routes of escape for the condensate while confining the steam. To be effective, three conditions must be met: the proper type of trap must be selected; the trap must be correctly sized for the load and application; and the trap must be maintained. Failure to meet any of these three conditions results in a system that either allows condensate to back up dangerously into the steam lines, or one that wastes energy by allowing steam to escape.

Selecting the Right Steam Trap

There are three general classifications of steam traps: thermostatic, mechanical, and thermodynamic. Within each classification are a number of different types of traps. Since the principles of operation of each trap type differ, each is best suited for particular applications that impose certain conditions on the trap and how it is expected to perform. There is no one universal trap suited for all applications. Figure 1.12 lists the most common trap types, their characteristics, and typical applications.

Thermostatic traps differentiate between steam and condensate by their temperatures. Condensate is typically cooler than steam, although in some systems, the temperature difference may be hard to detect. The thermostatic trap is designed to sense when cooler condensate is present and open, allowing it to pass. As soon as it comes in contact with the hotter steam, the trap closes.

Mechanical traps differentiate between steam and condensate by their density. The higher density condensate causes a mechanism, such as a float, to lift, opening a valve to pass the condensate. Once the condensate has been removed, the lower density steam cannot support the float, so it falls, closing the valve.

Thermodynamic traps differentiate between steam and condensate by their different velocities in the system. Steam, which has a higher velocity than condensate, exerts enough pressure on a disc valve to force it closed. Lower velocity condensate does not exert enough pressure so the disc opens, allowing the condensate to escape from the system.

Follow the guidelines given in the figure when selecting a trap for a new or existing installation.

Caution: Don't simply replace a failed trap with a new unit of the same type and size. The trap may have failed, in part, as the result of trying to use the wrong type of trap in that particular application.

Guidelines to Avoid Damage or Steam Loss

The selection of a properly sized steam trap for a particular application is a critical task. If the trap is sized too small, it will not pass condensate quickly enough during periods of heavy loads, resulting in condensate backing up into the steam equipment or line that it is draining. If enough condensate backs up, a slug of it could be carried downstream by the rapidly moving steam, resulting in water hammer damage when the slug hits an obstruction. If the trap is sized too large, its eventual failure would result in the loss of large amounts of steam.

Unfortunately trap sizing is more of an art than an exact science. Variations between systems in both design and performance result in significantly different production rates for condensate. For that reason most trap sizing operations make use of safety factors to insure that the trapping system is adequate to handle the condensate produced. If a sizing error is to be made, then it is far better to oversize than undersize the trap. While energy waste from a failed, oversized trap costs you money, the damage caused by water hammer in systems with inadequate trapping can be deadly as well as expensive to correct.

Use Worksheets 1.7 and 1.8 to approximate the size of steam traps in various applications: 1.7 to estimate the size for various steam loads, and 1.8 for those required on steam mains.

Sizing Steam Traps for Steam Mains

Traps for mains must be sized to remove the condensate during the highest pos-sible load. For steam mains this occurs during system start-up when the steam mains are cold. The worksheet sizes the traps for two different applications; supervised and unsupervised start-up.

A supervised start-up is used primarily in large systems that operate on a con-tinuous basis, being shut down only for maintenance or emergency. When these sys-tems are started, the steam traps are bypassed by manually opening valves until the initial surge of condensate has passed. For that reason, the traps are sized to handle the condensate produced in the main once it has reached its normal operating tem-perature. Use Section A of the worksheet to estimate the trap size in supervised start-up systems.

An unsupervised start-up is used in systems that are turned off on a regular basis, such as daily or weekly. Unsupervised start-up systems tend to be small and localized, such as in a laundry. The system uses no manual bypass to remove condensate pro-duced while the mains are heating up, so the traps must be sized to remove all con-densate during start-up. Use Section B of the worksheet to estimate the trap size in unsupervised start-up systems.

Trap Sizes in Supervised Start-Up Systems

Use Worksheet 1.8 to estimate the condensate load on steam traps during system startup as follows:

Step 1.   Figure 1.13 estimates the warm-up load in lbs of condensate pro-duced per 100 feet of steam main. Determine the warm-up load for the system operating pressure and the steam main size. If the steam main is to be located outdoors, above ground, multiply the load value from the figure by the 0°F correction factor from the last column of the figure. Enter the value in section B of the worksheet.

Step 2.   Divide the length of the steam main by 100 to determine the length in hundreds of feet. Enter the value in section B of the worksheet.

Step 3.   Figure 1.14 lists recommended safety factor ranges for sizing steam traps. The actual safety factor selected for a trap will depend on several elements, including confidence in the load esti-mate, system back pressure, and special or unusual conditions. If the confidence is low, the back pressure high, or special condi-tions exist, select a higher safety factor. For the type of trap being used in the application, select the most appropriate safety factor and enter the value in section A of the worksheet.

Step 4.   Since the trap is being sized for the load produced by normal system operation, the presence of insulation and the ambient temperature will impact the condensate load . If the main is insulated and indoors, use an insulation factor of 1.0. If the main is underground, use an insulation factor of 0.7. If the main is uninsulated, use an insulation factor of 0.5. Enter the insulation factor in section A of the worksheet.

Step 5.   Multiply the warm-up load by the main length and the safety factor, and divide by the insulation factor to determine the condensate load in lbs/hr. Enter the value in section A of the worksheet.

This is the condensate load that the trap must be capable of handling. Using manufacturer's capacity data for its traps, select the trap whose capacity is equal to or greater than the estimated condensate load.

Sizing Traps for Unsupervised Start-Up Systems

In supervised start-up systems, the heavy condensate load produced while the system is warming up is removed from the steam mains by the manual trap bypasses. In unsupervised start-up systems, there is no manual trap bypass. Therefore, the steam traps must be sized to remove the condensate from the system while it is warming up. This results in larger traps than would be required in a supervised start-up system.

Use part B of Worksheet 1.8 as follows to size steam traps in unsupervised systems.

Step 1.   Figure 1.13 estimates the load in lbs of condensate produced per hour per 100 feet of steam main. Determine from the figure the condensate produced for the system operating pressure and the steam main size. If the steam main is to be located outdoors, above ground, multiply the load value from the figure by the 0°F correction factor from the last column of the figure. Enter the value in section B of the worksheet.

Step 2.   Divide the length of the steam main by 100 to determine the length in hundreds of feet. Enter the value in section B of the worksheet.

Step 3.   Figure 1.14 lists recommended safety factor ranges for sizing steam traps. The actual safety factor selected for a trap will depend on several elements, including confidence in the load estimate, system back pressure, and special or unusual conditions. If the confidence is low, the back pressure high, or special conditions exist, select a higher safety factor. For the type of trap being used in the application, select the most appropriate safety factor and enter the value in section B of the worksheet.

Step 4.   Determine how long it takes for the system to warm up to normal operating temperature. For most small systems that use unsupervised start-up, this time will typically range between 15 and 60 minutes. Enter the heat-up time in minutes in section B of the worksheet.

Step 5.   Multiply the condensate production rate by the main length, the
                   number 60, and the safety factor, and divide by the heat-up time
                   to determine the condensate load during start-up. Enter the value
                   in section B.

This value is the condensate load that the trap must be capable of handling.
Using manufacturer's capacity data for its traps, select the trap whose capacity is
equal to or greater than the estimated condensate load.

AVOIDING WASTE OR SYSTEM DAMAGE THROUGH A STEAM TRAP MAINTENANCE PROGRAM

Although steam traps are relatively simple mechanisms, they are not maintenance
free. Surveys of facilities that have no systematic steam trap maintenance program
have shown that on the average, ten percent of the traps in the system are defective.
Regardless of whether the trap fails open or closed, both cases pose serious problems
for the facility. Traps failed open waste steam. Traps failed closed cause condensate to
backup in steam mains, resulting in potential damage to the steam system and the
equipment it is supplying.

Recording Data and Tracking Maintenance

A comprehensive steam trap maintenance program starts with a thorough survey of the entire steam system to identify and evaluate all steam traps. Use Figure 1.15
to record data from the survey and to track all maintenance performed on a particular trap. The maintenance log is important in diagnosing long term performance problems associated with a particular trap location, or with the performance of a particular trap type used on a system.

For each trap, record the data listed on the form. Tag each trap and note the location
on the figure so that it can be easily located in future inspections. Identification of the
equipment served by the trap will help in diagnosing problems with the trap or with the
performance of the equipment served as well as identify applications where the wrong type
of trap has been installed. Record other information, such as the size and manufacturer of
the trap, to help identify what replacement parts and traps need to be kept in stock.

During the survey, evaluate the performance of the trap. Trap testing is not simple. For some types of traps, you must remove and bench test the trap under particular conditions to determine if it is operating properly.

Steam Trap Troubleshooting

There are, however, several guidelines that can be followed in the field to determine if a trap may require maintenance. In Figure 1.16 look for the indicators of normal operation for the type of trap installed. If the trap appears to be malfunctioning,
it should be taken out of service as soon as possible and repaired.

Tip: Depending on the size of the trap, it is usually more economical to replace
the trap mechanism with a new or rebuilt unit rather than to rebuild the trap in the
field. The components removed can then be discarded or rebuilt and tested in the
shop. Replacing the entire trap mechanism also reduces the amount of time that the
system must be out of service.

FIGURE 1.1 Heating Values for Various Fuels

Type	Fuel	Heating Value
Oil	# 1 # 2 # 3 # 4 # 5 # 6	136,000 - 139,000 Btu/gal 139,000 - 141,000 Btu/gal 141,000 - 143,500 Btu/gal 144,000 - 146,000 Btu/gal 146,000 - 149,000 Btu/gal 149,000 - 152,000 Btu/gal
Gas	Natural Gas Propane Butane	$950 - 1,100$ Btu/ft^3 $2,600$ Btu/ft^3 $3,200$ Btu/ft^3
Coal	Anthracite Bituminous Sub-Bituminous Lignite	13,000 Btu/lb 10,000 - 14,000 Btu/lb 10,000 Btu/lb 7,000 Btu/lb
Distillates	Gasoline Kerosene Ethyl Alcohol Methyl Alcohol	20,600 Btu/gal 20,000 Btu/gal 12,800 Btu/gal 9,600 Btu/gal
Miscellaneous	Solid Waste Wood	4,000 - 9,000 Btu/lb 5,000 - 10,000 Btu/lb

Note: These figures represent typical heating values. Actual values depend on the source of the fuel and its moisture content.

FIGURE 1.2 Properties of Saturated Steam and Saturated Water

Abstracted from the 1993 ASME Steam Tables

Temp (°F)	Press. (psia)	Volume (ft³/lb)			Enthalpy (Btu/lb)			Entropy (Btu/lb, °F)			Temp (°F)
		Water v_f	Evap v_{fg}	Steam v_g	Water h_f	Evap h_{fg}	Steam h_g	Water s_f	Evap s_{fg}	Steam s_g	
32	0.08859	0.01602	3,305	3,305	- 0.02	1,075.5	1,075.5	0.0000	2.1873	2.1873	32
35	0.09991	0.01602	2,948	2,948	3.00	1,073.8	1,076.8	0.0061	2.1706	2.1767	35
40	0.12163	0.01602	2,446	2,446	8.03	1,071.0	1,079.0	0.0162	2.1432	2.1594	40
45	0.14744	0.01602	2,037.7	2,037.8	13.04	1,068.1	1,081.2	0.0262	2.1164	2.1426	45
50	0.17796	0.01602	1,704.8	1,704.8	18.05	1,065.3	1,083.4	0.0361	2.0901	2.1262	50
60	0.2561	0.01603	1,207.6	1,207.6	28.06	1,059.7	1,087.7	0.0555	2.0391	2.0946	60
70	0.3629	0.01605	868.3	868.4	38.05	1,054.0	1,092.1	0.0745	1.9900	2.0645	70
80	0.5068	0.01607	633.3	633.3	48.04	1,048.4	1,096.4	0.0932	1.9426	2.0359	80
90	0.6981	0.01610	468.1	468.1	58.02	1,042.7	1,100.8	0.1115	1.8970	2.0086	90
100	0.9492	0.01613	350.4	350.4	68.00	1,037.1	1,105.1	0.1295	1.8530	1.9825	100
110	1.2750	0.01617	265.4	265.4	77.98	1,031.4	1,109.3	0.1472	1.8105	1.9577	110
120	1.6927	0.01620	203.25	203.26	87.97	1,025.6	1,113.6	0.1646	1.7693	1.9339	120
130	2.2230	0.01625	157.32	157.33	97.96	1,019.8	1,117.8	0.1817	1.7295	1.9112	130
140	2.8892	0.01629	122.98	123.00	107.95	1,014.0	1,122.0	0.1985	1.6910	1.8895	140
150	3.718	0.01634	97.05	97.07	117.95	1,008.2	1,126.1	0.2150	1.6536	1.8686	150
160	4.741	0.01640	77.27	77.29	127.96	1,002.2	1,130.2	0.2313	1.6174	1.8487	160
170	5.993	0.01645	62.04	62.06	137.97	996.2	1,134.2	0.2473	1.5822	1.8295	170
180	7.511	0.01651	50.21	50.22	148.00	990.2	1,138.2	0.2631	1.5480	1.8111	180
190	9.340	0.01657	40.94	40.96	158.04	984.1	1,142.1	0.2787	1.5148	1.7934	190
200	11.526	0.01664	33.62	33.64	168.09	977.9	1,146.0	0.2940	1.4824	1.7764	200
210	14.123	0.01671	27.80	27.82	178.15	971.6	1,149.7	0.3091	1.4509	1.7600	210
212	14.696	0.01672	26.78	26.80	180.17	970.3	1,150.5	0.3121	1.4447	1.7568	212
220	17.186	0.01678	23.13	23.15	188.23	965.2	1,153.4	0.3241	1.4201	1.7442	220
230	20.779	0.01685	19.364	19.381	198.33	958.7	1,157.1	0.3388	1.3902	1.7290	230
240	24.968	0.01693	16.304	16.321	208.45	952.1	1,160.6	0.3533	1.3609	1.7142	240
250	29.825	0.01701	13.802	13.819	218.59	945.4	1,164.0	0.3677	1.3323	1.7000	250
260	35.427	0.01709	11.745	11.762	228.76	938.6	1,167.4	0.3819	1.3043	1.6862	260
270	41.856	0.01718	10.042	10.060	238.95	931.7	1,170.6	0.3960	1.2769	1.6729	270
280	49.200	0.01726	8.627	8.644	249.17	924.6	1,173.8	0.4098	1.2501	1.6599	280
290	57.550	0.01736	7.443	7.460	259.4	917.4	1,176.8	0.4236	1.2238	1.6473	290
300	67.005	0.01745	6.448	6.466	269.7	910.0	1,179.7	0.4372	1.1979	1.6351	300
310	77.67	0.01755	5.609	5.626	280.0	902.5	1,182.5	0.4506	1.1726	1.6232	310
320	89.64	0.01766	4.896	4.914	290.4	894.8	1,185.2	0.4640	1.1477	1.6116	320
340	117.99	0.01787	3.770	3.788	311.3	878.8	1,190.1	0.4902	1.0990	1.5892	340
360	153.01	0.01811	2.939	2.957	332.3	862.1	1,194.4	0.5161	1.0517	1.5678	360

FIGURE 1.2 (continued)

Temp (°F)	Press. (psia)	Volume (ft³/lb)			Enthalpy (Btu/lb)			Entropy (Btu/lb, °F)			Temp (°F)
		Water v_f	Evap v_{fg}	Steam v_g	Water h_f	Evap h_{fg}	Steam h_g	Water s_f	Evap s_{fg}	Steam s_g	
380	195.73	0.01836	2.317	2.335	353.6	844.5	1,198.0	0.5416	1.0057	1.5473	380
400	247.26	0.01864	1.8444	1.8630	375.1	825.9	1,201.0	0.5667	0.9607	1.5274	400
420	308.78	0.01894	1.4808	1.4997	396.9	806.2	1,203.1	0.5915	0.9165	1.5080	420
440	381.54	0.01926	1.1976	1.2169	419.0	785.4	1,204.4	0.6161	0.8729	1.4890	440
460	466.9	0.0196	0.9746	0.9942	441.5	763.2	1,204.8	0.6405	0.8299	0.4704	460
480	566.2	0.0200	0.7972	0.8172	464.5	739.6	1,204.1	0.6648	0.7871	1.4518	480
500	680.9	0.0204	0.6545	0.6749	487.9	714.3	1,202.2	0.6890	0.7443	1.4333	500
520	812.5	0.0209	0.5386	0.5596	512.0	687.0	1,199.0	0.7178	0.7013	1.4146	520
540	962.8	0.0215	0.4437	0.4651	536.8	657.5	1,194.3	0.7378	0.6577	1.3954	540
560	1,133.4	0.0221	0.3651	0.3871	562.4	625.3	1,187.7	0.7625	0.6132	1.3757	560
580	1,326.2	0.0228	0.2994	0.3222	589.1	589.9	1,179.0	0.7876	0.5673	1.3550	580
600	1,543.2	0.0236	0.2438	0.2675	617.1	550.6	1,167.7	0.8134	0.5196	1.3330	600
620	1,786.9	0.0247	0.1962	0.2208	646.9	506.3	1,153.2	0.8403	0.4689	1.3092	620
640	2,059.9	0.0260	0.1543	0.1802	679.1	454.6	1,133.7	0.8686	0.4134	1.2821	640
660	2,365.7	0.0277	0.1166	0.1443	714.9	392.1	1,107.0	0.8995	0.3502	1.2498	660
680	2,708.6	0.0304	0.0808	0.1112	758.5	310.1	1,068.5	0.9365	0.2720	1.2086	680
700	3,094.3	0.0366	0.0386	0.0752	822.4	172.7	995.2	0.9901	0.1490	1.1390	700

Courtesy of The American Society of Mechanical Engineers

FIGURE 1.3 Superheated Steam Tables

Abstracted from the 1993 ASME Steam Tables
v = specific volume, ft^3/lb; h = enthalpy, Btu/lb; s = entropy, Btu/lbm °R

Pressure, psia (sat temp, °F)		Temperature (°F)									
		100°	200°	300°	400°	500°	600°	700°	800°	900°	1,000°
1 (101.74)	v	0.01613	392.5	452.3	511.9	571.5	631.1	690.7	-	-	-
	h	68.00	1,150.2	1,195.7	1,241.8	1,288.6	1,336.1	1,384.5	-	-	-
	s	0.1295	2.0509	2.1152	2.1722	2.2237	2.2708	2.3144	-	-	-
5 (162.24)	v	0.01613	78.14	90.24	102.24	114.21	126.15	138.08	150.01	161.94	173.86
	h	68.01	1,148.6	1,194.8	1,241.3	1,288.2	1,335.9	1,384.3	1,433.6	1,483.7	1,534.7
	s	0.1295	1.8716	1.9369	1.9943	2.0460	2.0932	2.1369	2.1776	2.2159	2.2521
10 (193.21)	v	0.01613	38.84	44.98	51.03	57.04	63.03	69.00	74.98	80.94	86.91
	h	68.02	1,146.6	1,193.7	1,240.6	1,287.8	1,335.5	1,384.0	1,433.4	1,483.5	1,534.6
	s	0.1295	1.7928	1.8593	1.9173	1.9692	2.0166	2.0603	2.1011	2.1394	2.1757
15 (213.03)	v	0.01613	0.01664	29.899	33.963	37.985	41.986	45.978	49.964	53.946	57.926
	h	68.04	168.09	1,192.5	1,239.9	1,287.3	1,335.2	1,383.8	1,433.2	1,483.4	1,534.5
	s	0.1295	0.2940	1.8134	1.8720	1.9242	1.9717	2.0155	2.0563	2.0946	2.1309
20 (227.96)	v	0.01613	0.01664	22.356	25.248	28.457	31.466	34.465	37.458	40.447	43.435
	h	68.05	168.11	1,191.4	1,239.2	1,286.9	1,334.9	1,383.5	1,432.9	1,483.2	1,534.3
	s	0.1295	0.2940	1.7805	1.8397	1.8921	1.9397	1.9836	2.0244	2.0628	2.0991
25 (240.07)	v	0.01613	0.01664	17.829	20.307	22.740	25.153	27.557	29.954	32.348	34.740
	h	68.06	168.12	1,190.2	1,238.5	1,286.4	1,334.6	1,383.3	1,432.7	1,483.0	1,534.2
	s	0.1295	0.2940	1.7547	1.8145	1.8672	1.9149	1.9588	1.9997	2.0381	2.0744
30 (250.34)	v	0.01613	0.01664	14.810	16.892	18.929	20.945	22.951	24.952	26.949	28.943
	h	68.08	168.13	1,189.0	1,237.8	1,286.0	1,334.2	1,383.0	1,432.5	1,482.8	1,534.0
	s	0.1295	0.2940	1.7334	1.7937	1.8467	1.8946	1.9386	1.9795	2.0179	2.0543
40 (267.25)	v	0.01613	0.01664	11.036	12.624	14.165	15.685	17.195	18.699	20.199	21.697
	h	68.10	168.15	1,186.6	1,236.4	1,285.0	1,333.6	1,382.5	1,432.1	1,482.5	1,533.7
	s	0.1295	0.2940	1.6992	1.7608	1.8143	1.8624	1.9065	1.9476	1.9860	2.0224
50 (281.02)	v	0.01613	0.01663	8.769	10.062	11.306	12.529	13.741	14.947	16.150	17.350
	h	68.13	168.17	1,184.1	1,234.9	1,284.1	1,332.9	1,382.0	1,431.7	1,482.2	1,533.4
	s	0.1295	0.2940	1.6720	1.7349	1.7890	1.8374	1.8816	1.9227	1.9613	1.9977
60 (292.71)	v	0.01613	0.01663	7.257	8.354	9.400	10.425	11.438	12.446	13.450	14.452
	h	68.15	168.20	1,181.6	1,233.5	1,283.2	1,332.3	1,381.5	1,431.3	1,481.8	1,533.2
	s	0.1295	0.2939	1.6492	1.7134	1.7681	1.8168	1.8612	1.9024	1.9410	1.9774
70 (302.93)	v	0.01613	0.01663	0.01745	7.133	8.039	8.922	9.793	10.659	11.522	12.382
	h	68.18	168.22	269.72	1,232.0	1,282.2	1,331.6	1,381.0	1,430.9	1,481.5	1,532.9
	s	0.1295	0.2939	0.4372	1.6951	1.7504	1.7993	1.8439	1.8852	1.9238	1.9603
80 (312.04)	v	0.01613	0.01663	0.01745	6.218	7.018	7.794	8.560	9.319	10.075	10.829
	h	68.21	168.24	269.74	1,230.5	1,281.3	1,330.9	1,380.5	1,430.5	1,481.1	1,532.6
	s	0.1295	0.2939	0.4371	1.6790	1.7349	1.7842	1.8289	1.8702	1.9089	1.9454

Figure 1.3 (continued)

v = specific volume, ft³/lb; h = enthalpy, Btu/lb; s = entropy, Btu/lbm °R

Pressure, psia (sat temp, °F)		Temperature (°F)									
		400°	500°	600°	700°	800°	900°	1,000°	1,100°	1,200°	1,300°
90 (320.28)	v	5.505	6.223	6.917	7.600	8.277	8.950	9.621	10.290	10.958	11.625
	h	1,228.9	1,280.3	1,330.2	1,380.0	1,430.1	1,480.8	1,532.3	1,584.6	1,637.8	1,691.8
	s	1.6646	1.7212	1.7707	1.8156	1.8570	1.8957	1.9323	1.9669	2.0000	2.0316
100 (327.82)	v	4.935	5.588	6.216	6.833	7.443	8.050	8.655	9.258	9.860	10.460
	h	1,227.4	1,279.3	1,329.6	1,379.5	1,429.7	1,480.4	1,532.0	1,584.4	1,637.6	1,691.6
	s	1.6516	1.7088	1.7586	1.8036	1.8451	1.8839	1.9205	1.9552	1.9883	2.0199
120 (341.27)	v	4.0786	4.6341	5.1637	5.6813	6.1928	6.7006	7.2060	7.7096	8.2119	8.7130
	h	1,224.1	1,277.4	1,328.2	1,378.4	1,428.8	1,479.8	1,531.4	1,583.9	1,637.1	1,691.3
	s	1.6286	1.6872	1.7376	1.7829	1.8246	1.8635	1.9001	1.9349	1.9680	1.9996
140 (353.04)	v	3.4661	3.9526	4.4119	4.8588	5.2995	5.7364	6.1709	6.6036	7.0349	7.4652
	h	1,220.8	1,275.3	1,326.8	1,377.4	1,428.0	1,479.1	1,530.8	1,583.4	1,636.7	1,690.9
	s	1.6085	1.6686	1.7196	1.7652	1.8071	1.8461	1.8828	1.9176	1.9508	1.9825
160 (363.55)	v	3.0060	3.4413	3.8480	4.2420	4.6295	5.0132	5.3945	5.7741	6.1522	6.5293
	h	1,217.4	1,273.3	1,325.4	1,376.4	1,427.2	1,478.4	1,530.3	1,582.9	1,636.3	1,690.5
	s	1.5906	1.6522	1.7039	1.7499	1.7919	1.8310	1.8678	1.9027	1.9359	1.9676
180 (373.08)	v	2.6474	3.0433	3.4093	3.7621	4.1084	4.4508	4.7907	5.1289	5.4657	5.8014
	h	1,213.8	1,271.2	1,324.0	1,375.3	1,426.3	1,477.7	1,529.7	1,582.4	1,635.9	1,690.2
	s	1.5743	1.6376	1.6900	1.7362	1.7784	1.8176	1.8545	1.8894	1.9227	1.9545
200 (381.80)	v	2.3598	2.7247	3.0583	3.3783	3.6915	4.0008	4.3077	4.6128	4.9165	5.2191
	h	1,210.1	1,269.0	1,322.6	1,374.3	1,425.5	1,477.0	1,529.1	1,581.9	1,635.4	1,689.8
	s	1.5593	1.6242	1.6773	1.7239	1.7663	1.8057	1.8426	1.8776	1.9109	1.9427
220 (389.88)	v	2.1240	2.4638	2.7710	3.0642	3.3504	3.6327	3.9125	4.1905	4.4671	4.7426
	h	1,206.3	1,266.9	1,321.2	1,373.2	1,424.7	1,476.3	1,528.5	1,581.4	1,635.0	1,689.4
	s	1.5453	1.6120	1.6658	1.7128	1.7553	1.7948	1.8318	1.8668	1.9002	1.9320
240 (397.39)	v	1.9268	2.2462	2.5316	2.8024	3.0661	3.3259	3.531	3.8385	4.0926	4.3456
	h	1,202.4	1,264.6	1,319.7	1,372.1	1,423.8	1,475.6	1,527.9	1,580.9	1,634.6	1,689.1
	s	1.5320	1.6006	1.6552	1.7025	1.7452	1.7848	1.8219	1.8570	1.8904	1.9223
260 (404.44)	v	0.01864	2.0619	2.3289	2.5808	2.8256	3.0663	3.3077	3.5408	3.7758	4.0097
	h	375.11	1,262.4	1,318.2	1,371.1	1,423.0	1,474.9	1,527.3	1,580.4	1,634.2	1,688.7
	s	0.5666	1.5899	1.6453	1.6930	1.7359	1.7756	1.8128	1.8480	1.8814	1.9133
280 (411.07)	v	0.01863	1.9037	2.1551	2.3909	2.6194	2.8437	3.0655	3.2855	3.5042	3.7217
	h	375.13	1,260.0	1,316.8	1,370.0	1,422.1	1,474.2	1,526.8	1,579.9	1,633.8	1,688.4
	s	0.5666	1.5798	1.6361	1.6841	1.7273	1.7671	1.8043	1.8395	1.8730	1.9050
300 (417.35)	v	0.01863	1.7665	2.0044	2.2263	2.4407	2.6509	2.8585	3.0643	3.2688	3.4721
	h	375.15	1,257.7	1,315.2	1,368.9	1,421.3	1,473.6	1,526.2	1,579.4	1,633.3	1,688.0
	s	0.5665	1.5703	1.6274	1.6758	1.7192	1.7591	1.7964	1.8317	1.8652	1.8972

Figure 1.3 (continued)

v = specific volume, ft³/lb; h = enthalpy, Btu/lb; s = entropy, Btu/lbm °R

Pressure, psia (sat temp, °F)		Temperature (°F)									
		400°	500°	600°	700°	800°	900°	1,000°	1,100°	1,200°	1,300°
400 (444.60)	v	0.01862	1.2841	1.4763	1.6499	1.8151	1.9759	2.1339	2.2901	2.4450	2.5987
	h	375.27	1,245.1	1,307.4	1,363.4	1,417.0	1,470.1	1,523.3	1,576.9	1,631.2	1,686.2
	s	0.5663	1.5282	1.5901	1.6406	1.6850	1.7255	1.7632	1.7988	1.8325	1.8647
500 (466.96)	v	0.01861	0.99375	1.2065	1.3059	1.4421	1.5734	1.7020	1.8286	1.9538	2.0815
	h	375.38	1,231.2	1,299.1	1,357.7	1,412.7	1,466.6	1,520.3	1,574.5	1,629.1	1,684.4
	s	0.5660	1.4922	1.5596	1.6124	1.6579	1.6014.0	1.7372	1.7731	1.8070	1.8394
600 (486.20)	v	0.01860	0.7944	0.9456	1.0726	1.1892	1.3008	1.4093	1.5160	1.6211	1.7252
	h	375.49	1,215.9	1,290.3	1,351.8	1,408.3	1,463.0	1,517.4	1,571.9	1,627.0	1,682.6
	s	0.5657	1.4590	1.5329	1.5884	1.6351	1.6769	1.7155	1.7517	1.7859	1.8184
700 (503.08)	v	0.01858	0.0243	0.7928	0.9072	1.0102	1.1078	1.2023	1.2948	1.3858	1.4757
	h	375.61	487.93	1,281.0	1,345.6	1,403.7	1,459.4	1,514.4	1,569.4	1,624.8	1,680.7
	s	0.5655	0.6889	1.5090	1.5673	1.6154	1.6580	1.6970	1.7335	1.7679	1.8006
800 (518.21)	v	0.01857	0.02041	0.6774	0.7828	0.8759	0.9631	1.0470	1.1289	1.2093	1.2885
	h	375.73	487.88	1,271.1	1,339.3	1,399.1	1,455.8	1,511.4	1,566.9	1,622.7	1,678.9
	s	0.5652	0.6885	1.4869	1.5484	1.5980	1.6413	1.6807	1.7175	1.7522	1.7851
900 (531.95)	v	0.01856	0.02038	0.5869	0.6858	0.7713	0.8504	0.9262	0.9998	1.0720	1.1430
	h	375.84	487.83	1,260.6	1,332.7	1,394.4	1,452.2	1,508.5	1,564.4	1,620.6	1,677.1
	s	0.5649	0.6881	1.4659	1.5311	1.5822	1.6263	1.6662	1.7033	1.7382	1.7713
1,000 (544.58)	v	0.01855	0.02036	0.5137	0.6080	0.6875	0.7603	0.8295	0.8966	0.9622	1.0266
	h	375.96	487.79	1,249.3	1,325.9	1,389.6	1,448.5	1,505.4	1,561.9	1,618.4	1,675.3
	s	0.5647	0.6879	1.4557	1.5149	1.5677	1.6126	1.6530	1.6905	1.7256	1.7589
1,500 (596.20)	v	0.01849	0.02025	0.2820	0.3717	0.4350	0.4894	0.5394	0.5869	0.6327	0.6773
	h	376.56	487.63	1,176.3	1,287.9	1,364.0	1,429.2	1,490.1	1,549.2	1,607.7	1,666.2
	s	0.5634	0.6855	1.3431	1.4443	1.5073	1.5572	1.6004	1.6395	1.6759	1.7101
2,000 (635.80)	v	0.01844	0.02014	0.02332	0.2488	0.3072	0.3534	0.3942	0.4320	0.4680	0.5027
	h	377.19	487.53	614.48	1,240.9	1,335.4	1,408.7	1,474.1	1,536.2	1,596.9	1,657.0
	s	0.5621	0.6834	0.8091	1.3794	1.4578	1.5138	1.5603	1.6014	1.6391	1.6743
2,500 (668.11)	v	0.01838	0.02004	0.02302	0.1681	0.2293	0.2712	0.3068	0.3390	0.3692	0.3980
	h	377.82	487.50	612.08	1176.7	1,303.4	1,386.7	1,457.5	1,522.9	1,585.9	1,647.8
	s	0.5609	0.6815	0.8048	1.3076	1.4129	1.4766	1.5269	1.5703	0.6094	1.6456
3,000	v	0.01833	0.01995	0.02276	0.0982	0.1759	0.2161	0.2484	0.2770	0.3033	0.3282
	h	378.47	487.52	610.08	1,060.5	1,267.0	1,363.2	1,440.2	1,509.4	1,574.8	1,638.5
	s	0.5597	0.6796	0.8009	1.1966	1.3692	1.4429	1.4976	1.5434	1.5841	1.6214
4,000	v	0.0182	0.0198	0.0223	0.0287	0.1052	0.1463	0.1752	0.1994	0.2210	0.2411
	h	379.8	487.7	606.9	763.0	1,174.3	1,311.6	1,403.6	1,481.3	1,552.2	1,619.8
	s	0.5573	0.6760	0.7940	0.9343	1.2754	1.3807	1.4461	1.4976	1.5417	1.5812

Courtesy of The American Society of Mechanical Engineers

FIGURE 1.4 Effect of Intermittent Firing on Boiler Efficiency

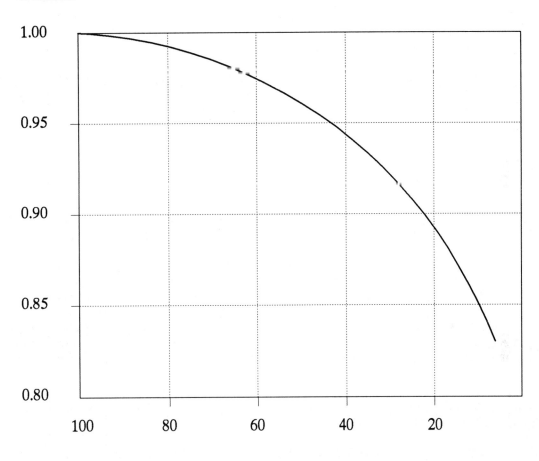

Efficiency
Multiplication
Factor

% Burner On Time

FIGURE 1.5 Excess Air and O$_2$ in Flue Gases

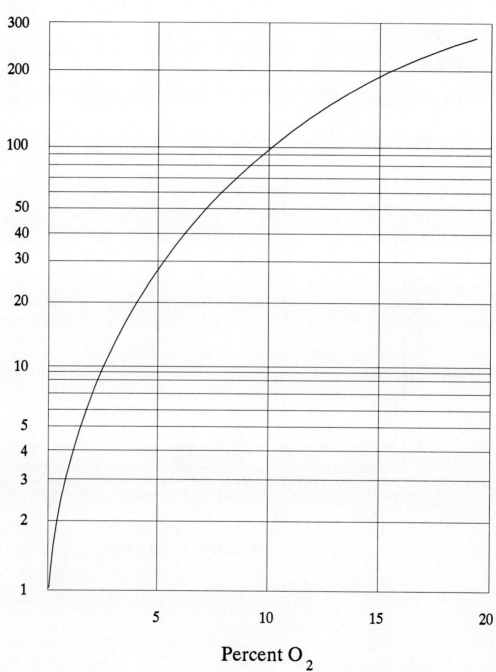

Percent
Excess Air

Percent O$_2$

FIGURE 1.6 Excess Air and CO$_2$ in Flue Gases

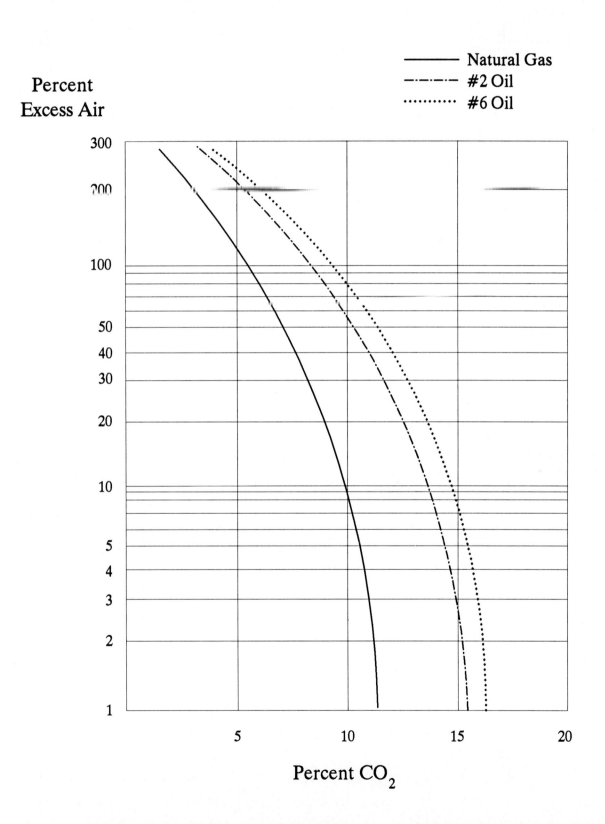

Percent
Excess Air

Percent CO$_2$

Legend:
— Natural Gas
—·—·— #2 Oil
·········· #6 Oil

FIGURE 1.7 Estimating Fuel Savings Through Reduced Excess Combustion Air

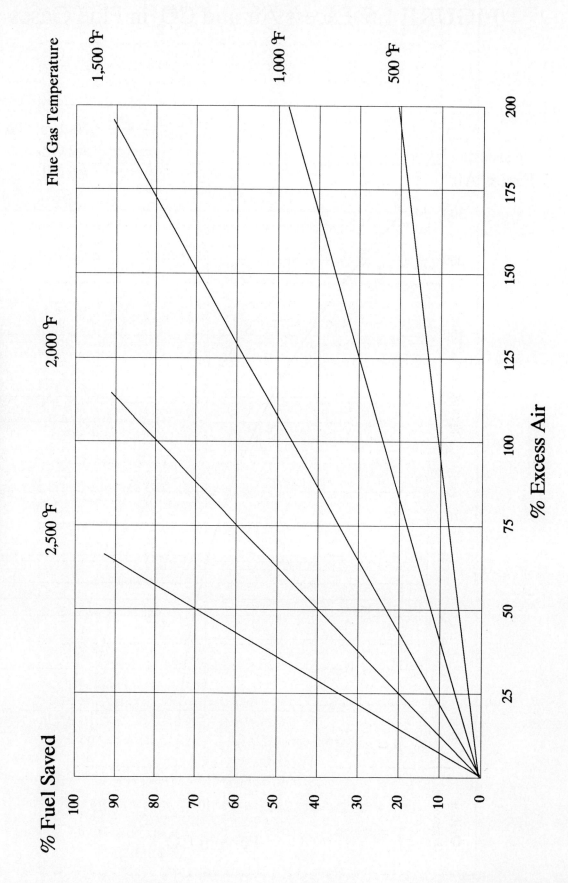

FIGURE 1.8 Steam Loss Through Failed Traps

Steam Loss (lb/hr)

Orifice Diameter (in)	2 psi	5 psi	10 psi	15 psi	25 psi	50 psi	75 psi	100 psi	125 psi	150 psi	200 psi	250 psi	300 psi
1/32	0.31	0.49	0.70	0.85	1.14	1.86	2.58	3.3	4.02	4.74	6.17	7.61	4.05
1/16	1.25	1.97	2.8	3.4	4.6	7.4	10.3	13.2	16.1	18.9	24.7	30.4	36.2
3/32	2.81	4.44	6.3	7.7	10.3	16.7	15.4	29.7	36.2	42.6	55.6	68.5	81.5
1/8	4.5	7.9	11.2	13.7	18.3	29.8	41.3	52.8	64.3	75.8	99.0	122	145
5/32	7.8	12.3	17.4	21.3	28.5	46.5	64.5	82.5	100	118	154	190	226
3/16	11.2	17.7	25.1	30.7	41.1	67.0	93.0	119	145	170	222	274	326
7/32	15.3	24.2	34.2	41.9	55.9	91.2	125	162	187	232	303	373	443
1/4	20.0	31.6	44.6	54.7	73.1	119	165	211	257	303	395	487	579
9/32	25.2	39.9	56.5	69.2	92.5	151	209	267	325	384	500	617	733
5/16	31.2	49.3	69.7	85.4	114	186	253	330	402	474	617	761	905
11/32	37.7	59.6	84.4	103	138	225	312	399	486	573	747	921	1,095
3/8	44.9	71.0	100	123	164	268	371	475	578	682	889	1,096	1,303
13/32	52.7	83.3	118	144	193	314	435	557	679	800	1,043	1,286	1,529
7/16	61.1	96.6	137	167	224	365	505	647	787	928	1,210	1,492	1,774
15/32	70.2	111	157	192	257	419	580	742	904	1,065	1,389	1,713	2,037
1/2	79.8	126	179	219	292	476	660	844	1,028	1,212	1,580	1,949	2,317

Courtesy of Spirax Sarco

FIGURE 1.9 Boiler Maintenance Requirements

Interval	Maintenance Activity
Daily	Inspect the operation of the water level control. Check the steam pressure. Measure the flue gas temperature. Visually inspect the burners. Visually inspect the operation of the boiler's motors and auxiliary equipment. Visually inspect the outside of the boiler. Test the low-water cutoff control. Inspect and test the main fuel shut-off valves
Weekly	Perform a complete exhaust gas analysis. Test the operation of all burner controls. Clean oil strainers and filters. Check the oil level in the control air compressor Test the operation of the boiler pressure controls.
Monthly	Test the boiler pressure safety valve. Clean and test the second low-water cutoff valve. Blow down all control air lines. Inspect for air leaks. Inspect the operation of the blowdown and water treatment systems. Inspect all belts.
Annually	Clean and inspect the water side of the boiler. Clean and inspect the fireside of the boiler. Inspect all fans and ducts. Inspect hydraulic and pneumatic valves. Clean the fuel system. Clean the feedwater system. Inspect and clean all electrical contacts on motors and starters. Check motor brush wear. Clean and rebuild all low-water cutoff controls. Inventory spare parts.

Note: The above listed maintenance activities are generalized activities that can be applied to most boilers. They represent a minimum level of maintenance that should be performed. Additional maintenance activities may be required by the manufacturer of a specific boiler. Always adhere to the manufacturer's requirements.

FIGURE 1.10 Pressure Drop in Schedule 40 Pipe
100 psig Saturated Steam
(For Other Pressures Use the Correction Factors)

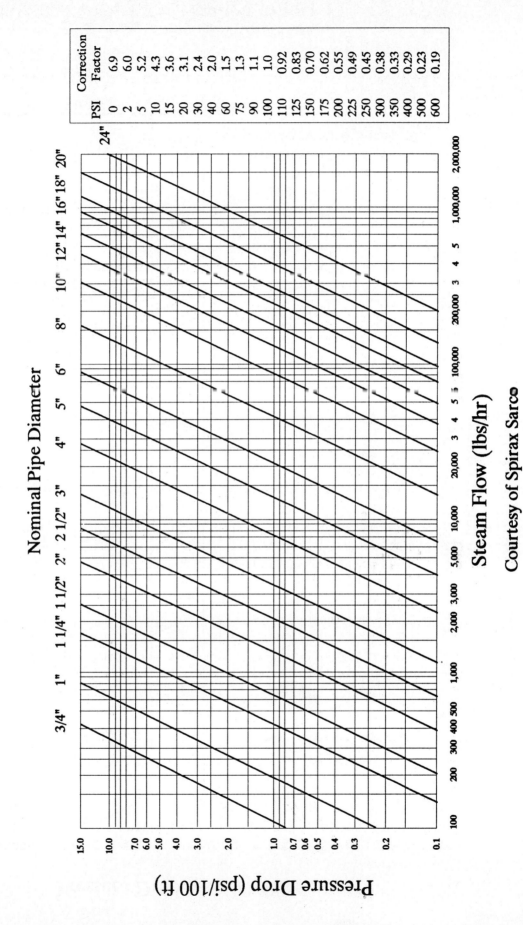

PSI	Correction Factor
0	6.9
2	6.0
5	5.2
10	4.3
15	3.6
20	3.1
30	2.4
40	2.0
60	1.5
75	1.3
90	1.1
100	1.0
110	0.92
125	0.83
150	0.70
175	0.62
200	0.55
225	0.49
250	0.45
300	0.38
350	0.33
400	0.29
500	0.23
600	0.19

Nominal Pipe Diameter

Steam Flow (lbs/hr)

Pressure Drop (psi/100 ft)

Courtesy of Spirax Sarco

FIGURE 1.11 Pressure Drop in Schedule 80 Pipe

100 psig Saturated Steam

(For Other Pressures Use the Correction Factors)

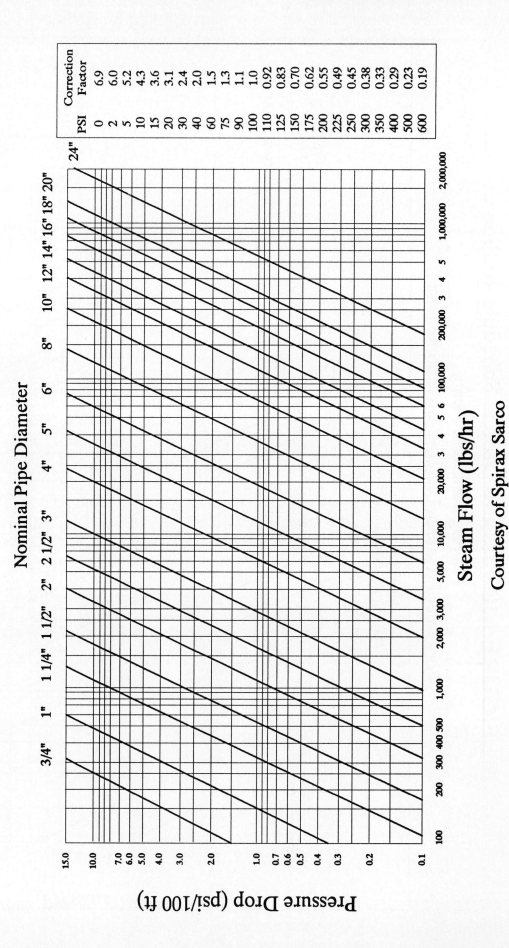

Courtesy of Spirax Sarco

PSI	Correction Factor
0	6.9
2	6.0
5	5.2
10	4.3
15	3.6
20	3.1
30	2.4
40	2.0
60	1.5
75	1.3
90	1.1
100	1.0
110	0.92
125	0.83
150	0.70
175	0.62
200	0.55
225	0.49
250	0.45
300	0.38
350	0.33
400	0.29
500	0.23
600	0.19

FIGURE 1.12 Steam Trap Application Guide

Steam Trap Type	Characteristics	Typical Applications
	Thermostatic Traps	
Balanced-Pressure	Available in sizes from 1/2 to 2 inches Intermittent operation Normal operation causes some condensate backup Discharges subcooled condensate Not suitable for operation with superheated steam Some elements are subject to damage from water hammer Good air venting capability Operation not impacted by back pressure May fail open or closed Best suited for light, steady loads on low pressure service	Radiators Convectors HVAC Coils Small Heat Exchangers
Bimetallic	Available in sizes from 1/2 to 2 inches Modulating or intermittent operation Normal operation causes some condensate backup Discharges subcooled condensate Not adversely affected by superheated steam Resistant to damage from water hammer Good air venting capability Operation affected by back pressure Usually fails open Suitable for high pressure applications Fair response to load and pressure changes	Steam tracers Storage Tanks

Figure 1.12 (continued)

Steam Trap Type		Characteristics	Typical Applications
		Thermostatic Traps (continued)	
Liquid-Expansion		Modulating operation Normal operation causes some condensate backup Discharges slightly subcooled condensate Not adversely affected by superheated steam Resistant to damage from water hammer Good air venting capability Operation affected by backpressure Usually fails open Suitable for pressures up to 300 psig Slow reaction to temperature changes	Storage Tank Heaters
		Mechanical Traps	
Float & Thermostatic		Available in sizes ranging from 1/2 to 2 inches Modulating discharge Normal operation causes no condensate backup Discharges condensate at steam temperature Not suitable for operation with superheated steam Readily damaged by water hammer Good air venting capability Operation not impacted by backpressure Can fail open or closed Suitable for applications up to 250 psig Good response to load and pressure changes	HVAC Coils Water Heaters Low-Pressure Drip Lines Unit Heaters

Figure 1.12 (continued)

Steam Trap Type	Characteristics	Typical Applications
	Mechanical Traps (continued)	
Inverted Bucket	Available in sizes from 1/2 to 3 inches Intermittent operation Normal operation causes no condensate backup Discharges condensate at steam temperature Suitable for operation with superheated steam under certain conditions Not readily damaged by water hammer Fair air venting capability Operation affected by backpressure Usually fails open Suitable for pressures up to 2,500 psig Moderate reaction to temperature changes Good response to load changes Some traps may require priming during system start-up	Low Pressure Systems Laundry Equipment Sterilizers Water Heaters
	Thermodynamic Traps	
Disc	Available in sizes from 1/2 to 2 inches Intermittent discharge Normal operation causes no condensate backup Discharges condensate at steam temperature Suitable for operation with superheated steam Not readily damaged by water hammer Poor air venting capability Operation impacted by backpressure Usually fails open Suitable for applications up to 1,500 psig Good response to load and pressure changes	Medium & High Pressure Drip Legs HVAC Coils

FIGURE 1.13 Steam Condensate Warm-Up Load

Warm-Up Load (lbs/100 feet of steam main)

Steam Pressure (psig)	Steam Main Size														0°F Correction Factor
	2"	2.5"	3"	4"	5"	6"	8"	10"	12"	14"	16"	18"	20"	24"	
0	6.2	9.7	12.8	18.2	24.6	31.9	48	68	90	107	140	176	207	308	1.50
5	6.9	11.0	14.4	20.4	27.7	35.9	48	77	101	120	157	198	233	324	1.44
10	7.5	11.8	15.5	22.0	29.9	38.8	58	83	109	130	169	213	251	350	1.41
20	8.4	13.4	17.5	24.9	33.8	43.9	66	93	124	146	191	241	284	396	1.37
40	9.9	15.8	20.6	29.3	39.7	51.6	78	110	145	172	225	284	334	465	1.32
60	11.0	17.5	22.9	32.6	44.2	57.3	86	122	162	192	250	316	372	518	1.29
80	12.0	19.0	24.9	35.3	47.9	62.1	93	132	175	208	271	342	403	561	1.27
100	12.8	20.3	26.6	37.8	51.2	66.5	100	142	188	222	290	366	431	600	1.26
125	13.7	21.7	28.4	40.4	54.8	71.1	107	152	200	238	310	391	461	642	1.25
150	14.5	23.0	30.0	42.8	58.0	75.2	113	160	212	251	328	414	487	679	1.24
175	15.3	24.2	31.7	45.1	61.2	79.4	119	169	224	265	347	437	514	716	1.23
200	16.0	25.3	33.1	47.1	63.8	82.8	125	177	234	277	362	456	537	748	1.22
250	17.2	27.3	35.8	50.8	68.9	89.4	134	191	252	299	390	492	579	807	1.21
300	25.0	38.3	51.3	74.8	104	143	217	322	443	531	682	854	1,045	1,182	1.20
400	27.8	42.6	57.1	83.2	116	159	241	358	493	590	759	971	1,163	1,650	1.18
500	30.2	46.3	62.1	90.5	126	173	262	389	535	642	825	1,033	1,263	1,793	1.17
600	32.7	50.1	67.1	97.9	136	187	284	421	579	694	893	1,118	1,367	1,939	1.16

Loads based on an ambient temperature of 70°F. For an outdoor temperature of 0°F, multiply the load values by the 0°F correction factor for that pressure. Values for pressures over 250 psig are for Schedule 80 pipe. Schedule 40 pipe used through 250 psig.

Figure 1.13 (continued)

Steam Pressure (psig)	Condensate Load (lbs/hr - 100 feet of insulated steam main) Steam Main Size														0°F Correction Factor
	2"	2.5"	3"	4"	5"	6"	8"	10"	12"	14"	16"	18"	20"	24"	
10	6	7	9	11	13	16	20	24	29	32	36	39	44	53	1.67
30	8	9	11	14	17	20	26	32	38	43	48	51	57	68	1.58
60	10	12	14	18	24	27	33	41	49	54	62	67	74	89	1.53
100	12	15	18	22	28	33	41	51	61	67	77	83	93	111	1.49
125	13	16	20	24	30	36	45	56	66	73	84	90	101	121	1.47
175	16	19	23	26	33	38	53	66	78	86	98	107	119	142	1.45
250	18	22	27	34	42	50	62	77	92	101	116	126	140	168	1.43
300	20	25	30	37	46	54	68	85	101	111	126	138	154	184	1.42
400	23	28	34	43	53	63	80	99	118	130	148	162	180	216	1.40
500	27	33	39	49	61	73	91	114	135	148	170	185	206	246	1.39
600	30	37	44	55	68	82	103	128	152	167	191	208	232	277	1.38

Loads based on an ambient temperature of 70°F. For an outdoor temperature of 0°F, multiply the load values by the 0°F correction factor for that pressure.
Loads based on an insulation efficiency of 80 %.
Schedule 40 pipe used through 250 psig. Values for pressures over 250 psig are for Schedule 80 pipe.

Courtesy of Spirax Sarco

FIGURE 1.14 Steam Trap Sizing Safety Factors

Type of Trap	Safety Factor
Balanced-Pressure	2 to 4
Bimetallic	2 to 4
Liquid-Expansion	2 to 4
Float & Thermostatic	1.5 to 2.5
Inverted Bucket	2 to 3
Disc	1.2 to 2

FIGURE 1.15 Steam Trap Maintenance Record

Application Information	

Trap ID Number: _____   Trap Type: _____

Location: _____   Size: _____

Equipment Served: _____   Manufacturer: _____

Date Installed: ____/____/____   Model #: _____

Inspection Log

	Date	Maintenance Performed	Initials
1.	____/____/____	_____	_____
2.	____/____/____	_____	_____
3.	____/____/____	_____	_____
4.	____/____/____	_____	_____
5.	____/____/____	_____	_____
6.	____/____/____	_____	_____
7.	____/____/____	_____	_____
8.	____/____/____	_____	_____
9.	____/____/____	_____	_____
10.	____/____/____	_____	_____
11.	____/____/____	_____	_____
12.	____/____/____	_____	_____
13.	____/____/____	_____	_____
14.	____/____/____	_____	_____
15.	____/____/____	_____	_____

FIGURE 1.16 Steam Trap Troubleshooting

Type of Trap	Indicators of Normal Operation	Causes for Indications of Malfunction	
		Open	Closed
Any Type of Trap	Should observe relatively high trap inlet temperature, but not superheat. Should observe flash on discharge to atmosphere and see normal characteristic discharge. Should hear normal, characteristic operation.	Excessive valve seat wear. Dirt on trap seat. Open bypass constantly blowing. Overloaded trap - discharging continuously.	Temperature control valve throttled, insufficient steam pressure. Overloaded trap, backing up cold condensate. Clogged strainer. Closed stop valve upstream. Closed return line stop valve or check valve.
Float or Float & Thermostatic	Normal discharge - continuous, but on light loads may be intermittent. Should see flash. Should hear continuous discharge. Should observe relatively high inlet temperature.	Thermal element leaking. Mechanism worn, broken or held open due to dirt/or oxides. Leaking internal seals or gaskets. See above - Any type of trap.	Thermal element failed closed. Float collapsed, main valve failed closed. Excessive pressure difference across disc. Worn oversized. See above - Any type of trap.
Thermostatic	Normal discharge - intermittent, or continuous depending on load, pressure, or type. Should see flash unless adjusted for subcooled operation. Should hear continuous or modulating flow. Should observe temperature near rated discharge temperature.	Thermal element failure (some types). Excessive backpressure (some types). Improper adjustment of setting. Worn valve or seat. Leaking gaskets. See above - Any type of trap.	Thermal element failed closed. Excessive backpressure (some types). See above - Any type of trap.
Inverted Bucket	Normal discharge - intermittent, can be continuous under some conditions of pressure and load. Should see flash. Should hear intermittent discharge - possibly rattle of bucket, or bubbling of vent flow. Should observe relatively high inlet temperatures.	Loss of prime (low load, fluctuating pressure differences). Worn mechanism, valve or seat. Leaking internal seals/gaskets. See above - Any type of trap.	Dirt-plugged vent. Excessive differential Pressure. Worn, oversized seat. Body filled with dirt. Air bound. See above - Any type of trap.
Disc	Normal discharge intermittent. Should see flash. Should hear intermittent discharge, possibly clicking of disc on seat. Should observe relatively high inlet temperatures.	Worn seat, disc, or bonnet. Leaking internal seals/gaskets. Excessive backpressure. See above - Any type of trap.	Installed backward. Air Bound. See above - Any type of trap.
Impulse Control Flow	Normal discharge - intermittent with continuous flow between discharges. Should hear continuous and intermittent flow. Should read relatively high inlet temperature.	Worn internals. Excessive backpressure. Condensate load too small. See above - Any type of trap	Excessive wear in control cylinder. Excessive dirt in control orifice Also, see above - Any type of trap.

Courtesy of Keystone Yarway Corporation

WORKSHEET 1.1 Fuel Cost Comparison

1. Fuel Option A

$$\frac{\boxed{} \times \boxed{} \times \boxed{} \times \boxed{}}{\boxed{1,000}} = \boxed{}$$

Fuel Unit Cost ($/unit) Heating Value (Btu/unit) Fuel Efficiency Factor Combustion Efficiency

Fuel Cost ($/10^3 Btu)

2. Fuel Option B

$$\frac{\boxed{} \times \boxed{} \times \boxed{} \times \boxed{}}{\boxed{1,000}} = \boxed{}$$

Fuel Unit Cost ($/unit) Heating Value (Btu/unit) Fuel Efficiency Factor Combustion Efficiency

Fuel Cost ($/10^3 Btu)

Typical Fuel Efficiency Factors	
Coal	0.7 - 0.9
Gas	0.95
Oil	0.8 - 0.9
Solid Waste	0.5 - 0.7
Wood	0.6 - 0.8

Combustion Efficiency

Fuel	Boiler Size	
	Small	Large
Coal	0.70	0.80
Gas	0.75	0.85
Oil	0.70	0.80
Solid Waste	0.60	0.75
Wood	0.70	0.80

WORKSHEET 1.2 Steam Production Efficiency

1. Steam Generator Data

Steam Generation Rate (lb steam/hr): _____
Steam Temperature (^{o}F): _____
Steam Pressure (psia): _____
Fuel Use Rate (lb or gal per hour): _____
Fuel Heating Value (Btu/lb or gal): _____
Feedwater Temperature (^{o}F): _____

2. Steam-Fuel Ratio

$$\frac{\boxed{} \text{ Steam Generation Rate (lb/hr)}}{\boxed{} \times \boxed{}} = \boxed{}$$

Steam Generation
Rate (lb/hr)

Fuel Use Rate   X   Fuel Heating Value   Steam-Fuel Ratio
(lb/hr, gal/hr   (Btu/lb, Btu/gal,   (lb steam/Btu fuel)
or ft^3/hr)   or Btu/ft^3)

3. Production Efficiency

$$\boxed{} \times \left[\boxed{} - \boxed{} \right] = \boxed{}$$

Steam-Fuel Ratio   Enthalpy of   Enthalpy of   Efficiency
(lb steam/Btu fuel)   Vapor   Feedwater   (%)
(Btu/lb)

WORKSHEET 1.3 Estimating Required Boiler Blowdown

1. Make-Up Water Requirements

[ ]	-	[ ]	=	[ ]	
Steam Produced (lb/hr)		Condensate Returned (lb/hr)		Makeup Water Rate (lb/hr)	

2. Blowdown Requirements

$$\frac{\boxed{} \; \times \; \boxed{}}{\boxed{} \; - \; \boxed{}} = \boxed{}$$

Solids in Makeup Water (ppm)   X   Makeup Water Rate (lb/hr)

ASME Solids Limit (ppm)   -   Solids in Makeup Water (ppm)

Boiler Blowdown Rate (lb/hr)

ASME Recommended Limits for Solids in Boiler Water

Boiler Steam Pressure (psig)	Total Dissolved Solids (ppm)
0 - 300	3,500
301 - 450	3,000
451 - 600	2,500
601 - 750	2,000
751 - 900	1,500
901 - 1,000	1,200

WORKSHEET 1.4 Boiler Horsepower/Capacity Conversion

1. System Characteristics

Rated Boiler Horsepower: _____
Rated Boiler Capacity (lb/hr): _____
Feedwater Temperature (^{o}F): _____
Steam Pressure (psig): _____
Superheat Temperature (^{o}F): _____

2. Horsepower to Pounds per Hour Conversion

$$\frac{33{,}475 \quad \text{X} \quad \boxed{} \text{ Boiler hp}}{\boxed{} - \boxed{}} = \boxed{}$$

Enthalpy of Feedwater (Btu/lb)   Enthalpy of Steam (Btu/lb)   Capacity (lb/hr)

3. Pounds per Hour to Horsepower Conversion

$$\frac{\left[\, \boxed{} - \boxed{} \,\right] \quad \text{X} \quad \boxed{}}{\boxed{33{,}475}} = \boxed{}$$

Enthalpy of Feedwater (Btu/lb)   Enthalpy of Steam (Btu/lb)   Capacity (lb/hr)   Boiler hp

WORKSHEET 1.5 The Cost of Steam

1. Generation Cost

$$\frac{\boxed{}\;+\;\boxed{}\;+\;\boxed{}\;+\;\boxed{}\;+\;\boxed{}}{\boxed{}}\;=\;\boxed{}$$

Fuel Cost ($)   Labor Cost ($)   Water Cost ($)   Chemical Cost ($)   Maintenance Cost ($)

Steam Generated (1,000 lbs)

Generation Cost ($/1,000 lb)

2. Point of Use Steam Cost

$$\frac{\boxed{}\;\times\;\boxed{}}{\boxed{}}\;=\;\boxed{}$$

Generation Cost ($/1,000 lb)   Distribution Factor

In-Plant Use Factor

Point of Use Cost ($/1,000 lb)

WORKSHEET 1.6 The Cost of Steam Leaks

1. Cost of Leaks

$$\frac{\boxed{} \text{ X } \boxed{} \text{ X } \boxed{}}{\boxed{1,000}} = \boxed{}$$

Leak Rate (lb/hr) X Point of Use Steam Cost ($/1,000 lb) X Hours Factor

Cost ($)

Hours Factor		
Time Interval	**Hours/Day**	**Factor**
Day	8 16 24	8 16 24
Week *	8 16 24	56 112 168
Month *	8 16 24	240 480 720
Year *	8 16	2,920 5,840

* Note: The hour factors given in the table for weekly, monthly, and annual calculations assume 7 days per week operation. If the steam system is used only 5 days per week, multiply the factors given in the table by 0.71.

WORKSHEET 1.7 Calculating Condensate Loads

1. Steam Lines

$$\frac{\boxed{} \times \boxed{} \times \boxed{}}{\boxed{}} = \boxed{}$$

Condensate (lbs/100 ft)   Pipe Length (100 ft)   Safety Factor

Insulation Factor

Condensate (lbs/hr)

2. Heating Water With Steam

$$\frac{\boxed{} \times \boxed{} \times \boxed{}}{\boxed{2}} = \boxed{}$$

Water Flow (gpm)   Temp. Rise   Safety Factor

Condensate (lbs/hr)

3. Heating Air With Steam

$$\frac{\boxed{} \times \boxed{} \times \boxed{}}{\boxed{900}} = \boxed{}$$

Air Flow (cfm)   Temp. Rise   Safety Factor

Condensate (lbs/hr)

4. Heating Air With Steam Convectors/Radiators

$$\frac{\boxed{2} \times \boxed{} \times \boxed{} \times \boxed{}}{\boxed{}} = \boxed{}$$

Area (sq ft)   Temp. Difference   Safety Factor

Latent Heat (Btu/lb)

Condensate (lbs/hr)

WORKSHEET 1.8 Steam Main Condensate Loads During Start-Up

A. Supervised Start-Up

$$\frac{\boxed{} \times \boxed{} \times \boxed{}}{\boxed{}} = \boxed{}$$

Warmup Load (lbs/100 ft) X Main Length (100 ft) X Safety Factor

Insulation Factor

Condensate Load (lbs/hr)

B. Unsupervised Start-Up

$$\frac{\boxed{} \times \boxed{} \times \boxed{60} \times \boxed{}}{\boxed{}} = \boxed{}$$

Condensate (lbs/hr-100 ft) X Main Length (100 ft) X 60 X Safety Factor

Heat-Up Time (minutes)

Condensate Load (lbs/hr)

Chapter 2

HOW TO OPERATE AND MAINTAIN CENTRAL CHILLED WATER EQUIPMENT AND DISTRIBUTION SYSTEMS

This chapter examines chilled water generation and distribution equipment typically found in central cooling systems. Material presented in this chapter can be used to estimate solutions to problems ranging from sizing central cooling equipment to improving the performance of specific pieces of equipment.

TYPES OF REFRIGERANTS

Refrigerants are the working fluids of air conditioning and refrigeration systems. Their purpose is to absorb heat by evaporation in one location, transport it to another location through the application of external work, then release it through condensation.

There is a wide range of commercially available refrigerants suitable for use in an equally wide range of applications. These refrigerants vary in chemical composition, boiling points, freezing points, critical temperatures, flammability, toxicity, chemical stability, chemical reactiveness, and cost. Selection of a particular refrigerant depends on the application and characteristics required. In most cases, the choice will be a compromise between different properties.

The different refrigerants are identified by a numbering system. Figure 2.1 lists the American Society of Heating, Refrigerating, and Air-Conditioning Engineers refrigerant numbering system, their chemical names and formulas, and their boiling points. Use the figure to identify the particular refrigerant in use.

In general, refrigerants with numbers less than 500 are classified as halocarbons. Refrigerants in the 500 series are azeotropes. Azeotropes are solutions that contain at least two chemical components that boil at the same pressure without undergoing a change in chemical composition. Six-hundred series refrigerants include hydrocarbons with oxygen, carbon, sulfur, or nitrogen compounds. Seven-hundred series refrigerants are inorganic compounds. Refrigerants whose numbers are greater than 1,000 are unsaturated hydrocarbons. One exception to these generalizations is refrigerant 500 which contains 26.2 percent of refrigerant 152 and 73.8 percent of refrigerant 12. Although this refrigerant is classified as an azeotrope, it is essentially in a class by itself.

The three most commonly used refrigerants in facility air conditioning and refrigeration systems are refrigerants 12, 22, and 502.

HOW TO ESTIMATE THE SIZE OF CENTRAL CHILLERS

The proper sizing of a central chilled water plant requires a detailed analysis of the cooling loads that will exist during peak cooling periods. Such an analysis is critical to the performance of the system, as a central plant that is undersized will not be able to meet cooling requirements during these peak periods. Similarly, a central plant that is oversized will not operate at peak efficiency.

There are a number of techniques used to accurately determine the peak cooling loads. Most are based on hourly load calculations, completed either manually or by computer, for all of the facilities being air conditioned during several peak cooling days that occur during the year. While these techniques give very accurate results in sizing systems, they are time consuming and are overkill for planning purposes.

Load range guides can be used to estimate the size of central cooling equipment for planning purposes and for a preliminary estimate of system size. While these guides do provide reasonable results, do not use them for the actual sizing of a new system.

Use Worksheet 2.1 to develop an estimate of the central cooling equipment size. The chiller size is based on estimated values for five components of the cooling load. These load components include heat gains through the walls and roof, through windows, and from introducing ventilation air into the conditioned space generated by the internal lighting systems, from the building occupants, and from equipment located within the space.

Use the worksheet as follows:

Step 1. Enter the total exterior wall area (excluding glass area) in thousands of square feet for the building in section #1 of the worksheet.

Step 2. Enter the total roof area in thousands of square feet in section #1.

Step 3. Add the wall and roof areas and multiply by the conversion factor of 0.4 to determine the walls and roof cooling load. Enter the value in section #1 of the worksheet.

Step 4. Enter the window area in thousands of square feet in section #2 of the worksheet.

Step 5.   The heat gain through windows depends on the solar transmissivity of the glass used. Typically it ranges from a value of 0.25 to 1.0 tons per thousand square feet. If the building has clear glass, use a value of 1.0. If the glass has a reflective film coating, use a value of 0.25. Most tinted glass will fall in the range of 0.50 to 0.75 depending on how dark the color is. Enter the window factor value that most closely matches the type of glass used in the building in section #2.

Step 6.   Multiply the window area by the window factor to determine the window cooling load. Enter the value in section #2 of the worksheet.

Step 7.   Enter the total floor area in thousands of square feet in section #3.

Step 8.   To provide fresh air for building occupants, outside air is introduced into the building at a set rate. How much air is introduced depends on the nature of the activities being performed in the occupied space. Typically the values range from 25 to 750 cfm per thousand square feet. Figure 2.2 lists typical ventilation rates for a number of different facilities. Select the facility type that most closely matches your particular installation. For mixed use facilities, use a best guess at an average ventilation rate based on the mix of activities being performed in the space. Enter the average value for the building in section #3.

Step 9.   Multiply the floor area by the ventilation rate and the factor 2.5 to determine the ventilation cooling load. Enter the value in section #3 of the worksheet.

Step 10.   Enter the total floor area in thousands of square feet in section #4.

Step 11.   If the average lighting load is known, enter the value in watts per square foot in section #4. If the value is not know, estimate it using Figure 2.2. The figure lists a range of lighting levels for various facilities. Select the type of facility that most closely matches your particular application, and select the lighting load from the range given for each facility type. Enter the value in section #4.

Step 12.   Multiply the floor area by the lighting load and the value 0.28 to determine the lighting cooling load. Enter the value in section #4 of the worksheet.

Step 13.   Enter the total floor area in thousands of square feet in section #5.

Step 14.   Figure 2.2 lists typical occupancy load factors in tons per 1,000 square feet for various types of facilities. Select the type of facility that most closely matches yours and enter the value in section #5.

Step 15. Multiply the floor area by the load factor to determine the occupant cooling load. Enter the value in section #5 of the worksheet.

Step 16. Enter the total floor area in thousands of square feet in section #6.

Step 17. The cooling load due to equipment located within the building typically ranges from two to seven watts per square foot of floor area. Offices with computers generally are in the range of three to five watts per square foot. Estimate the building equipment load factor and enter the value in watts per square foot in section #6.

Step 18. Multiply the floor area by the equipment factor and the value 0.28 to determine the equipment cooling load and enter the value in section #6 of the worksheet.

Step 19. The total cooling load that must be met by the central cooling plant is the sum of the load components. Enter the walls and roof cooling load from section #1, the window cooling load from section #2, the ventilation cooling load from section #3, the lighting cooling load from section #4, the occupant cooling load from section #5, and the equipment cooling load from section #6 into section #7. Add the component cooling loads to determine the total cooling load and enter the value in section #7 of the worksheet.

This value represents a first approximation of the size of the central chiller. It can be used to estimate the space requirement for the central plant as well as to provide an initial estimate of the plant requirements.

HOW TO ESTIMATE THE ELECTRICAL COST OF REFRIGERATION

There are many factors that influence how much energy is used in operating a facility's air conditioning system: the type of building construction; the type of mechanical systems installed; the operating condition of those mechanical systems; how the facility is operated; and the climate in which the facility is located. If a detailed study is required of the annual energy operating costs for an existing or a proposed system, there are a number of computer models that can calculate hour-by-hour energy use calculations for an entire year. If a detailed study is not required, however, such as in budgeting of energy costs for a proposed system, use the following method which is not as accurate but does provide reasonable energy cost estimates without the complexity.

Use Worksheet 2.2 to estimate the annual energy cost of providing air conditioning to a facility. Use the worksheet as follows:

Step 1. Enter the full-load capacity of the chiller in tons in section #1 of the worksheet. This capacity is the rating given to the chiller by the manufacturer for standard operating conditions and is listed on the chiller name plate. If two or more chillers are used simultaneously to meet the building cooling loads during peak cooling periods, sum the full-load capacities of each separate chiller to get the combined full-load capacity.

Step 2.   Enter the full-load kW per ton rating for electrically driven chillers in section #1 of the worksheet. This rating is provided by the manufacturer for standard operating conditions. Typically, the full-load rating ranges between 0.60 and 1.5 kW per ton. For steam absorption chillers, enter the full-load rating in 1,000 lbs of steam per ton. Typically this value is between 0.012 and 0.018 thousand pounds of steam per ton.

Step 3.   The equivalent full-load operating hours is used to estimate the amount of cooling required during a season for a facility. Figure 2.3 lists a range of equivalent full-load hours for air conditioning systems for a number of cities. Select the city closest to your location. The range listed for each location is for typical construction with average occupancy for eight to ten hours per day. If your facility is used eight hours per day, five days per week, select a number towards the lower portion of the range listed. If the facility is used 16 hours per day, or has a high occupancy load, select a value towards the top of the range given. Enter the value in section #1.

Step 4.   The energy cost rate for electrically driven chillers is the energy use charge in dollars per kWh from the facility's electrical bill. It does not include any demand charges. Determine the electrical rate from the utility bill or rate schedule and enter the value in section #1. The energy cost rate for steam absorption chillers is the energy charge in dollars per 1,000 pounds of steam delivered to the chiller. Enter the value in section #1.

Step 5.   The peak demand rate in dollars per kW load is the highest demand rate charge that is in effect for the facility. It can vary with season, time of day, or both. The demand rate that you need to use is the highest rate in effect during the cooling season as defined in the utility rate structure. Determine the peak demand rate and enter the value in section #1.

Step 6.   Enter the chiller capacity, chiller rating, equivalent full-load hours, and energy rate from section #1 of the worksheet into section #2.

Step 7.   Multiply the values in section #2 to determine the annual energy cost for operating the air conditioning system. Enter the value in section #2. For steam driven absorption chillers, this value is the total annual energy cost. Do not complete sections #3 and #4 for steam absorption chillers.

Step 8.   Enter the chiller capacity, chiller rating and peak demand from section #1 of the worksheet into section #3.

Step 9.	Multiply the values in section #3 to determine the monthly peak demand charge. Enter the value in section #3.
Step 10.	Enter the annual energy cost calculated in section #2 into section #4.
Step 11.	The peak demand charge for the facility will be increased during those months when the air conditioning is used heavily. To calculate the increased costs for these months, a multiplication factor is added to the monthly peak demand charge. That multiplication factor typically ranges from three to six, depending on the length of the air conditioning season. For your climate and how long the air conditioning system is typically operated, enter a multiplication factor (3 - 6) into section #4.
Step 12.	Enter the monthly peak demand charge calculated in section #3 into section #4.
Step 13.	Multiply the multiplication factor by the monthly peak demand charge and add the annual energy cost to determine the total annual cost of energy for operating the air conditioning system.

Note: Depending on the particular utility rate structure in effect, the total demand charges may equal or exceed the annual energy cost for the system.

THE CHARACTERISTICS OF CENTRAL CHILLERS

The performance of central air conditioning systems is greatly influenced by a number of operating characteristics that are independent of the equipment itself. To provide a uniform means of comparing system and component performance, standards have been established by which the units are rated. For example, the standard conditions under which chillers are rated are as follows:

Chilled water entering temperature:	54°F
Chilled water leaving temperature:	44°F
Condenser water entering temperature:	85°F
Condenser water leaving temperature:	95°F

When evaluating central chilled water systems and components, always make certain that the comparison is made on the basis of standard operating conditions. Systems or components that are rated at other than standard conditions may provide misleading performance characteristics with respect to other systems.

Major Types of Chillers

There are four basic types of chillers commonly used in facilities today: reciprocating; centrifugal; rotary or screw; and absorption. While all types can be used to provide chilled water for air conditioning, generally one type is best suited for a given application. Selection of a chiller type is based on several criteria, including the type and capacity of power available, energy efficiency, first costs, available space, required capacity, and maintenance requirements. Figure 2.4 gives chiller characteristics for the four primary chiller types. Use the figure to help match the type of chiller selected to the particular application.

Figure 2.5 shows the basic components of reciprocating, centrifugal, and rotary chiller systems. Their refrigeration effect is based on a vapor compression cycle that derives its energy from a rotary engine or motor. The cycle is efficient and typically results in chiller capacities in excess of one ton-hour of cooling per kW of electrical energy input.

Low pressure, refrigerant vapor is introduced to the compressor where the mechanical energy from the motor converts it to a high temperature, high pressure vapor. Heat is rejected from the refrigerant to the atmosphere, usually through a condenser water circuit, resulting in a moderate temperature, high pressure flow of refrigerant. The expansion valve causes the refrigerant to expand to a low pressure, low temperature mixture of liquid and vapor. Heat is picked up in the evaporator from the building's chilled water circuit, converting the refrigerant to a medium temperature vapor where it is then reintroduced into the compressor.

A characteristic of the operation of central chillers is a variance in operating efficiency with changing load. How much the efficiency varies depends on the type of chiller. Figure 2.6 shows the relationship between cooling load and electrical load for reciprocating, centrifugal, and rotary chillers. It can be seen from the figure that if chillers are to operate at peak efficiency, they need to be closely matched to the building load.

Reciprocating Chillers

Reciprocating chillers are positive displacement compressors. An electric motor-driven crankshaft powers one or more pistons in cylinders equipped with suction and discharge valves. R-22 is the most commonly used refrigerant.

Typical capacities for reciprocating chillers range from 10 to 200 tons, with most economical operation in the 20 to 100 ton range. Chiller efficiencies average between 0.84 and 1.00 kW per ton for most applications. Efficiency increases with machine capacity up to approximately 120 tons, as shown in Figure 2.7.

Reciprocating chillers can be of open or hermetically sealed construction. In open construction units, the motor and compressor sections are housed separately. Power is transmitted from the motor to the compressor section by direct drive or by a v-belt drive assembly. In general, open construction results in longer equipment life and lower maintenance requirements and costs than for hermetically sealed units.

Hermetically sealed units are the most commonly used reciprocating chillers. In these units, the motors are connected directly to the crankshaft assembly and sealed in a common enclosure. Refrigerant flowing through the chiller is directed through the motor for cooling, thus permitting the use of smaller motors for a given load.

Open units are typically ten percent more efficient than their hermetically sealed equivalent. This increase in efficiency is a result of the way in which heat is rejected from the motor. In hermetically sealed units, the motor's heat is carried away by the refrigerant, while in open units it is rejected to the atmosphere. It is this additional heat introduced into the refrigerant that results in an overall decrease in efficiency.

When compared to other chiller types, reciprocating chillers offer the advantage of a low initial cost for units under 700 tons. Their high condensing temperature makes them suitable for use with air cooled condensers or in low temperature refrigeration applications. Through the use of multiple machines, it is easy to match operating machine capacity to a varying load.

Reciprocating chillers are not readily suited for applications needing more than 200 tons cooling capacity. The space required and the initial costs for larger capacity units exceed that of other chiller types. Energy costs also are higher for large capacity units in comparison to other types of chillers.

Reciprocating chillers also generate excessive noise and vibration, requiring special precautions to isolate the units from the facility in which they are housed.

One of the major disadvantages of reciprocating chillers is their high maintenance requirement in comparison to other chiller types. Reciprocating chillers have more moving parts than centrifugal or rotary chillers, resulting in a greater need for wear- related maintenance activities.

Centrifugal Chillers

Centrifugal chillers are variable volume displacement machines. A drive unit (electric motor or steam turbine) powers one or more rotating impellers that use centrifugal force to compress the refrigerant vapor. Inlet vanes on the impeller section are used to control capacity down to approximately 25 percent of rated maximum capacity.

Capacities for centrifugal chillers range from 90 to 10,000 tons, with most units in use in the 150 to 300 ton range. Chiller efficiencies average between 0.60 and 0.70 kW per ton. Efficiency increases with machine capacity up to approximately 1,200 tons, as shown in Figure 2.8.

The higher capacities of centrifugal chillers make them most suitable for operation with water cooled condensers. Common refrigerants include R-113, R-11, R-500, and R-12. Although centrifugal chillers are available in both open and hermetically sealed configurations, hermetic units are the most common. Hermetic units are typically five to seven percent lower in efficiency than open units.

One of the reasons for the widespread application of centrifugal chillers is their low energy cost per ton in comparison to other chiller types, particularly for larger capacity machines. The physical size of large capacity machines is also small in comparison to reciprocating machines. The use of a rotary motion drive minimizes vibrations generated by the unit. However, the high speed centrifugal drive generates a relatively high level of high-pitched noise that can interfere with spaces located close to the chiller.

Although centrifugal chillers can provide stable operation from 25 to 100 percent of their rated capacity, operation at less than 25 percent rated capacity can cause surging and damage. Surging problems can be reduced or eliminated through the use of special controls, such as hot gas bypass, but use of these controls significantly reduces their operating efficiency.

Excessive electrical demand levels and charges can result from the unregulated start-up of larger capacity centrifugal chillers. Depending on the electrical rate structure in effect for the facility, these demand charges can more than offset the increased efficiency of the chiller over the air conditioning season.

Rotary Chillers

Rotary or screw chillers are positive displacement compressors. An electric motor drives two machined rotors, producing compression as the grooved lobes on the male and female rotors mesh. The rotary design results in fewer moving parts than for other chiller types. Units are available in open and hermetically sealed construction. The most commonly used refrigerant in rotary chillers is R-22.

Capacities for rotary chillers range from 20 to 2,000 tons, with most applications operating in the range of 175 to 750 tons. Chiller efficiencies average between 0.70 and 0.80 kW per ton for most applications, making them more efficient than reciprocating chillers for most applications, but slightly less efficient than centrifugal chillers. Typical full-load efficiencies are shown in Figure 2.9.

Rotary chillers offer the advantage of compact size and low weight. Their high compression ratios and few moving parts result in units that are smaller and lighter than comparable reciprocating or centrifugal units. Their rotary motion also results in quieter, smoother operation.

The relatively high operating temperatures of rotary chillers result in a high heat of rejection, making them well suited for air cooled applications.

Loads can easily be controlled down to ten percent of rated capacity. Since the chillers are positive displacement compressors, they do not encounter surging problems frequently associated with centrifugal chillers operating at low loads. Unlike reciprocating chillers, liquid refrigerant entering the compressor of a rotary chiller will not result in damage to the compressor. Part load efficiencies of rotary chillers typically exceed those of other chiller types.

The primary disadvantage of rotary chillers is their high first cost in smaller capacity machines. For loads up to approximately 350 tons, the reciprocating chiller is less expensive to install.

Absorption Chillers

While other types of compressors are driven by some form of mechanical energy, absorption chillers are driven by heat energy. Figure 2.10 shows the major components of an absorption chiller. A heat source, such as steam or hot water, vaporizes a refrigerant and separates it from the absorbent in the system. As the refrigerant vapor passes through the condenser section of the chiller, heat is transferred to the condenser water and the refrigerant is condensed. The refrigerant in the form of a relatively high-pressure liquid enters a low-pressure evaporator, expanding and vaporizing the refrigerant. The low-pressure refrigerant vapor is absorbed into the absorbent solution and pumped back to the generator. Chilled water is produced in the low-pressure evaporator.

For most building applications, water cooled absorption chillers use water as the refrigerant and lithium bromide as the absorbent. In air cooled applications, ammonia is the refrigerant and water is used as the absorbent. Water-ammonia machines have also been used in applications requiring low temperature brine for refrigeration.

Capacities for absorption chillers range from 100 to 5,000 tons, with most machines operating in the 300 to 500 ton range. Thermal efficiencies of the machines range between 11,000 and 19,000 Btu of heat input per ton-hour of cooling produced.

Absorption chillers are available in either direct or indirect-fired models. Direct-fired models use natural gas or heating oil as the heat source. The more common indirect models use low-pressure steam or hot water as the heat source.

The primary advantage of absorption chillers is their use of a power source other than electricity. Absorption chillers, since they derive their cooling energy from a heat source, draw a small fraction, typically ten percent, of the electricity required by other types of chillers. This use of an alternative energy source is particularly important in facilities where additional electrical capacity is not available, or where the additional electrical demand charges resulting from an electrically driven chiller would be too expensive.

Absorption chillers also offer the advantage of being powered by a wide range of heat sources, including process steam, waste heat, high temperature cooling water, and solar energy. If the facility has a heat source that it must dispose of, absorption offers a means of achieving low-cost cooling while reducing the exhaust temperature of the waste heat.

The three major disadvantages associated with absorption chillers are their low thermal efficiencies, their high maintenance requirements, and their high first cost.

The low thermal efficiency results in greater energy input requirements per ton of cooling produced than for electrically driven chillers. Typically, the energy costs (excluding demand charges) for operating the absorption chiller are 25 to 50 percent higher than those for electrical chillers. This low thermal efficiency gets even lower under part load operation, as shown in Figure 2.11.

Although there are few moving parts in absorption chillers, maintenance requirements are somewhat higher than for electrically driven chillers. The most serious of these can occur if the lithium bromide solution becomes crystallized. Crystallization occurs when a concentrated solution of lithium bromide is sub-cooled as a result of the absorber operating for an extended period of time under low load, the loss of the heat source, or a rapid drop in the condenser water temperature. Decrystallization is a slow process that, depending on the size of the absorber, may take several days to complete.

Absorption chillers are more expensive to install than electrically driven chillers. First costs run 10 to 20 percent greater because of the costs of both the absorber itself and the larger supporting components. For example, cooling towers and condenser water pumps serving absorption chillers are significantly larger than those required for equally sized electrically driven chillers.

For these reasons, absorption chillers are used primarily in applications where waste heat is readily available or where electrical demand charges are such that they offset the additional installation and operating costs.

Ways to Improve Central Chiller Efficiency

Since central chillers represent such a large energy load within a facility, attention has been focused on improving their operating efficiency. Among the techniques used to increase efficiency are improving heat transfer within the chiller by reducing scale, chilled and condenser water temperature reset, variable speed chiller drives, ice storage, heat recovery, evaporative cooling, and free cooling. Not all techniques are suitable for use with all chiller types or applications.

How to Keep Heat Transfer Surfaces Clean

During normal operation, a number of factors combine to reduce the operating efficiency of chillers by disturbing the heat transfer surfaces, primarily on the condenser water side of the chiller. There are four major causes for this disruption; scaling, fouling, biological growth, and corrosion.

SCALING. Scaling is the process by which soluble salts in the water are precipitated and deposited on heat transfer surfaces. The most common of these is calcium carbonate. Calcium carbonate is formed when calcium bicarbonate in the water breaks down as a result of the heating of the water while passing through the condenser side of the chiller. How rapidly it forms depends on the temperature rise in the condenser and the level of calcium hardness of the water.

Scaling can be controlled by one of three ways:

➤ removing the calcium bicarbonate from the makeup water prior to use,

➤ chemically treating the water to keep the calcium bicarbonate in suspension,

➤ treating the water with chemicals that react with the calcium bicarbonate to form a sludge that settles out of the water instead of forming a hard scale that attaches itself to heat transfer surfaces.

FOULING. Fouling is the process by which suspended solids in the water drop out of suspension and accumulate on heat transfer surfaces. These solids may occur within the water naturally, or may be introduced as a result of the operation of the system. Typical suspended solids include silt, rust, bacteria, and fibers from cooling tower fill material. The rate of fouling accelerates as water temperature increases or as water velocity decreases.

Fouling is controlled through:

➤ filtering,

➤ treating the water with chemicals,

➤ bleeding off and replacing a percentage of the water to limit the concentration of suspended solids.

Even with those measures, it is still necessary to open the system periodically and clean the condenser tubes by chemical or mechanical means.

BIOLOGICAL GROWTH. Biological growth can also greatly reduce the effectiveness of heat transfer surfaces. Two classes of growths need to be controlled: large and microscopic organisms. Large organisms include weeds and other floating debris that enter the system through the cooling tower. Microscopic organisms, such as algae, fungi, or bacteria, exist in the form of slime-like materials that adhere to heat transfer surfaces, often blocking tubes within chillers. In addition to reducing heat transfer, microscopic organisms can form corrosive byproducts that attack surfaces.

Biological growth is controlled through the use of screens added to tower sumps and chemical water treatment. If the biological growth becomes extensive, it is necessary to flush the system with chemicals to remove it.

CORROSION. Corrosion is the electrochemical process by which metal used in heat transfer surfaces deteriorates. Corrosion of the surface poses two problems to chiller operation. First, it reduces the heat transfer coefficient of the metal, resulting in less efficient operation. Second, corrosion eats away metal. Heat exchanger tubes used in chillers are typically less than 3/32 inches thick. It doesn't take corrosion long to completely eat through tube walls.

Corrosion is controlled primarily through the use of chemical water treatment that reduces the reactiveness of chemicals suspended in the water or coats the heat exchanger surface with a protective film. Corrosion can be removed by chemical or mechanical means.

Estimating the Savings Due to Decreased Fouling Factor

In order to operate at peak efficiency, all heat transfer surfaces in a chiller must be clean and free of deposits. Deposits on heat transfer surfaces result in thermal resistance, which in turn reduces the peak capacity of the chiller and increases the amount of compressor energy required to produce a given level of cooling.

Thermal resistance in a chiller's heat exchangers is measured in terms of its fouling factor. While new chillers typically operate with a fouling factor of 0.0002 or less, that factor rapidly increases with operation unless steps are taken to control it. A fouling factor of 0.0002 corresponds to a layer 0.002″ thick on the chiller's tubes. Most chiller manufacturers recommend limiting fouling to 0.005 or less (0.06″).

The reason why the fouling factor is so important to chiller operation is that even a small buildup can significantly reduce chiller performance. For example, if two identical chillers were operating, the first with a fouling factor of 0.00205 and the second with a fouling factor of 0.00230, the second chiller would require approximately 16 percent less energy to produce the same cooling.

Use Worksheet 2.3 to estimate for any water-cooled chiller the savings that can be achieved in a chiller system through the reduction of its fouling factor. Use the worksheet as follows:

Step 1.   Enter the full-load capacity of the chiller in tons in section #1 of the worksheet. This capacity is the rating given to the chiller by the manufacturer for standard operating conditions and is listed on the chiller name plate.

Step 2.   Enter the full-load kW per ton rating for electrically driven chillers in section #1 of the worksheet. This rating can be provided by the manufacturer for standard operating conditions. Typically, the full-load rating ranges between 0.60 and 1.5 kW per ton. For steam absorption chillers, enter the full-load rating in 1,000 lbs of steam per ton. Typically this value is between 0.012 and 0.018 thousand pounds of steam per ton.

Step 3.   The equivalent full-load operating hours is used to estimate the amount of cooling required during a season for a facility. Figure 2.3 lists a range of equivalent full-load hours for air conditioning systems for a number of cities. Select the city closest to your location. The range listed for each location is for typical construction with average occupancy for eight to ten hours per day. If your facility is used eight hours per day, five days per week, select a number towards the lower portion of the range listed. If the facility is used 16 hours per day, or has a high occupancy load, select a value towards the top of the range given. Enter the value in section #1.

Step 4.   The energy cost rate for electrically driven chillers is the energy use charge in dollars per kWh from the facility's electrical bill. It does not include any demand charges. Determine the electrical rate from the utility bill or rate schedule and enter the value in section #1. The energy cost rate for steam absorption chillers is the energy charge in dollars per 1,000 pounds of steam delivered to the chiller. Enter the value in section #1.

Step 5.   Enter the chiller capacity, chiller rating, equivalent full-load hours, and energy rate from section #1 of the worksheet into section #2 .

Step 6.   Multiply the chiller capacity by the chiller rating, the equivalent full-load hours, and the energy rate to determine the design annual energy cost for operating the chiller. This value assumes a standard fouling factor of 0.002. Enter the value in section #2.

Step 7.   Enter the design annual energy cost from section #2 into section #3.

Step 8.   Figure 2.12 shows the relationship between fouling factor and chiller efficiency based on the assumed design standard fouling factor of 0.002. Actual chiller fouling factor will deviate from this design standard. The amount of deviation depends on the level of maintenance performed on the chiller's condenser water system. While it is difficult to determine the actual fouling factor without measuring the thickness of the build-up on condenser tubes, several values can be assumed based on the level of maintenance performed. If the chiller's condenser water system has no or minimal water treatment, assume a fouling factor of 0.0030. If the system is operated with a good water treatment program, a tower water bleed-down system, and is cleaned on a regular basis, assume a fouling factor in the range of 0.00180 to 0.00210. Using Figure 2.12 for the fouling factor assumed, determine the efficiency loss over design conditions and enter the value as a decimal (0.0 - 0.30) in section #3.

Step 9.   Add the number one to the efficiency loss and multiply the sum by the design annual energy cost to determine the actual energy cost. Enter the value in section #3.

Step 10.   Enter the design annual energy cost from section #2 into section #4.

Step 11.   If you are implementing a maintenance program that includes semi-annual chiller tube cleaning, automatic water treatment, and tower water bleed-down, assume an improved fouling factor of 0.00180. If an automatic brush cleaning system is being installed in addition to a chemical maintenance program, assume an improved fouling factor of 0.0002. Using Figure 2.12, determine efficiency decrease from design conditions, and enter the value as a decimal (0.0 - 0.30) in section #4.

Step 12.   Add the number one to the efficiency loss and multiply the sum by the design annual energy cost to determine the improved annual energy cost. Enter the value in section #4.

Step 13.   Enter the actual annual energy cost from section #3 into section #5.

Step 14.   Enter the improved annual energy cost from section #4 into section #5.

Step 15.   Subtract the improved from the actual annual energy cost to determine the annual energy savings. Enter the value in section #5.

The savings produced by keeping the heat transfer surfaces clean in a chiller more than justifies the maintenance costs. Additional savings are realized through increased system performance and extended equipment life.

Estimating the Savings from Chilled Water Temperature Reset

The temperature of the chilled water supplied to a building is based on the capacity of the system and the maximum cooling load that must be met by the system. Over the years, chiller manufacturers and system design engineers have standardized on the use of set chilled water supply temperatures, typically 44°F. This supply temperature remains constant even though the load on the chiller varies and is below the maximum demand load approximately 95 percent of the time.

During periods of off-peak load operation, it is possible to meet the cooling loads imposed on the chilled water system with water temperatures in excess of 44°F. Raising chilled water supply temperatures offers the advantage of increased chiller efficiency. For example, a centrifugal chiller's efficiency is increased by nearly three percent by resetting the chilled water supply temperature from 44°F to 46°F. Figure 2.13 shows the typical efficiency increases by chiller type that can be expected through chilled water temperature reset.

A factor that must be considered when implementing chilled water temperature reset is the impact that it will have on space humidity conditions. If chilled water temperatures are raised too high, particularly on days when the humidity is high, the air conditioning system will not be able to adequately dehumidify the air being supplied to the space. Monitoring of humidity conditions in select areas will help prevent this condition.

Accurately estimating the annual energy savings that can be achieved through chilled water temperature reset requires a detailed analysis that takes into consideration, among other factors, how the load varies with outside temperature and humidity. In most cases, the analysis is completed by computer using hour-by-hour load calculations.

Use Worksheet 2.4 to complete a preliminary estimate of the savings that can be achieved through the use of chilled water temperature reset. Use the worksheet as follows:

Step 1.   Enter the full-load capacity of the chiller in tons in section #1 of the worksheet. This capacity is the rating given to the chiller by the manufacturer for standard operating conditions and is listed on the chiller name plate.

Step 2.   Enter the full-load kW per ton rating for electrically driven chillers in section #1 of the worksheet. This rating can be provided by the manufacturer for standard operating conditions. Typically, the full-load rating ranges between 0.60 and 1.5 kW per ton. For steam absorption chillers, enter the full-load 1,000 lbs of steam per ton rating. Typically this value is between 0.012 and 0.018 thousand pounds of steam per ton.

Step 3.   The equivalent full-load operating hours is used to estimate the amount of cooling required during a season for a facility. Figure 2.3 lists a range of equivalent full-load hours for air conditioning systems for a number of cities. Select the city closest to your location. The range listed for each location is for typical construction with average occupancy for eight to ten hours per day. If your facility is used eight hours per day, five days per week, select a number towards the lower portion of the range listed. If the facility is used 16 hours per day, or has a high occupancy load, select a value towards the top of the range given. Enter the value in section #1.

Step 4.   The energy cost rate for electrically driven chillers is the energy use charge in dollars per kWh from the facility's electrical bill. It does not include any demand charges. Determine the electrical rate from the utility bill or rate schedule and enter the value in section #1. The energy cost rate for steam absorption chillers is the energy charge in dollars per 1,000 pounds of steam delivered to the chiller. Enter the value in section #1.

Step 5.   Enter the chiller capacity, chiller rating, equivalent full-load hours, and energy rate from section #1 of the worksheet into section #2.

Step 6.   Figure 2.13 gives the seasonal average chiller efficiency increase by chiller type that can be achieved through chilled water temperature reset. Determine the maximum temperature at which chilled water will be supplied. For most applications, the maximum temperature will be between 50 and 52°F. For this temperature, and the type of chiller installed, determine the efficiency increase from the figure and enter the number as a decimal value (0 - 0.25) in section #2.

Step 7.   Section #3 of the worksheet gives a table of multiplication factors based on how many hours per day that a chiller is operated. This factor takes into consideration the percentage of time that the chilled water system will be operated at higher temperatures. Select the appropriate multiplication factor from the table and enter the value in section #2 of the worksheet.

Step 8.   Multiply the values in section #2 to determine the annual energy savings resulting from chilled water reset. Enter the value in section #2 of the worksheet.

When used aggressively, chilled water temperature reset can produce sufficient energy savings to pay for the investment in less than one year.

Estimating the Savings from Condenser Water Temperature Reset

Chiller manufacturers and system design engineers, in addition to developing systems to operate at a fixed chilled water supply temperature, operate them with a set design condenser water supply temperature. Tower fans and bypass valves are used to maintain this supply temperature as loads on the chiller and outside temperatures change.

Operating chillers at a constant condenser water supply temperature has been the accepted mode of operation for several reasons. First, it is widely used today because it has been widely used in the past. Operating at constant condenser water supply temperatures is also an accepted norm for manufacturers, designers, and operating engineers. In particular, there is a widespread belief that minimizing the operating hours of tower fans saves energy by reducing tower energy use. However, in a chiller system, cooling tower energy use (including pumps and fans) is typically ten percent of the overall system energy use. Saving tower fan energy is insignificant when compared to compressor energy savings.

A second factor that contributes to the practice of operating systems at constant temperature is the believed impact that varying temperatures will have on chiller performance and life. Operating a chiller at constant condenser water supply temperatures minimizes thermal stresses on the chiller's heat exchanger. A higher temperature also reduces the formation of scale on heat exchanger surfaces.

Thermal stresses will be increased by reducing condenser water supply temperatures, but there are no serious negative effects on the heat exchanger as long as those temperatures are maintained within the manufacturer's suggested operating range. The amount by which the temperatures can be reduced will vary with chiller type, but they can be reduced for all chillers. For example, absorption chillers are sensitive to condenser water temperatures. Too low a supply temperature can result in a salting-up of the chiller. However, few absorption chillers are required to operate with 85°F water.

Scaling may be a concern with lower condenser water temperatures, but it can be readily addressed with a water treatment program.

Use Worksheet 2.5 to calculate the energy savings that can be achieved through the use of condenser water temperature reset. Use the worksheet as follows:

Step 1.   Enter the full-load capacity of the chiller in tons in section #1 of the worksheet. This capacity is the rating given to the chiller by the manufacturer for standard operating conditions and is listed on the chiller name plate.

Step 2.   Enter the full-load kW per ton rating for electrically driven chillers in section #1 of the worksheet. This rating can be provided by the manufacturer for standard operating conditions. Typically, the full-load rating ranges between 0.60 and 1.5 kW per ton. For steam absorption chillers, enter the full-load 1,000 lbs of steam per ton rating. Typically this value is between 0.012 and 0.018 thousand pounds of steam per ton.

Step 3.   The equivalent full-load operating hours is used to estimate the amount of cooling required during a season for a facility. Figure 2.3 lists a range of equivalent full-load hours for air conditioning systems for a number of cities. Select the city closest to your location. The range listed for each location is for typical construction with average occupancy for eight to ten hours per day. If your facility is used eight hours per day, five days per week, select a number towards the lower portion of the range listed. If the facility is used 16 hours per day, or has a high occupancy load, select a value towards the top of the range given. Enter the value in section #1.

Step 4.   The energy cost rate for electrically driven chillers is the energy use charge in dollars per kWh from the facility's electrical bill. It does not include any demand charges. Determine the electrical rate from the utility bill or rate schedule and enter the value in section #1. The energy cost rate for steam absorption chillers is the energy charge in dollars per 1,000 pounds of steam delivered to the chiller. Enter the value in section #1.

Step 5.   Enter the chiller capacity, chiller rating, equivalent full-load hours, and energy rate from section #1 of the worksheet into section #2.

Step 6.   Figure 2.14 gives the seasonal average chiller efficiency increase by chiller type that can be achieved through condenser water temperature reset over a base temperature of 85°F. The actual temperature that can be achieved depends on the local climate and the chiller manufacturer's recommendations. In warm climates, the amount of reset might be limited to five degrees. In colder climates, the average reset might be as much as 15°F. Based on your local climate and the recommendations of the chiller manufacturer, select an average entering condenser water temperature. From Figure 2.14 for the entering condenser water temperature and the type of chiller determine the percent increase in efficiency. Enter the value as a decimal number (0 - 0.25) in section #2.

Step 7.   Section #3 of the worksheet gives a table of multiplication factors based on how many hours per day that a chiller is operated. This factor takes into consideration the percentage of time that the condenser water system will be operated at lower temperatures.

For the number of hours per day that the chiller will be operated, select the multiplication factor from the table and enter the value in section #2 of the worksheet.

Step 8.   Multiply the values in section #2 to determine the annual energy savings resulting from condenser water reset. Enter the value in section #2 of the worksheet.

Condenser water temperature reset, like chilled water temperature reset, can provide significant savings with a short payback period.

Estimating the Savings from Variable Speed Chiller Drives

Centrifugal chiller efficiency can be increased through the use of electronic variable speed controls. Centrifugal chillers operate at peak efficiency (minimum kW/ton) when they are fairly heavily loaded. Depending on the particular chiller design, this generally occurs at or above 75 percent of full-load capacity. However, the number of hours that the chiller actually operates in this range is low in comparison to the total number of operating hours. For example, chillers are sized to meet the largest cooling loads imposed on them during a cooling season, even though they may operate at full capacity for less than two percent of the time. This results in a chiller that generally operates at 75 percent capacity or less, more than 80 percent of the time. Since chiller efficiency decreases with decreasing load, chillers operate most of the time at below peak efficiency.

The reason why centrifugal chiller efficiency drops with decreasing load is the way in which the chiller's control system responds to decreasing loads. Centrifugal chillers regulate cooling capacity by closing prerotation vanes on the inlet to the compressor. These vanes restrict the flow of refrigerant to the compressor, thus reducing its capacity. While the kW draw of the chiller decreases with reduced refrigerant flow, the capacity of the chiller is reduced even quicker. This rapid fall off in chiller capacity is a result of the operation of the prerotation vanes.

Prerotation vanes are designed to induce a change in direction of refrigerant flow at full flow in the direction of the compressor's impeller rotation. As the vanes are closed in response to reduced cooling load on the chiller, their prerotation effects are reduced, thus resulting in a higher energy requirement on the compressor.

Variable speed drives do not suffer the losses associated with closing prerotation vanes. Instead of controlling capacity by closing the vanes and reducing refrigerant flow, these drives reduce the speed of the compressor. Prerotation vanes remain in the fully open position. Refrigerant flow is reduced by the lower compressor speed, but so is the power required to drive the compressor. The result is a chiller that at low load offers an increase in efficiency by as much as 50 percent over conventional prerotation vane controls. Figure 2.15 shows a comparison of operating efficiencies for prerotation vane controlled (constant speed) and variable speed controlled centrifugal chillers. It can be seen from the figure that the energy use per ton of cooling produced is much lower for variable speed chillers.

Variable speed centrifugal chillers offer the greatest savings in applications that require part-load cooling for a large number of hours during a year. Typical applications would include facilities that operate chillers 24 hours per day for four months or more. During this operating period, the variable speed chiller would be operating at higher efficiency than a constant speed unit at least 90 percent of the time.

In applications that use multiple centrifugal chillers, variable speed controls need to be installed on only one of the chillers. As the load varies, constant speed chillers can be operated at near full-load capacity, while the variable speed chiller is used to match the varying load.

Use Worksheet 2.6 to estimate the savings produced by the use of a variable speed centrifugal chiller in comparison to a constant speed chiller of the same size and kW per ton rating. Use the worksheet as follows:

Step 1.   Enter the full-load capacity of the chiller in tons in the System Data section of the worksheet. This capacity is the rating given to the chiller by the manufacturer for standard operating conditions and is listed on the chiller name plate.

Step 2.   Enter the full-load kW per ton rating of the chiller in the System Data section of the worksheet. This rating can be provided by the manufacturer for standard operating conditions. Typically, the full-load rating for centrifugal chillers ranges between 0.60 and 1.0 kW per ton.

Step 3.   The equivalent full-load operating hours is used to estimate the amount of cooling required during a season for a facility. Figure 2.3 lists a range of equivalent full-load hours for air conditioning systems for a number of cities. Select the city closest to your location. The range listed for each location is for typical construction with average occupancy for eight to ten hours per day. If your facility is used eight hours per day, five days per week, select a number towards the lower portion of the range listed. If the facility is used 16 hours per day, or has a high occupancy load, select a value towards the top of the range given. Enter the value in the System Data section.

Step 4.   The electrical rate in dollars per kWh is the energy use charge from the facility's electrical bill. It does not include any demand charges. Determine the electrical rate from the utility bill or rate schedule and enter the value in the System Data section.

Step 5.   Enter the chiller capacity, chiller rating, equivalent full-load hours, and electrical rate from the System Data section of the worksheet into the Annual Energy Savings section.

Step 6.   The bottom section of the worksheet gives a table of multiplication factors based on how many hours per day that a chiller is operated. This factor takes into consideration the percentage of time that the variable speed chiller will be operated at reduced speed and the efficiency increase that is achieved over constant speed operation. For the number of hours per day that the chiller will be operated, select the multiplication factor from the table and enter the value in the Annual Energy Savings section of the worksheet.

Step 7.   Multiply the values in the Annual Energy Savings section to determine the annual energy savings from operating the variable speed chiller. Enter the value in the Annual Energy Savings section of the worksheet.

This value represents the annual energy savings produced through the use of variable speed controls on a centrifugal chiller.

HOW TO USE ICE STORAGE TO REDUCE ELECTRICAL COSTS

The implementation of time-of-day rate structures by utility companies has resulted in significant increases in the cost of operating electrically driven air conditioning systems. Figure 2.16 presents a time-of-day rate structure in effect for a large institutional user. While the particular rate structures will vary by utility and by the type of customer connected, this particular structure can be used to illustrate the impact that time-of-day rates have on air conditioning costs and the potential benefits of ice storage systems.

In the rate structure presented in the figure, two separate rate schedules are in effect, one for the summer months and one for the winter months. During the summer months, electrical charges are broken down into three components: an energy charge; a production and transmission charge; and a distribution charge. The energy charge sets the cost per kilowatt-hour of electricity used during each of three periods based on the time of day. The difference between peak and off-peak rates is significant; in this example, the on-peak rate is two and one-half times the off-peak rate.

The production and transmission charges and the distribution charge make up the demand portion of the electrical bill. They are calculated based on the peak electrical load (demand) in kilowatts that the facility draws from the utility. While the distribution charge is based on the peak demand during the entire day, the peak production and transmission charge is based on the peak electrical demand during the on-peak billing period. However, in most commercial and institutional facilities, the two peaks occur at the same time; resulting in a demand charge in this example of $13.25 per kilowatt.

Unfortunately, this peak demand period occurs when the air conditioning load in the facility is reaching its maximum value. The resulting electrical load on the system produced by the chiller causes a significant increase in the cost of electricity. It is this high cost of electricity during periods of high cooling demand that has resulted in the increased application of ice storage systems.

Ice storage systems reduce the cost of operating air conditioning systems by shifting the electrical load from peak to off-peak hours. This shift produces two separate reductions in the cost of electricity. First, by operating the system during off-peak hours, the energy charge rate is reduced. Second, peak electrical demand for the facility is reduced. The two, depending on the particular rate schedule in effect, can combine to make ice storage a cost effective measure.

Figure 2.17 presents a schematic of a typical ice storage system. During intermediate and off-peak periods, the centrifugal chiller provides chilled water to the facility for air conditioning. During the off-peak period, a second chiller, typically a rotary unit, is operated to produce ice. This ice-producing chiller is shut down when the storage tank is fully charged, and before the on-peak period starts. During the on-peak period of the rate schedule, cold water is circulated between the ice bank and a high efficiency heat exchanger. The facility's chilled water system is circulated through the other side of the heat exchanger. The 32°F water from the ice bank cools the facility's chilled water supply to normal circulating temperatures of approximately 44°F.

When the ice storage is depleted, or when the on-peak period ends, the bypass valve is closed and chilled water is again generated by the centrifugal chiller. The rotary chiller is then started, and the ice storage system is recharged.

When to Use Ice Storage

Ice storage systems cannot be applied economically in all facilities; there are certain conditions that must be met first, such as:

1. There must be a time-of-day rate structure in effect for the facility. Ice storage systems save operating costs by shifting electrical loads from on-peak, high rate periods to off-peak, low rate periods. If the rate structure in effect does not offer a reduction for off-peak periods, the major cost benefit for ice storage will not be applicable.

2. The facility should have a cooling load profile that varies with the time of day. In an ideal application, it will be low in the morning until nine or ten o'clock, rise fairly rapidly between ten o'clock and noon, remain high for four to five hours in the afternoon with a peak occurring around three or four o'clock, and fall off rapidly around six o'clock in the evening. Night cooling loads would be low.

If these two conditions apply to a given facility further investigation of the suitability of an ice storage system is warranted. There are three areas that need to be investigated initially: the size of the potential ice storage system; the cost savings that would be produced by using the system; and the local utility rate structure that would be in effect when using the system.

How to Estimate the Size of an Ice Storage Tank

The largest single component in any ice storage system is the container or series of containers for the ice. In some applications, the physical size of the required storage system may make ice storage unfeasible.

Use Worksheet 2.7 to estimate the size of the storage tank required for an ice storage system. Use the worksheet as follows:

Step 1.   The size of the storage system depends on the total ton-hours of cooling that must be provided by the system during the on-peak demand billing period. This load can be determined several different ways. The most accurate method is by the use of Btu meters installed on the existing chiller. The load can also be estimated by recording the kWh used by the chiller during the on-peak demand period. If metering is not available, a computer load program can be used to estimate the total ton-hours of cooling produced. It is important in all three methods to measure or calculate the total ton-hours produced for the peak cooling load day of the year, and that the load be measured or calculated over the same hours that the on-peak demand rate is in effect. If the cooling load in ton-hours is known from the use of Btu meters or as the result of a computer load program, enter the value in ton-hours as the cooling load in section #1 and skip to step #5.

Step 2.   If the cooling load is to be estimated using measured kWh use by the chiller, enter the total kWh used during the on-peak demand period in section #1.

Step 3.   Enter the chiller rating in kWh per ton-hr in section #1.

Step 4.   Divide the chiller load by the chiller rating to determine the cooling load in ton-hours. Enter the value in section #1 of the worksheet.

Step 5.   Enter the cooling load from section #1 into section #2 of the worksheet.

Step 6.   The reserve capacity factor is used to increase the ice storage capacity to allow for load growth or to provide a margin of safety in system sizing. For most applications, it ranges from 1.10 to 1.25. A value of 1.0 would provide no reserve capacity. Determine the amount of reserve capacity required and enter the value in section #2.

Step 7.   Multiply the cooling load by the reserve capacity factor and the conversion factor of 13.1 to determine the storage capacity in gallons. Enter the value in section #2.

The worksheet gives an order of magnitude estimate of the storage system size required. It should be used only in determining the feasibility of applying an ice storage system given a set of physical constraints for a particular application. The final design storage size requires a detailed study of load characteristics of the facility and the system that will be using the ice.

How to Estimate the Savings from Ice Storage

Use Worksheet 2.8 to provide an estimate of the order of magnitude of savings that are associated with the use of an ice storage system. Use the worksheet as follows:

Step 1.   Enter the full-load capacity of the chiller in tons in the Installation Data section of the worksheet. This capacity is the rating given to the chiller by the manufacturer for standard operating conditions and is listed on the chiller name plate.

Step 2.   Enter the full-load kW per ton rating of the chiller in the Installation Data section of the worksheet. This rating can be provided by the manufacturer for standard operating conditions. Typically, the full-load rating for centrifugal chillers is between 0.60 and 1.0 kW per ton.

Step 3.   Enter the full-load kW per ton rating of the chiller that will be used to generate the ice. The rating that should be used for the chiller will be for producing brine at the temperature used in the manufacture of ice, typically 22 to 28°F, and at condensing temperatures that would be regularly experienced at night in the climate where the ice storage system is being installed.

Step 4.   The equivalent full-load operating hours is used to estimate the amount of cooling required during a season for a facility. Figure 2.3 lists a range of equivalent full-load hours for air conditioning systems for a number of cities. Select the city closest to your location. The range listed for each location is for typical construction with average occupancy for eight to ten hours per day. If your facility is used eight hours per day, five days per week, select a number towards the lower portion of the range listed. If the facility is used 16 hours per day, or has a high occupancy load, select a value towards the top of the range given. Enter the value in the Installation Data section.

Step 5.   Enter the summer on-peak energy charge for electricity. This is the straight kWh charge and does not include any demand charges.

Step 6.   Enter the summer off-peak energy charge for electricity. This is the straight kWh charge and does not include any demand charges.

Step 7.   Enter the summer on-peak demand charge for electricity.

Step 8.   Enter the full-load capacity for the conventional chiller, the full-load rating, the equivalent full-load hours, and the summer on-peak energy charge from the Installation Data section into section #2 of the worksheet.

Step 9.   Multiply the chiller capacity by the chiller rating, the equivalent full-load hours, the 0.75 daytime load factor, and the summer on-peak energy charge to determine the conventional system annual energy cost. Enter the value in section #2.

Step 10.   Enter the conventional chiller full-load capacity, the conventional chiller full-load rating, and the summer on-peak demand charge from the Installation Data section into section #3.

Step 11.   From the electricity rate structure in effect for the facility, determine the number of months that the summer demand rate is in effect. Enter the value in section #3.

Step 12.   Multiply the chiller capacity by the chiller rating, the summer on-peak demand charge, and the number of months that the peak demand rate is in effect to determine the conventional system annual demand cost. Enter the value in section #3.

Step 13.   Enter the conventional chiller full-load capacity, the ice storage system chiller full-load rating, the equivalent full-load hours, and the summer off-peak energy charge from the Installation Data section into section #4.

Step 14.   Multiply the chiller capacity by the chiller rating, the equivalent
                full-load hours, the 0.75 daytime load factor, and the summer off-
                peak energy charge to determine the ice storage system annual
                energy cost.

Step 15.   From section #2 enter the conventional system annual energy
                cost into section #5.

Step 16.   From section #3 enter the conventional system annual demand
                cost into section #5.

Step 17.   From section #4 enter the ice storage system annual energy cost
                into section #5.

Step 18.   Add the conventional system annual energy cost and the conven-
                tional system annual demand cost, and subtract the ice storage
                system annual energy cost to determine the annual ice system
                savings. Enter the value in section #5.

The savings calculated by using the worksheet will serve as an indicator of the
savings that can be achieved through the use of an ice storage system.

COOLING TOWERS

Early in their development, central air conditioning systems used city water to carry
away the heat generated within the chiller. City water, at 55 to 65°F readily absorbed
heat from the chiller and carried it down the drain. However, since these systems used
once-through cooling, the cost of supplying water soon became prohibitive.

Cooling towers were developed as an alternative to these early systems. Cooling
towers circulate water through the chiller to remove heat from the refrigerant, then
reject it to the atmosphere by means of heat and mass transfer.

Types of Cooling Towers

There are two basic types of cooling towers: natural and mechanical draft.
Natural draft towers are used primarily in operations where a large quantity of low
grade heat must be rejected to the atmosphere, such as in power plants. Air is moved
through the tower by natural convection arising from the difference in the entering
and leaving air densities.

The mechanical draft tower is the predominant type of cooling tower associated
with building air conditioning systems. It is available in forced and induced configurations. Forced draft towers use fans mounted in the air intake to force air through the
tower. Induced draft towers use propeller type fans located in the exhaust to draw air
through the tower.

Figure 2.18 shows the major components of a typical induced draft cooling tower.
Warm condenser water from the chiller is pumped to the tower where it is sprayed
over fill material and collected in the tower sump before being returned to the chiller.
Air enters the tower through a series of louvers and is passed over the fill material
where it picks up heat from the condenser water. Older towers use wooden slats as fill

material. Newer towers make use of a wide range of fill materials, including ceramic blocks, metal, and PVC. Conversion of older wooden fill to one of the newer materials can increase tower capacity by 10 to 20 percent.

Before being exhausted from the tower, the air is passed through the drift eliminator to reduce the amount of liquid water carried away from the tower. Under normal operating conditions, a well-designed and maintained drift eliminator can limit drift to less than one percent of the flow rate through the tower.

Sizing Cooling Towers

Cooling towers are matched to the size of the chiller and the ambient conditions under which they will be operating. Most operate with a constant water flow rate of three gallons per minute per ton of cooling load. Two rating factors that must be evaluated in selecting and operating the tower are its range and its approach. Range is the temperature difference between the entering and leaving water under design conditions. The most commonly used design practice is to size chillers for 95°F entering and 85°F leaving water, thus having a range of 10°F.

While the range is set for a tower at design conditions, the number of hours that the tower actually operates at design conditions is less than five percent of its total operating time. Rather than open the tower water bypass valve to maintain 85°F leaving water temperature, the temperature should be allowed to float. As the return water temperature falls, the efficiency of the chiller increases. For example, with centrifugal chillers, a drop in return water temperature from 85°F to 75°F results in a five percent increase in efficiency. Each chiller will have its lower limit for return water temperature, typically ten degrees above the condensing temperature.

Caution: Consult with the manufacturer of the particular chiller to determine the lowest safest return water temperature that can be employed.

Approach is how close the leaving water temperature is to the entering air wet bulb temperature under design conditions. Approach is an important value in determining the size of the tower. For example, decreasing the approach from 15°F to 7.5°F doubles the size of a tower for a given cooling load.

During normal operation, it is necessary to add water to the tower to replace water loss from drift and evaporation. An additional volume of water must be constantly bled from the tower in order to help control the build-up of solids as a result of evaporation. The combined effects of blowdown, drift, and evaporation losses result in the need to replace approximately three to five percent of the flow rate through the tower.

Air-Cooled Condensers

An alternative to the cooling tower is the air-cooled condenser. In systems using the air-cooled condenser, the refrigerant is piped directly into a heat exchanger where heat is removed by blowing air over the coils. With heat being rejected directly to the air from the refrigerant, there is no intermediate water loop as is the case with cooling towers.

Systems that use air-cooled condensers do require more energy to operate than their water-cooled counterparts, but there are a number of applications where they are readily employed. In general, systems under 300 tons are suitable for air-cooled condensers. While energy costs might be 10 to 20 percent higher for air-cooled systems, when the cost of the water, chemicals, and maintenance are factored in, particularly when there is no in-house maintenance staff, air-cooled condensers become an attractive alternative to cooling towers. Figures 2.19 and 2.20 list the advantages and disadvantages of both systems. Use the figures as a guide in selecting the type of system to be used in a particular application.

CHILLED WATER SYSTEM MAINTENANCE REQUIREMENTS

Maintenance strategies for central chilled water equipment range from that of a highly organized preventive maintenance program to one based on the philosophy that if it isn't broken, don't fix it. Of the two, the preventive maintenance program is the lowest cost in the long run. While simply doing just enough to keep equipment running has the appearance of lower costs, the true costs of such an approach are not so obvious.

Maintenance costs go far beyond the actual labor and material costs of the maintenance program to include the impact of maintenance or lack thereof on equipment life, energy costs, operating costs, and interruption of services. As a rule of thumb, the cost of repairs to central chilled water equipment typically runs ten times what it would have been to maintain the equipment through preventive maintenance. When one figures in the cost of the downtime resulting from the equipment failure, this factor grows even further.

In addition to increased repair costs, lack of proper maintenance on central chilled water equipment has significant implications on the operating efficiency of the equipment. The chiller is typically the single largest user of energy within a given facility. Chiller controls operating one degree out of proper calibration result in a decrease in operating efficiency of two to three percent. A build-up of scale of only 0.015 inches in the condenser increases chiller energy use by approximately ten percent. A cooling tower control system that is out of calibration and returns condenser water to the chiller at five degrees above the desired return temperature results in a five to ten percent increase in chiller energy use.

While the preventive maintenance program must be matched to the equipment and the application based on the level of reliability and efficiency desired, all programs have two common elements: periodic inspection and scheduled completion of certain maintenance activities. These maintenance activities are scheduled to be performed on a regular basis, such as daily, weekly, monthly, and annually. In addition, there will be several tasks, such as the scheduled cleaning of chiller condenser tubes, that must be performed on a regular basis of one every three to five years based on the conditions under which the chiller is operated.

Maintenance Tasks

The tasks required for chillers varies with the type of chiller. Use Figure 2.21 to identify the recommended minimum maintenance activities for centrifugal chillers, Figure 2.22 for rotary chillers, Figure 2.23 for reciprocating chillers, and Figure 2.24 for absorption chillers. The figures represent the minimum level of maintenance required for a standard installation. Additional maintenance tasks may be needed based on manufacturer's requirements and application factors. For example, chillers installed in health care or computer facilities with year-round critical cooling loads may require more frequent or additional maintenance tasks. Consult with the chiller manufacturer to determine the actual level of maintenance required for the application.

Cooling Tower Maintenance Requirements

Cooling towers are a relatively high maintenance item as a result of the operation that they perform and the environment in which they operate. For example, the efficiency of cooling towers depends to a great extent on the ability to keep surfaces within the tower clean and free of scale, dirt, and biological growths while operating in a warm, moist environment. The conditions under which a cooling tower is expected to operate are the very factors that result in rapid deterioration of mechanical and electrical equipment.

Deterioration of a cooling tower impacts the entire chilled water system. To a great extent, the condition of the tower determines the operating efficiency of the system. Towers that do not provide adequate heat transfer to the atmosphere result in increased energy requirements for the chiller. Dirt, corrosion, and biological growth within the tower are easily transferred to the chiller, collecting on the sides of the condenser water tubes and reducing their overall efficiency.

Cooling towers can be kept in good operating condition only through a comprehensive preventive maintenance program that combines regular inspections with maintenance activities that are performed on a regular basis. Use Worksheet 2.9 to assess the condition of an existing cooling tower. The worksheet should be completed annually at a regularly scheduled time, such as immediately following system shutdown at the end of the cooling season. Successive assessments will help to identify those elements in the tower that are deteriorating with time.

Figure 2.25 lists inspection and maintenance activities that are to be performed throughout the operating season. The figure represents the minimum level of maintenance required for a standard installation. Additional maintenance tasks may be required based on specifics of the application. Consult with the tower manufacturer to determine the actual level of maintenance required for the application.

FIGURE 2.1 Standard ASHRAE Refrigerant Designations

Refrigerant Number	Chemical Name	Chemical Formula	Boiling Point ($^{\circ}$F)
10	Carbontetrachloride	CCl_4	170.2
11	Trichlorofluoromethane	CCl_3F	74.8
12	Dichlorodifluoromethane	CCl_2F_2	-21.6
13	Chlorotrifluoromethane	$CClF_3$	-114.6
13 B1	Bromotrifluoromethane	$CBrF_3$	-72.0
14	Carbontetrafluoride	CF_4	-198.4
20	Chloroform	$CHCl_3$	142
21	Dichlorofluoromethane	$CHCl_2F$	48.1
22	Chlorodifluoromethane	$CHClF_2$	-41.4
23	Trifluoromethane	CHF_3	-119.9
30	Methylene Chloride	CH_2Cl_2	105.2
31	Chlorofluoromethane	CH_2ClF	48.0
32	Methylene Fluoride	CH_2F_2	-61.4
40	Methyl Chloride	CH_3Cl	-10.8
41	Methyl Fluoride	CH_3F	-109
50	Methane	CH_4	-259
110	Hexachloroethane	CCl_3CCl_3	365
111	Pentachlorofluoroethane	CCl_3CCl_2F	279
112	Tetrachlorodifluoroethane	CCl_2FCCl_2F	199.0
112A	Tetrachlorodifluoroethane	CCl_3CClF_2	195.8
113	Trichlorotrifluoroethane	CCl_2FCClF_2	117.6
113a	Trichlorotrifluoroethane	CCl_3CF_3	114.2
114	Dichlorotetrafluoroethane	$CClF_2CClF_2$	38.4
114a	Dichlorotetrafluoroethane	CCl_2FCF_3	38.5
114 B2	Dibromotetrafluoroethane	$CBrF_2CBrF_2$	117.5
115	Chloropentafluoroethane	$CClF_2CF_3$	-37.7
116	Hexafluoroethane	CF_3CF_3	-108.8
120	Pentachloroethane	$CHCl_2CCl_3$	324
123	Dichlorotrifluoroethane	$CHCl_2CF_3$	83.7
124	Chlorotetrafluoroethane	$CHClFCF_3$	10.4
124a	Chlorotetrafluoroethane	CHF_2CClF_2	14
125	Pentafluoroethane	CHF_2CF_3	-55
133a	Chlorotrifluoroethane	CH_2ClCF_3	43.0
134a	Tetrafluoroethane	CF_3CH_2F	-15.1
140a	Trichloroethane	CH_3CCl_3	165
142b	Chlorodifluoroethane	CH_3CClF_2	12.2
143a	Trifluoroethane	CH_3CF_3	-53.5
150a	Dichloroethane	CH_3CHCl_2	140
152a	Difluoroethane	CH_3CHF_2	-12.4
160	Ethyl Chloride	CH_3CH_2Cl	54.0

Figure 2.1 (continued)

Refrigerant Number	Chemical Name	Chemical Formula	Boiling Point ($^{\circ}$F)
170	Ethane	CH_3CH_3	-127.5
218	Octafluoropropane	$CF_3CF_3CF_3$	-36.4
290	Propane	$CH_3CH_2CH_3$	-44.2
C316	Dichlorohexafluorocyclobutane	$C_4Cl_2F_6$	140
C317	Chloroheptafluorocyclobutane	C_4ClF_7	77
C318	Octafluorocyclobutane	C_4F_8	21.1
500	Refrigerants 12/152a	CCl_2F_2/CH_3CHF_2	-28.0
501	Refrigerants 22/12	$CHCl_2F_2/CCl_2F_2$	-42
502	Refrigerants 22/115	$CHClF_2/CClF_2CF_3$	-50.1
503	Refrigerants 23/13	$CHF_3/CClF_3$	-127.6
504	Refrigerants 32/115	$CH_2F_2/CClF_2CF_3$	-71.0
505	Refrigerants 12/31	CCl_2F_2/CH_2ClF	-21.8
506	Refrigerants 31/114	$CH_2ClF/CClF_2CClF_2$	9.9
610	Ethyl Ether		94.3
611	Methyl Formate	$C_2H_5OC_2H_5$	89.2
		$HCOOCH_3$	
630	Methyl Amine		20.3
631	Ethyl Amine	CH_3NH_2	61.8
702	Hydrogen	$C_2H_5NH_2$	-423.2
704	Helium	H_2	-452.1
717	Ammonia	He	-28.0
		NH_3	
718	Water		212
720	Neon	H_2O	-410.9
728	Nitrogen	Ne	-320.4
729	Air	N_2	-318
732	Oxygen	$.21O_2, .78N_2, .01A$	-297.3
		O_2	
740	Argon		-302.6
744	Carbon Dioxide	A	-109
744A	Nitrous Oxide	CO_2	-127
764	Sulfur Dioxide	N_2O	14.0
1112a	Dichlorodifluoroethylene	SO_2	67
		$CCl_2 = CF_2$	
1113	Chlorotrifluoroethylene		-18.2
1114	Tetrafluoroethylene	$CClF = CF_2$	-105
1120	Trichloroethylene	$CF_2 = CF_2$	187
1130	Dichloroethylene	$CHCl = CCl_2$	118
1132a	Vinylidene Fluoride	$CHCl = CHCl$	-119
		$CH_2 = CF_2$	
1140	Vinyl Chloride		7.0
1141	Vinyl Fluoride	$CH_2 = CHCl$	-98
1150	Ethylene	$CH_2 = CHF$	-155.0
1270	Propylene	$CH_2 = CH_2$	-53.7
		$CH_3CH = CH_2$	

Reprinted by permission from 1993 ASHRAE Handbook Fundamentals

FIGURE 2.2 Estimated Cooling Loads

Type of Facility	Ventilation Rate (cfm/1,000 sq ft)	Lighting Load (Watts/sq ft)	Occupancy Load (tons/1,000 sq ft)
Hotels	30	1.5 - 3	0.5
Libraries	100	1 - 3	1.2
Manufacturing, Light	70	9 - 12	0.6
Manufacturing, Heavy	100	15 - 25	0.7
Office Buildings	35	2 - 8	0.5
Recreational Facilities	600	1 - 5	3.9
Restaurants	500	1.5 - 2	2.5
Retail Shops	150	3 - 6	1.0
Schools	250	4 - 5	1.2
Warehouses	25	1 - 1.3	0.15

FIGURE 2.3 Equivalent Full Load Hours for Air Conditioning Equipment

Location	Equivalent Full Load Hours	Location	Equivalent Full Load Hours
Albuquerque, NM	800 - 2,200	Indianapolis, IN	600 - 1,600
Atlantic City, NJ	500 - 800	Little Rock, AR	1,400 - 2,400
Birmingham, AL	1,200 - 2,200	Minneapolis, MN	400 - 800
Boston, MA	400 - 1,200	New Orleans, LA	1,400 - 2,800
Burlington, VT	200 - 600	New York, NY	500 - 1,000
Charlotte, NC	700 - 1,100	Newark, NJ	400 - 900
Chicago, IL	500 - 1,000	Oklahoma City, OK	1,100 - 2,000
Cleveland, OH	400 - 800	Pittsburgh, PA	900 - 1,200
Cincinnati, OH	1,000 - 1,500	Rapid City, SD	800 - 1,000
Columbia, SC	1,200 - 1,400	St. Joseph, MO	1,000 - 1,600
Corpus Christi, TX	2,000 - 2,500	St. Petersburg, FL	1,500 - 2,700
Dallas, TX	1,200 - 1,600	San Diego, CA	800 - 1,700
Denver, CO	400 - 800	Savannah, GA	1,200 - 1,400
Des Moines, IA	600 - 1,000	Seattle, WA	400 - 1,200
Detroit, MI	700 - 1,000	Syracuse, NY	200 - 1,000
Duluth, MN	300 - 500	Trenton, NJ	800 - 1,000
El Paso, TX	1,000 - 1,400	Tulsa, OK	1,500 - 2,200
Honolulu, HI	1,500 - 3,500	Washington, DC	700 - 1,200

Reprinted by permission from 1992 ASHRAE Handbook Systems and Equipment

FIGURE 2.4 Central Chiller Characteristics

	ABSORPTION	CENTRIFUGAL	RECIPROCATING	ROTARY
Source of Power	Steam, waste heat, solar	Electrical motor, steam turbine, engine	Electrical motor or engine	Electrical motor
Relative Energy Cost	Medium	Low	High	Medium
Relative Initial Cost	High	High	Low	Medium
Relative Physical Size	Large	Large	Small	Small
Capacity Range	50 - 1,500 tons	80 - 2,400 tons	1 - 200 tons	20 - 2,000 tons
Relative Maintenance Requirements	High	Medium	Low	Low
Refrigerant	Lithium Bromide, Ammonia-Water	R-11, R-12, R-22, R-113, R-114, R-500	R-12, R-22, R-500	R-12, R-22, R-502

FIGURE 2.5 Central Chiller Components

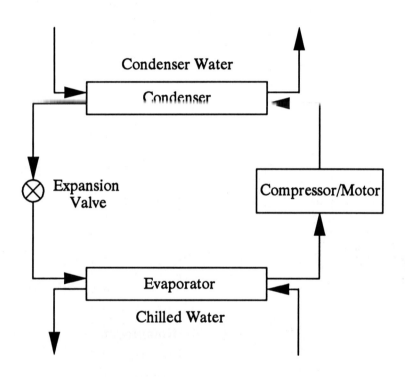

FIGURE 2.6 Part Load Chiller Performance

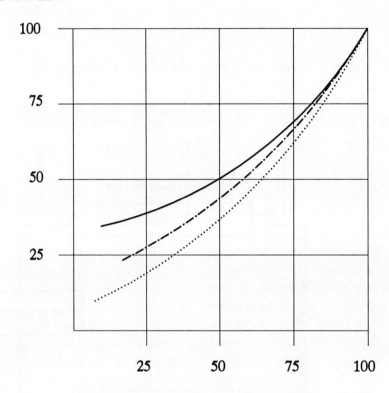

Percent
Full-Load KW

Percent Full-Load Capacity

——— Reciprocating
—·—·— Centrifugal
············ Rotary

FIGURE 2.7 Typical Full-Load Reciprocating Chiller Efficiency

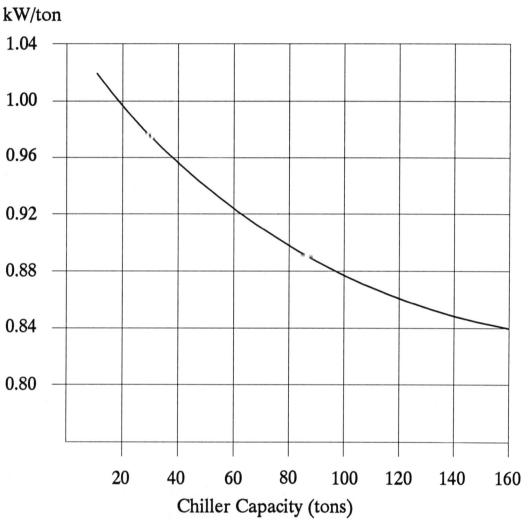

kW/ton

Chiller Capacity (tons)

95° leaving condenser water temperature
44° chilled water temperature

FIGURE 2.8 Typical Full-Load Centrifugal Chiller Efficiency

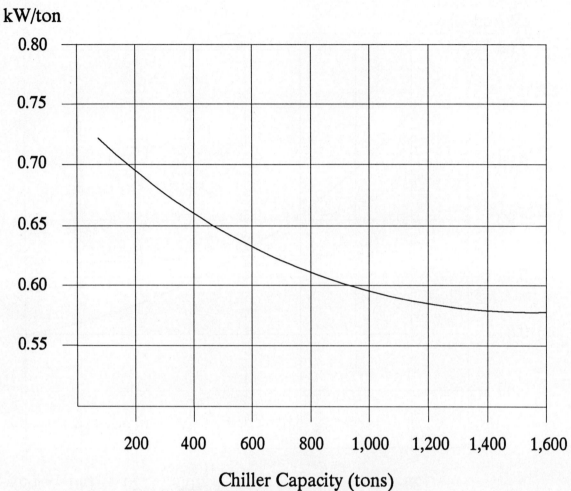

Chiller Capacity (tons)

95° leaving condenser water temperature
44° chilled water temperature

FIGURE 2.9 Typical Full-Load Rotary Chiller Efficiency

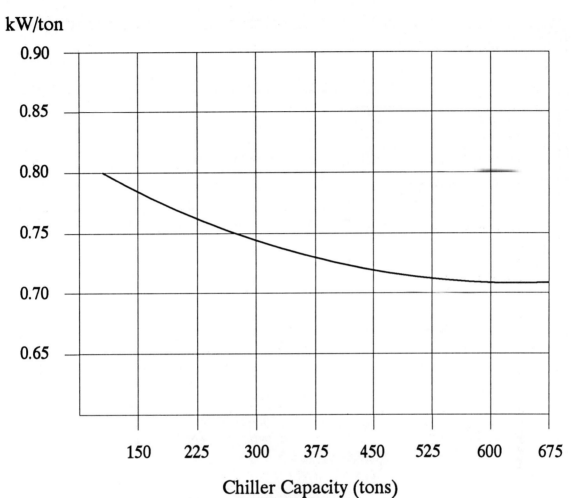

kW/ton

Chiller Capacity (tons)

95° leaving condenser water temperature
44° chilled water temperature

FIGURE 2.10 Absorption Chiller Components

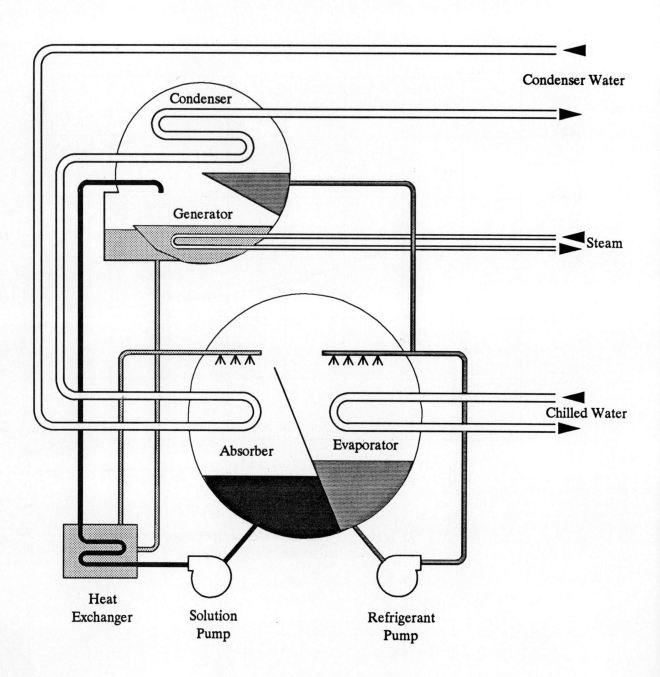

Condenser Water

Condenser

Generator

Steam

Absorber

Evaporator

Chilled Water

Heat
Exchanger

Solution
Pump

Refrigerant
Pump

FIGURE 2.11 Part-Load Absorption Chiller Efficiency

Percent Full-Load
Heat Requirement

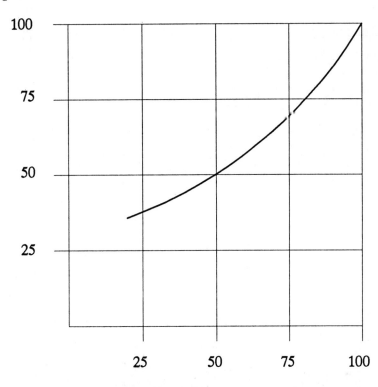

Percent Full-Load Capacity

FIGURE 2.12 Fouling Factor and Chiller Efficiency
Based on a design fouling factor of 0.0002

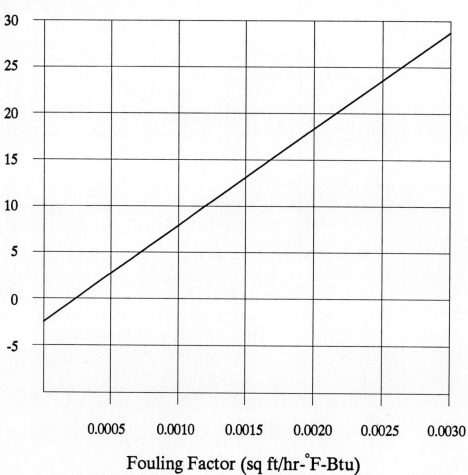

Efficiency Decrease (%)

Fouling Factor (sq ft/hr-°F-Btu)

FIGURE 2.13 Chilled Water Temperature and Chiller Efficiency

% Increase
In Efficiency

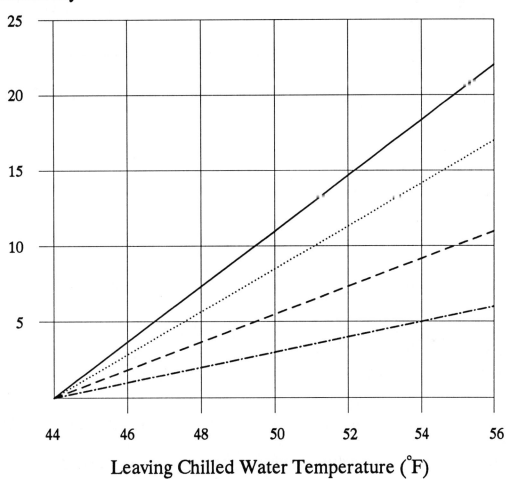

Leaving Chilled Water Temperature (°F)

——————— Rotary
.... Centrifugal
– – – – Reciprocating
–·–·–·– Absorption

Figure 2.14 Condenser Water Temperature and Chiller Efficiency

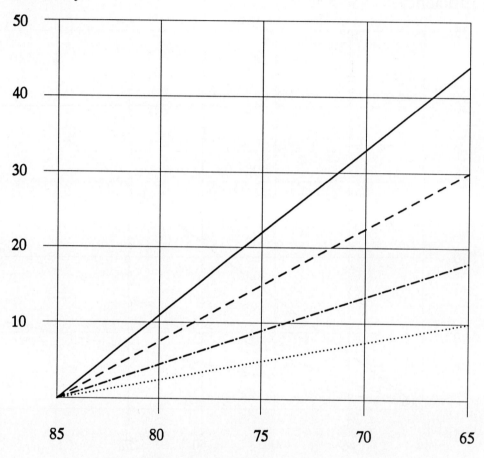

% Increase
In Efficiency

Entering Condenser Water Temperature (F)

——————— Rotary
– – – – – – Reciprocating
–·–·–·–· Absorption
················· Centrifugal

FIGURE 2.15 Variable Speed Chiller Performance

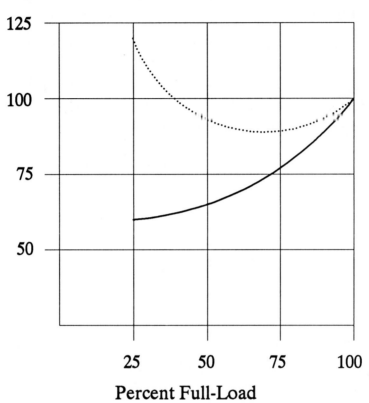

% Full-Load
kW/ton

Percent Full-Load

.... Constant Speed

———— Variable Speed

FIGURE 2.16 Typical Time-of-Day Rate Structure

Monthly Charge	Summer Months	Winter Months

Energy Charge
    On-Peak Period
    Intermediate Period
    Off-Peak Period
	
	2.962 ¢/kWh
	2.338 ¢/kWh
	0.859 ¢/kWh
		
		2.156 ¢/kWh
		1.636 ¢/kWh
		0.444 ¢/kWh

Production and Transmission Charge	$9.40/kW	-
Distribution Charge	$3.85/kW	$3.85/kW

Summer Months	June through October
Winter Months	November through May
On-Peak Period	Weekdays (excluding holidays), 12:00 noon through 8:00 p.m.
Intermediate Period	Weekdays (excluding holidays), 8:00 a.m. through 12:00 noon and 8:00 p.m. through 12:00 midnight
Off-Peak Period	Saturdays, Sundays, Holidays, and weekdays 12:00 midnight through 8:00 a.m.
Production and Transmission Charge	The maximum 30 minute demand measured during the on-peak period for the month. It is calculated during the summer months only.
Distribution Charge	The maximum 30 minute demand measured during the billing month.

FIGURE 2.17 Components of an Ice Storage System

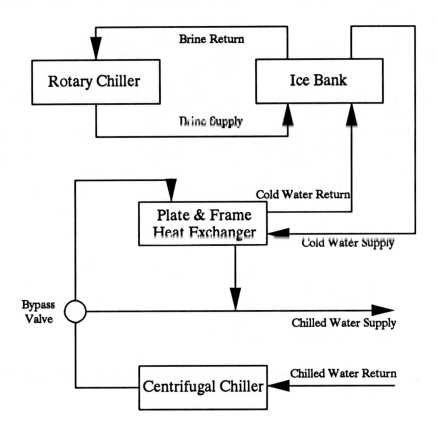

FIGURE 2.18 Cooling Tower Schematic

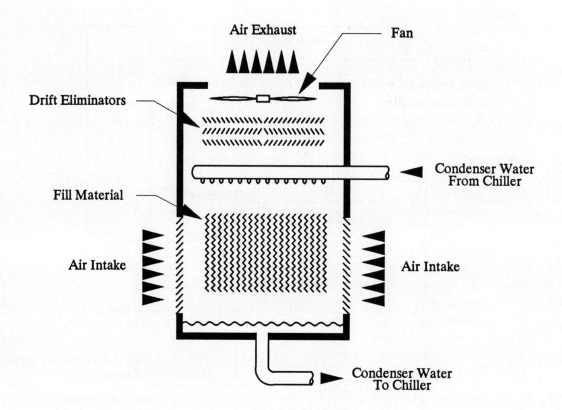

Air Exhaust

Fan

Drift Eliminators

Condenser Water From Chiller

Fill Material

Air Intake

Air Intake

Condenser Water To Chiller

FIGURE 2.19 Cooling Tower Characteristics

Advantages

1. Greater Chiller Efficiency - As a general rule of thumb, chiller systems using cooling towers are from 10 to 25% more efficient than comparable systems that use air-cooled condensers.
2. Lower Condenser Water Supply Temperature - As a result of evaporative cooling within the tower, the chiller condenser water supply is reduced resulting in lower head pressures within the chiller.
3. Towers can be Remotely Located - Condenser water can be piped to the best possible location for the tower, thus reducing the impact of tower noise and drift.
4. Potential for Free Cooling - With the installation of a high efficiency plate and frame heat exchanger in parallel with the chiller, the cooling tower can be used to produce chilled water whenever the outside temperature is below $50^{o}F$ without having to operate the chiller.

Disadvantages

1. Water Use - Cooling towers require that from 3 to 5% of their flow rate be replaced to make up for evaporation, drift, and blowdown.
2. Higher Maintenance Costs - In addition to routine maintenance requirements, towers must be treated to eliminate bacteria, algae, and scale. The operation of equipment in a warm environment exposed to water requires frequent inspections, cleaning, and painting.
3. Winterization - All towers that are to be operated through the winter must be sufficiently winterized in order to prevent freezing.
4. Higher Weight - Cooling towers impose a greater weight load than air-cooled condensers of the same capacity.
5. Plume Production - Operation of the tower in cool or humid weather can produce a significant plume.

FIGURE 2.20 Air-Cooled Condenser Characteristics

Advantages

1. No Water Use - Since the refrigerant is cooled directly by air, there is no water required for operation of the cooling system, nor is water treatment required.
2. No Winterization - Without the use of water, there are no special requirements for operation year-round. For systems that are used seasonally, there is no requirement to drain the system.
3. No Condenser Water Pump - With direct cooling by air, there is no need to pump condenser water. Condenser water pumping can be a significant maintenance and operating cost, particularly in installations where the tower is separated by a significant distance from the chiller.
4. Lower Maintenance Requirements - With fewer mechanical parts, and with mechanical parts that are not required to operate in a harsh environment, maintenance inspections and tasks are reduced.

Disadvantages

1. Higher Operating Cost - Air-cooled condensers cannot produce refrigerant temperatures as low as can be produced by cooling towers, thus increasing chiller head pressures and reducing overall system efficiency.
2. Siting - Air-cooled condensers must be located close to the chiller due to refrigerant piping restrictions.
3. System Size - Air-cooled condensers are not well suited for use with large chillers.
4. Noise - Air-cooled condensers require the use of fans to move air over the heat transfer surfaces, larger volumes of air than are required by comparably sized cooling towers. Operation of these cooling fans produces noise levels that can be objectionable to surrounding operations.

FIGURE 2.21 Centrifugal Chiller Maintenance Tasks

Daily Tasks

Log condenser and oil pressure readings.
Check general condition.
Check for excessive noise or vibration.
Inspect for oil leaks.
Inspect for water leaks.
Check oil level in sump.

Weekly Tasks

Check motor for overheating.
Check refrigerant level.
Check refrigerant system for leaks.
Inspect operation of purge system.
Log purge cycle counter reading.
Inspect water treatment system operation.

Monthly Tasks

Inspect all valves for leaks.
Check control system settings and operation.
Check filters and strainers.

Annual Tasks

Inspect all wiring, starters, and disconnects.
Test operation of all safety controls.
Meg motor windings.
Calibrate chiller controls.
Change purge unit dehydrators.
Change compressor oil and filter.
Check operation of purge system.
Inspect condenser tubes for scale and fouling.
Inspect chiller case for rust.
Inspect chiller and piping insulation.

FIGURE 2.22 Rotary Chiller Maintenance Tasks

Daily Tasks

Log condenser pressure readings.
Check general condition.
Check for excessive noise or vibration.
Inspect for oil leaks.
Inspect for water leaks.
Check oil level.

Weekly Tasks

Check motor for overheating.
Check refrigerant level.
Check refrigerant system for leaks.
Inspect water treatment system operation.

Monthly Tasks

Inspect all valves for leaks.
Inspect pump seals.
Check control system settings and operation.
Check filters.

Annual Tasks

Inspect all wiring, starters, and disconnects.
Calibrate chiller controls.
Test chiller safety controls.
Meg motor windings.
Inspect condenser tubes for scale and fouling.
Change compressor oil and filter.
Inspect chiller case for rust.
Inspect chiller and piping insulation.

FIGURE 2.23 Reciprocating Chiller Maintenance Tasks

Daily Tasks

Log operating pressures and temperatures.
Check general condition.
Check for excessive noise or vibration.
Check crankcase oil level.
Check oil pressure.

Weekly Tasks

Check oil color for contamination.
Check refrigerant level.
Check refrigerant system for leaks.
Check belts and coupling alignment.

Monthly Tasks

Check vibration isolators.
Check control system settings and operation.
Cycle controls and check operation of unloaders.
Check crankcase heaters.

Annual Tasks

Inspect all wiring, starters, and disconnects.
Test chiller safety controls.
Meg motor windings.
Calibrate operating controls.
Change compressor oil.
Inspect piping insulation.

FIGURE 2.24 Absorption Chiller Maintenance Tasks

Daily Tasks

Log operating temperatures.
Log boiler/steam pressure.
Check general condition.
Check for excessive noise or vibration.

Weekly Tasks

Check operation of purge unit.
Inspect purge unit belt.
Check solution pump motor.

Monthly Tasks

Check safety control settings.
Clean line strainers for lubricating pump.

Annual Tasks

Inspect all wiring, starters, and disconnects.
Test chiller safety controls.
Check operation of steam valve.
Check operation of temperature controllers.
Calibrate all controls.
Change purge unit pump oil.
Test lithium bromide solution.

FIGURE 2.25 Cooling Tower Maintenance Tasks

Tasks to be Performed Before System Start-up

Inspect structural members and fasteners.
Inspect safety railings, stairs, walkways, and access doors.
Inspect for rust and corrosion and repaint as needed.
Repair or replace sections of damaged drift eliminators.
Inspect tower fill material.
Clean debris from unit.
Clean air intake screens
Clean sump strainer.
Clean and flush sump.
Check and adjust operation of make-up water system.
Inspect and adjust all drive belts and pulleys.
Change oil in all gear boxes.
Inspect propeller and fan blades for damage.
Inspect all piping.
Inspect wiring and electrical controls.

Daily Tasks

Visually check general operation.
Check for unusual vibration or noise.
Check sump water level.
Check rate of water bleed-off.

Weekly Tasks

Inspect basin for debris.
Check drive motor for excessive heat or vibration.
Inspect gearbox for oil leaks.
Check oil level in gearbox.

Figure 2.25 (continued)

Monthly Tasks

Clean air intake screens.
Inspect drift eliminators for damage, dirt, and biological growth.
Flush debris from sump.
Clean sump strainer.
Inspect sump for leaks.
Inspect header for clogging and biological growth.
Inspect spray nozzles.
Inspect and adjust drive belts.
Lubricate drive bearings.

System Shutdown Tasks

Inspect general condition.
Inspect protective finishes.
Inspect tower fill material.
Inspect drift eliminators.
Drain sump and piping.
Cover and protect drive motors, shafts, and gearboxes.

WORKSHEET 2.1 Estimating Central Chiller Size

1. Walls & Roof Load

$$\left[\boxed{} + \boxed{} \right] \text{ X } \boxed{0.4} = \boxed{}$$

Wall Area   Roof Area   Walls & Roof
(1,000 sq ft)   (1,000 sq ft)   Load (tons)

2. Window Load

$$\boxed{} \text{ X } \boxed{} = \boxed{}$$

Window Area   Window Factor   Window Load
(1,000 sq ft)   (tons/1,000 sq ft)   (tons)

3. Ventilation Air Load

$$\boxed{} \text{ X } \boxed{} \text{ X } \boxed{2.5} = \boxed{}$$

Floor Area   Ventilation Rate   Ventilation
(1,000 sq ft)   (cfm/1,000 sq ft)   Load (tons)

4. Lighting Load

$$\boxed{} \text{ X } \boxed{} \text{ X } \boxed{0.28} = \boxed{}$$

Floor Area (1,000   Lighting Load   Lighting Load
sq ft)   (Watts/sq ft)   (tons)

Worksheet 2.1 (continued)

5. Occupant Load

[ ]	X	[ ]	=	[ ]	
Floor Area (1,000 sq ft)		Load Factor (tons/1,000 sq ft)		Occupant Load (tons)	

6. Equipment Load

[ ]	X	[ ]	X	0.28	=	[ ]	
Floor Area (1,000 sq ft)		Equipment Factor (Watts/sq ft)				Equipment Load (tons)	

7. Total Cooling Load

[ ] + [ ] + [ ] + [ ] +

Walls & Roof Load (tons)   Window Load (tons)   Ventilation Load (tons)   Lighting Load (tons)

[ ] + [ ] = [ ]

Occupant Load (tons)   Equipment Load (tons)   Cooling Load (tons)

WORKSHEET 2.2 Annual Cost of Refrigeration

1. Installation Data

Chiller Full-Load Capacity (tons): _____

Chiller Full-Load Rating (kW/ton, or 1,000 lb/ton): _____

Equivalent Full-Load Operating Hours (hr): _____

Energy Cost Rate ($/kWh, or $/1,000 lbs): _____

Peak Demand Rate ($/kW): _____

2. Annual Energy Cost

Chiller Capacity (tons)	X Chiller Rating (kW/ton) or (1,000 lb/ton)	X Equivalent Full-Load Hours (hr)	X Energy Rate ($/kWh) or ($/1,000 lb)	= Annual Energy Cost ($)

3. Monthly Demand Charges

Chiller Capacity (tons)	X Chiller Rating (kW/ton)	X Peak Demand Rate ($/kW)	= Monthly Peak Demand Charge ($)

4. Annual Energy Cost

Annual Energy Cost ($)	+ Multiplication Factor	X Monthly Peak Demand Charge ($)	= Total Annual Cost

WORKSHEET 2.3 Energy Savings From
Improved Chiller Fouling Factor

1. System Data

Chiller Full-Load Capacity (tons): _____
Chiller Full-Load Rating (kW/ton, or 1,000 lb/ton): _____
Equivalent Full-Load Operating Hours (hr): _____
Energy Cost Rate ($/kWh, or $/1,000 lb): _____

2. Annual Energy Cost - Design Conditions

$$\boxed{} \;X\; \boxed{} \;X\; \boxed{} \;X\; \boxed{} \;=\; \boxed{}$$

Chiller Capacity (tons)	Chiller Rating (kW/ton) or (1,000 lb/ton)	Equivalent Full-Load Hours (hr)	Energy Rate ($/kWh) or ($/1,000 lb)	Design Annual Energy Cost ($)

3. Annual Energy Cost - Actual Conditions

$$\boxed{} \;X\; \left[\; 1 + \boxed{} \;\right] \;=\; \boxed{}$$

Design Annual Energy Cost ($)   Efficiency Loss   Actual Annual Energy Cost ($)

4. Annual Energy Cost - Improved Fouling Factor

$$\boxed{} \;X\; \left[\; 1 + \boxed{} \;\right] \;=\; \boxed{}$$

Design Annual Energy Cost ($)   Efficiency Loss   Improved Annual Energy Cost ($)

5. Annual Energy Savings

$$\boxed{} \;-\; \boxed{} \;=\; \boxed{}$$

Actual Annual Energy Cost ($)   Improved Annual Energy Cost ($)   Annual Energy Savings ($)

WORKSHEET 2.4 Chilled Water Temperature Reset Savings

1. System Data

Chiller Full-Load Capacity (tons): _____
Chiller Full-Load Rating (kW/ton or 1,000 lb/ton): _____
Equivalent Full-Load Operating Hours (hr): _____
Energy Cost Rate ($kWh or $/1,000 lb): _____

2. Annual Energy Savings

[ ] X	[ ] X	[ ] X	[ ] X	[ ] X	[ ]
Chiller Capacity (tons)	Chiller Rating (kW/ton) or (1,000 lb/ton)	Equivalent Full-Load Hours (hr)	Energy Rate ($/kWh) or ($/1,000 lb)	Efficiency Increase	Chilled Water Reset Factor

= [   ]

Annual Energy
Savings ($)

3. Chilled Water Reset Factor

Operating Hours per Day	Multiplication Factor
8	0.25
16	0.40
20	0.55
24	0.70

WORKSHEET 2.5 Condenser Water Temperature Reset Savings

1. System Data

Chiller Full-Load Capacity (tons): _____
Chiller Full-Load Rating (kW/ton or 1,000 lb/ton): _____
Equivalent Full-Load Operating Hours (hr): _____
Energy Cost Rate ($kWh or $/1000 lb): _____

2. Annual Energy Savings

☐	X	☐	X	☐	X	☐	X	☐	X	☐
Chiller Capacity (tons)		Chiller Rating (kW/ton) or (1,000 lb/ton)		Equivalent Full-Load Hours (hr)		Energy Rate ($/kWh) or ($/1,000 lb)		Efficiency Increase		Condenser Water Reset Factor

= ☐

Annual Energy
Savings ($)

3. Condenser Water Reset Factor

Operating Hours per Day	Multiplication Factor
8	0.25
16	0.40
20	0.55
24	0.70

WORKSHEET 2.6 Variable Speed Chiller Savings

1. System Data

Chiller Full-Load Capacity (tons): _____
Chiller Full-Load Rating (kW/ton): _____
Equivalent Full-Load Operating Hours (hr): _____
Energy Rate ($kWh): _____

2. Annual Energy Savings

Chiller Capacity (tons)		Chiller Rating (kW/ton)		Equivalent Full-Load Hours (hr)		Electrical Rate ($/kWh)		Variable Speed Factor

$$\boxed{} \text{ X } \boxed{} \text{ X } \boxed{} \text{ X } \boxed{} \text{ X } \boxed{}$$

$$= \boxed{}$$

Annual Energy
Savings ($)

3. Variable Speed Factor

Operating Hours per Day	Multiplication Factor
8	0.05
16	0.13
20	0.18
24	0.28

WORKSHEET 2.7 Estimating Ice Storage System Size

1. Building Cooling Load

$$\frac{\boxed{}}{\boxed{}} = \boxed{}$$

Chiller Load (kWh) / Chiller Rating (kWh/ton-hr) = Cooling Load (ton-hr)

2. Required Storage Capacity

$$\boxed{} \times \boxed{13.1} \times \boxed{} = \boxed{}$$

Cooling Load (ton-hr) X 13.1 X Reserve Capacity Factor = Storage Capacity (gal)

WORKSHEET 2.8 Annual Savings From Ice Storage

1. Installation Data

Conventional Chiller Full-Load Capacity (tons): _____
Conventional Chiller Full-Load Rating (kW/ton): _____
Ice Storage System Chiller Full-Load Rating (kW/ton): _____
Equivalent Full-Load Operating Hours (hr): _____
Summer On-Peak Energy Charge ($/kWh): _____
Summer Off-Peak Energy Charge ($/kWh): _____
Summer On-Peak Demand Charge ($/kW): _____

2. Conventional Chiller System Energy Costs

[____]	X	[____]	X	[____]	X	[0.75]	X	[____]
Chiller Capacity (tons)		Chiller Rating (kW/ton)		Equivalent Full-Load Hours (hr)		Daytime Load Factor		Summer On-Peak Energy Charge ($/kWh)

= [____]

Conventional System
Annual Energy Cost ($)

3. Conventional Chiller System Demand Charges

[____]	X	[____]	X	[____]	X	[____]	=	[____]
Chiller Capacity (tons)		Chiller Rating (kW/ton)		Summer On-Peak Demand Charge ($/kW)		Number of Months Peak Demand Rate in Effect		Conventional System Annual Demand Cost ($)

Worksheet 2.8 (continued)

4. Ice Storage System Energy Costs

[ ]	X [ ]	X [ ]	X 0.75	X [ ]
Chiller Capacity (tons)	Chiller Rating (kW/ton)	Equivalent Full-Load Hours (hr)	Daytime Load Factor	Summer Off-Peak Energy Charge ($/kWh)

= [ ]

Ice Storage System
Annual Energy Cost ($)

5. Ice System Savings

[ ]	+ [ ]	- [ ]	= [ ]
Conventional System Annual Energy Cost ($)	Conventional System Annual Demand Cost ($)	Ice Storage System Annual Energy Cost ($)	Ice System Savings ($)

WORKSHEET 2.9 Cooling Tower Condition Assessment

1. Installation Data

Building: _____   Manufacturer: _____

Location: _____   Model: _____

Type of Tower: _____   Date Installed: _____

Rate each element from 0 to 5, with 0 for very poor and 5 for like new

Tower Component	Condition (0 - 5)	Comments
Structure		
Steel support	_____	_____
Tower casing	_____	_____
Access ladders & stairways	_____	_____
Fan deck	_____	_____
Tower basin	_____	_____
Fill material	_____	_____
Drift eliminators	_____	_____
Louvers and screens	_____	_____
Water System		
Inlet piping	_____	_____
Bypass valves	_____	_____
Spray nozzles	_____	_____
Makeup water valve	_____	_____
Outlet piping	_____	_____
Fan System		
Propeller/blower	_____	_____
Drive motor	_____	_____
Starters & disconnects	_____	_____
Speed reducer & driveshaft	_____	_____
Drive belts & pulleys	_____	_____
Fan guards	_____	_____
Control system	_____	_____

## Chapter 3

THE OPERATION OF AIR HANDLING UNITS

This chapter examines air handling systems and their components. Material presented in this chapter can be used to identify and solve problems ranging from poor system design to inadequate equipment performance.

Proper identification of the problem is critical to correcting the operation of air handling systems. Too often "quick fix" solutions are implemented on the symptoms rather than the cause. Their implementation generally serves only to further mask the root cause of the problem. Eventually, layer upon layer of quick fixes build up making it impossible for the system to operate as originally designed or as required for the application. Eventually the frustration level of the building manager reaches the point where the system is overhauled or completely replaced when all that was required was a thorough diagnosis of the existing conditions in the building and HVAC system.

Identification of the cause of the particular problem is also important as the performance of many building HVAC systems suffers not from a lack of maintenance, but rather because the system is incapable of performing as required. The original design may have been inadequate, or alterations may have been made to the conditioned space to render the system ineffective. In either case, no amount of maintenance will correct the problems. Changes will have to be made to the system. This chapter will help to identify situations where the system is being asked to perform beyond its capabilities.

FAN TYPES

There are two major types of fans used in building HVAC applications: centrifugal and axial. Of the two, centrifugal fans are more widely used because they can move a wider volume of air over a greater range of system static pressures than axial fans can.

Centrifugal Fans

Centrifugal fans move air by forcing it to rotate within a fan housing. The resulting centrifugal force and the kinetic energy imparted by the rotating impeller act on the air mass, developing pressure to move the air stream. It is this action that enables centrifugal fan systems to operate in systems having relatively high static pressure.

Centrifugal fans are of four types: forward curve, backward inclined, radial blade, and tubular centrifugal. Each fan type has its own characteristics, advantages, and disadvantages, summarized in Figure 3.1.

Axial Fans

Axial fans, although less efficient than centrifugal fans, are used effectively in numerous HVAC applications due to their flexibility and relatively low cost. They move air solely by the change in velocity induced by the rotating blades. There is no centrifugal force component contributing to the air flow. For this reason, static pressures produced by axial fans typically are much lower than those produced by centrifugal fans of the same capacity.

Axial fans are classified as propeller, tube axial, and vane axial. Each fan type has its own characteristics, advantages, and disadvantages, summarized in Figure 3.2.

FAN LAWS AND HVAC MAINTENANCE

All fans operate according to a set of physical rules known as fan laws. These laws dictate performance variables, such as static pressure, air flow, and horsepower requirements for a given set of fans. Variations in one performance variable result in predictable variations in other performance variables.

There are three fan laws that are of importance in maintaining HVAC systems: the relationship between air flow and fan speed, the relationship between static pressure and fan speed, and the relationship between fan horsepower requirements and fan speed.

For a given fan size, air density, and connected HVAC distribution system, the relationship between fan speed and air flow is as follows:

$$\frac{\text{cfm}_1}{\text{cfm}_2} = \frac{\text{rpm}_1}{\text{rpm}_2}$$

where: cfm_1 = the initial air flow rate
         cfm_2 = the final air flow rate
         rpm_1 = the initial fan speed
         rpm_2 = the final fan speed

You can see from the equation that one possible means of increasing the air flow from a fan system is to simply increase the operating speed of the fan. While this will increase the cfm supplied by a fan, it will also result in an increase in system static pressure and fan horsepower requirements.

For a given fan size, air density, and connected HVAC distribution system, the relationship between fan speed and system static pressure is as follows:

$$\frac{\text{sp}_1}{\text{sp}_2} = \left[\frac{\text{rpm}_1}{\text{rpm}_2}\right]^2$$

where: sp_1 = the initial system static pressure
         sp_2 = the final system static pressure
         rpm_1 = the initial fan speed
         rpm_2 = the final fan speed

The equation shows that a slight increase in the speed of the fan will result in a significant increase in the system static pressure. Where this becomes particularly important is in calculating the impact that increased air flow has on fan horsepower requirements.

For a given fan size, air density, and connected HVAC distribution system, the relationship between fan speed and fan horsepower requirements is as follows:

$$\frac{\text{bhp}_1}{\text{bhp}_2} = \left[\frac{\text{rpm}_1}{\text{rpm}_2}\right]^3$$

where: bhp_1 = the initial fan horsepower
         bhp_2 = the final fan horsepower
         rpm_1 = the initial fan speed
         rpm_2 = the final fan speed

A slight increase in fan speed results in a large increase in fan horsepower requirements. Therefore, before increasing fan speed to improve supply cfm, it is essential to monitor the line current supplying the fan motor to insure that it does not become overloaded.

In general it is not a good practice to simply increase fan speed to increase air flow. Most low air flow problems are a result of changes in the system resistance. The original static pressure design calculations may have been in error. The system may have been modified to such an extent that the overall system static pressure has changed significantly. Dampers in the system may have failed in either the open or closed position. The coils and filters may be sufficiently blocked to restrict air flow. For these reasons it is best to determine the cause of the low air flow before simply increasing fan speed.

FAN CURVES

The fan laws dictate the performance of a particular fan in an application. To aid designers and users of fan systems, manufacturers give the performance of their fans in a graph showing the relationship between pressure, efficiency, power, and fan capacity. These graphs, known as fan curves, are useful tools in diagnosing problems .

Figure 3.3 shows a typical fan performance curve. In the figure, the system curve represents the static pressure load that the HVAC system places on the fan system based on cfm delivery from the fan. As can be seen in the figure, static pressure increases rapidly with an increase in supply cfm.

The fan curve in the figure represents the cfm that the fan can deliver at various system static pressures. The curve is unique to the particular fan installed and is governed by the fan laws.

The intersection of the system curve and the fan curve is the operating point for the fan system in that particular application. Since fans can operate only along their fan curve, changes in the resistance of the system result in changes in the volume of air supplied by the fan. Figure 3.4 demonstrates the impact that an increase in system static pressure has on fan performance. The fan and HVAC system shown in the figure were designed to operate at a specific static pressure and supply cfm governed by the duct design and the fan curve for the fan selected. However, the actual static pressure present in the system is larger than anticipated, possibly as a result of design errors, closed system dampers, or clogged air filters. This increase in static pressure results in a decrease in supply cfm as shown in the figure.

When troubleshooting HVAC problems, particularly those involving low air flows, find the cause of the problem before simply trying to increase the output of the fan.

CONTROLLING HVAC NOISE LEVELS

Controlling noise in fan systems is nearly as important as controlling temperature, humidity, and air flow. Noise control is generally a function of good system design. However, a number of maintenance-related problems can result in excessive noise in fan systems.

Before investigating methods for reducing noise from fan systems, it is important to measure the noise level resulting from the fan system and determine if it is excessive. Nearly every measure taken to reduce noise generated by an HVAC system results in a reduction in system performance, so before measures are implemented, be certain that action is needed.

Noise Standards

Noise measurements can be taken using a sound level meter. Measurements should be taken using the "A-scale" to approximate the response of the human ear. Figure 3.5 lists OSHA recommended indoor background noise levels for a number of applications. The levels listed in the figure are total noise of which HVAC system noise is only a component. If the noise measurements taken in the space exceed those values listed in the figure, then some form of noise attenuation may be required.

Fan generated noise is a function of the design of the fan system, the volume of air flow, the total system pressure, fan efficiency, and the tip speed of the fan impeller. Of these, the most important and the most costly to correct is the fan system design. Fan systems that include sharp bends in ductwork and radical reducers in duct cross sectional areas are prone to noise problems that are not readily corrected without impacting system performance.

Ways to Reduce Noise Levels

Several generalities may be applied to fan systems when looking for ways to reduce system noise.

1. For a given system static pressure, the noise generated by the fan is proportional to the tip speed of the impeller. Increasing fan speed to increase air flow will result in a disproportionate increase in fan noise.

2. If noise is a problem in a fan system that is to be replaced, consider changing the type of fan used. Backward curved fans have better noise characteristics than radial blade fans, and radial blade fans have better noise characteristics than forward curved units.

3. A major source of fan noise is the fan wheel, and the major cause of wheel noise is an unbalanced fan wheel. Fan wheels can be unbalanced as a result of the manufacturing process, damage, or buildup of dirt.

4. Limiting duct velocities, while no guarantee of reducing system noise, is important. Figure 3.6 lists the recommended maximum supply and return duct velocities for typical applications. Use these values to determine if the existing ductwork is adequately sized for the current load.

5. Fan silencers should be considered only after all other reasonable attempts to reduce system noise have been implemented. Silencers result in a pressure drop in the system. The greater the noise attenuation of the silencer, the greater the pressure drop.

ESTABLISHING A FAN MAINTENANCE PROGRAM

HVAC fan systems achieve high reliability without imposing unusual or extensive maintenance requirements. Most of the required activities can be classified as routine scheduled or preventive maintenance. When performed on a regular basis these activities can help to insure equipment life ranging from 20 to 30 years or more.

Figure 3.7 lists the recommended monthly, semi-annual, and annual tasks generally required by fan systems. For specific applications, particularly those serving critical areas, there may be additional maintenance requirements. Consult with the fan system manufacturer to determine what additional maintenance activities might be required.

VENTILATION REQUIREMENTS

In order to maintain acceptable indoor air quality within buildings, HVAC systems introduce outdoor air, also known as ventilation air, into the conditioned space. Note that ventilation air is only a portion of the total air supplied to a particular space within the building by the HVAC system, the remainder being supplied by recirculated building air. The volume of ventilation air supplied depends on the particular needs of the building space. In general, the greater the need for maintaining a clean environment within the building, or the greater the quantity of contaminants produced within the building, the greater the requirement for ventilation air.

Building managers must be concerned with the quantity of ventilation air being supplied. Too little results in unacceptable or even dangerous levels of contaminants within the occupied space. Too much results in excessive energy use, as the HVAC system must heat or cool the ventilation air before it is delivered to the occupied spaces.

ASHRAE has established a set of standards for determining the quantity of ventilation air required for different applications. These ventilation standards are published in ASHRAE Standard 62-1989, *Standards for Natural and Mechanical Ventilation.* Figure 3.8 presents a condensed listing of the ventilation standards for a number of applications. Use the figure to determine the minimum acceptable ventilation rate for a particular application. Actual ventilation rates may have to be greater than those listed in the table as the result of special requirements for the application. For a more complete listing of applications, see the complete ASHRAE Standard.

HVAC system dampers are typically designed to provide a specific minimum ventilation air rate. Unfortunately, few systems are calibrated even when new. As they age, they become more and more inaccurate at regulating the amount of ventilation air being introduced into a building. Worksheet 3.1 provides a means of determining the percentage of outdoor air being supplied by a system and its ventilation rate.

To use the worksheet, three temperature measurements and one air flow measurement will have to be made. Measurements should be made only after the system has been operating for a long enough period of time for them to stabilize. Accuracy of the measurements is crucial to the accuracy of the calculations. Use the Worksheet as follows:

Step 1.	Set the outdoor air dampers to their minimum flow position. In this position, the measurements taken will show the minimum ventilation air being introduced into the system.
Step 2.	Insert the thermometer into the air flow in the return, mixed, and outdoor air sections of the HVAC system ductwork. Enter the readings in section #1 of the worksheet.
Step 3.	There are two methods for determining the total air flow in the system: measurement or design flow. If air flow measurements are used, they should be taken in the ductwork on the discharge side of the supply fan. If the design flow value is used, use the value that represents the total supply cfm for the fan system. Enter the value in section #1 of the worksheet.

Step 4.   Section #2 calculates the percent outdoor air being supplied to the conditioned spaces when the outside air dampers are in their minimum position. Enter the return, mixed, and outside air temperatures in section #2.

Step 5.   Subtract the mixed air temperature from the return air temperature, and divide by the difference between the return and outside air temperature to determine the percent outside air being supplied to the conditioned space.

Step 6.   Section #3 determines the ventilation rate for the conditioned space. Enter the total air flow from section #1 into section #3.

Step 7.   Enter the percent outside air calculated in section #2 into section #3.

Step 8.   Determine the number of people that normally occupy the space and enter the value in section #3.

Step 9.   Multiply the total air flow by the percent outside air and divide by the occupancy to determine the ventilation rate in cfm per person. Enter the value in section #3.

The ventilation rate determined by Worksheet 3.1, when compared to the ventilation standards listed in Figure 3.8 will indicate how over- or under-ventilated the space is. If the space is over-ventilated, it is possible to cut energy use by reducing the ventilation rate. Use Worksheet 3.2 to calculate the heating energy savings resulting from reducing ventilation air. While both heating and cooling costs will be reduced, the impact of excessive ventilation air on heating costs is much greater than it is on cooling costs in all but the most southern climates. Before Worksheet 3.2 can be used, Worksheet 3.1 will have to have been completed.

Use Worksheet 3.2 as follows:

Step 1.   Enter the actual ventilation rate determined by Worksheet 3.1 in section #1.

Step 2.   From Figure 3.8, determine the minimum ventilation rate for the application. Enter the value in section #1 of the worksheet.

Step 3.   Determine the number of people who normally occupy the space and enter the value in section #1 of the worksheet.

Step 4.   Figure 3.9 is a map of the annual number of heating degree days (65°F base). For the location of the facility, determine the annual number of heating degree days and enter the value in section #1 of the worksheet.

Step 5.   Determine the average occupied hours space temperature for the facility during the heating season and enter the value in section #1 of the worksheet.

Step 6.   Determine the number of hours that the HVAC systems operate each week and enter the value in section #1 of the worksheet.

Step 7.   Section #2 of the worksheet determines the ventilation cfm reduction that can be achieved. Enter the values from section #1 for the actual ventilation rate, the required ventilation rate, and the space occupancy in section #2 of the worksheet.

Step 8.   Subtract the required ventilation rate from the actual ventilation rate, and multiply by the space occupancy to determine the ventilation rate reduction. Enter the value in section #2 of the worksheet.

Step 9.   Section #3 of the worksheet determines the annual energy savings achieved. Enter the ventilation rate from section #2 into section #3.

Step 10.   Use Figure 3.10 to determine the annual energy use per thousand cfm of ventilation air. Enter the figure on the left side at the number of annual heating degree days for the application. Draw a line horizontally to the right across the figure until you intersect the line for the space temperature for the application. From the intersection of the two lines, draw a vertical line until you intersect the line for the hours of operation for the application. From that intersection, move horizontally to the left until you intersect the scale for annual energy use. Determine the use and enter the value in section #3 of the worksheet.

Step 11.   Multiply the ventilation rate reduction by the annual energy use and divide by 1,000 to determine the annual energy savings. Enter the value in section #3 of the worksheet.

Step 12.   Section #4 of the worksheet determines the annual heating cost savings achieved through ventilation air reduction. Enter the annual energy savings from section #3 into section #4.

Step 13.   Determine the fuel cost in dollars per million Btu for the fuel source that supplies the heating system. Enter the value in section #4 of the worksheet.

Step 14.   The conversion efficiency factor is used to correct for losses in the generation and distribution of heat to the system. For hot water systems, use a factor of 1.15. For steam systems use a factor of 1.30. Enter the conversion factor in section #4 of the worksheet.

Step 15.   Multiply the annual energy use by the fuel cost and the conversion efficiency factor to determine the annual heating cost savings.

This value represents the annual heating energy savings that would result from a reduction in ventilation rates. Additional savings will be achieved during the air conditioning season, but those savings will not be as large.

FILTERING SYSTEMS

In HVAC systems, air filters serve a number of different purposes. They help protect heating and cooling coils from an accumulation of dirt that would restrict air flow in the system and decrease the heat transfer efficiency of the coils. They help protect the ductwork from collecting material that could possibly serve as a breeding ground for bacteria and mold. They help protect special areas, such as clean rooms, from contamination.

The type of filtration system used and the degree to which the air is filtered depend primarily on the type of application performed in the space served by the unit, the level of cleanliness required, and the type and quantity of contaminants that exist in the air supply. For example, general industrial applications may require only that coarse particles be removed from the air supply, while clean room application may require that contaminants as small as 0.01 microns be removed.

There are two sources of contaminants that must be considered when evaluating filtration requirements: those introduced into the facility from the atmosphere, and those generated within the building itself. Atmospheric contaminants range from those as small as 0.01 microns to those as large as leaves. They come in all conceivable shapes and configurations. They vary with such factors as the location of the building, the surrounding environment, and the season. Typical atmospheric contaminants include pollen, dust, leaves, and gases.

The size of building-generated contaminants ranges from bacteria to lint, with the majority less than one micron in size. Their type and concentration depend primarily on the function of the building. Typical contaminants include dust, bacteria, hair, lint, and smoke.

Figure 3.11 lists typical air-entrained impurities commonly found in most buildings. Of these, the most common in general building applications are dust, smoke, microorganisms, gases, and vapors.

Filter Terminology

Before examining different air filtration methods, it is important to understand some of the terminology used in evaluating filter performance. ASHRAE has established a set of procedures that can be used to evaluate several key performance characteristics of air filters. The procedures are very exacting in order to provide a basis for comparison between filter types as well as between different manufacturers for the same type. Before evaluating filters for a particular application, all eligible filters must have been rated using the ASHRAE standards.

The two most important filter rating criteria for HVAC applications are how well the filter cleans the air, and how well the filter holds the dirt it has removed from the air stream. Two measures of a filter's ability to clean the air are its arrestance and efficiency. Figure 3.12 lists the arrestance and efficiency ratings for common filter types.

Arrestance, expressed as a percentage, measures the amount of dust particles by weight that the filter can remove from the air stream. It indicates the filter's ability to remove the larger, heavier particles.

Efficiency, also known as the dust spot efficiency, is measured in percentage and is the air filter's ability to remove particulate matter, generally smaller than a micron in diameter. Since the efficiency of a filter changes as it loads up with particulate matter, the most reasonable measure is its average efficiency over its expected life. Figure 3.13 lists commonly used efficiency ratings for HVAC filters.

Since arrestance and efficiency are measured in different ways, they seldom are the same for a given type of filter. For example, a typical two-inch disposable panel filter of medium efficiency might have an average efficiency rating of 15% and an arrestance rating of 90%. The level of arrestance and efficiency required varies with the application. Figure 3.14 shows typical values used in HVAC systems. Use the figure to select a particular filter efficiency rating based on the needs for a given application

How well a filter holds the dust it has removed from an air stream is measured by its dust-holding capacity. As a filter loads up with dust and other particles, the resistance to air flow through the filter increases. Each filter is designed to operate up to a maximum resistance value for a given air flow through the filter. Dust-holding capacity is the weight of the dust that the filter can hold before reaching this resistance value. Dust-holding capacity is most useful in evaluating the expected life of different manufacturers' filters. A more expensive filter with a higher dust holding capacity may be less expensive to operate than a cheaper one with a lower capacity since it would not have to be changed as often

Figure 3.15 lists the arrestance, efficiency, and dust-holding capacities for commonly used filter media. Use the figure to match filter characteristics to the needs of a particular application.

How to Select Filters

Factors that influence the selection of a filtration system for a particular application can be broken down into two categories: primary and secondary. Primary factors include the degree of cleanliness required and the concentration of particles to be removed from the air stream. They will determine both the efficiency and the dust-holding characteristics of the system.

Secondary factors include first and maintenance costs, system space requirements, and the velocity of the air stream. Higher filtration efficiencies result in filters that offer a greater resistance to the air stream. The greater resistance requires a higher capacity fan in order to move the same volume of air through the filter, resulting in increased first and operating costs. High efficiency filters typically cost more than lower efficiency units, again increasing operating costs.

The HVAC system imposes a number of restrictions on the type of filter that can be used. The duct size, the space available for filter installation, and the accessibility of the filter units for maintenance all to a great extent determine which type of filter is suitable for use. For example, roll filters do not require much space for installation, but they do require that the system be accessible on both sides for changing.

The velocity of the air stream also restricts the type of filtering system that can be used. For example, low cost panel filters typically operate in air velocities up to 800 feet per minute while electrostatic units operate best at velocities of 500 feet per minute or less.

Filter Types

There are four major types of filters used in building applications: panel, automatic or roll, extended surface, and electronic. Figure 3.16 lists characteristics of each type.

PANEL FILTERS. Panel filters are the lowest in first and replacement costs of the major filter types used in buildings. They also are the lowest in operating efficiency. Panel filters are available as disposable or permanent units, and typically range from one-half inch to four inches thick. As panel filters load up with particles, the pressure drop increases, resulting in the need for frequent monitoring.

The low efficiency of panel filters makes them suitable for use only in applications where removal of air stream contaminants is not a serious concern. They are frequently used upstream of more efficient filter types as a prefilter designed to remove large particles and thus extend the service life of the more expensive main filter.

AUTOMATIC FILTERS. Automatic or roll filters consist of a roll of filter medium that is fed from a supply reel across the air stream to a takeup roll. New filter medium is constantly fed across the air stream based on a measured pressure drop across the filter or on a timed interval. These filters have higher first costs than panel filters, but cost approximately the same to operate and maintain. They are higher in efficiency than panel filters and offer the advantage of nearly constant efficiency throughout their life. Since automatic filters are constantly supplying new filter medium, the pressure drop across the filter remains relatively constant.

EXTENDED SURFACE FILTERS. Extended surface filters, commonly called bag filters, use sections of filter material that has been shaped into elongated bags to increase the filtering surface area exposed to the air stream. The efficiency and pressure drop of extended surface filters exceed that of both panel and automatic filters, but the pressure drop is less than would be imposed by a panel or automatic filter of the same efficiency. First costs and maintenance costs also are higher.

The higher replacement cost for extended surface filters in most cases mandates the use of a low efficiency panel or automatic filter upstream to prefilter large particles.

ELECTRONIC FILTERS. While panel, automatic, and extended surface filters remove particles from the air stream by impingement or straining, electronic filters use electrostatic charges to attract particles to collecting plates. An ionizing wire imparts a charge to particles in the air stream. As the particles pass through a system of charged and grounded plates, they are attracted to the plates where they are held by an adhesive coating. Periodically the plates must be removed and cleaned.

Electronic filters are high in efficiency and offer low pressure drop. Efficiency is directly impacted by the velocity of the air. First costs exceed those for other filtering systems, and maintenance costs are low. Electronic filters are especially effective for filtering fine dust and smoke particles.

Special caution must be used when working with or around electronic filtering systems due to the high voltage present in the system. Typical units operate at a DC potential of 12 kV.

How to Establish a Filter Maintenance Program

Figure 3.17 lists weekly and biannual maintenance activities to be performed on filter systems which are generic in nature and will vary from system to system. For example, in systems that use 100 percent outside air, particularly in a location that has unusually large amounts of airborne contaminants, it may be necessary to increase the inspection frequency. Similarly, systems that use HEPA or other high efficiency filters may require more frequent inspections in order to prevent operation with dirt-loaded filters.

MAINTENANCE REQUIREMENTS OF HVAC SYSTEM COILS

Heating, cooling, and dehumidifying coils can be a major expense if they are not properly maintained. The failure of a medium- to large-sized coil in an HVAC system typically requires several days to replace once a suitable coil has been located and purchased. Replacement costs, particularly in installations where no provisions were made for coil replacement in the air handler design, often approach the original cost of the air handler. For these reasons, proper maintenance of HVAC system coils is important.

In order for coils to perform as designed, the internal and external heat transfer surfaces must be kept clean. Interior surfaces are kept clean through the use of a water treatment program designed to minimize scale and sludge. Exterior surfaces are kept clean through periodic cleaning with compressed air or water. Most important to the cleanliness of exterior coil surfaces is a program that regularly inspects and changes the system's air filters.

Most other maintenance activities related to coil maintenance involve regular inspections. Figure 3.18 lists and identifies the minimum required maintenance activities that must be completed on a monthly and annual basis. In performing these activities, pay particular attention to cooling coils and their condensate pans. As the result of their operation, these components are wet with condensate. Contaminants from the outside air, or from air recirculated from within the building become dissolved in the condensate, forming acids and other chemical compounds that can attack coil and pan surfaces.

Figure 3.18 also lists activities to be completed at the end of the air conditioning season in order to protect the cooling coil from freezing during winter. If a mixture of ethylene glycol and water is used to prevent freezing, it should be mixed in the right proportions for the lowest temperatures typically experienced in that climate. Figure 3.19 shows the ratio of ethylene glycol to water to prevent freezing for outside air temperatures down to -60°F. Use the figure to determine the quantity of ethylene glycol that must be added to the system to prevent freezing at the lowest expected temperature to which any component of the system will be exposed.

HOW TO MAINTAIN HVAC DUCTWORK

If HVAC ductwork is properly engineered and installed, it will function for the lifetime of the building with only minimal maintenance . However, if the design was not properly engineered or if the installation was not up to industry standards, there is little that maintenance can do to correct the situation. A poorly designed installation will cause continuous problems for building owners and occupants.

The goal of ductwork maintenance activities is to uncover minor problems before they develop into major, expensive ones. For that reason, most maintenance activities involve inspection. Figure 3.20 lists typical maintenance activities for HVAC ductwork. Special systems may have additional maintenance requirements based on the application and the system installed.

Even in systems well engineered and installed, problems may occur as the result of changes in the use of the occupied space. One of the most frequently cited complaints concerning HVAC systems is the noise that they transmit to the occupied spaces. Two methods can be readily employed to control duct-transmitted noise: reduction in the velocity of the air supply; and installation of acoustical insulation to the ductwork.

Figure 3.6 lists recommended maximum duct velocities in order to minimize noise generated by fan systems and the duct itself. If duct transmitted noise is a problem, determine that the supply and return air velocities are within the recommended limits. If the system velocities are higher than the recommended values, determine if the system is properly balanced. Rebalancing the system may reduce the air velocities sufficiently to eliminate the noise problem.

If the system is balanced and the velocities are within the accepted limits, then it may be necessary to add acoustical insulation. The effect that acoustical insulation has on noise varies with the frequency of the sound. In general, the lower the frequency of the noise, the less the impact that acoustical insulation will have. Figure 3.21 lists the impact that several types and thicknesses of interior duct acoustical insulation have on noise. Use the figure to determine the type and thickness of insulation needed to produce the required drop in noise levels.

FIGURE 3.1 Centrifugal Fan Characteristics

Type	Characteristics	Advantages	Disadvantages
Forward Curve	Produces high volume air flow at low static pressure.	Low first costs. Wide operating range. Low operating speed results in small shafts and bearings.	Not suited for applications with high static pressure. Motor can be overloaded if system static pressure is decreased.
Backward Inclined	Operates at a higher speed than forward curved.	Higher efficiency Non-overloading horsepower curve. Suitable for use in systems with higher static pressure.	Higher operating speed requires a larger shaft and bearings. System balance more critical than with forward curved fans.
Radial Blade	Produces low volume flows at high static pressures.	No fan surge region. Linear relationship between fan horsepower and cfm.	Lower operating efficiency. Higher first cost.
Tubular Centrifugal	Operates at low volume and pressure. Commonly used in return systems.	Small size as a result of straight through air flow.	No fan surge region. Linear relationship between fan horsepower and cfm.

FIGURE 3.2   Axial Fan Characteristics

Type	Characteristics	Advantages	Disadvantages
Propeller	Produces a high volume of air flow at a low static pressure, typically less than 3/4". Used primarily in applications that do not require ductwork.	Inexpensive. Small size.	Low efficiency. Small increases in static pressure result in large decreases in volume of air.
Tube Axial	Duct mounted. Operates at medium static pressure, up to 3".	Small size. More efficient than propeller.	Spiral air flow produces high duct and system losses.
Vane Axial	Tube axial fans with guide vanes. Operates at medium to high static pressures, up to 15".	Small size. Adjustable pitch of fan blades permits varying the volume of air supplied.	Relatively low efficiency at high static pressures.

FIGURE 3.3 Typical Fan Performance Curve

Static Pressure

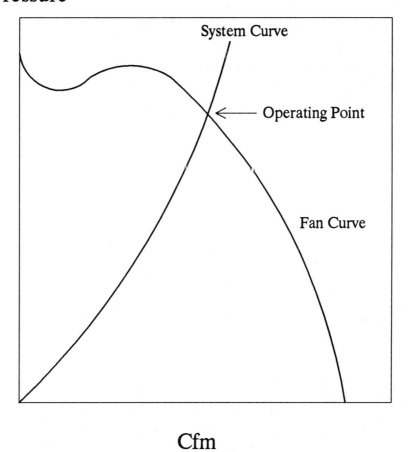

Cfm

FIGURE 3.4 Impact of System Resistance on Fan Performance

Static Pressure

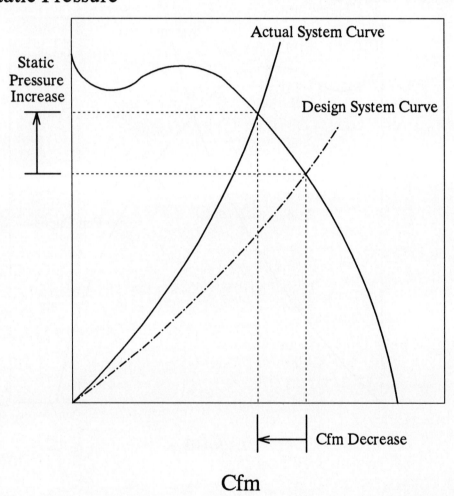

Cfm

FIGURE 3.5 Acceptable Indoor Background Noise

		dBA Level
Auditoriums	Concert & Opera Halls	30 - 34
	Lecture Halls	38 - 42
	Lobbies	42 - 52
	Movie Theaters	38 - 42
Hospitals	Laboratories	42 - 52
	Lobbies, Halls, Waiting Rooms	42 - 52
	Operating Rooms	38 - 47
	Private Rooms	34 - 42
Hotels	Ballrooms, Banquet Rooms	38 - 47
	Guest Rooms	42 - 52
	Lobbies, Halls	38 - 47
Offices	Conference Rooms	34 - 38
	Executive Offices	38 - 42
	General Open Offices	42 - 56
	Lobbies, Halls	42 - 61
Public Buildings	Court Rooms	38 - 47
	Libraries, Museums	38 - 47
	Post Offices	38 - 52
Restaurants	Cafeterias	47 - 56
	Lounges	42 - 56
	Restaurants	42 - 52
Schools	Classrooms	34 - 42
	Laboratories	42 - 52
	Libraries	34 - 42
	Lobbies, Halls	42 - 56
	Recreation Areas	42 - 56
Stores	Clothing	42 - 52
	Department	42 - 52
	Retail	47 - 56
	Supermarkets	47 - 56

Reprinted by permission from <u>1991 ASHRAE Handbook HVAC Applications</u>

FIGURE 3.6 Recommended Maximum Duct Velocities

Application	Velocity (fpm)	
	Supply	Return
Auditoriums	1,300	1,100
Banks	2,000	1,500
Cafeterias	2,000	1,500
Industrial Shops	3,000	1,800
Hospital Rooms	1,500	1,300
Libraries	2,000	1,500
Offices	2,000	1,500
Residences	1,000	800
Restaurants	2,000	1,500
Retail Stores	2,000	1,500
Theaters	1,300	1,100

Reprinted by permission from <u>1991 ASHRAE Handbook HVAC Applications</u>

FIGURE 3.7 Fan Maintenance Activities

Monthly Tasks

Lubricate fan and motor bearings.
Check fan for vibration.
Inspect drive sheaves for wear and tightness.
Inspect drive belt tension.
Test fan freeze-stat controls.

Semi-Annual Tasks

Inspect drive belt for wear.
Adjust drive belt tension.
Inspect tightness of the fan wheel on the drive shaft.
Check bearing alignment.

Annual Tasks

Inspect entire unit for rust.
Inspect fan blades for damage and excessive wear.
Clean fan wheel.
Inspect vibration isolators and motor mounts.
Inspect electrical connections and contactors.

FIGURE 3.8 ASHRAE Recommended
Outdoor Air Ventilation Rates

Application	cfm/person
Ballrooms	25
Classrooms	15
Conference Rooms	20
Dining Areas	20
Hospital Patient Rooms	25
Offices	20
Residences	0.35 *
Retail Stores	0.02 - 0.30 **
Spectator Areas	15
Theaters	15

*   air changes per hour
**   cfm per square foot of floor space

Reprinted by permission from ASHRAE Standard 62-1989,
Standards for Natural and Mechanical Ventilation

FIGURE 3.9 Annual Heating Degree Days (base 65°)

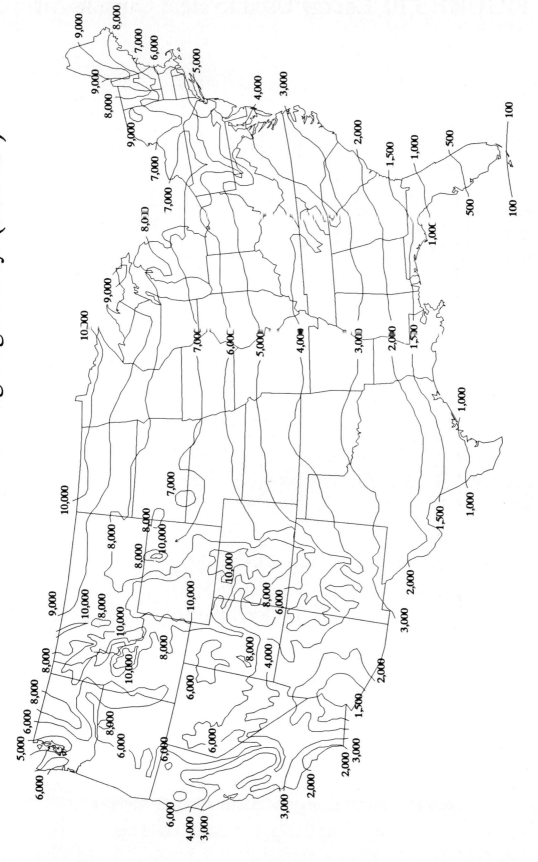

Source: Climatic Atlas of the United States, U.S. Department of Commerce

FIGURE 3.10 Energy Used to Heat Outside Air

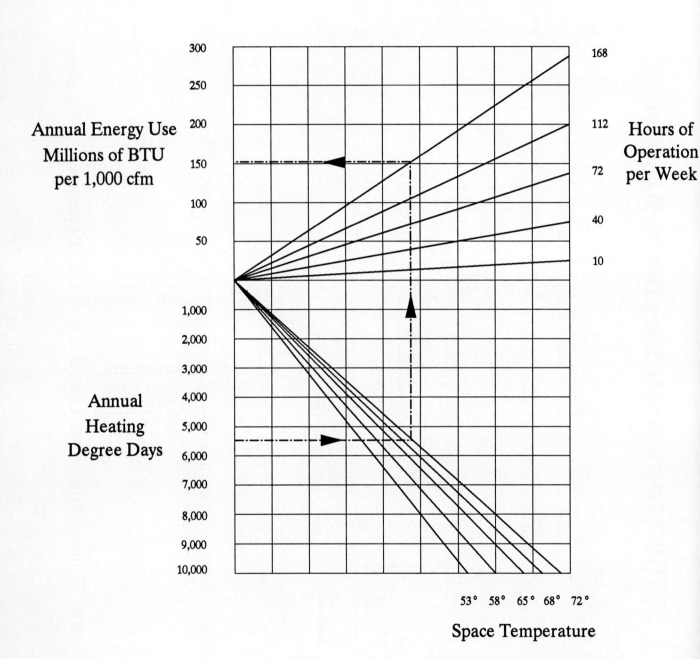

Annual Energy Use
Millions of BTU
per 1,000 cfm

Annual
Heating
Degree Days

Hours of
Operation
per Week

Space Temperature

Source: Federal Energy Administration, <u>Guidelines</u>
<u>for Saving Energy in Existing Buildings</u>

FIGURE 3.11 Air-Entrained Impurities

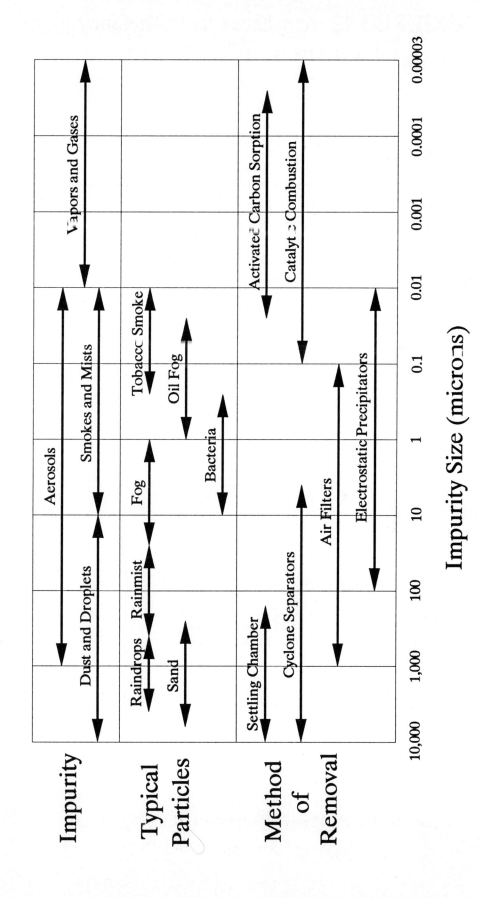

Reprinted with permission from 1981 ASHRAE Handbook Fundamentals

FIGURE 3.12 Arrestance and Efficiency
for Various Air Filter Types

Filter Type	Average Arrestance (%)	Average Efficiency (%)
Two inch disposable panel	80	20
Two inch media pad	80	20
Automatic roll media	85	20
Two inch extended-surface pleated	90	20
Extended surface pocket	98 - 99	50 - 90

Reprinted by permission from 1992 ASHRAE Handbook Equipment

FIGURE 3.13 Particulate Filter Efficiencies
(0.3 micron particle size)

Filter Description	ASHRAE Standard 52-76 Rating		Efficiencies (percent)		
	Dust Spot (percent)	Arrestance (percent)	Initial	Final	Average *
Medium efficiency	25 - 30	92	1	25	15
Medium efficiency	40 - 45	96	5	55	34
High efficiency	60 - 65	97	19	70	50
High efficiency	80 - 85	98	50	86	68
High efficiency	90 - 95	99	75	99	87
95 percent HEPA	-	-	95	99.5	99.1
99.97 percent HEPA	-	-	99.97	99.97	99.97

* Weighted average efficiency to 1 in. WG for medium efficiency filters, and 1.5 in. WG for high efficiency filters.

Reprinted by permission from 1983 ASHRAE Handbook Equipment

FIGURE 3.14 Typical Applications of Filters

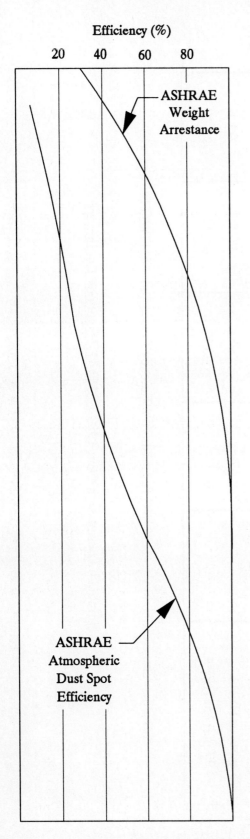

Efficiency (%)

Window air conditioners, protection of heat exchanger from lint accumulations; relatively ineffective on smoke, settling dust, and pollen.

Window air conditioners, packaged air conditioners, domestic warm air heating; effective on lint; somewhat effective on common ragweed pollen (generally under 70%); relatively ineffective on smoke and staining particles.

Air conditioners, domestic heating, central systems; fairly effective on ragweed pollen (generally over 85%); relatively ineffective on smoke and staining particles.

Same as immediately preceding but with greater degree of effectiveness; recommended minimum for makeup air for paint spray; somewhat effective in removing smoke and staining particulates.

Effective on finer airborne dust and pollen; reduce smudge and stain materially; slightly effective on fume and smoke; ineffective on tobacco smoke. Used in building recirculating and fresh-air systems; some types used in domestic heating and air conditioning; used as prefilters to high-efficiency types.

Effective on all pollens, majority of particles causing smudge and stain, fume, coal and oil smoke; partially effective on tobacco smoke. Used same as above but better protection. Some types reasonably effective on bacteria.

Very effective on particles causing smudge and stain, coal and oil smoke and fume. Highly effective on bacteria. Suitable for hospital surgeries, pharmaceutical preparation areas, and controlled areas. Quite effective on tobacco smoke.

Excellent protection against bacteria, radioactive dusts, toxic dusts, all smokes and fumes. Filters in this efficiency range are generally rated by the DOP test method. Uses include hospital surgeries, intensive care wards, clean rooms, pharmaceutical packaging.

Reprinted by permission from 1983 ASHRAE Handbook Equipment

FIGURE 3.15 Performance of Dry Media Filters

Filter Media Type	ASHRAE Weight Arrestance (%)	ASHRAE Atmospheric Dust Spot Efficiency (%)	MIL-STD 282 DOP Efficiency (%)	ASHRAE Dust-Holding Capacity Grams per 1000 cfm Cell
Finer open cell foams and textile denier non-wovens	70 - 80	15 - 30	0	180 - 425
Thin, paperlike mats of glass fibers, cellulose	80 - 90	20 - 35	0	90 - 180
Mats of glass fiber multi-ply cellulose, wool felt	85 - 90	25 - 40	5 - 10	90 - 180
Mats of 5 to 10 um fibers, 1/4 to 1/2 in. thickness	90 - 95	40 - 60	15 - 25	270 - 540
Mats of 3 to 5 um fibers, 1/4 to 1/2 in. thickness	95	60 - 80	35 - 40	180 - 450
Mats of 1 to 4 um fibers, mixture of various fibers and asbestos	95	80 - 90	50 - 55	180 - 360
Mats of 0.5 to 2 um fibers (usually glass fibers)	NA	90 - 98	75 - 90	90 - 270
Wet laid papers of mostly glass and asbestos fibers <1 um diameter (HEPA filters)	NA	NA	95 - 99.999	500 - 1,000
Membrane filters (membranes of cellulose acetate, nylon, etc., having holes 1 um diameter or less)	NA	NA	~ 100	NA

Reprinted with permission from 1983 ASHRAE Handbook Equipment

FIGURE 3.16 Characteristics of Various Filter Types

Filter Type	Pressure Drop	Efficiency	First Costs	Maintenance Costs	Space Requirements
Panel	Medium, increases with dust loading	Low - Medium	Low	Low	Small
Automatic	Medium, constant	Medium	Medium	Low	Medium
Extended Surface	High, increases with dust loading	High	Medium - High	Medium	Large
Electronic	Low, constant	High	High	Low	Large

FIGURE 3.17 Filter Maintenance Schedule

Weekly Maintenance Activities

Inspect for cleanliness and physical damage.
Record pressure drop across filter and replace filters if it exceeds maximum recommended values.
Inspect operation of automatic roll filters.
Test operation of dirty filter alarms
Inspect that all filter access panels are closed and secured.
Inspect for air leakage around filter media.

Biannual Maintenance Activities

Inspect, clean, and lubricate automatic filter drive equipment.
Recalibrate differential pressure manometers and alarms.
Inspect frames for rust.

Additional Maintenance Activities

(to be performed according to manufacturer's recommendations)

Replace disposable filter media.
Clean permanent filter media.
Clean electronic filter collection plates.

FIGURE 3.18 Heating & Cooling Coil
Maintenance Schedule

Monthly Activities

Record inlet and outlet air and water temperatures.
Inspect coil face for dirt accumulation.
Inspect coil tubes for leaking.
Inspect condensate pans for debris.
Check condensate pan for standing water.
In systems that add chemicals to the condensate pan, check chemical supply.

Annual Activities

Inspect coils and fins for corrosion and signs of leaking.
Inspect coil tubes for bulging and cracks
Clean coil fins and tubes with water or compressed air.
Inspect coil frames and casings for corrosion.

Winterizing Cooling Coils

Test automatic freeze protection system (where applicable).
Valve off coil and drain as required by installation.
Add a mixture of water and glycol to prevent freezing in coils that cannot be fully drained.

FIGURE 3.19 Freezing Point of Ethylene Glycol and Water Mixtures

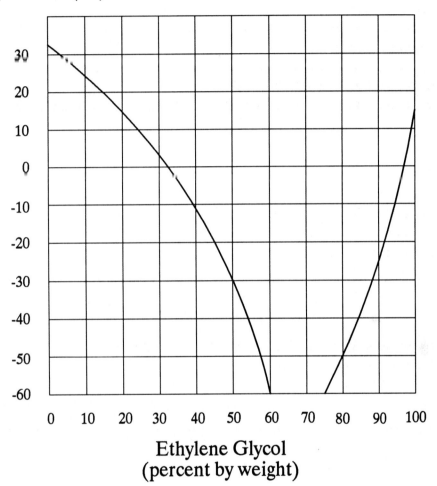

Temperature (° F)

Ethylene Glycol
(percent by weight)

FIGURE 3.20 Recommended HVAC Duct Maintenance Activities

Monthly Tasks

Inspect operation of outside, return, and mixed air dampers.
Lubricate all damper linkages.
Inspect dampers for proper sealing.
Clean outside air intake louver screens.

Annual Tasks

Inspect duct interior for dirt, dust, and lint.
Inspect fire damper positions.
Inspect duct interior downstream of cooling coils for signs of water damage.
Inspect duct exterior for corrosion, loose insulation, and separated connections.
Test for air leakage at joints.
Inspect flexible joints for splitting.

FIGURE 3.21 Acoustical Performance of Interior Duct Insulation

Type	Density (lbs/ft^3)	Thickness (inches)	Absorption Coefficient by Frequency (Hz)						
			125	250	500	1,000	2,000	4,000
Blanket	1.5	1.0	0.32	0.51	0.60	0.83	0.98	0.86
	2.0	0.5	0.16	0.53	0.41	0.60	0.84	0.87
		1.0	0.41	0.58	0.65	0.89	0.90	0.86
	3.0	0.5	0.15	0.51	0.44	0.77	0.92	0.87
		1.0	0.38	0.53	0.71	0.97	0.95	0.90
	3.0	1.0	0.24	0.49	0.65	0.93	0.99	0.99
		2.0	0.50	0.78	0.99	0.99	0.99	0.99
Rigid Board	4.2	1.0	0.24	0.52	0.66	0.88	0.97	0.95
		2.0	0.42	0.74	0.99	0.99	0.99	0.99
	6.0	1.0	0.26	0.47	0.66	0.96	0.99	0.96
		2.0	0.53	0.76	0.99	0.99	0.99	0.97

WORKSHEET 3.1 Determining Outside Air Ventilation Rate

1. Operating Parameters

Return Air Temperature (^{O}F): _____

Mixed Air Temperature (^{O}F): _____

Outside Air Temperature (^{O}F): _____

Total Air Flow (cfm): _____

2. Percent Outside Air

$$\frac{\boxed{}_{\text{Return Air Temp}} - \boxed{}_{\text{Mixed Air Temp}}}{\boxed{}_{\text{Return Air Temp}} - \boxed{}_{\text{Outside Air Temp}}} = \boxed{}_{\text{\% Outside Air}}$$

3. Ventilation Rate

$$\frac{\boxed{}_{\text{Total Air Flow (cfm)}} \ X \ \boxed{}_{\text{\% Outside Air}}}{\boxed{}_{\substack{\text{Area Occupancy} \\ \text{(\# of people)}}}} = \boxed{}_{\substack{\text{Ventilation Rate} \\ \text{(cfm/person)}}}$$

WORKSHEET 3.2 Annual Heating Cost of Ventilation Air

1. Application Data

Actual Vent. Rate (cfm/person): _____

Required Vent. Rate (cfm/person): _____

Area Occupancy (# of people): _____

Annual Heating Degree Days: _____

Space Temperature (^{o}F): _____

Weekly Hours of Operation: _____

2. Cfm Reduction

$$\left[\ \boxed{}\ -\ \boxed{}\ \right]\ \times\ \boxed{}\ =\ \boxed{}$$

| Actual Ventilation Rate (cfm/person) | Required Ventilation Rate (cfm/person) | Occupancy (# of people) | Ventilation Rate Reduction (cfm) |

3. Annual Heating Energy Savings

$$\frac{\boxed{}\ \times\ \boxed{}}{\boxed{1,000}}\ =\ \boxed{}$$

Ventilation Rate Reduction (cfm)   Annual Energy Use (10^{6} Btu/1000 cfm)

Conversion Factor

Annual Energy Savings (10^{6} Btu)

4. Annual Heating Cost Savings

$$\boxed{}\ \times\ \boxed{}\ \times\ \boxed{}\ =\ \boxed{}$$

| Annual Energy Use (10^{6} Btu) | Fuel Cost ($/$10^{6}$ Btu) | Conversion Efficiency Factor | Annual Heating Cost Savings ($) |

Chapter 4

How to Use and Maintain a Fluid Handling System and Its Components

This chapter examines several of the key fluid handling components found in buildings: piping, pumps, and valves. Material presented in this chapter can be used to estimate solutions to problems ranging from frequent component failures to inadequate flow.

The long term life of a piping system depends on the proper selection, sizing, and installation of the piping materials. The wrong piping material used in an application can be rapidly corroded or plugged as the result of chemical reactions with the fluid it is handling. Metallic piping, if in contact with components of dissimilar metals, can rapidly be destroyed by electrical currents set up between the two materials. Improper support of piping can result in unwanted movement and stresses that eventually will lead to piping failures.

STEEL AND COPPER PIPE

Until recently, all piping systems made use of steel pipe or copper tubing. While plastic pipe is widely used today, the vast majority of installed piping systems are of steel or copper.

Steel and copper piping systems are low maintenance, long life-expectancy systems. Both are available in a wide range of sizes and thicknesses suitable for many applications.

Most sizes of steel pipe are available in two different classes, schedule 40 and schedule 80. Schedule 80 pipe has a thicker wall diameter than schedule 40 and is generally used in applications subjected to higher pressures or stresses. Steel pipe may be connected by pipe threads, welds, welded flanges, or special compression fittings. Figure 4.1 lists physical characteristics of steel pipe for sizes ranging from one-half inch through 24 inches.

Copper tube is available in four classes: K, L, M, and DWV. Class K has the thickest wall and class DWV the thinnest. The majority of building HVAC applications use class K or class L copper tube. Class DWV is limited in use to drain, waste, and vent systems. Most sizes of copper tubing are connected by soldering or brazing. Smaller sizes often use compression fittings. Figure 4.2 lists physical characteristics of copper tube for sizes ranging from one-half inch through eight inches.

PLASTIC PIPE

Development in materials, manufacturing processes, and installation practices has led to the widespread installation of plastic piping. Contributing to the rapid growth in use of plastic pipe are the significant advantages that it offers over more conventional metal piping in certain applications. Applied properly, plastic pipe offers both lower first costs and lower maintenance costs over the life of the system. However, if it is used in unsuitable applications, or if the wrong type is used, the results can be disastrous.

A rule of thumb to follow when using any type of plastic pipe is to keep the maximum flow rate under five feet per second. Thermal expansion of plastic pipe also exceeds that for other piping materials and must be accounted for in the piping system design. This is particularly important in applications having piping runs of more than 100 feet or where the temperature change of the fluid being carried by the pipe varies by more than 30°F.

Figure 4.3 lists the general properties of commonly used plastic pipe. Two temperature ratings are given for each type of piping, one for pressurized systems, the other for non-pressurized systems. Use the figure to determine the most suitable type of piping to use in a particular application.

Figure 4.4 lists the maximum operating pressures for different types of plastic pipe. The pressure ratings given in the figure are for the standard operating temperature of 73°F. As the operating temperature of the fluids handled by the pipe increases, the maximum pressure that the pipe should be subjected to decreases. Figure 4.5 shows the pressure de-rating factors that should be applied for systems operating at elevated temperatures. Use the figure to determine the maximum working pressure for a plastic pipe operating at a given service temperature.

Polyvinyl chloride (PVC) piping is the most widely used plastic piping. It is available in schedule 40 and 80 strengths in sizes ranging from one-half inch through 12 inches. It is a good general service piping suitable for use in applications where the maximum service temperature does not exceed 140°F.

Chlorinated polyvinyl chloride (CPVC) has properties similar to those of PVC but is suitable for use in applications with service temperatures up to 210°F. CPVC pipe is available in both schedule 40 and 80 strengths in sizes ranging from one-half inch through 8 inches. CPVC is gaining acceptance for use in building heating and chilled water distribution systems.

Acrylonitrile-butadiene-styrene (ABS) is the lightest weight of all of the rigid or semi-rigid plastic pipes. It is available in both schedule 40 and 80 strengths, and has a maximum service temperature of 180°F. ABS pipe, available in sizes ranging from 1 $1/4$ inch through 6 inches, is used primarily in drain, waste, and vent applications.

Polyethylene (PE) pipe offers the advantage of extreme flexibility. It is available in schedule 40 and 80 strengths in sizes ranging from one-half inch through 48 inches. The flexibility of PE pipe allows sizes of up to two inches to be supplied in coils of up to 400 foot long. PE pipe is used primarily in low pressure applications that require good chemical resistance.

Polypropylene (PP) pipe offers properties similar to PVC but is more chemically resistant. It is available in both schedule 40 and 80 strengths in sizes ranging from one-half inch through 24 inches. PP pipe is widely used in the petroleum industry and chemical laboratories.

HOW TO MAINTAIN PIPE

The two most important elements of any piping maintenance program are good design and regular inspections. In order to be properly maintained, piping systems must be properly sized during the design stage. If the pipes are too small, the result will be higher than desired flow rates. High flow rates produce excessive noise and erosion to the piping system. In systems where the flow is intermittent, high flow rates can lead to water hammer damage to the piping and valves.

A good rule of thumb to follow when sizing pipe for a given flow rate is to limit flow velocities to four feet per second for pipe diameters of two inches or less. Flow velocities in larger pipes depend on the particular application, but should never exceed 15 feet per second.

Piping maintenance has two major elements: water treatment and regular inspections. Water treatment limits the damage to pipe interiors by removing or neutralizing the compounds that attack the metal surfaces. What type of water treatment program should be implemented depends on a number of factors including the type of pipe used and what type of equipment is connected to the system.

Figure 4.6 lists periodic maintenance inspections that should be conducted on piping systems. The inspection intervals listed are for typical installations. Applications that are critical in nature or are in areas where conditions are severe will require more frequent inspections. Use the figure to identify the inspection tasks and frequencies for the application.

PUMPS

Pumps used in building applications are classified by the pressure at which they operate and the flow rate they produce. The required flow rate of the application and its operating pressure will to a great extent determine the type of pump that is best suited for the application.

Installations where the systems pressure is less than or equal to 100 psi are considered to be low-pressure applications. Operating pressures between 100 and 500 psi are considered to be moderate pressure. Those with operating pressures in excess of 500 psi are classified as being high-pressure applications.

A similar classification system is used based on the system flow rate. Flows of less than 50 gpm are considered to be small volume applications. Flow rate between 50 and 500 gpm are classified as being moderate flow applications. Applications with flow rates in excess of 500 gpm are classified as large volume systems.

There are three primary types of pumps used in building applications: reciprocating, rotary, and centrifugal. Of these, the most dominant type is the centrifugal.

Reciprocating Pumps

Reciprocating pumps are positive displacement units that use a moving piston or diaphragm in combination with suction and discharge valves to produce flow. The pumps are self-priming and produce a relatively constant flow capacity over a wide operating pressure range. Reciprocating pumps are best suited for applications where the system pressure is high but the required flow rate is low.

The initial cost of reciprocating pumps is high in comparison to other pump types, but this higher first cost can often be justified by the pump's high operating efficiency. One of the most serious drawbacks of this type of pump is that it produces a pulsating flow as a result of its reciprocating action which also results in noisier operation than other pump types.

Rotary Pumps

Rotary pumps are positive displacement pumps that use one or more rotating elements, such as a vane, gear, lobe, or screw to scoop fluid from the pump chamber. The pumps are self-priming and, like reciprocating pumps, provide a nearly constant flow capacity over a wide range of operating pressures. Most are self-lubricating, using the fluid being pumped. Rotary pumps are typically used over an operating range of 25 to 500 psi.

Rotary pumps are used most in hydraulic, pumped lubricant, and oil burner applications.

Centrifugal Pumps

The most widely used type of pump in building applications is the centrifugal pump. Its simple design and flexibility make it well suited for a wide range of applications. Centrifugal pumps consist of a pump casing and an impeller wheel. Fluid enters the pump casing at the center of the impeller. The rotation of the impeller accelerates the fluid to a high velocity where centrifugal action forces it out of the casing through a discharge port.

The flow discharge from centrifugal pumps is continuous without the characteristic pulsations of reciprocating pumps. The flow rate produced by the pump is not constant under varying systems conditions; it varies inversely with system pressure. Additionally, the pump horsepower requirements vary directly with the fluid flow. Use Worksheet 4.1 to estimate various parameters for centrifugal pump applications. Use the worksheet as follows:

Step 1. Determine the density of the fluid that is being pumped by the system. For systems using water, use a density of 8.3 pounds per gallon. For systems using a mixture of water and glycol, the density will depend on the ratio of glycol to water. Consult with the glycol manufacturer to determine the density. Enter the value in section #1 of the worksheet.

Step 2.   Determine the desired flow rate for the system in gallons per minute. Enter the value in section #1 of the worksheet.

Step 3.   The system head is the sum of the static head created by the change in elevation of the fluid, the friction head created by friction losses in the piping system, and the velocity head that exists at the end of the discharge pipe. It is generally calculated by the engineer designing the pumping system. Enter the system head in feet in section #1 of the worksheet.

Step 4.   The efficiency of the pump varies by design and by size. From the manufacturer's data, determine the pump efficiency and enter the value in section #1 of the worksheet.

Step 5.   Enter the fluid density from section #1 into section #2 of the worksheet.

Step 6.   Enter the system flow rate from section #1 into section #2 of the worksheet.

Step 7.   Multiply the density by the flow rate and the conversion factor of 60 to determine the mass flow rate of the system. Enter the value in section #2 of the worksheet.

Step 8.   Enter the mass flow rate calculated in section #2 into section #3 of the worksheet.

Step 9.   Enter the system head from section #1 into section #3 of the worksheet.

Step 10.   Enter the pump efficiency from section #1 into section #3 of the worksheet.

Step 11.   Multiply the mass flow rate by the system head and the conversion factor of 0.00005 and divide by the pump efficiency to determine the power required by the pump. Enter the value in section #3 of the worksheet.

Step 12.   Enter the fluid density from section #1 into section #4.

Step 13.   Enter the system head from section #1 into section #4.

Step 14.   Multiply the fluid density by the system head and the conversion factor of 0.056 to determine the system pressure. Enter the value in section #4 of the worksheet.

Use the values calculated by the worksheet to determine the pumping system requirements for the application.

Controlling Centrifugal Pumps

The most common method of controlling flow through centrifugal pumps is through the use of throttling valves. In relatively small applications, a throttling valve located on the discharge side of the pump is closed partially until the desired flow rate is achieved. In more complex systems, such as those where heating or chilled water is distributed to a number of different air handlers, throttling or bypass valves are installed at each heating or cooling coil. If throttling valves are used, a centrally located bypass valve senses the change in differential pressure across the pump and opens or closes as required in order to maintain a constant flow rate through the pump.

One of the primary disadvantages of these constant volume systems is the energy required for pumping. Since the volume of fluid being circulated remains constant regardless of the heating or cooling load placed on the system, the pump energy requirements are the same at partial and full system loads. Even if the system is throttled back at partial loads, the pump horsepower requirements do not decrease very much.

An alternative means of operating centrifugal pumps is through the use of a variable speed drive unit connected to the pump. As the throttling valves close at the heating and cooling coils, the variable speed drive senses an increase in the system differential pressure and decreases the speed of the pump, thus maintaining a constant system differential pressure. Since the pump horsepower requirements vary directly as the cube of the pump speed, any decrease in pump operating speed results in a significant reduction in pump energy requirements. Figure 4.7 compares the typical horsepower requirements for part load operation under throttling and variable speed control.

Variable speed drive units offer another advantage over throttling control. In conventional drive systems, whenever the pump is started, its motor is stressed as it attempts to come up to full speed while loaded. In systems using variable speed drives, the pump motor experiences a soft start where it is brought up to speed slowly by the controller.

Establishing a Pump Maintenance Program

The amount of maintenance required by centrifugal pumps is limited but essential. Most pump failures are the result of neglect either to the pump itself or to the fluid that it is handling. Figure 4.8 lists typical maintenance requirements for centrifugal pumps. Pumps serving critical operations, or those handling corrosive or dirty fluids, will require more frequent inspections and service. Use the figure to identify maintenance tasks and their frequencies.

Most pump maintenance activities are concentrated in three areas: bearings, sealing devices, and alignment. Bearing maintenance consists of supplying the right type and quantity of lubricant to the bearing. Oil lubricated bearings must have their oil level kept in the normal range. Too little oil and the bearing may run dry and self-destruct. Too much oil results in overheating of the bearing. Similarly, grease lubricated bearings will burn out if run dry. If over-greased, the grease may prevent the ball bearings from rolling properly, damaging the bearing races.

There are two types of seals used in most centrifugal pumps, packing glands and mechanical seals. Packing glands require only periodic inspection and minor adjustment. Overtightening can damage both the seal and the pump shaft. The only maintenance that mechanical seals require is periodic inspection for leaking.

The two things that contribute the most to premature pump seal failure are dirt in the pumped fluid and misaligned pump couplings. When dirt and other material is in suspension in the pumped fluid, it gets between the seal and the rotating shaft resulting in wear. Misalignment places excessive stresses on seals.

Proper alignment of pumps and motors is important for other reasons. Misalignment results in vibrations, noisy operation, damage to couplings and bearings, and excessive wear to shafts and wear rings. While minor misalignments can be offset by the motor-pump coupling, the more accurate the alignment, the better the pump will operate. Accurate pump alignment requires the use of a dial indicator because the manufacturer's recommendations for maximum deviations are typically limited to several thousandths of an inch.

VALVES

Problems with the operation of building mechanical systems valves are so widespread in facilities that they have almost become accepted as the norm. Early failures, leaks, locked operation, inability to fully close off flow: all are common valve problems that result in system downtime and increased operating and maintenance costs. Most of these valve problems, particularly those that reoccur on a regular basis, can be traced back to four major causes: using the wrong type of valve for a particular application; improperly installing the valve; neglecting the valve while it is in operation; and using the valve in ways it was never designed to be used.

Proper valve selection is critical to the operation of the system. For example, exceeding the valve's operating temperature and pressure range can result in damage to internal components and contribute to early failure. Contaminants in the fluid flow are damaging to some valve types but have no effect on others. The operation of some valve types produces water hammer strong enough to damage piping and other components in the system. The pressure drop induced across some types of valves is severe enough to restrict the fluid flow while other types produce little or no pressure drop.

Poor installation practices lead to rapid valve failures. For example, using the flange bolts on a valve body to correct for improperly aligned piping places stress on the flanges and valve body, frequently resulting in cracks. Construction debris left in the system piping can damage valve seats as it passes through the valve body.

Poor maintenance practices involving valves are primarily the result of neglect. Many valves, particularly those used to isolate pieces of equipment, sit for months or years at a time without being operated. Then when they are needed, it is often found that the valve has frozen in the open position, or cannot fully shut off the flow. Periodic maintenance, including cycling the valve, can reduce valve-related problems and the expense of correcting them.

Each valve type has its own advantages and limitations. Some valves are designed to withstand frequent operation while others are not. Operating these valves too frequently can lead to premature valve failures. Similarly, not all valves can operate properly with fluid flows that contain suspended particles; the particles can erode or build up on valve seats resulting in leakage through the valve. To be successful, the valve must be matched to the application.

How to Select Valves

There are four use factors that must be considered when evaluating valves for applications: the function that the valve is expected to perform; the level and type of contamination found in the fluid passing through the valve; the working pressure of the fluid; and the working temperature of the fluid. Selecting the wrong type of valve for the application can result in early valve failure or poor system performance.

Valve Classification

Valves are classified according to the function that they are to perform. In mechanical systems there are three primary functions: on-off control, throttling, and prevention of back flow. On-off control is used primarily in the isolation of equipment and components, such as a building chiller. Throttling control is used to regulate the flow of the fluid, such as the flow of chilled water in a cooling coil. Back flow prevention is a concern in domestic water systems where the possibility exists for siphoning contaminated water back into the water supply.

FLUID CONTAMINATION. All fluid flows contain some quantity of suspended particles. The level of contamination and the velocity of the flow will determine to a great extent the type of valve that is suitable for use. In general, the greater the level of contamination and the higher the flow velocity, the lower the level of obstruction to flow must be presented by the valve.

VALVE WORKING PRESSURE. All valves are rated and marked on the valve body for the maximum pressure under which they should be operated. Higher operating pressures can result in failures of valve components. Two pressures are given: SP and WOG. The SP rating is the maximum operating pressure for the valve in steam systems. The WOG rating is maximum operating pressure in water, oil, or gas systems.

VALVE WORKING TEMPERATURE. The maximum temperature rating of a valve is an important consideration in selecting valves since operation above this point may result in damage to the valve from deformation or binding of the stem.

Figure 4.9 lists characteristics of the most commonly used valves in building applications. Use the figure to help in selecting the most appropriate type of valve to use in a particular application.

Isolation Valves

The purpose of the isolation valve is to separate sections of pipe or pieces of equipment from the rest of the system. It performs an on-off control function with no need to regulate or throttle the quantity of fluid passing through the system. In most valve designs, attempting to throttle the flow with an isolation valve results in erosion to valve seats and other internal components.

The major factors that must be considered when evaluating different isolation valve types include the speed of closure, how often the valve will be operated, and the level of resistance to the fluid flow when the valve is fully open. The most common isolation valves include the gate, butterfly, plug, and ball valves.

Gate valves use a vertical disk or gate that slides perpendicular to the flow direction to cut off the flow. Units are available with non-rising and rising stems. In non-rising stem gate valves, the screw mechanism that drives the gate is internal to the valve body and is exposed to the fluid flow. They are best suited for applications where the headroom is limited. Rising stem gate valves have the screw drive mechanism mounted external to the valve body and isolated from the flow. They are recommended for use in applications involving high temperature, corrosive fluids, or fluids with suspended solids.

Gate valves are a general purpose isolation valve that performs well in a wide range of application temperatures, pressures, and fluids. One of its greatest limitations is that frequent operation results in wear and improper sealing.

Butterfly valves control flow by means of a circular disk mounted to a pivot axis through the center of the valve. Turning the valve handle rotates the disk perpendicular to the flow, cutting it off. Sealing is provided by means of a compressible elastomers doughnut around the disk. Most butterfly valves are intended for use in low temperature and low pressure applications only.

Plug valves control flow by means of a tapered cylinder with a hold drilled through it. When the hole is lined up with the fluid flow path, full flow takes place. As the cylinder is rotated, the hole is closed off, restricting flow. The ball valve is similar in construction and operation, but uses a ball with a hole in it instead of a tapered cylinder.

Both the plug and ball valves are intended for use in low temperature and pressure applications. Neither functions well in steam lines.

Throttling Valves

The purpose of the throttling valve is to provide manual flow regulation. While the valves can fully close off the flow, they are generally used to limit the flow to some value between full-flow and no-flow. Due to their designs, most throttling valves present a relatively high flow resistance in the full-open position.

The major factors that must be considered when evaluating different throttling valve types include the speed of closure, how often the valve will be operated, the layout of the piping on either side of the valve, and the ease of maintenance. The two most common throttling valves are the globe and the angle valves. Two additional throttling valves, the diaphragm and the pinch valve, provide both isolation and throttling control.

The globe valve uses a moving disk or plug that presses against a seat in the valve body to choke off the flow. In the process, the fluid flow changes direction several times, resulting in turbulence and relatively high pressure drops through the valve. The turbulent flow through the valve body helps to keep disk and valve seat surfaces free of contaminants. Even when some particles do become lodged between the seat and the disk, frequently they can be cleared simply by partially closing the valve, fully opening it, then closing it.

Globe valves are well suited for applications requiring frequent adjustments to the flow rates. Maintenance is a relatively easy task as the seat and disk can be readily removed for repair or replacement.

The angle valve is identical in construction and operation to the globe valve with the exception of a 90-degree change of flow direction between the valve inlet and outlet. The inlet-to-outlet arrangement produces a slightly lower pressure drop in the angle valve.

The diaphragm valve makes use of a flexible diaphragm element that is pressed against a fixed seat to close off fluid flow. The diaphragm can be made from a variety of materials depending on the type of fluid. It can be used equally well as an isolation and a throttling valve. Construction of the valve permits easy maintenance or replacement of interior parts. It is ideal for use with corrosive and contaminated fluids because the mechanical valve operator is isolated from the fluid flow. Service is limited to low pressure applications.

The pinch valve, although used primarily in throttling applications, is suitable for use in applications requiring an isolation valve. Flow control is achieved by the use of one or more flexible elements that are pressed together to choke off the fluid flow. Like the diaphragm valve, the flexible elements can be made out of a variety of materials to handle a wide range of fluids. It is ideal for use with corrosive and contaminated fluids in low pressure applications.

Check Valves

Check valves are used in fluid handling systems to prevent the accidental reversal of flow of fluid. They perform an on-off control and are self-actuating. They readily permit fluid to flow in one direction, yet swing closed upon flow reversal. There are two major types of check valves used in building mechanical systems: the swing check valve and the lift check valve.

The swing check valve uses a hinged disk that is held open by normal fluid flow. When the flow stops or reverses, the disk swings closed, blocking flow. The valve does not provide tight shut-off of flow. It may be installed horizontally or in a vertical position as long as the flow is upward.

Swing check valves are not intended for applications that experience rapid changes in direction of flow. Such applications can result in excessive wear of the disk and the disk mounting mechanism. Rapid direction of flow changes can also result in cases of severe water hammer.

The lift check valve uses a disk that is lifted by normal fluid flow. Flow keeps the valve open. Two types of valves are manufactured, one for use in horizontal flows, the other in vertical flows. The two types are not interchangeable.

Lift check valves provide a tighter flow seal than do swing check valves, and they can be used in flows that rapidly change direction. Their major drawback is their relatively high pressure loss when in the full-open position.

How to Establish a Valve Maintenance Program

A thorough valve maintenance program begins with proper valve selection. If the wrong type of valve is used in a particular application, no amount of maintenance will correct the problem. In fact, the life of the valve will most likely be shorter than expected.

The next step in a valve maintenance program is insuring that the valves are properly installed. Overtightening, using the valve flange or connections to bring misaligned piping into proper alignment places stress on the valve body and internal components. Similarly, installing valves in vertical pipe runs that were intended for use in horizontal applications results in improperly functioning valves.

Finally, valves require attention. Even if the correct valve is properly installed, it will eventually come back to haunt you if it is ignored. One of the most common valve complaints from building managers is that when maintenance crews attempted to work on a piece of equipment and they tried to disconnect it from the heating or chilled water supply, the isolation valves would not hold. As a result, they had to shut down and drain the entire system, turning a job that should have lasted only a few hours into one that may have lasted days and caused major disruptions to the entire facility.

The level of maintenance that valves require depends on several factors, including the type of valve, the type of fluid it is handling, and how critical its operation is. Figure 4.10 lists the minimum valve maintenance activities required for typical applications. It is important to note that these are minimum maintenance requirements. Applications involving corrosive or highly contaminated fluids will require more frequent inspections and service. Applications where valves serve critical functions also will require more frequent testing and inspection.

Finally, one of the most important maintenance activities that can help to extend valve life and minimize maintenance problems is the use of a water treatment program. Most building valve applications are in systems that use water. The majority of these involve water used in heating and air conditioning systems. As the water is recirculated, over time contaminants build up and are suspended in the circulating water. It is these contaminants that erode valve seats, cause valves to seal improperly, and corrode valve operating mechanisms. Proper water treatment can significantly reduce the level of contamination in water systems, thus reducing its impact on valve operation and life.

FIGURE 4.1 Steel Pipe Dimensions and Properties

Nominal Pipe Size & Schedule		Dimensions (inches)			Pipe Weight (lb/ft)	Outside Surface Area (sq ft/ft)
		Outside Diameter	Inside Diameter	Wall Thickness		
1/2	40	0.840	0.622	0.109	0.850	0.220
	80	0.840	0.546	0.147	1.087	0.220
3/4	40	1.050	0.824	0.113	1.130	0.275
	80	1.050	.0742	0.154	1.473	0.275
1	40	1.315	10.49	0.133	1.678	0.344
	80	1.315	0.957	0.179	2.171	0.344
1 1/2	40	1.900	1.610	0.145	2.717	0.497
	80	1.900	1.500	0.200	3.631	0.497
2	40	2.375	2.067	0.154	3.65	0.622
	80	2.375	1.939	0.218	5.02	0.622
2 1/2	40	2.875	2.469	0.203	5.79	0.753
	80	2.875	2.323	0.276	7.66	0.753
3	40	3.500	3.068	0.216	7.58	0.916
	80	3.500	2.900	0.300	10.25	0.916
4	40	4.500	4.026	0.237	10.79	1.178
	80	4.500	3.826	0.337	14.98	1.178
6	40	6.625	6.065	0.280	18.97	1.73
	80	6.625	5.761	0.432	28.57	1.73
8	40	8.625	7.981	0.322	28.55	2.26
	80	8.625	7.625	0.500	43.39	2.26
10	40	10.750	10.020	0.365	40.48	2.81
	80	10.750	9.750	0.500	54.74	2.81
12	40	12.750	11.938	0.406	53.6	3.34
	80	12.750	11.374	0.688	88.6	3.34
14	30	14.000	13.250	0.375	54.6	3.67
16	30	16.000	15.250	0.375	63	4.19
	60	16.000	15.000	0.500	83	4.19
20	20	20.000	19.250	0.375	79	5.24
	30	20.000	19.000	0.500	104	5.24
24	20	24.000	23.250	0.375	95	6.28

Reprinted by permission from 1989 ASHRAE Handbook Fundamentals

FIGURE 4.2 Copper Tube Dimensions and Properties

Nominal Pipe Size & Type		Dimensions (inches)			Pipe Weight (lb/ft)	Outside Surface Area (sq ft/ft)
		Outside Diameter	Inside Diameter	Wall Thickness		
1/2	K	0.625	0.527	0.049	0.344	0.164
	L	0.625	0.545	0.040	0.285	0.164
	M	0.625	0.569	0.028	0.203	0.164
3/4	K	0.875	0.745	0.065	0.641	0.229
	L	0.875	0.785	0.045	0.455	0.229
	M	0.875	0.811	0.032	0.328	0.229
1	K	1.125	0.995	0.065	0.839	0.295
	L	1.125	1.025	0.050	0.654	0.295
	M	1.125	1.055	0.035	0.464	0.295
1 1/2	K	1.625	1.481	0.072	1.361	0.425
	L	1.625	1.505	0.060	1.143	0.425
	M	1.625	1.527	0.049	0.940	0.425
	DWV	1.625	1.541	0.042	0.809	0.425
2	K	2.125	1.959	0.083	2.063	0.556
	L	2.125	1.985	0.070	1.751	0.556
	M	2.125	2.009	0.058	1.459	0.556
	DWV	2.125	2.041	0.042	1.065	0.556
2 1/2	K	2.625	2.435	0.095	2.926	0.687
	L	2.625	2.465	0.080	2.479	0.687
	M	2.625	2.495	0.065	2.026	0.687
3	K	3.125	2.907	0.109	4.002	0.818
	L	3.125	2.945	0.090	3.325	0.818
	M	3.125	2.981	0.072	2.676	0.818
	DWV	3.125	3.035	0.045	1.687	0.818
4	K	4.125	3.857	0.134	6.510	1.080
	L	4.125	3.905	0.110	5.377	1.080
	M	4.125	3.935	0.095	4.661	1.080
	DWV	4.125	4.009	0.058	2.872	1.080
6	K	6.125	5.741	0.192	13.867	1.603
	L	6.125	5.845	0.140	10.200	1.603
	M	6.125	5.881	0.122	8.916	1.603
	DWV	6.125	5.959	0.083	6.105	1.603
8	K	8.125	7.583	0.271	25.911	2.127
	L	8.125	7.725	0.200	19.295	2.127
	M	8.125	7.785	0.170	16.463	2.127
	DWV	8.125	7.907	0.109	10.637	2.127

Reprinted by permission from 1989 ASHRAE Handbook Fundamentals

FIGURE 4.3 General Properties of Plastic Pipe

Type of Pipe	Properties	Typical Applications	Operating Temperature		Method of Joining
			Without Pressure	With Pressure	
ABS	Rigid, good impact strength at low temperatures, maintains rigidity at higher temperatures	Water Drain Waste Vent Sewage	180 °F	100 °F	Solvent cement Threading Transition fittings
PE	Flexible, good impact strength, good performance at low temperatures	Water Gas Chemical Irrigation	180 °F	100 °F	Heat fusion Insert and transition fittings
PVC	Rigid, self-extinguishing, high impact and tensile strength	Water Gas Sewage Process Irrigation	180 °F	110 °F	Solvent cement Threading Elastomeric seal Mechanical Transition fitting
CPVC	Rigid, self-extinguishing, high impact and tensile strength	Chemical Hot water Cold water	220 °F	180 °F	Solvent cement Threading Mechanical Transition fitting
PB	Flexible, good performance at high temperatures	Water Gas Irrigation	200 °F	130 °F	Insert fitting Heat fusion Transition fitting
PP	Rigid, light, high chemical resistance	Chemical waste Process	180 °F	100 °F	Threading Mechanical Heat fusion
SR	Rigid, moderate chemical resistance, fair impact resistance	Drainage Septic field	150 °F	-	Solvent cement Elastomeric seal Transition fitting

FIGURE 4.4 Pressure Ratings for Plastic Pipe

Nominal Pipe Size (inches)	PVC		CPVC		ABS		PE	
	Sch. 40	Sch. 80	Sch. 40	Sch. 80	Sch. 40	Sch. 80	Sch. 40	Sch. 80
1/2	600	850	600	850	476	678	188	267
3/4	480	690	480	690	385	550	152	217
1	450	630	450	515	360	504	142	199
1 1/2	330	470	330	470	264	376	104	148
2	280	400	280	400	222	323	87	127
3	260	370	260	370	211	297	83	118
4	220	320	220	320	177	259	70	102
5	190	290	-	-	-	-	61	91
6	180	280	180	280	141	222	55	88
8	160	250	-	250	-	-	50	-
10	140	230	-	-	-	-	-	-
12	130	230	-	-	-	-	-	-
14	130	220	-	-	-	-	-	-
16	130	220	-	-	-	-	-	-

Note: All pressure ratings are for water at 73°F

FIGURE 4.5 Plastic Pipe Pressure De-Rating Factors

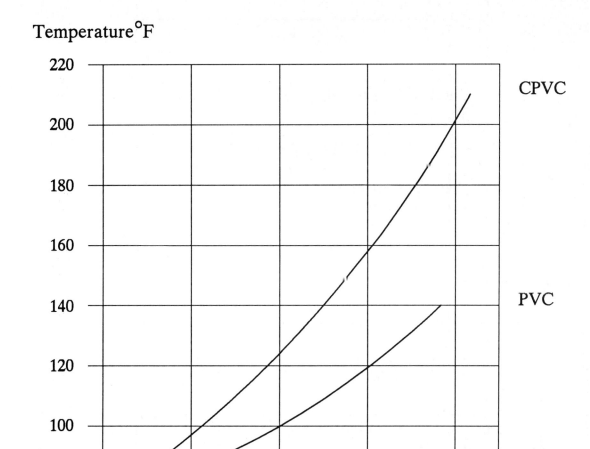

FIGURE 4.6 Piping Inspection Tasks

Weekly Tasks
Inspect for leaks Check for sweating pipes, valves, and fittings Test water treatment system
Quarterly Tasks
Clean pipe strainers Perform water treatment sample analysis
Annual Tasks
Inspect for rust Check for damaged or missing insulation Replace missing pipe and valve labels

FIGURE 4.7 Typical Horsepower Requirements for Throttling and Variable Speed Pump Flow Control

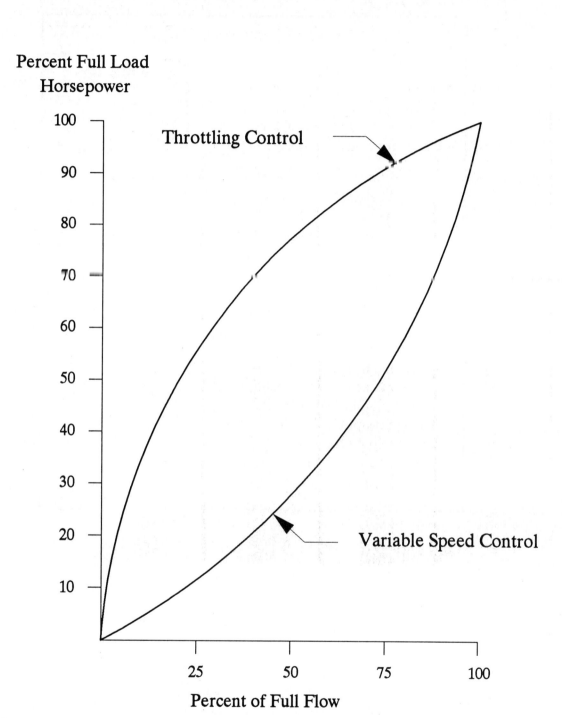

FIGURE 4.8 Centrifugal Pump Maintenance Activities

Periodic Maintenance Tasks	
Task	**Frequency**
Inspect packing glands for leaks	Daily
Check pump bearing oil level	Daily
Check for excessive noise	Daily
Check for excessive vibration	Daily
Clean strainers	Monthly
Grease bearings	Monthly

Annual Maintenance Tasks

Open casing and inspect casing and impeller for wear
Remove, clean, and inspect bearings
Remove packing and inspect shaft sleeve
Clean and repaint casing
Check casing and piping alignment
Inspect coupling for wear
Realign coupling
Meg pump motor
Inspect motor wiring, starter, and disconnect
Retorque mounting bolts

FIGURE 4.9 Valve Application Guide

Valve Type	Function	Frequency of Operation	Full-Open Pressure Drop	Closing Speed	Tightness of Shut-Off	Typical Applications
Gate	Isolation	Low	Low	Slow	Poor	General service, steam, oil, gas, air, heavy liquids
Globe	Throttling	Medium	High	Medium	Good	General service, liquids, gases
Angle	Throttling	Medium	Medium	Medium	Good	General service, liquids, gases
Butterfly	Isolation	High	Low	Fast	Good	General service, liquids, gases, liquids with suspended solids
Plug	Isolation	High	Low	Fast	Good	General service, liquids, gases
Ball	Isolation	High	Low	Fast	Good	General service, liquids, gases
Diaphragm	Isolation & Throttling	Medium	Medium	Medium	Good	Corrosive liquids, dirty liquids, sludges
Pinch	Isolation & Throttling	Medium	Low	Slow	Good	Low temperature and pressure slurries and liquids with suspended solids
Swing Check	Check Flow Reversal	Low	Low	Medium	Poor	Low-velocity liquids
Lift Check	Check Flow Reversal	High	High	Medium	Fair	Liquids or gases

FIGURE 4.10 Valve Maintenance Activities

Valve Type	Task	Frequency (months)
Gate	Cycle through operating range Inspect for leaks Lubricate stem packing Check/replace valve packing Check stem alignment	6 6 6 6 6
Globe and Angle	Cycle through operating range Inspect for leaks Adjust packing nut Test for tight shut-off	3 3 6 6
Butterfly	Cycle through operating range Inspect stem for leaks Test for tight shut-off	6 6 6
Plug	Cycle through operating range Inspect for leaks Lubricate	3 3 3
Ball	Cycle through operating range Inspect for leaks Lubricate packing gland	3 3 3
Diaphragm	Cycle through operating range Inspect valve stem Test for tight shut-off	6 6 6
Pinch	Cycle through operating range Inspect valve stem Test for tight shut-off	6 6 6
Swing and Lift Check	Disassemble and inspect Clean	24 24

WORKSHEET 4.1 Pump Parameters

1. System Parameters

Fluid Density (lb/gal): _____   System Head (ft): _____

Flow Rate (gpm): _____   Pump Efficiency (%): _____

2. Mass Flow Rate

[ ]	X [ ]	X [60]	=	[ ]
Density (lb/gal)	Flow Rate (gal/min)	Conversion Factor		Mass Flow Rate (lb/hr)

3. Power Requirements

$$\frac{[\quad] \times [\quad] \times [0.00005]}{[\quad]} = [\quad]$$

Mass Flow Rate (lb/hr)   System Head (ft)   Conversion Factor

Pump Efficiency

Power (hp)

4. System Pressure

[ ]	X [ ]	X [0.056]	=	[ ]
Density (lb/gal)	System Head (ft)	Conversion Factor		System Pressure (psi)

## Chapter 5

SELECTING AND OPERATING MISCELLANEOUS MECHANICAL EQUIPMENT

This chapter examines two components in HVAC systems: heat exchangers and air compressors. Both are key components in the operation of nearly all HVAC systems; yet both are often overlooked when maintenance requirements are considered. Compounding the difficulty is the fact that problems in heat exchangers and air compressors frequently show up in other areas and thus often go undiagnosed until the situation becomes acute.

Material presented in this chapter can be used to identify and solve problems with heat exchangers and air compressors. Additional information is presented to help establish maintenance activities designed to prevent or reduce the frequency of problems in these components.

HEAT EXCHANGERS

Heat exchangers are found throughout building HVAC systems. By definition, heat exchangers are any device that facilitates the exchange of heat from one medium to another medium while maintaining a physical separation of the two media. Steam converters, heating and cooling coils, hot water converters, boilers, and radiators are all examples of heat exchangers commonly found in building HVAC systems. For the purposes of this chapter, discussion of heat exchangers will be limited to two specific types: shell and tube heat exchangers, and plate and frame heat exchangers.

How to Estimate Heat Exchanger Parameters

Determining the operating parameters is made easier by the fact that the energy input into the heat exchanger equals the energy out of the exchanger. By knowing the energy supplied to a heat exchanger, it is possible to determine the temperature and flow rate parameters on the secondary side of the exchanger.

Use Worksheet 5.1 to estimate the heat transfer rate through a heat exchanger based on actual performance. Use the worksheet as follows:

Step 1.	For the heat source supplying a heat exchanger, determine the water flow rate in gallons per minute, the inlet water temperature, and the outlet water temperature. Enter the values in section #1 of the worksheet.
Step 2.	Enter the water flow rate from section #1 into section #2 of the worksheet.
Step 3.	Enter the inlet and outlet water temperatures from section #1 into section #2 of the worksheet.
Step 4.	Subtract the outlet temperature from the inlet temperature, multiply by the flow rate and the conversion factor of 500 to determine the heat transfer rate in Btu per hour. Enter the value in section #2 of the worksheet.

The worksheet calculates the heat transfer rate through the heat exchanger. The values can then be used to determine the parameters for the secondary side of the exchanger. For a given flow rate, the temperature rise can be determined, or for a given temperature rise, a flow rate can be calculated.

Use Worksheet 5.2 to estimate the temperature rise or flow rate parameters for the secondary side of a heat exchanger. Use the worksheet as follows:

Step 1.	Enter the heat transfer rate in Btu per hour for the heat exchanger in section #1 of the worksheet. If the actual heat transfer rate is known, use that value. If the actual rate is not known, use the name plate rating.
Step 2.	If the flow rate is known and you are estimating the temperature rise across the secondary side of the heat exchanger, enter the flow rate in section #1 of the worksheet. Skip to step #4.
Step 3.	If the temperature rise is known and you are estimating the flow rate, enter the temperature rise in section #1 of the worksheet. Skip to step #6.
Step 4.	To estimate the temperature rise, enter the heat transfer rate and the flow rate from section #1 of the worksheet into section #2.

Step 5.   Divide the heat transfer rate by the flow rate and the conversion factor of 500 to determine the temperature rise across the heat exchanger. Enter the value in section #2 of the worksheet.

Step 6.   To estimate the flow rate through the heat exchanger, enter the heat transfer rate and the temperature rise from section #1 of the worksheet into section #3.

Step 7.   Divide the heat transfer rate by the temperature rise and the conversion factor of 500 to determine the flow rate through the heat exchanger. Enter the value in section #3 of the worksheet.

The temperature rise and flow rate parameters calculated by use of the worksheet for the secondary side of the heat exchanger can be used to determine the capacity of the system.

Using Shell and Tube Heat Exchangers

Shell and tube heat exchangers have long been the workhorse of building HVAC systems. One fluid is passed through a series of tubes through the center of the heat exchanger. The second fluid surrounds the tubes and is contained by the unit's shell. Units are typically designed to have one, two, or four tube passes through the shell. Flow in the shell and tubes can be in the same direction or in opposite directions.

The tubes are made of a variety of materials, including copper, steel, stainless steel, and copper-nickel. Material selection depends on the fluid passing through the tubes and the shell.

An important factor in extending the life of shell and tube heat exchangers is limiting the velocity of the fluid in both the tubes and the shell. Shell fluid velocities should be limited to 4 feet per second. For copper tubes, the velocity in the tubes should be limited to 7.5 feet per second. For steel, stainless steel, or copper-nickel tubes, fluid velocity should be limited to 10 feet per second. These velocities represent the maximum recommended tube velocities for fluid that is free of contaminants. If the fluid that is being circulated through the tubes contains suspended solids, velocities should be further reduced to limit erosion in tube bends.

Using Plate and Frame Heat Exchangers

While shell and tube heat exchangers are considered to be the workhorse of HVAC system applications, a second type, the plate and frame heat exchanger, has been gaining widespread acceptance as an alternative. Plate and frame construction consists of a series of gasketed plates bolted together in a rigid steel frame. The two fluids pass through alternate layers in the heat exchangers, with the heat transfer taking place across the steel plates. The use of a number of plates creates a large area for heat transfer.

The simple construction of plate and frame heat exchangers has been designed to operate at pressures up to 300 psig and 300°F. A large unit, with an 18-inch inlet and outlet connection, can handle flow rates as high as 19,000 gpm.

Plate and frame heat exchangers offer several advantages for HVAC applications. Their footprint is significantly smaller than that of shell and tube heat exchangers of the same capacity. Their ability to be constructed of a wide range of materials permits the design of units that are corrosion-resistant to the fluids being handled. Their design permits flexibility in design capacity through the addition of plates.

Maintenance Problems in Heat Exchangers

The most common maintenance problems associated with both shell and tube and plate and frame heat exchangers are erosion, fretting, corrosion, and the build-up of deposits.

EROSION. Erosion is a problem primarily in shell and tube heat exchangers, but it occurs in plate and frame units as well. It is the thinning of tube walls and heat exchanger plates as the result of abrasive action by particles suspended in the fluid. The rate at which the material is eroded depends on the quantity and size of the suspended particles, the velocity of the particles, the angle at which the particles strike the heat exchanger surface, and the properties of the heat exchanger material.

In shell and tube units, erosion is most severe where the tubes bend at the ends of the tube bundle. In plate and frame units, most of the erosion takes place at the inlet areas of the plates where the fluid flow is forced to follow a sharp 90 degree bend.

The effects of erosion can be limited primarily through good design practices and proper water treatment. A well designed system will limit the flow rate to within the recommended limits for the materials used. A good water treatment program will limit the formation and accumulation of particles in the fluid.

FRETTING. Fretting is the wearing of surfaces and components as the result of relative motion. As the components of the heat exchanger expand and contract, they move. The relative movement between components results in wear at the point of movement. Its effects can be limited only through proper design of the heat exchanger.

CORROSION. Corrosion is the destruction of heat transfer surfaces by chemical reaction with contaminants in the fluid. In most HVAC heat exchanger applications, corrosion is the result of oxygen dissolved in the fluid, salts suspended in the fluid, or acids and alkalides formed in the fluid from chemical reactions elsewhere in the system. It is best controlled through a water treatment program.

DEPOSIT BUILD-UP. Deposits on heat transfer surfaces are the most common cause of performance loss in heat exchangers. Deposits are formed when soluble salts precipitate out of the fluid and are deposited on the heat transfer surfaces. The rate at which deposits form depends on the temperature difference between the fluid and the surface, the quantity of material suspended in the fluid, and the acidity or alkalinity of the fluid. They generally form as water temperatures are increased as they pass through the heat exchanger.

The rate at which deposits form is best controlled through a water treatment program designed to limit the quantity of material suspended in the fluid and control the pH of the fluid. Once formed, deposits must be removed by mechanical or chemical cleaning. Mechanical cleaning involves the use of soft brushes for the removal of soft deposits and biological growth. Chemical cleaning requires the application of chemicals designed to dissolve the deposits.

How to Establish a Heat Exchanger Maintenance Program

In order to keep heat exchangers performing as designed, proper maintenance is a necessity. Since most heat exchanger problems are related to the fluid that is circulated through the system, an ongoing water treatment program is the single most important maintenance activity. Water treatment will reduce the quantity of particles suspended in the fluid as well as regulate the pH of the fluid. The result will be a reduction of erosion of tubes, of corrosion of heat transfer surfaces, and of the formation of deposits on heat transfer surfaces.

In addition to a water treatment program, heat exchangers require an on-going maintenance inspection program. Figure 5.1 lists the frequency for maintenance activities for a typical shell and tube heat exchanger. Figure 5.2 lists the activities and their frequencies for plate and frame heat exchangers. The activities listed in both figures represent the minimum level of maintenance required. Use the figures as a starting point in establishing a preventive maintenance program. Additional activities may be required depending on the particular installation. Check with the heat exchanger manufacturer to determine the acceptable level of maintenance.

AIR COMPRESSORS

Air compressors serve three primary purposes in facilities: they supply compressed air for power, process, or control uses. Power air is used to drive equipment and motors, such as drills, air motors, and sprayers. Process air is used in plant applications ranging from aerating of chemicals to the mixing of food ingredients. Control air is used to power laboratory processes and building temperature control systems.

While the specific requirements for the air supply depend on the application, each of the three primary uses imposes general conditions on the quality of the air supplied. Power air must be free of liquid water that would corrode drive mechanisms; if it is used for spraying products, such as paint, it must also be free of oil. Process air must be free of contaminants, water, and oil, particularly when it is used with food ingredients. Control air must be free of contaminants, water, moisture, and oil to prevent damage and clogging of air ports in control devices.

The quality of an air compressor being produced today is easily capable of meeting these requirements for a very long period of time with proper maintenance, and with a little planning as to the installation concerning the compressor size and the environment in which it will operate.

Sizing Compressors

As a rule of thumb, air compressors should be slightly oversized for the application. In most instances this means a compressor with 20 to 40 percent more capacity than is required by the application. Application with high peak demands will require a greater degree of oversizing. Additional oversizing is required for compressors located at higher elevations. Figure 5.3 shows the impact that elevation has on compressor output. Use the figure to correct compressor capacity ratings for operation at higher elevations.

Locating Compressors

The environment in which the compressor operates will determine to a great extent its life and the frequency with which it must be serviced. Dirty environments with airborne dust and other contaminants require greater filtering protection on the air compressor intake to prevent fouling the air supply. Dirty environments also will require more frequent maintenance inspections and cleaning to prevent the buildup of dirt from interfering with cooling of the unit.

High temperature locations should also be avoided. Compressors generate heat and require cooling either by air or by water. Locating the compressor in a hot environment causes it to operate at a higher temperature, decreasing its operating life.

High temperature locations also decrease the capacity of the compressor. All air compressors are rated at standard operating conditions of 14.7 psig atmospheric pressure, 60°F, and zero percent relative humidity. Operating at a higher inlet temperature to the compressor will decrease the rated capacity. Figure 5.4 shows the effect that elevated temperatures will have on a compressor's SCFM rating. Use the figure to modify the compressor capacity rating for operation in areas with elevated temperatures.

High humidity locations also are to be avoided for similar reasons. High humidity promotes corrosion of compressor components, decreases operating capacity, and results in moisture and water contamination of the air supply system.

Air Compressor Types

There are two classes of air compressors: positive displacement and dynamic. Positive displacement compressors draw a quantity of air into a confined space. As the volume of the space is reduced, the pressure rises. The three most commonly used positive displacement types are the reciprocating, the sliding vane, and the screw compressor.

Reciprocating compressors use a piston connected to a rotating crankshaft to compress the air. Sliding vane compressors use rotating vanes mounted on an eccentrically positioned rotor. As the rotor turns, the space between it and the housing decreases, compressing the air. Screw compressors use two interlocking, rotating screws. As the screws turn, the volume of the space between them decreases, compressing the air. Both are well suited for applications requiring air at 60 to 100 psi at flow rates up to 300 cfm. Higher pressures and flow rates generally require a two-stage reciprocating unit.

The most widely used dynamic compressor is the centrifugal compressor. It uses a high speed rotating impeller to accelerate the air, then converts the induced velocity head to pressure head. Centrifugal compressors are best suited for applications where high pressures are required.

Most air compressors used in building applications are air-cooled. However, in some power and process applications requiring large volumes of compressed air, water-cooled units are common. Maintenance requirements for water-cooled units are similar to that of air-cooled with the exception of the cooling water system. Since deposits on the heat transfer surfaces of the compressor could severely limit cooling capacity, it is important that the cooling water be treated.

Air Treatment

Before air from a compressor is supplied to the application, it is treated. The method and quantity of treatment applied depend on how strong the need is for clean air. Clean air is particularly important in building HVAC control applications where contamination from dirt, water, and oil can clog air ports in controllers, destroying or decalibrating them.

There are three types of contamination that must be controlled for: dirt sucked into the compressor from the environment, oil introduced to the air system by the compressor, and moisture supplied to the system as a result of the compression of air. One exception is the lack of oil contamination in systems that use oil-less compressors.

DIRT CONTAMINATION. Dirt is controlled through placement and filtering. Placing the air intake in a dirty environment simply increases the volume of dirt that will be introduced into the air system. When a dirty environment is a problem, and the compressor cannot be relocated, try moving the air intake to a cleaner location.

Even when the intake is positioned in a relatively clean location, it will be necessary to filter the incoming air. Filtering removes contaminants that can cause problems in the air system fed by the compressor. The type and level of filtering depends on the application and the degree to which it can tolerate dirt. Once installed, it is important to establish a regularly scheduled inspection program to insure that the filters are changed on a regular basis.

OIL CONTAMINATION. Oil contamination of the compressed air is a result of oil from the compressor's crankcase being drawn into the system past compression seals and rings. It is particularly a problem in older, neglected reciprocating compressors that are suffering from worn internal parts. The problem is that oil is particularly damaging to controls and instruments connected to the air system. Even worse, once a system is contaminated with oil, it is extremely difficult to get it out of the system.

The most common method of preventing oil from entering the air system is the use of a coalescing air filter on the discharge side of the compressor. Coalescing filters use impingement and centrifugal action to remove up to 99 percent of all solid particles and droplets of oil from the air supply. While the filters are effective in removing oil, they must be inspected and serviced regularly if they are to maintain their effectiveness.

MOISTURE CONTAMINATION. Moisture is introduced into the air system as a normal part of the compression process. Air entering the compressor contains a certain quantity of water depending on the relative humidity. As the air is compressed, the volume of the moisture remains constant as it cannot be compressed. The concentration of moisture in suspension in the compressed air rises until the saturation point is reached. When the air cools as it leaves the compressor, a portion of the moisture condenses to water and is carried into the air system. A portion of the water collects in the bottom of the receiver where it is readily drained, but a portion is carried off by the compressed air.

To prevent the moisture and condensed water from entering the receiver and the air system, air dryers are generally installed between the compressor and the receiver. There are two type of air dryers: mechanical and chemical.

The most common mechanical air dryer is the refrigerated air dryer. This type uses mechanical refrigeration to cool the air below the dew point. Once it reaches the dew point, the moisture condenses and is readily removed by a separator.

There are, in turn, two types of chemical separators: desiccant and deliquescent. Desiccant separators contain chemicals, such as silica gel, that attract and hold water without chemically binding to the molecules. The chemicals can generally be regenerated by heating or by exposure to dry air. Desiccant air dryers are suitable for applications requiring a dew point of 32°F or less. To be effective they require a clean supply of air free of particles and oil.

Deliquescent separators contain chemicals, such as sodium chloride, that react with the molecules of water, binding to them. Deliquescent separator chemicals can not be reused. These separators are generally restricted to special applications, particularly where air lines are exposed to freezing conditions.

Compressor Maintenance

Building air compressors with proper maintenance are capable of reliable service for an extended period of time. Most maintenance activities are geared towards preventive maintenance and early detection of minor problems before they develop into expensive repairs. Figure 5.5 lists typical maintenance activities for air compressors. Use the figure to identify the tasks and their frequencies for a preventive maintenance program.

FIGURE 5.1 Shell and Tube Heat Exchanger Maintenance

Maintenance Activity	Frequency
Check inlet and outlet temperatures.	Daily
Inspect for leaks.	Weekly
Test operation of control valves.	Weekly
Disassemble heat exchanger	Annually
Inspect heat transfer surfaces for fouling and corrosion.	
Clean heat transfer surfaces.	
Inspect tubes for damage.	

FIGURE 5.2 Plate and Frame Heat Exchanger Maintenance

Maintenance Activity	Frequency
Check inlet and outlet temperatures.	Daily
Inspect gaskets for leaks.	Weekly
Test operation of control valves.	Weekly
Inspect frame for corrosion.	Annually

FIGURE 5.3 Altitude Effect on Compressor Rating

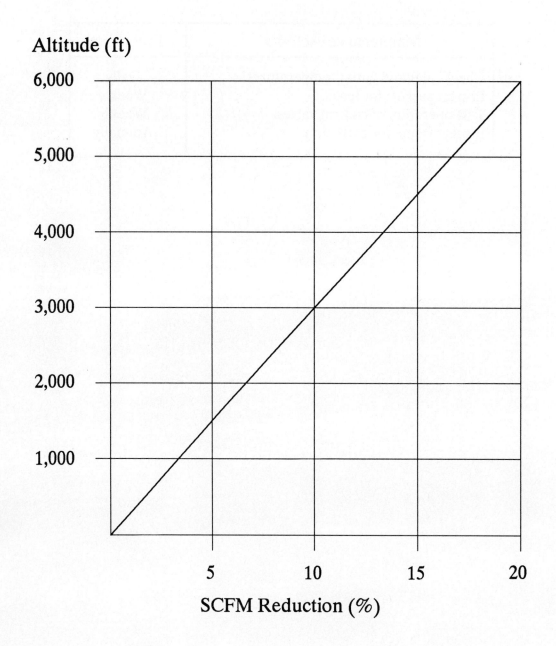

FIGURE 5.4 Temperature Effect on Compressor Rating

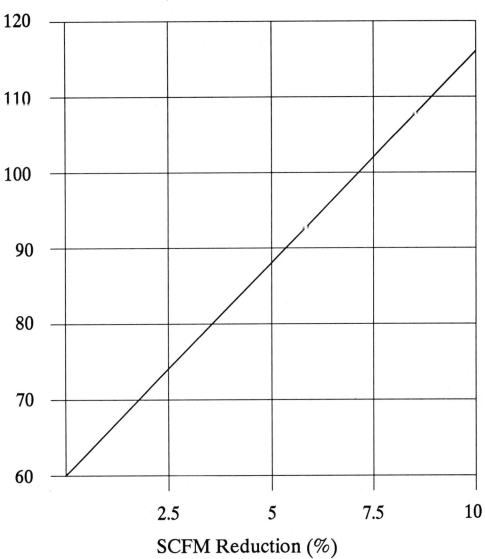

Ambient Temp. (^{0}F)

SCFM Reduction (%)

FIGURE 5.5 Air Compressor Maintenance

Weekly Tasks

Check regulator discharge pressure
Check oil level
Drain water from tank
Drain oil from separator
Check intake air filter
Inspect for oil leaks
Check for unusual noise and vibration

Monthly Tasks

Check suction and discharge pressures
Clean strainers
Clean oil separator

Three Month Tasks

Adjust belt tension
Test pressure relief valve
Test pressure switch controls
Change oil
Check motor for overheating
Lubricate motor

Annual Tasks

Inspect wiring for damage and loose connections
Inspect contacts for pitting and corrosion
Check belt guards
Check mounting bolts for tightness
Clean compressor cooling fins

WORKSHEET 5.1 Heat Exchanger Transfer Rates

1. Heat Exchanger Parameters

Water Flow Rate (gpm): _____

Inlet Temperature (°F): _____

Outlet Temperature (°F): _____

2. Heat Transfer Rate

$$\boxed{500} \quad X \quad \boxed{} \quad X \quad \left[\boxed{} \; - \; \boxed{} \right] \quad = \quad \boxed{}$$

Water flow rate (gpm) — Inlet Temp. (°F) — Outlet Temp. (°F) — Heat Transfer Rate (Btu/hr)

WORKSHEET 5.2 Estimating Heat Exchanger Parameters

1. Application Characteristics

Heat Transfer Rate (Btu/hr): _____

Flow Rate (gpm): _____

Temperature Rise (^{o}F): _____

2. Temperature Rise

$$\frac{\boxed{} \text{ Heat Transfer Rate (Btu/hr)}}{\boxed{} \text{ Flow Rate (gpm)} \quad X \quad \boxed{500}} = \boxed{} \text{ Temperature Rise } (^{o}F)$$

3. Flow Rate

$$\frac{\boxed{} \text{ Heat Transfer Rate (Btu/hr)}}{\boxed{} \text{ Temperature Rise } (^{o}F) \quad X \quad \boxed{500}} = \boxed{} \text{ Flow Rate (gpm)}$$

ELECTRICAL MAINTENANCE

DETERMINING CABLES AND WIRE FACTORS FOR A SAFE AND EFFICIENT DISTRIBUTION SYSTEM

This chapter addresses cabling, wiring, and protective devices typically found in facility power distribution systems. The material presented in this chapter is for general reference and estimating purposes only. While the tables in this chapter conform to the information presented in the National Electrical Code, they are not intended to be used as a replacement for federal, state, or local building codes. Where sections of local building codes are more restrictive than the National Electrical Code, the local building codes must be complied with.

CABLE AND WIRE BASICS

This section presents a discussion of and the working definitions for some of the more widely used terminology with regard to cable and wire. If you need a more precise definition, refer to those presented in The National Electrical Code.

A conductor is the device used to conduct electrical current from one point in the facility to another. While conductors come in many different configurations and can be made out of a wide range of materials, the two most common forms are the wire and the cable. **Wire** consists of a single conductor surrounded by a layer of insulation. **Cable** consists of two or more wires grouped together in a single enclosure. The most common materials used for conductors in both wire and cables are copper and aluminum.

The conductors in both wire and cable can be either solid or stranded. **Solid** conductors consist of a single piece of conducting material whereas **stranded** conductors

Wet Locations: Installations underground or in concrete slabs or masonry in direct contact with the earth, and locations subject to saturation with water or other liquids, such as vehicle washing areas, and locations exposed to weather and unprotected.[1]

HOW TO SELECT CABLE TYPES

Multi-conductor cables are identified by two numbers and a series of code letters. The first number gives the AWG number of the wire used for the conductors. The second number gives the number of conductors in the cable, exclusive of the grounding wire. The code letters designate the type of insulation used. If the cable includes a bare grounding wire, it is designated so on the cable. For example, 14-2 NM with ground indicates a cable with two 14 AWG wires and a ground wire enclosed in a nonmetallic sheathed enclosure.

Common cable types include the following:

AC   –   Armored Cable

NM   –   Nonmetallic Sheathed for Dry Locations

NMC   –   Nonmetallic Sheathed for Dry or Damp Locations

UF   –   Underground Feeder

USE   –   Underground Service Entrance

TWO FACTORS TO CONSIDER WHEN SELECTING WIRE SIZE

In addition to selecting the wire type suitable for the application, you must determine the size of the wire. There are two sizing considerations that you must examine: the voltage drop that will occur in the wire as a result of current drawn by the connected load, and the ampacity rating of the conductor.

Selecting Appropriate Ampacity Ratings

Ampacity ratings of both copper and aluminum conductors are given in tables in the National Electrical Code. Figure 6.3 lists the ampacity ratings for various cable types and sizes at several different ambient temperatures. Use the figures to determine the wire size required for the current and service conditions of the application.

How to Calculate Voltage Drop for Maximum Output

The voltage drop must be calculated for the particular load and the length of the cable to which it is connected.

Voltage drop is particularly important when considering the impact that voltage has on operating efficiency of connected loads. For example, a voltage drop of five percent in a circuit feeding an electric motor reduces the power output of that motor by approximately ten percent and decreases the expected life of the motor. Similarly,

---

[1] Reprinted from the NFPA 70-1987 National Electrical Code.

a voltage drop of five percent reduces the light output of an incandescent lamp by nearly 15 percent. The impact of voltage drop can be more significant on other types of loads such as computers and fluorescent or HID lights.

In determining how much voltage drop is acceptable, a good rule of thumb to follow is to limit voltage drop in the feeder to less than two percent, and an additional two percent in branch circuits measured at the furthest connected load. The National Electrical Code limits voltage drop to a maximum of five percent from the service to the furthest connected load. For a typical 120 volt system then, the maximum permissible voltage drop is six volts (three volts in each of the two conductors).

While you can use the above mentioned rule of thumb and the National Electrical Code limits as a guide, it may be necessary to reduce the voltage drop below these values as a result of special requirements of the connected load.

Use Worksheet 6.1 to calculate the minimum wire size needed to limit the voltage drop to a particular value for a given load or the voltage drop for a given wire size and length and load. You can use the worksheet with both single and three-phase loads.

Use the worksheet as follows:

Step 1.   In order to calculate the wire size needed for a particular voltage drop or the voltage drop in a circuit, it is first necessary to calculate the current in the wire for the connected load. If the current is known, skip to line #7 to determine the wire size or to line #13 to determine the voltage drop in a circuit.

Step 2.   Enter the connected load in kW and the voltage in section #1 of the worksheet.

Step 3.   If the circuit is single-phase, the phase factor is 1.0. If the circuit is three-phase, the phase factor is 1.73. Enter the phase factor in section #1.

Step 4.   Enter the power factor as a decimal value (0 - 1.0) in section #1.

Step 5.   Multiply the connected load by 1,000 and divide by the voltage, the phase factor, and the power factor to determine the current in the circuit. Enter the value in section #1.

Step 6.   If you are calculating the voltage drop in a circuit, skip to line #13.

Step 7.   To calculate the cmil area required for a given voltage drop, enter in section #2 the resistivity of the conductor material used. If the conductor is copper, use the value of 22 ohms per cmil-ft. If the conductor is aluminum, use the value of 36 ohms per cmil-ft. *Note:* these resistivity values take into account that the total conductor length is twice the actual wire length.

Step 8.   Enter the current calculated in section #1 or the value of the known current in amps in section #2.

Step 9.   The cable length used in the calculation is the length of the cable run, not the total length of the conductors. Do not multiply the length by two (for two conductors). Enter the cable length in feet in section #2.

Step 10.   The phase factor for single-phase circuits is 1.0. The phase factor for three-phase circuits is 1.73. Enter the phase factor for the type of service in section #2.

Step 11.   Enter the allowable voltage drop in section #2.

Step 12.   Multiply the resistivity by the current, the cable length, and the phase factor. Divide by the voltage and the percent voltage drop to determine the cmil area required for the cable. Using Figure 6.1, look up the calculated cmil area to determine the AWG wire size. Always select the wire that is one gauge higher than the calculated size. Although the selected cable size might meet the requirements concerning voltage drop, it might not meet the National Electrical Code requirements for conductor size based on load. Use Figure 6.3 to determine the wire size as required by the code. Use the larger of the two wire sizes.

Step 13.   To calculate the voltage drop in a given length of cable for a specific load, enter the cable length in feet, the current in amps, and the cmil area of the cable in section #3.

Step 14.   The resistivity of the cable depends on the material used in the conductor. If the conductor is copper, use the value of 22 ohms per cmil-ft. If the conductor is aluminum, use the value of 36 ohms per cmil-ft.
Note: these resistivity values take into account that the total conductor length is twice the actual wire length. Enter the resistivity value in section #3.

Step 15.   Multiply the cable length by the current and the resistivity. Divide by the cmil area to determine the voltage drop in the wire.

If the voltage drop calculated by the worksheet is greater than the maximum allowable voltage drop for that particular application, repeat the voltage drop calculation for a larger wire size.

HOW TO DETERMINE CONDUIT SIZE

The National Electrical Code establishes maximum values for conductors in conduit in new work, based on the size of the conductors and the type of insulation used on the wire. Figure 6.4 lists the maximum number of conductors as specified in the code. Use the figure to determine the minimum required conduit size for an application.

Tip: While the table lists the code requirements, it is often good practice to select even larger conduit sizes to provide space for future expansion.

Protecting Underground Cables

The most common type of wire used in underground applications is USE: Underground Service Entrance. It is available in single and multiconductors and may be buried directly in the ground. Other wire types with the letter W, designating suitable for use in a wet location, may also be used in suitable conduits or raceways.

Selecting Burial Depth to Protect the Cable

No matter what type of cable is used, you must take special precautions to protect it. Of these, the most important is the depth of burial. Figure 6.5 lists the National Electrical Code requirements for minimum burial depth for cables, conduits, and raceways. Use the figure to determine the minimum depth required for an application.

Protecting Wiring Against Overheating and Short Circuits

As current flows through a wire, it generates heat due to the resistance of the wire. The amount of heat generated varies with the square of the current. Doubling the current increases the heat generated within the wire by a factor of four. If the current is permitted to get high enough, the heat can melt the insulation on the wire and cause a short-circuit or start a fire. To prevent this, all wiring must be protected by current-limiting safety devices that are properly sized for the type and size of wire installed. Such safety devices are commonly known as **over current devices.** The most common types of over current devices are the fuse and the circuit breaker.

Types of Fuses and Their Uses

A fuse consists of a short length of metal alloy mounted within a protective housing. The metal alloy has a low melting point and is sized to carry a specified current without melting. Any currents over the specified size cause additional heating within the metal alloy. The heat melts the alloy and breaks the circuit, protecting the wire and the device connected to it.

There are two major classifications of fuses, standard and time-delay. **Standard fuses** are designed to melt immediately when subjected to any overload. **Time-delay fuses** are designed to melt immediately when subjected to short-circuits and continuous overloads, but do not fail when subjected to temporary overloads such as those that occur when a motor is started.

Tip: Since fuses fail as a result of heat, fuses installed in a hot location will fail before their rated current is achieved. While the wiring must be sized for the connected load, and the fuse must be sized for the installed wiring size, it is good practice not to have a connected load exceed 75% of the fuse's rating. Higher loads may result in nuisance fuse failures.

Figure 6.6 shows the three major fuse configurations: the plug, ferrule-contact cartridge, and knife-blade-contact cartridge. A fourth type, the renewable cartridge, resembles the knife-blade-contact cartridge in appearance but uses a replaceable fusible link.

The plug fuse is available in 15, 20, 25, and 30 amp ratings. It is suitable for use on circuits where the voltage to ground is less than 150 volts. Plug fuses are available with both standard and time-delay elements. Plug fuses are generally found only in older construction on branch circuits, having been replaced with the more popular and convenient circuit breaker.

The ferrule-contact cartridge fuses are available in ratings up to 60 amps, and come in both standard and time-delay configurations.

The knife-blade-contact cartridge fuse is available in ratings of 60 amps and up in both standard and time-delay configurations. Several classes of this type of cartridge fuse are available with varying current limiting, high-fault current interrupt, and time-delay characteristics.

Circuit Breakers and Their Ratings

A circuit breaker is a device that is designed to automatically interrupt a circuit at a preset overcurrent. Unlike a fuse, a circuit breaker can also be used manually to open and close the circuit. In operation, the circuit breaker performs the dual function of a switch and a resettable fuse.

Most circuit breakers have two trip elements: thermal and magnetic. The thermal element consists of a bimetallic strip that deflects with increasing current flow through the breaker. The strip is calibrated so that when the current reaches a predetermined value, the strip deflects enough to open the breaker's electrical contacts. The magnetic element is designed to sense a short-circuit and immediately open the electrical contacts.

There are two ratings used for circuit breakers: continuous current and interrupting capacity. The **continuous current** rating is the maximum current in amps that the breaker will carry without exceeding a set temperature rise. It must never exceed the current-carrying capabilities of the wire connected to it. The **interrupting capacity** rating is the maximum short-circuit current that will trip the breaker.

SIZING PROTECTIVE DEVICES FOR MOTORS

Motors, due to their high starting currents, present a particularly difficult design problem when sizing protective devices. The protective device must be capable of withstanding the short duration, high currents that occur during start-up, yet provide protection from faults in the branch circuit feeding the motor and within the motor itself. In addition, the protective device must protect against motor overloads that, if uncorrected, would result in damage to the motor and its wiring. To assist designers, the National Electrical Code has developed ratings for motor branch circuit protective devices. Figure 6.7 lists the maximum rating of protective devices for motor branch circuits.

SIZING EQUIPMENT AND SYSTEM GROUNDING WIRES

The purpose of electrical grounding is safety; it reduces the danger of electrical shock, equipment damage, fire, and lightning damage. Therefore, proper grounding is an essential characteristic of any electrical installation.

Grounding is the intentional connecting of components in an electrical system to a metal pipe of an underground water system, or a metal pipe or rod driven into the ground. There are two types of grounding: system and equipment grounding. **System grounding** is the connection of one of the electrical system's current-carrying conductors to ground. **Equipment grounding** is the connection to ground of non-current-carrying parts of the system, such as motors, breaker panels, or switch boxes.

The size of the grounding conductors is established by the National Electrical Code for both types of grounding systems. Figure 6.8 lists the required wire sizes for both copper and aluminum wire for equipment grounding. Figure 6.9 lists the required conductor sizes for copper and aluminum conductors for system grounding.

FIGURE 6.1 Characteristics of Copper Wire

Wire Size (AWG)	Diameter		DC Resistance (Ohms per 1000 feet)	Weight (lbs per ft)
	Nominal Inches	Circular Mils		
28	0.0126	159	65.3	0.481
27	0.0142	202	51.4	0.610
26	0.0159	253	41.0	0.765
25	0.0176	320	32.4	0.970
24	0.0201	404	25.7	1.22
23	0.0226	511	20.3	1.55
22	0.0253	640	16.2	1.94
21	0.0285	812	12.8	2.46
20	0.0320	1,020	10.1	3.10
19	0.0359	1,290	8.05	3.90
18	0.0403	1,620	6.39	4.92
17	0.0453	2,050	5.05	6.21
16	0.0508	2,580	4.02	7.81
15	0.0571	3,260	3.18	9.87
14	0.0641	4,110	2.52	12.4
13	0.0720	5,180	2.00	15.7
12	0.0808	6,530	1.59	19.8
11	0.0907	8,230	1.26	24.9
10	0.1019	10,380	0.9986	31.4
9	0.1144	13,090	0.7925	39.6
8	0.1285	16,510	0.6281	50.0
7	0.1443	20,820	0.4981	63.0
6	0.1620	26,240	0.3952	79.4
5	0.1819	33,090	0.3134	100
4	0.2043	41,740	0.2485	126
3	0.2294	52,620	0.1971	159
2	0.2576	66,360	0.1563	201
1	0.2893	83,690	0.1239	253
1/0	0.3249	105,600	0.09825	320
2/0	0.3648	133,100	0.07793	403
3/0	0.4096	167,800	0.06182	508
4/0	0.4600	211,600	0.04901	641

FIGURE 6.2 Characteristics of Aluminum Wire

Wire Size (AWG)	Diameter		DC Resistance (Ohms per 1000 feet)	Weight (lbs per ft)
	Nominal Inches	Circular Mils		
28	0.0126	159	106	0.146
27	0.0142	202	83.2	0.185
26	0.0159	253	66.4	0.233
25	0.0176	320	52.4	0.295
24	0.0201	404	41.5	0.371
23	0.0226	511	32.9	0.471
22	0.0253	640	26.2	0.590
21	0.0285	812	20.7	0.748
20	0.0320	1,020	16.4	0.943
19	0.0359	1,290	13.0	1.19
18	0.0403	1,620	10.3	1.50
17	0.0453	2,050	8.18	1.89
16	0.0508	2,580	6.50	2.37
15	0.0571	3,260	5.15	3.00
14	0.0641	4,110	4.08	3.77
13	0.0720	5,180	3.24	4.77
12	0.0808	6,530	2.57	6.02
11	0.0907	8,230	2.04	7.57
10	0.1019	10,380	1.616	9.56
9	0.1144	13,090	1.282	12.05
8	0.1285	16,510	1.016	15.20
7	0.1443	20,820	0.8060	19.16
6	0.1620	26,240	0.6395	24.15
5	0.1819	33,090	0.5072	30.47
4	0.2043	41,740	0.4021	38.40
3	0.2294	52,620	0.3189	48.44
2	0.2576	66,360	0.2529	61.08
1	0.2893	83,690	0.2005	77.02
1/0	0.3249	105,600	0.1590	97.14
2/0	0.3648	133,100	0.1261	122.5
3/0	0.4096	167,800	0.1000	154.4
4/0	0.4600	211,600	0.07930	194.7

FIGURE 6.3 Allowable Ampacities of Single Insulated Conductors

Size	Temperature Rating of Conductor						Size
	60°C (140°F)	75°C (167°F)	90°C (194°F)	60°C (140°F)	75°C (167°F)	90°C (194°F)	
AWG kcmil	Types *TW, UF*	Types *FEPW, *RH, *RHW, *THHW, *THW, *THWN, XHHW, *USE, *ZW	Types TA, TBS, SA, SIS, *FEP, *FEPB, MI, *RHH, RHW-2, *THHN, *THHW, THW-2, THWN-2, USE-2, XHH, *XHHW, XHHW-2, ZW-2	Types *TW *UF	Types *RH, *RHW, *THW, *THWN, *XHHW, *USE	Types TA, TBS SA, SIS, *THHN, *THHW, THW-2, THWN-2, *RHH, RHW-2, USE-2, XHH, XHHW-2, ZW-2	AWG kcmil
	Copper			Aluminum or Copper-Clad Aluminum			
18	-	-	14	-	-	-	-
16	-	-	18	-	-	-	-
14	20 *	20 *	25 *	-	-	-	-
12	25 *	25 *	30 *	20 *	20 *	25 *	12
10	30	35 *	40 *	25	30 *	35 *	10
8	40	50	55	30	40	45	8
6	55	65	75	40	50	60	6
4	70	85	95	55	65	75	4
3	85	100	110	65	75	85	3
2	95	115	130	75	90	100	2
1	110	130	150	85	100	115	1
1/0	125	150	170	100	120	135	1/0
2/0	145	175	195	115	135	150	2/0
3/0	165	200	225	130	155	175	3/0
4/0	195	230	260	150	180	205	4/0
250	215	255	290	170	205	230	250
300	240	285	320	190	230	255	300
350	260	310	350	210	250	280	350
400	280	335	380	225	270	305	400
500	320	380	430	260	310	350	500
600	355	420	475	285	340	385	600
700	385	460	520	310	375	420	700
750	400	475	535	320	385	435	750
800	410	490	555	330	395	450	800
900	435	520	585	355	425	480	900
1000	455	545	615	375	445	500	1000
1250	495	590	665	405	485	545	1250
1500	520	625	705	435	520	585	1500
1750	545	650	735	455	545	615	1750
2000	560	665	750	470	560	630	2000

Correction Factors

For ambient temperatures other than 30 °C (86 °F), multiply the allowable ampacities shown above by the appropriate factor shown below

Ambient Temp. °C								Ambient Temp. °F
21 - 25	1.08	1.05	1.04	1.04	1.08	1.05	1.04	70 - 77
26 - 30	1.00	1.00	1.00	1.00	1.00	1.00	1.00	79 - 86
31 - 35	0.91	0.94	0.95	0.96	0.91	0.94	0.95	88 - 95
36 - 40	0.82	0.88	0.90	0.91	0.82	0.88	0.90	97 - 104
41 - 45	0.71	0.82	0.85	0.87	0.71	0.82	0.85	106 - 113
46 - 50	0.58	0.75	0.80	0.82	0.58	0.75	0.80	115 - 122
51 - 55	0.41	0.67	0.74	0.76	0.41	0.67	0.74	124 - 131
56 - 60	-	0.58	0.67	0.71	-	0.58	0.67	133 - 140
61 - 70	-	0.33	0.52	0.58	-	0.33	0.52	142 - 158
71 - 80	-	-	0.30	0.41	-	-	0.30	160 - 176

Note: correction factor values continue for 90°C columns: 36-40: 0.91; 41-45: 0.87; 46-50: 0.82; 51-55: 0.76; 56-60: 0.71; 61-70: 0.58; 71-80: 0.41 (Aluminum 90°C).

* Unless otherwise specifically permitted elsewhere in this Code, the overcurrent protection for conductor types marked with an asterisk (*) shall not exceed 15 amperes for 14 AWG, 20 amperes for 12 AWG, and 30 amperes for 10 AWG copper; or 15 amperes for 12 AWG and 25 amperes for 10 AWG aluminum and copper-clad aluminum after any correction factors for ambient temperature and number of conductors have been applied..

Figure 6.3 (continued)

Size	Temperature Rating of Conductor						Size
	60°C (140°F)	75°C (167°F)	90°C (194°F)	60°C (140°F)	75°C (167°F)	90°C (194°F)	
AWG kcmil	Types *TW, UF*	Types *FEPW, *RH, *RHW, *THHW, *THW, *THWN, XHHW, *ZW	Types TA, TBS, SA, SIS, *FEP, *FEPB, MI, *RHH, RHW-2, *THHN, *THHW, THW-2, THWN-2, USE-2, XHH, *XHHW, XHHW-2, ZW-2	Types *TW *UF	Types *RH, *RHW, *THW, *THWN, *XHHW,	Types TA, TBS, SA, SIS, *THHN, *THHW, THW-2, THWN-2, *RHH, RHW-2, USE-2, XHH, *XHHW, XHHW-2, ZW-2	AWG kcmil
	Copper			Aluminum or Copper-Clad Aluminum			
18	-	-	18	-	-	-	-
16	-	-	24	-	-	-	-
14	25 *	30 *	35 *	-	-	-	-
12	30 *	35 *	40 *	25 *	30 *	35 *	12
10	40 *	50 *	55 *	35 *	40 *	40 *	10
8	60	70	80	45	55	60	8
6	80	95	105	60	75	80	6
4	105	125	140	80	100	110	4
3	120	145	165	95	115	130	3
2	140	170	190	110	135	150	2
1	165	195	220	130	155	175	1
1/0	195	230	260	150	180	205	1/0
2/0	225	265	300	175	210	235	2/0
3/0	260	310	350	200	240	275	3/0
4/0	300	360	405	235	280	315	4/0
250	340	405	455	265	315	355	250
300	375	445	505	290	350	395	300
350	420	505	570	330	395	445	350
400	455	545	615	355	425	480	400
500	515	620	700	405	485	545	500
600	575	690	780	455	540	615	600
700	630	755	855	500	595	675	700
750	655	785	885	515	620	700	750
800	680	815	920	535	645	725	800
900	730	870	985	580	700	785	900
1000	780	935	1055	625	750	845	1000
1250	890	1065	1200	710	855	960	1250
1500	980	1175	1325	795	950	1075	1500
1750	1070	1280	1445	875	1050	1185	1750
2000	1155	1385	1560	960	1150	1335	2000

Correction Factors

Ambient Temp. °C	For ambient temperatures other than 30 °C (86 °F), multiply the allowable ampacities shown above by the appropriate factor shown below							Ambient Temp. °F
21 - 25	1.08	1.05	1.04	1.04	1.08	1.05	1.04	1.04	70 - 77
26 - 30	1.00	1.00	1.00	1.00	1.00	1.00	1.00	1.00	79 - 86
31 - 35	0.91	0.94	0.95	0.96	0.91	0.94	0.95	0.96	88 - 95
36 - 40	0.82	0.88	0.90	0.91	0.82	0.88	0.90	0.91	97 - 104
41 - 45	0.71	0.82	0.85	0.87	0.71	0.82	0.85	0.87	106 - 113
46 - 50	0.58	0.75	0.80	0.82	0.58	0.75	0.80	0.82	115 - 122
51 - 55	0.41	0.67	0.74	0.76	0.41	0.67	0.74	0.76	124 - 131
56 - 60	-	0.58	0.67	0.71	-	0.58	0.67	0.71	133 - 140
61 - 70	-	0.33	0.52	0.58	-	0.33	0.52	0.58	142 - 158
71 - 80	-	-	0.30	0.41	-	-	0.30	0.41	160 - 176

* Unless otherwise specifically permitted elsewhere in this Code, the overcurrent protection for conductor types marked with an asterisk (*) shall not exceed 15 amperes for 14 AWG, 20 amperes for 12 AWG, and 30 amperes for 10 AWG copper; or 15 amperes for 12 AWG and 25 amperes for 10 AWG aluminum and copper-clad aluminum after any correction factors for ambient temperature and number of conductors have been applied..

Figure 6.3 (continued) Allowable Ampacities of Three Single Insulated Conductors

Size	Temperature Rating of Conductor									Size
	110 °C (125 °F)	125 °C (257 °F)	150 °C (302 °F)	200 °C (392 °F)	250 °C (482 °F)	110 °C (125 °F)	125 °C (257 °F)	150 °C (302 °F)	200 °C (392 °F)	
AWG MCM	Types AVA, AVL	Types AI, AIA	Type Z	Types A, AA, FEP, FEPB, PFA	Types PFAH, TFE	Types AVA, AVL	Types AI, AIA	Type Z	Types A, AA	AWG MCM
	Copper				Nickel or Nickel-Coated	Aluminum or Copper-Clad Aluminum				
14	29	31	34	36	39	-	-	-	-	14
12	36	39	43	45	54	25	27	30	35	12
10	46	50	55	60	73	37	40	44	47	10
8	64	69	76	83	93	48	52	57	65	8
6	81	87	96	110	117	63	68	75	86	6
4	109	118	120	125	148	85	92	94	98	4
3	129	139	143	152	166	96	104	109	119	3
2	143	154	160	171	191	111	120	124	133	2
1	168	181	186	197	215	131	141	145	154	1
1/0	193	208	215	229	244	150	162	169	183	1/0
2/0	229	247	251	260	273	179	193	198	208	2/0
3/0	263	284	288	297	308	205	221	227	238	3/0
4/0	301	325	332	346	361	235	253	260	275	4/0
250	345	372	-	-	-	270	291	-	-	250
300	391	422	-	-	-	306	330	-	-	300
350	436	470	-	-	-	342	369	-	-	350
400	468	505	-	-	-	368	397	-	-	400
500	531	573	-	-	-	421	454	-	-	500
600	588	634	-	-	-	471	508	-	-	600
700	645	696	-	-	-	520	561	-	-	700
750	673	726	-	-	-	545	588	-	-	750
800	699	754	-	-	-	566	610	-	-	800
1000	785	846	-	-	-	651	701	-	-	1000
1500	961	-	-	-	-	795	-	-	-	1500
2000	1109	-	-	-	-	919	-	-	-	2000

Ampacity Correction Factors										
Ambient Temp. °C	For ambient temperatures other than 40 °C (104 °F), multiply the ampacities shown by the appropriate factor below.									Ambient Temp. °F
41 - 50	0.93	0.94	0.95	0.97	0.98	0.93	0.94	0.95	0.97	106 - 122
51 - 60	0.85	0.87	0.90	0.94	0.95	0.85	0.87	0.90	0.94	124 - 140
61 - 70	0.76	0.80	0.85	0.90	0.93	0.76	0.80	0.85	0.90	142 - 158
71 - 80	0.65	0.73	0.80	0.87	0.90	0.65	0.73	0.80	0.87	160 - 176
81 - 90	0.53	0.64	0.74	0.83	0.87	0.53	0.64	0.74	0.83	177 - 194
91 - 100	0.38	0.54	0.67	0.79	0.85	0.38	0.54	0.67	0.79	195 - 212
101 - 120	-	0.24	0.52	0.71	0.79	-	0.24	0.52	0.71	213 - 248
121 - 140	-	-	0.30	0.61	0.72	-	-	0.30	0.61	249 - 284
141 - 160	-	-	-	0.50	0.65	-	-	-	0.50	285 - 320
161 - 180	-	-	-	0.35	0.58	-	-	-	0.35	321 - 356
181 - 200	-	-	-	-	0.49	-	-	-	-	357 - 392
201 - 225	-	-	-	-	0.35	-	-	-	-	393 - 437

Figure 6.3 (continued)

Size	Temperature Rating of Conductor									Size
	110 °C (125 °F)	125 °C (257 °F)	150 °C (302 °F)	200 °C (392 °F)	250 °C (482 °F)	110 °C (125 °F)	125 °C (257 °F)	150 °C (302 °F)	200 °C (392 °F)	
AWG MCM	Types AVA, AVL	Types AI, AIA	Type Z	Types A, AA, FEP, FEPB, PFA	Types PFAH, TFE	Types AVA, AVL	Types AI, AIA	Type Z	Types A, AA	AWG MCM
	Copper				Nickel or Nickel-Coated	Aluminum or Copper-Clad Aluminum				
14	39	42	46	54	59	-	-	-	-	14
12	51	55	60	68	78	40	43	47	54	12
10	67	72	80	90	107	53	57	63	71	10
8	90	97	106	124	142	70	75	83	96	8
6	121	131	155	165	205	95	102	112	128	6
4	160	172	190	220	278	125	135	148	171	4
3	180	194	211	252	327	144	155	170	196	3
2	215	232	255	293	381	167	180	198	222	2
1	247	266	293	344	440	193	208	228	267	1
1/0	286	309	339	399	532	222	239	263	310	1/0
2/0	329	355	390	467	591	257	277	305	363	2/0
3/0	380	410	451	546	708	296	319	351	443	3/0
4/0	446	481	529	629	830	347	374	411	490	4/0
250	493	532	-	-	-	384	414	-	-	250
300	552	595	-	-	-	431	464	-	-	300
350	611	659	-	-	-	477	514	-	-	350
400	663	715	-	-	-	518	559	-	-	400
500	767	827	-	-	-	600	647	-	-	500
600	860	928	-	-	-	674	727	-	-	600
700	953	1028	-	-	-	749	808	-	-	700
750	1000	1079	-	-	-	786	848	-	-	750
800	1039	1121	-	-	-	818	882	-	-	800
1000	1197	1291	-	-	-	947	1021	-	-	1000
1500	1465	1580	-	-	-	1160	1251	-	-	1500
2000	1692	1825	-	-	-	1340	1444	-	-	2000

Ampacity Correction Factors										
Ambient Temp. °C	For ambient temperatures other than 40 °C (104 °F), multiply the ampacities shown by the appropriate factor below.									Ambient Temp. °F
41 - 50	0.93	0.94	0.95	0.97	0.98	0.93	0.94	0.95	0.97	106 - 122
51 - 60	0.85	0.87	0.90	0.94	0.95	0.85	0.87	0.90	0.94	124 - 140
61 - 70	0.76	0.80	0.85	0.90	0.93	0.76	0.80	0.85	0.90	142 - 158
71 - 80	0.65	0.73	0.80	0.87	0.90	0.65	0.73	0.80	0.87	160 - 176
81 - 90	0.53	0.64	0.74	0.83	0.87	0.53	0.64	0.74	0.83	177 - 194
91 - 100	0.38	0.54	0.67	0.79	0.85	0.38	0.54	0.67	0.79	195 - 212
101 - 120	-	0.24	0.52	0.71	0.79	-	0.24	0.52	0.71	213 - 248
121 - 140	-	-	0.30	0.61	0.72	-	-	0.30	0.61	249 - 284
141 - 160	-	-	-	0.50	0.65	-	-	-	0.50	285 - 320
161 - 180	-	-	-	0.35	0.58	-	-	-	0.35	321 - 356
181 - 200	-	-	-	-	0.49	-	-	-	-	357 - 392
201 - 225	-	-	-	-	0.35	-	-	-	-	393 - 437

FIGURE 6.4 Maximum Number of Conductors
in Trade Sizes of Conduit or Tubing

Type Letters	Conductor Size AWG/kcmil	Conduit or Tubing Trade Size (inches)											
		1/2	3/4	1	1 1/4	1 1/2	2	2 1/2	3	3 1/2	4	5	6
TW, XHHW (14 through 8) RH (14 + 12)	14	9	15	25	44	60	99	142	-	-	-	-	-
	12	7	12	19	35	47	78	111	171	-	-	-	-
	10	5	9	15	26	36	60	85	131	176	-	-	-
	8	2	4	7	12	17	28	40	62	84	108	-	-
RHW and RHH (without outer covering), RH (10+8), THW, THHW	14	6	10	16	29	40	65	93	143	192	-	-	-
	12	4	8	13	24	32	53	76	117	157	-	-	-
	10	4	6	11	19	26	43	61	95	127	163	-	-
	8	1	3	5	10	13	22	32	49	66	85	133	-
	6	1	2	4	7	10	16	23	36	48	62	97	141
	4	1	1	3	5	7	12	17	27	36	47	73	106
	3	1	1	2	4	6	10	15	23	31	40	63	91
	2	1	1	2	4	5	9	13	20	27	34	54	78
	1	-	1	1	3	4	6	9	14	19	25	39	57
TW, THW, FEPB (6 through 2), RHW and RHH (without outer covering) RH,THHW	1/0	-	1	1	2	3	5	8	12	16	21	33	49
	2/0	-	1	1	1	3	5	7	10	14	18	29	41
	3/0	-	1	1	1	2	4	6	9	12	15	24	35
	4/0	-	-	1	1	1	3	5	7	10	13	20	29
	250	-	-	1	1	1	2	4	6	8	10	16	23
	300	-	-	1	1	1	2	3	5	7	9	14	20
	350	-	-	-	1	1	1	3	4	6	8	12	18
	400	-	-	-	1	1	1	2	4	5	7	11	16
	500	-	-	-	1	1	1	1	3	4	6	9	14
	600	-	-	-	-	1	1	1	3	4	5	7	11
	700	-	-	-	-	1	1	1	2	3	4	7	10
	750	-	-	-	-	1	1	1	2	3	4	6	9

Note 1. This table is for concentric stranded conductors only.
Note 2. Conduit fill for conductors with a -2 suffix is the same as for those types without the suffix

Figure 6.4 (continued)

This table is for concentric stranded conductors only.

Type Letters: THWN, THHN, FEP (14 through 2), FEPB (14 through 8), PFA (14 through 4/0), PFAH (14 through 4/0), Z (14 through 4/0), XHHW (4 through 500 kcmil)

Conductor Size AWG/kcmil	Conduit or Tubing Trade Size (inches)											
	1/2	3/4	1	1 1/4	1 1/2	2	2 1/2	3	3 1/2	4	5	6
14	13	24	39	69	94	154	-	-	-	-	-	-
12	10	18	29	51	70	114	164	-	-	-	-	-
10	6	11	18	32	44	73	104	160	-	-	-	-
8	3	5	9	16	22	36	51	79	106	136	-	-
6	1	4	6	11	15	26	37	57	76	98	154	-
4	1	2	4	7	9	16	22	35	47	60	94	137
3	1	1	3	6	8	13	19	29	39	51	80	116
2	1	1	3	5	7	11	16	25	33	43	67	97
1	-	1	1	3	5	8	12	18	25	32	50	72
1/0	-	1	1	3	4	7	10	15	21	27	42	61
2/0	-	1	1	2	3	6	8	13	17	22	35	51
3/0	-	1	1	1	3	5	7	11	14	18	29	42
4/0	-	1	1	1	2	4	6	9	12	15	24	35
250	-	-	1	1	1	3	4	7	10	12	20	28
300	-	-	1	1	1	3	4	6	8	11	17	24
350	-	-	1	1	1	2	3	5	7	9	15	21
400	-	-	-	1	1	1	3	5	6	8	13	19
500	-	-	-	1	1	1	2	4	5	7	11	16
600	-	-	-	1	1	1	1	3	4	5	9	13
700	-	-	-	-	1	1	1	3	4	5	8	11
750	-	-	-	-	1	1	1	2	3	4	7	11

XHHW

Conductor Size AWG/kcmil	1/2	3/4	1	1 1/4	1 1/2	2	2 1/2	3	3 1/2	4	5	6
6	1	3	5	9	13	21	30	47	63	81	128	185
600	-	-	-	1	1	1	1	3	4	5	9	13
700	-	-	-	-	1	1	1	3	4	5	7	11
750	-	-	-	-	1	1	1	2	3	4	7	10

Note 1. This table is for concentric stranded conductors only.

Note 2. Conduit fill for conductors with a -2 suffix is the same as for those types without the suffix

FIGURE 6.6 Common Fuse Types

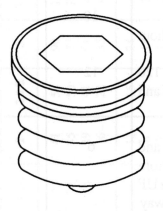

Plug

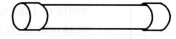

Ferrule - contact
Cartridge

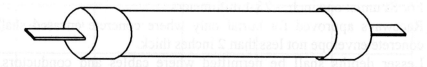

Knife - blade - contact
Cartridge

FIGURE 6.7 Maximum Rating or Setting of Motor Branch-Circuit Short-Circuit and Ground-Fault Protective Devices

Type of Motor	Percent of Full-Load Current			
	No Time Delay Fuse	Dual Element (Time-Delay)	Instantaneous Trip Breaker	Inverse Time Breaker *
Single-phase, all types				
No code letter	300	175	700	250
All A.C. single-phase and polyphase squirrel-cage and synchronous motors** with full-voltage, resistor or reactor starting:				
No code letter	300	175	700	250
Code letters F to V	300	175	700	250
Code letters B to E	250	175	700	200
Code letter A	150	150	700	150
All A.C. squirrel-cage and synchronous motors with autotransformer starting:				
No more than 30 amps				
No code letter	250	175	700	200
More than 30 amps				
Code letters F to V	200	175	700	200
Code letters B to E	250	175	700	200
Code letter A	200	175	700	200
High-reactance squirrel-cage	150	150	700	150
Not more than 30 amps				
No code letter	250	175	700	250
More than 30 amps				
No code letter	200	175	700	200
Wound-rotor				
No code letter	150	150	700	150
Direct current (constant voltage)				
No more than 50 hp				
No code letter	150	150	250	150
More than 50 hp				
No code letter	150	150	175	150

* The values given in the last column also cover the ratings of non adjustable inverse time types of circuit breakers that may be modified as in Section 430-52 of the National Electric Code.

** Synchronous motors of the low-torque, low-speed type (usually 450 rpm or lower), such as are used to drive reciprocating compressors, pumps, etc. that start unloaded do not require a fuse rating or circuit-breaker setting in excess of 200 percent of full-load current.

FIGURE 6.8 Minimum Size Equipment Grounding Conductors for Grounding Raceway and Equipment

Rating or Setting of Automatic Overcurrent Device in Circuit Ahead of Equipment, Conduit, etc., Not Exceeding (Amperes)	Size	
	Copper Wire No.	Aluminum or Copper-Clad Aluminum Wire No. *
15	14	12
20	12	10
30	10	8
40	10	8
60	10	8
100	8	6
200	6	4
300	4	2
400	3	1
500	2	1/0
600	1	2/0
800	0	3/0
1000	2/0	4/0
1200	3/0	250 kcmil
1600	4/0	350 kcmil
2000	250 kcmil	400 kcmil
2500	350 kcmil	600 kcmil
3000	400 kcmil	600 kcmil
4000	500 kcmil	800 kcmil
5000	700 kcmil	1200 kcmil
6000	800 kcmil	1200 kcmil

* Aluminum or copper-clad aluminum grounding conductors shall not be used where in direct contact with masonry or the earth or where subject to corrosive conditions. Where used outside, aluminum or copper-clad aluminum grounding conductors shall not be installed within 18 inches of the earth

FIGURE 6.9 Grounding Electrode Conductor for AC Systems

Size of Largest Service-Entrance Conductor or Equivalent Area for Parallel Conductors		Size of Grounding Electrode Conductor	
Copper	Aluminum or Copper-Clad Aluminum	Copper	Aluminum or Copper-Clad Aluminum *
2 or smaller	0 or smaller	8	6
1 or 0	2/0 or 3/0	6	4
2/0 or 3/0	4/0 or 250 kcmil	4	2
Over 3/0 through 350 kcmil	Over 250 kcmil through 500 kcmil	2	0
Over 350 kcmil through 600 kcmil	Over 500 kcmil through 900 kcmil	0	3/0
Over 600 kcmil through 1100 kcmil	Over 900 kcmil through 1750 kcmil	2/0	4/0
Over 1100 kcmil	Over 1750 kcmil	3/0	250 kcmil

* Aluminum or copper-clad aluminum grounding conductors shall not be used where in direct contact with masonry or the earth or where subject to corrosive conditions. Where used outside, aluminum or copper-clad aluminum grounding conductors shall not be installed within 18 inches of the earth.

WORKSHEET 6.1 Voltage Drop Calculations

1. Current in Wire

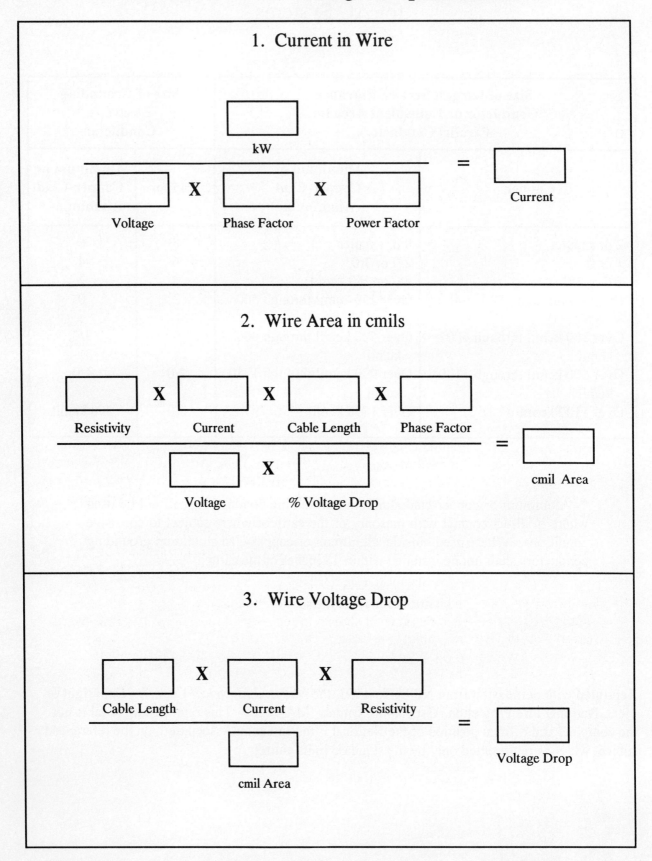

2. Wire Area in cmils

3. Wire Voltage Drop

Chapter 7

HOW TO SELECT AND OPERATE ELECTRIC MOTORS TO SAVE ENERGY

There is a nearly unlimited variety in the types of electric motors in use today. Chances are, dozens of different types can be found in the typical facility, in applications ranging from HVAC systems to computer equipment. Servo, stepping, hydraulic, synchronous, direct current, and induction motors represent the more popular types in widespread application.

Of these types, the one that is of most concern to the facility manager is the induction motor. While the other types can generally be classified as special application motors in facilities, the induction motor represents the class of motor most frequently used in facility applications. When a special application motor fails, it is generally replaced with an identical unit from the same manufacturer. When an induction motor fails, you have a wide range of choices in replacement; choices that permit the selection of the optimum motor for the application.

Fortunately, there has been a great deal of standardization in the manufacture of motors, primarily the result of the efforts of the National Electrical Manufacturers Association (NEMA). While NEMA standards are voluntary, they are widely accepted by the industry. NEMA standards apply to nearly all aspects of motor manufacture and use, including terminology, materials, dimensions, operating characteristics, and ratings. Without such standards, it would be difficult or impossible to find replacement for particular units without having to go back to the original motor manufacturer.

Induction Motors and How They Work

Of the types of motors used in facilities, the vast majority are induction motors. The most common type of induction motor in use is the squirrel cage induction motor. The simplicity, durability, and availability of the squirrel cage induction motor in a wide range of configurations has made it the standard for nearly every motor application.

Induction motors are essentially rotating transformers. The voltage applied to the stator windings generates a magnetic field in the stator which in turn induces a magnetic field in the rotor. The magnetic field in the stator rotates as a result of the applied alternating current. This rotating current interacts with the induced magnetic field in the rotor, causing it to turn.

One characteristic of the induction motor that is a result of the interaction between the stator and rotor fields results in a motor whose speed varies only slightly from no load to full load. The rotation or synchronous speed of the motor is set by the frequency of the current through the stator windings (generally 60 hertz) and the number of poles built into the motor.

Figure 7.1 gives some of the more commonly used formulas for induction motors. These formulas can be used in carrying out a wide range of calculations for single- and three-phase motors.

Factors to Consider when Selecting a Motor

The definitions given in this section are not meant to be the precise definitions as given by NEMA and other standards. Rather, the definitions given in this section are worded to give a general understanding of the more commonly used motor terms. If more precise definitions are required, refer to NEMA Standard MG-1.

Induction motors have two primary parts, the stator and the rotor. The stator is the stationary element in the motor that includes the primary windings, laminated core, and support frame. The stator produces the rotating magnetic fields that drive the rotor. The rotor is the rotating portion of the motor, including the motor shaft, secondary windings, and magnetic core.

The turning force developed by a motor is its torque and is expressed in pound-feet or ounce-inches. There are a number of different torque ratings for motors that you should consider when selecting one for a particular application. All torque ratings for motors assume that the motor is fed power at its rated voltage and frequency.

Figure 7.2 shows the different torques used to rate motors. Of these, the most commonly cited one is the motor's full load torque. A motor's full load torque is the torque produced by the motor while operating at its rated output and speed. Other torque ratings are generally given in terms of percent of full load torque.

The locked rotor torque (sometimes called the starting torque) is the minimum amount of torque developed by the motor for all angular positions of the rotor when the rotor is at rest and power is first applied. The locked rotor torque rating for a motor is an important consideration when selecting motors that are expected to start with a load connected. For those applications, the locked rotor torque of the motor must be greater than the resistance of the connected load.

The motor's pull up torque is the minimum torque developed during the period of acceleration from rest to the motor's rated operating speed. The motor's pull up torque rating must exceed the load's resistance at all times during the acceleration period.

The breakdown torque is the maximum torque that the motor will develop without a sudden drop in speed.

When operating at full load torque, the speed of an induction motor is less than when it is operating at no load, or synchronous speed (see Figure 7.2). The difference between the full load and synchronous speeds is the motor's slip and is generally expressed as a percentage of synchronous speed.

Induction Motor Classifications

Induction motors are classified a variety of ways depending on the criteria used to distinguish them. Some of the more commonly used classifications include size, electrical type, method of cooling, how it is used, how well it is protected from the environment in which it operates, and its variability of speed. For example, motors that meet the classification of being small include those that operate at 1,000 rpm and are rated at one horsepower or less. If the motor operates at 800 rpm or less, it must be rated at 1/3 horsepower or less.

Efficiency

A motor's efficiency is the ratio of the horsepower output to the power input and is expressed in percent or as a decimal value. Since motor efficiency varies with the load on the motor (see Figure 7.3), efficiency is rated at full load conditions.

Motor Service Factor

One other factor that is important in selecting a motor for a particular application is the motor's service factor. Service factor is a multiplier, ranging from 1.00 to 1.40, that can be applied to the motor's full load horsepower rating to determine an acceptable loading for that motor under certain conditions. Those conditions include operating the motor at its rated voltage and frequency values under normal environmental conditions.

Caution: While the concept of a motor service factor seems to imply that a motor can be intentionally undersized for a particular application with no consequences, that is not the case. Overloading a motor even within its normal service factor results in an increase in temperature within the motor windings. That temperature increase can significantly reduce the expected life of the insulation. For example, a 10°C increase in insulation temperature over design standards results in a decrease in the expected life of that insulation of 50%.

The service factor is better used to estimate the temporary overload that a motor can be subjected to without seriously shortening the expected motor life.

GUIDELINES FOR SELECTING MOTOR INSULATION

Motor manufacturers have established four classes for rating motor insulation: A, B, F, and H. The classes are used to define the maximum operating hot spot temperature that the motor's insulation can be subjected to without sustaining damage. Hot spot temperature is calculated based on a 40°C ambient temperature and the motor's temperature rise as a result of loading.

Figure 7.4 lists the insulation classes and their associated winding hot spot temperatures. Although Class A insulation is still used in some special purpose applications, it is essentially obsolete. Class H insulation is used primarily for special purpose motors. Classes B and F are the most commonly used insulation classes, with Class B being the basic standard.

The key to determining the required motor insulation class is the temperature rise in the motor's windings. The higher the temperature rise, the faster the insulation material deteriorates with time. A 10°C increase in winding temperature results in a 50 percent decrease in expected life of the insulating material. As long as the motor is operated at temperatures less than its rated hot spot temperature, the insulation can be expected to perform for the motor's rated service life and would not result in a premature motor failure. Installing a motor with a higher rated insulation under the same operating conditions would extend the expected service life of the insulation. There would be no guarantee that the motor would last longer though, as deteriorated motor insulation is only one factor that can lead to motor failure.

PERFORMANCE STANDARDS TO USE IN SELECTING MOTORS

In evaluating motors for a specific application, there are a number of performance factors for single- and three-phase motors that must be evaluated. These include minimum locked rotor torque, minimum breakdown torque, and maximum locked rotor current.

Figures 7.5 and 7.6 list the average full load, locked rotor, and breakdown torques for single- and three-phase induction motors. The table was compiled by averaging torque values given by a number of different manufacturers for motors of the same speed and horsepower ratings. The tables are intended to be used only as a guide in evaluating the torque needs of a particular application. When selecting a particular motor for a given application, always consult the manufacturer for specific data on that motor.

Figures 7.7 and 7.8 list average full load and locked rotor currents for single- and three-phase induction motors. As was the case with the torque tables, these tables were compiled by averaging data from a number of different manufacturers for motors of the same speed and horsepower ratings. Use the figures to estimate the current requirements for single- and three-phase motors. Again, consult the manufacturer for specific motor current data.

How Changes in Voltage and Frequency Affect Motor Performance

The published performance characteristics for motors all assume that the motor is operating at a specific voltage and frequency. NEMA standards require that the motor be capable of operating at rated load with a supply frequency variation of ± 5 percent, or a supply voltage variation (measured at the motor's terminals) of ± 10 percent.

Operating a motor at a voltage or frequency other than what it was designed to operate at not only changes its performance characteristics, but also can significantly reduce its expected life. How significantly a motor's performance and life are impacted depends on it's design. Figure 7.9 lists the general effects of voltage and frequency variation on the performance of induction motors.

In most applications, voltage variations are of more concern than frequency variations simply because the frequency of the power supplied in most utility systems is very stable while there may be large variations in the voltage. These variations are the result of changes in the supply voltage to the distribution systems as well as changes in the distribution voltage as a result of changes in system loading.

In general, a voltage higher than rated voltage is less harmful to the motor than one that is less than rated voltage. Operating a motor at less than rated voltage results in decreased motor efficiency, increased operating temperatures, and decreased locked rotor and full load torques.

Voltage Imbalance

A second voltage variation must be taken into consideration for polyphase induction motors—voltage imbalance. A voltage imbalance is a difference between phase voltages applied to the motor when measured at the motor's terminals. NEMA standards require that a motor perform at rated load with a voltage imbalance of one percent or less.

Voltage imbalance is particularly important because it results in the production of large current imbalances within the motor, typically five to ten times what the voltage imbalance is. These current imbalances result in increased losses, decreased torques, and decreased full load speed.

How to Estimate the Payback from High-Efficiency Motors

All induction motors are very efficient, particularly when compared to other energy conversion equipment. For example, the typical integral horsepower, squirrel cage induction motor has efficiencies ranging from the high 70s for motors in the five horsepower range, to the mid 90s for larger units. For a given horsepower rating, there is a certain amount of variability in efficiency as a result of variations between manufacturers in the design of the motor.

Manufacturers have also introduced a number of "high-efficiency" motor designs that while they cost more to purchase, can result in significant savings in operating costs over the life of the motor. These designs achieve their higher operating efficiencies by reducing eddy current losses, improving the conductivity of the stator, or decreasing the required magnetizing current. While all three methods improve the operating efficiency of the motor, all increase its manufacturing costs.

Use Worksheet 7.1 to estimate the savings resulting from the installation of a high-efficiency motor in a particular application. Use the worksheet as follows:

Step 1.   Determine the horsepower requirements of the load that will be driven by the motor.

Note: This may or may not equal the horsepower rating of the motor as it is common practice to slightly oversize the motor for an application. Enter the horsepower requirements in sections #1 and #2 of the worksheet.

Step 2. Estimate the number of hours that the motor will operate in a year and enter the value in sections #1 and #2 of the worksheet.

Step 3. Enter the average cost of electricity in dollars per kilowatt hour in sections #1 and #2 of the worksheet. If the facility is operated under a time-of-day rate schedule, estimate the average rate that will be in effect while the motor is operating.

Step 4. Determine the operating efficiency for a standard replacement motor from the manufacturer's data when the motor is operating at the connected load. Do not use the full load efficiency rating of the motor unless the motor is actually operating at full load. Enter the value in section #1.

Step 5. Similarly, determine the operating efficiency for a high-efficiency motor at the same rated load. Enter the value in section #2.

Step 6. Multiply the number 0.746 by the load horsepower, the number of annual operating hours, and the electric rate, and divide by the motor's efficiency to determine the annual operating cost for the standard motor. Enter the value in section #1.

Step 7. Multiply the number 0.746 by the load horsepower, the number of annual operating hours, and the electric rate, and divide by the motor's efficiency to determine the annual operating cost for the high-efficiency motor. Enter the value in section #2.

Step 8. Enter the standard motor's annual operating cost from section #1 into section #3. Enter the high efficiency motor's annual operating cost from section #2 in section #3. Subtract the annual operating cost for the high efficiency motor from the annual operating cost for the standard motor to determine the annual savings for the high-efficiency motor.

The calculated savings for the high-efficiency motor are based on average rates and do not fully reflect demand charges and time-of-day rate structures. However, the estimate is sufficiently accurate for a preliminary investigation of high-efficiency motors.

WORKSHEET FOR SELECTING THE BEST MOTOR FOR YOUR NEEDS

Matching a motor to your particular application requires consideration of a number of factors related to the required performance characteristics of the motor, service conditions, energy use, and maintenance requirements. In addition, you should consider several environmental factors, including the environment in which the motor will be operated, how it will be mounted, and how it will be connected to the load. Use

Worksheet 7.2 to list some of the most important considerations in selecting a motor for a particular application.

Caution: It is important that the motor size be properly matched to the connected load. Undersizing the load will result in inadequate performance and decreased motor life. Oversizing the motor will result in low system power factor.

Power factor is the ratio of the kilowatt (kW) input to the kilovolt-ampere (kVa) input to the motor. The kW component is the work producing component while the kVa component is the total power input to the motor. The difference between the two is the magnetizing current required for the motor to operate. Expressed in percentage, an induction motor's power factor typically ranges from 50 percent to 90 percent, depending on the motor horsepower and load.

The importance in selecting a motor that is not oversized is that power factor decreases with decreasing load for a given motor as shown in Figure 7.3. Operating a facility with a number of low power factor electrical loads increases the losses within the facility's electrical distribution systems as well as decreases the system's capacity.

The best method of avoiding the penalties of low power factor, is to install properly sized induction motors. However, even with proper sizing, factors such as varying loads on motors can result in low power factor within a facility. While there are a number of different techniques for correcting low power factor, the most commonly used one is the installation of capacitors. See Chapter 12 for information on how to size and install power factor correction capacitors for induction motors.

HOW TO CYCLE MOTORS TO SAVE ENERGY WITHOUT REDUCING MOTOR LIFE

An increased concern over energy costs has led to the practice of cycling motors. Since motors represent some of the largest electrical loads in a facility, significant energy savings can be achieved by shutting down motor driven equipment, such as air handlers or compressors.

Two approaches have been taken towards equipment shutdown. First, equipment is shut off during off hours when it simply isn't needed. These shutdowns generally last for several hours.

The second approach involves the turning off of motor driven equipment as a means of limiting the facility's peak electrical demand. Under demand limiting, equipment is turned off for a short period of time, typically for no more than five or ten minutes. With most facilities operating on a 15 or 30 minute demand period, some facility managers turn motors off and on up to four times per hour during peak demand periods.

While there is no question that turning motors off when they aren't needed and cycling motors during peak demand periods will save energy and demand charges, the savings may be offset by decreased motor life as the result of frequent motor starts.

Every time a motor is started, it is subjected to stresses that shorten its life. The problem is heat. During motor start-up, there is a tremendous heat build-up within the motor. This heat build-up is particularly critical in motors that are starting high inertial loads typically found in HVAC equipment. This heat causes stresses in the insulation that eventually will result in the loss of insulating properties due to chemical reactions that take place within the insulating materials. The higher the temperature and the longer the motor is operated at those temperatures (i.e., the more often it is started), the faster the insulation will lose its insulating properties.

While all starts contribute to this deterioration of insulation, it is the successive starting and stopping of a motor without sufficient time for the temperature to return to normal between starts that results in the most damage. Too frequent duty cycling results in sustained operation at elevated temperatures and will significantly shorten motor life.

NEMA standards call for a motor to be capable of withstanding two starts from rest when initially at ambient temperature or one restart from rated load operation without exceeding its rated load operating temperature. Even under those conditions, NEMA recommends that the number of motor starts be kept to a minimum as they impact the life of the motor.

A rule of thumb to follow when determining duty cycle periods for motors that have been operating under load is to allow the motor to remain off for the following times:

HORSEPOWER	MINIMUM OFF PERIOD
1 – 5	5 minutes
5 – 25	1 minute/horsepower
26 and over	Consult the manufacturer

CHECKLIST FOR PROPER MOTOR MAINTENANCE

An important but often overlooked aspect of motor maintenance is record keeping. The failure of a motor represents significant costs in both the labor and material for the replacement motor installation as well as the impact of the downtime on the operation of the facility. In spite of these costs, few facilities keep complete records of motor maintenance.

Good motor maintenance records will accomplish two things. First, they will show if there is a problem with inadequate maintenance. Complete records will show what maintenance activities were performed when. If a motor fails before the end of its expected life, you can review the records to determine if the maintenance activities for that application were appropriate.

Second, good maintenance records will help to flag application problems where the wrong size or type of motor has been installed. Without records, it is difficult to remember when a particular motor was last replaced. Therefore, there is no way of determining if the failure is due to the age of the motor or to an improper application. Without that information, most failed motors are simply replaced in kind.

Instead of simply replacing a prematurely failed motor with a similar unit that may also fail prematurely, records would indicate that there was a problem with premature motor failure and that the installation of that particular motor in that application should be evaluated.

Worksheet 7.3 presents a means of recording important motor characteristics as well as all maintenance activities. Use a separate copy of the worksheet for each motor.

Use Figure 7.10 as a checklist of important maintenance activities for general purpose motors. The figure is intended to identify minimum maintenance requirements. Motors that perform critical functions may require additional maintenance activities.

FIGURE 7.1 Motor Formulas

1 Horsepower = 0.746 kW

Power Factor $= \dfrac{\text{kW Input}}{\text{kVA Input}}$

Single-Phase Power $\quad$ kVa $= \dfrac{\text{Voltage X Current}}{1,000}$

Three-Phase Power $\quad$ kVa $= \dfrac{1.73 \text{ X Voltage X Current}}{1,000}$

Torque (ft-lb) $= \dfrac{\text{Horsepower X 5250}}{\text{rpm}}$

Synchronous Speed $= \dfrac{120 \text{ X Frequency}}{\text{Number of Poles}}$

Slip $= \dfrac{\text{Synchronous Speed - Full Load Speed}}{\text{Synchronous Speed}}$

FIGURE 7.2 Motor Torque Designations

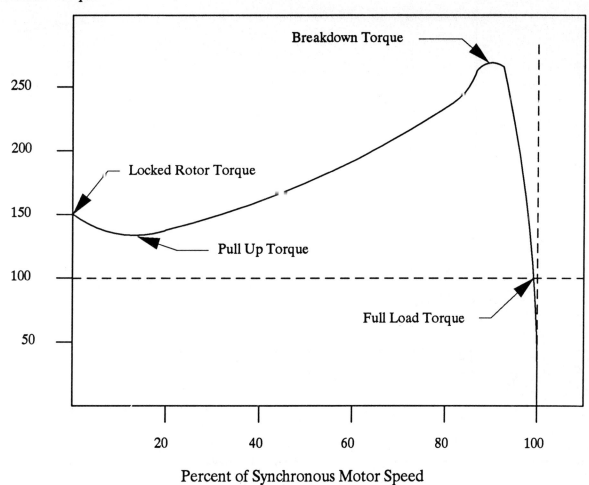

Percent of
Full Load Torque

Breakdown Torque

Locked Rotor Torque

250

Pull Up Torque

200

150

Full Load Torque

100

50

20   40   60   80   100

Percent of Synchronous Motor Speed

FIGURE 7.3 Efficiency and Power Factor vs. Load

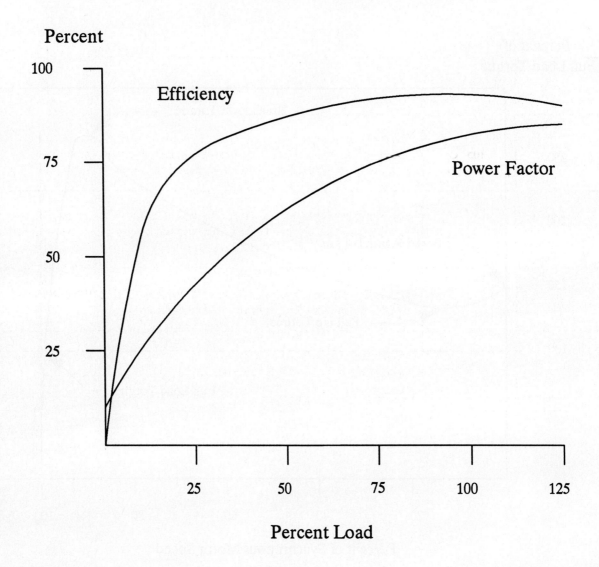

FIGURE 7.4 Motor Insulation Classes

Class	Hot Spot Temperature	Description
A	105 °C	Insulating materials such as cotton or paper impregnated or coated with a variety of materials. Class A insulation was once the most common insulation for small motors but is now considered to be obsolete.
B	130 °C	Insulating materials such as glass fibers, polyester laminates, and mica, with suitable bonding agents. Class B insulation is the most common class of insulating materials used in general purpose motors.
F	155 °C	Insulating materials similar to those used in Class B motors, but capable of operation at higher temperatures without damage.
H	180 °C	Insulating materials such as glass fibers, polyester laminates, mica, and silicone elastomers, with suitable bonding agents.

FIGURE 7.5 Average Torque for Single-Phase Induction Motors

Horsepower	Synchronous Speed (rpm)	Torque (ft-lbs)		
		Full Load	Locked Rotor	Break Down
1/2	3600	0.8	1.7	2.1
	1800	1.5	5.1	4.3
	1200	2.3	6.3	5.2
	900	3.0	5.3	7.7
3/4	3600	1.1	2.3	3.3
	1800	1.2	7.4	6.1
	1200	3.5	8.2	6.9
	900	4.5	8.8	11.5
1	3600	1.5	2.9	4.2
	1800	3.1	9.3	7.3
	1200	4.6	9.8	9.2
	900	6.1	9.5	14.4
1.5	3600	23.	3.9	5.4
	1800	4.6	12.6	10.2
	1200	6.9	13.5	13.8
	900	9.1	14.0	20.0
2	3600	3.0	4.3	7.5
	1800	6.1	16.4	13.0
	1200	9.2	16.7	18.0
	900	12.1	19.0	27.0
3	3600	4.5	7.6	8.6
	1800	9.1	22.7	19.0
	1200	13.7	23.5	25.8
5	3600	7.5	11.3	13.5
	1800	15.1	32.5	30.0
	1200	22.9	40.0	40.5
7.5	3600	11.2	16.0	20.0
	1800	22.7	47.0	45.0
	1200			
10	3600	14.9	20.0	27.0
	1800	30.1	58.5	60.0
	1200			

FIGURE 7.6 Average Torque for 3-Phase Induction Motors

Horsepower	Synchronous Speed	Torque (ft-lbs)		
		Full Load	Locked Rotor	Break Down
1/2	3600	0.8	1.3	3.1
	1800	1.5	5.4	7
	1200	2.3	5.3	8.0
	900	3.1	4.6	9.0
3/4	3600	1.1	1.9	4.0
	1800	2.3	7.2	9.7
	1200	3.4	7.2	10.3
	900	6.9	8.5	11.5
1	3600	1.5	2.7	5.2
	1800	3.0	8.5	9.4
	1200	4.6	11.0	15.1
	900	6.1	13.0	15.2
1.5	3600	2.3	5.8	6.7
	1800	4.6	12.7	17.4
	1200	6.9	14.0	20.8
2	3600	3.1	7.2	8.2
	1800	6.1	16.7	27.0
	1200	9.0	18.4	25.5
3	3600	4.5	11.1	12.7
	1800	9.1	25.0	27.1
	1200	13.6	29.0	38.3
5	3600	7.5	13.7	19.8
	1800	15.2	38.4	41.6
	1200	22.4	43.8	56.2
7.5	3600	11.3	19.2	27.4
	1800	22.4	48.2	54.0
	1200	33.6	73.4	79.0
10	3600	14.9	31.8	34.7
	1800	30.0	63.1	69.4
	1200	44.7	87.6	99.7
15	3600	22.4	48.8	51.4
	1800	44.8	86.3	101
	1200	66.9	114	141
20	3600	29.9	48.5	64.5
	1800	59.6	119	137
	1200	89.3	162	202

FIGURE 7.6 (continued)

Horsepower	Synchronous Speed	Torque (ft-lbs)		
		Full Load	Locked Rotor	Break Down
25	3600	37.3	57.0	88.5
	1800	74.1	140	169
	1200	111	184	227
30	3600	44.4	65.6	93.0
	1800	89.0	161	198
	1200	134	246	296
40	3600	59.3	87.8	132
	1800	119	217	265
	1200	178	306	377
50	3600	74.3	100	150
	1800	148	272	335
	1200	223	281	488
60	3600	89.3	118	182
	1800	178	294	411
	1200	268	464	568
75	3600	111	132	233
	1800	222	360	503
	1200	333	620	732
100	3600	148	211	323
	1800	297	512	664
	1200	445	819	997
125	3600	185	308	386
	1800	370	670	850
	1200	554	864	1285
150	3600	222	264	447
	1800	444	755	915
	1200	665	1190	1403
200	3600	296	554	660
	1800	590	915	1330
	1200	897	1435	1880
250	3600	370	555	850
	1800	738	2015	1970
	1200	1117	2130	2300

FIGURE 7.7 Average Full-Load Current Ratings for Single-Phase Induction Motors

Horsepower	Synchronous Speed (rpm)	115 V		230 V	
		Full Load Current (amps)	Locked Rotor Current (amps)	Full Load Current (amps)	Locked Rotor Current (amps)
1/2	3600	7.0	43.6	3.5	21.8
	1800	8.2	45.0	4.1	22.5
	1200	11.0	40.0	5.5	20.0
	900	13.2	40.0	6.6	20.0
3/4	3600	9.8	64.6	4.9	32.3
	1800	11.2	63.6	5.6	31.8
	1200	14.6	61.0	7.3	30.5
	900	17.8	60.0	8.9	30.0
1	3600	12.0	76.4	6.0	38.2
	1800	14.0	75.8	7.0	37.9
	1200	16.8	70.0	8.4	35.0
	900	20.8	70.0	10.4	35.0
1.5	3600	17.0	109	8.5	54.3
	1800	19.0	105	9.5	52.3
	1200	23.0	100	11.5	50.0
	900	28.0	100	14.0	50.0
2	3600	18.6	131	9.3	65.3
	1800	23.0	130	11.5	65.0
	1200	30.0	130	15.0	65.0
	900	31.0	130	15.5	60.0
3	3600	30.0	180	15.0	90.0
	1800	33.6	189	16.8	94.5
	1200	36.0	180	18.0	90.0
5	3600	44.0	270	22.0	135
	1800	46.0	234	23.0	117
	1200	51.0	270	25.5	135
7.5	3600	62.0	350	31.0	175
	1800	64.0	350	32.0	175
	1200	70.0	350	35.0	175
10	3600	82.0	460	41.0	230
	1800	88.0	460	44.0	230
	1200	92.0	460	46.0	230

FIGURE 7.8 Average Current for 3-Phase Induction Motors

Horsepower	Synchronous Speed	230 V		460 V	
		Full Load Current (amps)	Locked Rotor Current (amps)	Full Load Current (amps)	Locked Rotor Current (amps)
1/2	3600	1.2	15.0	0.6	7.5
	1800	1.9	16.6	0.9	8.3
	1200	1.9	15.3	0.9	7.7
	900	2.8	20.0	1.4	10.0
3/4	3600	2.3	18.8	1.2	9.4
	1800	2.4	21.3	1.3	10.6
	1200	3.0	20.9	1.5	10.5
	900	3.7	22.7	1.9	11.3
1	3600	3.7	4.9	1.9	12.5
	1800	3.5	25.8	1.7	12.9
	1200	3.9	26.3	1.9	13.1
	900	4.5	28.0	2.2	14.0
1.5	3600	4.5	37.0	2.2	18.6
	1800	4.7	35.5	2.4	17.8
	1200	5.1	36.5	2.5	18.3
2	3600	5.6	44.8	2.8	22.4
	1800	6.0	45.5	3.0	22.8
	1200	6.8	45.8	3.4	22.9
3	3600	7.8	54.3	3.9	27.1
	1800	8.7	60.8	4.3	30.4
	1200	10.0	60.0	5.0	30.0
5	3600	13.1	91.0	6.6	45.5
	1800	13.7	91.0	6.8	45.4
	1200	15.5	88.3	7.8	44.1
7.5	3600	19.0	125	9.5	62.4
	1800	20.4	122	10.2	61.1
	1200	21.4	124	10.7	62.1
10	3600	25.5	158	12.7	79.1
	1800	26.1	156	13.1	78.1
	1200	28.2	156	14.1	78.1
15	3600	37.4	229	18.7	114
	1800	38.5	225	19.3	112
	1200	41.5	221	20.7	111
20	3600	49.0	285	24.5	142
	1800	50.8	289	25.4	145
	1200	54.5	290	27.3	145

FIGURE 7.8 (continued)

Horsepower	Synchronous Speed	230 V		460 V	
		Full Load Current (amps)	Locked Rotor Current (amps)	Full Load Current (amps)	Locked Rotor Current (amps)
25	3600	59.7	361	29.9	180
	1800	63.1	362	31.6	181
	1200	67.0	355	33.5	178
30	3600	72.7	432	36.4	216
	1800	74.7	432	37.4	216
	1200	78.8	432	39.4	216
40	3600	94.6	577	47.3	289
	1800	100	577	50.0	289
	1200	107	577	53.7	278
50	3600	118	688	58.9	344
	1800	124	723	62.2	362
	1200	132	724	66.1	362
60	3600	140	823	69.9	412
	1800	149	853	74.3	427
	1200	150	850	75.0	425
75	3600	175	1022	87.5	511
	1800	184	1077	91.9	538
	1200	185	1053	92.4	527
100	3600	227	1383	113	691
	1800	235	1402	118	701
	1200	244	1426	122	713
125	3600	288	1683	144	842
	1800	292	1777	146	887
	1200	302	1807	151	904
150	3600	346	2084	173	1042
	1800	340	2135	170	1068
	1200	354	2083	177	1041
200	3600	466	2684	233	1342
	1800	444	2751	222	1376
	1200	468	2900	234	1450
250	3600	559	3650	279	1825
	1800	547	3419	273	1709
	1200	583	3650	292	1825

FIGURE 7.9 Effect of Voltage and Frequency Variation on Induction Motor Characteristics

Voltage and Frequency Variation		Starting and Maximum Running Torque	Synchronous Speed	Percent Slip	Full Load Speed	Efficiency		
						Full Load	75 % Load	50 % Load
Voltage Variation	120 % Voltage	Increase 44 %	No Change	Decrease 30 %	Increase 1.5 %	Small Increase	Decrease 0.5 to 2 %	Decrease 7 to 20 %
	110 % Voltage	Increase 22 %	No Change	Decrease 17 %	Increase 1 %	Increase 0.5 to 1 %	Practically No Change	Decrease 1 to 2%
	Function of Voltage	$(\text{Voltage})^2$	Constant	$\dfrac{1}{(\text{Voltage})^2}$	(Synchronous Speed Slip)	-	-	-
	90 % Voltage	Decrease 19 %	No Change	Increase 23 %	Decrease 1.5 %	Decrease 2 %	Practically No Change	Increase 1 to 2 %
Frequency Variation	105 % Frequency	Decrease 10 %	Increase 5 %	Practically No Change	Increase 5 %	Slight Increase	Slight Increase	Slight Increase
	Function of Frequency	$\dfrac{1}{(\text{Frequency})^2}$	Frequency	-	(Synchronous Speed Slip)	-	-	-
	95 % Frequency	Increase 11 %	Decrease 5 %	Practically No Change	Decrease 5 %	Slight Decrease	Slight Decrease	Slight Decrease

FIGURE 7.9 (continued)

Voltage and Frequency Variation		Full Load Current	Starting Current	Full Load Temperature Rise	Maximum Overload Capacity	Magnetic Noises, No Load in Particular	Power Factor		
							Full Load	75 % Load	50 % Load
Voltage Variation	120 % Voltage	Decrease 11 %	Increase 25 %	Decrease 5 to 6° C	Increase 44 %	Noticeable Increase	Decrease 5 to 15 %	Decrease 10 to 30 %	Decrease 15 to 40 %
	110 % Voltage	Decrease 7 %	Increase 10 to 12 %	Decrease 3 to 4° C	Increase 21 %	Increase Slightly	Decrease 3 %	Decrease 4 %	Decrease 5 to 6 %
	Function of Voltage	-	Voltage	-	$(Voltage)^2$	-	-	-	-
	90 % Voltage	Increase 11 %	Decrease 10 to 12 %	Increase 6 to 7° C	Decrease 19 %	Decrease Slightly	Increase 3 %	Increase 2 to 3 %	Increase 4 to 5 %
Frequency Variation	105 % Frequency	Decrease Slightly	Decrease 5 to 6 %	Decrease Slightly	Decrease Slightly	Decrease Slightly	Slight Increase	Slight Increase	Slight Increase
	Function of Frequency	-	$\dfrac{1}{Frequency}$	-	-	-	-	-	-
	95 % Frequency	Increase Slightly	Increase 5 to 6 %	Increase Slightly	Increase Slightly	Increase Slightly	Slight Decrease	Slight Decrease	Slight Decrease

Reproduced from the ASHRAE Handbook Equipment

FIGURE 7.10 Motor Maintenance Checklist

In Service Inspection

_____ Proper protection of all rotating parts
_____ Dripping oil, water, or other fluids
_____ Noisy operation
_____ Excessive vibrations
_____ High frame temperatures (> 80°C for open frame
         motors, > 90°C for enclosed frames)
_____ Excessive sparking
_____ Physical damage to motor frame
_____ Accumulation of dust or dirt on motor frame
_____ Rust on motor frame or supports

Out of Service Inspection

_____ Clogged air ventilation slots
_____ Damaged or loose motor mounts
_____ Improper alignment
_____ Excessive rotor end play
_____ Exposed or damaged wiring
_____ Pitted or damaged starter contacts
_____ Low insulation resistance

WORKSHEET 7.1 Evaluating Energy Savings From High-Efficiency Motors

1. Standard Motor Operating Costs

$$\frac{0.746 \; \times \; \boxed{} \; \times \; \boxed{} \; \times \; \boxed{}}{\boxed{}} \; = \; \boxed{}$$

0.746 X [Horsepower] X [Operating Hours] X [Electricity Rate]

÷ [Efficiency] = [Annual Operating Cost ($)]

2. High-Efficiency Motor Operating Costs

0.746 X [Horsepower] X [Operating Hours] X [Electricity Rate]

÷ [Efficiency] = [Annual Operating Cost ($)]

3. Annual Cost Savings

[Standard Motor Annual Operating Costs ($)] − [High-Efficiency Motor Annual Operating Costs ($)] = [Annual Savings ($)]

WORKSHEET 7.2 Motor Selection Criteria

1. Power Supply

Voltage:	_____	Volts
# of phases:	_____	
Frequency:	_____	Hz

2. Horsepower: _____ Hp

3. Frame Size: _____

4. Speed:

☐	Constant	Speed:	
☐	Varying	Max. Speed:_____	rpm
☐	Adjustable	Range:_____	rpm
☐	Adjustable/Varying	Range:_____ rpm to _____ rpm
☐	Multispeed	Speeds:_____ rpm to _____ rpm

5. Duty Cycle:

   ☐ Low
   ☐ Average
   ☐ High

6. Starting Torque:

   ☐ Low
   ☐ Average
   ☐ High

7. Environmental Requirements:

☐ Open	☐ Enclosed, Non-ventilated
☐ Drip Proof	☐ Enclosed, Ventilated
☐ Splash Proof	☐ Explosion Proof
☐ Guarded	☐ Dust-Ignition Proof
☐ Enclosed	☐ Water Proof

WORKSHEET 7.3 Motor Record Keeping

Identification # : _____	NEMA Frame# : _____
Location: _____	Voltage: _____
Manufacturer: _____	# of Phases: _____
Serial # : _____	Current: _____
Horsepower: _____	Speed: _____

Date	Maintenance Activity

Chapter 8

SELECTING, OPERATING, AND MAINTAINING TRANSFORMERS FOR MAXIMUM PERFORMANCE

There are two primary uses of power transformers in facilities: to step down the incoming voltage from the utility company to the desired distribution voltage within the facility, and to further step down the distribution voltage to match the voltages required by the various equipment loads within the facility. Other special application transformers used within facilities include current transformers for metering, isolation transformers for connection to critical loads, and low-voltage transformers for control and signaling.

HOW POWER TRANSFORMERS WORK

A power transformer is a static piece of equipment that links two or more independent electrical circuits through a magnetic circuit. The transformer has two major components: a magnetic steel core, and at least two coils. The coils are divided into two sets, primary and secondary. The primary coils are connected to the incoming or service electrical lines. The secondary coils are connected to the electrical loads within the facility. The ratio of the number of turns in the primary and secondary coils determines whether the service voltage is stepped up, stepped down, or held constant.

Power transformers operate on the principle of magnetic induction. An alternating current flowing through the primary coils generates a magnetic field within the transformer's steel core. The magnetic field, in turn, induces a voltage in the secondary coils. The output voltage of the transformer varies with the ratio of the turns in the primary and secondary coils.

How to Measure Transformer Capacity

A power transformer's capacity, expressed in thousands of volt-amperes (kVA) is the product of the voltage, the current, and the power factor in its secondary coils. For rating purposes, the power factor is assumed to be equal to 1.0. Figures 8.1 and 8.2 list the full load current ratings for single and three-phase transformers. Use these figures to estimate the current capacity for installed transformers.

Transformers can be loaded beyond their rating for short periods of time without experiencing serious damage. Repeated or lengthy overloads, however, will increase the rate of deterioration of the insulation and will shorten the transformer's expected life.

How to Increase Transformer Capacity

For naturally cooled dry type and oil filled transformers, you can increase the rated capacity by adding fans for forced air cooling. Properly installed, the fans can supplement the heat transfer by natural convection without resulting in hot spots within the windings that damage the insulation. For dry type transformers, the rated capacity can be increased by 30%. For oil filled transformers, the capacity can be increased by 15 to 20%. While the use of external cooling fans should not be factored into the process of sizing a transformer, they can help during emergency conditions such as an unusual peak load, or when one transformer must pick the load normally shared by two.

How Transformer Efficiency Is Calculated

The heat generated within the transformer is a product of inefficiencies that give rise to energy losses. The two major sources for losses within the transformer are copper losses and core losses. Copper loss within a transformer is the energy loss in the windings due to their resistance. Copper loss increases with the temperature of the windings and with the square of the current flowing through the winding.

Core loss is the energy loss due to the induction of magnetic currents within the iron core of the transformer. Its magnitude depends on the construction of the transformer, the voltage, and the frequency of the current. Since these factors are independent of load, core loss remains constant from no load to full load for a particular transformer.

The efficiency of a transformer is the ratio of its output to its input. Since the losses within a transformer are drawn from the primary supply, the efficiency can be calculated from:

$$\text{Efficiency} = \frac{\text{Output}}{\text{Output} + \text{Copper Loss} + \text{Core Loss}}$$

Because copper losses increase with increasing load drawn from the transformer, the efficiency of a unit varies with its load. For most power transformers, efficiencies vary

242   CHAPTER 8

between 95 and 99% when the units are loaded to at least 25% of their rated capacity. An important consequence of the losses in a transformer is that all lost energy eventually shows up in the form of heat. Figure 8.3 shows typical full load losses for transformers up to 2,000 kVA.

GENERAL TRANSFORMER CLASSIFICATIONS

Transformers are loosely classified into four groups on the basis of their size and secondary voltage rating. Figure 8.4 lists the characteristics of the four main groups. There is considerable overlapping between transformer groups since different manufacturers name units of the same capacity and voltage differently.

Transformers with a capacity of 10,000 kVA or more fall into the category of main substation transformers which typically have secondary voltages greater than 2,400 volts. Distribution transformers typically have capacities between 300 and 10,000 kVA and secondary voltages ranging up to 600 volts. Load center transformers typically have capacities less than 750 kVA and secondary voltages ranging from 120 to 600 volts. Fourth, general purpose transformers range in size up to 100 kVA with secondary voltages of 480 volts or less.

Although the basic transformer is a static piece of equipment, it often uses auxiliary equipment that includes a number of electromechanical devices. Integral cooling systems on main and secondary substation transformers use pumps and fans. Main and secondary substation transformers also make use of manual or automatic tap changers. Tap changers make use of multiple taps on either the primary or secondary windings to adjust the voltage of the system to compensate for varying primary voltages or varying secondary voltages that result from widely changing loads.

COOLING OF TRANSFORMERS

In spite of the high efficiency of transformers, provisions must be made for removing the heat generated from both copper and core losses and dissipating it to the surrounding air. If it is not removed quickly enough, the transformer's insulation, windings, and core will be damaged.

Depending on the size of the transformer and the application where it is being used, different cooling methods have been developed. Dry transformers are typically air cooled, using natural, forced, or combined natural and forced air circulation. Oil filled transformers also use natural and forced air circulation for cooling combined with natural or forced circulation of the insulating oil.

CHARACTERISTICS OF OIL-FILLED SYSTEMS

There are two basic classifications of cooling systems: oil-filled and dry. In oil-filled units, the entire core and coil assembly are immersed in a tank filled with insulating oil. Heat generated within the core and coils is carried away by convection of the oil. The oil then transfers the heat to the atmosphere by conduction and convection through the transformer tank or through a heat exchanger.

Figures 8.5 and 8.6 list the characteristics of pole and pad mounted oil-filled transformers. The values given in the tables are averages for units of those ratings. Actual characteristics will vary from manufacturer to manufacturer. Use the figures to estimate the physical characteristics for transformers required to meet certain load conditions.

Advantages

Oil-filled transformers have long-rated lives and are considered to be very reliable. Part of the reason for the reliability is the operation of the coils in a controlled environment where they can be protected from the effects of dust, dirt, and moisture. Oil-filled units are smaller and lower in first costs than their dry type counterparts.

Disadvantages

In comparison to dry type transformers, oil-filled units require more maintenance to insure that the insulating oil is properly filled, clean, and free of moisture.

CHARACTERISTICS OF DRY COOLING SYSTEMS

Dry type transformers use no liquid for cooling. Rather, they depend on natural or forced convection of the surrounding air to carry away the heat generated by the transformer. Figure 8.7 gives the characteristics of the most common dry type transformers. The values given in the table are averages for units of that capacity. Exact values will vary from manufacturer to manufacturer. Use the table to estimate the physical characteristics for transformers required to meet certain load conditions.

Dry type transformers are classified by the ability of their insulation to withstand elevated temperatures without breaking down. The three most commonly used classes are Class B - 80°C temperature rise, Class F - 115°C temperature rise, and Class H - 150°C temperature rise.

Figure 8.8 lists the temperatures associated with the different classes of transformers. For example, a transformer with a Class A insulating material is designed to have a full load temperature rise in the windings of not more than 55°C over the ambient temperature, with a maximum hot spot temperature rise of an additional 10°C. Therefore, the maximum allowable spot conductor temperature in a Class A transformer is 105°C.

Efficiency Factors to Consider

One of the advantages of the Class B and Class F transformers over Class H units is their efficiency. For units operating at 25% full-load or more, internal losses in Class F transformers are approximately 15% less than those in a Class H transformer. Class B transformers over the same load range operate with losses 30 to 35 percent less than those in a Class H transformer. This increase in operating efficiency is usually enough to justify the higher initial costs of the transformers.

Advantages

Dry type transformers are widely used in facilities despite several limitations. Their lack of an oil-based insulating fluid minimizes the potential for a transformer fire or explosion and reduces the maintenance required to test the units.

Disadvantages

To facilitate heat transfer, dry types in general have larger coils and cores than oil filled units. They are bulkier, operate less efficiently, and cost more than dry type transformers. Since the units depend on the efficient transfer of heat for proper cooling, it is important that the coils be cleaned periodically.

HOW TO SELECT A SUITABLE TRANSFORMER FOR YOUR APPLICATION

In selecting a transformer for a particular application, there are four factors you should consider: the primary voltage and number of phases, the secondary voltage, the kVA load on the transformer, and the future growth expected. The first two will be defined by the type of service to the facility and the type of equipment that is to be powered.

Use Worksheet 8.1 to estimate the kVA requirements for a transformer installation based on the kVA load requirements and the anticipated growth in electrical demand for the facility. Use the worksheet as follows:

Step 1.   Resistance loads are those loads such as incandescent lights and resistance heaters that have a power factor equal to 1.0. Sum the wattage of all resistance loads and enter the value in section #1 of the worksheet. Enter the voltage of the resistance loads (typically 120 volts) in section #1 of the worksheet.

Step 2.   Multiply the total wattage of the resistance loads by their voltage to determine the resistance kVA load. Enter the value in section #1.

Step 3.   Fluorescent lights typically operate at a power factor of 0.90 to 0.95 and therefore must be treated differently from resistance loads. Sum the wattage of all fluorescent lights to be powered by the transformer and enter the value in section #2. Enter the voltage at which the lights will be operated (typically 120 volts) in section #2.

Step 4.   Multiply the total watts by the voltage and the power factor of 0.9 to determine the lighting kVA load. Enter the value in section #2.

Step 5.   Enter the total wattage for all miscellaneous loads in section #3. Enter the voltage at which those loads will be operated in section #3. If the power factor of those loads is known, enter the value in section #3. If the power factor is not known, assume one of 0.85.

Step 6.   Multiply the total watts by the voltage and the power factor to determine the miscellaneous kVA load on the transformer and enter the value in section #3.

Step 7.   A motor loads the electrical system approximately one kVA per horsepower. For motors ranging from $1/4$ to one horsepower, assume a value of 1 kVA per motor. Sum the kVA load for all motors and enter the value in section #4.

Step 8.　　　Enter the resistance, lighting, miscellaneous, and motor kVA loads from sections #1 through 4 in section #5.

Step 9.　　　Add the resistance, lighting, miscellaneous, and motor kVA loads to determine the base kVA load on the transformer. Enter the value in section #5.

Step 10.　　The base kVA load represents the estimated load placed on the transformer by the existing equipment in the facility. To account for future growth, a growth factor must be entered into the calculations. Typical growth factors range from 1.5 to 2.0. Enter the growth factor in section #6 or #7 depending on whether a single or three-phase transformer is used.

Step 11.　　Multiply the base kVA by the growth factor for single-phase transformers to determine the kVA capacity. Enter the value in section #6. For three-phase transformers, multiply the base kVA by the growth factor and the number 1.73 to determine the kVA capacity. Enter the value in section #7.

This value represents the minimum kVA requirements for the transformer.

HOW TO KEEP TRANSFORMER NOISE AT AN ACCEPTABLE LEVEL

An important consideration in developing a site plan for locating the transformers serving a facility is the impact that the noise they generate will have on the operation. The noise level produced varies both with the size and capacity of the transformers, and without careful planning can easily reach unacceptable levels. The transformer itself generates noise as a natural by-product of its operation. Through good design and installation practices, it can be reduced, but it can never be fully eliminated. Although several components contribute to the noise generated within the transformer, the major source is its laminated core. The magnetic fields generated within the transformer subject the metal layers within the core to minute periodic variations in length which, in turn, cause vibrations that are transmitted from the laminated core through its supporting structure and insulation to the transformer case. The fundamental frequency of the vibrations is twice the frequency of the electrical system (120 hertz for a standard 60 hertz electrical system). The amplitude of the vibrations varies with the power drawn from the transformer.

The impact that the noise generated by a transformer will have in a particular application depends on three factors: the sound level of the noise generated by the transformer; the average ambient noise level where the transformer is installed; and the way in which it is installed.

NEMA Recommended Sound Levels

The sound level of the noise produced by a transformer is rated by its manufacturer using standard test procedures. Figure 8.9 lists the NEMA recommended maximum average sound level produced for transformers. Manufacturers typically publish sound level data for particular transformers which generally meet or exceed the levels recommended by NEMA.

Selection Rule of Thumb

A rule of thumb to follow in selecting a particular transformer for an installation is to select one whose sound level rating is less than the average ambient noise level where it is being installed. For example, in office areas, the typical ambient noise level ranges from 45 to 70 dB depending on the use of equipment in the area. In retail sales areas, the ambient noise level typically ranges from 40 to 50 dB.

Five Ways to Reduce Noise Levels

The way in which a transformer is installed will determine to a great extent how much of the noise it generates is transmitted to the surrounding areas. Good installation practices can reduce sound levels by 10 to 15 decibels (db). Since each 3 db decrease in sound level results in a decrease in volume of approximately 50 percent, proper installation techniques can easily make the difference between an acceptable and an unacceptable installation.

Suggested installation practices that can reduce the sound transmission include the following:

➤ Install the transformer in a location where its noise will have little impact on surrounding operations.

➤ Mount the transformer to a solid foundation using vibration isolators to dampen the sound transmission.

➤ Use flexible connections and vibration dampers on all electrical connections to the transformer to reduce vibrations transmitted through the cabling.

➤ Place the units as far away from walls and ceilings as possible for transformers mounted inside facilities. If units must be mounted close to a solid surface, install a sound absorbing material on that surface to reduce sound transmission. Avoid installing the units in stairways and hall areas where walls can resonate and echo.

➤ Construct a solid barrier between the transformer and the area being protected for units installed outside facilities. The barrier's size depends on where it is located between the transformer and the area to be protected.

A rule of thumb to follow for barriers located close to transformers is to extend the barrier at least twice the length of the transformer and one and one-half times its height. Small transformers can be shielded by using shrubbery.

RECOMMENDED MAINTENANCE ACTIVITIES FOR TRANSFORMERS

Transformers require periodic maintenance to insure proper operation over their design life of 25 to 30 years. The need for maintenance results from the effects that the environment has on the operation of the unit. For larger units, a second need arises from the use of auxiliary cooling equipment that must be inspected and tested.

Although the insulating and cooling oil used in transformers is very stable, it will react slowly with oxygen and moisture that it comes in contact with. The oil absorbs oxygen from the air which becomes distributed throughout the transformer's tank and, as the oxygen slowly reacts with the oil, forms acids that can greatly reduce the oil's insulating properties. The rate of oxidization increases with increasing oil temperature.

Moisture absorbed into the oil from the air has a similar effect on the dielectric strength of the insulating materials within the transformer. By testing the oil periodically you can detect the effects of moisture and oxidation before it leads to a failure of the transformer.

Heat generated within the transformer also has a long-term effect on its life. Under normal operating conditions, when the transformer is operated below its rated capacity, the effects of heat will be minimal. However, most transformers are periodically subjected to overload conditions. While an occasional, short-term overload will have little impact on the transformer's operation, the heat generated by repeated or prolonged overloads breaks down the insulating materials through a process called depolymerization which, as it progresses, reduces both the mechanical strength and the insulating properties of the materials. Test the transformer's insulation periodically to detect the effects of depolymerization before it results in a transformer failure.

The auxiliary equipment associated primarily with larger transformers also requires periodic maintenance. To ensure proper operation, you should examine and evaluate tap changers, cooling fans, cooling pumps, and protective relays on a regular basis.

Factors to Consider when Establishing a Maintenance Program

Most of the maintenance activities associated with transformers involve periodic inspection and testing. How frequently you perform these activities depends on the size and type of the transformer as well as the particular application. For example, you should test large power transformers that serve entire facilities at least once a year. Smaller transformers serving specific loads within a facility, such as lighting, can be tested only once every two to five years.

When establishing a maintenance schedule for transformers, follow this rule of thumb: The more costly the transformer is to replace and the more critical the loads it serves, the more frequently you should test and inspect it. You should balance inspection and testing costs against the total cost of a transformer failure.

A transformer maintenance program must begin early in the design stages of the facility. There must be adequate room for personnel who will be performing the inspection and testing activities to gain access to the transformer while maintaining adequate clearance from other high-voltage gear in the area that may still be live.

An additional factor to consider during the design stage is how the facility will be operated while the maintenance is being performed on a particular transformer. Most maintenance activities require that the transformer be taken out of service. To do so without disrupting the operation of the facility requires the ability to switch the connected load to another unit. If additional transformers are not available, you will have to schedule an interruption of electrical service.

Figure 8.10 lists the suggested maintenance activities for medium- to large-power transformers. The recommended maintenance intervals given in the table are for typical applications and may have to be adjusted for specific requirements.

FIGURE 8.1 Single-Phase Full-Load Current Ratings

kVA	AMPERES			
	120 V	240 V	480 V	600 V
1	8.33	4.16	2.08	1.6
1.5	12.5	6.24	3.12	2.4
2	16.66	8.33	4.16	3.2
3	25	12.5	6.1	4.8
5	41	21	10.4	8.3
7.5	62	31	15.6	12.5
10	83	42	21	16.5
15	124	62	31	25
25	208	104	52	42
37.5	312	156	78	62
50	416	208	104	84
75	624	312	156	124
100	830	415	207	168
167	1,390	695	348	278
200	1,660	833	416	336
250	2,080	1,040	520	420
333	2,780	1,390	695	555
500	4,160	2,080	1,040	840

FIGURE 8.2 Three-Phase Full-Load Current Ratings

AMPERES

kVA	208 V	240 V	480 V	600 V	2,400 V	4,160 V	7,200 V	12,000 V	12,470 V	13,200 V
30	83.3	72.2	36.1	28.9	7.22	4.16	2.41	1.44	1.39	1.31
45	125	108	54.1	43.3	10.8	6.25	3.61	2.17	2.08	1.97
75	208	180	90.2	72.2	18.0	10.4	6.01	3.61	3.47	3.28
112	312	271	135	108	27.1	15.6	9.02	5.41	5.21	4.92
150	416	361	180	144	36.1	20.8	12.0	7.22	6.94	6.56
225	625	541	271	217	54.1	31.2	18.0	10.8	10.4	9.84
300	833	722	361	289	72.2	41.6	24.1	14.4	13.9	13.1
500	1,388	1,203	601	481	120	69.4	40.1	24.1	23.1	21.9
750	2,082	1,804	902	722	180	104	60.1	36.1	34.7	32.8
1,000	2,776	2,406	1,203	962	241	139	80.2	48.1	46.3	43.7
1,500	4,162	3,608	1,804	1,443	361	208	120	72.2	69.4	65.6
2,000	-	4,811	2,406	1,925	481	278	160	96.2	92.6	87.5
2,500	-	-	3,007	2,406	601	347	200	120	116	109
3,000	-	-	3,609	2,887	722	416	241	144	139	131
3,750	-	-	4,511	3,608	902	520	301	180	174	164
5,000	-	-	-	4,811	1,203	694	401	241	231	219
7,500	-	-	-	-	1,804	1,041	601	361	347	328
10,000	-	-	-	-	2,406	1,388	802	481	463	437

FIGURE 8.3 Typical Full-Load Transformer Losses

Load Losses kVa

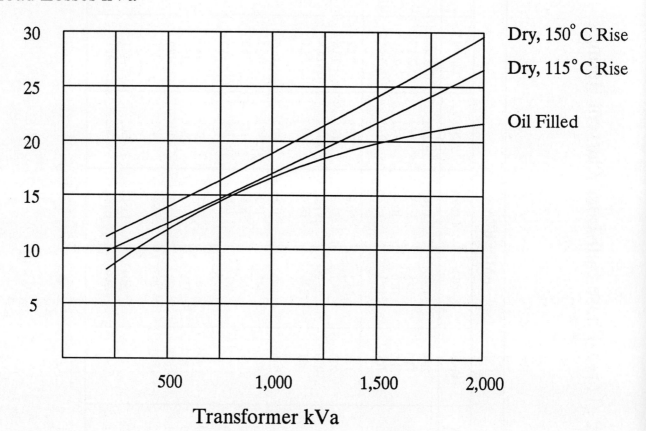

Dry, 150° C Rise

Dry, 115° C Rise

Oil Filled

Transformer kVa

FIGURE 8.4 General Transformer Classifications

Transformer Type	Capacity (KVA)	Cooling Method	Voltage			
			Primary		Secondary	
General Purpose	1 - 100	Air, Natural Circulation	120 208 240	480 600	120 208 240	480
Load Center	10 to 750	Air & oil, natural or forced circulation	2,400 4,160 7,200	11,000 13,200 13,800	120 208 240	480 600
Distribution	300 to 10,000	Oil, natural or forced circulation	2,400 4,160 7,200	13,200 13,800	480 600	
Main Substation	10,000 and up	Oil, forced circulation	7,200 12,470 13,200 22,900	34,400 43,800	2,400 4,160	

FIGURE 8.5 Three-Phase Pole Mounted Transformers

kVA	Height (in)	Diameter (in)	Weight (lb)
Less Than 5,000 Volt Primary			
10	29	20	245
15	29	20	270
30	42	26	620
45	46	29	920
75	51	32	1,100
100	47	35	1,250
150	55	35	1,550
250	55	48	1,950
500	72	55	3,500
5,000 to 12,000 Volt Primary			
10	32	20	250
15	32	20	290
30	47	21	680
45	49	24	850
75	55	29	1,200
100	51	34	1,200
150	58	37	1,600
250	64	43	2,050
500	74	55	3,600
12,000 to 19,000 Volt Primary			
10	41	19	320
15	41	19	330
30	47	21	700
45	51	24	985
75	56	30	1,140
100	51	34	1,225
150	58	37	1,650
250	65	45	2,100
500	76	55	3,500
Greater Than 19,000 Volt Primary			
25	41	21	500
50	57	26	995
100	57	35	1,175
150	59	43	1,590
250	69	50	2,330
500	73	62	3,200

FIGURE 8.6 Three-Phase Oil Filled Transformers

kVA	Height (in)	Width (in)	Depth (in)	Weight (lb)
Less Than 5,000 Volt Primary				
500	84	67	42	4,500
750	84	76	50	7,500
1,000	90	85	57	8,000
1,500	92	90	64	10,100
2,000	92	100	60	11,800
2,500	92	120	60	13,700
5,000 to 15,000 Volt Primary				
500	84	67	43	4,700
750	88	76	52	6,800
1,000	92	82	62	7,500
1,500	92	92	66	10,400
2,000	96	92	66	12,600
2,500	96	96	70	15,000
5,000	110	96	80	28,000
7,500	120	96	86	38,000
10,000	130	100	100	48,500
Greater Than 15,000 Volt Primary				
750	72	77	75	9,000
1,000	87	77	80	10,900
1,500	90	77	80	13,400
2,000	94	79	86	15,900
2,500	100	80	88	16,500
5,000	120	90	90	29,500
7,500	130	90	90	41,000
10,000	140	96	100	52,000

FIGURE 8.7 Three-Phase Dry Transformers

80° C Rise

kVA	Height (in)	Width (in)	Depth (in)	Weight (lb)
Less Than 5,000 Volt Primary				
225	90	60	56	2,600
300	90	60	56	3,200
500	90	60	56	4,000
750	90	72	56	5,300
1,000	90	72	56	7,500
1,500	90	72	56	9,500
2,000	100	100	56	11,500
2,500	100	100	56	13,000
5,000 to 15,000 Volt Primary				
225	90	60	54	3,400
300	90	60	54	3,500
500	90	60	54	5,100
750	90	72	54	6,000
1,000	90	72	54	8,000
1,500	90	72	54	10,800
2,000	100	100	54	13,400
2,500	100	100	54	15,000
Greater Than 15,000 Volt Primary				
225	90	60	54	3,700
300	90	60	54	4,300
500	100	70	60	6,000
750	100	70	60	6,900
1,000	100	96	60	10,000
1,500	110	96	70	12,800
2,000	120	100	70	14,000
2,500	120	100	70	18,000

FIGURE 8.7 (continued)

115° C Rise

kVA	Height (in)	Width (in)	Depth (in)	Weight (lb)
Less Than 5,000 Volt Primary				
225	68	56	36	2,300
300	68	56	36	2,600
500	90	72	38	3,400
750	90	72	56	5,000
1,000	90	84	58	5,500
1,500	90	84	58	8,000
2,000	100	108	58	10,900
2,500	110	108	58	12,200
5,000 to 15,000 Volt Primary				
225	68	60	54	2,800
300	90	72	54	3,300
500	90	72	54	4,500
750	90	84	54	6,000
1,000	90	84	54	7,400
1,500	90	96	54	9,000
2,000	110	108	54	10,900
2,500	110	108	54	12,500
Greater Than 15,000 Volt Primary				
225	92	70	62	3,000
300	92	70	62	3,500
500	100	100	70	5,000
750	100	100	70	6,000
1,000	100	100	70	7,500
1,500	110	110	70	10,000
2,000	120	110	70	12,000
2,500	120	120	70	14,000

FIGURE 8.7 (continued)

150° C Rise

kVA	Height (in)	Width (in)	Depth (in)	Weight (lb)
Less Than 5,000 Volt Primary				
225	68	50	36	2,000
300	68	50	36	2,400
500	90	50	56	3,200
750	90	68	56	4,600
1,000	90	68	56	5,300
1,500	90	80	58	7,100
2,000	95	90	58	9,700
2,500	105	100	58	12,000
5,000 to 15,000 Volt Primary				
225	68	56	36	2,600
300	90	65	54	3,500
500	90	65	54	4,300
750	90	65	54	5,100
1,000	90	80	60	6,500
1,500	90	70	60	8,200
2,000	100	100	60	10,500
2,500	105	100	60	12,700
Greater Than 15,000 Volt Primary				
225	90	70	60	4,000
300	90	70	60	5,000
500	110	110	70	7,200
750	110	110	70	7,600
1,000	110	110	70	8,700
1,500	120	120	70	10,900
2,000	120	120	70	12,800
2,500	120	120	70	14,500

FIGURE 8.8 Transformer Temperature Rise Classification

Transformer Insulation Class	Ambient Temperature (°C)	Winding Temperature Rise (°C)	Hot Spot Temperature Rise (°C)	Transformer Temperature Rise (°C)
A	40	55	10	105
B	40	80	30	150
F	40	115	30	185
H	40	150	30	220

FIGURE 8.9 Single- and Three-Phase Transformer Noise Levels

Up to 600 V

kVA	Noise Level (db)
0 - 9	40
10 - 50	45
51 - 150	50
151 - 300	55
301 - 500	60

Over 600 V

kVA	Noise Level (db)
51 - 150	55
151 - 300	58
301 - 500	60
501 - 700	62
701 - 1,000	64
1,001 - 1,500	65
1,501 - 2,000	66
2,001 - 3,000	68

FIGURE 8.10 Recommended Maintenance Activities

	Activity	**Frequency**
General	Inspect for structural integrity of the foundation, anchor bolts, supporting frame, and the transformer case.	Annually
	Inspect for dirt and debris on or around insulators, bushings, cable entrances, and all transformer cooling surfaces.	Annually
	Inspect for rust on all metal surfaces of the transformer case and its supporting frame.	Annually
	Inspect all liquid filled transformers for signs of leaking	Monthly
	Inspect all bushings, insulators, and cables for signs of cracks, discoloring, or burned or broken connections.	Annually
	For dry type transformers, vacuum dust from all windings	Annually
	For transformers using a nitrogen gas cushion, check the transformer and gas cylinder pressures.	Monthly
Insulation	Draw a sample of the insulating oil and have it tested for dielectric strength and acidity.	Annually
	Test the resistance of the insulation between windings in the transformer, and between each winding and ground.	Annually
Protective Devices	Inspect all alarm wiring for loose or corroded components.	Annually
	Test calibration of all temperature indicators and alarms.	Annually
	Inspect all liquid level gauges for clear indication of actual liquid levels.	Annually
	For inert gas systems, check calibration of pressure gauges.	Monthly
	Inspect overcurrent devices for evidence of damage, corrosion, dirt, or overheating.	Annually
	Test the operation of all manual and automatic circuit breakers and switches.	Annually
	Inspect and clean all lightning arresters. Replace any units showing signs of cracks or burns.	Annually
	Inspect the dehydrating breathers for moisture saturation.	Monthly
	Test the operation of the pressure relief valves.	Annually
Auxiliary Equipment	Clean, inspect, and test all auxiliary motors, fans, and pumps for proper operation and calibration.	Annually
	Inspect all mechanical parts of the tap changers for corrosion, dirt, wear, and proper lubrication. Rotate the tap changer through its entire range to assure proper surface contact and tension.	Annually

WORKSHEET 8.1 Sizing Transformers

1. Resistance Loads

[ ]	X [ ]	X 1.0	= [ ]	
Total Watts	Voltage	Power Factor	Resistance kVA	

2. Fluorescent Lighting Load

[ ]	X [ ]	X 0.9	= [ ]	
Total Watts	Voltage	Power Factor	Lighting kVA	

3. Miscellaneous Loads

[ ]	X [ ]	X [ ]	= [ ]	
Total Watts	Voltage	Power Factor	Misc. kVA	

4. Motor Loads

[ ]

Motor kVA

5. Base Load

[ ]	+ [ ]	+ [ ]	+ [ ]	= [ ]
Resistance kVA	Lighting kVA	Misc. kVA	Motor kVA	Base kVA

WORKSHEET 8.1 (continued)

6. Single-Phase Capacity

[ ]	X	[ ]	=	[ ]
Base kVA		Growth Factor		kVA Capacity

7. Three-Phase Capacity

[ ]	X	[ ]	X	1.73	=	[ ]
Base kVA		Growth Factor				kVA Capacity

## Chapter 9

MAINTAINING BATTERY SYSTEMS TO IMPROVE THEIR EFFICIENCY AND RELIABILITY

Central battery banks are frequently used as standby or emergency power sources for building lighting systems, communication equipment, telephone switching stations, electrical switchgear, computer system uninterruptible power supplies, and other critical electrical loads that require a temporary, reliable source of power during an electrical outage. Systems can be configured to power loads ranging from a few watts to several thousand watts for periods of time ranging from seconds to 24 hours or more.

Two types of loads are served by the systems: those requiring direct current, and those requiring alternating current. In systems powering direct current loads, there are two basic components: the battery and the battery charger. Systems requiring alternating current add a third component, a static inverter to convert the direct current into alternating current.

HOW BATTERIES WORK

A battery is a group of electrical cells connected in series to provide power to an electrical load. Each cell is a physically separate unit consisting of a positive and a negative plate placed in an electrolyte solution, generally a mixture of sulfuric acid and water. A chemical reaction between the electrodes and the electrolyte produces 1.2 or 2.0 volts across the electrodes depending on the type of cell. Passing an electrical current through the cell reverses the chemical process, storing electrical energy as chemical energy within the cell. The voltage of the battery is the sum of the voltages produced by each of its cells connected in series. The current produced by the battery is the current-producing capacity of a single cell.

How Battery Chargers Work

The battery charger serves three purposes: recharging the battery after use; maintaining a full charge in the battery between periods of use; and insuring that all cells within the battery are charged to their full capacity. Recharging is the process of converting electrical energy into chemical energy for storage within the individual cells. Recharging is accomplished by the charger passing a current through the battery at a higher voltage than is produced by the battery itself. For acid based cells, the recharging voltage is typically 2.33 volts for a 2.00 volt cell.

When the battery is fully charged, the voltage applied by the charger is reduced to a float voltage, typically 2.17 volts for a 2.00 volt cell. The purpose of the float voltage is to compensate for chemical reactions that are taking place within the cells that would result in a decreased cell capacity. The float voltage is always higher than the battery's rated nominal voltage, but less than the normal recharge voltage to prevent overcharging of the cells. Overcharging results in high water use through excessive gassing; the release of hydrogen and oxygen gas by electrolysis within the cells.

To keep all cells within the battery equally charged, the battery charger passes an equalizing current through the cells. Due to slight variations in both manufacturing and aging, no two cells are exactly the same. As a result, under normal float charging, some cells may not be kept at full capacity. The charge in these cells can be enhanced by periodically passing a prolonged charge at a voltage higher than is used for float charging through the battery. For most applications, the voltage used to pass the equalizing current is the same as is used for recharging the battery. Depending on how often the batteries are used, equalizing currents may be applied at intervals ranging from once a month to once a year.

How Battery Capacity Is Determined

The capacity of a battery is a measure of its ability to produce an electrical current over a period of time. Capacity is rated in ampere-hours and is determined by multiplying the current drawn by the connected load (in amps) by the length of time (in hours) that the battery can produce that current. Battery ampere-hour ratings are based on the current that the battery can produce over an eight-hour time period at 77°F.

A convenient measure of the state of a cell's charge is its specific gravity reading as measured on a hydrometer. Specific gravity is the ratio of the density of the electrolyte within the cell to the density of pure water. Since the density of the electrolyte varies with the charge of the cell, you can use specific gravity to measure the level of charge within a cell. Figure 9.1 shows the relationship between the specific gravity in a typical cell and its percent discharge. Use the figure to determine the percent discharge state of a battery cell based on the specific gravity reading taken on that cell.

Advantages and Disadvantages of Common Battery Types

Figure 9.2 lists characteristics of the three most commonly used types of cells in standby power systems: lead-antimony, lead-calcium, and nickel-cadmium. The values given in the table are typical for that type of cell. Actual cell characteristics will vary from manufacturer to manufacturer.

Lead-Antimony Cells

Of the three types of cells, the lead-antimony or lead-acid cell is the most popular for medium to large battery systems. Lead-antimony cells offer good performance at a relatively low first cost. Cells operate at a nominal 2.00 volts, with a float voltage of 2.17 volts. Periodic equalizing charges are required to keep all cells at their full potential. As the cells age, the float current required to maintain the charge in the cells increases, resulting in increased water use.

Lead-Calcium Cells

Lead-calcium cells offer a longer life than lead-antimony, but at a higher first cost. The cells operate at a nominal 2.00 volts, with a float voltage of 2.25 volts. In spite of this higher float voltage, the water use of lead-calcium cells is relatively low and does not increase with cell age. Lead-calcium cells, partly because of their higher float voltage, do not require equalizing charges as often as is required by lead-antimony cells. One major drawback of the cells is their susceptibility to permanent damage during deep discharges.

Nickel-Cadmium Cells

Nickel-cadmium cells offer a life expectancy similar to that of lead-calcium cells, but at an even higher cost. Cells operate at a nominal 1.20 volts, with a float voltage of 1.42 volts. This lower float voltage requires the installation of more cells to obtain the same system voltage.

An advantage of the nickel-cadmium cells is their flexibility. The cells can be recharged without damage at a wide range of recharging rates, from a fast charge of less than four hours to an overnight charge lasting ten or more hours. Nickel-cadmium cells perform well in applications having a high discharge rate.

MEASURING BATTERY PERFORMANCE

As energy is drawn from the cells, chemical reactions take place within the cells that change their characteristics. One of the most important considerations is the variation in cell voltage with discharge. Figure 9.3 shows the decrease in cell voltage with respect to percent discharge for a typical lead-antimony cell. From the figure it can be seen that you must consider variations in cell voltage when establishing the upper and lower system operating voltages needed to match equipment requirements.

Correcting for Changes in Temperature

The changes in cell characteristics with discharge are most easily determined by measuring the specific gravity of the cell. As the cell is discharged, its specific gravity decreases from between 1.28 and 1.30 for a fully charged lead-antimony cell, to approximately 1.1 for a fully discharged cell. Figure 9.1 shows the change in specific gravity for a lead-antimony cell operating at 77°F. If the cell is operating at any temperature other than 77°F, the hydrometer reading must be corrected to give the true specific gravity. Figure 9.4 lists the correction values for various temperatures. For the temperature at which the battery is stored, add or subtract the hydrometer correction values given in the chart to the readings taken to determine the true value.

Estimating the Time Required to Recharge a Battery

A cell's specific gravity can also be used as an indication of how much time will be required to recharge the cell to full capacity. For a cell operating at 77°F with the conventional recharge period of eight hours, use Figure 9.5 to estimate the time required to return a lead-antimony cell to full charge.

PROTECTING CELLS FROM FREEZING

Since the cell electrolyte contains a mixture of acid and water, cells that are operated in a cold environment must be protected from freezing. Although the electrolyte will not freeze solid under normal operating conditions, an icy slush will form that can permanently damage cell plates. The temperature at which that slush forms depends on the level of charge within the cell. Figure 9.6 shows the relationship between specific gravity and the temperature at which the slush will form.

Use the figure to determine the minimum ambient room temperature that can be tolerated by batteries at various levels of charge.

HOW TO SIZE A BATTERY SYSTEM

One of the most critical operations in designing a battery system is the proper sizing of the battery to be used, including both the number of cells required and their rated capacity. The factors that are most important in determining these characteristics are the maximum operating system voltage, the minimum operating system voltage, the load placed on the battery, and the temperature at which the battery will be operated.

DETERMINING HOW MANY CELLS ARE NEEDED

In applications involving banks of batteries, a number of identical cells are connected in series. In series-connected applications, the total voltage of the battery is equal to the voltage of a single cell times the number of cells in the battery. The amp-hr capacity of the battery is equal to the amp-hr capacity of a single cell.

Use Worksheet 9.1 to estimate the number of cells required for a particular application. Use the worksheet as follows:

Step 1.   Determine the maximum operating voltage for the equipment to be powered by the battery system. For 120 volt equipment, the typical maximum voltage is 130 volts. Enter the maximum permissible operating voltage in sections #1 and #2 of the worksheet.

Step 2.   Determine the minimum operating voltage for the equipment to be powered by the battery system. For 120 volt equipment, the typical minimum voltage is 105 volts. Enter the minimum allowable operating voltage in section #1 of the worksheet.

Step 3.   Figure 9.2 lists the float voltage for various types of cells. For the type of cell to be installed, determine the float voltage from the figure and enter the value in section #2.

Step 4.   Divide the maximum operating voltage by the float voltage per cell to determine the number of cells required. Round off the value to the next highest whole number and enter the value in section #2.

Step 5.   Enter the minimum operating voltage from section #1 into section #3.

Step 6.   Enter the number of cells estimated from section #2 into section #3.

Step 7.   Divide the minimum operating voltage by the number of cells to determine the discharge state voltage per cell. Enter the value in section #3.

Step 8.   Use Figure 9.3 to determine the percent discharged state of the cell as a function of the cell voltage. As a rule of thumb, for maximum life the cells should never be discharged by more than 80 percent. For the discharge voltage per cell calculated in section #3, determine the percent discharge state of the cell. If the value is greater than 0.80, use the number from the chart. If the value is less than 0.80, use 0.80. Enter the value in section #4.

The number of cells calculated by using the worksheet is based on both the maximum operating voltage and minimum operating voltage required by the connected load.

ESTIMATING BATTERY CAPACITY

Once you have determined the number of cells needed in the battery and the discharge limit established, you can size the battery capacity. Use Worksheet 9.2 to estimate the amp-hr capacity required for the battery. Use the worksheet for applications having typical duty cycles where the loads are evenly spaced over the entire cycle.

Caution: If a particular application has widely varying loads, particularly at the end of the duty cycle, or if the entire capacity of the battery is needed in a short period of time, use the worksheet only as a first approximation. You can achieve more accurate sizing for those applications by using the procedures given in the *IEEE Standard, Recommended Practice for Sizing Large Lead Storage Batteries for Generating Stations and Substations.*

Use the worksheet as follows:

Step 1.   If the load to be connected to the battery system is constant, only one line of section #1 is required. Enter the load in amps and the time it will operate in hours in section #1. If the load is not constant, divide the load into its individual load and time components and enter the values in section #1.

Step 2.   Multiply each load in section #1 by its operating time to determine the amp-hr requirements. Sum the amp-hr components to get the total load and enter the value in section #1.

Step 3.   Enter the load in amp-hr from section #1 into section #2.

Step 4.   Enter the percent discharged limit from section #4 of Worksheet 9.1 as a decimal value (0   1.0) in section #2.

Step 5.   The temperature of the electrolyte of the cells will impact their capacity. Electrolyte temperature will closely follow room temperature, except during periods of heavy charging. To correct for temperatures other than 77°F, a temperature correction factor is introduced. Use Figure 9.4 to determine the temperature correction factor. For the temperature of the room where the cells will be installed, select the temperature correction factor and enter the value in section #2. If the room temperature is allowed to vary widely, use the temperature correction factor for the lowest temperature expected.

Step 6.   As cells age, their capacity slowly decreases. To compensate for this decline in capacity, extra capacity must be built into the original design. For most applications, an age factor of 1.25 is sufficient. Enter the age factor in section #2.

Step 7.   Multiply the load in amp-hr by the temperature factor and the age factor, and divide by the percent discharged state of the battery to determine the required capacity of the battery system in amp-hr. Enter the value in section #2.

The value calculated by the worksheet represents the total electrical capacity of the battery system that can be drawn during the expected life of the batteries, assuming that they are properly maintained.

How to Size the Battery Charger

The battery charger serves two functions: to recharge the cells after their energy has been used, and to maintain the charge within the cells by passing a small current through the cells while they are fully charged. To accomplish these functions, the charger must have sufficient capacity to provide the high current required to recharge the battery within a reasonable period of time, and sufficient voltage regulation to prevent the overcharging of a cell. Overcharging results in excessive production of hydrogen gas, increases water use within the cells, and reduces cell life and performance.

Most of the chargers available today are of the constant voltage design with sufficient voltage regulation to maintain a float voltage of ± 0.5 volts over the entire rated current range of the charger. Typical voltages include 12, 24, 32, 48, 120, and 240 volts. For the higher voltages, chargers are available in both single and three-phase units.

You should select the charger for a specific application after you define the load to be powered by the battery and after you have selected the particular cell. For most applications, the charger is sized based on the capacity of the battery and the time required to fully recharge the cells. In applications where the load floats on line with the battery, such as in an uninterruptible power supply, the charger must be capable of simultaneously recharging the battery and supplying power to the load.

Use Worksheet 9.3 to estimate the capacity of a battery charger for a particular application. To use this worksheet, first determine the number of cells from Worksheet 9.1 and the battery capacity from Worksheet 9.2. Use the worksheet as follows:

Step 1.	Enter the battery capacity in amp-hrs from section #2 of Worksheet 9.2 into section #1.
Step 2.	Enter the percent discharge limit from section #4 of Worksheet 9.1 as a decimal value (0 - 1.0) in section #1.
Step 3.	Section #1 of Worksheet 9.2 lists the load components powered by the battery. Sum the individual loads in amps and enter the value in section #1.
Step 4.	Enter the battery capacity in amp-hrs and the percent discharge limit from section #1 into section #2.
Step 5.	If the load is to be powered by the battery charger while it is recharging the batteries, enter the load from section #1 into section #2. If the load is not to be powered by the charger during the recharge period, set the load in section #2 equal to zero.
Step 6.	Typical times to fully recharge the battery range from eight to 24 hours. Determine the number of hours that you want it to take to recharge the battery, and enter the value in section #2.
Step 7.	Multiply the battery capacity by the percent discharge limit and the number 1.1. Divide the product by the hours it takes to recharge the battery. Add the load connected to the charger during the recharging operation to determine the base capacity requirements for the charger. Enter the value in sections #2 and #3.

Step 8. The base capacity of the battery charger must be corrected for operating temperatures that are in excess of 100°F. If the room in which the battery charger is located operates at 100°F or less, the temperature factor is 1.0. If the room temperature is between 100 and 120°F, the temperature factor is 0.80. If the room operates in excess of 120°F, the temperature factor is 0.65. Enter the correct temperature factor in section #3.

Step 9. To allow for variations in battery characteristics and environmental factors, a safety factor is added into the calculation. For most applications, a safety factor of 1.1 is adequate. Enter the value selected in section #3.

Step 10. Multiply the base capacity by the temperature and safety factors to determine the charger capacity in amps. Round off the value to the next highest whole number. Enter the value in section #3.

The value calculated by the worksheet represents the minimum size of charger that should be installed for that application.

HOW TO DETERMINE THE VENTILATION RATE FOR A BATTERY ROOM

Nearly all battery cell types produce hydrogen gas during charging. The gas is produced as a result of electrolysis taking place in the cell and is vented to the battery room through the cell vent plug.

The period of highest hydrogen gas production, or "gassing," occurs when the cells are fully or nearly fully charged and are subjected to a high charging current. For a room temperature of 77°F, most cells produce approximately 0.016 ft^3 of hydrogen gas per hour per cell for each ampere of charging current applied.

For small battery systems, such as wall mounted emergency lighting units, the amount of hydrogen gas produced is small and is readily dissipated by air infiltration. However, the volume of hydrogen gas produced by larger batteries can be significant. The risk of explosion becomes critical when the gas is permitted to build to a concentration greater than three percent of the room air by volume.

To eliminate this risk, ensure that mechanical ventilation is provided to dilute the volume of hydrogen gas present and remove it from the battery room. The ventilation rate required depends on the rate at which hydrogen gas is produced and the volume of the room. Under normal operation, the battery charger will limit the current through the cells when they are fully or near fully charged, thus reducing gassing and the volume of hydrogen gas produced. The ventilation system should be designed, however, to keep the concentration of hydrogen gas well below the three percent concentration safety limit should the battery charger malfunction and operate at full charging current when the batteries are fully charged.

Use Worksheet 9.4 to calculate the minimum required ventilation rate for a battery room. Use the worksheet as follows:

Step 1.   Enter the number of cells, the room dimensions (in feet), and the maximum current (in amps) that the battery charger can produce in section #1 of the worksheet.

Step 2.   Enter the charging current and the number of cells from section #1 into section #2. Multiply the charging current by the number of cells and the number 0.016 to determine the volume of hydrogen gas produced in cubic feet per hour. Enter the value in section #2.

Step 3.   Enter the volume of hydrogen gas produced from section #2 into section #3. Multiply the room length by its width and height to determine the room volume. Enter the number in section #3.

Step 4.   Divide the hydrogen produced by the room volume multiplied by the number 0.03 to determine the number of air changes per hour in room air required to keep the concentration of hydrogen below the safety limit of three percent.
               Rule of Thumb: The ventilation rate should never be less than three air changes per hour. Enter the larger value in section #3 as the required air changes per hour.

Step 5.   Enter the air changes per hour from section #3 into section #4. Enter the room volume in section #4.

Step 6.   Multiply the air changes per hour by the room volume and the number 0.0167 to determine the required ventilation rate in cubic feet per minute. Enter the value in section #4.

The value calculated by the worksheet represents the minimum ventilation rate required for the battery room. Specific battery/charger configurations may result in the need for additional ventilation. Check with the battery manufacturer to ensure that sufficient ventilation will be provided.

HOW TO MAINTAIN BATTERY SYSTEMS FOR PEAK PERFORMANCE AND LONG LIFE

To ensure maximum performance and long life of the battery cells and system components, several maintenance activities must be performed on a regular basis.

Recommended Maintenance

Figure 9.7 lists suggested maintenance activities and their frequencies. The activities and schedule presented in the figure are for typical installations. You may have to modify them to match the conditions present in your application.

Battery Inspection Log

Use Worksheet 9.5 as a cell inspection sheet to record individual cell voltages and specific gravities. Since specific gravity is a function of cell temperature, you should correct the reading taken for each cell based on the actual cell temperatures. Figure 9.4 lists the correction factors for cell temperatures ranging from 35°F to 110°F. For each cell, add the correction values to the hydrometer reading to determine the cell's actual specific gravity.

Completing the worksheet on a regular basis will identify problems within specific cells when they occur as well as long-term trends in cell performance.

Three Critical Activities

1. Add water. Of the activities listed, the single most important is the addition of water to the cells in the battery. As part of the normal charging process, electrolysis breaks down the water in the cells into hydrogen and oxygen. The gases can be seen bubbling through the electrolyte primarily during charging periods when the batteries are almost fully charged. Both the hydrogen and the oxygen escape to the battery room air through the vent located on the top of each cell.

   Water must be periodically added to replace that lost to electrolysis. How often it must be added depends on the float current through the cells, the frequency and duration of the equalizing current, the temperature of the electrolyte, and the design of the cell. In addition, as antimony cells age, their demand for water increases.

   Keep the level of the water in the cells between the high and low marks on the cell case. Over-filling the cells can result in the electrolyte overflowing the cell through the vent. Under-filling exposes the tops of the plates within the cells, resulting in decreased cell capacity and permanent cell damage. To limit damage resulting from impurities in the water, use distilled water.

2. Adjust float voltages. The second most important maintenance activity is the regular inspection and adjustment of the battery charger float voltage. To pass a current through the battery and charge it, the output voltage of the charger must be greater than the open circuit voltage of the battery. The greater the difference in voltage, the greater the current that will be passed through the battery.

   Adjust the charger so that its output voltage is just high enough to maintain the minimum current through the cells required to keep them fully charged. Too high a current results in overcharging, decreased battery life, and increased water use by the cells.

3. Clean cells and connectors regularly. The accumulation of dust and dirt as well as spilled and splashed electrolyte creates a conductive path between the cell terminals that impacts the cell's charge rate and full charge capacity.

Under normal operation where the cells remain fairly clean and dry, brushing off the dirt periodically will prevent the accumulation that could affect cell performance. If electrolyte or water is spilled or splashed on the cell tops, neutralize it with a solution of baking soda and water. Mix one pound of soda for each gallon of water. Liberally apply the solution to the cell tops, using a brush to insure that it is worked under the cell connections. Hose off the solution with a low-pressure hose, and wipe dry.

FACTORS TO CONSIDER DURING INSTALLATION

To facilitate maintenance of the battery system, carefully consider how the cells are to be installed. In a well designed installation, all cells are easily accessible for specific gravity testing, adding water, cleaning, and tightening of cable terminals. To provide easy access, provide a minimum of three feet of clearance between racks of cells. If cells are installed in racks with more than one level, the minimum clearance between levels is one and one-half times the cell height.

Finally, the battery room should be equipped with a floor drain and a water supply for cleaning the cell tops. For personnel safety, most building codes require the installation of an emergency eye wash system.

FIGURE 9.1 Specific Gravity vs. Percent Discharge

Specific Gravity

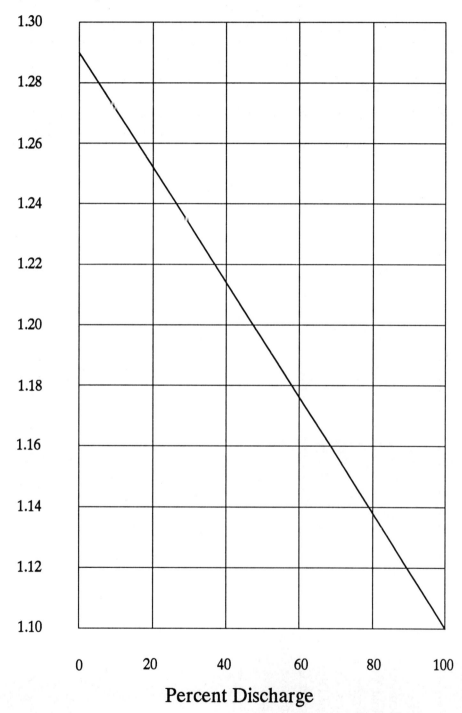

Percent Discharge

FIGURE 9.2 Characteristics of Common Battery Types

Battery Characteristic	Lead-Antimony	Lead-Calcium	Nickel-Cadmium
Life	7-10 years	15-20 years	15-20 years
Nominal Volts per cell	2.00	2.00	1.20
Float Voltage	2.17	2.25	1.42
Discharged Voltage	1.75	1.75	1.14
Float Current	300 ma	40 ma	100 ma
Self Discharge Rate	5% per month	1% per month	1% per month
Water Use	630 cc per month	130 cc per year	-
Relative Cost	1.0	1.5	3.0
Relative Weight	1.0	1.0	0.8

FIGURE 9.3 Battery Voltage vs. Percent Discharged

% Discharged

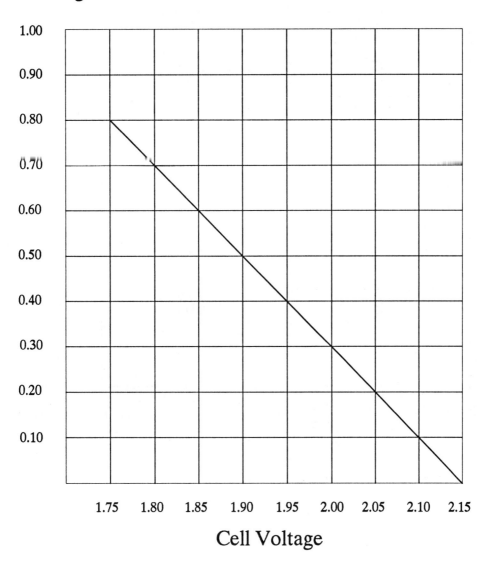

Cell Voltage

FIGURE 9.4 Temperature Correction Chart for Specific Gravity

Temperature (^{o}F)	Hydrometer Correction
110	+ 0.0100
105	+ 0.0085
100	+ 0.0070
95	+ 0.0055
90	+ 0.0040
85	+ 0.0025
80	+ 0.0010
77	0
75	- 0.0006
70	- 0.0021
65	- 0.0036
60	- 0.0051
55	- 0.0066
50	- 0.0081
45	- 0.0096
40	- 0.0101
35	- 0.0116

FIGURE 9.5 Specific Gravity vs. Recharging Time

Specific Gravity

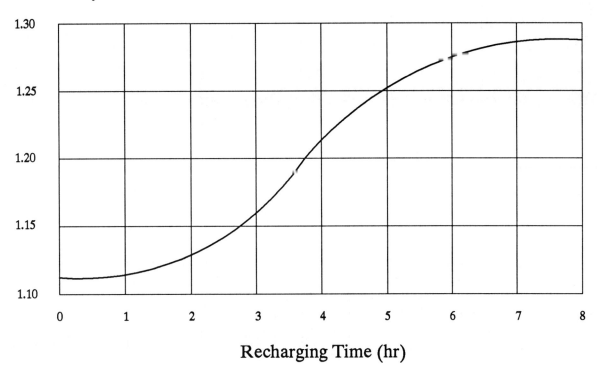

Recharging Time (hr)

FIGURE 9.6 Battery Specific Gravity vs. Slush Point

Specific Gravity

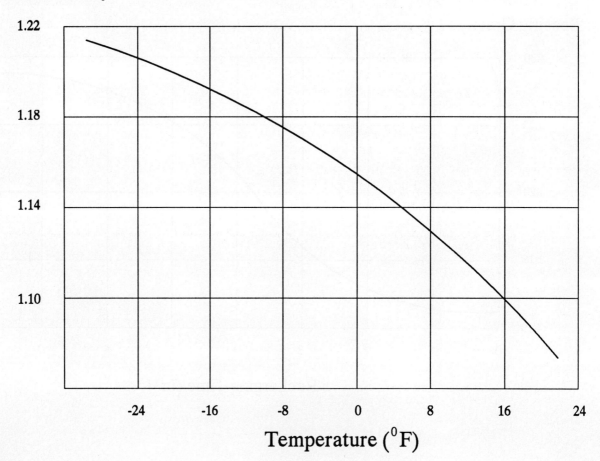

Temperature (^{0}F)

FIGURE 9.7 Battery Maintenance Activities

Activity	Monthly	Biannual
1. Check general appearance	X	
2. Check battery room temperature	X	
3. Inspect connections for corrosion	X	
4. Check individual cell voltages	X	
5. Check individual cell specific gravity	X	
6. Add water to cells as required	X	
7. Adjust float and equalizing voltages		X
8. Check terminals for proper torque		X
9. Clean cell tops and connections		X

WORKSHEET 9.1 Estimating the Number of Cells

1. System Characteristics

Maximum System Voltage: _____ Volts
Minimum System Voltage: _____ Volts

2. Number of Cells

$$\frac{\boxed{} \text{ Maximum Operating Voltage}}{\boxed{} \begin{array}{c}\text{Float}\\\text{Voltage/cell}\end{array}} = \boxed{} \text{ Number of Cells}$$

3. Cell Discharge Voltage Estimate

$$\frac{\boxed{} \text{ Minimum Operating Voltage}}{\boxed{} \text{ Number of Cells}} = \boxed{} \begin{array}{c}\text{Discharge}\\\text{Voltage/cell}\end{array}$$

4. Cell Data

Number of Cells: _____
Percent Discharge Limit: _____

WORKSHEET 9.2 Battery Capacity

Load Estimation

	Load (amps)		Time (hr)		Amp-hr
1.	_____	X	_____	=	_____
2.	_____	X	_____	=	_____
3.	_____	X	_____	=	_____
4.	_____	X	_____	=	_____
5.	_____	X	_____	=	_____
6.	_____	X	_____	=	_____

1.

Total _____

Battery Capacity

2.

$$\frac{\boxed{} \; \text{Load (amp-hr)}}{\boxed{} \; \text{Percent Discharged}} \; X \; \boxed{} \; \text{Temperature Factor} \; X \; \boxed{} \; \text{Age Factor} \; = \; \boxed{} \; \text{Capacity (amp-hr)}$$

WORKSHEET 9.3 Sizing the Charger

1. System Characteristics

Battery Capacity: _____ amp-hr
Discharge Limit: _____ %
Load: _____ amps

2. Base Charger Capacity

$$\left[\boxed{1.1} \times \frac{\boxed{} \times \boxed{}}{\boxed{}} \right] + \boxed{} = \boxed{}$$

1.1 × Battery Capacity (amp-hr) × % Discharge Limit / Hours to Recharge + Load (amps) = Base Capacity (amps)

3. Charger Capacity

$$\boxed{} \times \boxed{} \times \boxed{} = \boxed{}$$

Base Capacity (amps) × Temperature Factor × Safety Factor = Charger Capacity (amps)

WORKSHEET 9.4 Battery Room Ventilation Needs

1. Installation Characteristics

Number of Cells: _____
Room Dimensions: L _____, W _____, H _____
Maximum Charging Rate: _____ amps

2. Volume of Hydrogen Produced

0.016	X		X		=	
		Charging Current per Cell (amps)		Number of Cells		Hydrogen Produced (cu ft/hr)

3. Air Changes Required

$$\frac{\text{Hydrogen Produced (cu ft/hr)}}{0.03 \quad X \quad \text{Room Volume (cu ft)}} = \boxed{} \text{ Air Changes per Hour}$$

4. Ventilation Rate

0.0167	X		X		=	
		Air Changes per Hour		Room Volume (cu ft)		Ventilation Rate (cfm)

WORKSHEET 9.5 Battery Inspection Log

Location: _____   Room Temperature: _____ °F

Date: ___/___/___   Inspector: _____

Cell	Voltage	Specific Gravity Reading	Corrected	Cell	Voltage	Specific Gravity Reading	Corrected
1				31			
2				32			
3				33			
4				34			
5				35			
6				36			
7				37			
8				38			
9				39			
10				40			
11				41			
12				42			
13				43			
14				44			
15				45			
16				46			
17				47			
18				48			
19				49			
20				50			
21				51			
22				52			
23				53			
24				54			
25				55			
26				56			
27				57			
28				58			
29				59			
30				60			

HOW TO SELECT A LIGHTING SYSTEM THAT MEETS YOUR NEEDS AND MINIMIZES ENERGY USE

There are three basic considerations that you should take into account when working with facility lighting systems:

➤ using the right light source for the application

➤ providing the proper lighting level for the activity being performed

➤ developing a planned lighting maintenance program to insure that the lighting system will perform as intended

Unfortunately it isn't as simple as it might sound. Finding the proper light source requires considering not only the wattage, but also the efficiency, color output, mounting height, spacing, and location. Providing the proper lighting level requires additional consideration of the activity to be performed in the illuminated space, who is performing the activity, and the level of maintenance that will be carried out on the lighting system. Compounding the process is the fact that the planned level of maintenance helps determine what the initial design lighting levels should be as well as what type of light sources and fixtures are to be used. When you consider these factors, the facility will obtain a maximum rate of return on your lighting investment.

A QUICK REFERENCE GUIDE TO THE TERMINOLOGY OF LIGHTING

As with most areas of specialization, the lighting field has developed its own terminology. Rather than give precise, detailed definitions and explanations of the more common terms of lighting, a simplified discussion is presented here. If you need a more in-depth discussion, refer to the IES Lighting Handbook.

There are two major categories into which most lighting terminology can be classified: quantity of light, and quality of light.

Quantity of Light

The basic unit of measure for the quantity of light produced by a source of light is the **lumen.** It is a measure of the total flow of light from the source, independent of direction and area. To help illustrate the lumen and many other lighting terms, consider a frequently used analogy of flow of water in a hose. The rate at which water flows from the hose is measured in gallons per minute. Similarly, the rate at which light flows from a light source is measured in *lumens.*

Since, as we have said, the lumen is a measure of the flow of light that is independent of direction and area, it can serve as a means of comparing the energy efficiency, or **efficacy,** of one light source with another. Calculated in terms of lumens per watt, it can be used to compare the efficiency of similar light sources with different wattages as well as the efficiency of different types of light sources. For example, a 25 watt incandescent lamp has an efficacy rating of approximately eight lumens per watt, while an 18 watt low-pressure sodium lamp has an efficacy rating of greater than 60 lumens per watt. When calculating the efficacy of any light source that uses a ballast, include the wattage losses of the ballast in the calculation.

While the lumen tells you how much light a source is producing, it gives no indication of how much of that light is striking a surface. That measure is known as the **illuminance.** Measured in lumens per square foot, it is comparable in the water hose analogy to the flow rate of water over a given area: gallons per minute per square foot.

The measure of illuminance most commonly used is the **footcandle.** One footcandle is equal to an illuminance of one lumen per square foot.

Quality of Light

Two of the most important issues concerning the quality of light produced by a source are the whiteness of the source and the ability of the source to render the color of objects correctly. The whiteness or **color temperature** of a source sets the "tone" of the space: warm (yellow and pink) or cool (blue and green). As a material is heated, it radiates energy back to its environment. If the temperature of the material is increased enough, it will begin to glow visibly. As the temperature increases further, the color of the glow changes. For a perfect or black-body radiator, there is a direct relationship between the color of the light radiated and the absolute temperature of the body measured in **degrees Kelvin.** Although one temperature is specified, the body is actually radiating energy over a fairly wide spectrum. Where that spectrum is centered is what gives the body its color.

Applying the black-body radiator principle to lighting, the relative color of a light source can be rated based on its spectral distribution. The color temperature of the light source in degrees Kelvin serves as a means of comparing the spectral distribution of the light produced by one light source with that of another. Figure 10.1 shows the relative color temperature of a number of light sources.

Color Temperature Rating for Non-Incandescent Lighting

The color temperature rating system as described above is accurate only for incandescent light sources that produce a continuous spectrum of light, as the color temperature system represents both the color of light produced and the spectral distribution of that light. Non-incandescent sources, such as electric discharge lamps, tend to produce light in narrow bands rather than a wide spectrum. To apply the system to these light sources, a correlated or apparent color temperature is used.

Note: Even though such lamps are rated at specific temperatures, the spectrum of light that they produce is narrower than that produced by incandescent lights. When objects are illuminated by these light sources, they do not appear in their natural color. How closely that natural color is produced is a function of the source's color perception and color discrimination capabilities.

Color perception is the ability to detect the color of an object. An object appears to be a particular color because it reflects light of that color. Under daylight and some light sources such as incandescent, all colors can be easily perceived as those sources generate light of all colors across the visible spectrum. But not all sources generate all colors of light; objects of the color missing from the source will appear as varying shades of gray.

Color discrimination is the ability to see all colors in their true hues and intensities as they would appear in daylight. Not all lighting applications require having the ability to discriminate colors; simple color perception may be sufficient. On the other hand, correctly rendering the color of an object is critical in some applications that involve color matching or discrimination. How well a light source renders colors is measured by its Color Rendering Index (CRI). The CRI, expressed as a number between 0 and 100, compares the source to a reference source of the same color temperature. The higher the CRI, the more natural the colors will appear.

Finally, two terms that are closely related to the quality of light are the **lamp expected life** and the **lamp lumen depreciation factor.** Although both terms are maintenance-related, how well they are taken into account greatly impacts the quality of light delivered by the system.

Measuring the Life of a Bulb

The life of all light sources is finite. To indicate how long a particular lamp can be expected to burn before failing, manufacturers make use of an **expected life** rating. To rate a particular bulb, the manufacturer tests a number of the same bulb type under "standard" operating conditions. The expected life rating is the number of operating hours it took for 50% of the lamps to burn out. Figure 10.2 shows a typical failure curve for incandescent and fluorescent lamps.

Lamp performance will vary from application to application depending on the local conditions, such as the temperature at which the bulbs are operated, the design of the lighting fixture, and how frequently they are turned on and off. Therefore, actual lamp life can vary widely from the expected life. In spite of this limitation, the lamp expected life is an important factor to take into account when considering different light sources or when establishing a group relamping interval.

Determining when to Relamp

The lamp depreciation factor is defined as the ratio of the light output of a source when it reaches its expected life to its light output when it was new. As most lamps age, their light output decreases from the initial lumens per watt value. This decrease in light output is especially important to lighting system designers who want to maintain a minimum lighting level in an area over the life of the light source. To do so requires knowing how much the source will deteriorate and then overdesigning the system to take this depreciation into account.

The lamp depreciation factor is also important when establishing a group relamping program. By picking the correct relamping interval, the lamps can be replaced before their light output has decreased to the point where the space has become underlit. Selecting the right interval also enables the facility manager to set lower initial lighting levels knowing that the lamps will be replaced before their output falls below a predetermined level.

CHARACTERISTICS OF COMMONLY USED LIGHT SOURCES

Lamp characteristics vary widely both between different types of light sources, and among sources of the same type. These variations must be taken into consideration when selecting a light source for a particular application. Figure 10.3 lists the ranges of wattages, efficacy, rated life, and color temperature for commonly used light sources. Use the table to help in selecting the most suitable light source for your application.

You should consider other factors specific to the application. For example, the light output of fluorescent lamps drops off significantly with decreasing temperature. Without the use of special, temperature-compensating ballasts, outdoor use of fluorescent lamps may prove to be unacceptable in colder climates. Similarly, while low-pressure sodium lamps have the highest efficacy rating of commonly used sources, they have the poorest color rating and therefore would not be suitable for use in applications where color discrimination is important.

Incandescent Lights

The size and shape of incandescent bulbs is designated by a letter-number code. The letter indicates the shape (see Figure 10.4) and the number indicates the diameter of the bulb in eighths of an inch. For example, a PAR-38 lamp is a parabolic lamp with a diameter of four and three-quarter inches.

BULB SHAPES AND TYPES. The most common incandescent bulb shapes and types are as follows:

A	–	General service
C and F	–	Flame
G	–	Globe
PAR	–	Parabolic
PS	–	Pear shape
R	–	Reflector
S	–	Straight
T	–	Tubular

BULB BASES. Bases of incandescent bulbs vary with the wattage and application. Figure 10.5 shows typical bases. Common bases include Admedium, bayonet, candelabra, disc, intermediate, medium prefocus, medium skirted, medium 2-pin, mogul, mogul bipost, and 2-pin. Most general purpose lamps use medium screw bases. Other screw bases are used for low and high-wattage lamps. Prefocus and bipost lamp bases are used primarily in applications where the lamp filament must be carefully aligned, or where heat dissipation is critical.

Figure 10.6 lists the characteristics of commonly used incandescent bulbs. The values given in the table are typical for that size of bulb and will vary from manufacturer to manufacturer. Use the table to help determine the most appropriate bulb for your application.

Fluorescent Bulb Shapes and Types

Fluorescent bulbs are designated by a letter number combination similar to the one used for incandescent bulbs. The letter indicates the shape (see Figure 10.7) and the number indicates the maximum diameter of the bulb in eighths of an inch. A T-12 bulb therefore would indicate a tubular bulb with a diameter of $12/8$ inches, or $1\,1/2$ inches. The length of the bulb as indicated in manufacturer's data includes the actual bulb length plus the thickness of the standard lampholders.

The most common shapes for fluorescent bulbs include:

C	–	Circline
PL	–	Compact Twin-tube
SL	–	Compact, Double-folded, Bent-tube
T	–	Tubular U
"U"	–	Bent Lamp

BULB BASES. In addition to providing electrical contact to the fluorescent tube, the lamp bases provide physical support for the tube. Base design varies with the type of lamp used. Instant start lamps generally use a single pin connection at both ends of the tube. Preheat and rapid start lamps use a dual pin connection at both ends. Circline lamps use a single four-pin connector. The miniature PL lamps use a two-pin, keyed base. The SL lamp, designed as a direct replacement for the incandescent bulb, uses a standard screw-in base. Typical fluorescent lamp bases are shown in Figure 10.8.

CHARACTERISTICS. Figure 10.9 lists the characteristics of commonly used fluorescent bulbs. The values given in the table are typical for that size of bulb and will vary from manufacturer to manufacturer. Other parameters that influence the performance of fluorescent lights include:

> ➤ the color of the light produced
> ➤ the temperature at which the lamps are operated
> ➤ the lamp lumen depreciation factor
> ➤ how often the lamps are turned on and off

Fluorescent lamps are classified based on the color of the light they produce. There are four major classifications: cool white, deluxe cool white, warm white, and deluxe warm white. Figure 10.10 lists characteristics of these four lamp classifications. Use the figure to help select a particular bulb type based on the needs of your application. Selection of one type over another is generally based on the preferences of those occupying the space as well as the desired effect that the lighting system is to achieve.

COMPENSATING FOR TEMPERATURE DIFFERENCES. The performance of fluorescent lamps is significantly influenced by the ambient temperature. All ratings for fluorescent lamps are made for operation in a 76°F ambient, which corresponds to the optimum tube wall temperature of about 100°F. As the wall temperature deviates from the optimum point, the light output of the tube decreases. Figure 10.11 shows the impact that the ambient operating temperature has on the light output of a typical fluorescent tube. A good rule of thumb to follow is that the light output decreases one percent for every two degree Fahrenheit deviation in ambient temperature from 76°F. Use the figure to predict the difference in light output based on off-standard operating temperatures.

DETERMINING WHEN TO RELAMP. As a fluorescent tube is operated, its light output decreases with time. By the time the lamp reaches its rated life (typically 15,000 hours), the light output has decreased to approximately 80% of the initial lumens even though the lamp is still drawing the same amount of current. This decrease in operating efficiency becomes an important factor when establishing a group relamping interval based on the most efficient time to replace the lamps.

The rated fluorescent lamp life, as shown in Figure 10.9, is based on the lamps operating for three hours each time they are turned on. Every time a lamp is started, some of the coating is eroded from the lamp filament. When enough of the material has eroded, the lamp will no longer start. Therefore, fluorescent lamp life is determined in part by how often the lamps are turned on and off. The effect of starting frequency on lamp life is shown in Figure 10.12.

SHOULD YOU TURN OFF LIGHTS TO SAVE ENERGY? Since the operating life of a fluorescent lamp depends in part on how often it is turned on and off, the idea of turning off the lights in an area to save energy when it is not occupied has been questioned. If the lights are switched often enough, the decrease in energy use will be offset by the decrease in lamp life. However, the breakeven point for average labor and electricity rates is in the range of two and one-half to three minutes.

Rule of thumb: Turn off the lights if the area is to be unoccupied for more than five minutes.

Mercury Vapor Lamps

Mercury vapor lamps fall into the classification of high-intensity discharge lamps that operate on the principle of producing an electric arc. Mercury vapor lamps, like fluorescent lamps, require the use of a current limiting ballast.

Caution: Most bulbs use external ballasts, but some manufacturers offer lamps with built-in ballasts. These self-ballasted lamps offer a lower operating efficiency than comparable lamps with external ballasts and should be used only as a direct replacement for incandescent lamps in applications where lamp replacement is difficult and external ballasting is impractical.

BULB SIZES AND SHAPES. Mercury vapor bulbs are available in sizes ranging from 50 to 1,000 watts. The shape and size of the lamp are designated by a letter and number code, with the letter indicating the shape of the bulb and the number indicating the diameter of the bulb in eighths of an inch. An R-40 bulb therefore would indicate a reflector bulb with a diameter of 40/8 inches, or five inches. Figure 10.13 shows the most common bulb shapes for mercury vapor lamps.

BASES. The most common bases for mercury lamps include medium, mogul, medium side prong, and skirted (see Figure 10.14).

Mercury vapor lamps consist of an inner tube that contains the arc and an outer tube that is coated with phosphors. The phosphors serve to filter the ultraviolet light emitted by the arc and convert it to visible light.

Warning: The lamps can pose a potential health hazard should the outer tube become broken as the arc will continue to operate and emit ultraviolet light. Special lamps are available that will automatically extinguish the arc in the event that the outer tube becomes damaged. Use these lamps wherever the potential exists for exposing people to the unshielded ultraviolet radiation for more than just a few minutes.

CHARACTERISTICS. Figure 10.15 lists characteristics of common mercury vapor lamps. The values given in the table are typical for that size of bulb and will vary from manufacturer to manufacturer. Use the table to identify the particular bulb needed for your application based on the required illumination level.

The composition of the phosphors used on the outer tube is varied slightly to produce different bulb colors and temperatures. The three most common are the standard white coating (5,900°K), the deluxe coating (4,000°K), and the white deluxe coating (3,600°K). All offer very good color detection capabilities. Color discrimination varies with the particular coating used.

DETERMINING WHEN TO RELAMP. Mercury vapor lamps have a poor lamp lumen depreciation factor. Light output steadily decreases throughout the lamp's life, resulting in a light output at the lamp's rated life of only 40% of the initial light output when the lamp was new. Although this value is low in comparison with that for fluorescent lamps, most users feel it is offset by the exceptionally long-rated lamp life. In applications where maintenance of a set level of illumination is important, you can decrease the group relamping interval so that lamps would be replaced before their light output decreased below acceptable levels.

Another factor influencing the relamping interval for mercury vapor lamps is the shift in color of the light produced by the lamp as it ages. The older the lamp, the more its color spectrum is shifted towards the green-blue portion of the spectrum, further reducing the quality of the light produced.

Metal Halide Lamps

Metal halide lamps fall into the classification of high-intensity discharge lamps that operate on the principle of producing an electric arc. Metal halide lamps, like fluorescent lamps, require the use of a current limiting ballast.

BULB AND BASE SIZES AND SHAPES. Metal halide bulbs are available in sizes ranging from 175 to 1,500 watts. The shape and size of the lamp are designated by a letter and number code, with the letter indicating the shape of the bulb and the number indicating the diameter of the bulb in eighths of an inch. A BT-280 bulb, therefore, would indicate a Bulb Tubular bulb shape with a diameter of 28/8 inches, or 3 and $1/_2$ inches.

The most common bulb shapes for metal halide lamps are the Bulb Tubular (BT) and the Tubular (T). All lamps use a mogul base. Lamp shapes and bases are shown in Figure 10.16.

Metal halide lamps use a temperature-sensitive switch to disconnect the starting electrode within the lamp once the arc has been established. For the switch to operate properly, it must be located at the hottest portion of the lamp. Therefore separate lamp designs have been developed for different burning positions: horizontal, base up, and base down. To get the best performance and life out of the bulb, you should select bulbs based on the burning position of the lamp.

Metal halide lamps consist of an inner tube that contains the arc and an outer tube. Bulbs are available with either clear or phosphor-coated outer tubes. Use clear finish bulbs only in enclosed fixtures.

Hazard Warning: The lamps can pose a potential health hazard should the outer tube become broken because the arc will continue to operate and emit ultraviolet light. Special lamps are available that will automatically extinguish the arc in the event that the outer tube becomes damaged. Use these lamps wherever the potential exists for exposing people to the unshielded ultraviolet radiation for more than just a few minutes.

CHARACTERISTICS. Figure 10.17 lists characteristics of common metal halide lamps. The values given in the table are typical for that size of bulb and will vary from manufacturer to manufacturer. Use the figure to match lamp characteristics to the needs of your application.

ADVANTAGES OF METAL HALIDE LAMPS. Metal halide lamps offer very good color perception and discrimination characteristics. While the average lamp life is shorter than that for mercury vapor lamps, their lamp lumen depreciation factor is much less. At their rated life, most metal halide lamps emit roughly 70% of their initial lumens.

High-Pressure Sodium Lamps

High-pressure sodium lamps are classified as high-intensity discharge lamps that operate on the principle of producing an electric arc. They, like fluorescent lamps, require the use of a current limiting ballast.

BULB SIZES AND SHAPES. High-pressure sodium bulbs are available in sizes ranging from 35 to 1,000 watts. The shape and size of the lamp are designated by a letter and number code, with the letter indicating the shape of the bulb and the number indicating the diameter of the bulb in eighths of an inch. A B-17 bulb, therefore, would indicate a bulb shape with a diameter of $^{17}/_8$ inches, or $2 ^1/_8$ inches.

The most common bulb shapes (see Figure 10.18) for high-pressure sodium lamps are the following:

B   –   Bulb shape
E   –   Elongated Bulb
PAR   –   Parabolic reflector

Figure 10.19 shows the bases typically used with the lamps.

CHARACTERISTICS. Figure 10.20 lists the characteristics of commonly used high-pressure sodium lamps. The values given in the table are typical for that size of bulb and will vary from manufacturer to manufacturer.

ADVANTAGES OF HIGH-PRESSURE SODIUM LAMPS. Although high-pressure sodium lamps emit light in narrow bands across most of the visible spectrum, emissions are stronger in the red, orange, and yellow regions. As a result, the lamp offers fair to good color perception characteristics, but only fair color discrimination.

They also offer an exceptionally long-rated life (24,000 hours for most bulbs), and a very low lamp lumen depreciation factor. Light output at the rated life is typically 90% of the initial light output.

Tip: Some lighting manufacturers make high-pressure sodium lamps that are direct replacements for a number of mercury vapor bulbs without having to replace the ballast. Consult with the manufacturer for the suitability of a particular replacement as improper substitution will impact the performance and life of the bulb and its ballast. Properly matched, the substitution of a high-pressure sodium lamp will nearly double the operating efficiency of the light.

Low-Pressure Sodium Lamps

Low-pressure sodium lamps are the most efficient light source in widespread use. Efficacies range up to 150 lumens per watt, including ballast requirements. They are another member of the high-intensity discharge family of lamps and require a current limiting ballast in order to operate.

BASE AND BULB SIZES AND SHAPES. Low-pressure sodium bulbs are available in sizes ranging from 18 to 180 watts. The shape and size of the lamp are designated by a letter and number code, with the letter indicating the shape of the bulb and the number indicating the diameter of the bulb in eighths of an inch. A T-17 bulb, therefore, would indicate a Tubular shape with a diameter of $^{17}/_8$ inches, or 2 $^1/_8$ inches.

Most low-pressure sodium lamps use the tubular shape bulb and the double contact bayonet base shown in Figure 10.21.

CHARACTERISTICS. Figure 10.22 lists the characteristics of commonly used low-pressure sodium lamps. The values given in the table are typical for that size of bulb and will vary from manufacturer to manufacturer. Use the table to select the proper wattage lamp to meet your lighting requirements.

DRAWBACKS OF LOW-PRESSURE SODIUM LAMPS. Most of the light output from low-pressure sodium lamps is concentrated in two narrow bands in the yellow region of the spectrum. Therefore, all colors other than yellow will be misrepresented under their light. Both color detection and color discrimination qualities of the light are poor.

Light output does not decrease much with lamp age, but the current increases as the bulbs age, resulting in only a fair lamp lumen depreciation characteristic.

GUIDELINES FOR SELECTING THE RIGHT LIGHT SOURCE FOR YOUR NEEDS

Selecting a light source for a particular application must be based on the characteristics of the source and the needs of the application. Figure 10.23 shows a decision-making process that you can use to select the suitable sources for the application. When more than one source is applicable, consider the total operating cost for the system, including the energy cost and the maintenance cost of bulb changes. In comparison, the cost of the bulb will be rather small.

Keep Starting Time in Mind

One important factor to remember when selecting one of the HID sources is that, unlike incandescent and fluorescent bulbs, HID sources do not start immediately as soon as the power is applied. Depending on the particular HID system used, the bulbs can take anywhere from one to ten minutes to come up to full illumination levels when first started, and after a momentary power outage. Consider this time delay when selecting the light source for a particular application. If the activity is such that the area cannot be without light during that interval, you can either avoid using HID systems or provide supplemental incandescent or fluorescent lamps for use only while the HID lamps are restarting.

THREE KEY FACTORS TO CONSIDER WHEN DETERMINING INTERIOR LIGHTING NEEDS

When determining the level of illumination required for performing a particular task, consider the following:

➤ the average age of the people working in the area

➤ the importance of speed and accuracy to the operation

➤ the reflectance of the task background.

It is because of how these factors influence the need for light that the Illuminating Engineering Society has revised its recommended illumination tables for specific tasks from a single value to a range of values for a given task. This change acknowledges the importance of these factors in lighting system design.

Average Age of Workers

As the eye ages, its ability to see decreases as a result of both decreased focusing ability and reduced ocular efficiency. For example, at age 60, the average worker requires almost 25% more light than a 20-year-old coworker in order to achieve the same visual acuity. Using the average age of the workers to determine the illumination level is a compromise that means some younger workers will have more light than they need while some older workers will have less than ideal lighting. If levels were established based on the needs of only the older workers, the area would be overilluminated for the majority of the workers and system installation and operating costs would be increased.

Importance of Speed and Accuracy

The need to factor into the lighting system design the importance of speed and accuracy in the operation is fairly obvious. The higher the lighting levels, the quicker a worker can visually distinguish objects and tasks, with decreased chance for error. There is a limit, though, to what increased lighting levels can do for speed and accuracy. Once the illumination is sufficient for workers to perform their tasks accurately and quickly, further increases in lighting levels will produce only slight improvements at best.

Contrast

The reflectance of task background to a great extent affects the worker's ability to see. The greater the contrast between the object and its background, the easier it is to see. If the contrast is poor, the illumination levels should be increased in order to compensate. For example, black objects or type against a white background are much easier to see than black objects against a dark gray background.

Figure 10.24 lists the recommended reflectances for typical backgrounds. Note: The table lists the maintained values, not initial reflectance values. With time, dirt accumulation on surfaces can greatly alter the reflectance of those surfaces. How rapidly that dirt will alter the surface reflectance must be taken into consideration during the design of the lighting system.

DETERMINING HOW MUCH ILLUMINATION YOU NEED

Figure 10.25 lists the Illuminating Engineering Society's recommended illumination ranges based on the activity for a particular area. Three values are given in footcandles: low, medium, and high. For most applications where the worker's average age is between 40 and 50, the required speed and accuracy of the activity is average, and the background surface reflectances fall in the ranges given in Figure 10.25, the medium illuminance value should be used. If conditions in the area differ, then you should modify the design illuminance within the range set in the table.

HOW TO ESTIMATE THE NUMBER OF FIXTURES YOU NEED FOR INTERIOR LIGHTING

Use Worksheet 10.1 to estimate the number of fixtures required to provide a given level of illumination in an area. While this worksheet can provide a reasonable first estimate of the requirements for a given area, it is an estimating method only. You should not use it as an exacting design tool. Use the worksheet as follows:

Step 1. Determine the type of lamps to be used (fluorescent, incandescent, etc.) and enter the type and bulb size in section #1 of the worksheet. The bulb size can be determined using the figures provided earlier in this chapter.

Step 2. Determine the maintained illuminance in footcandles from Figure 10.25 for your application. Enter the value in section #2 of the worksheet.

Step 3. Enter the gross square footage of the area in section #2.

Step 4. Figure 10.26 lists lamp lumen maintenance factors for different lamp types. If the area is to be group relamped, use the value listed in the table. If the area is to be spot relamped, multiply the value by 0.95. Enter the value as a decimal number (0 - 1.0) in section #2.

Step 5. Figure 10.26 lists lamp dirt depreciation factors for typical applications. Select the environment that most closely matches the conditions in the area. If the area is to be group relamped, use the value given in the table. If the area is to be spot relamped, multiply the value in the table by 0.95. Enter the value as a decimal number (0 - 1.0) in section #2.

Step 6. A Utilization Factor must be added to the calculations to account for light given off by the fixture that does not reach the work surface due to absorption by the walls, ceiling, and floor. For an average room, set the Utilization Factor at 0.75. For a room with dark colors, set the Utilization Factor at 0.60. Enter the value in section #2.

Step 7. For the particular bulb that you have selected, use the figures provided earlier in this chapter to determine the initial lumens for that bulb. Enter the initial lumens per bulb in section #2 of the worksheet.

Step 8.	Multiply the maintained footcandles by the room area, the lumen maintenance factor, the dirt depreciation factor, and the Utilization Factor. Divide the product by the initial lumens per bulb to determine the total number of bulbs required in the area.
Step 9.	Enter the number of bulbs from section #2 of the worksheet into section #3.
Step 10.	Enter the number of bulbs per fixture for the particular fixture selected in section #3.
Step 11.	Divide the number of bulbs by the number of bulbs per fixture to determine the number of fixtures required in the area.

This value represents the first approximation of the number of fixtures needed to provide the level of illumination required.

DETERMINING YOUR EXTERIOR LIGHTING NEEDS

Two basic types of lighting fixtures are used in exterior lighting applications: fixed and variable aiming. Which type you select depends on your lighting application, the area to be illuminated, and the desired lighting effect.

Fixtures that have a fixed aiming generate a set pattern of light distribution that cannot be changed. The fixtures are typically wall or pole mounted and aimed downwards to illuminate an area with a radius from the base of the pole or wall of two to three times the mounting height. Fixtures can be mounted individually or in clusters on low, medium, or high poles.

Fixtures that can be aimed make use of lenses and baffles to control the beam spread so that only a specific area is illuminated. Fixtures are distinguished by their bulb type, wattage, and the distribution or beam spread of the light produced. The beam spread of a fixture is the angle measured from the center of the beam pattern where the illumination levels decrease to 10% of the maximum measured value in the pattern. Fixtures are available in a wide range of beam spreads from ten to 130 degrees.

While most fixed-aiming fixtures are used to illuminate horizontal surfaces such as parking lots, those whose light output can be aimed are used primarily on vertical surfaces, such as building exteriors. The fixtures are commonly mounted at ground level or on short poles.

Rules of Thumb for Exterior Lighting

There are several rules of thumb that can be followed to make exterior lighting system design easier while at the same time producing an effective lighting system.

WHERE TO SET FIXED-AIMING FIXTURES. For fixed-aiming fixtures, the radius of the area illuminated is approximately two to three times the mounting height. Therefore, for effective area lighting with uniform illumination levels, set the distance between poles at four times the mounting height. Do not set any pole more than two mounting heights from the edge of the area being lighted.

SETBACK FOR VARIABLE-AIMING FIXTURES. In applications where fixtures that can be aimed are used to floodlight buildings, signs, or other vertical surfaces, set back the fixture from the surface approximately two-thirds of the vertical height to be illuminated. You can emphasize architectural details and surface features by moving the fixture closer, but you will sacrifice uniformity in illumination levels. For uniform lighting, set the distance between fixtures no more than two times the setback from the vertical surface.

Fixtures that can be aimed can also be used to illuminate areas where both horizontal and vertical illumination is important. In these applications, fixtures are usually installed around the perimeter of the area. Aim the lights two-thirds to three-fourths of the distance across the illuminated area. Depending on the beam spread of the particular fixture selected, most can effectively illuminate an area of radius of two times the mounting height of the fixtures. Separate poles by no more than two times their mounting heights.

How to Estimate Your Exterior Lighting Requirements

Two methods are given for estimating the requirements for lighting exterior areas. The first method estimates the number of lamps of a given type and wattage that are required to illuminate an area. You would then lay out the poles and determine the mounting heights required to provide the required distribution of illumination.

The second method starts with a layout of pole locations based on a selected mounting height. The method then calculates the lamp wattage required to provide the desired level of illumination based on the pole and fixture layout.

ESTIMATING THE NUMBER OF FIXTURES REQUIRED. Use Worksheet 10.2 to estimate the number of fixtures required to provide a given level of illumination in an area. Use the worksheet as follows:

Step 1. Figure 10.27 lists the recommended minimum illuminance level in footcandles for outdoor areas. Select the application from the table that most closely matches the design application and enter the value in section #1.

Step 2. Calculate the square footage of the area to be illuminated and enter the value in section #1. If the area is irregular, use the gross square footage or break it into two or more separate areas, completing a separate calculation for each one.

Step 3. Multiply the illumination level by the area to determine the total lumens required and enter the value in section #1.

Step 4. For the particular lamp selected, use the figures listed earlier in this chapter to determine the initial lumens per lamp. Enter the value in section #2.

Step 5.   If manufacturer's data is available for the particular fixture selected, use the fixture's utilization factor for the selected mounting height and aiming pattern. If no data is available, estimate the utilization factor to be 50% if the width of the area is less than twice the mounting height. For wider areas, estimate the utilization factor to be 40%. Enter the value as a decimal number (0 - 1.0) in section #2.

Step 6.   If the lamps are to be group relamped, use the value listed in Figure 10.26, which lists lamp lumen maintenance factors for different lamp types. If the lamps are spot replaced, multiply the value by 0.95. For the type of light selected, enter the lumen maintenance factor as a decimal value (0.60 - 0.95) in section #2.

Step 7.   Multiply the initial lumens per lamp by the utilization factor and the lumen maintenance factor to determine the effective lumens produced per lamp. Enter the value in section #2.

Step 8.   Enter the total lumens required from section #1 into section #3. Enter the effective lumens per lamp from section #2 into section #3. Divide the total lumens required by the effective lumens per lamp to determine the total lamps required. Round the value up to the nearest whole number and enter the value in section #3.

The value calculated by the worksheet represents the minimum number of lamps that will be required to provide the required illumination level. Use the figure for budgetary and preliminary planning purposes.

DETERMINING THE LAMP SIZE. Use Worksheet 10.3 to determine the type and wattage of the lamps required to provide a given level of illumination and a set number of fixtures. Use the worksheet as follows:

Step 1.   Figure 10.27 lists the recommended minimum illuminance level in footcandles for outdoor areas. Select the application from the table that most closely matches the design application and enter the value in section #1.

Step 2.   Calculate the square footage of the area to be illuminated and enter the value in section #1. If the area is irregular, use the gross square footage or break it into two or more separate areas, completing a separate calculation for each one.

Step 3.   Using the rules of thumb cited in the previous section, make a layout of the poles and fixtures needed to provide uniform coverage for the area. From the layout, determine the number of fixtures required and enter the value in section #1.

Step 4.   Multiply the illumination level by the area and divide by the total number of lamps to determine the effective lumens per lamp required. Enter the value in sections #1 and #2.

Step 5.   Estimate the utilization factor to be 50% if the width of the area is less than twice the mounting height. For wider areas, estimate the utilization factor to be 40%. Enter the value as a decimal number (0 - 1.0) in section #2.

Step 6.   If the area will be group relamped, estimate the lumen maintenance factor to be 0.90. If the area will be spot relamped, estimate the factor to be 0.80. Enter the value in section #2.

Step 7.   Divide the effective lumens per lamp by the utilization factor multiplied by the lumen maintenance factor to determine the initial lumens per lamp required. Enter the value in section #2.

Step 8.   Select a particular lamp type, such as metal halide or high-pressure sodium, and enter the selection in section #3.

Step 9.   Using the lamp characteristics figures given earlier in this chapter, select the figure that matches the particular lamp type you are using. From the figure, select the wattage of the lamp that most closely matches the calculated initial lumens per lamp from section #2. If the calculated initial lumens per lamp falls between two values on the table, select the higher table value.

THREE MAINTENANCE ACTIVITIES THAT REDUCE LIGHT LOSS

No matter how well designed the lighting system is, its performance will suffer over time unless it is properly maintained. Dirt builds up on lamps and lenses. Lamp light output decreases as the lamps age. Lamps burn out. Even factors such as dirt build-up on room surfaces can decrease the amount of light reaching the task being illuminated. The result is a significant decrease in effective light output over time.

There are three maintenance activities that will work together to reduce the amount of light loss that occurs in a system: scheduled room repainting, scheduled lamp and fixture cleaning, and scheduled or group lamp replacement. Figure 10.28 shows how a scheduled maintenance program for a typical office fluorescent lighting system can help to reduce light loss from the system. While the light loss in the example is still significant, it would be even greater if there were no planned maintenance program.

Scheduled Room Repainting

Most organizations have an interior painting schedule for their facilities. Although these schedules are typically established for aesthetic purposes, the schedule should take into consideration the impact that dirt accumulation on walls and ceilings will have on space lighting.

Scheduled Lamp and Fixture Cleaning

Scheduled lamp and fixture cleaning is a task that is often overlooked in lighting maintenance, and yet it can significantly increase the useful light output of the system. Depending on the type of fixture used and the environment in which it is located, dirt build-up on bulbs and the reflective surfaces of fixtures can reduce useful light output by as much as 35% over a two-year period. Figure 10.26 lists typical depreciation factors resulting from dirt.

How often lamps and fixtures should be cleaned depends on the cleanliness of the environment, the type of fixture used, and how much light loss is acceptable. Rule of thumb: If a group relamping program is implemented, clean the fixtures at every relamping interval or at alternate relamping intervals.

Group Lamp Replacement

Scheduled or group relamping has gained in popularity but is still not widely accepted. In group relamping programs, all of the lamps within a given area are replaced at the same time on a set interval. Although some useful life of the lamps is sacrificed by replacing them before they burn out, that cost is more than offset by the labor savings achieved by group rather than spot replacement. Burned out lamps will still have to be replaced, but the number of burnouts will be reduced by a factor of ten or more.

Benefit: Scheduled relamping provides better lamp lumen maintenance. As lamps age, their light output decreases. When lamps are replaced on a spot basis, their average light output is less than that which could be obtained through a group replacement program.

The key to a successful group relamping program is setting the relamping interval to balance the value of lamps removed before they burned out against the cost of spot replacing burned-out lamps. Programs typically target lamps for replacement when they have reached 60 to 80% of their rated life. For example, a group relamping program designed to replace fluorescent lamps when they have reached 60% of their rated life would find that approximately five percent of the tubes had burned out prior to the relamping interval. A similar program that replaces lamps at 80% of their rated life would have experienced failure of 18% of the tubes prior to relamping. Replacing lamps earlier wastes useful lamp life, while replacing lamps later results in an increased number of burned-out lamps.

ESTIMATING THE RELAMPING INTERVAL. Use Worksheet 10.4 to determine the optimum group relamping interval for incandescent, fluorescent, and HID sources. Use the worksheet as follows:

Step 1.   Enter the type of lamp in section #1. Using the lamp characteristics figures given earlier in this chapter, determine the rated life in hours for the lamp selected. Enter the rated life in sections #1 and #3.

Step 2.   Since the rated life of most lamps is based on an average burn time per start, it must be corrected to match the particular application. Select the Percent Full Life Factor (FLF) from section #2 of the worksheet for the type of lamp used and the average hours of operation per start of the lamp and enter it in section #3.

Step 3.   Multiply the Rated Life by the Percent Full Life Factor to get the estimated average Operating Hours for the lamps. Enter the value in sections #3 and #4.

Step 4.   Enter the average number of hours that the lamps are operated per day and the average number of days per month in section #4.

Step 5.   Divide the Operating Hours by the number of Hours Operated per Day multiplied by the number of Days Operated per Month to determine the group Replacement Interval in months. Enter the value in section #4.

The figure calculated by the worksheet is the recommended replacement interval for lamps under the conditions identified for your installation.

ESTIMATING THE GROUP RELAMPING SAVINGS. Group relamping programs increase lamp costs as lamps are removed before they have operated their full life. If the programs are to be cost effective, the labor savings achieved must more than offset this increase. Use Worksheet 10.5 to estimate the cost savings achieved by initiating a group relamping program. The worksheet calculates the cost differential between a conventional spot relamping program and a group relamping program over a period of time that includes two relamping intervals. During that period, it can be expected that 100% of the lamps in a spot relamping program will have burned out.

Use the worksheet as follows:

Step 1.   Enter the purchase Cost per Lamp for the bulbs in section #1 of the worksheet.

Step 2.   Enter the Number of Lamps in the area being considered for group relamping in section #1.

Step 3.   Multiply the Cost per Lamp by the Number of Lamps to determine the Spot Relamping Lamp Cost and enter the value in section #1.

Step 4.   Enter in section #2 the Labor Rate in $/hr for the personnel who change light bulbs.

Step 5.   Estimate the time required to change a light bulb. Include travel, setup, cleanup, and return time. Enter the value (in hours) in section #2. (Note: typical times to change a single fluorescent bulb are 20 to 30 minutes.)

Step 6.   Enter the Number of Lamps in the area in section #2.

Step 7.   Multiply the Labor Rate by the Time per Lamp and the Number of Lamps to get the Spot Relamping Labor Costs. Enter the value in section #2.

Step 8. Enter the Spot Relamping Lamp Cost from section #1 and the Spot Relamping Labor Costs from section #2 into section #3. Add the two values together to get the Spot Relamping Total Costs. Enter the value in section #3.

Step 9. Enter the purchase Cost per Lamp and the Number of Lamps (the same values used in section #1) in section #4.

Step 10. Multiply the Cost per Lamp by the Number of Lamps and by the number 2 (a total of two relamping intervals) to get the total Group Relamping Lamp Costs. Enter the value in section #4.

Step 11. Enter the Labor Rate and the Number of Lamps (the same values used in section #2) in section #5.

Step 12. Estimate the time required to change a light bulb while group relamping. Enter the value in hours in section #5. (Note: typical times to change a fluorescent bulb during group relamping are two to five minutes.)

Step 13. Multiply the Labor Rate by the Time per Lamp, the Number of Lamps, and the number 2 to determine the Group Relamping Labor Costs. Enter the value in Section #5.

Step 14. Even with group relamping, there will be a number of lamps that burn out between the relamping periods. How many burn out depend on the period of time between relamping intervals. If the relamping interval is set at 60% of the lamp's rated life, approximately 5% of the lamps will have already failed. At 70% of rated life, the failure rate is 10%. At 80% of rated life, the failure rate is 18%. Set the Relamp Interval Factor equal to the percentage of lamps that fail between relamping intervals, and enter the number as a decimal value (0.05 - 0.18) in section #6.

Step 15. Enter the Spot Relamping Labor Costs from section #2 into section #6. Multiply the Relamping Interval Factor by the Spot Relamping Labor Costs and the number 2 to get the Burnout Replacement Labor Costs. Enter the value in section #6.

Step 16. Enter the Group Relamping Lamp Costs from section #4, the Group Relamping Labor Costs from section #5, and the Burnout Replacement Labor Cost from section #6 all into section #7.

Step 17. Add the three group relamping costs in section #7 to get the Group Relamping Total Cost. Enter the value in section #7.

The savings achieved by group relamping over the two-cycle interval is the difference between the Spot Relamping Total Costs and the Group Relamping Total Costs.

FIGURE 10.1 Color Temperature of Various Light Sources

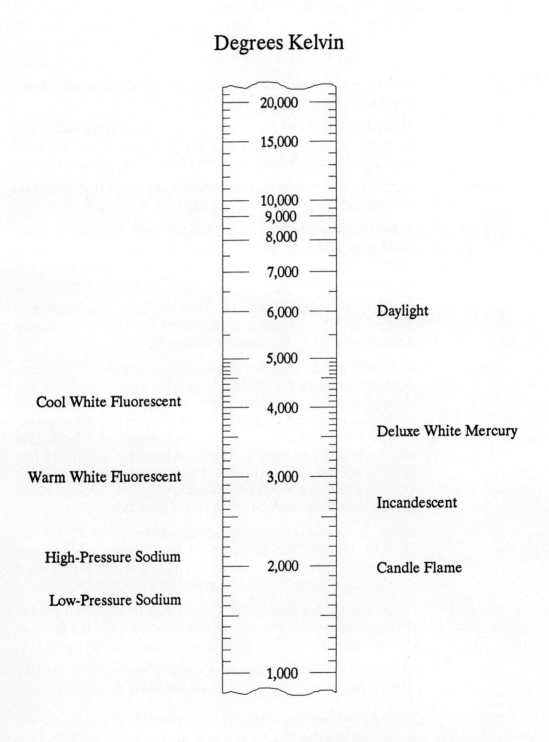

Degrees Kelvin

Courtesy of the Illuminating Engineering Society of North America
120 Wall Street, 17th Floor, N.Y., NY 10005

FIGURE 10.2 Fluorescent and Incandescent Lamp Mortality Curve

Percent Failed

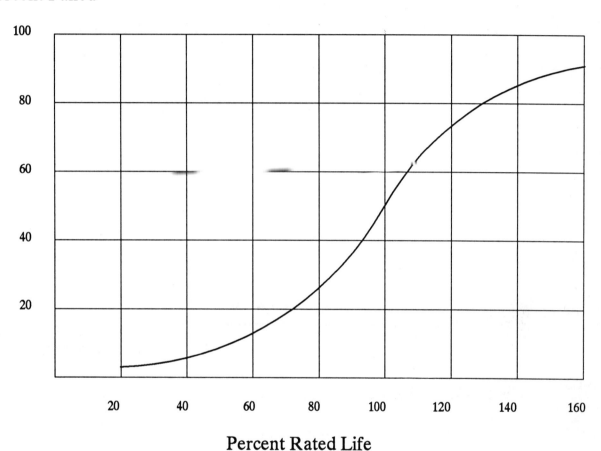

Percent Rated Life

FIGURE 10.3 Lamp Characteristics

Lamp	Wattage	Initial Lumens/Watt *	% Lumen Maintenance	Avg. Rated Life (hr)
Incandescent	60 - 1,500	17 - 24	90 - 95	750 - 3,500
Fluorescent (Standard)	20 - 215	63 - 95	80 - 90	9,000 - 20,000
Fluorescent (Self-Ballasted)	8 - 44	22 - 50	70 - 90	7,500 - 18,000
Mercury Vapor (Standard)	40 - 1,000	24 - 60	60 - 80	12,000 - 24,000
Mercury Vapor (Self-Ballasted)	160 - 1,250	14 - 25	60 - 80	12,000 - 20,000
Metal Halide	175 - 1,500	69 - 115	70 - 80	7,500 - 20,000
High-Pressure Sodium	35 - 1,000	51 - 130	90 - 95	7,500 - 24,000
Low-Pressure Sodium	18 - 180	62 - 150	90 - 95	12,000 - 18,000

* Lamp lumen/watt rating includes ballast losses

FIGURE 10.4 Incandescent Lamp Shapes

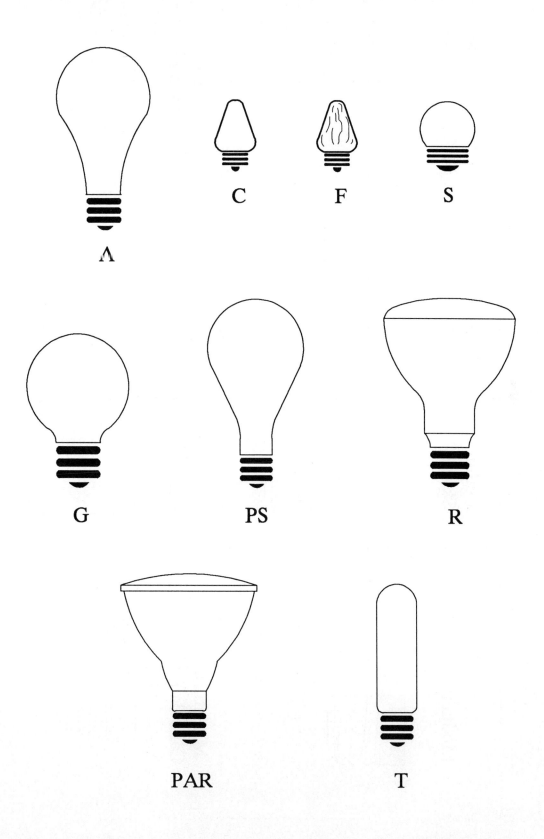

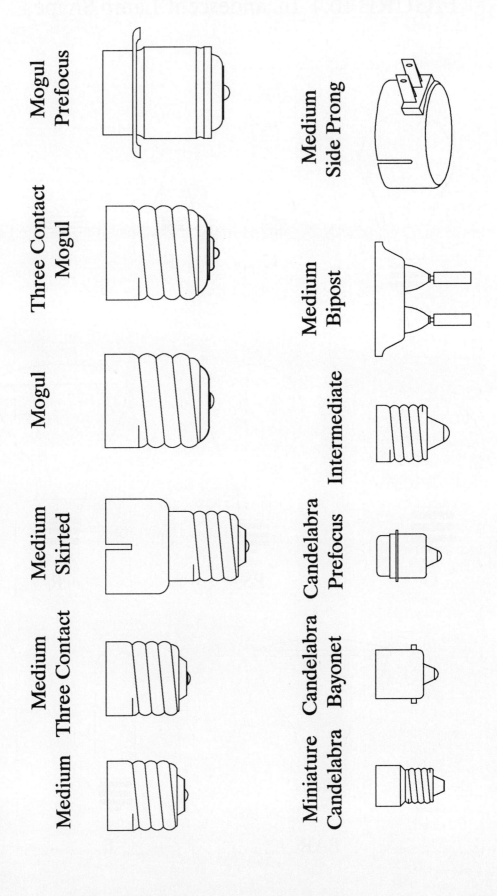

FIGURE 10.5 Common Incandescent Lamp Bases

FIGURE 10.6 Incandescent Lamp Characteristics

Wattage	Bulb Size	Initial Lumens	Life (hr)
Standard Incandescent			
5	C-7	21	2,000
7	C-7	46	3,000
10	C-7	40	5,000
10	S-14	76	1,500
15	A-15	125	2,500
25	A-19	235	2,500
25	F-15	179	1,500
25	G-25	190	1,500
45	A-19	505	1,000
40	A-15	455	1,500
40	B-13	455	1,500
40	F-15	455	1,500
40	G-25	370	1,500
40	G-40	440	2,500
60	A-19	870	1,000
60	G-25	660	1,500
75	A-19	1,190	750
100	A-21	1,280	1,000
100	G-40	1,280	2,500
150	A-21	2,850	750
150	PS-25	2,680	750
200	A-21	4,010	750
200	PS-30	3,710	750
250	A-23	4,500	750
300	PS-35	5,820	1,000
500	PS-35	10,850	1,000
750	PS-52	17,040	1,000
1,000	PS-52	23,740	1,000
1,500	PS-52	34,400	1,000

Figure 10.6 (continued)

Wattage	Bulb Size	Initial Lumens	Life (hr)
R Incandescent			
15	R-14	140	1,000
25	R-14	230	2,000
75	R-30	900	2,000
100	R-40	1,190	2,000
150	R-40	1,900	2,000
250	R-40	3,700	5,000
300	R-40	3,750	2,000
500	R-40	6,500	2,000
750	R-52	13,000	2,500
1,000	R-52	21,000	2,000
PAR Incandescent			
100	PAR-38	1,280	2,500
150	PAR-38	1,740	2,000
200	PAR-46	2,270	2,000
300	PAR-56	3,840	2,000
500	PAR-64	6,500	2,000
Quartz			
20	MR-16	260	3,000
50	MR-16	895	3,000
75	MR-16	1,300	3,500
100	T-4	1,600	750
150	T-4	2,800	2,000
150	PAR-38	2,000	4,000
200	T-3	3,400	1,500
250	PAR-38	3,325	6,000
250	T-4	4,850	2,000
300	T-4	5,650	2,000
400	T-4	7,850	2,000
500	T-3	11,100	2,000
500	PAR-56	8,000	4,000
1,000	T-6	23,400	2,000
1,000	PAR-64	19,400	4,000
1,500	T-3	35,800	2,000

FIGURE 10.7 Fluorescent Bulb Shapes

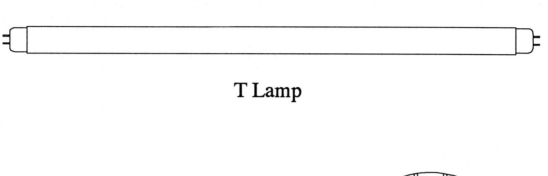

T Lamp

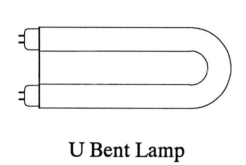

U Bent Lamp

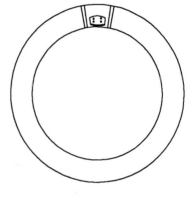

Circline Lamp

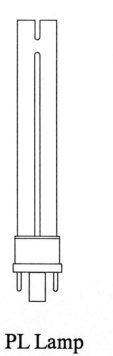

PL Lamp

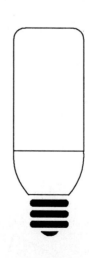

SL Lamp

FIGURE 10.8 Common Fluorescent Lamp Bases

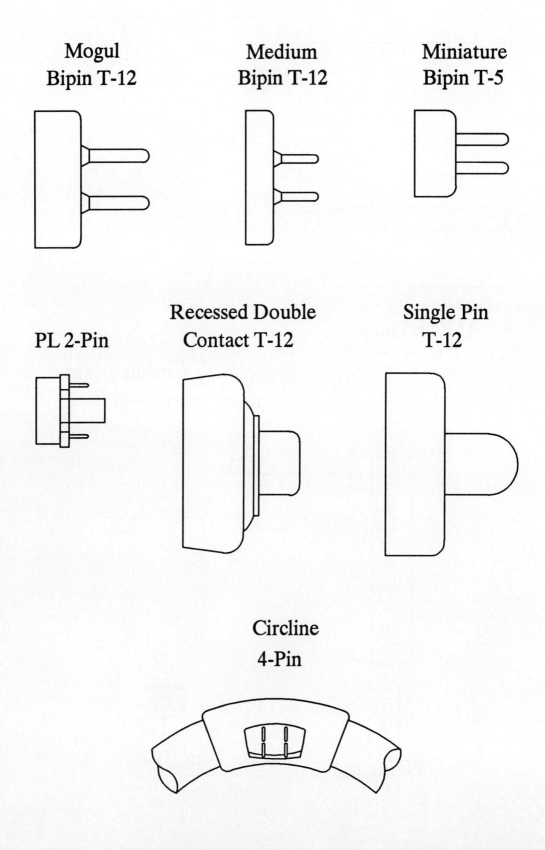

Mogul
Bipin T-12

Medium
Bipin T-12

Miniature
Bipin T-5

PL 2-Pin

Recessed Double
Contact T-12

Single Pin
T-12

Circline
4-Pin

FIGURE 10.9 Fluorescent Lamp Characteristics

Wattage	Bulb Size	Initial Lumens	Life (hr)
Preheat			
4	F4T5	135	6,000
6	F6T5	295	7,500
8	F8T5	385	7,500
14	F14T8	675	7,500
15	F15T8	870	7,500
20	F20T12	1,250	9,000
30	F30T8	2,200	7,500
90	F90T17	6,000	9,000
Rapid Start			
25	F30T12	2,000	18,000
30	F30T12	2,300	18,000
34	F40T12	2,750	20,000
40	F40T12	3,250	15,000
Instant Start			
40	F40T12	3,100	7,500
40	F40T17	2,680	7,500
Circline			
20	FC6T9	800	12,000
22	FC8T9	1,050	12,000
32	TC12T9	1,900	12,000
40	TC16T9	2,600	12,000
U-Shaped			
20	F20T12	1,120	9,000
35	F40T12	2,730	12,000
40	F40T12	2,925	12,000

Figure 10.9 (continued)

Wattage	Bulb Size	Initial Lumens	Life (hr)
Biaxial			
7	F7BX	400	10,000
9	F9BX	600	10,000
13	F13BX	850	10,000
18	F18BX	1,080	10,000
Slimline			
20	F24T12	1,150	7,500
30	F36T12	2,000	7,500
35	F72T8	3,000	7,500
40	F48T12	3,000	9,000
40	F64T6	2,800	7,500
50	F60T12	3,550	12,000
50	F96T8	4,200	7,500
60	F96T12	5,800	12,000
75	F96T12	6,300	12,000
High Output			
35	F24T12	1,700	9,000
45	F36T12	2,400	9,000
55	F42T12	3,000	9,000
60	F48T12	4,300	12,000
75	F60T12	5,400	12,000
85	F72T12	6,650	12,000
110	F96T12	9,200	12,000
110	F96T12	9,200	12,000
Self-Ballasted			
7	FLA7	400	10,000
9	FLA9	600	10,000
15	FCL15	700	9,000
22	FCA22	870	12,000
44	FCA44	1,750	7,500
16\44	FCA44	580\1,750	7,500

Courtesy of North American Philips Lighting Corporation

FIGURE 10.10 Fluorescent Lamp Color Characteristics

Color Rating	Color Temperature (Degrees K)	CRI	Colors Strengthened	Colors Weakened
Cool White	4,100	62	Orange, yellow, blue	Red
Deluxe Cool White	4,200	89	All nearly equally	None
Warm White	3,000	52	Orange, yellow	Red, blue, green
Deluxe Warm White	3,000	77	Red, orange, yellow, green	Blue

FIGURE 10.11 The Effect of Temperature on Fluorescent Light Output

Percent of Rated
Light Output

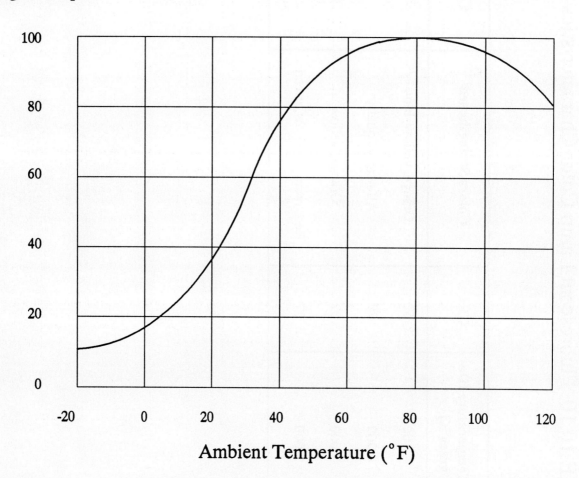

Ambient Temperature (°F)

FIGURE 10.12 The Effect of Starting Frequency on Lamp Life

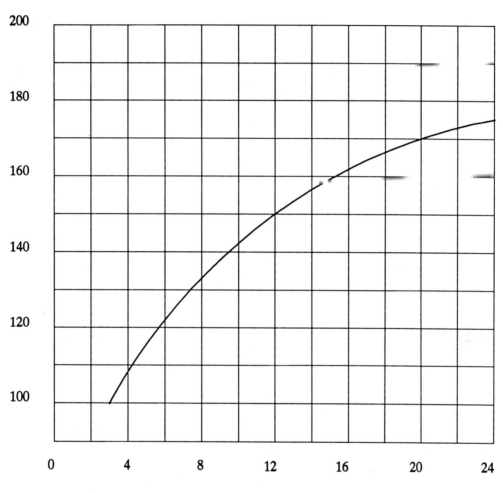

Percent of
Rated Life

Hours Operated per Start

FIGURE 10.13 Mercury Vapor Lamp Shapes

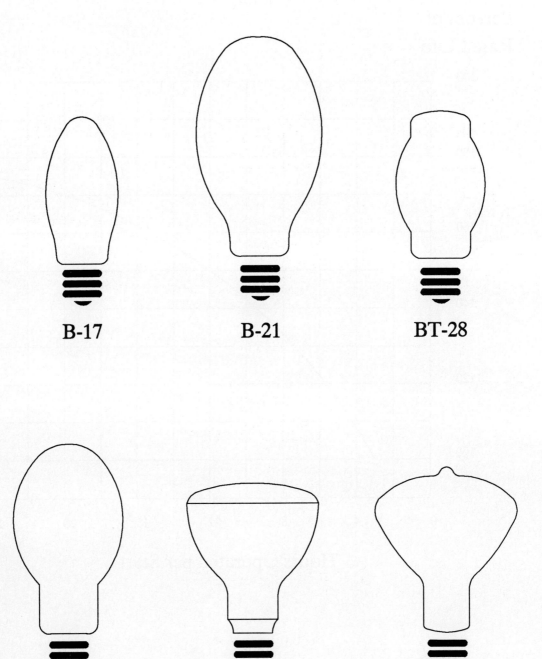

B-17   B-21   BT-28

E-37   R-40   R-60

FIGURE 10.14 Mercury Vapor Lamp Bases

Medium

Mogul

**Medium
Side Prong**

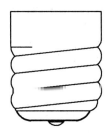
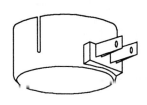

**Mogul

Skirted Clamp**

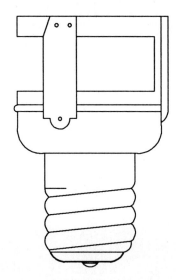

FIGURE 10.15 Mercury Vapor Lamp Characteristics

Wattage	Bulb Size	Initial Lumens	Life (hr)
40	E-17	1,140	16,000
50	E-17	1,575	16,000
75	E-17	2,800	16,000
75	PAR-38	1,600	12,000
100	E-23 1/2	4,200	24,000
100	R-40	2,850	24,000
100	PAR-38	2,450	12,000
175	E-28	8,600	24,000
175	R-40	5,700	24,000
250	E-28	12,100	24,000
400	E-37	22,500	24,000
400	BT-37	21,000	24,000
400	R-52	22,000	24,000
400	R-60	15,500	24,000
700	BT-46	42,000	24,000
1,000	BT-56	63,000	24,000
1,000	R-80	42,000	24,000

Courtesy of North American Philips Lighting Corporation

FIGURE 10.16 Metal Halide Lamp Shapes and Bases

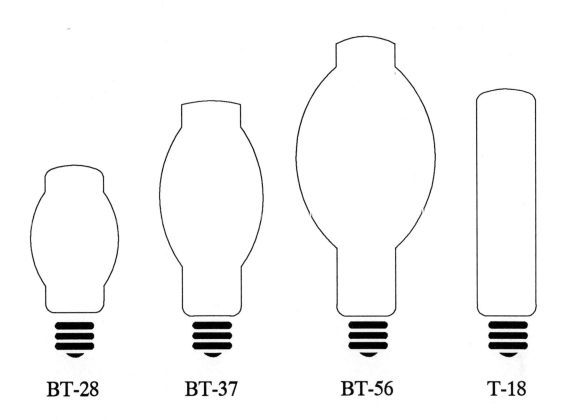

BT-28   BT-37   BT-56   T-18

Mogul

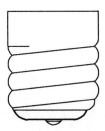

FIGURE 10.17 Metal Halide Lamp Characteristics

Wattage	Bulb Size	Initial Lumens		Life (hr)
32	E-17	2,500		7,500
175	E-23 1/2	16,000		10,000
175	E-28	14,000		10,000
250	E-28	10,000	V	14,000
250	E-28	6,000	H	12,000
400	E-37	36,000	V	20,000
400	E-37	32,000	H	20,000
1,000	BT-56	110,000	V	12,000
1,000	BT-56	108,000	H	12,000

V - Vertical Burning Position
H - Horizontal Burning Position

Courtesy of North American Philips Lighting Corporation

FIGURE 10.18 High-Pressure Sodium Lamp Shapes

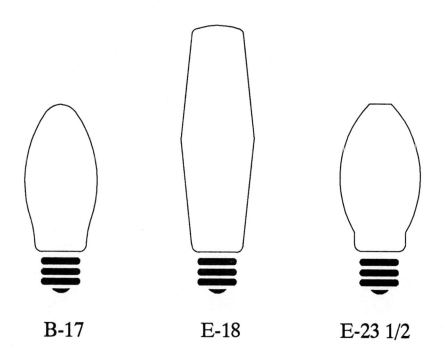

B-17   E-18   E-23 1/2

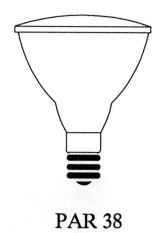

PAR 38

FIGURE 10.19 High-Pressure Sodium Lamp Bases

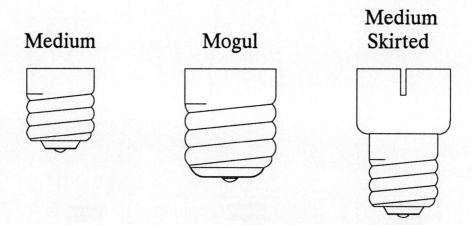

Medium   Mogul   Medium
                                Skirted

FIGURE 10.20 High-Pressure Sodium Lamp Characteristics

Wattage	Bulb Size	Initial Lumens	Life (hr)
35	E-17	2,250	16,000
35	R-38	1,400	16,000
50	E-23 1/2	3,800	24,000
50	E-17	3,800	24,000
70	E-23 1/2	5,400	24,000
70	E-17	5,400	24,000
70	R-38	3,400	16,000
100	E-23 1/2	9,000	24,000
100	E-17	9,000	24,000
150	E-23 1/2	16,000	24,000
150	E-17	16,000	24,000
150	E-28	15,000	24,000
200	E-18	22,000	24,000
250	E-18	27,500	24,000
250	E-28	26,000	24,000
400	E-18	50,000	24,000
405	E-37	47,500	24,000
1,000	E-25	140,000	24,000

FIGURE 10.21 Low-Pressure Sodium Lamps and Bases

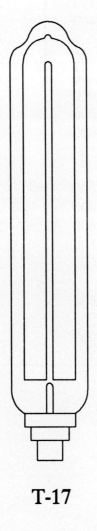

T-17

Double Contact
Bayonet

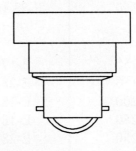

FIGURE 10.22 Low-Pressure Sodium Lamp Characteristics

Wattage	Bulb Size	Initial Lumens	Life (hr)
18	T-17	1,800	14,000
35	T-17	4,800	18,000
55	T-17	8,000	18,000
90	T-21	13,500	18,000
135	T-21	22,500	18,000
180	T-21	22,500	18,000

Courtesy of North American Philips Lighting Corporation

FIGURE 10.23 Light Source Selection Guide

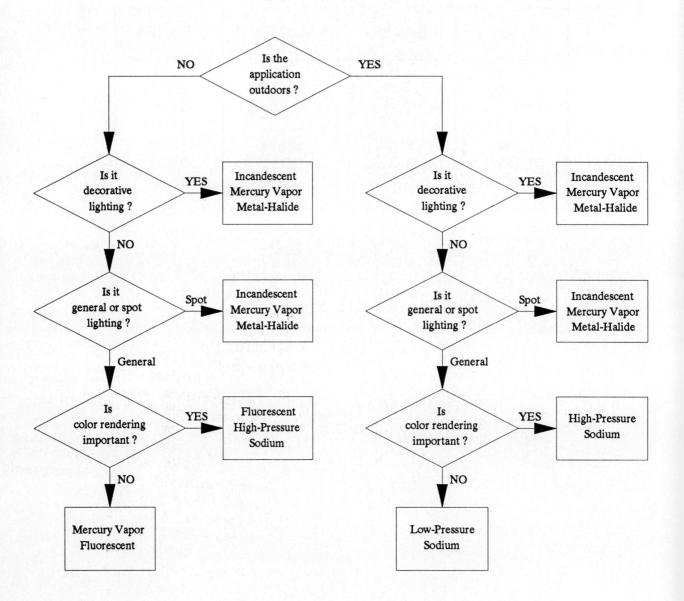

FIGURE 10.24 Recommended Maintained Reflectance Values

Surface	Reflectance (%)
Ceiling	80 to 90
Walls	40 to 60
Desk & bench tops	25 to 40
Equipment	25 to 45
Floors	Greater than 20

FIGURE 10.25 Recommended Ranges of Illuminance

Type of Activity	Illuminance (fc)	Typical Applications
Public areas with dark surroundings	2 - 3 - 5	Unoccupied storage areas, night lighting of hallways
Simple orientation for short occupancy	5 - 7.5 - 10	Restaurant dining areas, inactive storage rooms, service elevators, stairways
Occasional, simple visual tasks	10 - 15 - 20	Auditoriums, passenger elevators, lobbies, corridors
Execution of visual tasks having high contrast or large size	20 - 30 - 50	Conference rooms, book stacks, active storage rooms, rough bench or machine work, simple inspections
Execution of visual tasks having medium contrast or small size	50 - 75 - 100	Mail sorting, reading poor copy, high contrast drafting, medium bench or machine work
Execution of visual tasks having low contrast or small size	100 - 150 - 200	Proofreading, low contrast drafting, difficult inspection
Execution of visual tasks having low contrast and small size, for a long period of time	200 - 300 - 500	Very difficult assembly, inspection, or machine work
Execution of sustained and exacting visual tasks	500 - 750 - 1,000	Exacting assembly or inspection, extra-fine bench or machine work
Execution of special and exacting visual tasks having low contrast and small size	1,000 - 1,500 - 2,000	Surgical procedures

Courtesy of the Illuminating Engineering Society of North America, 120 Wall Street, 17th Floor, N.Y., NY 10005

FIGURE 10.26 Lamp Depreciation Factors

Environment	Lamp Dirt Depreciation Factors		
	Bare Bulb	Open Louver	Enclosed
Clean	0.95	0.95	0.88
Average	0.85	0.85	0.78
Dirty	0.78	0.80	0.70
Very Dirty	0.60	0.74	0.65

Lamp Lumen Depreciation Factors

Incandescent	0.86
Fluorescent	0.77
Mercury Vapor	0.68
High-Pressure Sodium	0.73
Low-Pressure Sodium	0.86

The above values assume a group relamping interval of 24 months or less. If lamps are spot replaced, multiply the above values by 0.95.

FIGURE 10.27 Recommended Minimum Illuminance Levels
for Outdoor Areas

Application	Footcandles
Building Exteriors	
Entrances (active)	5
Entrances (inactive)	1
Critical Areas	5
Buildings & Monuments	
Bright Surroundings, Light Surfaces	15
Bright Surroundings, Dark Surfaces	50
Dark Surroundings, Light Surfaces	5
Dark Surroundings, Dark Surfaces	20
Bulletin Boards & Signs	
Bright Surroundings, Light Surfaces	50
Bright Surroundings, Dark Surfaces	100
Dark Surroundings, Light Surfaces	20
Dark Surroundings, Dark Surfaces	50
Loading Docks	20
Parking Facilities	
Open, Low Activity	0.5
Open, High Activity	2
Covered, General Parking	5
Covered, Ramps	10
Covered, Entrances	50
Roadways	1
Storage Yards	
Active	20
Inactive	1
Walkways	
General	0.5
Stairways	4.0

Courtesy of the Illuminating Engineering Society of North America,
120 Wall Street, 17th Floor, N.Y., NY 10005

FIGURE 10.28 The Impact of Maintenance on Lighting Levels

Useful Light

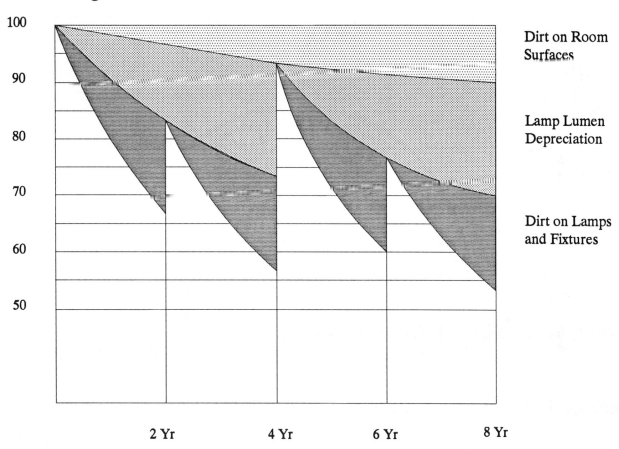

Eight year room surface repainting interval
Four year group relamping interval
Two year lamp cleaning interval

WORKSHEET 10.1 Interior Lighting Fixture Calculation

1. Application Information

Lamp Type: _____
Bulb Size: _____

2. Number of Bulbs Required

$$\cfrac{\boxed{}\;\times\;\boxed{}\;\times\;\boxed{}\;\times\;\boxed{}}{\boxed{}}\;=\;\boxed{}$$

Maintained Footcandles Area (sq ft) Lumen Maintenance Factor Dirt Depreciation Factor

Initial Lumens/Bulb

Bulbs

3. Number of Fixtures

$$\cfrac{\boxed{}}{\boxed{}}\;=\;\boxed{}$$

Bulbs

Bulbs/Fixture

Fixtures

WORKSHEET 10.2 Exterior Lamp Requirements

1. Lumens Required

[ ]	X	[ ]	=	[ ]	
Illumination Level (footcandles)		Area (sq ft)		Total Lumens Required	

2. Effective Lumens per Lamp

[ ]	X	[ ]	X	[ ]	=	[ ]
Lumens/Lamp		Utilization Factor		Lamp Lumen Maintenance Factor		Effective Lumens/Lamp

3. Number of Lamps

$$\frac{\text{Total Lumens Required}}{\text{Effective Lumens/Lamp}} = \boxed{} \text{ Total Lamps}$$

WORKSHEET 10.3 Exterior Lamp Sizing

1. Effective Lumens per Lamp

$$\frac{[\text{Illumination Level (footcandles)}] \times [\text{Area (sq ft)}]}{[\text{Total Lamps}]} = [\text{Effective Lumens/Lamp}]$$

Illumination Level (footcandles)

X

Area (sq ft)

Total Lamps

= Effective Lumens/Lamp

2. Initial Lamp Lumens

$$\frac{[\text{Effective Lumens/Lamp}]}{[\text{Utilization Factor}] \times [\text{Lumen Maintenance Factor}]} = [\text{Initial Lumens/Lamp}]$$

Effective Lumens/Lamp

Utilization Factor

X

Lumen Maintenance Factor

= Initial Lumens/Lamp

3. Lamp Data

Wattage: _____

Lamp Type: _____

WORKSHEET 10.4   Optimum Group Relamping Interval

1. Lamp Data

Lamp Type: _____
Rated Life (hr): _____

2. % Full Life Factor

Incandescent: FLF = 1.0 for all applications

Fluorescent	HID
For < 3 hr/start, FLF = 0.6	For < 6 hr/start, FLF = 0.6
For 3 to 6 hr/start, FLF = 0.7	For 6 to 10 hr/start, FLF = 0.7
For > 6 hr/start, FLF = 0.8	For > 10 hr/start, FLF = 0.8

3. Operating Hours to Replacement

$$\boxed{} \quad X \quad \boxed{} \quad = \quad \boxed{}$$

Rated Life (hr) 　　% Full Life Factor (FLF) 　　Operating Hours

4. Replacement Interval

$$\frac{\boxed{} \text{ Operating Hours}}{\boxed{} \text{ Hours Operated per Day} \quad X \quad \boxed{} \text{ Days Operated per Month}} = \boxed{} \text{ Replacement Interval (months)}$$

WORKSHEET 10.5   Group Vs. Spot Relamping Costs

1. Lamp Cost - Spot Relamping

[ ]	X	[ ]	=	[ ]	

Cost per Lamp   Number of Lamps   Spot Relamping
                                                Lamp Cost

2. Labor Cost - Spot Relamping

[ ]	X	[ ]	X	[ ]	=	[ ]

Labor Rate   Time per Lamp   Number of Lamps   Spot Relamping
$/hr   (hr)   Labor Cost

3. Total Cost - Spot Relamping

[ ]	+	[ ]	=	[ ]

Spot Relamping   Spot Relamping   Spot Relamping
Lamp Cost   Labor Cost   Total Cost

Worksheet 10.5 (continued)

---

4. Lamp Cost - Group Relamping

2 X [___] X [___] = [___]

Cost per Lamp   Number of Lamps   Group Relamping
Lamp Cost

---

5. Labor Cost - Group Relamping

2 X [___] X [___] X [___] = [___]

Labor Rate   Time per Lamp (hr)   Number of Lamps   Group Relamping
($/hr)   Labor Cost

---

6. Burnout Replacement Labor Cost - Group Relamping

2 X [___] X [___] = [___]

Relamp Interval   Spot Relamping   Burnout Replace-
Factor   Labor Cost   ment Labor Cost

---

7. Total Cost - Group Relamping

[___] + [___] + [___] = [___]

Group Relamping   Group Relamping   Burnout Replace-   Group Relamping
Lamp Cost   Labor Cost   ment Labor Cost   Total Cost

Chapter 11

USING UNINTERRUPTIBLE POWER SUPPLIES TO PROTECT COMPUTERS AND ELECTRONIC EQUIPMENT

Uninterruptible power supplies have gained in popularity as a result of the widespread use of computers and other sensitive electronic equipment. Unlike conventional electrical loads, such as motors and lights, the performance of computers and electronic equipment can be adversely affected by small irregularities in the power supply. Operation can be disrupted by voltage fluctuations, frequency deviations, power line noise, brownouts, momentary dropouts, and blackouts.

ELECTRICAL SUPPLY REQUIREMENTS FOR COMPUTERS

Figure 11.1 identifies typical electrical supply voltage and frequency requirements for computers, electronic, and telecommunications equipment. The figure also lists typical voltage and frequency characteristics of power supplied by utility companies to a facility and those same characteristics at the connected load. From the figure it can be seen that actual power conditions, particularly with respect to voltage, do not meet the exacting requirements of computers. As a result, you may be called on to improve the level of electrical service through the use of an uninterruptible power supply.

The purpose of the uninterruptible power supply (UPS) is to filter voltage and frequency variations from the line feeding the critical load, and to provide power during momentary outages. When backed up by a motor-generator set, the UPS can provide continued operation even during long periods of power blackouts. UPS systems are available in sizes ranging from a few hundred volt-amps through several thousand kVa.

CAUSES OF POWER SUPPLY IRREGULARITIES

The types of fluctuations occurring on an electrical supply vary with the following:

- ➤ the location of the facility
- ➤ the types of loads connected within the facility
- ➤ the time of day
- ➤ the season of the year

Utility companies operate within strict standards of performance on the power they generate, including limits on the amount the frequency can deviate from the 60 Hz standard, the duration of momentary dropouts, and variations from the nominal voltage they supply. But even these limits can be too broad for computer and telecommunication equipment.

For example, load switching at a utility can cause momentary variations in voltage and dropouts of 30 milliseconds or less. While such deviations from the standard pose no problems to most building equipment, they can result in disruption of program execution, loss of memory, and even damage to computer and telecommunication equipment components.

Not all power line problems originate at the utility. Some are induced in the power lines between the utility and the facility as a result of the operation of other loads, or weather factors. Additional problems originate within the facility itself. Potentially damaging voltage fluctuations can be induced by any of the following:

- ➤ the starting or stopping of motors
- ➤ the arcing of contacts in motor starters and brushes
- ➤ the opening of electrical contacts under load
- ➤ the operation of an arc welder
- ➤ a grounding fault within the system.

HOW THE UPS SYSTEM WORKS

Although a number of different UPS architectures are used by system manufacturers, one of the most commonly used configurations is the AC-to- DC-to-AC UPS as shown in Figure 11.2. This particular configuration has the capability of supplying clean, continuous power to equipment under all types of power fluctuations and interruptions.

The system has four major components: a rectifier/charger unit; a static inverter; a bank of batteries; and a static switch. A fifth component, a standby engine-generator set can be added to provide power during prolonged power outages.

Under normal operation, the rectifier/charger unit converts the commercial electricity supply from alternating current to direct current. The direct current is used to keep the battery bank at full charge and to power the static inverter. The static inverter converts the direct current back to alternating current that then passes through the static switch to the protected load.

If the commercial utility supply is interrupted or falls below the minimum voltage needed to operate the system, the batteries supply the needed power to the inverter. Since the batteries are floating on the line between the rectifier and the inverter, there is no momentary loss of power during changeover. The computer load never sees a power blackout, brownout, or momentary outage.

The UPS also provides protection for the computer equipment from other power line problems, such as noise on the line and voltage spikes. All such irregularities are filtered out by the process of converting the utility supply to direct current and back to alternating current.

Caution: The only noise that would not be filtered out by the process is noise generated by equipment on the load side of the UPS, such as an air conditioning compressor. For that reason, users of UPS systems must be careful in selecting and isolating loads to be fed by a UPS.

FIVE FACTORS TO CONSIDER BEFORE INVESTING IN A UPS SYSTEM

Although UPS systems offer the highest level of protection for computer and telecommunications equipment, their application is limited by their expense. Other methods, such as the use of surge suppressors and noise filters, may provide the level of protection needed without having to invest in a UPS. To determine the level of protection needed for your application, consider the following questions:

➤ What are the tolerance limits of the equipment in terms of voltage regulation and surges? If the equipment is readily damaged by voltage variations of five percent or less, or if momentary surges of 20 percent will damage equipment, a UPS system is justified.

➤ Momentary outages typically cause computer operations to stop processing. For a desktop computer user, the momentary outage may result in the loss or corruption of data entered but not yet recorded to disk. For a mainframe system, the momentary outage may result in having to restart the entire system. For a telecommunications system, momentary outages may shut down all or part of the system.

If the operation of the equipment will be disrupted by momentary outages of 30 milliseconds and the resulting disruption of service cannot be tolerated, a UPS system is justified.

➤ Although power blackouts generally last less than ten minutes, they can continue for days. During a blackout, the entire facility is disrupted. A UPS system, backed up with a standby generator, can provide continuous power to the computer or telecommunications system over the duration of the power outage. If providing power to those systems enables critical functions to continue during periods when the remainder of the facility is without power, a UPS system is the only option.

➤ Computer-based systems are often used for critical life safety functions in buildings, such as fire alarm and security system monitoring. If disruption of power to those systems will endanger personnel or property, a UPS system is justified.

➤ In addition to providing power during blackouts, UPS systems filter out nearly all types of power line problems that can disrupt computer operation or damage sensitive electronic components. If the disruption caused by having computer and electronic equipment out of service cannot be tolerated in the facility, a UPS system is justified.

Unless a UPS system is absolutely essential to the operation of your facility, you should consider alternatives. For example, power line filters and surge suppressors can provide protection to computer systems at a fraction of the cost of a UPS system. While they cannot provide power during brownouts and blackouts, not all installations need such protection.

TWO KEY FACTORS TO CONSIDER WHEN SELECTING A UPS SYSTEM

If you determine that a UPS system is essential, consider the following factors before selecting a particular system or systems:

➤ If there are several computer installations in a particular building, consider installing one UPS system sized to serve all installations. A single large unit, complete with a standby generator, is more cost effective than several smaller systems. Smaller, independent UPS systems are best suited for use where the individual loads that must be protected are small and widely scattered throughout the facility. Small-load UPS systems are available to provide full line filtering and battery backup for 15 to 30 minutes for a typical computer system.

➤ Consider future changes that will impact the use of computers and computer-based equipment in the facility and the need to have those systems protected by a UPS system. Computer-based systems are the most rapidly growing technology in buildings today. Not only will the number of systems increase, but also the dependence on computers will grow significantly, a dependence that will result in the need to have the systems protected by a UPS system.

HOW TO SIZE THE UPS SYSTEM

Three major components need to be properly sized in a UPS installation: the inverter/rectifier unit; the standby batteries; and the backup generator. For a system to operate properly, all three must be properly matched to the load connected to the system.

Sizing the UPS Unit

Two ratings must be taken into consideration when sizing a UPS system: the system's continuous rating and its overload rating. The continuous rating, given in terms of kilovolt amperes (kVa) or kilowatts (kW), is a measure of the total steady state load that will be connected to the system. To find this rating, sum the power requirements of the individual loads connected to the system (see Worksheet 11.1).

The UPS can also supply more power than this continuous rating for a short period of time. Expressed as a percent of the continuous rating, this overload rating is the maximum load that can be powered by the system without damaging the UPS system or having the output voltage fall below the specified value. Overload ratings are important with respect to equipment inrush currents. Although such currents typically last less than a second, the UPS system components must be properly sized to handle them or they will be damaged.

Calculating the System Load Ratings

Use Worksheet 11.1 to determine both the continuous and the instantaneous loads that the UPS system must be capable of powering. Use the worksheet as follows:

Step 1. Identify each piece of equipment that will be powered by the UPS system.

Step 2. For each piece of equipment, determine the operating voltage and the rated current. The voltage and current data are listed on the name plate of the equipment or are available from the manufacturer. Enter the voltage and current ratings for each piece of equipment on the worksheet.

Step 3. For each piece of equipment determine the inrush current (the start-up current draw). Inrush current is listed on the equipment nameplate or is available from the manufacturer and is always equal to or greater than the rated operating current. Enter the inrush current for each piece of equipment on the worksheet.

Step 4. For each piece of equipment, multiply the voltage by the current to determine the equipment's apparent power in kVa. Enter the apparent current for each piece of equipment.

Step 5. When all equipment has been listed, add the values for the apparent power, and divide by 1,000 to convert the units to kVa. Enter the value at the bottom of the worksheet.

Step 6. Add the values for the inrush current and enter the value at the bottom of the worksheet.

These values—the total apparent power and the peak inrush currents—are the minimum ratings required for the rectifier/inverter unit. They represent an approximation of the load size that the UPS system must be capable of handling. The actual size of the UPS system includes this minimum load rating, growth factors, and overload ratings.

Calculating Steady State and Overload Ratings

Use Worksheet 11.2 to determine the steady state kVa rating for the UPS system based on these factors. Use the worksheet as follows:

Step 1. Enter the total apparent power in kVa from Worksheet 11.1 in section #1 of the worksheet.

Step 2. The total apparent power represents the load of the current equipment. Over time, additional equipment will be installed, increasing the load on the system. To take into account this future growth, a growth multiplication factor is introduced, typically a value between 1.3 and 2.0. Enter the growth factor in section #1.

Step 3. Multiply the total apparent power by the growth factor to determine the first approximation of the steady state kVa requirement for the system.

Step 4. Enter the peak inrush current in amps from the bottom of Worksheet 11.1 in section #2.

Step 5. If the UPS is a single-phase system, enter the value of 0.001414 for the multiplication factor. If the UPS is a three-phase system, enter the value of 0.00245 for the multiplication factor.

Step 6. Enter the system voltage in section #2.

Step 7. Multiply the peak inrush current by the multiplication factor and the system voltage to determine the inrush kVa needed. Enter the value in section #2.

Step 8. Enter the inrush kVa from section #2 into section #3.

Step 9. Enter the first approximation of the steady state kVa from section #1 into section #3.

Step 10. Add the inrush kVa and the first approximation of the steady state kVa to determine the overload rating kVa. Enter the value in section #3.

Step 11. The second approximation of the steady state kVa system requirements is, by rule of thumb, equal to the system's overload rating divided by 1.25. Enter the overload rating kVa from section #3 into section #4. Divide by 1.25 to get the second approximation of the steady state kVa system requirements. Enter the value in section #4 of the worksheet.

Step 12. Compare the first approximation of the steady state system requirements in section #1 with the second approximation in section #4. Enter the larger of the two values in section #5. This value represents the steady state rating in kW that the UPS must be capable of supplying for system power factors in the range of 0.80 to 1.00.

The steady state kVa rating determines the overall current handling capacity of the system. An additional sizing factor that must be determined is the size of the battery.

Sizing the UPS System Battery

In planning a UPS system, consideration must be given to sizing the batteries in terms of their electrical and physical characteristics. An undersized battery system won't allow sufficient time to start and stabilize the standby generator or for the operators to complete an orderly shutdown of the protected load. Too large a battery system wastes money both in the initial installation cost and in increased maintenance expenses.

The physical characteristics of the battery system are equally important to UPS system planners. The battery portion of the UPS in all but the smallest of systems is its largest and heaviest component. For systems having a reserve capacity exceeding five kVa-hr, batteries are generally housed in specially constructed rooms capable of carrying the heavy floor loading generated. Batteries are arranged on racks within these rooms, racks that have one, two, or three tiers of batteries. Although the racks are typically two feet deep, the need to perform routine maintenance on the batteries requires that the room be designed with a minimum of four feet clearance between racks.

GUIDELINES FOR SETTING UP A BATTERY SYSTEM. Selecting a site for the battery room requires consideration. Batteries are heavy, producing a floor loading that can exceed the capacity of typical building construction. As a result, most battery rooms are located on the lowest level of a building.

Tip: Since cable losses are an important factor at the current levels typical in UPS installations, locate the UPS unit as close as possible to the battery room.

Battery rooms also require a ventilation system to remove hydrogen gas generated during the charging process. Rule of thumb: Provide from 1 to $1\,^1/_2$ air changes per hour. At this rate, the hydrogen content of the battery room air will be kept well below the critical level. The ventilation system should be designed to exhaust air from near the battery room ceiling since hydrogen is lighter than air. All ventilation air from the room should be exhausted to the outside rather than returned to the building's air distribution system.

The average temperature of the battery room can significantly impact the battery performance which is rated at 77°F. Figure 11.3 shows the effect on capacity when batteries are operated at less than 77°F. Operating batteries at temperatures higher than 77°F does not significantly increase battery capacity, but does result in increased maintenance requirements as well as decreased battery life. Use the figure to estimate the additional capacity required due to space temperatures that are below 77°F.

Carefully consider the site for the UPS unit. Although lighter and smaller than the batteries, the UPS unit also can exceed floor loading limits. In addition, the inverter and charger units produce a loud, 60 Hz hum that is readily transmitted to adjacent spaces unless the room has been acoustically treated.

THREE FACTORS TO CONSIDER WHEN SIZING BATTERIES FOR A UPS SYSTEM. Three major factors must be considered when sizing the batteries for a UPS installation: the kVa-hr capacity rating of the batteries; the physical size of the racks of batteries; and the weight of the batteries and racks. Use Worksheet 11.3 to estimate all three factors for a particular UPS installation.

Step 1.   Enter in section #1 the steady state kVa rating from Worksheet 11.2.

Step 2.   Most UPS systems, particularly those backed up with a standby generator, are designed to operate on battery power for about fifteen minutes. Longer operating times are required for systems with no backup generator. Estimate the operating time in minutes that the batteries must be capable of carrying the full load connected to the system and enter the value in section #1.

Step 3.   Multiply the steady state kVa rating by the operating time and the conversion factor of 0.0167 to determine the capacity of the battery system in kVa-hr. This value represents the battery capacity necessary to power the full system load for the desired operating time. If the actual load is less, the operating time will be increased. Enter the value in section #1 of the worksheet.

Step 4.   If the average battery room temperature is 77°F, skip to step #8.

Step 5.   Enter the calculated capacity from section #1 into section #2 of the worksheet.

Step 6.   For the design room temperature, determine from Figure 11.3 the percent of rated output. Enter the value as a decimal (0 - 1.0) in section #2 of the worksheet.

Step 7.   Divide the battery capacity by the percent of rated output to determine the corrected capacity at 77°F rating. Enter the value in section #2 of the worksheet.

Step 8.   Figure 11.4 gives an estimate of the length of the battery rack based on the kVa-hr capacity of the battery system. For the battery capacity determined in section #1 (or section #2 for off-temperature rooms), and for the number of tiers in the battery rack, use Figure 11.4 to determine the estimated length of the battery rack. Enter the value in section #3 of the worksheet.

Step 9.   Figure 11.5 estimates the weight of the batteries based on capacity. For the battery capacity determined in section #1 (or section #2 for off-temperature rooms), use Figure 11.5 to estimate the weight of the battery system. Enter the value in section #4 of the worksheet.

The three factors estimated by the worksheet—battery capacity, battery rack size, and battery weight—will determine the physical requirements for the battery room as well as the number of batteries required to power the UPS system during an outage.

HOW TO SIZE THE UPS GENERATOR

Two sources of power can provide extended operation of the UPS system during a power outage: batteries and a standby generator. The problem with batteries is that their cost per kVa-hr is high compared to standby generators for all but the smallest systems. For that reason, medium to large systems typically use batteries to provide power only until the standby generator can be started and brought on line.

How to Estimate the Generator Capacity You Need

When estimating the size of the generator needed, two loads must be considered: the load from the UPS system and its connected equipment, and the load resulting from recharging the batteries. Both are essential because the batteries will be partially discharged when the generator comes on line.

Use Worksheet 11.4 to estimate the rating of the generator needed to power the system. Use the worksheet as follows:

Step 1.	Enter the total apparent power of the load from Worksheet 11.1 in section #1. Multiply the value by 2.5 to determine the first approximation of the standby generator capacity. Enter the value in section #1 of the worksheet.
Step 2.	Determine the battery capacity from Worksheet 11.3, section #1, or section #2 for non-standard room temperatures. Enter the value in section #2 of the worksheet.
Step 3.	The battery load depends in part on the recharge time for the batteries. For a recharge time of four hours, use a multiplication factor of 1.268. For a recharge time of eight hours, use a factor of 0.552. For a recharge time of 12 hours, use a factor of 0.367. Enter the recharge multiplication factor in section #2 of the worksheet.
Step 4.	Multiply the battery capacity by the recharge multiplication factor to determine the battery component of the load and enter the value in section #2.
Step 5.	Enter the battery load component from section #2 into section #3.
Step 6.	Determine the steady state kVa rating for the UPS system from section #5 of Worksheet 11.2. Enter the value in section #3 of the worksheet.
Step 7.	Add the battery load component and the steady state kVa rating. Multiply by 1.2 to determine the second estimate of system capacity. Enter the value in section #3 of the worksheet.
Step 8.	Determine the larger of the two system capacity estimates calculated in sections #1 and #3. Enter the value in section #4.

The figure estimated by the worksheet will determine the minimum generator capacity for the system. If other loads will be connected to this generator, the generator capacity will have to be increased to reflect those loads.

HOW TO CREATE A SUMMARY SPECIFICATION OF THE UPS SYSTEM

Use Worksheet 11.5 to specify system characteristics in planning a UPS system installation. While the summary does not provide all of the information necessary to specify a system for bidding purposes, it does provide enough information for you to obtain a budget price from a system supplier. In addition, the information included in the summary will help you develop specifications later.

Most of the information included in the summary comes from the worksheets in this chapter. Complete the worksheet as follows:

Step 1.	Determine the required system voltage, number of phases, and frequency from the components that will be connected to the system. Enter the values in section #1 of the worksheet. For example, a typical system would have to provide power to equipment at 120/208 volts, single phase, and at 60 Hz.
Step 2.	Determine the steady state system rating from section #5 of Worksheet 11.2. Enter the value in section #2 of the worksheet.
Step 3.	Determine the overload rating from section #3 of Worksheet 11.2. Enter the value in section #2 of the worksheet.
Step 4.	Determine the capacity of the battery system from section #2 of Worksheet 11.3. Enter the value in section #3 of the worksheet.
Step 5.	Determine the generator rating from section #4 of Worksheet 11.4. Enter the value in section #4 of the worksheet.
Step 6.	The static transfer switch must be capable of carrying the full load of the system, both at installation time and at some point in the future when the system has grown. Rule of thumb: Size the switch to be at least 1.3 times the capacity of the UPS system. Multiply the steady state UPS output (section #2) by 1.3 and enter the value in section #5.

The characteristics listed on the worksheet will determine the overall capacities for the UPS system.

MAINTENANCE GUIDELINES FOR A RELIABLE UPS SYSTEM

One of the main reasons for installing a UPS system is to enhance the reliability of the electrical system feeding critical loads. To insure that the system can do that, you should perform certain maintenance activities regularly. Without such maintenance, there is no insurance that the system will perform as required during momentary or prolonged power interruptions.

Cleaning Requirements

The UPS system itself is a static device and requires little maintenance other than a routine cleaning and testing of the system's inverter and charger units. Dust, if it is permitted to accumulate on cooling fins in these units, will cause them to operate at above-normal temperatures, and could eventually lead to component failure.

Key Battery Inspection and Testing Procedures

Inspect and test the batteries regularly. Routine battery maintenance and monitoring will insure maximum performance and life of the battery component of the UPS system. Use Worksheet 11.6 to record and monitor battery performance. All readings should be performed when the batteries are fully charged. The worksheet has space for monitoring up to 50 battery cells. Use the worksheet as follows:

Step 1.   Measure and record the voltage across each cell. Slight variations (±0.15 volts) between cells and between monthly readings for the same cell are normal. Large variations are an indication that something is wrong with that cell.

Step 2.   Conduct hydrometer readings for each cell in the battery system. Since hydrometer readings are temperature-dependent, the value must be corrected to the standard rating of temperature of 77°F before recording the value. Use the hydrometer temperature correction factor table listed at the bottom of the worksheet. Slight variations (±0.020) are normal.

There are three additional maintenance activities that should be completed while filling out the worksheet.

1. After the voltage and hydrometer readings have been taken, add distilled water to the cell as required.

2. Clean the tops of all cells to remove dust and dirt.

3. Tighten all cell connectors to manufacturer-specified torques.

FIVE VITAL MAINTENANCE PROCEDURES FOR KEEPING STANDBY GENERATORS PROBLEM FREE

Of all components in the UPS system, the one that gives users the most problems is the standby generator. Generators are notorious for not starting when needed, overheating during operation, and stalling due to water in the fuel. Fortunately, almost all of these problems can be avoided though proper maintenance:

➤ Test the battery for the standby generator twice monthly to insure it is capable of starting the system.

➤ Record voltage and hydrometer readings.

➤ Equip all batteries with a charging system that does not depend on the operation of the generator.

➤ Test run the generator at least twice a month to insure that the entire starting system is capable of actually starting the generator. To test the system further, run the generator under load for a minimum of fifteen minutes.

➤ Test the entire UPS system in a power failure mode at least twice a year, preferably during a time when demand on the computer system is low. Pull the main disconnect on the utility line feeding the UPS system. If it is operating properly, the batteries will immediately pick up the load, and the generator will start and come on line. Then run the generator for a minimum of two hours to thoroughly test its cooling system.

These are the minimum maintenance requirements for operating a UPS system. The frequency at which tests and inspections are carried out depends on the critical nature of the load being protected by the system.

FIGURE 11.1 Electrical Supply Characteristics

Characteristic	Typical Computer Requirements	Typical Service From Utility	Typical Supply at Load
Steady state voltage	120/208 volts + or - 10%	120/208 volts + or - 5%	120/208 volts + 1%, - 9%
Transient voltage	No surges or dips greater than 20% for longer than 30 milliseconds	Switching of large loads can easily exceed the limits imposed by computers	Surges as high as 2,700 volts can be induced by loads within the facility
Voltage outages	Limited to 15 milliseconds or less	Outages of 30 milliseconds or more daily as the result of load switching	More frequent outages as a result of load switching in the facility
Frequency	60 Hertz + or - 1/2 Hertz	60 Hertz with little or no variation	60 Hertz with little or no variation

FIGURE 11.2 UPS System Components

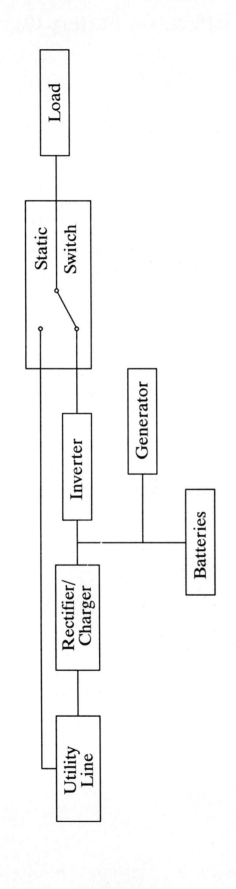

FIGURE 11.3 Temperature Effects on Battery Capacity

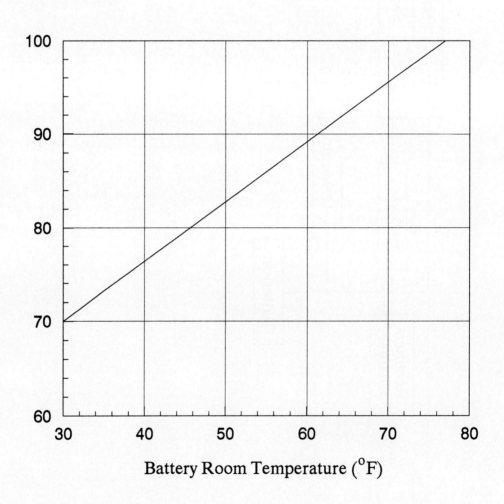

FIGURE 11.4 UPS Battery Rack Size
as a Function of Capacity

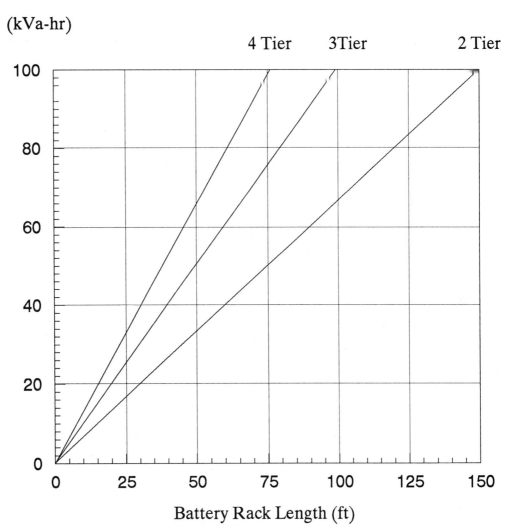

Battery Capacity

(kVa-hr)

4 Tier   3Tier   2 Tier

100

80

60

40

20

0

0   25   50   75   100   125   150

Battery Rack Length (ft)

FIGURE 11.5 UPS Battery Weight as a Function of Capacity

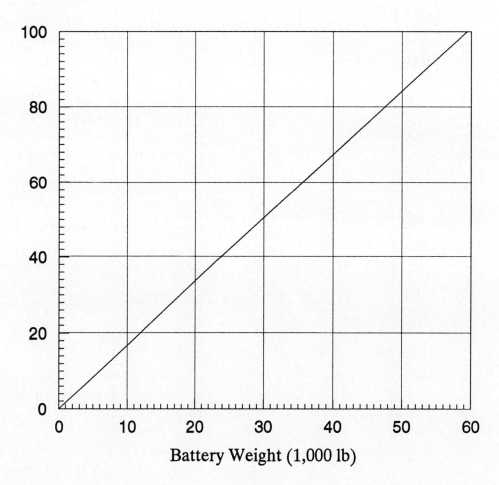

Battery Capacity
(kVa-hr)

Battery Weight (1,000 lb)

WORKSHEET 11.1 UPS System Load Ratings

Equipment	Voltage	Current (amps)	Apparent Power (kVa)	Inrush Current (amps)

Total Apparent Power: _____   Peak Inrush Current (amps): _____

WORKSHEET 11.2 Steady State and Overload Ratings

1. Annual Electricity Cost Savings

[ ]	X [ ]	= [ ]
Total Apparent Power (kVa)	Growth Factor	First Approximation Steady State kVa

2. Inrush Current

[ ]	X [ ]	X [ ]	= [ ]
Peak Inrush Current (amps)	Multiplication Factor	System Voltage (Volts)	Inrush Current (kVa)

3. Overload rating

[ ]	+ [ ]	= [ ]
Inrush kVa	First Approximation Steady State kVa	Overload Rating (kVa)

4. Steady State Rating, Second Approximation

$$\frac{\boxed{\qquad}\;\text{Overload Rating (kVa)}}{\boxed{1.25}} = \boxed{\qquad}$$

Second Approximation
Steady State kVa

5. Steady State kVa Rating

[ ]

Steady State kVa
Rating

WORKSHEET 11.3 Battery Characteristics

1. Battery Capacity

	X		X	0.0167	=	

Steady State kVa Rating   Operating Time (minutes)   Capacity (kVa-hr)

2. Temperature Corrected Battery Capacity

$$\frac{\text{Capacity (kVa-hr)}}{\text{Correction Factor}} = \boxed{}$$

Corrected Capacity (kVa-hr)

3. Battery Rack Size

Rack size from Figure 11.4

4. Battery Weight

Battery weight from Figure 11.5

WORKSHEET 11.4 UPS Generator Rating

1. First Estimate of Capacity

$$\boxed{} \quad \text{X} \quad \boxed{2.5} \quad = \quad \boxed{}$$

Total Apparent
Power (kVa)

First Estimate of
Capacity (kVa)

2. Battery Load Component

$$\boxed{} \quad \text{X} \quad \boxed{} \quad = \quad \boxed{}$$

Battery Capacity
(kVa)

Recharge
Multiplication
Factor

Battery Load
Component (kVa)

3. Second Estimate of Capacity

$$\left[\; \boxed{} \quad + \quad \boxed{} \;\right] \quad \text{X} \quad \boxed{1.2} \quad = \quad \boxed{}$$

Battery Load
Component (kVa)

UPS Rating
(kVa)

Second Estimate
of Capacity (kVa)

4. Generator Capacity

$$\boxed{}$$

kVa Rating

WORKSHEET 11.5 UPS System Characteristics Summary

1.   System Voltage (Volts): _____

                                  Phase: _____

                     Frequency (Hz): _____

2.   UPS Output Steady State kVa: _____

                    Overload kVa: _____

3.   Battery Capacity (kVa-hr): _____

4.   Generator Capacity (kVa): _____

5.   Static Transfer Switch Capacity (kVa): _____

WORKSHEET 11.6 UPS Battery Maintenance Report

Date: _____   Time: _____

Bus Voltage: _____   Cell _____   Temperature: _____

Inspector: _____

Cell	Volts	Hydrometer	Cell	Volts	Hydrometer
1			26		
2			27		
3			28		
4			29		
5			30		
6			31		
7			32		
8			33		
9			34		
10			35		
11			36		
12			37		
13			38		
14			39		
15			40		
16			41		
17			42		
18			43		
19			44		
20			45		
21			46		
22			47		
23			48		
24			49		
25			50		

Hydrometer Temperature Correction	
Temp ($^{\circ}$F)	Factor
110	+ 0.010
100	+ 0.007
90	+ 0.004
80	+ 0.001
77	0.000
70	-0.002
60	-0.003
50	-0.005

1. Check the electrolyte temperature within several cells. Use the average temperature to determine the hydrometer temperature correction factor.
2. Record the temperature-corrected hydrometer reading.
3. Add water (if required) after all hydrometer readings have been taken.

## Chapter 12

How to Increase Capacity and Save Money by Correcting Your Facility's Power Factor

A facility's power factor is one of the most frequently misunderstood characteristics of its electrical system. As a result, millions of dollars are wasted each year paying penalties in the form of reduced system capacity, increased electric rates, and poor system performance. Yet correcting a facility's power factor is one of the most straightforward tasks that you can perform to reduce operating expenses.

Quick Reference Guide to Power Factor Basics

The electrical power supplied to facilities by the utility company is an alternating current, with both the voltage and the current varying in the form of a sine wave. If the electrical loads of the facility were purely resistive, such as incandescent lights and resistance heaters, the voltage and the current in the electrical system would vary in phase with each other. Whenever one would hit a minimum or maximum, so would the other. Figure 12.1 shows the relationship between voltage and current when the load is purely resistive.

In practice, no facility has a purely resistive load. Facilities are filled with electrical equipment that make use of inductive currents. Induction motors, transformers, welders, induction furnaces, and fluorescent and other ballasted lights all use a portion of the electrical current they draw to create the magnetic fields that the devices require to operate. One effect of these magnetic fields is the changing of the relationship between the current and the voltage in the circuit.

Figure 12.2 shows the current and voltage in an electrical system with inductive loads. The voltage, no longer in phase with the current, reaches its minimum and maximum values before the current does. In this case, the current is said to lag the voltage.

Actual Versus Apparent Power

If a watt meter, a volt meter, and an ammeter were connected to a system with a purely resistive load, the reading on the watt meter, known as actual power, would equal the product of the voltage reading on the volt meter and the current reading on the ammeter. This product of system voltage and current is called the apparent power. For purely resistive loads, the actual power in a system is equal to the apparent power.

If the same meters were connected to a system with an inductive load, the reading of actual power from the watt meter would be less than the value for the apparent power calculated from the voltage and current readings. The reason for the difference in power levels is the shift in phase between current and voltage. In the system with purely resistive loads, the system voltage and the current are both positive or both negative at the same time. The instantaneous power in the system, which is defined as the product of the voltage and current, therefore is always positive (see Figure 12.1).

In a system with inductive loads, the voltage and the current are not in phase with each other. Most of the time, both are positive or both are negative; however, there is a period during a portion of each cycle when one is positive and the other is negative. The resulting power during these periods is negative as shown in Figure 12.2. This negative power, also known as reactive power, produces no useful work but is a direct result of the current used by inductive loads to produce the magnetic fields they require to operate.

In a system with inductive loads, the actual power used (the power for which a user is billed by the utility company) is the difference between the positive and negative power areas. Power factor is defined as the ratio of this actual power (watts) to the power which is apparently being drawn from the utility company lines (volt-amps).

$$\text{Power Factor} = \frac{\text{Actual Power}}{\text{Apparent Power}} \qquad (12.1)$$

If the loads in the system were purely resistive, the voltage and the current in the system would be in phase with each other and the system power factor would be equal to one. If the loads were purely reactive, the voltage and the current would always be opposite in sign resulting in a system power factor of zero. In practice, there are no systems with purely resistive or reactive loads since facility loads typically consist of a combination of both. The greater the inductive component, the lower the power factor.

Problems Caused by Low Power Factor

Low power factor causes problems for both the user of the electricity and the utility company that supplies it. Consider what happens when two similar loads are connected to an electrical system. Assume that the two loads are identical with the exception that the first load has been fitted with a power factor correction capacitor. Also assume that the power factor of the uncorrected load is 0.45 and that the power factor of the corrected load is 0.90.

Since the loads are identical, the actual power drawn by each is the same. Rearranging equation 12.1;

$$\text{Apparent Power} = \frac{\text{Actual Power}}{\text{Power Factor}} \qquad (12.2)$$

With the power factor of the corrected load being twice that of the uncorrected load, using equation 12.1, it can be seen that the uncorrected load has an apparent power that is twice that of the corrected load. Since apparent power is the product of the system voltage and current drawn by the load, and the voltage in the two systems is the same, the current for the uncorrected load is twice that of the corrected load.

In the above example, both customers would pay the same amount for the power used even though one load draws twice the current of the other. The utility company must therefore invest in additional equipment to generate and transmit the current without being able to recover its expenses through power use charges. To the customer, the additional current that is drawn by equipment with a poor power factor results in decreased system capacity. Plant wiring systems have a limited current-carrying capacity. The more current that is carried by the system as the result of poor power factor equipment, the less capacity that is available for power-producing equipment.

Utility companies recover their expenses for low power factor primarily through penalties charged to customers whose power factor falls below some set minimum value, typically 0.85. These penalties can be very expensive for large users of electricity whose power factor has fallen below the minimum.

Power Factor Ratings of Typical Loads

All inductive loads will draw a component of reactive power, thus causing the system power factor to drop below 1.00. How much the power factor drops depends on the size of the system's reactive power component in relation to its actual power component. Figure 12.3 lists the power factor ratings of typical loads found within a facility.

INDUCTION MOTORS: THE BIGGEST CULPRITS. Of these loads, the one that contributes most to a system's low power factor is the induction motor. Figure 12.4 shows the relationship between power factor and loading for a typical induction motor. Depending on the type of induction motor and its rated horsepower, the full load power factor typically ranges from 0.75 to 0.90. As the load on the motor drops, so does the work producing component of the power (actual power) drawn by the motor. But the magnetizing component remains nearly constant regardless of load. Therefore a lightly loaded induction motor will have a large ratio of apparent power to actual power—a low power factor.

HOW TO CORRECT FOR LOW POWER FACTOR

The key to correcting for low power factor is to find a source other than the utility company for the magnetizing current needed by inductive devices.

Using a Capacitor to Boost the Power Factor

Capacitive devices are one such source. While inductive loads cause the voltage to lag the current in the system, capacitive loads have exactly the opposite effect; current in the system lags the voltage. When combined in the proper ratio, the two effects cancel each other out. In this case, the power factor correction device, such as a capacitor, serves as the source for magnetizing current.

Figure 12.5 demonstrates how you can use a capacitor to supply the magnetizing current to an inductive load. With the capacitor installed, the load draws the magnetizing current from the capacitor rather than from the utility company's line. The utility company then supplies only the power-producing current of the motor, resulting in an increased system power factor measured at the power meter.

Tip: The capacitor installation as shown in Figure 12.5 improves the system power factor and frees current-carrying capacity only from the point where the capacitor is connected to the system on back towards the utility company meter. For that reason, you should generally install capacitors as close to the inductive load as possible.

TWO TECHNIQUES FOR USING CAPACITORS. The two most common techniques for using capacitors as power factor correctors are installing the capacitors on individual motors, and installing them in central banks.

In individual motor applications, capacitors are wired directly to the motor so that the capacitor may be switched with the motor, thereby preventing overcorrection of the system power factor when the motor isn't operating.

Tip: Installing capacitors on all induction motors within a facility is not economically feasible because the cost of capacitors for small motors is large in comparison to the savings produced. In practice, capacitors are rarely installed on motors of less than five horsepower. Similarly, it is not economical to correct the power factor to 1.00. Rather, a target value of a corrected power factor of 0.95 is used for most applications.

When the installation of individual capacitors is impractical, such as in a facility having a large number of inductive loads, system power factor can be corrected through the use of a central bank of capacitors. Centrally located capacitors are also an economical alternative to the installation of individual capacitors in systems where the load and, therefore, the system power factor remains fairly constant. In group installations, a bank of capacitors is installed across the main electrical feed to the facility, on the facility side of the utility company meter. The capacitors supply the magnetizing current to the inductive loads within the facility, thus reducing the current drawn through the utility company line. Since the magnetizing current still flows within the electrical system within the facility, the improvement in power factor is limited to the meter side of the capacitor bank. Central capacitor banks solve the problem of penalties imposed by utility companies due to low power factor, but they do not free system capacity because the magnetizing current must still flow between the central capacitor bank and the individual inductive loads.

Central capacitor banks require additional hardware, including disconnect switches, protection and discharge devices, and an automatic switching device to vary the amount of correction applied as the inductive load varies. The additional hardware costs are offset by the reduced costs for capacitors since fewer are needed.

SIZING CAPACITORS FOR INDIVIDUAL MOTOR INSTALLATIONS. Figures 12.6 and 12.7 list the suggested maximum capacitor ratings in kVar for induction motors. The capacitor ratings listed in the tables raise the full load power factor of the motor to approximately 95%. Select the table that corresponds with the particular type of motor being corrected. Use the figures to size capacitors for induction motors.

SIZING CAPACITORS FOR CENTRAL BANK LOCATIONS. Figure 12.8 lists kW multipliers to be used in sizing central capacitor banks for power factor correction. To use the table, read down the first column to the measured power factor for the facility, then read across the table to get the kW multiplier listed for the target corrected power factor. The capacitor kVar rating is determined from the following:

$$\text{Capacitor Rating (kVar)} = \text{Average Facility Load (kW)} \times \text{Multiplier}$$

Example

A facility has an average uncorrected power factor of 0.70. The average connected load for the facility is 600 kW. The utility company has a penalty clause in the rate structure that becomes effective whenever a customer's power factor falls below 0.85. To be safe, this facility manager set a target value of 0.90 for the corrected power factor.

In Figure 12.8, you see that the kW multiplier corresponding to raising the power factor from 0.70 to 0.90 is 0.536. The size of the capacitor bank required is found by multiplying the average load by the kW multiplier:

$$\text{Capacitor Rating} = 0.536 \times 600 \text{ kW}$$
$$= 321.6 \text{ kVar}$$

SIZING CAPACITOR AUXILIARY EQUIPMENT. Use Figure 12.9 to determine recommended sizes for switches, wiring, and fuses used in the capacitor circuit.

RELEASING SYSTEM CAPACITY THROUGH POWER FACTOR IMPROVEMENT

One of the benefits of improving a facility's power factor is that it releases system capacity that may then be used for work-producing loads. Transformers, switchgear, and distribution systems all are limited in their capacity to carry current. To those components, there is no difference between reactive and power-producing current. Thus the more reactive current that must be carried by a system, the less capacity there will be for work-producing current.

When capacitors are installed close to inductive loads, they serve as sources of the reactive power required by those loads to operate, reactive power that would otherwise be drawn from the utility line and distributed through the facility's electrical system. The wiring between the capacitor location and the inductive load must still carry both the power-producing current and the reactive current, but when capacitors are installed close to the loads, the length of the wiring is limited.

The system capacity that is released by power factor correction is directly related to the improvement in power factor and can be calculated from the following:

$$\text{Released capacity} = \text{kVa}_{(\text{original PF})} - \text{kVa}_{(\text{improved PF})} \quad (12.3)$$

Substituting equation 12.2 for the two kVa terms:

$$\text{Released capacity} = \frac{\text{KW}}{\text{PF}_{(\text{original})}} - \frac{\text{KW}}{\text{PF}_{(\text{corrected})}} \quad (12.4)$$

Example

The power factor in an electrical feeder serving a portion of a facility is measured to be 0.75. The measured load on the feeder is 100 kW. The system capacity that would be released by raising the system power factor to 0.95 through capacitors installed at the individual loads would be calculated as follows:

$$\text{Released capacity} = \frac{100}{0.75} - \frac{100}{0.95}$$

$$= 133.3 - 105.3$$

$$= 28 \text{ kW}$$

HOW TO CALCULATE THE SAVINGS FROM POWER FACTOR IMPROVEMENT

Although utility companies must supply both work-producing and reactive power to their customers, only the work-producing component registers on the utility meter. Even though reactive power uses available capacity of generators, transformers, switchgear, and distribution systems, the utility company cannot bill the customer through conventional meter readings. Therefore, to compensate for their additional expenses arising from the lost capacity, utility companies build power factor clauses into the rate structures of industrial, commercial, and institutional users. Depending on the rate structure in effect for a particular customer, power factor charges can be a significant portion of the monthly utility bill. In these applications, installing capacitors, or taking other steps to improve the facility's power factor can produce substantial savings.

How a utility company charges its customers for low power factor varies from utility to utility. In some rate structures, the power factor clause is applied only when the average monthly power factor for the facility falls below a set minimum, typically 0.85. In other rate structures, the power factor clause is always in effect. In both cases, the charges for low power factor are calculated using the monthly peak billing demand for the facility.

Two of the most common methods of how utility companies bill for low power factor are presented here. Check with your local utility company to determine which method is in effect for your rate structure.

Method 1: KVA Demand Billing

Under a kVa demand billing rate structure, the customer pays for both the reactive and work-producing current drawn by the facility regardless of the power factor. The demand charges under this rate structure are calculated as follows:

$$\text{Demand Charge} = (\text{kVa Demand}) \times (\text{Demand Rate}) \qquad (12.5)$$

Where: kVa demand = the peak demand for the month
demand rate = the $/kVa charge from the rate structure

Example

For a given month, a facility has a peak demand of 2,000 kVa, with an average power factor of 0.85. The rate structure specifies a demand rate of $5.50/kVa. The facility manager wants to know the impact of raising the power factor to 0.95. From equation 12.1:

$$\text{Power factor} = \frac{(\text{Actual Power})}{(\text{Apparent Power})}$$

Rearranging and substituting the values for the month:

$$\text{Actual Power} = (\text{Power Factor}) \times (\text{Apparent Power})$$
$$= (0.85) \times (2,000)$$
$$= 1,700 \text{ kW}$$

At the rate of $5.50/kVa, the demand charge for the month would be $11,000.

Since the actual power would remain the same after power factor correction, the new apparent power can be calculated using the corrected power factor and equation 12.1:

$$\text{Apparent Power} = \frac{(\text{Actual Power})}{(\text{Power Factor})}$$

$$= \frac{1,700 \text{ kW}}{0.95}$$

$$= 1,789 \text{ kVa}$$

At the billing rate of $5.50/kVa, the charge for the same month if the power factor had been corrected to 0.95 would be $9,842, a savings of $1,158 for the month.

Method 2: Minimum Power Factor Charges

In cases where power factor charges are imposed only when the average monthly power factor falls below a specified minimum value, they serve as a penalty clause in the utility rate structure. As long as the customer corrects the facility's power factor to some value above the set minimum value, there is no power factor charge. A commonly specified minimum power factor is 0.85.

The most common method of assessing power factor penalty charges under this type of rate structure is through the use of a rider charge applied to the monthly demand charge as follows:

$$\text{Billing Demand} = (\text{kW Demand}) \times (\text{Power Factor Rider}) \qquad (12.6)$$

Where: kW Demand = peak demand for the month
Power Factor Rider = multiplier from the rate structure

The demand charge for the month is then calculated as follows:

$$\text{Demand Charge} = (\text{Billing Demand}) \times (\text{Demand Rate}) \qquad (12.7)$$

Where: the demand rate ($/kW) is specified in the rate structure

Example

For a given month, a facility has a peak demand of 1,500 kW. During that month, the average power factor was measured to be 0.80. The rate schedule in effect specifies a demand rate of $7.90 per kW, and imposes a power factor rider of 1.111 whenever the average monthly power factor falls below 0.85. The facility manager wants to determine the savings that would result from increasing the average power factor to 0.85.

Since the power factor for the billing period is below the specified minimum value, the demand charge includes the power factor rider.

$$
\begin{aligned}
\text{Billing Demand} &= (\text{kW Demand}) \times (\text{Power Factor Rider}) \\
&= (1{,}500 \text{ kW}) \times (1.111) \\
&= 1{,}667 \text{ kW}
\end{aligned}
$$

At the rate of $7.90/kW, the demand charge for the month would be $13,169.

If the power factor were raised to a value above 0.85, the billing demand would be the peak demand of 1,500 kW. At $7.90/kW, the charge for the month would be $11,850, a savings of $1,319 for the month.

THREE WAYS TO GET THE MAXIMUM BENEFIT AND LONGEST LIFE FROM CAPACITORS

Capacitors used for power factor correction are static devices and require very little maintenance. To insure proper operation over the rated life of the units, you should perform the following during installation:

➤ Install capacitors as close as possible to the loads they are serving to get the largest benefit in terms of released system capacity. Power factor correction occurs from the point of application back towards the utility meter.

➤ Keep room temperatures below 105°F. During normal operation, capacitors give off heat; therefore you should prevent the heat within the capacitor from becoming excessive.

➤ Avoid operating capacitors continuously at higher than rated voltages which can result in excessive heating, increased kVar production, and decreased capacitor life. Capacitors are rated at specific operating voltages and can continue to operate during short periods when the line voltage rises above normal.

During operation, the only additional requirement is that the capacitors be inspected periodically for proper operation. During normal operation, capacitors will be warm to the touch. If a capacitor is cold, check to see if the fuse has blown or if the disconnect has been accidentally left open. *Tip:* Before replacing blown fuses, inspect the case of the capacitor for signs of bulging. If any surface shows bulging, the capacitor is defective and you should replace it immediately.

FIGURE 12.1 Voltage, Current, and Power in a Circuit with a Purely Resistive Load

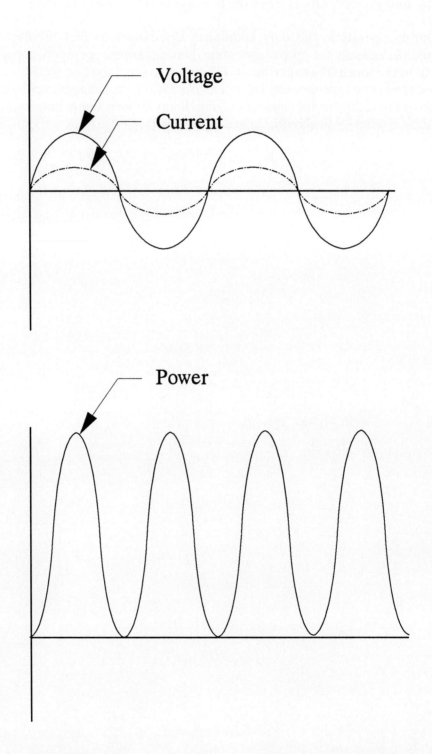

FIGURE 12.2 Voltage, Current, and Power in a Circuit with an Inductive Load

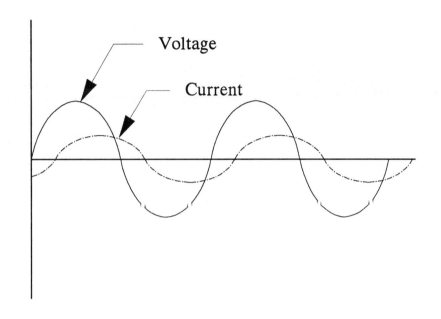

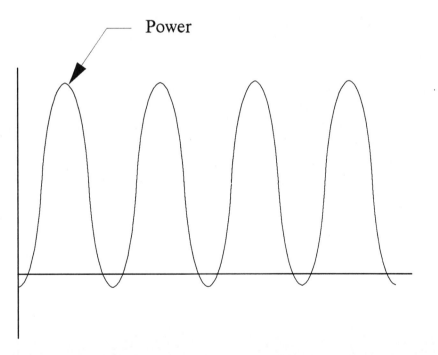

FIGURE 12.3 Power Factor Characteristics of Electrical Loads

Load	Power factor
Fluorescent Lamps	0.95 - 0.97
Incandescent Lamps	1.00
Resistance Heaters	1.00
Induction Motors	
Split Phase (fractional horsepower)	0.55 - 0.75
Split Phase (1 - 10 horsepower)	0.75 - 0.85
Split Phase (10 horsepower and larger)	0.75 - 1.00
Polyphase Squirrel Cage Motors	
High Speed (1 - 10 horsepower)	0.75 - 0.90
High Speed (10 horsepower and larger)	0.85 - 0.92
Low Speed	0.70 - 0.85
Wound Rotor	0.80 - 0.90
Welders	0.50 - 0.70
Arc Furnaces	0.80 - 0.90
Induction Furnaces	0.60 - 0.70

FIGURE 12.4 Power Factor as a Function of Motor Load

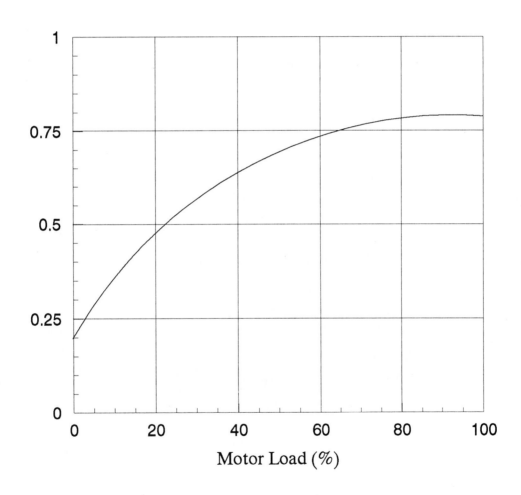

FIGURE 12.5 Capacitors as Sources for Magnetizing Current

Work Producing
Current

Current
Supplied
by Utility

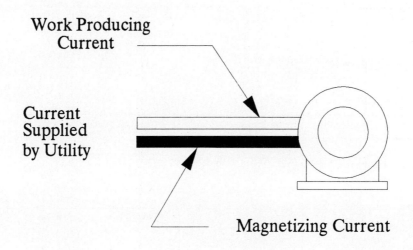

Magnetizing Current

Work Producing
Current

Current
Supplied
by Utility

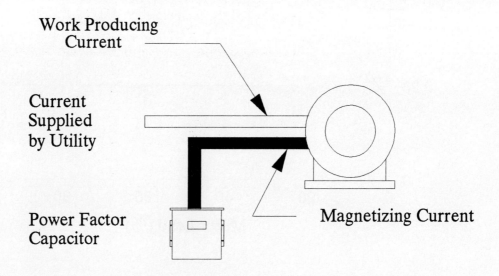

Power Factor
Capacitor

Magnetizing Current

FIGURE 12.6 Suggested Maximum Capacitor Ratings for High Efficiency and Older Design Motors (Pre T-Frame)

Induction Motor Horsepower	Capacitor Rating (kVar)					
	Motor Speed (rpm)					
	3,600	1,800	1,200	900	720	600
3.0	1.5	1.5	1.5	2.0	2.5	3..0
5.0	2.0	2.0	2.0	3.0	4.0	4.0
7.5	2.5	2.5	3.0	4.0	5.0	6.0
10.0	3.0	3.0	3.0	5.0	6.0	7.5
15.0	4.0	4.0	5.0	6.0	8.0	9.0
20.0	5.0	5.0	6.0	7.5	9.0	12.5
25	6.0	6.0	7.5	9.0	10.0	15.0
30	7.0	7.0	9.0	10.0	12.5	17.5
40	9.0	9.0	10.0	15.0	15.0	20.0
50	12.5	10.0	12.5	12.5	20.0	25.0
60	15.0	15.0	15.0	17.5	22.5	27.5
75	17.5	17.5	17.5	20.0	25.0	35.0
100	22.5	20.0	25.0	27.5	35.0	40.0
125	27.5	25.0	30.0	30.0	40.0	50.0
150	32.0	30.0	35.0	37.5	50.0	50.0
200	40.0	37.5	40.0	50.0	60.0	60.0
250	50.0	45.0	50.0	60.0	70.0	75.0
300	60.0	50.0	60.0	60.0	80.0	90.0
350	60.0	60.0	75.0	75.0	90.0	95.0
400	75.0	60.0	75.0	85.0	95.0	100.0
450	75.0	75.0	80.0	90.0	100.0	110.0
500	75.0	75.0	85.0	100.0	100.0	120.0

Courtesy of Vishay Sprague Company

FIGURE 12.7 Suggested Maximum Capacitor Ratings for T-Frame NEMA Design B Motors

Induction Motor Horsepower	Capacitor Rating (kVar)					
	Motor Speed (rpm)					
	3,600	1,800	1,200	900	720	600
2.0	1.0	1.0	1.5	2.0	2.0	3.0
3.0	1.5	1.5	2.0	3.0	3.0	4.0
5.0	2.0	2.5	3.0	4.0	4.0	5.0
7.5	2.5	3.0	4.0	5.0	5.0	6.0
10.0	4.0	4.0	5.0	6.0	7.5	8.0
15.0	5.0	5.0	6.0	7.5	8.0	10.0
20.0	6.0	6.0	7.5	9.0	10.0	12.5
25	7.5	7.5	8.0	10.0	12.5	17.5
30	8.0	8.0	10.0	15.0	15.0	20.0
40	12.5	15.0	15.0	17.5	20.0	25.0
50	15.0	17.5	20.0	22.5	22.5	30.0
60	17.5	20.0	22.5	25.0	30.0	35.0
75	20.0	25.0	25.0	30.0	35.0	40.0
100	22.5	30.0	30.0	35.0	40.0	45.0
125	25.0	35.0	35.0	40.0	45.0	50.0
150	30.0	40.0	40.0	50.0	50.0	60.0
200	35.0	50.0	50.0	70.0	70.0	90.0
250	40.0	60.0	60.0	80.0	90.0	100
300	45.0	70.0	75.0	100	100	120
350	50.0	75.0	90.0	120	120	135
400	75.0	80.0	100	130	140	150
450	80.0	90.0	120	140	160	160
500	100	120	150	160	180	180

Courtesy of Vishay Sprague Company

FIGURE 12.8 Multipliers to Determine Capacitor Kilovars Required for Power Factor Correction

Original Power factor	Corrected Power Factor														
	0.86	0.87	0.88	0.89	0.90	0.91	0.92	0.93	0.94	0.95	0.96	0.97	0.98	0.99	1.00
0.50	1.139	1.165	1.192	1.220	1.248	1.276	1.306	1.337	1.369	1.403	1.440	1.481	1.529	1.589	1.732
0.51	1.094	1.120	1.147	1.175	1.203	1.231	1.261	1.292	1.324	1.358	1.395	1.436	1.484	1.544	1.687
0.52	1.050	1.076	1.103	1.131	1.159	1.187	1.217	1.248	1.280	1.314	1.351	1.392	1.440	1.505	1.643
0.53	1.007	1.033	1.060	1.088	1.116	1.144	1.174	1.205	1.237	1.271	1.308	1.349	1.397	1.457	1.600
0.54	0.966	0.992	1.019	1.047	1.075	1.103	1.133	1.164	1.196	1.230	1.267	1.308	1.356	1.416	1.559
0.55	0.926	0.952	0.979	1.007	1.035	1.063	1.093	1.124	1.156	1.190	1.227	1.268	1.316	1.376	1.519
0.56	0.887	0.913	0.940	0.968	0.996	1.024	1.054	1.085	1.117	1.151	1.188	1.229	1.277	1.337	1.480
0.57	0.849	0.875	0.902	0.930	0.958	0.986	1.016	1.047	1.079	1.113	1.150	1.191	1.239	1.299	1.442
0.58	0.812	0.838	0.865	0.893	0.921	0.949	0.979	1.010	1.042	1.076	1.113	1.154	1.202	1.262	1.405
0.59	0.776	0.802	0.829	0.857	0.885	0.913	0.943	0.974	1.006	1.040	1.077	1.118	1.166	1.226	1.369
0.60	0.740	0.766	0.793	0.821	0.849	0.877	0.907	0.938	0.970	1.004	1.041	1.082	1.130	1.190	1.333
0.61	0.706	0.732	0.759	0.787	0.815	0.843	0.873	0.904	0.936	0.970	1.007	1.048	1.099	1.156	1.299
0.62	0.673	0.699	0.726	0.754	0.782	0.880	0.840	0.871	0.903	0.937	0.974	1.015	1.066	1.123	1.266
0.63	0.640	0.666	0.693	0.721	0.749	0.777	0.807	0.838	0.870	0.904	0.941	0.982	1.033	1.090	1.233
0.64	0.608	0.634	0.661	0.689	0.717	0.745	0.775	0.806	0.838	0.872	0.909	0.950	0.998	1.068	1.201
0.65	0.576	0.602	0.629	0.657	0.685	0.713	0.743	0.774	0.806	0.840	0.877	0.918	0.966	1.026	1.169
0.66	0.545	0.571	0.598	0.626	0.654	0.682	0.712	0.743	0.775	0.809	0.846	0.887	0.935	0.995	1.138
0.67	0.515	0.541	0.568	0.596	0.624	0.652	0.682	0.713	0.745	0.779	0.816	0.857	0.905	0.965	1.108
0.68	0.485	0.511	0.538	0.566	0.594	0.622	0.652	0.683	0.715	0.749	0.786	0.827	0.875	0.935	1.078
0.69	0.456	0.482	0.509	0.537	0.565	0.593	0.623	0.654	0.686	0.720	0.757	0.798	0.846	0.906	1.049
0.70	0.427	0.453	0.480	0.508	0.536	0.564	0.594	0.625	0.657	0.691	0.728	0.769	0.817	0.877	1.020
0.71	0.399	0.425	0.452	0.480	0.508	0.536	0.566	0.597	0.629	0.663	0.700	0.741	0.789	0.849	0.992
0.72	0.371	0.397	0.424	0.452	0.480	0.508	0.538	0.569	0.601	0.635	0.672	0.713	0.761	0.821	0.964
0.73	0.343	0.369	0.396	0.424	0.452	0.480	0.510	0.541	0.573	0.607	0.644	0.685	0.733	0.793	0.936
0.74	0.316	0.342	0.369	0.397	0.425	0.453	0.483	0.514	0.546	0.580	0.617	0.658	0.706	0.766	0.909
0.75	0.289	0.315	0.342	0.370	0.398	0.426	0.456	0.487	0.519	0.553	0.590	0.631	0.679	0.739	0.882
0.76	0.262	0.288	0.315	0.343	0.371	0.399	0.429	0.460	0.492	0.526	0.563	0.604	0.652	0.712	0.855
0.77	0.236	0.262	0.289	0.317	0.345	0.373	0.403	0.434	0.466	0.500	0.537	0.571	0.626	0.686	0.829
0.78	0.209	0.235	0.262	0.290	0.318	0.346	0.376	0.407	0.439	0.473	0.510	0.558	0.599	0.659	0.802
0.79	0.183	0.209	0.236	0.264	0.292	0.320	0.350	0.381	0.413	0.447	0.484	0.525	0.573	0.633	0.776
0.80	0.157	0.183	0.210	0.238	0.266	0.294	0.324	0.355	0.387	0.421	0.458	0.499	0.547	0.609	0.750
0.81	0.131	0.157	0.184	0.212	0.240	0.268	0.298	0.329	0.361	0.395	0.432	0.473	0.521	0.581	0.724
0.82	0.105	0.131	0.158	0.186	0.214	0.242	0.272	0.303	0.335	0.369	0.406	0.447	0.495	0.555	0.698
0.83	0.079	0.105	0.132	0.160	0.188	0.216	0.246	0.277	0.309	0.343	0.380	0.421	0.469	0.529	0.672
0.84	0.053	0.079	0.106	0.134	0.162	0.190	0.220	0.251	0.283	0.317	0.354	0.395	0.443	0.503	0.646
0.85	0.027	0.053	0.080	0.108	0.136	0.164	0.194	0.225	0.257	0.291	0.328	0.396	0.417	0.477	0.620
0.86	0.000	0.026	0.053	0.081	0.109	0.137	0.167	0.198	0.230	0.264	0.301	0.342	0.390	0.450	0.593
0.87		0.000	0.027	0.055	0.083	0.111	0.141	0.172	0.204	0.244	0.275	0.316	0.364	0.427	0.567
0.88			0.000	0.028	0.056	0.084	0.114	0.145	0.177	0.211	0.248	0.289	0.337	0.394	0.540
0.89				0.000	0.028	0.056	0.086	0.117	0.149	0.188	0.220	0.261	0.309	0.369	0.512
0.90					0.000	0.028	0.058	0.089	0.121	0.155	0.192	0.233	0.281	0.341	0.484
0.91						0.000	0.030	0.061	0.093	0.133	0.164	0.205	0.253	0.313	0.456
0.92							0.000	0.031	0.063	0.097	0.134	0.175	0.223	0.283	0.426
0.93								0.000	0.032	0.066	0.103	0.144	0.192	0.252	0.395
0.94									0.000	0.044	0.071	0.112	0.160	0.220	0.363
0.95										0.000	0.037	0.079	0.126	0.186	0.329
0.96											0.000	0.041	0.089	0.149	0.292
0.97												0.000	0.048	0.108	0.251
0.98													0.000	0.060	0.203
0.99														0.000	0.143

Courtesy of Vishay Sprague Company

FIGURE 12.9 Recommended Wire Sizes, Switches, and Fuses for Three-Phase, 60 Hz Capacitors

KVAR	240 Volts Current (amps)	240 Volts Wire Size Type THW, THWN, XHHW	240 Volts Fuse (amps)	240 Volts Switch (amps)	480 Volts Current (amps)	480 Volts Wire Size Type THW, THWN, XHHW	480 Volts Fuse (amps)	480 Volts Switch (amps)	600 Volts Current (amps)	600 Volts Wire Size Type THW, THWN, XHHW	600 Volts Fuse (amps)	600 Volts Switch (amps)
0.5	1.20	14	3	30	-	-	-	-	-	-	-	-
1.0	2.41	14	6	30	1.20	14	3	30	0.96	14	3	30
1.5	3.61	14	6	30	1.80	14	3	30	1.44	14	3	30
2.0	4.81	14	10	30	2.41	14	6	30	1.92	14	6	30
2.5	60.1	14	10	30	3.00	14	6	30	2.41	14	6	30
3.0	7.22	14	15	30	3.61	14	6	30	2.89	14	6	30
4.0	9.62	12	20	30	4.81	14	10	30	3.85	14	10	30
5.0	12.0	12	20	30	6.02	14	10	30	4.81	14	10	30
6.0	14.4	10	25	30	7.22	14	15	30	5.77	14	10	30
7.5	18.0	10	30	30	9.02	14	15	30	7.22	14	15	30
8.0	19.2	8	35	60	9.62	12	20	30	7.69	14	15	30
10	24.1	8	40	60	12.0	12	20	30	9.62	12	20	30
12.5	30.0	8	50	60	15.0	10	25	30	12.0	12	20	30
15	36.1	6	60	60	18.0	10	30	30	14.4	10	25	30
17.5	42.2	6	80	100	21.0	8	40	60	16.8	10	30	30
20	48.1	4	80	100	24.1	8	40	60	19.2	8	35	60
22.5	54.2	4	100	100	27.1	8	50	60	21.6	8	40	60
25	60.2	4	100	100	30.1	8	50	60	24.1	8	40	60
30	72.2	2	125	200	36.1	6	60	60	28.9	8	50	60
35	84.4	1/0	150	200	42.4	6	80	100	33.6	8	60	60
40	96.2	1/0	175	200	48.1	4	80	100	38.5	6	35	100
45	108	1/0	200	200	54.1	4	100	100	43.3	6	40	100
50	120	2/0	200	200	60	4	100	100	48	4	100	100
60	144	3/0	250	400	72	2	125	200	58	4	100	100
75	180	250M	300	400	90	1/0	150	200	72	2	125	200
80	192	250M	350	400	96	1/0	175	200	77	2	150	200
90	216	350M	400	400	108	1/0	200	200	86	1/0	150	200
100	241	350M	400	400	120	2/0	200	200	96	10/	175	200
120	289	(2) 3/0	500	600	144	3/0	250	400	115	2/0	200	200
125	300	(2) 3/0	500	600	150	4/0	250	400	120	2/0	200	200
150	361	(2) 250M	600	600	180	250M	300	400	144	3/0	250	400
180					216	350M	400	400	173	4/0	300	400
200					241	350M	400	400	192	250M	350	400
240					289	(2) 3/0	500	600	231	350M	400	400
250					300	(2) 3/0	500	600	241	350M	400	400

Courtesy of Vishay Sprague Company

How to Use Standby Generators to Improve the Reliability of Your Electrical System

This chapter examines standby electrical generators commonly found in facilities. Material presented in this chapter can be used to establish preventive and scheduled maintenance programs for generators to insure that they operate when needed. An additional section provides information to estimate the economic benefits of using standby generators to reduce peak electrical loads during periods of high electrical demand.

THE NEED FOR STANDBY POWER

Buildings and operations have become so dependent on electricity that nearly every facility has a need for standby electrical power even though most electrical utility companies operate with a reliability in excess of 99.9%. Although code requirements often mandate the installation of standby power systems, there frequently is a need for standby power based on how the facility is used. Utility system failures are not the only cause for power outages; failures in the facility's primary and distribution systems can be the cause as well.

In smaller facilities where the primary purpose of a standby system is to provide sufficient illumination for safe egress, most standby power requirements can be met through the use of battery-powered lights and exit signs. In facilities where particular loads cannot tolerate even a momentary interruption of electrical power, uninterruptable power supplies (UPS) are installed. However, most facilities fall between these extremes. The power requirement is greater than can be met through batteries alone, but a UPS system is not required and cannot be justified. In these facilities, the standby emergency generator is the best option.

WHY GENERATORS ARE INSTALLED

Before you can establish a maintenance program for your standby electrical generator, it is important to understand the reasons why it was installed in the first place. The purposes that the generator serves will to a great extent determine the level of maintenance efforts that you should expend. For example, most standby generator manufacturers recommend that their equipment be test run at least once a month. If the generator serves critical loads, it will be necessary to test run the unit once a week or once every two weeks.

Understanding why the emergency generator is installed is also critical to the timing of the test run periods. Transferring from utility power to standby power even on a test basis results in a momentary interruption in electrical supply to the connected loads. Even such momentary interruptions can cause HVAC systems to trip off-line, chillers to shut down, and computers to crash. In these applications it will be necessary to schedule the timing of the test so as to minimize the disruption to the facility's operation.

One of the main reasons why standby power systems are installed in facilities is to provide emergency lighting for safe egress in the event of a failure of the utility supply. Exit lights, stairway lighting, and a portion of the corridor lighting systems are typically connected to a standby generator.

Fire and safety equipment often is connected to the standby power system to assist in emergency operations. Fire pumps, communications systems, fire detection and alarm systems, and security systems remain operational in the event of a disruption of the normal electrical supply.

Critical pieces of mechanical equipment, such as building sump pumps, are connected to the standby system to protect the facility from damage if the equipment were out of service during an electrical outage.

Standby power systems are frequently used to permit operation of at least a portion of the facility during a power outage. Typical facilities include manufacturing plants, communication centers, and public safety centers.

Standby power systems, when connected to UPS systems, permit operation of critical electrical loads during lengthy outages. Most UPS systems use batteries to supply power during outages, but only for a short period of time such as from 15 minutes to less than two hours. The cost of larger battery systems is generally greater than that of a standby electrical generator.

Finally, with the widespread use of time-of-day billing and peak demand charges by utility companies, standby generators have been used successfully as a means of reducing peak demand charges. An estimation of the economics of peak shaving using standby generators is presented later in this chapter.

FOUR TYPES OF STANDBY GENERATORS

Standby generators are typically classified according to the type of engine used to drive the generator. There are four major types used in facilities: gasoline, Diesel, gaseous fuel, and gas turbine. Selection of the type for a particular application depends on a number of factors including the following:

- ➤ the size of the connected load
- ➤ the expected hours of operation per year
- ➤ fuel availability
- ➤ the impact that generator noise will have on the operation

Gasoline Generators

Gasoline-driven standby generators offer the lowest initial cost per kW capacity. In most applications, they are economical for connected loads of 100 kW or less. The engines are easy starting and quickly come up to operating speed.

The two most significant problems with gasoline-driven units are their relatively short operating life and fuel storage. Gasoline is highly explosive and requires precautions for safe storage. Additionally, gasoline deteriorates with age and can cause problems in both starting and running the engine.

Diesel Generators

Diesel engine driven generators are more expensive to purchase than gasoline generators of the same capacity. In general, they are economical in capacities ranging from 25 to 2,000 kW. They offer the advantages of economical operation, low maintenance, and reliability.

Diesel fuel does not present the same storage problems associated with gasoline. It is not explosive and its rate of deterioration is much slower. One drawback is the need to protect it from contamination with water. Water, if drawn into the injection system, can damage the fuel injectors and the injection pump. Additionally, if there is water present in the Diesel fuel and the ambient temperature drops below 20°F, the fuel and water react to form a jell that can plug the entire fuel system.

One additional problem experienced in Diesel fuel systems is the growth of bacteria. Unless the generator is used on a regular basis, the Diesel fuel tends to remain in the storage tank for a lengthy period of time. During this time, bacteria can enter the system and feed on the nitrogen, sulfur oxides, and iron oxides found in the fuel. If there is sufficient growth, the bacteria will result in blocked fuel filters and fouled injectors. This can be controlled through the use of biocides. Systems, particularly those that are used infrequently and do not turn over the fuel supply, should be periodically tested for bacterial growth and treated as required.

Diesel engine-driven generators are slower in coming up to operating speed than gasoline units. If installed in areas where the ambient temperature falls below 40°F, the units typically require the use of crankcase heaters to ease starting.

Gaseous Fuel Generators

Gaseous fuel-driven generators are comparable to Diesel units. Most are fueled by either natural gas or propane. A few special applications, such as waste treatment plants or landfills, power the generators wholly or partially with methane gas, a byproduct of their operation.

Gaseous fuel-based generators are more expensive than Diesel units for large capacity units. They offer reliable service with low maintenance and a long service life. Fuel storage problems are minimal, although an alternative fuel may be required by building codes for particular applications in the event of a disruption of service, particularly when powered by natural gas.

Gas Turbine Generators

Gas turbine generators have the highest initial cost of the four major generator types in small to medium load applications. This high initial cost restricts their application to large loads, typically 500 kW and larger. Units are available that can burn a variety of liquid or gaseous fuels.

In spite of their higher initial cost, gas turbine generators offer several major advantages in standby generator applications. They are small in size, lighter in weight, and more vibration free than any other generator type. They provide the longest service life and lowest maintenance requirements between major overhauls of the different generator types.

The major disadvantages of gas turbine generators relate to the operation of the turbine itself. The turbine operates at a relatively high speed and is slow starting. The high speed also results in large volumes of exhaust gas that must be safely ducted away from the facility. Gas turbines also are noisy and typically require sound isolation from the remainder of the facility.

WHY GENERATORS REQUIRE MAINTENANCE

One of the problems with standby generators is that they must be 100% reliable; yet they typically sit idle for more than 99% of the time. It is not uncommon to find that a standby generator was required to operate for one hour or less in a given year. Compounding the problem is the fact that the failure of a single component in the standby system can render the entire system inoperative.

Since the purpose of standby generator systems is to provide power immediately upon the failure of utility power, the entire system must be reliable. Reliability requires that each component be serviced and kept in operating condition at all times. Working against this required reliability is the length of time that the system remains inactive. Inactivity results in deterioration of the fuel, lubricants, coolants, and battery electrolytes, and the absorption of moisture, a major cause of damage to electrical windings and contacts.

To insure that the systems perform as required when required, a maintenance program must be established that accomplishes two primary tasks: testing of the entire system and components, and regularly scheduled maintenance of system components.

HOW TO TEST STANDBY GENERATORS

Without regularly scheduled test running, there is no way to know that the generator will perform when needed. Even something as simple as a dead starting battery can render the entire system inoperative. Regular test runs of the generator will detect problems so that corrective action can be taken before the generator is needed in an emergency situation.

Two Types of Scheduled Generator Tests

There are two types of scheduled test runs that should be performed on standby generators: a standard-load test run and a full-load, stress test run. Some facilities test run the generator under no-load conditions. However, such test runs only fully test the generator's starter and battery and give no assurance that the system will perform properly when loaded. Its speed and voltage regulator systems, load transfer switch, and fuel systems are only partially tested when the generator is operated under no-load conditions.

STANDARD-LOAD TEST. The standard-load test consists of the following:

➤ simulating a power failure

➤ permitting the generator to sense the failure, start, and reach operating speed and voltage

➤ transferring and carrying the connected load

Run the unit long enough to reach normal operating temperature, typically 30 to 60 minutes. The frequency of the standard-load test depends on the critical nature of the loads connected to the system. Facilities such as hospitals might require testing once a week while office facilities might require only monthly testing.

Operating the system under load until normal operating temperatures are reached is important in order to evaluate the condition of the cooling system, but it is particularly important for Diesel units. The piston rings in Diesel engines don't fully expand and provide a proper seal until they reach normal operating temperatures. Until they seal, they allow crankcase oil to leak past into the combustion chamber where it forms deposits and fouls the injectors. While the engine will appear to operate properly under light loads, the power output will be greatly reduced. This condition, commonly called "wet stacking," severely reduces engine power output, possibly making full-load operation impossible.

FULL-LOAD TEST. In addition to the standard-load test, standby generators should be full-load tested once a year. Most standby generators are oversized for the application and therefore never reach full-load capabilities during standard-load testing. Full-load testing stresses the entire generator system and can provide early warning of defects and problems. For example, a restricted radiator may adequately cool the generator during the regularly scheduled test run when the unit is not fully loaded and is operated for only a short period of time. However, the restriction might be sufficient to cause overheating should there be an extended power outage. The annual full-load test would detect the restriction.

The full-load test typically requires loading the generator to its rated capacity for a several hour period. In most cases, the electrical load consists of resistor banks connected in place of the building load. The unit should be operated long enough to allow the generator and the room in which it is located to stabilize in temperature.

GENERATOR PERIODIC MAINTENANCE REQUIREMENTS. In addition to scheduled load testing of the generator, periodic maintenance must be performed on the generator and its support components. Figure 13.1 lists typical maintenance activities that are performed on standby generators. The most convenient time to perform these activities is while the generator is being test run. Some activities will be performed prior to starting the unit, others while the unit is running. Still others must be performed after the unit has been stopped. On the average it will take one hour to perform the required maintenance on a typical generator system.

A log of maintenance activities performed during each load testing will help determine long-term trends in the performance of the generator. Use Figure 13.2 to log generator maintenance activities.

Generators require that additional maintenance activities be performed on a regular basis, generally monthly or annually. Figure 13.3 lists generator maintenance activities that are required in addition to those performed during the weekly test run.

STANDBY GENERATORS AND PEAK LOAD SHAVING

During the past ten years, electric utility companies have moved to a rate structure that uses time-of-day rates and peak demand charges. In large facilities, where electricity use closely matches the building occupancy, monthly peak demand charges can exceed monthly use charges. Since the peak demand charge is based on the period of highest electrical use during a given month, reducing the electrical load during this period can produce significant savings. Figure 13.4 shows a peak demand curve for a typical office building. Even though the peak demand occurred for only a short period of time, the monthly billing for peak demand is based on that peak. For a detailed discussion of peak demand charges see Chapter 14.

A number of facilities have successfully used their standby generators to reduce their electrical demand during periods of peak electrical use. When used properly, the savings in demand charges more than offset the fuel costs, maintenance costs, and depreciation of the standby generator systems.

Requirements for Peak Load Shaving

There are three requirements in order to successfully use standby generators to reduce the facility's peak electrical demand:

➤ an accurate means of monitoring the facility's electrical demand

➤ a means of remotely starting the standby generator and transferring the loads to the generator

➤ sufficient loads connected to the generator to make an impact on the facility's electrical demand

While the standby generator is operating, it will also reduce the facility's electrical use. While these savings are significant, they are not sufficient to justify generating electrical power on-site because the efficiency of a standby generator is lower than that of the generators used by utility companies.

Use Worksheet 13.1 to estimate the savings that can be produced by using standby generators to reduce the facility's peak load. The worksheet estimates both the reduction in demand charges and the savings in electrical energy use. In order to use the worksheet, you will need a copy of the rate structure in effect for your facility and also the manufacturer's data on the generator system. Use the worksheet as follows:

Step 1.	The rate structure indicates peak demand rates ($/kW) in effect for the facility. Typically there will be two peak rates, one for summer months and one for winter months. The rate structure will also indicate energy use rates ($/kWh) for peak billing periods during summer and winter months. Enter in section #1 of the worksheet the peak summer demand rate ($/kW), the peak summer energy use rate ($/kWh), the peak winter demand rate ($/kW), the peak winter energy use rate ($/kWh), the number of months that the summer rates are in effect, and the number of months that the winter rates are in effect.
Step 2.	Determine the electrical load in kW that is connected to the generator and enter the value in section #1 of the worksheet.
Step 3.	From the manufacturer's data sheets, determine the fuel burn rate for the generator when operating at the electrical load determined above. For gasoline or Diesel units, use gallons per hour. For natural gas units, use thousands of cubic feet per hour. Enter the value in section #1 of the worksheet.
Step 4.	In order to determine the maintenance costs associated with running the generator, it will be necessary to determine the maintenance run cost in $/kWh. Most manufacturers can provide this data. If the information is unavailable use the default value of $0.02/kWh. Enter the value in section #1 of the worksheet. *Note:* these are maintenance costs only and do not include depreciation or fuel costs.
Step 5.	The number of hours that the generator will operate during a typical month will depend on the ability to sense demand levels, and how long use remains at peak levels. In a typical non-manufacturing operation, the peak demand period will be approached fewer than 20 hours per month. Unless a detailed analysis of the facility's electrical energy use is performed, use 20 hours as the default value. Enter the value in section #1 of the worksheet.
Step 6.	Enter the summer demand rate, the generator loading, and the number of months in the summer rate schedule from section #1 into section #2 of the worksheet.
Step 7.	Enter the winter demand rate, the generator loading, and the number of months in the winter rate schedule from section #1 into section #2 of the worksheet.
Step 8.	Multiply the summer demand rate by the generator loading and the number of months in the summer rate schedule. Multiply the winter demand rate by the generator loading and the number of months in the winter rate schedule. Add the two numbers to determine the electrical demand savings and enter the value in section #2 of the worksheet.

Step 9.　　From section #1 of the worksheet, determine the generator loading, the hours of operation per month, the summer energy use rate, the number of months in the summer rate schedule, the winter energy use rate, and the number of months in the winter rate schedule.

Step 10.　　Multiply the summer energy use rate by the number of months in the summer rate schedule. Multiply the winter energy use rate by the number of months in the winter rate schedule. Add the two values and multiply by the generator loading and the hours of operation per month to determine the annual energy use savings. Enter the value in section #3 of the worksheet.

Step 11.　　From section #1, determine the generator fuel burn rate, the hours of operation per month, and the fuel cost in $/gallon or $/mcf. Enter the values in section #4 of the worksheet.

Step 12.　　Multiply the generator fuel burn rate, the hours of operation per month, and the fuel cost by the conversion factor of 12 to determine the annual fuel cost. Enter the value in section #4 of the worksheet.

Step 13.　　From section #1, determine the generator run cost, the generator loading, and the hours of operation per month. Enter the values in section #5 of the worksheet.

Step 14.　　Multiply the generator run cost by the generator loading, the hours of operation per month, and the conversion factor of 12 to determine the annual maintenance cost. Enter the value in section #5 of the worksheet.

Step 15.　　From section #2, determine the annual demand savings. From section #3, determine the annual energy savings. From section #4 determine the annual fuel cost. From section #5 determine the annual maintenance cost. Enter the values in section #6 of the worksheet.

Step 16.　　Subtract the fuel cost and the maintenance cost from the demand savings added to the energy savings to determine the annual savings. Enter the value in section #6 of the worksheet.

The annual savings produced by using the generator to reduce peak electrical loads will be offset somewhat by increased wear and tear on the generator. However, most generators fail due to neglect and inoperation, not overuse. Leaving a generator idle for long periods of time is more damaging than using it regularly.

FIGURE 13.1 Weekly Generator Maintenance Tasks

Before Test Run

Inspect system for debris and missing guards
Inspect for fuel, oil, and water leaks
Check all belts for tension and condition
Check engine oil level
Check engine coolant level
Check air filter
Check operation of engine block heaters
Check battery specific gravity
Check battery electrolyte level
Check fuel level
Drain water from Diesel fuel filters

During Test Run

Measure engine cranking time
Check for noise and vibration
Check oil pressure
Check fuel pressure
Check generator frequency and voltage
Inspect exhaust system for leaks
Check operation of radiator louvers
Check engine operating temperature

After Test Run

Inspect for heat damage to areas around the exhaust system
Drain the exhaust system condensate trap
Check battery charge rate
Reset start switch to automatic position
Check fuel level

FIGURE 13.2 Generator Maintenance Log

Manufacturer: _____

Serial #: _____

Location: _____

Generator Capacity (kVa): _____

Date	Crank Time (sec)	Oil Pressure	Water Temp	Voltage	Freq.	Amps	Run Time (min)	Notes

FIGURE 13.3 Periodic Generator Maintenance Activities

Monthly

Clean battery connections
Inspect drive belts for wear and tightness
Inspect starter connections
Inspect battery charger connections
Inspect coolant lines
Test coolant strength
Inspect condition of flexible coolant hoses
Test fuel for contamination

Annually

Inspect and tighten wiring
Test safety switches and relays
Inspect transfer switch contacts
Inspect generator brushes
Clean slip rings
Inspect fuel system
Inspect cooling system
Clean radiator exterior
Change air filter
Replace fuel filter
Adjust engine valves
Change engine oil
Perform extended operation, full-load test

FIGURE 13.4 Typical Facility Electrical Demand Plot

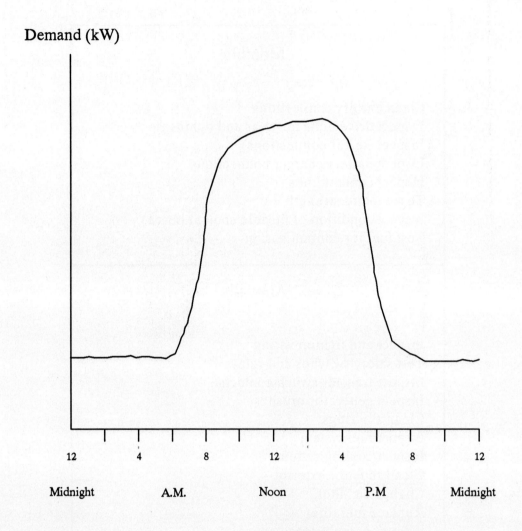

Demand (kW)

12   4   8   12   4   8   12

Midnight   A.M.   Noon   P.M   Midnight

WORKSHEET 13.1 Estimating Generator Peak Shaving Savings

1. System Parameters

Summer peak demand rate ($/kW):_____   # of months at the winter rate:_____

Summer energy use rate ($/kWh):_____   Generator loading (kW):_____

Winter peak demand rate ($/kW):_____   Hours of operation per month:_____

Winter energy use rate ($/kWh):_____   Generator burn rate (gal/hr):_____

# of months at the summer rates:_____   Generator run cost ($/kWh):_____

2. Demand Charge Savings

$$\left[\boxed{} \times \boxed{} \times \boxed{} \right] + \left[\boxed{} \times \boxed{} \times \boxed{} \right] = \boxed{}$$

Summer De-mand Rate ($/kW)	Generator Loading (kW)	# of Summer Months		Winter De-mand Rate ($/kW)	Generator Loading (kW)	# of Winter Months		Demand Savings ($)

3. Energy Use Savings

$$\boxed{} \times \boxed{} \times \left[\boxed{} \times \boxed{} + \boxed{} \times \boxed{} \right] = \boxed{}$$

Generator Loading (kW)	Hours of Operation per Month		Summer Use Rate ($/kWh)	# of Summer Months	Winter Use Rate ($/kWh)	# of Winter Months		Energy Use Savings ($)

4. Fuel Cost

$$\boxed{} \times \boxed{} \times \boxed{} \times \boxed{12} = \boxed{}$$

Generator Burn Rate	Hours of Operation per Month	Fuel Cost			Fuel Cost ($/yr)

Worksheet 13.1 (continued)

5. Maintenance Cost

☐	X	☐	X	☐	X

☐ X ☐ X ☐ X 12 = ☐

Generator Run Cost ($/kWh)   Generator Loading (kW)   Hours of Operation per Month   Annual Maintenance Cost ($)

6. Annual Savings

☐ + ☐ - ☐ - ☐ = ☐

Demand Savings ($)   Energy Use Savings ($)   Fuel Cost ($)   Annual Maintenance Cost ($)   Annual Savings ($)

Chapter 14

UNDERSTANDING THE ELEMENTS OF YOUR POWER BILL TO HELP CONTROL OPERATING COSTS

This chapter examines electrical rate structures commonly used in facilities and measures that can be used to limit their impact on the facility's operation. Material presented in this chapter can be used to determine the cost to the facility for a kWh of electricity, the benefits of owning the electrical substation serving the facility, and the economics of controlling electrical demand.

ELECTRICAL RATE STRUCTURES

In 1978, Congress passed the National Energy Act. A portion of that bill, the Public Utility Regulatory Policies Act (PURPA), was designed to encourage state regulatory policies for electric utilities that would, in turn, promote energy conservation, encourage efficient utility operation, and establish equitable rates for residential, commercial, and industrial consumers. Six rate-making standards were included in the Act. While their implementation was not mandatory, the Act did mandate that the utility regulatory bodies consider each. One of the rate-making standards was time-of-day rates.

Time-of-Day Rates

Prior to the implementation of time-of-day rates, electricity users paid a set rate for electricity use. While the rate varied with volume of use, such as four cents for the first 10,000 kWh and 3.5 cents for the next 50,000 kWh, the rates were fixed with respect to time of day and season of year. The utilities also included a fuel charge and a demand charge. The fuel charge was the mechanism for passing on increases in fuel costs to their customers. The demand charge was an attempt to pass on the cost of running additional generating facilities during peak demand times.

Time-of-day rates do away with the set rate concept in electricity pricing. The basis for these rates is that the demand for electricity and the costs incurred by the utilities are not constant. Both vary with the time of day, the day of the week, and the season of the year. During an operating day, the utility can base load its operation with its most efficient and lowest cost generating facilities. As the demand increases, it must bring facilities on line that have higher operating costs, raising the incremental cost of electricity. How high that incremental cost goes depends on how many additional units must be brought on line to meet the demand.

The driving force behind the incremental cost of electricity is the demand placed on the generating facilities. Over a year, that demand varies with season, typically peaking during the hottest months when air conditioning use peaks. If electrical heating systems are common in the region, a second seasonal peak may occur during the coldest months.

Demand varies not only with season, but also with the day of the week and the time of the day. Saturday and Sunday as well as holidays tend to be low peak demand days. Use tends to peak between the hours of 10:00 A.M. and 4:00 P.M. These variations in the demand for electricity produce the variations in the cost of generation that the time-of-day rates are designed to pass on to the utility's largest users, the ones that generate the largest portion of the varying demand rate.

Passing on the high cost of generation during peak intervals was only one objective of the PURPA legislation. Another was to reduce the need for peaking stations by lowering the demand peaks. Peaking stations have two major drawbacks. First, since they are for the most part oil- or gas-fired, they tend to be expensive to run in terms of cost per kWh produced. Second, since the plants operate for only a fraction of the year, the rate of return on the utility's investment is either small or nonexistent. Therefore, the PURPA legislation sought to flatten out the daily, weekly, and seasonal variations in the demand curve to reduce the need for construction of peaking plants.

Flattening the demand peaks could only be accomplished by the users of the electricity. Therefore, the legislation directed the state regulatory bodies to consider time-of-day rates that would charge customers a higher rate during peak hours, and would charge the customers who contribute the most to those peaks an even higher rate.

TIME-OF-DAY RATE STRUCTURES. The major components of a time-of-day rate structure include eligibility, monthly charge schedule, season designation, and rating periods. Figure 14.1 shows a typical rate structure that is based on time-of-day rates. The particular rate structure that applies to your facility will be somewhat different since it was developed by the state regulatory body having jurisdiction in your area. However, the concept will be the same. To determine what your charges would be under the time-of-day rate schedule, contact your local utility company and ask for a copy of the rate schedule that is applicable to your facilities.

Figure 14.1 presents a number of charges that appear on each month's bill as calculated under a typical time-of-day rate structure.

THE MINIMUM CHARGE. The minimum charge is the base cost for connecting to the utility system. If for some reason the facility did not use any electricity in a particular month, it would still be charged this fee.

THE ENERGY CHARGE. The energy charge is divided into three periods: the on-peak period, the intermediate period, and the off-peak period. Each period is divided into two seasons, summer and winter. The charge for each kilowatt hour of electricity used varies with both the season and the period. For this example, the cost ranges from a low of 0.444 cents per kilowatt hour during the winter off-peak period, to a high of 2.962 cents per kilowatt hour during the summer on-peak period.

The billing periods under this rate schedule are defined as follows. The on-peak period lasts from noon until 8:00 P.M. on weekdays. The intermediate period is split into two sections, 8:00 A.M. to noon, and 8:00 P.M. until midnight on weekdays. The off-peak period is from midnight to 8:00 A.M. on weekdays as well as all day Saturday, Sunday and holidays.

The summer period under this time-of-day rate structure is defined to include the months of June through October. Winter rates apply to all other months.

THE PRODUCTION CHARGE. A third charge under the time-of-day schedule is the Production Charge. The Production Charge is based on the maximum 15- or 30-minute demand experienced by the user during the on-peak period for that month. Unlike other charges, it is calculated only during the summer billing period. In this example rate structure, the Production Charge is $9.40 per kilowatt of demand.

THE DISTRIBUTION CHARGE. Another portion of the monthly charge schedule is the Distribution Charge. The Distribution Charge is similar to the demand charge found in other non-time-of-day rate schedules. It is based on the maximum 15- or 30-minute demand experienced during the month. It may occur during the on-peak, off-peak, or intermediate peak periods. It applies to both the summer and winter rating periods. In this rate structure example, the Distribution Charge is $3.85 per kilowatt of demand.

Figure 14.2 presents a sample bill calculated under the time-of-day rate schedule for the month of July. The total use for the facility was 8.8 million kilowatt hours: 2.5 million during the on-peak period, 2.3 million during the intermediate period, and 4.0 million during the off-peak period. The peak demand for the month was 12,000 kilowatts, and it occurred during the on-peak billing period. Using the rates of the example rate structure, the monthly bill would be $321,434 excluding fuel and other surcharges. In this example, the demand charges equal approximately 49% of the total monthly charge.

HOW TO CALCULATE THE UNIT COST FOR ELECTRICITY

The traditional method used to calculate the cost of electricity is to divide the total bill by the number of kilowatt hours of electricity used to determine the unit cost in cents per kWh. While this method provides an index of the average unit cost, it does not reflect the true cost of electricity because it does not consider time-of-day rates and demand charges.

For example, consider the sample bill shown in Figure 14.2. The facility used a total of 8,800,000 kWh of electricity for the month. The total cost of electric service for the month was $321,434. Dividing the cost by the kWh use results in an average unit cost of 3.653 cents per kWh. But average cost does not reflect the actual cost due to the time-of-day rates and demand charges. There are three different unit costs for electricity under this billing schedule: one for on-peak period use, a second for intermediate period use, and a third for off-peak period use.

The true electrical cost to operate a piece of equipment under a time-of-day billing structure depends on when that equipment was operated. If electricity cost calculations are being made or if tenants in a facility are being billed for electricity use at the average unit cost for electricity, those with a high on-peak load are being subsidized by those whose loads are relatively flat throughout the day. A more accurate way to determine true electrical costs would be to install time-of-day metering with peak demand indicators, and to calculate costs at the same rates used in the utility company rate schedule.

On-peak costs may be estimated by using the on-peak period rate plus a portion of the demand component of the bill. Under the rate structure shown in Figure 14.2, the on-peak period unit cost for electricity would be 2.962 cents per kWh for use plus the demand charge component. The demand charge component can be calculated by dividing the sum of the production and distribution charges, $159,000 by the kilowatt hour use of 2,500,000. The resulting demand component of 6.36 cents per kWh should be added to the on-peak period rate. In this example, the unit cost for electricity during on-peak use would be 10.01 cents per kWh.

DETERMINING THE ECONOMICS OF SUBSTATION OWNERSHIP

Electrical utility companies distribute power at voltages higher than can be used directly by their customers. Distributing power at these higher voltages decreases distribution losses, decreases first costs, and increases system reliability for the utility companies. The disadvantage is that equipment must be installed at the customer's site to reduce the voltage to the needs of the facility, equipment that requires an investment on the part of the utility company as well as on-going maintenance. These costs are passed on to the customer through the rate structure.

In order to reduce their capital investment and maintenance costs, utility companies are willing to offer incentives to customers to install, operate, and maintain their own primary electrical substations. In most cases, these incentives come in the form of a rider attached to the rate structure that reduces the total bill, excluding fuel charge, by a specified percentage. The reduction is sufficient to provide a return on investment in two to five years.

Qualifying for Rate Reductions

To qualify for the rate reduction, the customer must do the following:

➤ accept service at a minimum voltage, typically 13 kV or greater
➤ provide the primary power transformers, switchgear, disconnects, regulators, and protective equipment

➤ assume responsibility for maintenance of the equipment

Typical substation maintenance includes two major areas: transformer maintenance and routine maintenance.

Transformer Maintenance

Transformer maintenance consists of annual or biannual testing of the transformer windings and oil, and cleaning of the bushings. Periodically, transformer oil will need reprocessing. Air-cooled transformers have additional maintenance requirements in the testing of the operation of the cooling fans and their controls.

Routine Maintenance

Routine substation maintenance includes painting of equipment enclosures and steel structures, inspection and cleaning of disconnects, and annual or biannual testing of all circuit breakers and protective relays. Rule of thumb: The total annual maintenance costs for a substation range from one to two percent of the initial equipment investment.

In evaluating the economics of substation ownership several factors need to be considered. The installation of a new electrical substation or the purchase of an existing substation from the utility company is an expensive proposition. For new facilities, the cost of getting the power from the utility company lines to the substation and from the substation to the facility must be factored into the initial costs. Annual maintenance costs and the maintenance capabilities of the organization must be evaluated. If in-house personnel cannot perform the required maintenance tasks, substation maintenance can be contracted out to companies that specialize in substation maintenance and testing.

The most important factor to consider is the discount rate that is being offered by the utility. For service supplied at 13 kV, the discount rate is typically five percent. At 69 kV, the discount rate is generally 10%. The actual rate will vary from utility company to company, so it is important to contact the utility before investing significant time in investigating the feasibility of substation ownership. Use Worksheet 14.1 to estimate the annual savings achieved by substation ownership. Use the worksheet as follows:

Step 1.   The only portion of the electrical bill that will not be impacted by substation ownership is the monthly fuel charge. Therefore, it must be subtracted out of the monthly electrical bill. Sum the remaining charges for a twelve-month period and enter the value in section #1 of the worksheet.

Step 2.   The utility company offers a discount rate for customers who own and maintain their own substations. For service voltages of 13 kV, the discount rate is usually five percent. For service voltages of 69 kV, the discount rate is usually ten percent. Use these default values or contact your local utility to determine the actual discount rate. Enter the value as a decimal number (0 - 1.0) in section #1 of the worksheet.

Step 3.   Estimate the cost of the substation that is to be installed or purchased from the utility company. Enter the value in section #1 of the worksheet.

Step 4.   From section #1, enter the annual electrical cost and the discount rate in section #2 of the worksheet.

Step 5.   Multiply the annual electrical cost by the discount rate to determine the annual electricity cost savings. Enter the value in section #2 of the worksheet.

Step 6.   If the substation maintenance is to be contracted out, determine the annual contract price and enter the value in section #3 of the worksheet. Skip to step #8. If the contract price for the substation maintenance is not known, it can be estimated from the value of the substation. From section #1, enter the substation cost in section #3 of the worksheet.

Step 7.   Multiply the substation cost by the number 0.02 to determine the annual maintenance cost. Enter the value in section #3 of the worksheet.

Step 8.   From section #2, enter the annual electricity savings in section #4 of the worksheet.

Step 9.   From section #3, enter the annual maintenance cost in section #4 of the worksheet.

Step 10.   Subtract the annual maintenance cost from the annual electricity savings to determine the annual savings for substation ownership. Enter the value in section #4 of the worksheet.

This value represents the annual savings through reduced electrical rates that would result from owning and maintaining your own electrical substation.

THREE METHODS FOR ELECTRICAL DEMAND CONTROL

In the rate example used earlier in this chapter, approximately 49% of the $321,434 monthly electricity bill was for demand charges. In non-manufacturing facilities, summer demand charges typically run between $1/3$ and $1/2$ of the total monthly electrical bill. Since the demand charge is based on the single highest peak rate of use for the month that may have occurred for no more than 30 minutes, it represents a stiff penalty for the customer for a one-time use.

Electrical demand charges can be reduced through the implementation of a demand control program. The goal of the program is to reduce the facility's peak demand charge without disrupting operations. This reduction is accomplished through the shedding of electrical loads. In most cases, the load is turned off for only a short period of time, typically 10 or 15 minutes.

Types of Electrical Loads

Electrical loads in all facilities can be divided into two categories: critical and non-critical. Critical loads are those that are essential to the operation of the facility and cannot be turned off. In manufacturing and industrial facilities, critical loads might include certain production and process equipment. In commercial and institutional facilities, critical loads typically include elevators, escalators, certain lighting systems, and specific HVAC systems.

Non-critical loads include those pieces of equipment that would not disrupt the operation of the facility or compromise safety if they were turned off for a short period of time. Air conditioners, chillers, fan systems, electric water heaters, and certain lighting systems can be considered to be non-critical loads depending on the functions and areas that they support.

Shedding Non-Critical Loads

Non-critical loads may be shed either manually or automatically. In practice, only the automatic systems can provide an effective means of controlling electrical demand because they continually monitor the facility's level of demand. As that demand approaches a predetermined level, loads are shed until the 15- or 30-minute demand interval ends or until the level of demand falls.

Manual systems cannot track demand levels closely enough to respond quickly to any increase. However, manual procedures can be very effective in reducing the facility's peak demand. For example, limiting the hours of operation of specific pieces of equipment to off-peak billing periods can keep those loads from contributing to the facility's overall peak demand cost. Similarly, training maintenance personnel to turn off all unneeded equipment and lighting, particularly during the on-peak billing period, will help to reduce the connected load when the demand peak occurs.

On-Site Generation

A third way used to limit a facility's peak electrical demand is on-site generation of electrical power. With this method, both critical and non-critical loads can be shed from the utility system.

Under a peak shaving program that makes use of on-site generation, power from the utility company is supplemented with electricity generated on site during the peak demand period. No attempt is made to generate a large volume of electricity, as the user is interested only in lowering the peak demand, not supplying all of the electricity needed by the facility.

How much can a facility efficiently shave from the electrical demand through on-site generation? In most applications, the relatively high cost of operating your own generators limits practical peak shaving to no more than ten percent of the peak demand. The actual target value would be determined by several factors, including the shape of the facility's peak demand curve and the cost of the equipment that must be purchased in order to generate and switch on-site power. Facilities with relatively flat peak demand curves, except for a sharp spike at the point of highest peak demand, can economically shave a lot more of the load through on-site generation than can facilities with only gradual variations. Trying to reduce a flat peak demand curve requires lengthy run time for on-site generators, a mode of operation that is not economical.

Would your facility benefit from peak shaving through on-site generation? It depends on the load factor for the facility. The load factor is equal to the monthly average demand divided by the peak demand for the month. If your facility has a load factor of 0.50 or less it can benefit.

How to Determine if Your Facility Would Benefit from Peak Shaving

Use Worksheet 14.2 to estimate the savings that would result from the use of an electrical demand control program. The worksheet may be used with manual load shedding, automatic load shedding, or on-site generation programs. Use the worksheet as follows:

Step 1. From the rate schedule in effect for the facility, determine the summer production charge, summer distribution charge, the number of months the summer rate schedule is in effect, the winter production charge, the winter distribution charge, and the number of months that the winter rate schedule is in effect. Enter the values in section #1 of the worksheet.

Step 2. In order to reduce the level of demand on the utility system, non-critical electrical loads will have to be temporarily disconnected. For the facility, identify the loads that can be interrupted and total their connected kW. Enter the value in section #1 of the worksheet.

Step 3. The non-critical winter electrical load will differ from the summer load, primarily as a result of air conditioning systems not operating. Identify the non-critical winter electrical loads and total their connected kW. Enter the value in section #1 of the worksheet.

Step 4. The summer demand charge is the sum of the summer production charge and the summer distribution charge. Add the two charges and enter the value in section #2 of the worksheet.

Step 5. Enter the summer controllable load from section #1 into section #2 of the worksheet.

Step 6. Not all non-critical electrical loads will be able to be disconnected at the same time. Typically, only 25 to 50% will be turned off at the time the peak demand is experienced. Estimate this load factor and enter the value in section #2 of the worksheet.

Step 7. Enter the number of months that the facility is on the summer rate schedule from section #1 into section #2 of the worksheet.

Step 8. Multiply the summer demand charge by the summer controllable load, the load factor, and the number of months at the summer rate to determine the summer demand savings. Enter the value in section #2 of the worksheet.

Step 9. The winter demand charge is the sum of the winter production charge and the winter distribution charge.
Note: there may be no winter production charge in some rate schedules. Add the two charges and enter the value in section #3 of the worksheet.

Step 10. Enter the winter controllable load from section #1 into section #3 of the worksheet.

Step 11. Not all non-critical electrical loads will be able to be disconnected at the same time. Typically, only 25 to 50% will be turned off at the time the peak demand is experienced. Estimate this load factor and enter the value in section #3 of the worksheet.

Step 12. Enter the number of months that the facility is on the winter rate schedule from section #1 into section #3 of the worksheet.

Step 13. Multiply the winter demand charge by the winter controllable load, the load factor, and the number of months at the winter rate to determine the winter demand savings. Enter the value in section #3 of the worksheet.

Step 14. Enter the summer demand savings from section #2 into section #4 of the worksheet.

Step 15. Enter the winter demand savings from section #3 into section #4 of the worksheet.

Step 16. Add the summer and winter demand savings to determine the total demand savings. Enter the value in section #4 of the worksheet.

This value represents the savings that could be expected to result from the implementation of an average demand limiting program. More aggressive programs will produce additional savings.

CURTAILMENT SERVICE

As part of the efforts of utility companies to limit electrical demand, many are offering a Curtailment Service Program for their customers. Under the program, you agree to establish a firm peak demand level, and to reduce your demand for electricity to that level of demand upon the request of the utility. Participation in the program is voluntary. Programs offer incentives to the customers in the form of a credit during the curtailment period, but the programs also impose penalties if you fail to achieve the level of curtailment that you agreed to.

The details of these programs vary from utility company to utility company, but most are similar in structure. The programs establish a maximum demand level under which you must stay when the utility activates the curtailment. When the utility company notifies you that it is entering a curtailment situation, you have from 30 to 60 minutes to reduce the demand for electricity below this level. The number of curtailments that the utility can request is typically limited to 15 or less, and is limited to the on-peak period during the summer billing months.

Most curtailment periods last from four to six hours, during which time you must stay below the agreed-upon level of demand. The benefit to you is a credit for each billing month when a curtailment was requested. The amount of the credit depends on the particulars of the curtailment program, but usually is a reduction in the demand charges equal to a percentage of the curtailed load. However, if you fail to reduce the demand level sufficiently, you must pay a penalty to the utility company based on the number of kW above the agreed-upon level that you failed to curtail. Most penalty clauses in curtailment programs set the penalty rate at approximately twice that of the credit rate.

While the risks for participating in a curtailment program are great, so are the potential benefits. However, before agreeing to participate in such a program, you should determine if there are loads that can be turned off during periods of peak demand, what the connected kW of these loads is, what the impact of curtailing these loads would be, and if there is a way to respond within the time frame established by the utility company's curtailment program. Without the ability to curtail the required loads quickly, participation in such a program will increase, not decrease, electricity costs.

FIGURE 14.1 Typical Time-of-Day Rate Structure

	Summer	Winter
Minimum Charge	$250	$250
Energy Charge		
On-Peak Period	2.962 ¢/kWh	2.156 ¢/kWh
Intermediate Period	2.338 ¢/kWh	1.636 ¢/kWh
Off-Peak Period	0.859 ¢/kWh	0.444 ¢/kWh
Production Charge	$9.40/kW	-
Distribution Charge	$3.85/kW	$3.85/kW

Rating Period

Weekdays (excluding holidays)

On-Peak Period	12:00 noon - 8:00 PM
Intermediate Period	8:00 AM - 12:00 noon
	8:00 PM - 12:00 midnight
Off-Peak Period	12:00 midnight - 8:00 AM

Saturdays, Sundays, and holidays

   All hours are considered to be off-peak

FIGURE 14.2 Sample Time-of-Day Bill

Type of Charge	Use	Rate	Cost
Minimum Charge			$ 250
Energy Charge			
On-Peak Period	2,500,000 kWh	2.962 ¢/kWh	74,050
Intermediate Period	2,300,000 kWh	2.338 ¢/kWh	53,774
Off-Peak Period	4,000,000 kWh	0.859 ¢/kWh	34,360
Production Charge	12,000 kW	$9.40/kW	112,800
Distribution Charge	12,000 kW	$3.85/kW	46,200
		Total:	$ 321,434

WORKSHEET 14.1 Substation Ownership Savings

1. Application Parameters

Annual Electrical Bill, Excluding Fuel Charge ($): _____

Discount Rate (%): _____

Substation Installed/Purchase Cost ($): _____

2. Annual Electricity Cost Savings

$$\boxed{} \ \times \ \boxed{} \ = \ \boxed{}$$

Annual Electrical   Discount Rate   Annual Electricity
Cost ($)   Cost Savings ($)

3. Annual Maintenance Costs

$$\boxed{} \ \times \ \boxed{0.02} \ = \ \boxed{}$$

Substation   Annual
Cost ($)   Maintenance
Cost ($)

4. Annual Savings

$$\boxed{} \ - \ \boxed{} \ = \ \boxed{}$$

Annual Electricity   Annual   Annual Savings
Cost Savings ($)   Maintenance   ($)
                      Cost ($)

WORKSHEET 14.2 Demand Control Savings

1. Application Data

Summer Production Charge ($/kW): _____   Winter Production Charge ($/kW): _____

Summer Distribution Charge ($/kW): _____   Winter Distribution Charge ($/kW): _____

Number of months at summer rate: _____   Number of months at winter rate: _____

Summer Controllable Load (kW): _____   Winter Controllable Load (kW): _____

2. Summer Demand Savings

[ ] X	[ ] X	[ ] X	[ ] =	[ ]
Summer Demand Charge ($/kW)	Summer Controllable Load (kW)	Load Factor	Number of Months at Summer Rate	Summer Demand Savings ($)

3. Winter Demand Savings

[ ] X	[ ] X	[ ] X	[ ] =	[ ]
Winter Demand Charge ($/kW)	Winter Controllable Load (kW)	Load Factor	Number of Months at Winter Rate	Winter Demand Savings ($)

4. Total Demand Savings

[ ] +	[ ] =	[ ]
Summer Demand Savings ($)	Winter Demand Savings ($)	Total Demand Savings ($)

Part III

Buildings and Grounds Maintenance

Using Paint and Protective Coatings to Reduce Maintenance Costs

This chapter examines a variety of types of paint and protective coatings commonly used in facilities. Characteristics of components are examined and recommendations are made for their use in different applications. Material presented in this chapter can be used to diagnose paint and protective coating problems, to identify the most suitable paint or coating for a given application, to estimate the life expectancies of various coatings, and to estimate the material required for a particular application.

Paint Characteristics

Paint manufacturers provide a seemingly endless range of paint options. In additional to the traditional oil- and latex-based paints, a variety of specialty paints have been formulated for application on specific surfaces or under set service conditions. If maximum performance is to be achieved by a coating, it must be selected based on your application's particular requirements, including surface material, environmental conditions, and exposure to abrasion and other wear-causing elements. Selection of the wrong type of paint can lead to both short- and long-term problems with the application.

Common Paint Types

Figure 15.1 lists the most common types of paints used in facilities, their composition, and how they are used. Use the figure to match the type of paint to the needs of your application. In addition to these types, manufacturers have developed a range of specially formulated coatings for particular applications. Consult with the manufacturer on their use.

Properties of Paint

Four major paint properties help to determine the type of paint to use in a particular application:

➤ adhesion
➤ corrosion protection
➤ film thickness
➤ film density

In addition to varying with the type of paint used, the properties are also influenced by the application process. Figure 15.2 lists coating performance factors for a number of paint types.

ADHESION. Adhesion is a measure of how tightly the paint bonds to the surface or to other coats of paint. It is determined by molecular attraction and physical contact between the paint film and the surface to which it has been applied. For adhesion to be of a high value, the paint must be compatible with the surface or existing paint layer.

CORROSION PROTECTION. Paint provides corrosion protection by two methods: physical isolation of the surface from the environment, and electrochemical neutralization of corrosive elements. Physical isolation protection is a result of the paint's film providing separation between the surface and oxygen, water, and other corrosive elements in the surrounding environment. The level of protection is a function of the paint's film thickness.

Electrochemical corrosive protection is the result of a process that takes place within the paint itself. In zinc-rich paints, a galvanic cell is set up by the presence of dissimilar metals. The zinc in the paint acts as the sacrificial metal, protecting the metal in the surface. Other paints contain pigments that help create an alkaline environment to neutralize acidic electrolytes, thus preventing electron flow and its resulting corrosion.

FILM THICKNESS. The thickness of the paint film is determined by both the properties of the paint and the procedures used to apply it. It is important because it helps determine the level of protection against corrosion by separating the underlying surface from oxygen, water, and other corrosive elements in the environment. In general, the thicker the film, the greater the level of protection.

FILM DENSITY. The paint's film density is the measure of the quantity of voids present in the paint film. It is determined by the components of the film and the degree of dispersion achieved during manufacture. The denser the film, the tighter the surface particles are compacted, providing greater protection to the surface.

THE THREE MAJOR COMPONENTS OF PAINT

There are three basic components in all paint systems: pigment, binder, and thinner. The pigment is what gives the paint its color, covering power, and finish. The binder determines the paint's hardness, adhesion, and resistance to abrasion and chemical attack. The thinner determines the ease with which the paint can be applied, its viscosity, and the odor given off during curing.

Paint Pigment

The sheen of the finish is determined by varying the level of pigment in the paint. Higher pigment levels result in a flatter, rougher finish. Finishes are available in five sheens: flat, eggshell, satin, semi-gloss, and gloss.

Paint Binder

The binder causes the pigment particles to fuse together into a uniform protective film. While pigment gives the paint its color, the binder determines its washability, adhesion, and resistance to abrasion, chemicals, weathering, and ultraviolet light. In solvent-based paints, the most commonly used binders are varnishes, linseed oil, soy oil, and dehydrated castor oil. In water-based paints, butadiene-styrene, polyvinyl acetate, and acrylic resins are commonly used binders.

Paint Thinner

The thinner serves to reduce the viscosity of the paint so that it can be readily spread to a uniform thickness. As the paint dries, the thinner evaporates leaving behind a solid paint film. In solvent-based paints, organic materials, such as turpentine, naptha, and mineral spirits, are used as the thinner. It is the evaporation of these materials that generates much of the odor during drying. Water is the thinner used in water-based paint.

MATCHING INTERIOR PAINT TYPES AND APPLICATION REQUIREMENTS

When selecting interior paint, more attention is typically given to color than to the type of paint. Unfortunately, the long-term performance of the paint is determined by the type of paint used in that particular application. For example, a flat finish applied to corridor walls in a public area of a building may last only one year, while a semi-gloss finish applied to the same area will typically last at least four years.

Figure 15.3 lists paints recommended for a number of interior applications. Use the figure to determine painting options based on the material to be painted and the type of finish.

When selecting the type of paint for interior application, you must consider safety and environmental factors. Advances in paint formulation have led to the development of water-based coatings that perform as well as or better than their solvent-based alternatives. One of the major advantages of water-based coatings in interior applications is their lack of solvent vapors that can disrupt occupancy. It is the evaporation of the organic thinner in solvent-based paints that gives off most of the odor while the paint is drying.

An additional advantage of water-based coatings is their rapid drying time. Most water-based coatings can be recoated within two to four hours, while solvent-based coatings may require two days or more in between.

MATCHING EXTERIOR PAINT TYPES AND APPLICATION REQUIREMENTS

Figure 15.4 lists paints recommended for a range of exterior applications. Use the figure to determine painting options based on the material to be painted and the type of finish you want.

The two most commonly used exterior paints are alkyd (oil) and water-based (latex). An alkyd-based exterior paint offers the advantage of drying to a hard, dense finish that resists weathering and mildew. Its penetrating properties help it to bond tightly to both new and old surfaces, including those that are weathered or coated with a paint that is chalking. Alkyd-based paints are not alkali-resistant and therefore should not be used on masonry without the use of an alkali-resistant primer.

HOW TO SELECT PAINT COLORS

Selection of the paint color for a space within a building has a direct impact on a number of factors, including the energy required for lighting, employee morale and productivity, and safety. Additionally, the use of color can help to direct or draw the attention of visitors and others unfamiliar with the space to certain areas.

The most obvious way in which color impacts a facility is through the lighting system. The quantity and quality of light delivered to work surfaces is determined in part by the reflectance of the room's surfaces. Darker surfaces absorb more light, requiring a higher number of lighting fixtures to deliver a given illumination level measured at the work surface. Similarly, if the reflectance of the room's surfaces is increased, the number of lighting fixtures can be reduced, decreasing the lighting energy requirements for the space.

Figure 15.5 lists recommended paint reflectance values for interior surfaces for both industrial and office spaces. Use the figure to select colors to minimize lighting energy use while avoiding overly bright, glaring spaces.

Tip: Ceilings should be white to provide the maximum reflectance of light, and walls should be light colors to brighten the space.

Color can also be used in interior spaces to create other effects, such as a particular mood, or the enhancement of safety. Figure 15.6 lists the effects that various colors have on occupants and where they can be used most effectively. Use the table to select particular colors based on the desired effect.

Diagnosing Paint-Related Problems

The failure of protective coatings costs maintenance operations millions of dollars annually in maintenance costs and equipment and facility downtime. For that reason, steps must be taken to insure that the best suited paint be applied in the recommended manner to a properly prepared surface. These factors are particularly important when you consider that the three major causes of paint failure are inadequate surface preparation, mis-application of a particular type of paint, and improper use of a paint.

Figure 15.7 identifies the most common paint failures in exterior applications and the steps that should be taken to prevent future paint failures. Figure 15.8 lists common paint failures and corrective action for interior applications. Use the figures to help diagnose existing paint problems and to identify steps to be taken to prevent their return.

The Need for Good Surface Preparation

The single leading cause of early paint failure is inadequate surface preparation. It is estimated that nearly 80% of all coating failures can be traced back to this single cause. Inadequate surface preparation results in a weak adhesion of the coating to the surface. It is this weak adhesion that increases the chances of environmental factors damaging or destroying the coating. As an absolute minimum, the surface must be clean, dry, and free of corrosion, mold, and mildew. But this is not sufficient to guarantee good performance from the coating; additional surface preparation is required.

What is needed depends on the type of material being coated and the level of protection required. It is important to recognize that the performance of the applied coating is directly related to the time and effort put into surface preparation. Figure 15.9 lists commonly used surface preparation techniques for various materials.

The Need for Good Application Techniques

The second leading cause of premature paint failure is the improper application of a paint. This type of paint failure can usually be avoided simply by following the manufacturer's recommended application procedures. Use Figure 15.10 to help identify application-related paint problems and their causes.

How to Estimate Paint Material Requirements

There are only two factors needed to estimate the quantity of paint required for an application: the coverage rate of the coating being applied and the square footage of the area being painted.

Paint Coverage Rate

The coverage rate for a coating depends on the type of coating being applied, and the method used to apply it. Determine the coverage rate in square feet per gallon for the material being used from the manufacturer's published data.

Calculating Surface Areas

It is not always easy to calculate the square footage of an application since not all surfaces are flat or regular. However, it is possible to estimate areas using a number of different rules of thumb.

1. Walls. Multiply the length of the wall by its height. Do not subtract the areas of doors, windows, or other openings that are less than 100 square feet each.

2. Doors. For plain finish doors, multiply the door width by its height and the multiplication factor of 2.1 to account for both sides and all edges.

   For doors with one to three panels, multiply the door width by its height and the multiplication factor of 3.0.

   For doors with four to six panels, multiply the door width by its height and the multiplication factor of 4.0.

3. Round, square or rectangular columns (plain finish). Multiply the column's circumference by its height.

4. Fluted Columns. Multiply the column's circumference by its height and the multiplication factor of 1.5.

5. Paneled Columns. Multiply the column's circumference by its height and the multiplication factor of 2.0.

These rules of thumb are sufficiently accurate to estimate paint material requirements for most applications, as long as the paint is applied according to its manufacturer's recommended application procedures.

FIGURE 15.1 Types of Paint

Paint Type	Composition	Application Notes
Oil	Pigments suspended in a linseed oil binder, a drier to control drying time, and a thinner to control flow. As the thinner evaporates and the oil absorbs oxygen, the pigment and oil mixture dries to an elastic skin.	Interior and exterior applications. Bonds well to new and previously painted surfaces.
Alkyds	Similar in composition to oil-based paints, but uses a synthetic resin instead of linseed oil as the binder. Dries by evaporation and oxidation.	Interior and exterior applications. Good bonding properties. Produces a harder finish than oil paint.
Latex	A dispersion of fine synthetic resin particles and pigments in water. As the water evaporates, the latex particles coalesce into a film.	Interior and exterior applications. Produces a surface with better color and gloss retention than alkyd or oil paints and better alkali, blistering, and peeling resistance. Does not bond as well as alkyd paint.
Epoxy	A two-part coating consisting of a hardener and an epoxy base that is mixed just prior to application. The hardener reacts chemically with the epoxy to produce an extremely hard, durable film.	Used primarily in interior applications. Provides excellent hardness and chemical resistance
Polyurethane	A blend of urethanes, drying oils, and alkyds that dries by evaporation and oxidation.	Used primarily in interior applications. Provides good abrasion resistance on wood surfaces. Resists water, grease, and alcohol.
Aluminum	A blend of varnish and aluminum flake pigment. As the paint dries, the flakes float to the surface and form a reflective surface.	Used primarily in exterior applications. Produces a surface that is resistant to weathering.
Varnish	A solution of resins in a drying oil with no pigment. It dries by evaporation and oxidation.	Interior and exterior applications. Produces a hard, glossy finish that resists moisture.

Figure 15.1 (continued)

Paint Type	Composition	Application Notes
Polyester-Epoxy	Like epoxy paint, polyester-epoxy uses a two-part formula that is mixed just prior to use.	Available in both gloss and semi-gloss finish. Produces a finish that is durable like epoxy, but with the color retention of polyester
Polyamide-Epoxy	A two-component formula that must be mixed prior to use.	Produces a hard finish that is resistant to abrasion, acid, and alkali. Used to protect interior concrete floors subjected to heavy traffic. Not recommended for exterior applications as it chalks and loses gloss with prolonged exposure.
Acrylic-Urethane	A one-component coating that is suited for use in industrial and commercial applications.	Produces a finish that is chemical- and stain-resistant while providing good color and gloss retention. Excellent resistance to scratching, marring, and chipping. Used on steel, aluminum, and masonry in interior and exterior applications, particularly those exposed to oil, steam, grease, coolants, and solvents.

FIGURE 15.2 Coating Performance Factors

Paint Type	Adhesion	Corrosion Protection	Typical Film Thickness (mils)	Film Density	Coverage (sq ft)
Acrylic Latex	Medium	Fair	1.2	Low	400
Alkyd	Medium	Very Good	2.0	Medium	400
Epoxy	Very High	Very Good	3.5	High	250
Oil-Alkyd	Medium	Very Good	2.5	High	350
Urethane	High	Very Good	2.0	Medium	500
Zinc (organic)	Low	Excellent	2.2	Medium	400
Zinc (inorganic)	Low	Excellent	2.2	Medium	350

FIGURE 15.3 Interior Paint Application Chart

Material	Surface	Finish	Coating Type
Wood	Doors Trim Wall Panels Cabinets	Flat Enamel	Alkyd Resin
		Eggshell Enamel	Alkyd Resin
		Semi-Gloss Enamel	Alkyd Resin
		Gloss Enamel	Alkyd Resin
		Clear (open-grain wood)	Stain-Varnish
		Gloss, Satin or Flat (close-grain wood)	Stain-Varnish
		Gloss Enamel	Alkyd Resin
	Floors	Clear	Polyurethane Resin
			Oleoresinous
		Sealer	Penetrating Sealer
	Gymnasium Floors	Clear	Polyurethane Resin
Metal	Structural Beams, Columns and Trusses	Flat	Dry Fog Spray
			Alkyd Resin
		Eggshell	Dry Fog Spray
			Alkyd Resin
		Semi-Gloss	Dry Fog Spray
			Alkyd Resin
	Ornamental Iron Railings Windows	Gloss	Alkyd Resin
			Catalyzed Epoxy
			Catalyzed Polyester Epoxy
	Doors, Partitions, Cabinets and Lockers	All Sheens	Alkyd Resin
	Galvanized	All Sheens	Alkyd Resin

Figure 15.3 (continued)

Material	Surface	Finish	Coating Type
Drywall	Walls & Ceilings	Flat	Alkyd Resin
			Vinyl Latex
		Eggshell	Alkyd Resin
			Vinyl Acrylic Latex
			Acrylic Latex
		Semi-Gloss	Alkyd Resin
			Vinyl Acrylic Latex
			Acrylic Latex
		Gloss	Alkyd Resin
	Ceilings	Flat	Alkyd Resin
		Matte	Vinyl Latex Ceiling
Acoustic Tile	Ceilings	Flat	Oil Flat
			Vinyl Latex
Masonry	Walls & Ceilings	Flat	Alkyd Resin
			Vinyl Latex
		Spray Flat Dry Fog	Alkyd Resin
		Eggshell	Alkyd Resin
			Vinyl Acrylic Latex
			Acrylic Latex
		Semi-Gloss	Alkyd Resin
			Vinyl Acrylic Latex
			Acrylic Latex
		Gloss	Alkyd Resin
	Floors	Gloss	Catalyzed Polyester Epoxy or Catalyzed Polyamide Epoxy
			Urethane Modified Alkyd Enamel (not for vehicular use areas)

Figure developed with assistance from Duron, Inc.

FIGURE 15.4 Exterior Paint Application Chart

Material	Surface	Finish	Coating Type
Wood	Siding	Gloss	Oil-Alkyd House Paint
		Flat	Oil-Alkyd House Paint
			Latex House Paint
		Semi-Gloss	Latex House Paint
	Trim, Shutters & Sash	Gloss	Oil-Alkyd House Paint
		Clear	Spar Varnish (small Surface areas only)
	Shingles & Shakes	Flat	Oil-Alkyd House Paint
			Latex House Paint
		Gloss	Oil-Alkyd House Paint
	Floors, Steps & Porches	Gloss	Urethane Modified Alkyd Enamel
Transite	Shingles, Siding & Soffits	Flat	Latex House Paint
Porous Brick, Stucco	Walls, Ceilings	Flat	Latex House Paint
Concrete Block	Walls	Flat	Latex House Paint
Concrete	Floors	Gloss	Urethane Modified Alkyd Enamel (not for vehicular use areas)
			Catalyzed Polyester Epoxy
Concrete Concrete Block	Walls	Gloss	Catalyzed Polyester Epoxy
			Catalyzed Acrylic, Aliphatic Urethane
Metal	Structural Sash Bridges Towers Fences Fire Escapes Railings	Gloss	Oil-Alkyd House Paint
			Alkyd Enamel
			Urethane Modified Alkyd Enamel
			Catalyzed Acrylic, Aliphatic Urethane
			Aluminum Paint
Galvanized Metal	Roofs, Gutters Downspouts, Flashing	All Sheens	Oil-Alkyd House Paint
			Latex House Paint

Figure developed with assistance from Duron, Inc.

FIGURE 15.5 Recommended Paint Reflectance Values

Surface	Reflectance (%)	
	Industrial	Office
Ceiling	80 - 90	80 - 90
Walls	55 - 65	60 - 70
Floors	15 - 30	25 - 40
Equipment Surfaces	30 - 50	-
Desk Tops	-	40 - 50

Courtesy of The Sherwin-Williams Company

FIGURE 15.6 Use of Color

Color	Effect on Occupants	Suggested Applications
Warm Colors		
Red Orange Yellow	Attract attention Promote cheerfulness Stimulate action	Employee entrances Corridors Lunch rooms Locker rooms
Cool Colors		
Blue Turquoise Green	Cool, Relaxing Quieting Encourage Concentration	Production areas Maintenance shops Boiler rooms
Light Colors		
Off-whites Pastel tints	Make rooms seem larger Create a psychological lift	Production areas Small rooms Hallways Warehouse & storage areas
Dark Colors		
Deep tones Gray Black	Make objects appear heavier Rooms seem smaller	Not recommended for large areas Use only for contrast in small background areas
Bright Colors		
Yellow Yellow green Red orange	Attract attention Make objects appear larger Create excitement	Small objects Columns, graphics Areas where contrast is needed
White		
White	Cleanliness Highly reflective	Ceilings Overhead structures Small objects Areas where reflectance is needed

Courtesy of The Sherwin-Williams Company

FIGURE 15.7 Causes of Paint Failure: Exterior Applications

Surface	Failure	Corrective Action
	Peeling. Caused by improper surface preparation or moisture trapped behind the paint film.	Identify and eliminate the source of any moisture. Remove all loose paint, dirt, and any surface contamination, sand, prime all bare wood, and repaint with a latex-based paint.
	Blistering. Blistering is the beginning stage of peeling as the result of moisture or heat. Moisture-caused blisters generally lift all paint, exposing bare wood. Heat-caused blisters typically lift only the top paint layer.	Remove the blisters by scraping and sanding. To prevent the formation of new moisture blisters, the source of the moisture must be identified and corrected. Heat blisters are prevented by avoiding painting a surface that is too hot.
Wood	**Checking.** Checking is the development of short, narrow breaks in the paint that form as the result of a loss in elasticity. It is most prevalent on plywood surfaces.	Remove all lose paint with a scraper or wire brush, prime, and repaint.
	Alligatoring. The development of advanced cracking that takes on the appearance of alligator skin. It is the result of weathering, a top coat that is incompatible with an undercoat, or a build-up of paint.	All old paint must be removed by scraping or sanding. Prime the bare wood with an oil-base primer and paint with a quality latex- or oil-based paint.
	Chalking. Chalking is the development of a fine powder on the surface of the paint. It is the result of the binder breaking down due to weathering. All exterior oil paints chalk to some extent.	Use a stiff brush and water under pressure to remove the chalk residue. After drying, apply an alkyd primer if the chalk cannot be completely removed or a quality acrylic latex if the surface is clean.
Concrete, Cement Blocks, and Brick	**Efflorescence.** Moisture in the substrate dissolves some of the salts in the masonry and carries them to the surface where they are deposited. These salts can leave an unsightly deposit on the surface and can cause the paint to peel.	Remove all flaking paint and efflorescence by wire brushing, prime with an alkali resistant primer, and repaint. To prevent the formation of new efflorescence, identify and correct the source of moisture.

Courtesy of The Sherwin-Williams Company

FIGURE 15.8 Causes of Paint Failure: Interior Applications

Surface	Failure	Corrective Action
Plaster	**Efflorescence.** Moisture in the substrate dissolves some of the salts in the plaster and carries them to the surface where they are deposited.	Remove all flaking paint and efflorescence by wire brushing. Prime with an alkali-resistant primer and repaint. To prevent new formations, the source of the moisture must be identified and removed.
	Peeling. The failure of the paint to adhere to the surface.	Remove the existing paint by sanding or scraping, fill holes and cracks, and prime with an alkali-resistant primer. Allow new plaster to cure for a minimum of 30 days before painting.
	Flaking. Occurs when plaster with a high alkalinity content reacts with paint applied to it.	Remove all flaking paint by wire brushing or sanding. Prime with a alkali-resistant primer to seal the surface. Allow new plaster to cure for a minimum of 30 days before painting.
	Color Variation. Caused by not priming or the incorrect primer being used. The topcoat absorbs at varying degrees causing variation in color and gloss.	Prime the surface with an alkali-resistant primer and recoat.
Dry Wall	**Alligatoring.** The formation of a scale pattern of cracks at the joints caused by low humidity during drying.	Stabilize the space temperature and humidity, then apply an additional float coat over the joint.
	Photographing. The condition where tape joints and nail holes show on a painted wall. Generally caused by improper drying of the joint compound, or an inadequate primer being used.	In new work, allow sufficient time for the joint compound to dry before painting. In existing work, reseal and repaint.
	Paint Discoloration at Joints. Caused by darkening of paint applied over wet joints.	Reseal and repaint.

Courtesy of The Sherwin-Williams Company

FIGURE 15.9 Surface Preparation Techniques

Material	Removal Technique	Notes
Steel	White Metal Blast Cleaning	Recommended for metal exposed to highly corrosive environments. Uses a wheel or nozzle (wet or dry) and sand, grit, or shot to remove all visible rust, mill scale, paint, and foreign matter. The most expensive and effective removal method.
	Near-White Metal Blast Cleaning	Similar to the white metal blast cleaning, but leaves shadows from previous corrosion on no more than 5% of the blasted area.
	Commercial Blast Cleaning	Recommended for applications where a high degree of cleanliness is required but where it is not necessary to provide a perfect surface. Uses an abrasive to remove all rust, mill scale, and other debris, but may leave some shadows from previous corrosion on up to 33% of the blasted area.
	Brush-Off Blast Cleaning	One of the most cost effective methods of preparing metal surfaces for protective coatings. Uses an abrasive to remove loose mill scale, dirt, rust, and paint. Small quantities of tightly adhering coating may remain.
	Power Tool Cleaning	Uses power tools to sand, chip, grind, or wire brush loose rust and mill scale. Requires removal of oil and grease prior to application, and thorough cleaning of the surface by vacuuming or with compressed air.
	Hand Tool Cleaning	Recommended for use in interior applications with no abnormal environmental exposures. Removes loose rust, mill scale, paint, and other foreign matter.
	Solvent Cleaning	Consists of wiping or immersing the object in a solvent. Limited effectiveness for removing grease, oil, dirt, salts, and organic compounds.

Figure 15.9 (continued)

Material	Removal Technique	Notes
Masonry	Water Blast Cleaning	Uses medium- to high-pressure water with or without a light detergent sprayed on the masonry surface. Effectively removes dirt and loose foreign material. May result in damage to interior surfaces or may produce efflorescence and staining on the masonry surface.
	Chemical Cleaning	Uses a chemical cleaner suspended in a low-pressure water stream to remove dirt and loose foreign material. As with water blast cleaning, care must be used to prevent damage to interior surfaces or staining of masonry surfaces.
	Mechanical Cleaning	Uses grit blasters, grinders, or sanding disks to remove dirt and foreign materials. May result in significant surface erosion.
	Water Cleaning	Uses a water spray to remove most surface dirt. Remaining dirt is removed by scrubbing with a mild detergent solution. Mildew is removed using a bleach solution.
Wood	Sanding/Scraping	Recommended for applications where the paint has cracked, crazed, or blistered. Uses hand or mechanical sanding and scraping to produce a smooth finish.
	Stripping	Mechanical or chemical removal of all layers of paint. Recommended for applications where interior or exterior moisture has caused portions of the total coating to fail. Entire affected area must be stripped to bare wood, primed, and recoated.

Courtesy of The Sherwin-Williams Company

FIGURE 15.10 Common Paint Application Problems

Problem	Description
Cratering	The formation of small depressions in the dried paint film. The depressions are the result of air bubbles that were trapped during application and later burst. The bubbles are formed in the paint by overshaking the paint can, using a new roller without properly squeezing out trapped air, or by applying paint to a hot surface.
Crawling	The formation of drops, pools, and uncovered areas as the result of oil, wax, grease, or other non-compatible substance on the surface.
Lap Marks	The formation of defects on the fresh paint surface as the result of re-brushing. Lap marks are caused by a too rapid drying of the paint due to improper application techniques, including painting in direct sunlight, painting when the temperature is too high, and spreading the paint too thin.
Poor Hiding	Insufficient covering of the surface. It is the result of a number of different causes, including excessive thinning, spreading the paint too thin, inadequately sealed surfaces, and too radical a color change.
Sagging	The formation of curtain-like streaks. Sagging can result when paint is applied over a glossy finish, the temperature is above or below the recommended application temperature, or when the paint is too thick.
Slow Drying	Cool temperatures, high humidity, and inadequate ventilation contribute to slow drying times.
Spotting	The loss of gloss or color consistency. Spotting results from spreading the paint too thin, moisture condensing on the paint surface before it has fully dried, and the use of low quality paint.
Wrinkling	The formation of a leather-like texture on the surface. Wrinkling is the result of interfering with a paint's drying time. Applying a second coat before the first has fully dried, applying too heavy a coat, and painting over a glossy finish without sanding all can lead to wrinkling.

Courtesy of PPG Industries, Inc.

Chapter 16

HOW TO SELECT FLOOR COVERINGS FOR LONG LIFE AND LOW MAINTENANCE

This chapter examines commonly used types of resilient flooring and carpet. The material presented in this chapter can be used to determine the most suitable floor covering material to use in a particular application, to establish an effective maintenance program for floor coverings, and to estimate material requirements for applications.

RESILIENT FLOORING APPLICATIONS

The properties of resilient flooring make it ideally suited for use in facilities. It provides a durable surface that is low in maintenance, has low first costs, and provides a long product life. It resists damage from grease, oil, alkali, and dilute chemicals. Its natural resiliency gives it the ability to recover with no permanent damage from indentations caused by chairs, table legs, and other objects. Equally important, it can be manufactured to imitate the look of nearly any material, thus giving designers an almost unlimited range of appearance options.

Depending on the type of flooring, materials are available in sheet or tile form, with the 12-by-12-inch tile the most widely used format. Resilient flooring materials are available in a range of thicknesses or gauges. Patterns generally extend through the entire tile material. Figure 16.1 lists the physical properties of the most commonly used resilient flooring materials.

Resilient flooring covers a wide variety of materials including linoleum, asphalt tile, cork, vinyl tile, vinyl composition tile, sheet vinyl, and rubber tile. Of these, the most commonly used include sheet vinyl, vinyl composition tile, vinyl tile, and rubber tile. Linoleum was the first synthetic resilient flooring material to be widely used. Manufactured primarily in sheet form, its use is limited to industrial and other heavy duty applications. Asphalt tile, once widely used in facilities, has been replaced by the various synthetic materials. Although it is very durable and hard, it is brittle and prone to breakage.

Selection of a particular type of resilient flooring for an application is determined by a number of factors including:

- ➤ the activities being performed in the space
- ➤ the expected level of traffic through the space
- ➤ the type and weight of equipment and furniture that can be found in the space
- ➤ the degree of waterproofing required
- ➤ the cost of the tile

Figure 16.2 lists the properties of commonly used resilient flooring. Use the figure to help determine the best suited flooring for an application based on the performance characteristics needed.

Sheet Vinyl Characteristics

Sheet vinyl is manufactured in rolls that are typically six, nine, or twelve feet wide and up to 120 feet long. It comes in a number of different thicknesses; the most common is about 85 mils. Material is available in backed or non-backed construction. In backed construction, the color and pattern typically extend to a depth of 50 mils. In non-backed construction, they extend throughout the entire thickness. For applications requiring a non-slip surface, sheet vinyl can be manufactured using an aggregate-impregnated surface. Sheet vinyl has an average expected life of 20 to 25 years.

Sheet vinyl offers two primary advantages over vinyl tile: lower labor costs for installation, and the elimination of seams. Of these the most important is the seamless construction. In addition to improving the appearance of an area, seamless construction enhances sanitation by eliminating areas where dust, dirt, and bacteria can accumulate. In applications where two sheets of vinyl must be joined together, the seams can be heat-welded to create an effective seal. Additional protection can be achieved by turning the sheet vinyl up at walls, thus creating a watertight flash coving.

Composite Vinyl Tile Characteristics

Composite vinyl tile consists of vinyl resins, plasticizers, stabilizers, fillers, and pigments combined into a layer typically $3/32$ or $1/8$ of an inch thick. The most common tile size is twelve inches. The combination of good performance and low installed cost has made it widely accepted for use in facilities even though it is outperformed by solid vinyl tile. Composite tile has an average expected life of 10 to 15 years. It is well suited for use in areas not subjected to high volumes of pedestrian traffic or areas where frequent changes in the operation, such as in retail facilities, make the added performance and life expectancy of solid vinyl tile unnecessary.

Solid Vinyl Tile Characteristics

Solid vinyl tile is constructed from the same materials as composite vinyl tile. However, the binder content in solid vinyl tile is kept to less than 34 percent, while for composite vinyl tile there is no maximum level requirement. This limiting of the use of binders in manufacturing the tile results in a higher cost product, but also creates one that is more flexible, has a higher resistance to abrasion, and resists impact damage better. The average expected life of solid vinyl tile is 20 to 25 years.

It provides a surface that is easy to maintain. Its resistance to wear makes it well suited for high traffic areas. Available in an extensive selection of colors and patterns, solid vinyl tile can be used in a wide range of applications. Its flexibility allows it to conform to slight irregularities in the subflooring.

Solid vinyl tile is manufactured primarily in nine- and twelve-inch square tiles. Other sizes are available for special applications or to be used as borders, striping, or other visual enhancements. The most common tile thickness is one-eighth inch. Tile color and patterns extend throughout the entire depth of the tile. It is best suited for use in applications subjected to high pedestrian traffic or those areas where the long-term performance of the floor tile is a major concern.

Rubber Tile Characteristics

Rubber tile has gained popularity rapidly as the result of a need for a high performance, low cost surface that provides superior protection against slipping. Typically made of 100 percent rubber, the tile is available in sizes ranging from 12 to 19 inches and in thickness from one-eighth to three-sixteenths of an inch. It is easily recognized by its characteristic pattern of raised disks, diamonds, or squares.

Rubber tile produces a surface that is durable, long-wearing, resilient, and easy to maintain. It retains its natural shine without requiring the use of floor polish.

Rubber tile is best suited for use in high pedestrian traffic areas where slipping is a concern. Building entrances, lobbies, ramps, stairway landings, elevators, and hazardous areas are typical applications for rubber tile, particularly if those areas are subject to water from foot traffic.

RESILIENT FLOOR MAINTENANCE

One of the main advantages of resilient flooring is its low maintenance requirement. Nevertheless, some maintenance is still required on a regular basis if the materials are to perform as expected. Although the surfaces of resilient floor products are durable, their finishes can be permanently damaged by excessive quantities of dirt and grit ground into them.

Routine Maintenance

To minimize the buildup of damaging particles on the surface, all resilient floors should be vacuumed, swept, or dust mopped on a regular basis. The frequency with which surfaces are cleaned depends on the level of pedestrian traffic experienced and the quantity and type of material being tracked into the facility. Weather conditions will determine the frequency required for many areas, particularly those near building entrances.

During good weather, most areas need a light cleaning only once per day. During wet weather, or if construction activities near the building cause large amounts of dirt to be tracked into the facility, additional cleanings will be required. In addition to this light cleaning, resilient floors should be damp mopped using a dilute neutral cleaner on a weekly basis.

Preventive Maintenance

One of the most important maintenance activities that can be undertaken to enhance the life and performance of resilient flooring is preventive maintenance. While the materials are durable, they are subject to damage by compression. In most cases, compression damage is the result of exceeding the material's rated load carrying capacity. For composite vinyl tile, the maximum load that can be placed on the tile without permanent damage is 75 pounds per square foot. For solid vinyl tile and sheet vinyl, the maximum load is 125 pounds per square foot. For rubber tile it is 150 pounds per square foot.

While these values may seem high considering the weight of most objects and furniture placed on tile, you must also consider the contact area between the object and the tile. Even a light weight chair may exceed the load capacity of the resilient material when the weight of the person sitting in the chair is added, particularly if the chair has feet with a small cross-sectional area.

To protect against compression damage, install large, flat protectors or glides on the bottom of all equipment and furniture. Add large plastic castors to equipment and furniture that is frequently moved.

CARPET OPTIONS

The number of options you have when selecting carpet for a particular application has grown in recent years. Selecting the right carpet involves quite a few decisions, some obvious, some not so obvious. There are the choices of broadloom vs. modular tiles, pile density, pile construction, and type of fiber. There is no optimum carpet for all applications. Each has its own advantages and disadvantages which lend it to use in particular installations. In general, carpet selection must be made taking into consideration where it will be used, how long it is expected to be in service, how important appearance is, how the carpet will be maintained, and what the budget is for the installation.

Two Basic Forms: Broadloom and Modular Tiles

Carpet for use in facilities comes in two basic forms: broadloom and modular tiles. Both are available in many fibers, pile weights, constructions, colors, patterns, and textures. Both are suitable for use in a wide range of applications, each having its own advantages and disadvantages.

BROADLOOM. Broadloom carpet is manufactured in rolls with widths of six or twelve feet, and is sold by the square yard. It is lower in cost than modular tiles. It can be installed directly over the subfloor or over padding, tacked or glued down.

The primary disadvantage of broadloom carpet is its all-or-nothing nature. Even if only a portion of the carpet in a given area is in need of replacement, all of it must be replaced at the same time. Replacement generally means disrupting the operations of that area as people, furniture, and equipment must all be moved out.

With the growth of the use of computers and telecommunications equipment, the number of cables that must be run to workstations in a facility has increased significantly. Once the carpet has been installed, changes in the layout of workstations generally means cutting and patching the carpet as cables must be moved to match the new layout. Such procedures are costly, time consuming, and contribute to the carpet's ultimate failure.

MODULAR TILES. Modular tiles are manufactured in twelve-inch squares and sold by the box. They generally are installed directly over the subfloor with no padding. Tiles may be laid loose, permanently glued in place, or held down by a strippable adhesive for easy removal. Modular tiles are significantly higher in cost than broadloom, but offer several advantages.

Because of their modular construction, it is possible to carry out partial replacement of tile in heavy traffic areas, or of tile that has been damaged by staining or heavy soiling. Some facilities, to extend the life of their modular carpet, have developed a rotation system where tile installed in heavy traffic areas is rotated to areas with lower traffic on a regular basis.

Modular tiles also offer greater flexibility to operations that undergo frequent changes. As workstations are relocated, the modular tiles can be easily removed and replaced to gain access to underfloor wiring. Even when a total replacement project is undertaken, the disruption to the operation can be minimized by working in relatively small areas at a time.

Selection of a broadloom or modular tile carpet is determined by the requirements of the application. If the flexibility provided by modular tiles is a benefit, the additional expense often can be justified. However, if the facility cannot make use of the flexibility, it will be difficult to justify the increased expense.

THREE IMPORTANT CARPET PHYSICAL CHARACTERISTICS

When selecting carpet material for an application, there are three major physical characteristics that you must consider: the density of the carpet pile, the construction of the pile, and the type of fiber used to make the carpet. These three physical characteristics will impact its initial cost, its lifetime performance, and the level of maintenance effort.

Pile Density

The pile density of carpet is measured in the number of tufts per square inch. The higher the number, the more dense the carpet. Rule of thumb: The more dense the carpet, the longer it will retain its appearance. Pile density becomes particularly important in areas that experience high levels of pedestrian traffic. It is one of the most important factors that determines how well a carpet will perform long-term.

In a fairly dense carpet, the pile yarns are close enough together to help support each other. In carpets of low pile density, the yarns tend to lay over easily, resulting in a worn appearance.

Pile Construction

There are two major configurations for carpet pile construction: cut and loop. Of the two, loop pile is the most durable, particularly in areas subjected to heavy pedestrian traffic. When subjected to loads, it flexes and bounces back.

Cut pile with two or three ply yarns will perform well under heavy traffic only if the fibers have been properly twisted and heat set. Without this treatment, the yarns tend to open and unravel. Once unraveled, the pile ends separate and compress, creating the appearance of wear.

Type of Carpet Fiber

There are four major materials used for fibers: acrylic, nylon, olefin, and wool. Each fiber has its own performance characteristics that will to a great extent determine how well it will perform in a given application. Figure 16.3 lists properties of the four most common carpet fibers.

In addition to carpet properties varying by fiber, the way in which the carpet is constructed also varies. These variations are the result of the different properties of the fiber material and how well they perform in different configurations. Typical variations exist in weight, pitch, density, and construction as shown in Figure 16.4.

ACRYLIC FIBERS. Acrylic fibers are manufactured from a polymer-based synthetic. Carpet using acrylic fibers is available in a wide range of pile weight, construction, and color.

Acrylic fibers have a high bulk to weight ratio, resulting in good coverage and a high level of crush resistance. As the fiber material is a synthetic, it resists moisture and the growth of mildew and mold.

The two major drawbacks to acrylic fibers are their low abrasion resistance and their low alkali resistance. As a result of low abrasion resistance, the fibers are readily damaged by soil tracked into the carpet. Unless the soil is removed regularly and thoroughly, it scratches the fiber faces, creating additional areas for even more soil to attach itself to the fibers.

The low alkali resistance of the fibers indicates that they can be readily damaged by spills of common food products.

NYLON FIBERS. Nylon is the most widely used material in carpet fiber construction today. It has a naturally hard surface that resists abrasion and scratching. As a result, soil does not bond well to the fibers. Nylon fibers are not naturally resilient, but are made resilient by crimping, bending, and twisting them. The result is a fiber that retains its shape and appearance well. Nylon's abrasion and soil resisting properties make it well suited for use in high-soil areas.

One of the major drawbacks of nylon fibers is their inability to dissipate static electricity. Nylon fiber carpet can easily generate static charges in excess of 12,000 volts. The threshold of human sensitivity is approximately 3,500 volts. The recommended maximum value for sensitive electronic equipment, such as computers and telecommunication equipment, is much lower. To control static buildup, manufacturers add a carbonized fiber to the yard or a conductive surface coating. These help to dissipate static charges before they reach levels where they can be noticed or damage equipment. If carpeting is to be installed in areas where computers will be used, it is important that low-static carpeting be specified.

OLEFIN FIBERS. Olefin fibers are a synthetic polymer produced from a petroleum base. Of the four most popular fibers for carpet, they are the lightest and the lowest in cost. Carpet of olefin fibers is available in a wide range of yarn weights and pile densities. Most are of loop pile. While olefin fiber carpets are available in a broad range of colors, the selection is not as great as that for nylon fiber carpet.

One of the primary advantages of olefin fiber is its ability to resist moisture. As a result, staining agents cannot penetrate the surface of the fiber, making it extremely stain-resistant. However, the chemical structure of the fibers results in a molecular attraction for oily substances, making soil removal difficult.

Olefin fibers are softer than nylon and lack nylon's resiliency. They are prone to pile crush, and once crushed cannot be lifted. Unlike nylon, olefin fibers do not produce static electricity when new. However, as they wear the amount of static buildup increases. To prevent static buildup, manufacturers add conductive fibers and carbonized latex backings.

WOOL FIBERS. Of the four most commonly used fibers, wool is the only natural fiber. It is also the most expensive. Wool has long been regarded as the fiber of elegance. No synthetic fiber has been able to duplicate its appearance and feel. The surface of the wool fiber scatters light well, thus helping to hide dirt. Dirt does not bind to the fibers, making cleaning a relatively easy task. In spite of its superior appearance and dirt-hiding capabilities, wool has been widely replaced as the fiber of choice.

Wool fibers have a number of disadvantages that have contributed to its decrease in popularity, including low abrasion resistance and the ease with which they can be stained. These two properties have limited its use to special areas where elegance is required, the volume of foot traffic is low, and the chances for staining are also low.

How to Select a Carpet Fiber

In selecting a fiber for a particular application, it is important to determine first the performance characteristics required. If the area is to be subjected to heavy pedestrian traffic, the fiber should have properties of resilience, crush resistance, soil resistance, and wearability: properties found in acrylic and nylon fibers. If the area is not quite so performance-demanding, and if the area is expected to undergo a major remodeling within five years or less, olefin fibers offer a good balance between low cost and performance. If appearance is the primary function, the area is not subjected to heavy pedestrian traffic, and cost is not the dominating factor, wool fibers can be used effectively.

Carpet Soiling vs. Staining

In evaluating the performance of carpet fibers and the tasks required to maintain them, a distinction must be made between soiling and staining. Soiling is a problem common to all carpet fibers and remains fairly constant throughout the life of the carpet. Problems with staining vary with the type of fiber, the level of wear, and the level of maintenance performed on the carpet.

CARPET SOIL. Carpet soil is a combination of dust and dirt that either settles out of the air or is tracked onto the carpet. Typically, 80 to 90 percent of all carpet soil is the result of pedestrian traffic and as such, contains a high level of oil and is concentrated near building entrances. Soil particles, while small, are abrasive and readily scratch and dull carpet fibers. Scratched fibers have more attachment points that trap and hold additional soil, leading to more accumulation and carpet fiber damage. As soil builds in the carpet, it will cause fibers to cling and stick together, producing a matted or worn appearance.

The best defense against soil damage to fibers is regular vacuuming and cleaning. Areas subject to more soil should be vacuumed and cleaned more frequently.

CARPET STAINS. Staining, and the defense against it, is a completely different matter. Staining is the result of liquids penetrating the surface of the fibers, causing a change of appearance. The extent to which a carpet can be stained depends on how well moisture can penetrate the fiber. Nylon and acrylic fibers, which have a low penetration rate for moisture, are more stain-resistant than wool which is easily penetrated by moisture. Olefin fibers, which cannot be penetrated by moisture, are almost totally stain-resistant.

Stain resistance should not be confused with soil resistance. A carpet fiber can have excellent stain resistance simply because it cannot be penetrated by moisture, but it still will be subject to soiling. How well it resists soiling depends on properties of the fiber that are not related to its stain resistance properties.

The best defense against staining is to have the spill cleaned up before it is allowed to dry. Few carpet fibers, including wool, will be permanently damaged by staining materials if those materials are cleaned promptly and properly.

THE NEED FOR ON-GOING CARPET MAINTENANCE

Successful carpet maintenance programs are those that address the causes of carpet failure. Years ago, when wool was the dominant fiber, a carpet was considered to be worn out when a certain level of pile-thickness loss was achieved. Unlike wool, synthetic fibers lose little pile. Today, a carpet is considered to be worn out when its appearance has changed.

The two primary causes for carpet appearance change are soil accumulation and pile pack-down. Soil coats the fibers with oily residue that attracts and holds additional dirt. As the dirt level builds, the fibers clump together and become packed-down. Good maintenance practices can reduce the level of soil accumulation.

Pile pack-down is the result of heavy pedestrian traffic. It creates changes in the appearance of the carpet that look like wear. While nothing can be done to reduce the level of traffic, pile pack-down can be minimized through a careful maintenance program.

Elements of a Carpet Maintenance Program

There are two elements to a carpet maintenance program: preventive maintenance and routine maintenance. Preventive maintenance starts with the selection of the right type of carpet fiber and pile for the application. Even the color selection will influence its wear appearance. Multicolored or patterned carpets hide soil better than solid light or dark shades.

In general, nylon fibers will perform better than olefin fibers in heavy wear areas and areas subject to heavy soiling. Loop pile outperforms cut pile, hiding textural changes better.

Preventive maintenance for carpets should also include measures to limit a carpet's exposure to soiling. Since the vast majority of carpet soil is tracked into the facility on foot, all entrances should include walk-off mats or recessed grid systems for soil collection. Rule of thumb: Mats and grids should be large enough so that each foot of persons entering the facility would come in contact with the mat at least three times before the person steps onto carpet.

Routine maintenance for carpets consists of vacuuming, spot cleaning, and general chemical cleaning. The frequency of each activity depends on the type of carpet installed, the level of pedestrian traffic experienced, and the type and level of soil exposure. Figure 16.5 lists suggested maintenance schedules for various areas in a facility. The frequencies listed in the figure are minimum frequencies based on a typical installation and may have to be adjusted based on high-exposure levels to soil and traffic. Saving money by reducing the frequency of routine carpet maintenance activities only serves to shorten the life of the carpet.

HOW TO ESTIMATE CARPET MATERIAL REQUIREMENTS

Estimating material requirements for a carpet installation is straightforward. For large, open spaces, determine the square footage of the area and divide by 9 to determine the area in square yards. For roll carpet, multiply the square yards by 1.2 to account for waste. For carpet tile, multiply the square yards by 1.1.

For smaller areas, or areas of unusual shape, multiply the square yards by 1.3 for roll carpet and 1.1 for carpet tile.

FIGURE 16.1 Resilient Flooring Construction

Feature	Vinyl Sheet	Solid Vinyl Tile	Vinyl Composition Tile	Rubber Tile
Common Sizes	6, 9 and 12 foot wide rolls	9 x 9 inch 12 x 12 inch	9 x 9 inch 12 x 12 inch	12 x 12 inch $17^{13}/_{16}$ x $17^{13}/_{16}$ inch $19^5/_8$ x $19^5/_8$ inch
Thickness (inches)	3/32	1/8	3/32 1/8	1/8 5/32 3/16
Maximum Weight (lb/sq in)	125	125	75	150
Pattern Depth (%)	60 - 100	100	60 - 100	N/A

FIGURE 16.2 Resilient Flooring Properties

Characteristic	Vinyl Sheet	Solid Vinyl Tile	Vinyl Composition Tile	Rubber Tile
Alkali Resistance	Excellent	Excellent	Very Good	Good
Burn Resistance	Fair	Fair	Fair	Very Good
Durability	Very Good	Very Good	Good	Very Good
Ease of Cleaning	Excellent	Excellent	Good	Very Good
Indentation Resistance	Very Good	Very Good	Good	Excellent
Resilience	Excellent	Excellent	Good	Excellent
Stain Resistance	Very Good	Very Good	Very Good	Excellent
Wear Resistance	Excellent	Excellent	Very Good	Excellent

FIGURE 16.3 Carpet Fiber Properties

Characteristic	Acrylic	Nylon	Olefin	Wool
Abrasion Resistance	Poor	Very Good	Good	Fair
Alkali Resistance	Poor	Very Good	Good	Poor
Appearance Retention	Very Good	Very Good	Good	Very Good
Cleaning Ability	Good	Good	Fair	Very Good
First Cost	Medium	Medium	Low	High
Flame Resistance	Good	Good	Poor	Fair
Mildew Resistance	Good	Good	Good	Poor
Resilience	Fair	Good	Poor	Very Good
Soil Resistance	Very Good	Good	Good	Very Good
Stain Resistance	Good	Good	Very Good	Poor
Static Buildup Resistance	Good	Poor	Good	Fair

FIGURE 16.4 Carpet Construction

Characteristic	Acrylic	Nylon	Olefin	Wool
Pile Weight (ounces/sq yd)	25 - 40	18 - 50	18 - 28	30 - 50
Pile Density (tufts/sq in)	Medium	Medium to High	Medium	Medium to High
Pile Construction	Cut Loop Cut/Loop	Cut Loop Cut/Loop	Cut Loop Cut/Loop	Cut Loop
Backing	Jute Synthetic	Jute Synthetic	Synthetic	Jute

FIGURE 16.5 Carpet Maintenance Activities

Area	Vacuuming	Spot Removal	Chemical Cleaning
Corridors	Daily	Daily	Monthly
Entrances	Twice Daily	Daily	Weekly
High Traffic Areas	Daily	Daily	Weekly
Lobbies	Twice Daily	Daily	Weekly
Meeting Rooms	Weekly	As Required	Annually
Offices	Weekly	As Required	Annually

## Chapter 17

SELECTING ROOFING SYSTEMS THAT MEET THE NEEDS OF YOUR FACILITY

This chapter presents information on the most commonly installed roofing systems. The material presented in this chapter can be used to evaluate roofing options, determine the condition of existing roofing systems, and establish a roofing inspection program.

THE NEED FOR ROOFING MAINTENANCE

Roofing has long been a major source of maintenance problems for the facility manager. Surveys of building owners show that one-third of new roofs develop major maintenance problems within one year of installation. By the time the roof is five years old, that number has increased to nearly 90 percent.

When you consider that roofs are exposed to greater environmental extremes than any other building component, it is easy to understand why they have so many problems. These problems are further compounded because, unlike many other building systems, most roof components are fabricated at the building site while exposed to the same elements that they are designed to protect the building against: heat, cold, wind, ultraviolet light, rain, dirt, and foot traffic.

The importance of maintaining a good roof is readily demonstrated by the consequences of a roof failure. Not only does a failed roof require replacement, it also results in damage to the building it was designed to protect. Rule of thumb: For every dollar of damage done to a roof, there will be an additional ten dollars damage to the building and its contents.

A thorough maintenance program will help insure that the investment made in a roofing system will be protected. But maintenance is not the only requirement for a long service life. Good roofing performance begins with the selection of the proper type of roof for the application. Next, the roof must be properly installed. Once installed, it must be inspected on a regular basis to identify minor problems before they develop into major ones. It is these four elements—good design, proper installation, frequent inspections, and routine maintenance—that are required in order to maximize the performance of a roofing system.

SIX MAJOR ROOFING SYSTEMS: THEIR CHARACTERISTICS, STRENGTHS, AND WEAKNESSES

There are six major categories of roofing systems used in facilities today: built-up, single-ply, modified bitumen, shingle, metal, and foam. Selection of a particular type depends on the design characteristics of the facility, the desired roof performance, the money budgeted, and the previous experience that the building designer and/or owner has had with a particular roof type. Pay particular attention to matching the roofing system to the facility since not all systems are compatible with all applications. The selection of roof type will also determine what maintenance activities must be performed and how frequently they are required to keep the roof in new condition.

Roof type selection must take into consideration such factors as the rate of expansion and contraction that the roof will be subjected to, wind exposure, the volume of foot traffic it will be exposed to, the desired insulating value, insurance and fire code requirements, and the appearance of the roof.

Characteristics of Built-Up Roofing

Built-up roofing has long been the roofing system standard for facilities with low slope roofs. Its success and popularity can be attributed to its inherent redundancy: three or four alternating layers of reinforcing felts and waterproofing bitumens. A properly installed, well-maintained built-up roof has an expected service life of between 15 and 20 years depending on the number of layers of felts used. A built-up roof is well suited for applications where the roof is exposed to frequent foot traffic.

A typical built-up roof consists of a supporting deck covered by several layers of saturated roofing felts and surfaced with a layer of aggregate. The supporting deck can be made of wood, steel, or concrete. The surfacing aggregate typically is a layer of one-half inch diameter or smaller gravel.

The roofing felts used in built-up roofs are made from fiberglass, polyester, cotton rag, or wood pulp fabric that has been saturated in a bitumen, typically asphalt or coal tar. Each layer of felt is applied individually and bonded to the surface through the application of a saturating layer of asphalt or coal tar. Since each layer of felt is bonded to the surface, all built-up roofs are classified as being fully adhered.

Coal Tar Versus Asphalt

The selection of asphalt or coal tar is determined by the characteristics of the application. Coal tar resists water better than asphalt, but melts at a lower temperature. This relatively low melting temperature can cause it to become plastic at temperatures experienced during the summer. On roofs with only a slight pitch, this flow helps the roof to reseal itself, repairing minor damage. However, when applied to a roof with a pitch greater than one-half inch per foot, the plasticity of coal tar can cause sufficient flow to weaken and damage the roof.

Asphalt, the main alternative to coal tar, can be used on any roof pitch without concerns for plasticity and flow. While it is not self-patching, flaws are easier to spot than with coal tar, and the finish surface is smoother.

Figure 17.1 identifies common defects associated with built-up roofs. Use the figure to determine the most likely cause for the defect and to identify measures that can be implemented to correct it. Rules of thumb for built-up roof installations:

1. The minimum roof pitch for built-up roofs is 1/2 inch per foot for proper water drainage. Lower roof pitches will result in ponding.

2. The standard number of plies used in built-up roof is three. A three-ply roof, properly installed and maintained, will last 20 years. If the number of plies is reduced, the expected service life will be reduced by five years for each ply reduction.

3. If there is no comprehensive inspection and routine maintenance program in place, the service life of a built-up roof will be reduced by 50 percent.

4. The annual cost to inspect and properly maintain a built-up roof is approximately two percent of the replacement cost of the roof.

Characteristics of Single-Ply Roofing

The use of single-ply roofing has increased dramatically during the past fifteen years. Initially promoted as a low-cost alternative to petroleum product-based built-up roofs, particularly when petroleum products were costly and scarce, single-ply roofing has become widely accepted today more for its performance characteristics.

One of the main advantages of a single-ply membrane is its ability to stretch and match the structural and thermal movement of the underlying materials. These properties make single-ply roofing particularly well suited for areas that experience extremes in climate.

Another advantage of single-ply roofing is the ease and speed with which it can be installed. Unlike built-up roofing, which must be fully field fabricated, single-ply roofing membranes are pre-manufactured in a variety of widths and brought to the site for installation. In addition to speeding installation, manufacturing the membranes under controlled conditions helps to insure that the materials delivered to the application site are uniform in quality and performance.

It is relatively easy to detect defects in single-ply roofing because the membrane lies on top of the roof and can be easily inspected. However, placing the membrane on top of the roof exposes it to damage from environmental factors and foot traffic.

CLASSES OF SINGLE-PLY ROOFING. There are two classes of single-ply roofing: thermoset and thermoplastic. Thermoset roofing materials are installed in sheets with widths of 20 to 30 feet, making them well suited in applications having large open spaces with few roof penetrations. Depending on the chemical composition of the material, seams are solvent-welded, hot-air welded, or joined with adhesive.

Thermoset roofing materials are divided into two sub-categories, cured and uncured elastomers. Cured elastomers are vulcanized products that are chemically cross-linked during the manufacturing process, resulting in a material that cannot be molded or reshaped during application by heat. The most commonly used cured elastomer roofing materials are Neoprene and ethylene propylene diene monomer (EPDM).

Uncured elastomer roofing products are similar materials that remain uncured during the manufacturing process. Complete curing does not occur until the materials have been installed and exposed to heat and the atmosphere. Since the materials are uncured, they can be molded, reshaped, and heat-welded during installation. Since the materials gradually cure after installation, their properties slowly change, becoming similar to those of cured elastomers. The most commonly used uncured elastomer roofing material is cholosulfonated polyethylene (CSPE).

Thermoset membranes can be installed fully adhered, mechanically fastened, or ballasted. In general, thermoset roofing materials offer good resistance to the effects of ozone and weathering. The materials offer a very low level of water vapor permeability, but are not resistant to petroleum products.

Thermoplastic roofing materials contain polymer plastics that are not cross-linked during manufacture nor do they become cross-linked after installation. As a result, the roofing material can be repeatedly softened for repairs or modifications through the use of heat. The most common types are polyvinyl chloride (PVC) and ethylene interpolymer (EIP). Most thermoplastic membranes are installed mechanically fastened although some installations are ballasted.

Thermoplastic roofing materials are installed in narrower sheets than thermoset materials, typically ten feet wide or less. The narrower rolls makes thermoplastic a better suited selection for applications where there are a large number of roof penetrations. Sheets are typically joined by heat welding.

Most thermoplastic roofing materials offer good resistance to acids and alkalis, but must be protected from ultraviolet rays and petroleum products. One problem with the materials is that as they age, they experience a loss in chemical plasticizers, resulting in shrinkage and cracking. While the materials can be patched, care must be used in matching the repair materials to the materials used in the roofing membrane to avoid incompatibility problems.

When selecting a single-ply roofing material, it is important to consider the type of discharges from building vents and exhausts that the roof will be exposed to. For example, air from kitchen exhausts typically contains animal fats, grease, and solvents that attack some types of single-ply roofing membranes. Other discharges, particularly from rooftop-mounted mechanical systems, may expose the roofing membrane to damaging petroleum-based products.

Figure 17.2 identifies common defects associated with single-ply roofs. Use the figure to determine the most likely cause for the defect and to identify measures that can be implemented to correct it.

Several general rules should be followed when considering single-ply roof installations:

1. Membrane Seams. Most problems in single-ply roofing occur at the seams. Problems range from adhesive failure to separation of heat welds. Most are the result of improper installation techniques. Particular attention should be paid to

selecting a qualified roofing contractor experienced in the type of roof being installed. Materials must also be applied when temperatures and humidity levels are within the range specified by the manufacturer.

2. Ponding. While all roofing systems should be designed to provide positive drainage within a maximum of 24 hours after a rainfall, single-ply roofs are not as readily damaged by ponding as are built-up roofs.

3. Foot Traffic. It is essential that the membrane in single-ply roofs be protected from puncture and wear of foot traffic on the roof. If foot traffic takes place in a particular area more frequently than once a month, protective walkways must be provided.

4. Ballasting. If ballasting is used with a single-ply roof, the stone used as ballast material should not have sharp edges, such as with crushed stone. If river stone is unavailable, then a system of pavers should be used as ballast. In addition to holding the membrane in place, pavers provide protection from foot traffic.

Characteristics of Modified Bitumen Roofing

Modified bitumens are a hybrid of built-up and single-ply roofing. First developed in Europe, the roofing has gained widespread acceptance here by providing performance characteristics that fall between built-up and single-ply roofing. It offers the durability of multiple plies found in built-up roofing and the ease of installation of single-ply due to its factory-laminated construction. A properly installed and well-maintained modified bitumen roof has an expected service life of between 15 and 20 years.

A modified bitumen roof consists of a supporting deck covered with insulation and surfaced with a composite sheet membrane that has the look of asphalt roofing products. The membrane is a multi-layer sheet made from asphalt, polyester or fiberglass reinforcement, and plastic or rubber modifiers. The sheet is similar in construction to built-up roofing, but is laminated at the manufacturing plant rather than on site. Membranes can be fully adhered or ballasted. Seams typically are bonded by adhesives or by heat torching.

The most common types of modified bitumen membranes are styrene butadiene styrene (SBS) and atactic polypropylene (APP). SBS materials are applied in moppings of hot asphalt, similar to built-up roofing construction. APP materials are lapped and joined with a propane torch.

Modified bitumen roofs are well suited in applications that require puncture resistance. Modified bitumen membranes that are granular surfaced offer excellent resistance to foot traffic and other abuse. Maintenance is relatively easy through the use of fiberglass mesh and reinforcing cement. However, caution must be used when patching because the materials must be welded through the use of a propane torch.

As is the case with other single-ply roofing systems, the most common problem with modified bitumen roof installations is seam failure. Most seam failures can be traced back to improper installation techniques, including overstressing of membranes during installation and inadequate heating of seams during torch welding.

Another common problem results from inadequate attachment or ballasting of the roof membrane. All roofing materials are subject to wind-induced lifting, particularly at the building corners and along the perimeter. Ballasted roofs require a minimum of ten pounds of ballast per square foot. Additional ballast may be required along the perimeter, particularly in areas that experience high winds on a regular basis. Mechanically fastened roofs require adequate attachment points to a decking material that is structurally sound.

Figure 17.3 identifies common defects associated with modified bitumen roofs. Use the figure to determine the most likely cause for the defect and to identify measures that can be implemented to correct it.

Several general rules may be applied when considering modified bitumen roof installations:

1. Seam Failures. Since seam failures are the most common defect in modified bitumen roofs, it is essential that proper installation methods be followed to prevent overstressing seams at the time of installation.

2. Ponding. As with single-ply roofing, ponding rapidly destroys the integrity of the roof by stressing seams. Roofs must be inspected frequently to detect and correct areas that pond before their integrity is impacted.

3. Ballast. The typical weight of the ballasting used is ten pounds per square foot.

Characteristics of Shingle and Tile Roofing

Shingle and tile roofing materials are widely used in applications having decks sloped at least three inches per foot. Materials that have been used include asphalt, clay tile, masonry tile, slate, and wood. Life expectancies range from 20 to 30 years for asphalt and wood shingles to 75 years and more for slate and tiles.

Shingle and tile roofing consists of a wood or masonry supporting deck, covered with a layer of asphalt-impregnated building paper, and surfaced with a layer of shingles or tile. The shingles and tile are held in place by nails or a wide variety of fasteners.

One of the primary advantages of shingle and tile roofing is its low level of required maintenance. During the life of the roof, the primary maintenance activity consists of regular inspections for damaged or missing shingles and tiles. The relatively high pitch of the roofs completely eliminates the problems associated with ponding frequently found in other types of roofing. Most leaks, other than those caused by missing shingles and tiles, are the result of failures in flashings along roof valleys, sidewalls, and roof penetrations.

The biggest drawback of shingle and tile roofing is its inability to support mechanical equipment as a result of the high roof pitch. Cooling towers, air handlers, exhaust fans, and other equipment commonly found on low-pitch roofs must be located elsewhere.

Figure 17.4 identifies common defects associated with shingle and tile roofs. Use the figure to determine the most likely cause for the defect and to identify measures that can be implemented to correct it.

Rule of thumb: The minimum pitch that should be used for shingle and tile roofs is three inches per foot.

Characteristics of Metal Roofing

In the past, metal roofing has been used in commercial applications primarily for decorative reasons. Today it has become accepted as a low-maintenance system suitable for use in applications having a relatively high pitch. A well-installed and maintained metal roof has an expected life of 30 to 40 years.

There are two basic types of metal roofs: structural and architectural. In structural metal roofs, the supporting deck and the waterproofing layer are combined into a single component. In architectural metal roofs, the waterproofing layer and the supporting deck are separate components. Minimum roof slopes are one-quarter inch per foot for structural metal roofs and three inches per foot for architectural.

The most common materials used in constructing metal roofs are galvanized steel, painted steel, stainless steel, natural aluminum, painted aluminum, and copper. Typical roof weights range from one to three pounds per square foot.

Metal roofs can be installed using a number of different types of seams, including flat, batten, and standing seams. Batten and standing seams offer the advantage of elevating the joint one to three inches above the roof deck. The high pitch and elevated seams of metal roofs minimize leaking, eliminate ponding, and reduce maintenance.

Most problems in metal roofs occur as a result of loosening fasteners. During installation, fasteners can be overtightened and stripped. Wind-induced vibrations can result in fatigue cracking and ultimate failure of fasteners. Galvanic corrosion caused by contact between dissimilar metals weakens fasteners. Prolonged exposure to water, particularly in areas where the rain is acidic, also corrodes fasteners; as this happens, the metal panels loosen and become more readily damaged by wind.

Figure 17.5 identifies common defects associated with metal roofs. Use the figure to determine the most likely cause for the defect and to identify measures that can be implemented to correct it.

Several rules of thumb may be applied to metal roof installations:

1. Most metal roof problems involve failures of the fasteners, many of which can be traced to improper installation practices.

2. To limit the possibility of leaking from standing seams, elevate seams at least two inches from the panel surfaces.

3. The minimum pitch varies with the type of metal roof installed and the height of the seam. In general, roof pitch should be a minimum of $1/2$ inch per foot.

Characteristics of Foam Roofing

One of the newer roof types is the spray-on polyurethane foam roof. Applied as a seamless, monolithic coating, the foam roof eliminates the problems of seam leaks common to other types of roofing. A properly installed and maintained foam roof has an expected life in excess of 20 years.

There are two basic components to the foam roof: the foam roofing material and a protective coating. Foam is sprayed onto a prepared roofing deck to a depth of one to two inches. Once the foam has hardened, a 20 to 30 mil coating of urethane or silicone is applied to protect it from the sun's ultraviolet light. The total weight of the roofing system is approximately one-half pound per square foot.

The foam roof offers several advantages over other types of roofing. The foam material has a high thermal resistance, making it a good insulator. Its rate of thermal expansion and contraction is low, allowing it to respond well to temperature extremes without becoming stressed and cracked.

One of the most serious drawbacks of the foam roof is that it is readily damaged and punctured by impact. Even if the damage isn't sufficient to allow water to enter the building, damaging the protective coating will result in fairly rapid deterioration of the underlying foam from exposure to ultraviolet light. To protect the roof from damage it is essential that pads and walkways be installed for foot traffic. Conduct frequent inspections to identify and correct damaged areas before the foam deteriorates.

Successful application of a foam roof requires that the installer be well trained and experienced in that particular type of roofing. Maintaining the proper chemical mixtures and temperatures of the components that generate the foam is critical. Allowances must be made for such environmental factors as temperature, humidity, wind speed, and moisture content of the surface being covered.

Two of the major advantages of the foam roof are its low level of required maintenance and the ease with which that maintenance can be performed. The majority of foam roof problems occur on the surface where they are easily identified and corrected. Other than frequent inspections for surface damage, the only other major maintenance requirement is the periodic reapplication of the protective coating.

Foam roofs are well suited for applications where there is minimal equipment and access to the roof is limited. They are also well suited for re-roofing applications as they can be applied directly over an existing roof, do not add a significant amount of weight to the structure, increase the insulating value of the existing roof, and can be varied in thickness to give positive slope towards existing roof drains.

Figure 17.6 identifies common defects associated with foam roofs. Use the figure to determine the most likely cause for the defect and to identify measures that can be implemented to correct it.

Several general rules may be applied when considering foam roof installations:

1. Application Conditions. Foam roofs are constructed by mixing chemicals at the time of application whose physical properties are determined by the current conditions. For that reason, manufacturers specify a range for temperature, humidity, and wind velocity when their materials can be applied. If the roof is to perform as expected, the building owner must see that the contractor complies with those environmental conditions set by the manufacturer.

2. Installer. The success or failure of a foam roof depends to a great extent on the performance of the installer. To increase the chances of a good installation, require that the installer be certified by the manufacturer.

3. UV Coating Inspection. Since the foam material is attacked by ultraviolet light, it is essential that the roof be inspected frequently for damage to the protective coating. Any areas where the coating is found to be thin or otherwise damaged must be repaired immediately to prevent damage to the underlying foam.

4. Training. Although foam roofs are easy to maintain, maintenance personnel must be trained in how to work around them. In particular, the foam material is damaged by impact. Maintenance personnel who work on equipment located on the roof must be instructed to stay on walkways whenever possible. Storing

materials and equipment, even for short periods of time, should be discouraged unless measures are taken to protect the roof.

5. Insulation. Foam roofs are natural insulators. As a rule of thumb, foam roofs can be considered to reduce heat transmission through the roof by 20 to 40 percent.

THE THREE MAJOR CAUSES OF ROOFING FAILURE

In establishing a preventive maintenance program that will protect roofing materials from premature failure, it is important to understand the causes of roofing failures. Knowing what attacks the roof and how it damages roofing materials will permit the building manager to tailor the program to the particular application.

There are three categories of causes for roofing failures: chemical attack, heat and radiation effects, and physical abuse. All are related to the environment in which the roof is installed and must perform. Figure 17.7 summarizes the most common elements that attack a roof and what can be done to reduce their impact.

Chemical Attack

Chemical attack on roofing materials is a process that takes place over an extended period of time with a slow deterioration of the materials. Gradually chemical and physical properties of the roofing materials are changed until they can no longer perform and the roof fails. Most sources of chemical attack can be minimized through preventive measures. Common sources for chemical attack include ultraviolet light, oxidation, volatilization, and exposure to exhaust fumes.

UV LIGHT. Ultraviolet light from the sun attacks most roofing materials by triggering chemical reactions within the materials. In synthetic materials, ultraviolet light can break down the complex chemical chains that determine the materials' physical properties, such as tensile strength and flexibility. Similar reactions take place in natural roofing materials.

The best protection against ultraviolet light is the addition of a layer to block the sun's rays from the roofing material. In the case of sprayed-on foam roofing and some single-ply roofing, a protective coating is applied to the surface of the roof. In other single-ply and built-up roofing, ballast is an effective blocker of ultraviolet light.

OXIDATION. Oxidation occurs in materials ranging from the roofing deck to the protective coating applied to the membrane. In metal decks, oxidation weakens the deck materials resulting in increased movement and separation of overlying roofing layers. In synthetic roofing plies and membranes, oxidation can lead to polymerization and cross-linking of complex chemicals. The result is materials that are harder and less flexible and therefore more readily damaged by thermal and structural movement.

Oxidation rates are higher for asphalt-based products than for synthetic materials, but the effects are similar. As asphalt-based roofing products oxidize, they lose flexibility and tensile strength. In all materials, the rate of oxidation accelerates with higher temperatures.

Oxidation rates of roofing materials are greatly increased with exposure to water and high temperatures. Keeping water from penetrating the surface of the roof will help to reduce the oxidation of the materials lying under the surface. Material temperatures can be reduced by applying a light-colored finish to the upper surface or by installing a light colored layer of ballast.

VOLATILIZATION. Many roofing products, such as asphalt, have low volatility at normal roof temperatures. Their evaporation rates over time are not enough to damage their performance, but many synthetic roofing materials have components that are high in volatility; plasticizers, hardeners, and other additives do evaporate with time resulting in materials whose properties of strength and flexibility significantly decrease

The rate at which roofing products volatilize can be reduced primarily by reducing their temperature. Temperatures can be reduced by applying a light-colored finish to the upper surface or by installing a light-colored layer of ballast.

EXPOSURE TO EXHAUST FUMES. Building exhausts that discharge onto roofs often contain products that chemically attack roofing materials. Of particular concern are single-ply membranes that are exposed to kitchen exhausts. A number of these membranes are particularly susceptible to damage from vegetable and animal oils commonly used in food preparation. In selecting a new roof, you should consider the chemicals that may be discharged onto it. For existing roofs, precautions should be taken to insure that harmful discharges are ducted away from roof surfaces.

Heat and Radiation

Roofs do not wear out, they dry out. Heat from the sun evaporates volatile elements from asphalt, tar, and synthetic roof membranes. High temperatures increase the rate of oxidation of roofing materials. Heat-induced cycles of thermal expansion and contraction introduce stresses in roofing materials. Over time, these factors take their toll.

In asphalt-based products, a skin eventually forms on the surface. This skin, as the result of exposure to high temperatures, does not have the same thermal expansion properties as the underlying materials. As the sun heats the roof and the materials expand, the skin is unable to expand at the same rate. The result is the formation of hairline cracks. With repeated cycles of thermal expansion and contraction, these cracks grow until they reach deep into the underlying material.

In synthetic materials, heat increases the rate at which chemical reactions take place, accelerating the attack on the roofing materials.

Protective coatings, light-colored finishes, and light-colored ballast can all be used to help reflect sunlight from the roof, lowering its surface temperature.

Physical Abuse

There are four primary causes of physical damage to a roof: ponding, foot traffic, movement, and wind. When water is allowed to pond on a roof surface, it starts a process that accelerates rapidly and results in extensive damage to large areas.

Rule of thumb: If areas of water remain on a roof more than 24 hours after the rain has ended, the roof has a ponding problem.

PONDING. Ponding destroys roofs in two ways. First, the weight of the water causes a deflection in the surface of the roof, thus promoting even more ponding. A one-inch-deep pond measuring ten feet by ten feet weighs approximately 530 pounds, enough to induce a slight sag in roofing materials. The sag in turn stresses the materials. As this sag grows, the pond expands, increasing the stress. Eventually the stress is sufficient to tear surface and underlying materials, allowing water to enter.

The second way in which ponding destroys a roof is more indirect. Many roofing materials lose some of their strength as the result of prolonged exposure to water. Water also promotes the growth of biological agents that can attack roofing materials. If the water freezes, particularly if it has worked its way beneath the surface, its expansion will accelerate the splitting of materials.

Limiting roof damage from ponding requires frequent roof inspections. Ponding areas are readily identified by conducting a roof inspection within 24 hours of the end of a significant rainfall. Areas having ponded water should be identified and marked on a roof plan. If there are drains close by, check to see that they are clear and are located below the roof level. If the drains are clear and properly operating, then install additional roof drains or make modifications to raise the roof surface.

FOOT TRAFFIC DAMAGE. One of the most common causes of physical abuse to a roof is foot traffic to and from mechanical equipment. Frequent traffic to particular pieces of equipment results in paths worn in the roof's upper layer; ballast becomes displaced, ultraviolet blocking coatings become damaged, and membranes become stressed. Additional damage occurs when tools are dropped, heavy service equipment is rolled or dragged across the roof, and lubricating oils and grease drip on unprotected surfaces.

Minimize damage from foot traffic by limiting access to the roof to only those maintenance personnel who have duties to perform there. Once the volume of traffic has been reduced, install pads and walkways to permit access to all mechanical equipment located on the roof. Instruct maintenance personnel to stay on the pads as much as possible.

DAMAGE FROM MOVEMENT. Movement in the roofing materials and the supporting structure causes the roofing materials to crack, split, and delaminate. Movement can be in the form of thermal expansion and contraction, equipment-generated vibrations, or settlement of supporting structures.

Thermal and vibration-induced movement causes roofing failures through the process of fatigue. Materials are repeatedly stressed until small cracks form. Movement through settlement generally results in low spots that pond.

Damage from movement can be minimized by taking several steps. Use a light-color finish to reduce the temperature of the roof, thus reducing thermal movement. Reduce the transmission of equipment vibrations to the roof by installing vibration isolators on all roof mounted mechanical equipment. Settlement is best detected at the time of re-roofing by thoroughly inspecting and measuring the elevation of the supporting structure.

WIND DAMAGE. Wind damage is most often thought of as the result of a major storm. However, much lower velocity winds can cause significant physical damage to a roof over time. Wind-induced damage is primarily the result of lifting forces similar to those produced by a wing. As air flows over the flat surface of a roof, its pressure changes. That pressure change causes the roof surface to try and lift away from the remaining structure. If the roof is not properly attached or ballasted, the lifting action stresses seams and membranes. Even if the lifting is relatively minor, over time the materials will be come fatigued and will fail.

Proper attachment and ballasting is the best way to avoid wind damage to a roof. For facilities exposed to frequent high winds, roof pads along the perimeter of the roof may help to reduce wind damage.

THE NEED FOR ROOF MAINTENANCE

The importance of a good roof maintenance program is demonstrated by the difference in life expectancies for roofs that are aggressively maintained and those that are allowed to decay. A roof that has been ignored will typically fail in less than one-half of its rated life. With the annual cost of a complete maintenance program running between one and two percent of the replacement cost, maintenance can double the service life of a typical roof for roughly ten to twenty percent of the replacement cost.

Maintenance is also a requirement of roofing warranties. To remain in effect, most roofing companies require that specific maintenance activities be performed on a regular basis by the building owner. Damage caused by the owner or occupants, such as the improper installation of roof-mounted equipment, will void most roof warranties unless the installation is rapidly detected and corrected.

The key to a successful maintenance program is prompt identification and repair of defects while they are minor. Prompt identification requires that good documentation be kept, periodic inspections be completed, and questionable areas be tested. The information provided by such a program can provide the basis for both short- and long-term roof maintenance planning.

The best time to implement a roofing maintenance program is when the roof is new. Deferring the program until the roof has aged several years only serves to increase future maintenance costs.

Maintenance Records

One of the most important elements in a roofing maintenance program is documentation. Documentation provides a history from its installation through any required repairs. By keeping accurate records on what was installed and how it has been maintained, you will have the information required to make maintenance/replacement considerations.

Data that is important to a roof maintenance program ranges from installation information to repairs made to the roof. It includes a listing of who the manufacturer and installer were, a detailed description of what was installed and how it was installed, what the warranty terms are, when inspections were conducted, what conditions were found during those inspections, and what action was taken to correct defects. Keeping these records will assist in demonstrating compliance with warranty requirements as well as providing a means for insuring that detailed inspections are completed.

The maintenance records for a roof should start with data from the time of the original installation. Use Figure 17.8 to record data on a new or replacement roof. Complete separate data sheets for each building. If a particular building has two or more roof types or roof sections that were installed at different times, complete a separate data sheet for each section.

Detailed descriptions of the roof construction will assist you when it is necessary to make repairs to a particular roof. They also will help you to evaluate the performance of a particular roof. The information required varies with roof type. Use the following figures to record roofing construction details:

Figure 17.9   - Built-up
Figure 17.10 - Single-ply
Figure 17.11 - Modified Bitumen
Figure 17.12 - Shingle
Figure 17.13 - Metal
Figure 17.14 - Sprayed-On Foam

Match the data sheets to the type of roof that is installed. If a particular building has two or more roof types or roof sections that were installed at different times, complete a separate data sheet for each section.

For each building in the facility, establish a separate file. All information associated with that particular roof should be placed in that file for easy reference.

THREE TYPES OF ROOF INSPECTIONS

The roof inspection is the primary means of gaining feedback on the condition of a roof. With a complete inspection program, you can detect defects while they are still small, well before they develop into roof leaks. If you wait for an occupant's call to report a leaking roof, the extent of the damage and the costs to make the needed repairs will be much greater than if the problem had been identified during a routine roof inspection.

There are three types of inspections to be conducted: visual, core sampling, and non-destructive testing. Of these, visual inspections are the most important and should be conducted most often. If problems are found during a visual inspection, such as a damaged membrane, then it may be necessary to conduct core sampling or non-destructive roof testing in order to determine the extent of the problem.

Visual Inspections

Carry out visual inspections of each roof twice a year. Complete one inspection in the early fall after the roof has experienced the high temperatures of the summer. By conducting the inspection then, you can identify and correct summer-related damage while the temperature is still high enough for repairs to be made. Complete the second inspection in early spring after the last winter freeze. This inspection identifies damage from ice and freezing before it can be made worse by high summer temperatures.

In addition to the two annual inspections, make spot checks of roofs throughout the year, particularly after severe weather, including heavy rains, heavy snows, and wind storms. Spot check for ponding after a heavy rain.

Record and file inspection information for future reference, particularly when looking for long-term trends in roofing problems. Use the following figures to record roofing construction details:

Figure 17.15 - Built-up

Figure 17.16 - Single-ply

Figure 17.17 - Modified Bitumen

Figure 17.18 - Shingle or Tile

Figure 17.19 - Metal

Figure 17.20 - Sprayed-On Foam

Match the inspection form to the type of roof installed. If a particular building has two or more roof types or roof sections that were installed at different times, use a separate data sheet for each section.

Use Figure 17.21 to sketch the outline of the roof being inspected. Note all equipment penetrations on the grid for future reference. Roofs have a way of growing equipment and antennas that were installed without the knowledge of those who maintain the roof. By noting the location of existing equipment, it will be easy to determine when new units are added so that they may be inspected for proper installation. In addition, note on the figure defects found during the inspection along with a description of each. Use separate sheets for each section of a roof.

Photographs are particularly helpful in identifying and tracking defects. By comparing photographs from previous inspections, you can determine the rate of deterioration. Photographs also will help in demonstrating warranty-related problems.

Keep all data sheets for a particular roof or roof section in a file for that building. Past inspection reports will help you keep track of conditions as they change over time. They also will help you to identify a roof that is approaching the end of its expected life and is in need of replacement.

Core Sampling

The visual inspection provides detailed information on the condition of the membrane, the integrity of the flashing, and the extent of obvious damage. It does not, however, provide an indication of the amount and location of moisture that has already penetrated the membrane and entered the underlying layers. Visual inspections also do not give an indication of how well the roof layers are secured. Core sampling provides a mechanism for determining the extent of moisture damage and evaluating how well the membrane and insulation are attached.

Core sampling involves cutting through the roofing materials and removing a sample for inspection. If wet insulation or separated components are found, note their location on the roof sketch. By completing a pattern of samples, it will be possible to determine the extent of the wet or damaged materials. To complete the repairs, remove and replace all of the wet and damaged components. *Rule of thumb:* If 25% of the insulation is found to contain moisture, the roof is in need of replacement rather than repair.

Non-Destructive Testing

One of the problems with core sampling is that it is an invasive process. Each cut made into the roof must be patched to prevent the entry of water. For that reason, core sampling is generally limited to a relatively small number of test locations. As a result, core sampling may or may not identify all areas where moisture has penetrated the membrane.

Non-destructive testing techniques offer an alternative. They can, without any damage to the roof, determine the location and extent of wet insulation. Because they are non-destructive, enough readings can be taken to develop a map of moisture content of the roof. Typically a grid pattern is laid over the roof and measurements are taken at each point of the grid. For most open applications, a five-foot grid is sufficient to measure water penetration. The pattern should be decreased to two and one-half feet around any roof penetration and along the roof perimeter.

There are three types of non-destructive testing instruments that are used on roofs: nuclear gauges, electrical capacitance gauges, and infrared cameras.

Nuclear gauges use a weak radiation source to indirectly detect the presence of water in underlying layers of a roof. The instruments are most sensitive to water near the surface and cannot be used on all roof types or with all roofing materials. Since the instrument emits radiation, a licensing and periodic testing of the unit is required. Nuclear gauges are best suited for use on single-ply and built-up roofs.

Electrical capacitance gauges measure the dielectric constant of roofing materials. Wet materials indicate a higher value than dry materials. Like nuclear gauges, electrical capacitance gauges are more sensitive to moisture located near the surface. The roof surface must be dry in order to use the gauge. They cannot be used with certain roofing materials, such as foil-covered insulation.

Infrared roof inspections detect water in roofing materials by measuring the surface temperature. Areas with dry insulation and roofing materials cool more rapidly than areas where moisture has penetrated the surface. As a result, areas of the roof that are wet show in thermal images as being hotter. Unlike other non-destructive tests that rely on a sample grid, infrared inspections are continuous, providing a thermal image of the complete roof. To be effective, thermal testing of roofs must take place at night, well after the sun's thermal effects have been conducted and radiated away. Caution must be used to insure that the thermal image is not distorted by roof exhausts and other heat sources.

MAINTENANCE ACTIONS

The final element in developing documentation for a roof maintenance program is the tracking of all maintenance activities performed on that roof. Maintaining these records will help you to identify reoccurring problems as well as to track problems that are getting worse with time. Use Figure 17.22 to record a separate sheet for each maintenance action taken.

FIGURE 17.1 Built-Up Roofing Defects

Defect	Most Likely Cause	Recommended Maintenance Action
Ponding	Improper design or installation resulting in in-adequate slope for proper drainage, building or roof deck settlement, or insufficient or improp-erly placed roof drains.	Little can be done to correct roofs that do not have sufficient slope, are lacking adequate roof drains, or have settled. The impact of ponding in these cases can be minimized by pumping down the ponded areas after rainfall. Most ponding problems can be corrected only at the time of re-roofing.
Missing Aggregate	Insufficient ballast installation, use of a ballast material that is too small in diameter, high lev-els of foot traffic, and wind.	Install additional ballast to provide adequate coverage of the surface. Install concrete or synthetic foot pads from access areas to me-chanical equipment installed on the roof to prevent damage from foot traffic. If wind is removing ballast from certain areas, install con-crete pads instead of gravel.
Surface Blisters	Moisture trapped below the surface of the up-per roofing layer or insufficient ballast to pro-tect the roof surface from direct sunshine.	Slice and remove the entire blister. Patch the area and cover with a layer of ballast.
Alligatoring	As the roofing materials age, they dry out and crack, particularly if they are not protected from direct sunlight by a protective coating or ballast.	Once alligatoring has started, little can be done to save the membrane. Eventually the cracks will grow through the entire depth of the mem-brane, resulting in leaks. Alligatoring is best prevented by periodic recoating of the mem-brane and insuring it is sufficiently covered with ballast.

459

Figure 17.1 (continued)

Defect	Most Likely Cause	Recommended Maintenance Action
Deep Blisters	Moisture trapped between the plies from leaks or when the roof was applied.	Remove the membrane, slice and remove the entire blister, patch the damaged felts, and apply a new section of membrane.
Membrane Ridges	Thermally-induced movement of the felts or roofing deck that shows up at weak or stressed spots in the felts or membrane.	Requires removal and replacement of that section of the roof down to the deck. Unless the cause of the thermal movement is identified and corrected, the problem will reoccur.
Membrane Splits	Usually occur over joints in the insulation and deck as the result of improper attachment of the membrane and the insulation to the deck. May also occur near the edges of roof ponds due to the induced stress.	The source of the stress must be identified and corrected to complete repairs. In most cases, the section of the roof must be removed down to the deck. In the case of ponding, additional roof drains must be installed or the roof must be built up level with the surrounding roof surface.
Fishmouths	Gaps formed in membrane seams as the result of improperly stretching the felt during installation.	Cut the unattached membrane along the fishmouth until attached membrane is reached. Reattach the membrane sections to the felts, adding patches as required.

FIGURE 17.2 Single-Ply Roofing Defects

Defect	Most Likely Cause	Recommended Maintenance Action
Ponding	Improper design or installation resulting in inadequate slope for proper drainage, building or roof deck settlement, or insufficient or improperly placed roof drains.	Little can be done to correct roofs that do not have sufficient slope, are lacking adequate roof drains, or have settled. The impact of ponding in these cases can be minimized by pumping down the ponded areas after rainfall. Most ponding problems can be corrected only at the time of re-roofing.
Missing Aggregate	Insufficient ballast installation, use of a ballast material that is too small in diameter, high levels of foot traffic, and wind.	Install additional ballast to provide adequate coverage of the surface. Install concrete or synthetic foot pads from access areas to mechanical equipment installed on the roof to prevent damage from foot traffic. If wind is removing ballast from certain areas, install concrete pads instead of gravel.
Blisters	Moisture trapped below the surface of the membrane or insufficient ballast to protect the roof surface from direct sunshine.	Slice and remove the entire blister. Patch the area and recoat with a protective covering.
Alligatoring	As the roofing membrane ages, it dries out and cracks, particularly if it is not protected from direct sunlight by a protective coating or ballast.	Once alligatoring has started, little can be done to save the membrane. Eventually the cracks will grow through the entire depth of the membrane, resulting in leaks. Alligatoring is best prevented by periodic recoating of the membrane or insuring it is sufficiently covered with ballast.

Figure 17.2 (continued)

Defect	Most Likely Cause	Recommended Maintenance Action
Membrane Punctures	Most puncture damage is the result of foot traffic on the roof.	Limit access to the roof. Train maintenance personnel in how to work on roof-located equipment without damaging the roof membrane.
Split Seams	Split seams are generally the result of improper seaming techniques.	The quality of the seam installation is directly related to the qualifications and performance of the installer. Require that the installer be certified by the roofing system manufacturer. Monitor the installation.
Lifted Membrane	Lifting of the membrane around the building perimeter is usually the result of wind.	If the membrane is lifting at the perimeter, install pads. For adhered systems, inspect attachment points for deterioration. For ballasted systems, check depth of ballast.

FIGURE 17.3 Modified Bitumen Roofing Defects

Defect	Most Likely Cause	Recommended Maintenance Action
Ponding	Improper design or installation resulting in inadequate slope for proper drainage, building or roof deck settlement, or insufficient or improperly placed roof drains.	Little can be done to correct roofs that do not have sufficient slope, are lacking adequate roof drains, or have settled. The impact of ponding in these cases can be minimized by pumping down the ponded areas after rainfall. Most ponding problems can be corrected only at the time of re-roofing.
Split Seams	Split seams are usually the result of improper installation techniques, including stressing the seam during installation and inadequate heat and/or pressure.	Follow proper installation techniques to insure that seams are not stressed during installation.
Billowing	On windy days, if the roofing billows, the substrate has lost its adhesion. Smaller areas can be detected if ridges form on the surface when the edge of your shoe is dragged across the surface.	Determine the extent of the damage. In ballasted installations, insure that sufficient ballast has been installed to keep the membrane in place. In adhered roofs, that portion that has become detached will have to be removed and replaced.

FIGURE 17.4 Shingle and Tile Roofing Defects

Defect	Most Likely Cause	Recommended Maintenance Action
Curled Shingles	With age and exposure to heat, asphalt-based shingles shrink and curl up at the edges.	Curling is an indication that the asphalt shingles have reached the end of their useful life and are in need of replacement.
Cracked Shingles/Tiles	Cracking is caused by physical damage to the roof or by stress resulting from installing the fasteners too tightly.	Remove all overhanging tree branches that can come in contact with the roof. Fastener-related problems can be corrected only at the time of installation by following the manufacturer's recommended installation techniques.
Missing Shingle/Tiles	Wind is the most common cause of missing shingles and tiles. In tile roofs, failure and corrosion of the fasteners, aided by wind, can also lead to missing tiles.	Individual shingles and tiles can be replaced as required. However, if a large number of tiles are noted as being excessively loose, the fasteners are most likely failing and the roof will have to be replaced.

FIGURE 17.5 Metal Roofing Defects

Defect	Most Likely Cause	Recommended Maintenance Action
Lifting Panels	Corrosion or failure of the fasteners.	Fastener failures are generally the result of improper installation practices. Corrosion is the result of age or the use of the wrong type of material. Replace all damaged fasteners using care to not overtighten them.
Panel Corrosion	Failure of the protective coating.	All metal roofing panels will corrode to some extent. However, when the protective coating fails, the corrosion will accelerate. Depending on the type of roof, panels may be recoated or they may have to be replaced.
Panel Warping	Insufficient room for thermal expansion or overtightening of the fasteners.	Buckled panels should be removed and replaced. Insure that new panels are installed correctly to permit thermal movement.

FIGURE 17.6 Sprayed-On Foam Roof Defects

Defect	Most Likely Cause	Recommended Maintenance Action
Rough Surface	Rough and uneven foam roof surfaces are the result of incorrect chemical mixtures, improper application temperatures and humidity, or high wind conditions at the time of installation.	Installers should be limited to those firms and individuals that are certified by the roofing manufacturer. Roofs should be applied only when temperature, humidity, and wind conditions are within the ranges specified by the manufacturer.
Foam Degradation	Exposure of the roof foam to ultraviolet light.	Inspect the protective coating on the foam roof frequently. Reapply the coating every three to five years, or more frequently if the coating shows indications of wear.
Punctures	Most punctures are the result of worker carelessness and debris, such as tree branches, blown on the roof from surrounding areas.	Limit access to the roof to minimize foot traffic. Train maintenance personnel how to work on equipment located on the roof without damaging the roof surface. Inspect the roof frequently and remove all debris promptly.

FIGURE 17.7 Causes of Roof Failure

Element	Materials Damaged	Impact on Roofing Materials	Protective Measures
Ultraviolet Light	Damages nearly all roofing materials.	Causes chemical reactions that reduce flexibility and strength.	Insure that the upper surface is coated with an ultraviolet light-resistant coating, and that the coating is properly maintained.
Heat	Damages nearly all roofing materials.	Causes evaporation of volatile components resulting in a reduction in flexibility.	Use a light-colored finish or light-colored ballast to help reflect sunlight.
Oxidation	Damage varies with roofing material, ranging from relatively high for asphalt, moderate for coal tar, and low for most synthetics. The rate of oxidation increases with increased roof temperature.	Causes chemical reactions that reduce flexibility and strength.	Use a light-colored finish or light-colored ballast to reduce surface temperatures.
Movement	Structural, thermal, and vibration-induced movement impacts all roofing materials, but is most damaging to older materials that have lost some of their flexibility and elasticity.	Results in splits, cracks, and delaminations.	Use light-colored surface finishes to minimize temperature exposures. Insure that all roof penetrations are properly flashed. Mechanical equipment should be installed on vibration isolators and periodically checked for excessive vibrations.

Figure 17.7 (continued)

Element	Materials Damaged	Impact on Roofing Materials	Protective Measures
Moisture	Most synthetic and coal tar materials are highly moisture-resistant. While asphalt-based roof plies are moisture-resistant, they are less resistant than the synthetic materials. All materials will be damaged if water is allowed to pond on the surface.	When moisture penetrates some asphalt-based roofing materials, it can reduce the material's strength. If water is allowed to pond on any roof surface, the additional weight will cause the material to deflect, resulting in additional ponding. Eventually, the weight of the water will cause failures in the roofing materials.	Frequent inspections after rains will identify areas where ponding is taking place. Non-destructive testing techniques will identify areas where moisture has penetrated the roofing membrane.
Physical Abuse	All roofing surfaces can be easily damaged by excessive foot traffic, dropped tools, and other physical causes.	The damage usually extends well beyond the area of the surface damage, particularly once moisture penetrates the roofing membrane.	Provide sufficient roof pads to allow easy access to all roof installed mechanical equipment. Periodic inspections of roofs will help to identify areas that have been damaged before moisture has been able to extend the damage to other areas.

FIGURE 17.8 Roof Installation Data

1. General

Building: _____

Roof Section: _____

Roof Type: _____

Date Installed: _____ Area (sq ft): _____

Warranty Expiration
Date: _____ Cost: _____

2. Manufacturer

Company: _____

Address: _____

City: _____ State: _____ Zip: _____

Contact: _____

Phone: (_____) - _____ - _____

3. Installer

Company: _____

Address: _____

City: _____ State: _____ Zip: _____

Contact: _____

Phone: (_____) - _____ - _____

FIGURE 17.9 Built-Up Roof Construction Details

Building: _____ Section: _____ Area: _____

Deck Material

☐ Metal   ☐ Precast Concrete Slab
☐ Wood   ☐ Gypsum Slab
☐ Poured Concrete   ☐ Other _____

Insulation

Thickness: _____   Method of Attachment: _____

☐ Fiberglass Board   ☐ Perlite Sheet
☐ Mineral Fiberboard   ☐ Polystyrene Sheet
☐ Foamglass Board   ☐ Other _____

Felts
Number of Felts: _____

Felt Material   Bonding Agent
☐ Fiberglass   ☐ Asphalt
☐ Organic   ☐ Coal Tar
☐ Asbestos   ☐ Other _____
☐ Other _____

Surface

☐ Gravel   ☐ Cap Sheet
☐ Slag   ☐ Pavers
☐ Mineral Granules   ☐ Other _____

Flashing
Length (feet): _____

☐ Aluminum   ☐ PVC
☐ Copper   ☐ Stainless Steel
☐ Galvanized   ☐ Other _____

FIGURE 17.10 Single-Ply Roof Construction Details

Building: _____ Section: _____ Area: _____

Deck Material

- ☐ Metal
- ☐ Wood
- ☐ Poured Concrete

- ☐ Precast Concrete Slab
- ☐ Gypsum Slab
- ☐ Other _____

Insulation

Thickness: _____ Method of Attachment: _____

- ☐ Fiberglass Board
- ☐ Mineral Fiberboard
- ☐ Foamglass Board

- ☐ Perlite Sheet
- ☐ Polystyrene Sheet
- ☐ Other _____

Membrane

Material

- ☐ Cured Elastomer
- ☐ Modified Bitumen
- ☐ Thermoplastic
- ☐ Uncured Elastomer
- ☐ Other _____

Seam Sealing Method

- ☐ Adhesive
- ☐ Hot Air Gun
- ☐ Self-Sealing
- ☐ Solvent
- ☐ Torch Heating

Method Of Attachment

- ☐ Ballasted
- ☐ Fully Adhered
- ☐ Mechanically Fastened
- ☐ Partially Adhered

Flashing

Length (feet): _____

- ☐ Aluminum
- ☐ Copper
- ☐ Galvanized

- ☐ PVC
- ☐ Stainless Steel
- ☐ Other _____

FIGURE 17.11 Modified Bitumen Roof Construction Details

Building: _____ Section: _____ Area: _____

Deck Material

☐ Metal   ☐ Precast Concrete Slab
☐ Wood   ☐ Gypsum Slab
☐ Poured Concrete   ☐ Other _____

Insulation

Thickness: _____   Method of Attachment: _____

☐ Fiberglass Board   ☐ Perlite Sheet
☐ Mineral Fiberboard   ☐ Polystyrene Sheet
☐ Foamglass Board   ☐ Other _____

Membrane

Material

☐ Styrene Butadiene Styrene (SBS)
☐ Atactic Polypropylene (APP)
☐ Other _____

Seam Sealing Method   Method Of Attachment

☐ Adhesive   ☐ Ballasted
☐ Hot Asphalt   ☐ Fully Adhered
☐ Self-Sealing   ☐ Mechanically Fastened
☐ Torch Heating

Flashing

Length (feet): _____

☐ Aluminum   ☐ PVC
☐ Copper   ☐ Stainless Steel
☐ Galvanized   ☐ Other _____

FIGURE 17.12 Shingle Roof Construction Details

Building: _____ Section: _____

Slope: _____ Area: _____

Sheathing

☐ Plywood - Thickness: _____
☐ Wood Board - Thickness: _____
☐ Wood Lath
☐ Other: _____

Underlayment

☐ None
☐ Saturated Felt
☐ Other: _____

Shingles

☐ Asbestos   ☐ Aluminum Tile
☐ Fiberglass   ☐ Clay Tile
☐ Cedar   ☐ Mission Tile
☐ Cypress   ☐ Concrete Tile
☐ Pine   ☐ Steel Tile
☐ Slate   ☐ Other: _____

Flashing

Length (feet): _____

☐ Aluminum   ☐ PVC
☐ Copper   ☐ Stainless Steel
☐ Galvanized   ☐ Other _____

FIGURE 17.13 Metal Roof Construction Details

Building: _____ Section: _____ Area: _____

General

Type of Roof
- ☐ Architectural
- ☐ Structural

Type of Seam
- ☐ Batten
- ☐ Standing
- ☐ Flat

Slope of Roof (Inches per foot): _____

Deck Material

- ☐ Metal
- ☐ Wood
- ☐ Concrete
- ☐ Gypsum Slab
- ☐ None
- ☐ Other _____

Roofing Material

Material
- ☐ Aluminum
- ☐ Copper
- ☐ Steel
- ☐ Other: _____

Finish
- ☐ Galvanized
- ☐ Painted
- ☐ Natural
- ☐ Other: _____

Flashing

Length (feet): _____

- ☐ Aluminum
- ☐ Copper
- ☐ Galvanized
- ☐ PVC
- ☐ Stainless Steel
- ☐ Other _____

FIGURE 17.14 Sprayed-On Foam Roof Construction Details

Building: _____ Section: _____ Area: _____

Deck Material

☐ Metal   ☐ Precast Concrete Slab
☐ Wood   ☐ Gypsum Slab
☐ Poured Concrete   ☐ Other _____

Foam

☐ Polyurethane
☐ Other _____   Thickness (inches): _____

Protective Coating

☐ Elastomer   ☐ Butyl Rubber
☐ Acrylic   ☐ Vinyl
☐ Silicone   ☐ Other _____

Thickness (mils): _____

Flashing

Length (feet): _____

☐ Aluminum   ☐ PVC
☐ Copper   ☐ Stainless Steel
☐ Galvanized   ☐ Other _____

FIGURE 17.15 Built-Up Roofing Condition

Building: _____ Section: _____

Inspector: _____ Date: _____

General Condition
(Note defects on detail grid)

Evidence of Leaking: ☐ Yes   ☐ No
Reported Leaks: ☐ Yes   ☐ No
Evidence of Ponding: ☐ Yes   ☐ No
Physical Damage: ☐ Yes   ☐ No

Aggregate

☐ Poor   ☐ Good
☐ Fair   ☐ Excellent
☐ Other: _____

Surface Coating
(Check all that apply)

☐ Good, no defects   ☐ Buckled
☐ Alligatored   ☐ Cracked
☐ Blistered   ☐ Fishmouths
☐ Other: _____
Percent of surface exposed (0 - 100): _____

Felts
(Check all that apply)

☐ Good, no defects   ☐ Separated
☐ Fair   ☐ Curling
☐ Exposed
☐ Other: _____

Base Flashing
(Check all that apply)

☐ Good, no defects   ☐ Separated from wall
☐ Fair   ☐ Open joints
☐ Corroded   ☐ Loose
☐ Other: _____

Counter Flashing
(Check all that apply)

☐ Good, no defects   ☐ Separated from wall
☐ Fair   ☐ Open joints
☐ Corroded   ☐ Loose
☐ Other: _____

Figure 17.15 (continued)

Equipment/Vent Flashing (Check all that apply)	☐ Good, no defects ☐ Fair ☐ Corroded ☐ Other: _____	☐ Separated ☐ Open joints ☐ Loose
Expansion Joints (Check all that apply)	☐ Good, no defects ☐ Fair ☐ Surface cracks ☐ Other: _____	☐ Deteriorated membranes ☐ Damaged flashings ☐ Damaged blocking
Drains (Check all that apply)	☐ Good, no defects ☐ Fair ☐ Incorrect height ☐ Other: _____	☐ Separated from membrane ☐ Loose clamps ☐ Debris guard missing

Comments:

_____

_____

_____

_____

_____

_____

FIGURE 17.16 Single-Ply Roofing Condition

Building: _____ Section: _____

Inspector: _____ Date: _____

General Condition
(Note defects on detail grid)

Evidence of Leaking:	☐ Yes	☐ No
Reported Leaks:	☐ Yes	☐ No
Evidence of Ponding:	☐ Yes	☐ No
Physical Damage:	☐ Yes	☐ No

Ballast
(Ballasted systems only)

☐ Good
☐ Fully covered but thin
☐ Only partially covered
☐ Percent of surface exposed (0 - 100): _____
Other: _____

Surface Coating
(Check all that apply)

☐ Good, no defects   ☐ Peeling
☐ Alligatored   ☐ Cracked
☐ Blistered   ☐ Fishmouths
☐ Other: _____

Membrane
(Check all that apply)

☐ Good, no defects   ☐ Cracked
☐ Torn   ☐ Split seams
☐ Punctured
☐ Detached (0 - 100 %): _____
☐ Other: _____

Base Flashing
(Check all that apply)

☐ Good, no defects   ☐ Separated from wall
☐ Fair   ☐ Open joints
☐ Corroded   ☐ Loose
☐ Other: _____

Counter Flashing
(Check all that apply)

☐ Good, no defects   ☐ Separated from wall
☐ Fair   ☐ Open joints
☐ Corroded   ☐ Loose
☐ Other: _____

Figure 17.16 (continued)

Equipment/Vent Flashing (Check all that apply)	☐ Good, no defects ☐ Fair ☐ Corroded ☐ Other: _____	☐ Separated ☐ Open joints ☐ Loose
Expansion Joints (Check all that apply)	☐ Good, no defects ☐ Fair ☐ Surface cracks ☐ Other: _____	☐ Deteriorated membranes ☐ Damaged flashings ☐
Drains (Check all that apply)	☐ Good, no defects ☐ Fair ☐ Incorrect height ☐ Other: _____	☐ Separated from membrane ☐ Loose clamps ☐ Debris guard missing

Comments:

_____

_____

_____

_____

_____

_____

_____

FIGURE 17.17 Modified Bitumen Roofing Condition

Building: _____   Section: _____

Inspector: _____   Date: _____

General Condition
(Note defects on detail grid)

Evidence of Leaking: ☐ Yes   ☐ No
Reported Leaks: ☐ Yes   ☐ No
Evidence of Ponding: ☐ Yes   ☐ No
Physical Damage: ☐ Yes   ☐ No

Ballast
(Ballasted systems only)

☐ Good
☐ Fully covered but thin
☐ Only partially covered
☐ Percent of surface exposed (0 - 100): _____
Other: _____

Membrane
(Check all that apply)

☐ Good, no defects   ☐ Cracked
☐ Alligatored   ☐ Fishmouths
☐ Blistered   ☐ Split seams
☐ Other: _____

Base Flashing
(Check all that apply)

☐ Good, no defects   ☐ Separated from wall
☐ Fair   ☐ Open joints
☐ Corroded   ☐ Loose
☐ Other: _____

Counter Flashing
(Check all that apply)

☐ Good, no defects   ☐ Separated from wall
☐ Fair   ☐ Open joints
☐ Corroded   ☐ Loose
☐ Other: _____

Equipment/Vent Flashing
(Check all that apply)

☐ Good, no defects   ☐ Separated
☐ Fair   ☐ Open joints
☐ Corroded   ☐ Loose
☐ Other: _____

Figure 17.17 (continued)

Expansion Joints (Check all that apply)	☐ Good, no defects ☐ Fair ☐ Surface cracks ☐ Other: _____	☐ Deteriorated membranes ☐ Damaged flashings ☐ Damaged blocking
Drains (Check all that apply)	☐ Good, no defects ☐ Fair ☐ Incorrect height ☐ Other: _____	☐ Separated from membrane ☐ Loose clamps ☐ Debris guard missing

Comments:

_____

_____

_____

_____

_____

_____

_____

FIGURE 17.18 Shingle and Tile Roofing Condition

| Building: _____ | Section: _____ |
| Inspector: _____ | Date: _____ |

General Condition
(Note defects on detail grid)

Evidence of Leaking: ☐ Yes   ☐ No
Reported Leaks: ☐ Yes   ☐ No
Physical Damage: ☐ Yes   ☐ No

Type of Shingles

☐ Asbestos   ☐ Clay Tile
☐ Cedar   ☐ Mission Tile
☐ Cypress   ☐ Concrete Tile
☐ Pine   ☐ Steel Tile
☐ Slate
☐ Aluminum Tile
☐ Other: _____

Sheathing

☐ Good, no defects
☐ Water stained
☐ Rotted (sq ft): _____
☐ Other: _____

Flashing
(Check all that apply)

☐ Good, no defects   ☐ Separated from wall
☐ Fair   ☐ Open joints
☐ Corroded   ☐ Loose
☐ Other: _____

Gutters
(Check all that apply)

☐ Good, no defects   ☐ Missing Hangers
☐ Fair   ☐ Split Seams
☐ Corroded   ☐ Debris
☐ Other: _____

Figure 17.18 (continued)

Downspouts (Check all that apply)	☐ Good, no defects ☐ Fair ☐ Corroded ☐ Other: _____	☐ Separated Joints ☐ Detached ☐ Clogged

Comments:

_____

_____

_____

_____

_____

_____

_____

FIGURE 17.19 Metal Roofing Condition

Building: _____ Section: _____

Inspector: _____ Date: _____

General Condition
(Note defects on detail grid)

Evidence of Leaking: ☐ Yes   ☐ No
Reported Leaks: ☐ Yes   ☐ No
Physical Damage: ☐ Yes   ☐ No

Metal Roofing
(Check all that apply)

☐ Good, no defects   ☐ Moderate Corrosion
☐ Fair   ☐ Advanced Corrosion
☐ Cracks
☐ Other: _____

Seams

☐ Good, no defects   ☐ Moderate Corrosion
☐ Fair   ☐ Advanced Corrosion
☐ Detached
☐ Other: _____

Base Flashing
(Check all that apply)

☐ Good, no defects   ☐ Separated from wall
☐ Fair   ☐ Open joints
☐ Corroded   ☐ Loose
☐ Other: _____

Counter Flashing
(Check all that apply)

☐ Good, no defects   ☐ Separated from wall
☐ Fair   ☐ Open joints
☐ Corroded   ☐ Loose
☐ Other: _____

Equipment/Vent Flashing
(Check all that apply)

☐ Good, no defects   ☐ Separated
☐ Fair   ☐ Open joints
☐ Corroded   ☐ Loose
☐ Other: _____

Figure 17.19 (continued)

Expansion Joints (Check all that apply)	☐ Good, no defects ☐ Fair ☐ Surface cracks ☐ Other: _____	☐ Deteriorated membranes ☐ Damaged flashings ☐ Damaged blocking
Gutters (Check all that apply)	☐ Good, no defects ☐ Fair ☐ Corroded ☐ Other: _____	☐ Missing Hangers ☐ Split Seams ☐ Debris
Downspouts (Check all that apply)	☐ Good, no defects ☐ Fair ☐ Corroded ☐ Other: _____	☐ Separated Joints ☐ Detached ☐ Clogged

Comments:

_____

_____

_____

_____

_____

_____

FIGURE 17.20 Sprayed-On Foam Roofing Condition

Building: _____ Section: _____

Inspector: _____ Date: _____

General Condition
(Note defects on detail grid)

Evidence of Leaking: ☐ Yes ☐ No
Reported Leaks: ☐ Yes ☐ No
Evidence of Ponding: ☐ Yes ☐ No
Physical Damage: ☐ Yes ☐ No

Surface Coating
(Check all that apply)

☐ Good, no defects   ☐ Exposed Foam
☐ Blistered   ☐ Peeling
☐ Cracked   ☐ Worn
☐ Other: _____

Foam
(Check all that apply)

☐ Good, no defects   ☐ Dented
☐ Brittle   ☐ Deteriorated
☐ Cracked   ☐ Soft
☐ Other: _____

Base Flashing
(Check all that apply)

☐ Good, no defects   ☐ Separated from wall
☐ Fair   ☐ Open joints
☐ Corroded   ☐ Loose
☐ Other: _____

Counter Flashing
(Check all that apply)

☐ Good, no defects   ☐ Separated from wall
☐ Fair   ☐ Open joints
☐ Corroded   ☐ Loose
☐ Other: _____

Equipment/Vent Flashing
(Check all that apply)

☐ Good, no defects   ☐ Separated
☐ Fair   ☐ Open joints
☐ Corroded   ☐ Loose
☐ Other: _____

Figure 17.20 (continued)

Expansion Joints (Check all that apply)	☐	Good, no defects	☐	Deteriorated membranes
	☐	Fair	☐	Damaged flashings
	☐	Surface cracks	☐	Damaged blocking
	☐	Other: _____		

Drains (Check all that apply)	☐	Good, no defects	☐	Separated from membrane
	☐	Fair	☐	Loose clamps
	☐	Incorrect height	☐	Debris guard missing
	☐	Other: _____		

Comments:

_____

_____

_____

_____

_____

_____

_____

FIGURE 17.21 Roofing Detail Grid

Building: _____   Section: _____

FIGURE 17.22 Roof Maintenance Activity

Building: _____

Roof Section: _____

Problem Location: _____

Description of Problem: _____

_____

_____

_____

_____

_____

Action Taken: _____

_____

_____

_____

_____

_____

Cost of Repairs: _____

Comments: _____

_____

_____

_____

## Chapter 18

HOW TO ESTABLISH A HOUSEKEEPING PROGRAM THAT SAVES MONEY AND INCREASES PERFORMANCE

This chapter presents information that you can use in establishing or improving housekeeping programs. Material is presented to assist in such activities as establishing time standards, assigning housekeeping task frequencies, and developing a quality control inspection program. The material presented in this chapter is intended to serve as the foundation for housekeeping programs in a wide range of facilities. To make the most use of this information, you can modify it to meet the particular needs of your given application.

Housekeeping represents one of the most noticeable areas of facilities maintenance. How well your organization performs housekeeping tasks often serves as the basis for the first impression that visitors form of your organization. A clean, well-maintained facility promotes a positive image for both you and the people who work for you.

Housekeeping also has a very direct link to the morale and well-being of your employees. In addition to providing a healthy working environment, good housekeeping practices can significantly reduce the number and frequency of employee-generated complaints, thus improving employee morale.

Finally, good housekeeping practices enhance the investment in your facility by prolonging the service life of surfaces and finishes. For example, frequent vacuuming of carpet removes abrasive particles and dirt before they can damage the carpet fibers. Similarly, frequent damp and wet mopping of floor tile limits the damage caused by dirt being ground into the tile finish.

How to Promote Housekeeping Maintainability

Good housekeeping performance begins with maintainability planning. In new construction, the planning for housekeeping must be part of the overall design process. Don't rely solely on the architectural and engineering design team to incorporate housekeeping maintainability features; few design professionals have experience in running facilities once they have been completed. Fewer still have experience in housekeeping activities.

Housekeeping Space

Housekeeping maintainability begins with providing adequate space of the right type in locations suitable for housekeeping. Rule of thumb: At least one dedicated, fully equipped housekeeping space should be provided on each floor of a facility. In larger facilities, more than one space is required per floor. Special use areas with particular housekeeping requirements, such as gymnasiums and research labs, should be provided with their own housekeeping areas.

Rule of thumb: A standard housekeeping room should be a minimum of 60 square feet. Rooms that serve as storage areas for bulk supplies or ones that contain specialized housekeeping equipment will need to be larger.

Features included in housekeeping areas need to be matched to the requirements of the facility being served. As a minimum, each housekeeping area needs to be a dedicated, secured area that includes adequate lighting, an independent ventilation system, electrical outlets, hot and cold water, a floor-mounted utility sink with splash curbs, storage shelves, and storage areas for housekeeping equipment.

Selecting Finishes to Minimize Maintenance

Another key element in housekeeping maintainability is the selection of finish materials and surfaces suitable for the areas in which they are being installed. Select materials and surfaces based in part on their level of exposure to soil, their ability to withstand that exposure, and the level of housekeeping needed to maintain an acceptable appearance.

Limiting Exposure to Soil

Finally, housekeeping maintainability involves taking steps to limit the exposure to soil. Limiting exposure begins outside the facility with the design of walkways that are sloped sufficiently to drain water from entrances rapidly. Walkways near building entrances should have rough surfaces or be sufficiently textured to help remove dirt from peoples' shoes before they enter the facility.

Once in the facility, provide walk-off mats at each entrance. Rule of thumb: Make mats large enough so that each foot of a person entering the facility comes in contact with the walk-off mat at least three times before the person steps off onto the finished floor.

THREE TYPES OF HOUSEKEEPING STANDARDS

The task of setting standards for housekeeping is the responsibility of the facility manager who, however, cannot set them working alone. Housekeeping standards must take into consideration the expectations and needs of the facility occupants, the skill and experience of those performing the housekeeping activities, and those who provide the housekeeping funds.

The task of setting standards is one of achieving a balance among these groups. The housekeeping expectations of the building occupants may be greater than can be achieved given the resources that you have to work with. Similarly, you might be providing a higher level of service than expected or required by the occupants.

Your people who are performing the housekeeping tasks know the most about what is required to perform at a given level. They also would have the best understanding of achievable and unachievable performance levels.

Finally, the budget will, to a great extent, determine the level of standards that can be achieved. You must work closely with budgeting personnel to insure that they understand the impact that funding or lack of funding will have on housekeeping standards.

There are three major types of standards that need to be established to insure performance: task frequency standards, time standards, and performance or quality standards. There are no universal standards that can be applied to all facilities. If they are to be used effectively, they must be matched to the operation by taking into consideration factors such as the age and condition of the facility, the type of operations taking place in the facility, and the level and type of staffing available.

Task Frequency Standards

Task frequency standards are specific target periods for completion of housekeeping activities. For example, a frequency standard for vacuuming a carpet in an office might be once per week. Similarly, a frequency standard for the general cleaning of a conference room might be "after each use." By setting specific frequency standards for completing tasks, the facility manager avoids the ambiguity often associated with general directions, such as "clean when required."

Match task frequency standards to the particular areas within the given facility. Vary frequencies according to the type and use of an area, the particular housekeeping task being performed, the level of traffic to which the area is exposed, and the type and condition of the material being maintained.

Initial task frequencies can be established using a number of different sources, including the manufacturer's recommendations and past history. Figure 18.1 lists typical frequencies for a number of housekeeping tasks. Use the figure as a first approximation of the required frequencies, adjusting them to match the needs of your facility. Once the task frequency standard has been in place for some time, it may be necessary to adjust it based on the result of area inspections. If some areas consistently have poor inspection results, the solution may be a different task frequency standard.

Time Standards

Time standards attempt to establish the amount of time it should take to perform specific housekeeping tasks under standard conditions, using typical equipment and supplies, with average employees. Various methods have been used to establish time standards for housekeeping activities, including time studies by qualified evaluation personnel and the review of historical housekeeping records. While both methods can be useful, they, or any other method of establishing time standards, must be used with caution. Too often facility managers copy standards being used in a different type of facility and attempt to use them in their own facility without any modifications.

Time studies are general in nature and their results can be applied directly only to other organizations that are very similar in operation. Differences, such as the type of equipment used, the layout of the facility, and the level of experience of the housekeeping staff, have significant impact on the time required to complete tasks.

Similarly, the results of studying historical housekeeping records must also be used with caution. Setting standards based solely on past performance does nothing more to insure that past levels of performance will continue. To be useful, past performance must be evaluated in terms of current effectiveness and efficiency.

In spite of these problems, time standards can be an effective tool in establishing performance standards for housekeeping, if they are correctly established and applied. The key is adaptation. Whatever method is used to establish the standards must include adaptation of those standards to the needs of your facility.

Use Figure 18.2 as a starting point in establishing time standards. The figure lists housekeeping tasks and their estimated time for completion based on standard working conditions. Do not use the times from the figure without modification for specific conditions that exist in your facility.

Performance Standards

Performance standards establish the level of housekeeping that is to be maintained within different areas of the facility. They are best thought of as the quality of housekeeping or level of cleanliness maintained. Performance standards are non-judgmental. They simply indicate what you have accepted as the level of housekeeping desired for the facility.

Performance standards determine what housekeeping tasks are to be performed and how often they are to be performed. When housekeeping activities in practice are not living up to the performance standards, it becomes necessary to modify the tasks and or increase their frequency.

If the quality of housekeeping were the only factor to consider when establishing performance standards, then both the number of tasks performed and their frequencies would be nearly limitless. However, budget and other practical limitations restrict both. You must take into consideration all constraints when establishing initial performance standards. Those constraints will limit both the number of tasks being completed and their frequency. Conduct regular inspections to insure that the housekeeping standards are maintained under those conditions.

HOUSEKEEPING INSPECTION PROGRAMS

One of the most important elements in a housekeeping program is feedback. Without it, it is difficult to determine if you are maintaining the facility according to the desired standards. Similarly, without feedback it is nearly impossible for you to provide employees with a means of evaluating their performance relative to the standards set for the facility.

While tracking complaints received from building occupants provides some information, it is not sufficient. One of the most serious drawbacks with using complaints as the basis for feedback on performance is that complaints are based on the subjective standards of the occupant, not the housekeeping standards established for the facility.

Inspections, based on established performance criteria, provide a mechanism for evaluating housekeeping performance. Since the inspections are based on specific criteria that you establish for that area within the facility, the program can be custom tailored. In addition to evaluating housekeeping performance, inspection forms can be used to help uncover situations requiring change. When using inspections with housekeeping programs, use caution to insure that the purpose of the inspection is positive. Inspections are most effective when used to gather information needed to improve performance. They are least effective when used to punish poor performance.

Use Figures 18.3 through 18.10 as inspection forms to rate the housekeeping effectiveness for different areas within facilities. Forms are included for classrooms, conference rooms, elevators, entrances and hallways, offices, restrooms, stairwells, and waiting rooms. Select the form that most closely matches the area you are inspecting.

Use the forms as follows:

Step 1.   Rate each item listed on the form as satisfactory or unsatisfactory according to the housekeeping standards established for the facility. Leave items blank for those that are not applicable for that particular area.

Step 2.   Sum the satisfactory and unsatisfactory ratings and enter the totals in the ratings portion of the form.

Step 3.   Enter the number of satisfactory and unsatisfactory ratings in the lower portion of the form.

Step 4.   To determine the rating score for the area, multiply the number of satisfactory responses by 100, and divide by the sum of the number of satisfactory and unsatisfactory responses.

Use the rating score for an area to evaluate housekeeping performance both across areas within a facility and for the same area over time. Consistently low scores are an indication that frequency standards may need to be revised, additional training of custodial employees may be required, the cleaning procedures being used may be inappropriate for that application, or the wrong type of cleaning equipment may be in use.

Other Housekeeping Feedback

While regular and thorough inspections are a good source of feedback on performance, additional sources of feedback are available to you. One of these is the telephone complaint log. Telephone complaints provide direct feedback from building occupants on specific housekeeping activities. Formally logging complaints provides a mechanism for tracking custodial problems and the action taken to correct them. Over time, the complaint log provides additional information on how well the organization is meeting performance standards, and if those standards are effective. A formal complaint log also shows your customers that you are serious about maintaining housekeeping standards.

Use Figure 18.11 to log telephone complaints. To provide a means for getting feedback to building occupants, as well as identifying a contact if additional information should be required, caller information should be completely filled out. In addition, include the initials of the person receiving the call. Complete detailed descriptions for both the specifics of the complaint and the action taken to correct it.

Once completed, the complaint log forms should be filed by area or by building. Periodically review the files to determine if changes in housekeeping procedures are required.

FIGURE 18.1 Recommended Housekeeping Task Frequencies

Daily

Empty trash receptacles
Empty and wipe ash receptacles
Police floors for litter
Vacuum carpet
Spot clean carpet
Vacuum and spot clean elevators
Dust mop/sweep tile floors
Wet mop lobbies and entrances

Clean walk-off mats (wet weather)
Spot clean floors
Clean chalkboards
Sanitize restroom fixtures
Wet mop restroom floors
Restock restroom supplies
Clean glass doors

Weekly

Spot clean walls
Wet mop corridors
Clean walk-off mats (dry weather)
Wipe down baseboards
Wet mop stairs

Dust railings
Spray buff floors
Dust building surfaces
Dust furniture surfaces

Monthly

Dust window blinds
Wash windows
Steam clean lobby and entrance carpet
Spot clean woodwork

Vacuum draperies
Clean waste receptacles
Police storage areas

Annually

Clean lighting fixtures and diffusers
Clean HVAC diffusers

Clean draperies
Shampoo carpets

FIGURE 18.2 Housekeeping Time Standards

Area	Task	Time
General	Dust mopping - Open area Dust mopping - Offices Damp mopping - Manual Damp mopping - Machine Wet mopping - Manual Wet mopping - Machine Buffing Vacuuming Waxing	10 min/1,000 sq ft 20 min/1,000 sq ft 45 min/1,000 sq ft 10 min/1,000 sq ft 30 min/1,000 sq ft 10 min/1,000 sq ft 15 min/1,000 sq ft 20 min/1,000 sq ft 60 min/1,000 sq ft
Stairway	Dust and sweep Wet mopping	10 min/flight 20 min/flight
Restroom	Sanitize fixtures Wet mop floors Wipe down partitions	10 min/fixture 45 min/1,000 sq ft 10 min/stall
Glass	Door Window Store front	15 min/door 10 min/window 5 min/100 sq ft
Special	Elevator cleaning Escalator cleaning Venetian blind Fluorescent fixture Exterior grounds policing	20 min/cab 20 min/floor 10 min/unit 15 min/fixture 100,000 sq ft/day

FIGURE 18.3 Classroom Inspection Form

Building: _____   Room # : _____

Inspector: _____   Date: _____

Ratings

Rate each item below yes or no based on whether or not its condition meets the standards. For items that are not applicable for a particular area, leave that rating blank.

Item	Yes	No	Comments
Entry Door	_____	_____	_____
Door Hardware	_____	_____	_____
Windows	_____	_____	_____
Walls	_____	_____	_____
Floor	_____	_____	_____
Baseboard	_____	_____	_____
Lights	_____	_____	_____
HVAC Vents	_____	_____	_____
Student Desks & Chairs	_____	_____	_____
Instructor Desk & Chair	_____	_____	_____
Chalk Board & Tray	_____	_____	_____
Projector Screen	_____	_____	_____
Waste Receptacle	_____	_____	_____
Total:	_____	_____	

Score

Yes Rating Total	X	100

———————————————————————————— = [Score (%)]

[Yes Rating Total] + [No Rating Total]

FIGURE 18.4 Conference Room Inspection Form

Building: _____ Room # : _____

Inspector: _____ Date: _____

Ratings

Rate each item below yes or no based on whether or not its condition meets the standards. For items that are not applicable for a particular area, leave that rating blank.

Item	Yes	No	Comments
Entry Door	_____	_____	_____
Door Hardware	_____	_____	_____
Lights	_____	_____	_____
HVAC Diffusers	_____	_____	_____
Ceiling	_____	_____	_____
Walls	_____	_____	_____
Windows	_____	_____	_____
Blinds/Drapes	_____	_____	_____
Pictures	_____	_____	_____
Chalkboard	_____	_____	_____
Baseboard	_____	_____	_____
Floor	_____	_____	_____
Chairs	_____	_____	_____
Table	_____	_____	_____
Ash Trays	_____	_____	_____
Waste Receptacle	_____	_____	_____
Total:	_____	_____	

Score

[_____] X [100]

Yes Rating Total

[_____] + [_____]   = [_____]

Yes Rating Total   No Rating Total   Score (%)

FIGURE 18.5 Elevator Inspection Form

Building: _____ Room #: _____

Inspector: _____ Date: _____

Ratings

Rate each item below yes or no based on whether or not its condition meets the standards. For items that are not applicable for a particular area, leave that rating blank.

Item	Yes	No	Comments
Floor Call Buttons	_____	_____	_____
Floor Side Doors	_____	_____	_____
Cab Side Doors	_____	_____	_____
Door Tracks	_____	_____	_____
Floor	_____	_____	_____
Walls	_____	_____	_____
Control Panel	_____	_____	_____
Ceiling	_____	_____	_____
Lights	_____	_____	_____
Vent	_____	_____	_____

Total: _____ _____

Score

$$\frac{\boxed{} \times \boxed{100}}{\boxed{} + \boxed{}} = \boxed{}$$

Yes Rating Total

Yes Rating Total   No Rating Total   Score (%)

FIGURE 18.6 Entrance/Hallway Inspection Form

Building: _____ Room # : _____

Inspector: _____ Date: _____

Ratings

Rate each item below yes or no based on whether or not its condition meets the standards. For items that are not applicable for a particular area, leave that rating blank.

Item	Yes	No	Comments
Entry Door	_____	_____	_____
Door Hardware	_____	_____	_____
Windows	_____	_____	_____
Walk-off Matting	_____	_____	_____
Flooring	_____	_____	_____
Furniture/Seating	_____	_____	_____
Lighting	_____	_____	_____
Wall Decorations/Pictures	_____	_____	_____
Waste Receptacles	_____	_____	_____
Telephones	_____	_____	_____
Interior Doors	_____	_____	_____
Total:	_____	_____	

Score

$$\boxed{} \; X \; \boxed{100}$$

Yes Rating Total

$$\frac{\boxed{}}{\boxed{} \; + \; \boxed{}} \; = \; \boxed{}$$

Yes Rating Total   No Rating Total   Score (%)

FIGURE 18.7 Office Inspection Form

Building: _____ Room # : _____

Inspector: _____ Date: _____

Ratings

Rate each item below yes or no based on whether or not its condition meets the standards. For items that are not applicable for a particular area, leave that rating blank.

Item	Yes	No	Comments
Entry Door	_____	_____	_____
Door Hardware	_____	_____	_____
Lights	_____	_____	_____
HVAC Diffuser	_____	_____	_____
Walls	_____	_____	_____
Pictures	_____	_____	_____
Windows	_____	_____	_____
Blinds/Drapes	_____	_____	_____
Baseboard	_____	_____	_____
Floor	_____	_____	_____
Desk	_____	_____	_____
Chairs	_____	_____	_____
Furniture	_____	_____	_____
Waste Receptacle	_____	_____	_____
Total:	_____	_____	

Score

$$\frac{\boxed{} \text{ X } \boxed{100}}{\boxed{} + \boxed{}} = \boxed{}$$

Yes Rating Total

Yes Rating Total   No Rating Total

Score (%)

FIGURE 18.8 Restroom Inspection Form

Building: _____ Room # : _____

Inspector: _____ Date: _____

Ratings

Rate each item below yes or no based on whether or not its condition meets the standards. For items that are not applicable for a particular area, leave that rating blank.

Item	Yes	No	Comments
Entry Door	_____	_____	_____
Door Hardware	_____	_____	_____
Lights	_____	_____	_____
Vent	_____	_____	_____
Ceiling	_____	_____	_____
Walls	_____	_____	_____
Windows	_____	_____	_____
Mirrors	_____	_____	_____
Towel Holders	_____	_____	_____
Sinks/Fixtures	_____	_____	_____
Soap Dispensers	_____	_____	_____
Stalls	_____	_____	_____
Commodes	_____	_____	_____
Urinals	_____	_____	_____
Floor	_____	_____	_____
Waste Receptacle	_____	_____	_____
Total:	_____	_____	

Score

$$\boxed{} \text{ X } \boxed{100}$$

Yes Rating Total

_____   = $\boxed{}$

$\boxed{} + \boxed{}$ Score (%)

Yes Rating Total   No Rating Total

FIGURE 18.9 Stairwell Inspection Form

Building: _____   Room # : _____

Inspector: _____   Date: _____

Ratings

Rate each item below yes or no based on whether or not its condition meets the standards. For items that are not applicable for a particular area, leave that rating blank.

Item	Yes	No	Comments
Entry Door	_____	_____	_____
Door Hardware	_____	_____	_____
Windows	_____	_____	_____
Stairs	_____	_____	_____
Landings	_____	_____	_____
Banisters	_____	_____	_____
Lighting	_____	_____	_____
Walls	_____	_____	_____
Total:	_____	_____	

Score

$$\frac{\boxed{} \;X\; \boxed{100}}{\boxed{} \;+\; \boxed{}} = \boxed{}$$

Yes Rating Total

Yes Rating Total   No Rating Total   Score (%)

FIGURE 18.10 Waiting Room/Lounge Inspection Form

Building: _____ Room # : _____

Inspector: _____ Date: _____

Ratings

Rate each item below yes or no based on whether or not its condition meets the standards. For items that are not applicable for a particular area, leave that rating blank.

Item	Yes	No	Comments
Entry Door	_____	_____	_____
Door Hardware	_____	_____	_____
Lights	_____	_____	_____
HVAC Diffusers	_____	_____	_____
Ceiling	_____	_____	_____
Walls	_____	_____	_____
Windows	_____	_____	_____
Blinds/Drapes	_____	_____	_____
Pictures	_____	_____	_____
Baseboard	_____	_____	_____
Floor	_____	_____	_____
Chairs/Couches	_____	_____	_____
Furniture	_____	_____	_____
Ash Trays	_____	_____	_____
Waste Receptacle	_____	_____	_____
Total:	_____	_____	

Score

$$\boxed{} \ \text{X} \ \boxed{100}$$

Yes Rating Total

$$\frac{\boxed{}}{\boxed{} \ + \ \boxed{}} \ = \ \boxed{}$$

Yes Rating Total   No Rating Total   Score (%)

FIGURE 18.11 Housekeeping Telephone Complaint Log

Caller Information

Name: _____   Phone: _____

Building: _____   Room: _____

Date: _____   Initials: _____

Description of Complaint

_____

_____

_____

_____

_____

_____

_____

Action Taken

_____

_____

_____

_____

_____

_____

_____

Chapter 19

PROMOTING THE APPEARANCE OF YOUR FACILITY THROUGH A GROUNDS MAINTENANCE PROGRAM

This chapter presents information you can use to establish a comprehensive grounds maintenance program. Material is presented that will aid in diagnosing problems with materials used outside of the facility, setting up a grounds maintenance inspection program, standards for grounds maintenance, and grounds maintenance time standards.

This chapter's material can be adapted to a wide range of facilities, thus permitting you to establish a grounds maintenance program that addresses your standards and needs.

THE ROLE OF GROUNDS MAINTENANCE

By the time that any visitor, client, or employee enters your facility, they have already formed an impression both of the facility itself and of the people who run it from the appearance of the grounds. That first impression, right or wrong, is the one that frequently sticks with that person throughout the visit, interaction with people in the facility, or employment. With so much riding on first impressions and the image they create, effective grounds maintenance can and does make a difference. Good grounds maintenance projects an image of a well-run facility and a positive image of the businesses located there.

Moreover, effective grounds maintenance accomplishes more than projecting a good image. A well-maintained facility exterior is also an important element in providing a healthy working environment for your employees and visitors. Poorly maintained roadways, parking lots, and walkways, as well as overgrown underbrush and low hanging or dead tree limbs pose threats to the health and safety of people even before they enter a facility.

A well-maintained grounds complex also helps to promote your facility. It attracts business in the form of tenants, and customers for those tenants. It can help lease or rent space as well as help sell the facility itself.

A thorough grounds maintenance program also reduces costs. Good maintenance practices promote the health of plants, trees, and shrubs resulting in decreased replacement and emergency maintenance costs. Preventive maintenance activities help to extend the life of paved surfaces, thus reducing the frequency with which they must be replaced.

To be effective, the grounds maintenance program must be tailored to meet the requirements of your facility. As is the case with all other maintenance activities, a balance must be achieved between the level of effort dedicated to grounds maintenance and the funds available.

GROUNDS MAINTENANCE STANDARDS

In order to maintain the desired quality level of the grounds of a given facility, you must establish maintenance standards. These standards provide a basis for determining what activities must be performed by the maintenance crews, how frequently they are to be performed, and when additional efforts are required. Without established standards, the appearance of the grounds and the identification of the maintenance activities to be performed, as well as their frequency, are subject to interpretation by the individual. What might be considered a requirement by one person may be viewed as unimportant or extravagant by another.

To be effective, grounds maintenance standards must be concretely worded with little room for interpretation by the individual. Statements such as "Grass should be cut as frequently as required" are to be avoided. Instead, use statements like "Grass height not to exceed six inches." The first statement is subject to a wide range of interpretation. The second is not.

Figure 19.1 lists common grounds maintenance tasks and standards associated with those tasks. The standards presented in the figure are to be used as a starting point for establishing a set of grounds maintenance standards for your facility. The tasks identified and the actual standards adopted will vary from facility to facility based on the resources available, the type of facility, the site design, the climate, and the horticulture practices common for that location.

HOW TO ESTABLISH A GROUNDS INSPECTION PROGRAM

The most accurate means of determining how well a grounds maintenance program is performing is through an inspection program. Inspections evaluate the performance not only of the maintenance program, but also of plants and surfaces that the program is designed to maintain. By conducting periodic and thorough inspections, problems can be identified and corrected before they become serious. And for the items that grounds maintenance programs are designed to protect, early detection is essential.

If an inspection program is to be effective, it must be designed to evaluate an area or an item based on established criteria, the grounds maintenance standards.

Programs that are established on vague criteria are not as thorough and cannot provide comparable feedback.

Rating the condition of a particular grounds item can be very subjective. While condition rating scales, ranging from zero for poor to five for excellent, are effective in many activities, they are not of much value in grounds maintenance. Too much depends on the person completing the inspection. It is difficult to find two people who would rate a particular item exactly the same way. To be of any value, any inspection program must have consistency. Instead, therefore, of evaluating the condition of a grounds item, the inspection program should examine whether or not the item meets the grounds maintenance standards of your facility. If it does, the item should be rated acceptable; if it does not, then unacceptable.

Simply completing inspection forms won't lead to improved performance. The results of the inspections must be shared with employees not to rate performance but rather to give the information needed to improve performance. Inspections also need to be tracked over time to determine if there are any trends that may impact the area.

Use Figures 19.2 through 19.8 as inspection forms to rate the effectiveness of your grounds maintenance program. Forms are included for annuals, asphalt, playgrounds, retaining walls, shrubs, trees, and turf. Select the form that most closely matches the item or area being inspected.

Use the inspection forms as follows:

Step 1. Rate each item listed on the form as to whether or not it meets the grounds maintenance standards established for your facility. For items rated as not meeting the standards, note the reason why in the comments area. Leave items blank for those that are not applicable.

Step 2. Sum the "yes" and "no" ratings and enter the totals in the ratings portion of the form.

Step 3. Enter the number of "yes" and "no" ratings in the score portion of the form.

Step 4. To determine the rating score for the area, multiply the number of "yes" responses by 100, and divide by the sum of the number of "yes" ratings and "no" ratings.

Ratings that are consistently decreasing with time are an indication that conditions are deteriorating, and a significant facility renewal effort may be required if the area is to improve and meet maintenance standards.

GROUNDS TIME STANDARDS

The purpose of using time standards in a grounds maintenance operation is to establish a baseline from which time requirements for performing specific tasks can be estimated and evaluated. Grounds time standards, like most other maintenance time standards, are most effective when they are used to evaluate the time requirements of specific tasks, not the performance of individual employees.

Standards have been developed for a wide range of grounds maintenance activities, including cutting grass, weeding, pruning, and leaf removal. These standards are generally the result of extensive time studies by qualified evaluation personnel in a number of different facilities and under a wide range of conditions. To make them suitable for use in as wide a range of facilities as possible, the standards have been normalized. Therefore the times listed for specific tasks are the average times required to perform the task under normal operating conditions using the most appropriate equipment.

Before adopting a given set of time standards for use in a particular facility, you must first evaluate the conditions that exist. Are the conditions where the task is to be performed comparable to most other facilities? For example, cutting grass or raking leaves on a steeply sloped area or an area with numerous trees will take longer to complete than suggested by the time standards.

You will also have to take into consideration the equipment available for use by your grounds maintenance personnel. If the grounds maintenance operation does not have the quantities, type, and size of equipment commonly used in other facilities, the times indicated by the standards will again be too low.

The training and experience levels of the grounds maintenance personnel will similarly affect the time required to complete tasks. Since time standards assume an average level of experience and adequate training, any variations from these expected levels will impact performance.

In spite of these limitations, time standards can be an effective tool in grounds maintenance. Once it is realized that they are not hard and fast standards, but rather a starting point that will require adaptation, they can be used effectively to evaluate effectiveness and estimate manpower requirements.

Figure 19.9 lists performance standards for common grounds maintenance activities. All times listed are for average conditions. Use this figure as a starting point in establishing a program of time standards, modifying the actual times based on the given conditions in a facility.

LIFE EXPECTANCIES

Nearly every component within a facility has a finite life span. Mechanical and electrical equipment wears out or breaks down. Architectural finishes deteriorate with use and time. Roofs leak and fail. Even building structural components eventually fail.

The same holds true for items outside the facility. Living things give in to old age, the elements, disease, and abuse. Nonliving components, such as paved surfaces, also eventually fail. While the life expectancy of each of these grounds components can be extended through good maintenance practices, there will come a time when each will have to be replaced.

Figure 19.10 can be used by the facility manager to estimate the expected life span for trees, shrubs, and turf. By knowing how long each type of plant is expected to live, the facility manager can better estimate the need for and the time of replacement, thus permitting better planning and budgeting. The life expectancies given in the figure are for healthy plants under normal conditions. For plants subject to extreme weather conditions or abnormal abuse, such as turf that is regularly driven on, the life expectancies will be significantly decreased.

Figure 19.11 lists the average life expectancies for miscellaneous site items. As with Figure 19.10, the life expectancy values listed in the figure are based on normal use conditions. Areas subjected to abuse, weather extremes, and heavy vehicular traffic will have shorter lives than those indicated in the figure.

Two Approaches to Paved Area Maintenance

One of the major tasks in exterior maintenance is the upkeep of paved areas including roadways, parking lots, sidewalks, plazas, and bike paths. In general, one of two approaches is taken by facility managers towards this problem: reactive or preventive maintenance.

Reactive Maintenance

The reactive maintenance approach for paved areas attempts to minimize day-to-day maintenance costs by performing only the absolutely necessary maintenance tasks: cleaning, restriping, patching, etc. While this approach does minimize the short-term operating costs, it also significantly decreases the effective life of the paved surfaces. The result is that many paved areas will require replacement in a relatively short time.

Preventive Maintenance

The preventive maintenance approach for paved areas attempts to maximize the life of paved surfaces by annually spending three to five percent of the replacement costs on maintenance activities, including those designed to eliminate the conditions that lead to pavement failure. Its success depends on early detection and repair of problems while they are still minor. Through a regular program of inspection, preventive maintenance can extend the useful life for some paved areas by as much as 100 percent.

The Causes of Pavement Failure

The key to the successful development of a preventive maintenance program for paved areas is an understanding of the causes of pavement failure. The single leading cause of pavement failure is poor drainage. Water, if allowed to remain on the pavement, accelerates its deterioration. For concrete surfaces, the water lies in minute surface cracks. As the concrete undergoes freeze-thaw cycles, the water expands in the cracks, making them deeper, wider, and longer. Water lying on the surface of asphalt pavement accelerates the process by which oils are lost, thus contributing to a reduction in flexibility and the development of cracks.

Subsurface water, if not adequately drained away from the pavement, weakens the substrate. Sufficiently weakened, the substrate will no longer be capable of supporting the pavement, resulting in accelerated deterioration. Eventually, it will result in the failure of the pavement through the formation of potholes and uplifted areas.

Surface water is best removed from pavement through proper design techniques. Design all paved areas with a minimum slope of one to two percent. Mount all drains sufficiently below the level of the surface to provide drainage. Inspect drains on a regular basis to insure that they are clear of debris.

Subsurface water damage is best controlled through a combination of good design practices and good maintenance. Providing a supportive base that also rapidly drains water from subsurface materials is a design requirement. But even properly designed and installed subsurface materials are easily damaged by water that works its way through cracks in the pavement. Therefore, it is important to inspect the pavement on a regular basis for cracks, and to seal them while they are small.

Regular preventive maintenance is important for all paving materials, but especially for asphalt surfaces. While concrete is forgiving, asphalt is not. Without proper maintenance, asphalt surfaces rapidly deteriorate and fail. Figure 19.12 lists defects found in asphalt pavement, their causes, and recommended corrective action.

The single most important preventive measure that can be taken to prolong the life of asphalt surfaces is to protect the surface and the substrate from water penetration. The application of a seal coat every two to three years will help to minimize oil evaporation from the pavement, reduce the impact of ultraviolet light on the asphalt materials, and prevent water penetration. Apply the seal coating when the surface is warm and dry.

Clean and fill all cracks during cool, dry weather to further limit the amount of water that can penetrate the surface.

Rule of thumb: Inspect asphalt pavement twice per year, once in the spring before exposure to high summer temperatures, and once in the fall before the winter freeze.

By following these relatively simple maintenance techniques, it will be possible to greatly extend the life of most paved areas.

FIGURE 19.1 Grounds Maintenance Standards

Task	Standard
Turf Cutting	Grass height not to exceed a height of six inches. Minimum of one cutting per week during growing season.
Edging	Grass not to extend more than two inches over paved surface. Minimum of two edgings per year.
Turf Restoration	Grass coverage not to be less than 75%. Restoration to be completed in early spring or early fall as required.
Grounds Policing	Grounds to be kept clear of readily visible quantities of litter. Minimum of one policing per week.
Leaf Removal	A minimum of two bulk removals per fall. One additional bulk removal in early spring.
Pruning	One pruning to be completed during late summer or early fall.
Annual Beds	Beds to be maintained free of visible weeds year round.
Storm Drain Cleaning	Inspect all storm drains at least trice a year. Drains should be cleaned when there is visible debris present.
Parking Lot Striping	Restripe parking areas once a year or when 10 % of the lines are no longer visible.
Crosswalk Striping	Restripe crosswalks once a year or when 10 % of the markings have been worn away.

FIGURE 19.2 Annuals Inspection Form

Location: _____ Date: _____

Inspector: _____

Type of Plants: _____

Ratings

Rate each item below yes or no based on whether or not its condition meets the standards. For items that are not applicable for a particular area, leave that rating blank.

Item	Yes	No	Comments
General Appearance	_____	_____	_____
Health of Plants	_____	_____	_____
Fullness	_____	_____	_____
Foliage	_____	_____	_____
Color	_____	_____	_____
Insect Damage	_____	_____	_____
Weeding	_____	_____	_____
Mulch	_____	_____	_____
Edging	_____	_____	_____
Litter	_____	_____	_____
Total:	———	———	

Score

$$\frac{\boxed{} \text{ X } \boxed{100}}{\boxed{} + \boxed{}} = \boxed{}$$

Yes Rating

Yes Rating   No Rating

Score (%)

FIGURE 19.3 Asphalt Pavement Inspection Form

Location: _____ Area (sq ft): _____

Inspector: _____ Date: _____

Ratings

Rate each item below yes or no based on whether or not its condition meets the standards.
For items that are not applicable for a particular area, leave that rating blank.

Item	Yes	No	Comments
General Appearance	_____	_____	_____
Surface Condition	_____	_____	_____
Surface Wear	_____	_____	_____
Surface Evenness	_____	_____	_____
Cracking	_____	_____	_____
Drainage	_____	_____	_____
Curbs	_____	_____	_____
Pavement Markings	_____	_____	_____
Total:	_____	_____	_____

Score

$$\frac{\boxed{} \text{ X } \boxed{100}}{\underset{\text{Yes Rating}}{\boxed{}} + \underset{\text{No Rating}}{\boxed{}}} = \underset{\text{Score (\%)}}{\boxed{}}$$

Yes Rating

FIGURE 19.4 Playground Inspection Form

Location: _____ Date: _____

Inspector: _____

Ratings

Rate each item below yes or no based on whether or not its condition meets the standards. For items that are not applicable for a particular area, leave that rating blank.

Item	Yes	No	Comments
General Appearance	_____	_____	_____
Fence & Gates	_____	_____	_____
Loose Base Material	_____	_____	_____
Synthetic Base Material	_____	_____	_____
Steel Structures	_____	_____	_____
Wood Structures	_____	_____	_____
Finishes	_____	_____	_____
Drainage	_____	_____	_____
Weeding	_____	_____	_____
Litter	_____	_____	_____
Total:	____	____	

Score

$$\frac{\boxed{} \text{ X } \boxed{100}}{\boxed{} + \boxed{}} = \boxed{}$$

Yes Rating X 100

Yes Rating + No Rating = Score (%)

FIGURE 19.5 Retaining Wall Inspection Form

Location: _____   Height (ft): _____

Inspector: _____   Length (ft): _____

Date: _____   Material: _____

Ratings

Rate each item below yes or no based on whether or not its condition meets the standards. For items that are not applicable for a particular area, leave that rating blank.

Item	Yes	No	Comments
General Appearance	_____	_____	_____
Overall Condition	_____	_____	_____
Masonry Joints	_____	_____	_____
Expansion Joints	_____	_____	_____
Timber Sections	_____	_____	_____
Timber Anchors	_____	_____	_____
Horizontal Alignment	_____	_____	_____
Vertical Alignment	_____	_____	_____
Total:	_____	_____	

Score

$$\frac{\boxed{} \text{ X } \boxed{100}}{\boxed{} + \boxed{}} = \boxed{}$$

Yes Rating

Yes Rating   No Rating   Score (%)

FIGURE 19.6 Shrub Inspection Form

Location: _____

Inspector: _____ Date: _____

Ratings

Rate each item below yes or no based on whether or not its condition meets the standards. For items that are not applicable for a particular area, leave that rating blank.

Item	Yes	No	Comments
General Appearance	_____	_____	_____
Color	_____	_____	_____
Fullness	_____	_____	_____
Height	_____	_____	_____
Pruning	_____	_____	_____
Health	_____	_____	_____
Weeding	_____	_____	_____
Mulch	_____	_____	_____
Total:	_____	_____	_____

Score

$$\frac{\boxed{} \; X \; \boxed{100}}{\boxed{} \; + \; \boxed{}} = \boxed{}$$

Yes Rating

Yes Rating   No Rating   Score (%)

FIGURE 19.7 Tree Inspection Form

Location: _____   Height: _____

Inspector: _____   Diameter: _____

Tree Type: _____   Date: _____

Ratings

Rate each item below yes or no based on whether or not its condition meets the standards. For items that are not applicable for a particular area, leave that rating blank.

Item	Yes	No	Comments
General Appearance	_____	_____	_____
Fullness	_____	_____	_____
Pruning	_____	_____	_____
Insect Damage	_____	_____	_____
Trunk Damage	_____	_____	_____
Broken Branches	_____	_____	_____
Dead Limb Removal	_____	_____	_____
Low Branches	_____	_____	_____
Foliage	_____	_____	_____
Leaf Drop	_____	_____	_____
Total:	_____	_____	

Score

$$\frac{\boxed{} \text{ X } \boxed{100}}{\boxed{} + \boxed{}} = \boxed{}$$

Yes Rating

Yes Rating   No Rating   Score (%)

FIGURE 19.8 Turf Inspection Form

Location: _____   Area (sq ft): _____

Inspector: _____   Date: _____

Ratings

Rate each item below yes or no based on whether or not its condition meets the standards. For items that are not applicable for a particular area, leave that rating blank.

Item	Yes	No	Comments
General Appearance	____	____	_____
Grass Height	____	____	_____
Thickness of Grass	____	____	_____
Color of Grass	____	____	_____
Weeding	____	____	_____
Edging	____	____	_____
Trash & Debris	____	____	_____
Mower Damage	____	____	_____
Vehicle Damage	____	____	_____
Erosion	____	____	_____
Total:	____	____	_____

Score

$$\frac{\boxed{} \text{ X } \boxed{100}}{\boxed{} + \boxed{}} = \boxed{}$$

Yes Rating   X   100

Yes Rating   +   No Rating   =   Score (%)

FIGURE 19.9 Grounds Performance Standards

Activity	Unit	Average Time (hr)
Mowing (hand)	Acre	8.0
Mowing (deck 60" or less)	Acre	1.8
Mowing (deck greater than 60")	Acre	0.8
Dethatching	Acre	12.0
Edging Walkways	100 ft	0.1
Edging Beds	100 ft	0.1
Weeding Shrub Beds	1,000 sq ft	0.5
Weeding Flower Beds	1,000 sq ft	1.5
Pruning Shrubs	Acre	15.0
Shearing Hedges	100 ft	0.5
Leaf Removal - Beds	Acre	1.2

FIGURE 19.10 Typical Plant Life Expectancies

Plant	Type	Life Expectancy (yr)
Tree	Evergreen	25 - 30
	Small Deciduous	15
	Large Deciduous	35 - 50
Shrub	Evergreen	15
	Deciduous	15
Turf	General Use	15 - 20
	Recreational	8 - 10
	Athletic	3 - 5

FIGURE 19.11 Miscellaneous Site Item Life Expectancy

Item	Material	Life Expectancy (years)
Roadways	Bituminous Concrete Pavers Crushed Stone	5 - 7 20 30 10
Walkways	Bituminous Concrete Pavers Organic	10 30 40 3
Retaining Walls	Masonry Metal Wood	40 25 20
Fences	Metal Wood	15 10
Furniture	Metal Wood Plastic	10 5 3 - 5

FIGURE 19.12 Asphalt Defects

Defect Type	Causes	Corrective Action
Alligatoring	Small, interconnected surface cracks that form as a result of an unstable subgrade or lower course of pavement. May also be caused by repeated instances of exceeding the load-carrying capacity of the pavement.	Unstable subgrades are generally the result of inadequate drainage and can be corrected only by removing the unstable material, installing adequate drainage, and replacing the pavement.
Potholes	Breaking of the pavement into small, separate sections as the result of weaknesses in the pavement, failure of the subgrade, or insufficient drainage.	Permanent repair requires removing material from around the hole until solid material is reached on the bottom and all sides. The hole is then filled with hot base or surface material.
Shrinkage Cracks	A series of cracks that are interconnected into a series of large blocks. They are generally the result of volume changes in the surface or base mix.	Remove all debris and loose material by compressed air and apply a tack coat of asphalt emulsion by hand into the crack.
Bleed-Through Cracks	Cracks in the pavement that match cracks in the material underneath. The cracks form as the result of movement caused by thermal expansion and contraction.	Fill the cracks with a mixture of emulsified asphalt and sand.

Part IV

FACILITY ENERGY USE

## Chapter 20

WEATHER AND CLIMATE FACTORS AND THEIR IMPACT ON ENERGY USE IN YOUR FACILITY

This chapter presents data related to weather and climate that you can use in looking at the impact that weather has on the operation of a facility. Weather data is presented for a number of different cities. Additional material presented in this chapter can be used to convert temperatures between the Fahrenheit and Centigrade scales, calculate wind chill temperatures, determine the relative humidity at which water vapor will condense on windows, estimate the average daily solar radiation, and estimate the average well water temperature.

TWO FACTORS THAT IMPACT HEATING SYSTEM DESIGN AND PERFORMANCE

Two of the most commonly used factors when working with facility HVAC equipment or estimating the influence of weather on facility energy use are the winter design temperature and the heating degree day.

The Winter Design Temperature

The winter design temperature, expressed in degrees Fahrenheit, is defined as a value below which the temperature will fall less than one percent of the time during an average winter. It can be thought of as one of the coldest temperatures that will be experienced during an average winter, although it is not the absolute coldest temperature since it will be exceeded slightly during an average winter and exceeded even more during an extremely cold winter.

Winter design temperature is particularly important in sizing facility HVAC equipment. While heating equipment can be designed to heat a facility during the lowest expected outside temperature, that temperature occurs so infrequently that the cost of the larger heating equipment is not justified. Additionally, since larger units operate most of the time at lower loads where their operating efficiency is also lower, energy costs would increase. Instead, heating systems are designed to adequately heat a facility based on the heating design temperature for that climate.

The Heating Degree Day

The heating degree day is a term used to quantify the weather component in a facility's heating load. It is defined as the product of one day and the number of degrees that the daily mean temperature was below 65°F. For example, if the mean temperature for a given day was 50°F, the number of heating degree days for that day is 15.

Heating degree days are useful in a number of calculations, including those that examine the efficiency of heating equipment. Since weather conditions vary and are an influence on the quantity of heat required by a facility, it is difficult to evaluate the performance of equipment without first removing the influence of weather conditions. The heating degree day provides a means for removing these variations.

Another way in which the heating degree day is used is in projecting future energy use. If the energy use of a facility is known for given temperature conditions, then it can be estimated for a range of weather conditions using different values for the number of heating degree days.

Figure 20.1 lists winter design temperatures and average heating degree days for a number of cities. If your location is not listed in the figure, use the closest city. The data in the figure was taken from a compilation of weather data by the Engineering Meteorology Section of the USAF Environmental Technical Applications Center and published in the handbook *Engineering Weather Data*.

THREE FACTORS THAT IMPACT COOLING SYSTEM DESIGN AND PERFORMANCE

The impact of weather on the sizing and performance of cooling equipment can be measured by three factors similar to those used during the heating season; the summer design temperature, the cooling degree day, and the cooling degree hour.

Summer Design Temperature

The summer design temperature, expressed in degrees Fahrenheit, is comparable to the winter design temperature. It is the temperature that during a normal summer will be exceeded one percent of the time. Comparable to its winter counterpart, the summer design temperature can be thought of as close to the hottest temperature that will be experienced during an average summer, but not the absolute hottest temperature since it will be exceeded slightly during an average summer and exceeded even more during an extremely hot summer.

Summer design temperature is particularly important in sizing cooling and air conditioning equipment. While equipment ideally should be designed to adequately cool a facility during the hottest expected weather, that weather occurs so infrequently that the cost of the larger units cannot be justified. Also, similar to larger heating units, larger cooling units would operate most of the time at lower loads where efficiencies would also be lower, resulting in an increase in energy costs. Instead, cooling systems are sized to cool a facility based on the summer design temperature for that climate.

The Cooling Degree Day

The cooling degree day is a term used to quantify the temperature portion of the weather component in a facility's cooling load. It is defined as the product of one day and the number of degrees that the daily mean temperature was above 65°F. For example, if the mean temperature for a given day was 90°F, the number of cooling degree days for that day is 25.

While the cooling degree day gives an indication of the cooling load created by the outside temperature, it does not attempt to quantify an equally important weather-related cooling load, humidity. With dehumidification amounting to one-third to one-half of the annual weather-related cooling load for a facility, this limitation can seriously impact the use of cooling degree days in projecting annual cooling energy use within a facility. However, it is still a useful indicator of the relative severity of summer weather.

The Cooling Degree Hour

The third indicator of the cooling load produced by outside temperature is the cooling degree hour. It measures the number of hours that the outside temperature is above a base temperature during an average year. Any base temperature can be used, although the most commonly used base is 78°F.

Figure 20.2 lists summer design temperatures, average cooling degree days, and the number of degree hours when the temperature was above 78°F for a number of cities. The data in the figure was taken from a compilation of weather data by the Engineering Meteorology Section of the USAF Environmental Technical Applications Center and published in the handbook *Engineering Weather Data*. If your city is not listed in the figure, use the closest location to determine the summer design temperature and the number of cooling degree days.

HOW TO ESTIMATE COOLING DEGREE HOURS. The listing for degree hours above a base temperature of 78°F is not as complete as the other listings simply because not all facilities record and compile the data required. Since later chapters make extensive use of the 78°F degree hour value, an alternative method is used to calculate it for locations where data is missing.

Figure 20.3 shows the relationship to the base of 78°F between the two variables of cooling degree days and degree hours . Data was plotted for cities where both the numbers of cooling degree days and degree hours were known. A fairly high correlation was found between the two variables for cooling degree day values less than 4,000. While the correlation was high, there is also a fairly high level of variability between the two values, so use Figure 20.3 only when the actual number of degree hours is not known.

Use the figure to determine the number of degree hours as follows:

Step 1.   Determine the number of cooling degree days for the location.

Step 2.   From the number of cooling degree days, move horizontally across the graph until you intersect the line.

Step 3.   Drop vertically from the line to the horizontal axis. Read the number of degree hours from the axis.

The number of degree hours can also be calculated directly from the equation used to develop the figure:

$$DH = (6.2) * (CDD) - 402$$

Where: DH = the number of degree hours, base 78°F
    CDD = the number of cooling degree days, base 65°F

TRACKING DEGREE DAYS

The data presented in Figures 20.1 and 20.2 represent averages taken over a twenty-year span. Data for individual years are available from several government agencies, including the National Climatic Data Center. Data for the current year are also available from those same agencies as well as from private sources, including newspapers.

The number of degree days for a month can be calculated for any location. All that is required are accurate readings of the daily high and low temperatures. Use Figure 20.4 to calculate the number of heating and cooling degree days for any month if the daily high and low temperatures are known. Use the figure as follows:

Step 1.   Log the daily high and low temperature in degrees Fahrenheit.

Step 2.   Calculate the mean temperature for the day by subtracting the daily low temperature from the daily high.

Step 3.   If the mean temperature is less than 65°F, there were heating degree days. Subtract the mean temperature from 65°F to determine the number of heating degree days for that day.

Step 4.   If the mean temperature is greater than 65°F, there were cooling degree days. Subtract 65 from the mean temperature for the day to determine the number of cooling degree days for that day.

Calculating Degree Days for Other Bases

While 65°F is the traditional standard base for calculating both heating and cooling degree days, other base temperatures have often been used. One of the advantages of using a different base value is that better estimates of the influence of weather on energy use can be achieved.

All buildings have a balance point where the heat generated within the facility offsets the heat loss to the outside. For a well-constructed facility, this balance point is well below 65°F. If you calculate heating and cooling degree days based on a building's balance point, you will have a more accurate estimate of the weather-related energy component.

Use Figure 20.4 to calculate the number of heating and cooling degree days to any base simply by using the new base value in place of the standard 65°F.

WIND DATA

An additional factor that influences how much energy is used for heating and cooling is the speed of the wind. Figure 20.5 lists three wind-related factors for various cities: the wind direction that occurs most frequently when the temperature is close to the winter design temperature; the average wind speed when the temperature is close to the winter design temperature; and the wind direction that occurs most frequently when the temperature is close to the summer design temperature.

If your location is not listed in the figure, use the closest city. The data in the figure was taken from a compilation of weather data by the Engineering Meteorology Section of the USAF Environmental Technical Applications Center and published in the handbook *Engineering Weather Data.*

How to Determine the Wind Chill Temperature

The wind chill temperature widely used today in weather reporting is derived from research conducted during the 1940s. That research was designed to determine the combined effect of wind and temperature on exposed skin. By exposing a water-filled flask to various wind and temperature conditions, the researchers developed a wind chill index that attempted to quantify the additional cooling effect of wind.

In order to make the wind chill index more useful, it was modified and expressed as a temperature—the wind chill temperature. The wind chill temperature is a measure of the cooling rate produced by the combination of temperature and wind. Its value expressed in degrees Fahrenheit is the equivalent temperature that would produce the same cooling effect if there were no wind present. It is most meaningful when used to estimate the effect of wind and temperature on exposed skin.

There are limitations on applying wind chill temperature:

1. It cannot be applied for wind speeds below four miles per hour.

2. It cannot be applied for wind speeds greater than 55 miles per hour.

Use Figure 20.6 to determine the wind chill temperature for a range of temperatures and wind speeds. Use the figure as follows:

Step 1.   Enter the figure on the left side at the actual temperature.

Step 2.   Move horizontally across the chart until you intersect the average speed of the wind.

Step 3.   Drop vertically from this intersection point until you reach the bottom axis. Read the wind chill temperature from the bottom axis.

CONVERTING BETWEEN THE FAHRENHEIT AND CENTIGRADE TEMPERATURE SCALES

There are two different temperature scales widely used in facility operations today, the Fahrenheit (°F) and the Centigrade scales. On the Fahrenheit scale, the freezing point of water is 32°F and the boiling point is 212°F. On the Centigrade scale, the freezing point of water is 0°C and the boiling point is 100°C.

Although the Fahrenheit scale has been the most widely used temperature scale in facility management, the Centigrade scale is gaining gradual acceptance. Conversion between the two scales is by using formulas or tables. Use Figure 20.7 to convert temperature readings for values ranging from -30°F to +269°F. The values listed in the table have been rounded off to the nearest whole number. If more accurate values are required, or if values are needed beyond the range of the table, the Fahrenheit values can be converted to Centigrade by the following equation:

$$C = (F - 32) * 0.555$$
where C = the Centigrade temperature
F = the Fahrenheit temperature

Similarly, Centigrade values can be converted to Fahrenheit by the equation:

$$F = (C + 17.78) * 1.8$$
where F = the Fahrenheit temperature
C = the Centigrade temperature

THE RELATIONSHIP BETWEEN TEMPERATURE, RELATIVE HUMIDITY, AND CONDENSATION

For most heated facilities, the moisture content of the air within the building is higher than that of the air outside the building. The increase in moisture content is a result of the people, plants, and processes that are found within the facility. Additional moisture may be added to the building air through the use of HVAC humidification equipment.

While maintaining elevated moisture levels helps to promote a more healthy environment and reduce the effects of static electricity, there is a point at which high moisture levels in building air can cause damage to building surfaces through condensation. Condensation occurs when air is cooled to its dew point and water vapor condenses out of the air onto the cold surface.

In most buildings during the heating season, the coldest surface exposed to warm, moist room air is the glass in windows. Due to the relatively high thermal conductivity of window glass, the interior surface of the innermost glass layer is well below room temperature. If it is cold enough and the moisture content of the room air high enough, water will condense out of the air onto the window glass. As this water comes into contact with other materials, it will promote wood rot, paint peeling, and mildew formation.

The formation of condensation on building interior surfaces is determined by several factors including the outside temperature, the wind speed blowing across the outside surface, the speed of the air blowing across the inside surface, the inside air temperature, and the relative humidity of the inside air.

The first three of these factors determine the temperature of the inside surface. Of these, the most important are the outside air temperature and wind speed. For most applications, unless there is an HVAC unit specially designed to blow air across the inside surface, the interior air speed will be zero. If this inside surface temperature is below the dew point of the inside air for its given temperature and relative humidity, condensation will take place.

Figure 20.8 shows the point at which condensation will form on single-glazed windows for various outside temperatures, inside temperatures, and inside relative humidities. The figure can be used to determine the inside relative humidity that will result in condensation for a given inside and outside temperature. It can also be used to determine the outside temperature that will cause the formation of condensation for a given inside temperature and relative humidity.

Use Figure 20.9 for dual-glazed windows. In developing both figures, several assumptions were made. The coefficient of heat transfer of single-glazed windows was assumed to be 1.13 Btu/(hr-ft^2-°F). The coefficient of heat transfer for dual-glazed windows was assumed to be 0.61 Btu/(hr-ft^2-°F). There was no air movement across the interior window surface.

Three Methods to Avoid Condensation

If the figures show that condensation will occur in a facility, there are three methods that can be used to prevent its formation. The first method reduces condensation by lowering the interior relative humidity. As can be seen from the figures, a reduction in relative humidity will result in a reduction in the outside air temperature at which condensation will form.

The second method to reduce condensation is to decrease the thermal conductivity of the window so that the interior window surface temperature will increase. If it is increased above the dew point temperature for the interior temperature and relative humidity, condensation will not form. Additional glazing, either through storm windows or replacement dual- or triple-glazed windows, will decrease thermal conductivity.

The third method involves directing a flow of room air across the interior window surface. By so doing, the interior window surface temperature can be raised above the dew point temperature and condensation eliminated.

SOLAR RADIATION

Figure 20.10 shows the annual mean daily solar radiation received on a horizontal surface. The figure was originally produced by Dubin - Mindell - Bloome Associates in the Federal Energy Administration publication, *Guidelines for Saving Energy in Existing Buildings.*

The isolines shown are of Langleys per day, where one Langley equals one gram calorie per square centimeter. Solar radiation values for specific locations can be determined from the isoline located closest to that location. If the location is not close to an isoline, interpolate between the two closest isolines. The figure will be used in estimating energy requirements in later calculations presented in this book, such as the estimation of the solar heating load component on a roof. It can also be used in other energy calculations that require measurements in Btu per square foot by multiplying the Langley value by 3.68.

WELL WATER TEMPERATURE

Figure 20.11 shows average well water temperature. Data presented in the figure was compiled by the U.S. Geological Survey. The isolines shown are in degrees Fahrenheit and represent the average well water temperature for wells between 60 and 100 feet in depth. Well water temperatures for specific locations can be determined from the isoline located closest to that location. If the location is not close to an isoline, interpolate between the two closest isolines.

The figure will be used in estimating energy requirements in later calculations presented in this book, such as the estimation of the potential of using ground water for cooling.

FIGURE 20.1 Heating Data by City

State	City	Winter Design Temperature ($^\circ$F)	Heating Degree Days
Alabama	Birmingham	17	2,844
	Huntsville	11	3,302
	Mobile	25	1,684
	Montgomery	22	2,269
Alaska	Anchorage	-23	10,911
	Barrow	-45	20,265
	Fairbanks	-51	14,345
Arizona	Flagstaff	-2	7,322
	Phoenix	31	1,552
	Tucson	28	1,707
Arkansas	El Dorado	18	2,645
	Fort Smith	12	3,336
	Little Rock	15	3,354
California	Bakersfield	30	2,185
	Fresno	28	2,650
	Los Angeles	41	1,819
	Monterey	35	3,556
	Redding	29	2,688
	Sacramento	30	2,843
	San Diego	42	1,507
	San Francisco	35	3,042
Colorado	Colorado Springs	-3	6,473
	Denver	-5	6,016
	Grand Junction	2	5,605
	Pueblo	-7	5,394
Connecticut	Bridgeport	6	5,461
	Hartford	3	6,105
	New Haven	3	5,793
	New London	5	6,150
	Waterbury	-4	6,672
Delaware	Dover	11	4,756
	Wilmington	10	4,940

Figure 20.1 (continued)

State	City	Winter Design Temperature (^{0}F)	Heating Degree Days
District of Columbia	Washington	14	4,211
Florida	Daytona Beach	32	897
	Gainesville	28	1,081
	Jacksonville	29	1,327
	Key West	55	64
	Miami	44	206
	Orlando	35	704
	Pensacola	25	1,513
	Tallahassee	27	1,563
	Tampa	36	718
	West Palm Beach	41	299
Georgia	Atlanta	17	3,095
	Augusta	20	2,547
	Macon	22	2,240
	Savannah	24	2,029
Hawaii	Hilo	61	0
	Honolulu	62	0
	Lihue	58	2
	Wahiawa	58	10
Idaho	Boise	3	5,833
	Idaho Falls	-11	7,888
	Lewiston	-1	5,464
	Pocatello	-8	7,063
Illinois	Chicago	-5	6,127
	Decatur	-3	5,344
	Peoria	-8	6,098
Indiana	Evansville	4	4,624
	Fort Wayne	-4	6,209
	Gary	-4	6,165
	Indianapolis	-2	5,577
	Terre Haute	-2	5,351

Figure 20.1 (continued)

State	City	Winter Design Temperature (^{0}F)	Heating Degree Days
Iowa	Cedar Rapids	-10	6,601
	Des Moines	-10	6,710
	Sioux City	-11	6,953
	Waterloo	-15	7,415
Kansas	Dodge City	0	5,046
	Goodland	-5	6,119
	Kansas City	2	4,846
	Topeka	0	5,243
	Wichita	3	4,687
Kentucky	Covington	1	5,070
	Lexington	3	4,729
	Louisville	5	4,640
Louisiana	Alexandria	23	2,200
	Baton Rouge	25	1,670
	New Orleans	29	1,465
	Shreveport	20	2,167
Maine	Augusta	-7	7,826
	Bangor	-11	8,034
	Caribou	-18	9,632
	Portland	-6	7,498
Maryland	Annapolis	15	4,548
	Baltimore	10	4,729
	Cumberland	6	5,012
	Frederick	8	5,059
	Hagerstown	8	5,152
Massachusetts	Boston	6	5,621
	Nantucket	14	5,929
	New Bedford	5	5,395
	Pittsfield	-8	7,580
	Springfield	1	5,844
	Worcester	0	6,848

Figure 20.1 (continued)

State	City	Winter Design Temperature ($^{\circ}$F)	Heating Degree Days
Michigan	Alpena	-11	8,518
	Benton Harbor	1	6,296
	Detroit	3	6,228
	Grand Rapids	1	6,801
	Lansing	-3	6,904
	Saginaw	0	7,143
Minnesota	Bemidji	-31	10,203
	Duluth	-21	9,757
	International Falls	-29	10,547
	Minneapolis	-16	8,310
Mississippi	Columbus	15	2,890
	Gulfport	28	1,496
	Jackson	21	2,300
	Meridian	19	2,388
Missouri	Jefferson City	3	4,486
	Kansas City	2	4,711
	St. Joseph	-3	5,440
	St. Louis	2	4,750
	Springfield	3	4,570
Montana	Billings	-15	7,265
	Butte	-24	9,719
	Great Falls	-21	7,652
	Kalispell	-31	11,024
	Missoula	-13	7,931
Nebraska	Grand Island	-8	6,420
	Lincoln	-5	6,218
	North Platte	-8	6,743
	Omaha	-8	6,049
	Scottsbluff	-8	6,774
Nevada	Elko	-8	7,483
	Las Vegas	25	2,601
	Reno	5	6,022
	Winnemucca	-13	8,100

Figure 20.1 (continued)

State	City	Winter Design Temperature (°F)	Heating Degree Days
New Hampshire	Concord	-8	7,360
	Manchester	-8	7,101
	Portsmouth	-2	6,846
New Jersey	Atlantic City	10	4,946
	Camden	10	4,865
	Newark	10	5,034
	Trenton	11	4,947
New Mexico	Albuquerque	12	4,337
	Carlsbad	13	2,835
	Farmington	1	5,713
	Las Cruces	15	3,194
New York	Albany	-6	6,888
	Buffalo	2	6,927
	Ithaca	-5	7,052
	New York	12	5,184
	Syracuse	-3	6,772
	Utica	-12	7,299
	Watertown	-11	7,376
North Carolina	Cape Hatteras	25	2,731
	Charlotte	18	3,218
	Greensboro	14	3,825
	Raleigh	16	3,514
	Winston-Salem	16	3,679
North Dakota	Bismarck	-23	9,044
	Dickinson	-21	8,942
	Fargo	-22	9,271
	Grand Forks	-26	9,963
	Minot	-24	9,625

Figure 20.1 (continued)

State	City	Winter Design Temperature (^{0}F)	Heating Degree Days
Ohio	Akron	1	6,224
	Cincinnati	1	5,070
	Cleveland	1	6,154
	Columbus	0	5,702
	Dayton	-1	5,641
	Toledo	-3	6,381
	Youngstown	-1	6,426
Oklahoma	Oklahoma City	9	3,695
	Tulsa	8	3,680
Oregon	Astoria	25	5,295
	Eugene	17	4,739
	Klamath Falls	4	6,987
	North Bend	29	4,688
	Pendleton	-2	5,240
	Portland	17	4,792
	Salem	18	4,852
Pennsylvania	Allentown	4	5,827
	Altoona	0	6,192
	Erie	4	6,851
	Harrisburg	7	5,315
	Philadelphia	10	4,865
	Pittsburgh	1	5,930
	Scranton	3	6,114
	State College	3	6,132
	Williamsport	2	5,981
Rhode Island	Newport	5	5,840
	Providence	5	5,972
South Carolina	Charlestown	24	2,146
	Columbia	20	2,598
	Florence	22	2,566
	Greenville	18	3,163

Figure 20.1 (continued)

State	City	Winter Design Temperature (°F)	Heating Degree Days
South Dakota	Aberdeen	-19	8,617
	Huron	-18	8,055
	Rapid City	-11	7,324
	Sioux Falls	-15	7,838
Tennessee	Chattanooga	13	3,505
	Knoxville	13	3,478
	Memphis	13	3,227
	Nashville	9	3,696
Texas	Abilene	15	2,610
	Austin	24	1,737
	Corpus Christi	31	930
	Dallas	18	2,290
	El Paso	20	2,678
	Houston	27	1,434
	San Antonio	25	1,570
	Waco	20	2,081
Utah	Cedar City	-2	6,137
	Provo	1	5,720
	Salt Lake City	3	5,983
Vermont	Burlington	-12	7,876
Virginia	Charlottesville	14	4,162
	Lynchburg	12	4,233
	Norfolk	20	3,488
	Richmond	14	3,939
	Roanoke	12	4,307
Washington	Aberdeen	25	5,316
	Bellingham	10	5,738
	Richland	5	4,892
	Seattle	21	5,185
	Spokane	-6	6,835
	Yakima	-2	6,009

Figure 20.1 (continued)

State	City	Winter Design Temperature ($^\circ$F)	Heating Degree Days
West Virginia	Charleston	7	4,590
	Huntington	5	4,374
	Martinsburg	6	5,231
	Wheeling	1	5,930
Wisconsin	Green Bay	-13	8,098
	La Crosse	-13	7,417
	Madison	-11	7,730
	Milwaukee	-8	7,444
	Oshkosh	-14	7,602
Wyoming	Casper	-11	7,555
	Cheyenne	-9	7,255
	Rock Springs	-9	8,410

FIGURE 20.2 Cooling Data by City

State	City	Summer Design Temp (^{0}F)	Cooling Degree Days	Degree Hr > 78^{0}F
Alabama	Birmingham	96	1,928	11,934
	Huntsville	95	1,808	11,011
	Mobile	95	2,577	-
	Montgomery	96	2,238	13,569
Alaska	Anchorage	71	0	0
	Barrow	57	0	0
	Fairbanks	82	52	227
Arizona	Flagstaff	95	140	942
	Phoenix	109	3,308	40,376
	Tucson	104	2,896	25,352
Arkansas	El Dorado	98	2,204	-
	Fort Smith	101	2,022	15,307
	Little Rock	96	1,925	12,131
California	Bakersfield	104	2,179	18,172
	Fresno	102	1,671	-
	Los Angeles	83	615	928
	Monterey	75	32	-
	Redding	105	1,904	-
	Sacramento	101	1,159	12,298
	San Diego	83	722	529
	San Francisco	74	108	597
Colorado	Colorado Springs	91	461	3,494
	Denver	93	625	4,049
	Grand Junction	96	1,140	8,475
	Pueblo	97	981	8,773
Connecticut	Bridgeport	84	735	-
	Hartford	88	605	-
	New Haven	84	573	-
	New London	88	376	-
	Waterbury	85	547	-
Delaware	Dover	92	1,115	4,649
	Wilmington	92	992	4,673

Figure 20.2 (continued)

State	City	Summer Design Temp. (°F)	Cooling Degree Days	Degree Hr > 78°F
District of Columbia	Washington	93	1,415	5,336
Florida	Daytona Beach	92	2,919	-
	Gainesville	95	2,906	-
	Jacksonville	96	3,059	13,651
	Key West	90	4,888	22,375
	Miami	91	4,038	16,351
	Orlando	94	3,447	13,652
	Pensacola	94	2,562	12,932
	Tallahassee	94	2,563	12,755
	Tampa	92	3,366	15,855
	West Palm Beach	92	3,786	-
Georgia	Atlanta	94	1,589	8,464
	Augusta	97	1,995	13,115
	Macon	98	2,294	12,102
	Savannah	93	2,372	11,331
Hawaii	Hilo	84	3,066	-
	Honolulu	87	4,221	-
	Lihue	85	3,719	-
	Wahiawa	86	2,821	-
Idaho	Boise	96	714	9,042
	Idaho Falls	89	286	4,955
	Lewiston	96	657	5,483
	Pocatello	94	437	4,955
Illinois	Chicago	91	664	3,950
	Decatur	94	1,197	6,989
	Peoria	91	968	-
Indiana	Evansville	95	1,364	8,911
	Fort Wayne	92	748	-
	Gary	91	859	-
	Indianapolis	95	974	-
	Terre Haute	95	1,110	6,305

Figure 20.2 (continued)

State	City	Summer Design Temp (^{0}F)	Cooling Degree Days	Degree Hr > 78^{0}F
Iowa	Cedar Rapids	91	812	-
	Des Moines	94	928	5,279
	Sioux City	95	932	6,011
	Waterloo	91	675	-
Kansas	Dodge City	100	1,411	11,445
	Goodland	99	925	8,812
	Kansas City	99	1,420	7,490
	Topeka	99	1,361	7,490
	Wichita	101	1,673	10,399
Kentucky	Covington	92	1,080	7,767
	Lexington	93	1,197	-
	Louisville	95	1,268	-
Louisiana	Alexandria	95	2,193	14,225
	Baton Rouge	95	2,585	-
	New Orleans	93	2,706	12,082
	Shreveport	99	2,538	13,588
Maine	Augusta	88	271	-
	Bangor	86	304	1,117
	Caribou	84	128	-
	Portland	87	252	757
Maryland	Annapolis	91	1,155	5,418
	Baltimore	94	1,115	-
	Cumberland	92	828	-
	Frederick	94	948	-
	Hagerstown	94	981	-
Massachusetts	Boston	91	661	2,645
	Nantucket	79	284	-
	New Bedford	85	635	842
	Pittsfield	87	317	-
	Springfield	92	740	-
	Worcester	87	387	-

Figure 20.2 (continued)

State	City	Summer Design Temp (^{0}F)	Cooling Degree Days	Degree Hr > 78^{0}F
Michigan	Alpena	89	208	1,555
	Benton Harbor	91	638	-
	Detroit	91	743	2,570
	Grand Rapids	91	575	1,632
	Lansing	90	535	2,700
	Saginaw	91	487	-
Minnesota	Bemidji	88	241	-
	Duluth	85	176	814
	International Falls	85	176	1,037
	Minneapolis	92	527	3,437
Mississippi	Columbus	94	2,039	11,513
	Gulfport	94	2,682	15,485
	Jackson	97	2,321	14,658
	Meridian	97	2,231	11,804
Missouri	Jefferson City	98	1,640	8,621
	Kansas City	99	1,420	6,058
	St. Joseph	96	1,334	-
	St. Louis	97	1,475	9,263
	Springfield	96	1,382	8,223
Montana	Billings	94	498	4,417
	Butte	86	58	-
	Great Falls	91	339	-
	Kalispell	89	9	-
	Missoula	92	188	2,644
Nebraska	Grand Island	97	1,036	7,205
	Lincoln	99	1,148	-
	North Platte	97	802	6,403
	Omaha	94	1,173	-
	Scottsbluff	95	666	5,697
Nevada	Elko	94	342	-
	Las Vegas	108	2,946	35,710
	Reno	95	329	3,745
	Winnemucca	88	407	8,079

Figure 20.2 (continued)

State	City	Summer Design Temp (^{0}F)	Cooling Degree Days	Degree Hr > 78^{0}F
New Hampshire	Concord	90	349	-
	Manchester	91	378	-
	Portsmouth	88	252	1,952
New Jersey	Atlantic City	92	864	-
	Camden	93	1,104	-
	Newark	94	1,024	5,019
	Trenton	91	968	4,190
New Mexico	Albuquerque	96	1,394	9,591
	Carlsbad	103	1,993	-
	Farmington	95	749	7,857
	Las Cruces	99	1,585	13,858
New York	Albany	91	574	2,939
	Buffalo	88	437	2,322
	Ithaca	88	384	-
	New York	92	861	3,853
	Syracuse	90	591	2,809
	Utica	88	467	2,006
	Watertown	86	461	-
North Carolina	Cape Hatteras	87	1,550	7,269
	Charlotte	95	1,596	-
	Greensboro	93	1,341	6,703
	Raleigh	94	1,394	-
	Winston-Salem	94	1,543	7,100
North Dakota	Bismarck	95	487	4,093
	Dickinson	94	399	-
	Fargo	92	473	-
	Grand Forks	91	400	2,492
	Minot	92	398	3,021

Figure 20.2 (continued)

State	City	Summer Design Temp (^{0}F)	Cooling Degree Days	Degree Hr > 78^{0}F
Ohio	Akron	89	634	2,599
	Cincinnati	92	1,080	5,459
	Cleveland	91	613	-
	Columbus	92	809	-
	Dayton	91	936	4,734
	Toledo	90	685	3,478
	Youngstown	88	518	-
Oklahoma	Oklahoma City	100	1,876	11,970
	Tulsa	101	1,949	15,659
Oregon	Astoria	75	13	97
	Eugene	92	239	2,677
	Klamath Falls	90	228	-
	North Bend	69	0	-
	Pendleton	97	656	5,439
	Portland	89	300	1,546
	Salem	92	232	-
Pennsylvania	Allentown	92	772	-
	Altoona	90	617	-
	Erie	88	373	-
	Harrisburg	94	1,025	5,374
	Philadelphia	93	1,104	-
	Pittsburgh	87	647	2,950
	Scranton	90	630	2,723
	State College	90	583	-
	Williamsport	92	698	3,807
Rhode Island	Newport	88	690	2,009
	Providence	89	532	1,829
South Carolina	Charlestown	93	2,078	9,475
	Columbia	97	2,087	10,513
	Florence	94	1,952	-
	Greenville	93	1,573	8,010

Figure 20.2 (continued)

State	City	Summer Design Temp (^{0}F)	Cooling Degree Days	Degree Hr > 78^{0}F
South Dakota	Aberdeen	94	566	-
	Huron	96	716	5,623
	Rapid City	97	661	4,784
	Sioux Falls	94	719	4,825
Tennessee	Chattanooga	96	1,636	-
	Knoxville	94	1,569	8,135
	Memphis	98	2,029	10,905
	Nashville	97	1,694	8,955
Texas	Abilene	101	2,466	17,444
	Austin	100	2,908	19,860
	Corpus Christi	92	3,474	18,763
	Dallas	102	2,755	20,131
	El Paso	100	2,098	-
	Houston	96	2,889	15,017
	San Antonio	99	2,994	19,519
	Waco	101	2,878	22,162
Utah	Cedar City	93	615	-
	Provo	98	892	-
	Salt Lake City	97	927	6,026
Vermont	Burlington	88	369	-
Virginia	Charlottesville	94	1,263	-
	Lynchburg	93	1,100	6,267
	Norfolk	93	1,441	5,828
	Richmond	95	1,353	7,974
	Roanoke	93	1,030	6,267
Washington	Aberdeen	80	13	-
	Bellingham	81	44	-
	Richland	99	826	-
	Seattle	84	129	751
	Spokane	93	388	3,334
	Yakima	96	479	-

Figure 20.2 (continued)

State	City	Summer Design Temp (°F)	Cooling Degree Days	Degree Hr > 78°F
West Virginia	Charleston	92	1,055	5,568
	Huntington	94	1,098	6,350
	Martinsburg	93	922	-
	Wheeling	89	647	-
Wisconsin	Green Bay	88	386	1,834
	La Crosse	91	695	3,194
	Madison	91	460	3,308
	Milwaukee	90	450	-
	Oshkosh	89	547	-
Wyoming	Casper	92	458	4,218
	Cheyenne	89	327	2,300
	Rock Springs	86	227	1,467

FIGURE 20.3 Estimating Degree Hours Above 78 °F

Cooling
Degree Days

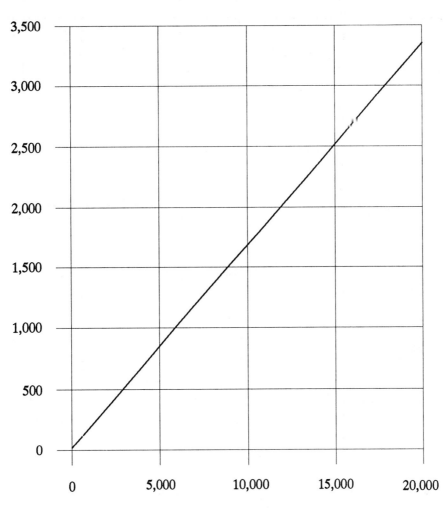

Degree Hours Greater Than 78°F

FIGURE 20.4 Monthly Degree Day Log

Month: _____

Date	High Temp (°F)	Low Temp (°F)	Mean Temp (°F)	Heating Degree Days	Cooling Degree Days
1	——	——	——	——	——
2	——	——	——	——	——
3	——	——	——	——	——
4	——	——	——	——	——
5	——	——	——	——	——
6	——	——	——	——	——
7	——	——	——	——	——
8	——	——	——	——	——
9	——	——	——	——	——
10	——	——	——	——	——
11	——	——	——	——	——
12	——	——	——	——	——
13	——	——	——	——	——
14	——	——	——	——	——
15	——	——	——	——	——
16	——	——	——	——	——
17	——	——	——	——	——
18	——	——	——	——	——
19	——	——	——	——	——
20	——	——	——	——	——
21	——	——	——	——	——
22	——	——	——	——	——
23	——	——	——	——	——
24	——	——	——	——	——
25	——	——	——	——	——
26	——	——	——	——	——
27	——	——	——	——	——
28	——	——	——	——	——
29	——	——	——	——	——
30	——	——	——	——	——
31	——	——	——	——	——
Total:				——	——

FIGURE 20.5 Wind Data by City

State	City	Winter		Summer Direction
		Direction	**Speed (Kn)**	
Alabama	Birmingham	NNW	8	WNW
	Huntsville	N	9	SW
	Mobile	N	10	N
	Montgomery	NW	7	W
Alaska	Anchorage	SE	3	WNW
	Barrow	SW	8	SE
	Fairbanks	N	3	WSW
Arizona	Flagstaff	NE	5	SW
	Phoenix	E	4	W
	Tucson	SE	6	WNW
Arkansas	El Dorado	S	6	SE
	Fort Smith	NW	8	SW
	Little Rock	N	7	S
California	Bakersfield	ENE	5	WNW
	Fresno	E	4	WNW
	Los Angeles	E	4	WSW
	Monterey	SE	4	NW
	Redding	NW	6	SSE
	Sacramento	ESE	6	SW
	San Diego	NE	3	WNW
	San Francisco	W	5	NW
Colorado	Colorado Springs	NE	7	SSE
	Denver	S	8	SE
	Grand Junction	ESE	5	WNW
	Pueblo	W	5	SE
Connecticut	Bridgeport	NNW	13	WSW
	Hartford	N	5	SSW
	New Haven	NNE	7	SW
	New London	NW	10	SW
	Waterbury	N	8	SW
Delaware	Dover	W	9	SW
	Wilmington	WNW	9	WSW

Figure 20.5 (continued)

State	City	Winter		Summer Direction
		Direction	Speed (Kn)	
District of Columbia	Washington	WNW	11	S
Florida	Daytona Beach	NW	8	E
	Gainesville	W	6	W
	Jacksonville	NW	7	SW
	Key West	NNE	12	SE
	Miami	NNW	8	SE
	Orlando	NNW	9	SSW
	Pensacola	NNE	7	S
	Tallahassee	NW	6	NW
	Tampa	N	8	W
	West Palm Beach	NW	9	ESE
Georgia	Atlanta	NW	11	NW
	Augusta	W	4	WSW
	Macon	NW	8	WNW
	Savannah	WNW	6	W
Hawaii	Hilo	SW	6	NE
	Honolulu	NW	5	ENE
	Lihue	W	6	NE
	Wahiawa	WNW	5	E
Idaho	Boise	SE	6	NW
	Idaho Falls	N	9	S
	Lewiston	W	3	WNW
	Pocatello	NE	5	W
Illinois	Chicago	WNW	11	SW
	Decatur	NW	10	SW
	Peoria	WNW	8	SW
Indiana	Evansville	NW	9	SW
	Fort Wayne	WSW	10	SW
	Gary	SW	11	SSW
	Indianapolis	WNW	10	SW
	Terre Haute	NNW	7	SSW

Figure 20.5 (continued)

State	City	Winter		Summer Direction
		Direction	Speed (Kn)	
Iowa	Cedar Rapids	NW	9	S
	Des Moines	NW	11	S
	Sioux City	NNW	9	S
	Waterloo	NW	9	S
Kansas	Dodge City	N	12	SSW
	Goodland	WSW	10	S
	Kansas City	NW	9	SSW
	Topeka	NNW	10	S
	Wichita	NNW	12	SSW
Kentucky	Covington	W	9	SW
	Lexington	WNW	9	SW
	Louisville	NW	8	SW
Louisiana	Alexandria	N	7	S
	Baton Rouge	ENE	8	W
	New Orleans	NNE	9	SSW
	Shreveport	N	9	S
Maine	Augusta	NNE	10	WNW
	Bangor	WNW	7	S
	Caribou	WSW	10	SW
	Portland	W	7	S
Maryland	Annapolis	WNW	9	S
	Baltimore	W	9	WSW
	Cumberland	WNW	10	W
	Frederick	N	9	WNW
	Hagerstown	WNW	10	W
Massachusetts	Boston	WNW	16	SW
	Nantucket	NW	14	SW
	New Bedford	NW	10	SW
	Pittsfield	NW	12	SW
	Springfield	N	8	SSW
	Worcester	W	14	W

Figure 20.5 (continued)

State	City	Winter		Summer Direction
		Direction	Speed (Kn)	
Michigan	Alpena	W	5	SW
	Benton Harbor	SSW	8	WSW
	Detroit	W	11	SW
	Grand Rapids	WNW	8	WSW
	Lansing	SW	12	W
	Saginaw	WSW	7	SW
Minnesota	Bemidji	N	8	S
	Duluth	WNW	12	WSW
	International Falls	W	7	S
	Minneapolis	NW	8	S
Mississippi	Columbus	N	8	S
	Gulfport	NNW	6	S
	Jackson	NNW	6	NW
	Meridian	N	6	WSW
Missouri	Jefferson City	NW	9	S
	Kansas City	NW	9	S
	St. Joseph	NNW	9	S
	St. Louis	NW	9	S
	Springfield	NNW	10	S
Montana	Billings	NE	9	SW
	Butte	S	5	NW
	Great Falls	SW	7	WSW
	Kalispell	NW	15	W
	Missoula	ESE	7	NW
Nebraska	Grand Island	NNW	10	S
	Lincoln	N	8	S
	North Platte	NW	9	SSE
	Omaha	NW	8	S
	Scottsbluff	NW	9	SE
Nevada	Elko	E	4	SW
	Las Vegas	W	7	SW
	Reno	SSW	3	WNW
	Winnemucca	SE	5	W

Figure 20.5 (continued)

State	City	Winter		Summer Direction
		Direction	Speed (Kn)	
New Hampshire	Concord	NW	7	SW
	Manchester	NNW	11	SW
	Portsmouth	W	8	W
New Jersey	Atlantic City	NW	11	WSW
	Camden	WNW	10	WSW
	Newark	WNW	11	WSW
	Trenton	W	9	SW
New Mexico	Albuquerque	N	7	W
	Carlsbad	N	6	SSE
	Farmington	ENE	15	SW
	Las Cruces	SE	5	SE
New York	Albany	WNW	8	S
	Buffalo	W	10	SW
	Ithaca	W	6	SW
	New York	WNW	15	SW
	Syracuse	WNW	7	WNW
	Utica	NW	12	W
	Watertown	E	7	WSW
North Carolina	Cape Hatteras	NNW	11	SSW
	Charlotte	NNW	6	SW
	Greensboro	NE	7	SW
	Raleigh	N	7	SW
	Winston-Salem	NW	8	WSW
North Dakota	Bismarck	WNW	7	S
	Dickinson	WNW	12	SSE
	Fargo	NNW	9	S
	Grand Forks	N	8	S
	Minot	WNW	10	S

Figure 20.5 (continued)

State	City	Winter		Summer Direction
		Direction	Speed (Kn)	
Ohio	Akron	SW	9	SW
	Cincinnati	W	9	SW
	Cleveland	SW	12	N
	Columbus	W	8	SSW
	Dayton	WNW	11	SW
	Toledo	WSW	8	SW
	Youngstown	SW	10	SW
Oklahoma	Oklahoma City	N	14	SSW
	Tulsa	N	11	SSW
Oregon	Astoria	ESE	7	NNW
	Eugene	N	7	N
	Klamath Falls	N	4	W
	North Bend	SE	7	NNW
	Pendleton	NNW	6	WNW
	Portland	ESE	12	NW
	Salem	N	6	N
Pennsylvania	Allentown	W	11	SW
	Altoona	WNW	11	WSW
	Erie	SSW	10	WSW
	Harrisburg	NW	11	WSW
	Philadelphia	WNW	10	WSW
	Pittsburgh	WSW	8	WSW
	Scranton	SW	8	WSW
	State College	WNW	8	WSW
	Williamsport	W	9	WSW
Rhode Island	Newport	WNW	10	SW
	Providence	WNW	11	SW
South Carolina	Charlestown	NNE	8	SW
	Columbia	W	6	SW
	Florence	N	7	SW
	Greenville	NW	8	SW

Figure 20.5 (continued)

State	City	Winter		Summer Direction
		Direction	Speed (Kn)	
South Dakota	Aberdeen	NNW	8	S
	Huron	NNW	8	S
	Rapid City	NNW	10	SSE
	Sioux Falls	NW	8	S
Tennessee	Chattanooga	NNW	8	WSW
	Knoxville	NE	8	W
	Memphis	N	10	SW
	Nashville	NW	8	WSW
Texas	Abilene	N	12	SSE
	Austin	N	11	S
	Corpus Christi	N	12	SSE
	Dallas	N	11	S
	El Paso	N	7	S
	Houston	NNW	11	S
	San Antonio	N	8	SSE
	Waco	N	11	S
Utah	Cedar City	SE	5	SW
	Provo	SE	5	SW
	Salt Lake City	SSE	6	N
Vermont	Burlington	E	7	SSW
Virginia	Charlottesville	NE	7	SW
	Lynchburg	NE	7	SW
	Norfolk	NW	10	SW
	Richmond	N	6	SW
	Roanoke	NW	9	SW
Washington	Aberdeen	ESE	6	NNW
	Bellingham	NNE	15	WSW
	Richland	WNW	5	SW
	Seattle	E	9	N
	Spokane	NE	6	SW
	Yakima	W	5	NW

Figure 20.5 (continued)

State	City	Winter		Summer Direction
		Direction	Speed (Kn)	
West Virginia	Charleston	SW	8	SW
	Huntington	W	6	SW
	Martinsburg	WNW	10	W
	Wheeling	WSW	10	WSW
Wisconsin	Green Bay	W	8	SW
	La Crosse	NW	10	S
	Madison	NW	8	SW
	Milwaukee	WNW	10	SSW
	Oshkosh	WNW	8	SSW
Wyoming	Casper	NE	10	SW
	Cheyenne	N	11	WNW
	Rock Springs	WSW	10	W

FIGURE 20.6 Wind Chill Temperature

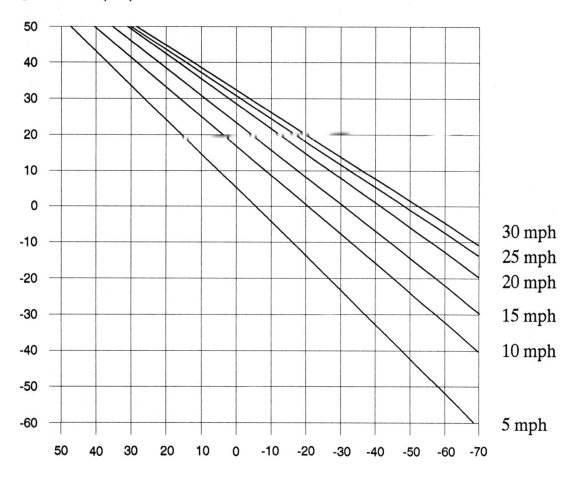

Wind Chill Temperature (°F)

FIGURE 20.7 Fahrenheit - Centigrade Conversion

Deg F	Deg C	Deg F	Deg C	Deg F	Deg C	Deg F	Deg C
-30	-34	0	-18	30	-1	60	16
-29	-34	1	-17	31	-1	61	16
-28	-33	2	-17	32	0	62	17
-27	-33	3	-16	33	1	63	17
-26	-32	4	-16	34	1	64	18
-25	-32	5	-15	35	2	65	18
-24	-31	6	-14	36	2	66	19
-23	-31	7	-14	37	3	67	19
-22	-30	8	-13	38	3	68	20
-21	-29	9	-13	39	4	69	21
-20	-29	10	-12	40	4	70	21
-19	-28	11	-12	41	5	71	22
-18	-28	12	-11	42	6	72	22
-17	-27	13	-11	43	6	73	23
-16	-27	14	-10	44	7	74	23
-15	-26	15	-9	45	7	75	24
-14	-26	16	-9	46	8	76	24
-13	-25	17	-8	47	8	77	25
-12	-24	18	-8	48	9	78	26
-11	-24	19	-7	49	9	79	26
-10	-23	20	-7	50	10	80	27
-9	-23	21	-6	51	11	81	27
-8	-22	22	-6	52	11	82	28
-7	-22	23	-5	53	12	83	28
-6	-21	24	-4	54	12	84	29
-5	-21	25	-4	55	13	85	29
-4	-20	26	-3	56	13	86	30
-3	-19	27	-3	57	14	87	31
-2	-19	28	-2	58	14	88	31
-1	-18	29	-2	59	15	89	32

Note: All temperatures are rounded off to the nearest whole number.

Figure 20.7 (continued)

Deg F	Deg C	Deg F	Deg C	Deg F	Deg C	Deg F	Deg C
90	32	120	49	150	66	180	82
91	33	121	49	151	66	181	83
92	33	122	50	152	67	182	83
93	34	123	51	153	67	183	84
94	34	124	51	154	68	184	84
95	35	125	52	155	68	185	85
96	36	126	52	156	69	186	86
97	36	127	53	157	69	187	86
98	37	128	53	158	70	188	87
99	37	129	54	159	71	189	87
100	38	130	54	160	71	190	88
101	38	131	55	161	72	191	88
102	39	132	56	162	72	192	89
103	39	133	56	163	73	193	89
104	40	134	57	164	73	194	90
105	41	135	57	165	74	195	91
106	41	136	58	166	74	196	91
107	42	137	58	167	75	197	92
108	42	138	59	168	76	198	92
109	43	139	59	169	76	199	93
110	43	140	60	170	77	200	93
111	44	141	61	171	77	201	94
112	44	142	61	172	78	202	94
113	45	143	62	173	78	203	95
114	46	144	62	174	79	204	96
115	46	145	63	175	79	205	96
116	47	146	63	176	80	206	97
117	47	147	64	177	81	207	97
118	48	148	64	178	81	208	98
119	48	149	65	179	82	209	98

Note: All temperatures are rounded off to the nearest whole number.

Figure 20.7 (continued)

Deg F	Deg C	Deg F	Deg C
210	99	240	116
211	99	241	116
212	100	242	117
213	101	243	117
214	101	244	118
215	102	245	118
216	102	246	119
217	103	247	119
218	103	248	120
219	104	249	121
220	104	250	121
221	105	251	122
222	106	252	122
223	106	253	123
224	107	254	123
225	107	255	124
226	108	256	124
227	108	257	125
228	109	258	126
229	109	259	126
230	110	260	127
231	111	261	127
232	111	262	128
233	112	263	128
234	112	264	129
235	113	265	129
236	113	266	130
237	114	267	131
238	114	268	131
239	115	269	132

Note: All temperatures are rounded off to the nearest whole number.

FIGURE 20.8 Window Condensation Temperatures
Single Glazing

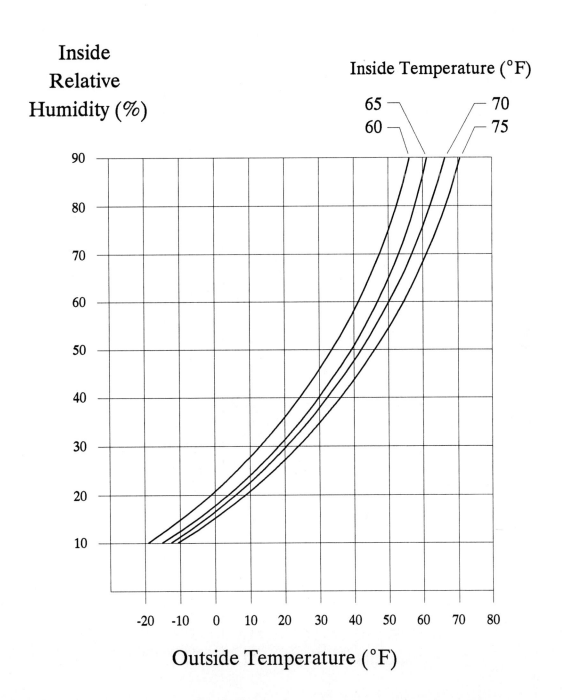

FIGURE 20.9 Window Condensation Temperatures
Dual Glazing

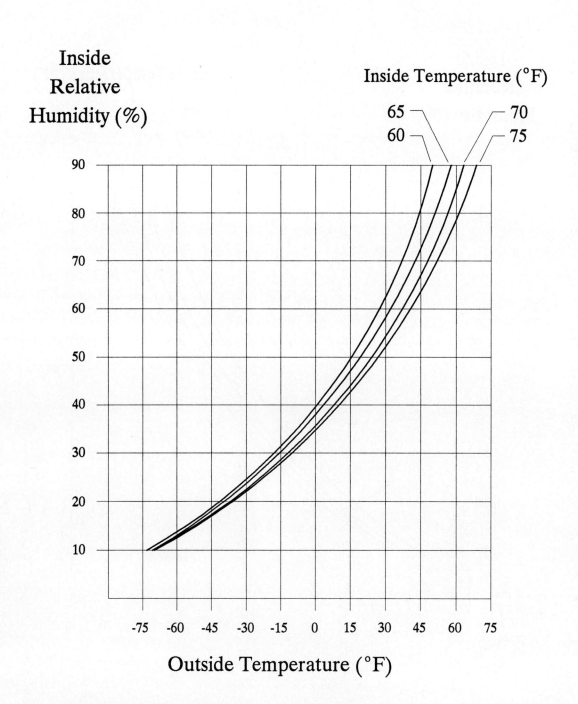

Inside Relative Humidity (%)

Inside Temperature (°F)

65 — — 70
60 — — 75

Outside Temperature (°F)

FIGURE 20.10 Annual Mean Daily Solar Radiation (Langleys)

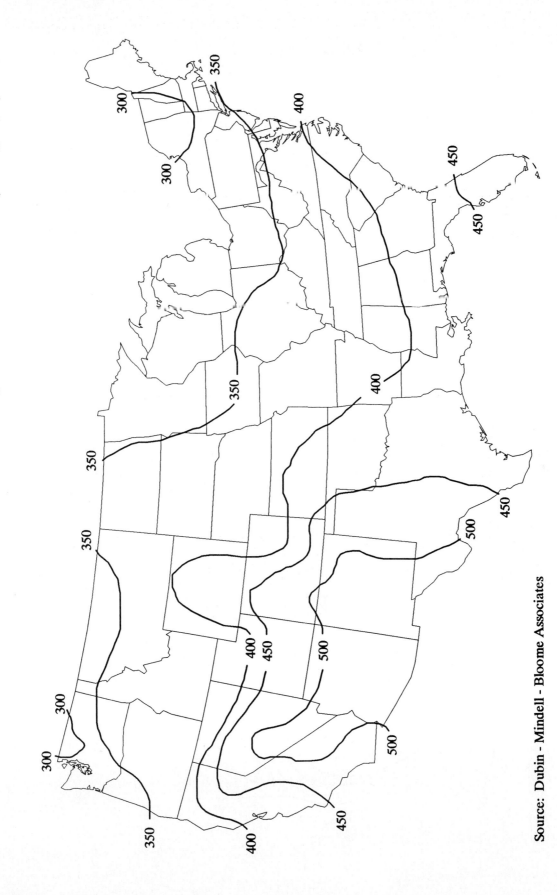

Source: Dubin - Mindell - Bloome Associates

FIGURE 20.11 Well Water Temperatures (°F)

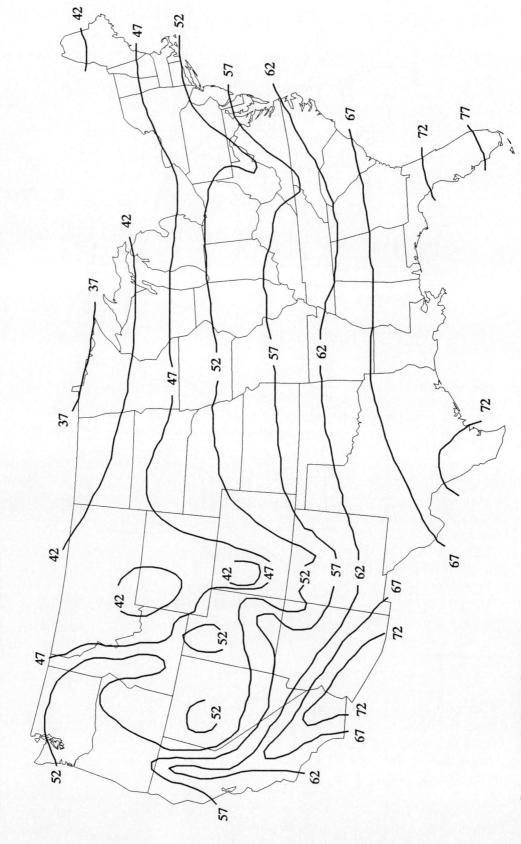

Source: U.S. Geological Survey

How to Estimate the Energy Savings of Modifications to the Building Envelope

The energy calculation procedures outlined in this chapter can be used to give the order of magnitude of savings that would result from implementing a number of different energy saving measures. They are sufficiently accurate to determine whether or not investigation is justified. They are not intended to give the exact values needed to make funding decisions. If you need more accurate estimates, you will need to complete a detailed computer-based analysis, one that makes use of hour-by-hour calculations for an entire year's weather.

There are three figures that are used to derive cost data for the energy calculation procedures given in this and later chapters. Use Worksheet 21.1 to determine heating energy unit costs. Use Worksheet 21.2 to determine cooling energy unit costs. Use Worksheet 21.3 to determine the cost savings associated with implementing specific energy conservation measures.

How to Estimate Building Component Heating Energy Costs

To estimate the component costs of building heating energy use, it is necessary to first estimate the cost of the energy that is being delivered to the conditioned space. There are three primary factors that determine the cost of the heating energy: the type of fuel being used; the rate structure under which the fuel is purchased; and the efficiency of the system used to convert the energy to heat and deliver it to the conditioned space.

Use Worksheet 21.1 to estimate the cost of heating energy as delivered to the conditioned space. This cost includes the inefficiencies and losses associated with converting the energy source to heat and delivering the heat to the conditioned space. The worksheet has three sections, one for each primary heating fuel source. Complete only the section for the heating fuel used in your facility. Use the worksheet as follows:

Step 1.   Determine the energy source (electricity, natural gas, or oil) used to generate heat for the facility.

Step 2.   For the energy source being used, determine the average rate charged for that type of energy. The average rate is determined by dividing the total cost for that utility by the number of units used (kWh, therms, or gallons). If there are separate rate structures in effect for summer and winter use, use a recent winter month's billing to calculate the average rate. Enter the value in the appropriate section in the worksheet.

Step 3.   From the table given at the bottom of the worksheet, for the type of heating system that you have, determine the efficiency factor. Enter the efficiency factor value in the section for the type of energy being used.

Step 4.   If the energy source is electricity or natural gas, skip to step 5. For oil heat, determine the oil conversion factor from the table given at the bottom of the worksheet for the type of oil burned. Enter the value in section #3 of the worksheet.

Step 5.   Multiply the average rate by the conversion factor and the efficiency factor to determine the unit cost for heating energy in dollars per million Btu. Enter the value in the section for the type of energy being used.

This unit cost of heating energy will be used in calculating the cost savings for various energy conservation measures presented in this and other chapters.

HOW TO ESTIMATE BUILDING COMPONENT COOLING ENERGY COSTS

Use Worksheet 21.2 to estimate the cost of cooling energy as delivered to the conditioned space. This cost includes the inefficiencies and losses associated with converting the energy source to air conditioning and delivering the conditioned air to the space. It also includes the seasonal coefficient of performance for the type of system installed in the facility. Use the worksheet as follows:

Step 1.   Determine the energy source, electricity or natural gas-fired absorption.

Step 2.   For the energy source being used, determine the average rate charged for that type of energy. The average rate is determined by dividing the total cost for that utility by the number of units used (kWh or therms). If there are separate rate structures in effect for summer and winter use, use a recent summer month's billing to calculate the average rate. Enter the value in either section #1 or #2 of the worksheet.

Step 3.   From the table given at the bottom of the worksheet, for the type of cooling system that you have, determine the efficiency factor. Enter the efficiency factor value in the section for the type of energy being used.

Step 4.   Multiply the average rate by the conversion factor and the efficiency factor to determine the unit cost for cooling energy in dollars per million Btu. Enter the value in the section for the type of energy being used.

This unit cost of cooling energy will be used in calculating the cost savings for various energy conservation measures presented in this and other chapters.

How to Estimate Energy Conservation Cost Savings

The procedures presented in this chapter can be used to estimate the energy savings that would result from modifying portions of the building envelope. To determine the savings that would result from the implementation of a particular measure, it is necessary to calculate the annual heating and cooling energy use for both the existing and the improved envelope component. By multiplying the annual heating and cooling energy requirements by their respective unit costs, the estimated annual savings can be determined.

Use Worksheet 21.3 to estimate the annual heating and cooling cost savings for each measure being investigated. Complete the figure as follows:

Step 1.   For the existing building envelope and using the appropriate worksheet from this chapter, determine the annual heating energy use for that building envelope component. Enter the value in section #1.

Step 2.   From Worksheet 21.1 determine the unit cost for the type of energy used to generate heat. Enter the value in sections #1 and #2 of the worksheet.

Step 3.   For the existing building envelope and using the appropriate figure from this chapter, determine the annual cooling energy use for that building envelope component. Enter the value in section #1. If no procedure is given to estimate the cooling energy use, enter a value of zero.

Step 4.   From Worksheet 21.2 determine the unit cost for the type of energy used for cooling. Enter the value in sections #1 and #2 of the worksheet.

Step 5.   Multiply the annual heating energy use by the heating energy unit cost, and the annual cooling energy use by the cooling energy unit cost. Add the two values to determine the annual component cost for the existing building construction. Enter the value in section #1 of the worksheet.

Step 6.   For the modified building envelope, determine the annual heating energy use for that building envelope component. Enter the value in section #2.

Step 7.   For the modified building envelope, determine the annual cooling energy use for that building envelope component. Enter the value in section #2.

Step 8.   Multiply the annual heating energy use by the heating energy unit cost, and the annual cooling energy use by the cooling energy unit cost. Add the two values to determine the annual component cost for the modified building construction. Enter the value in section #2 of the worksheet.

Step 9.   Enter the annual cost for the existing construction from section #1 into section #3 of the worksheet.

Step 10.   Enter the annual cost for the modified construction from section #2 into section #3 of the worksheet.

Step 11.   Subtract the modified construction annual cost from the existing construction annual cost to determine the annual cost savings. Enter the value in section #3 of the worksheet.

The estimate of annual savings is an estimate only. It should be used only as a first approximation of the savings that would result from implementation of that particular energy conservation measure. Its primary benefit is to help identify potential energy conservation measures for further study through a more detailed analysis.

HOW TO DETERMINE U-VALUES

The rate at which heat is conducted into or out of a facility is determined by the thermal conductance, or U-value, of the walls, ceiling, and floor. It is the inverse of the thermal resistance of that building component. The higher the thermal resistance, the lower the U-value. For example, a particular wall construction with a thermal resistance of 5.0 would have a U-value of 0.2.

The U-value is measured in Btu per hour per square foot per degree Fahrenheit temperature difference between the interior and exterior surfaces. The value for a particular wall, ceiling, or floor depends on the materials from which it was constructed. Each component, such as exterior siding or face brick, has a particular conductivity. The overall wall, ceiling, or floor conductivity is the combined effect of each component and can be calculated accurately knowing the properties of the individual components.

The simplest method to calculate the U-value for a particular type of construction is to work with the components' thermal resistances. Figure 21.1 lists the thermal resistances for common wall materials, and Figure 21.2 lists thermal resistances for ceiling, and floor materials. The total thermal resistance for a given wall, ceiling, or floor is determined by summing those for the individual components. The overall U-value is then calculated by inverting the value for the calculated thermal resistance.

Use Worksheet 21.4 to determine the U-value for walls, floors, and ceilings. Use the figure as follows:

Step 1.   The air film R-value takes into account the inside and outside air film resistance. Use the following air film R-values:

Walls:	1.02
Floors:	0.90
Ceilings:	0.90

Step 2.   For the type of construction, use Figures 21.1 and 21.2 to determine the R-values of the materials used to construct the walls. Enter the values in section #1 of the worksheet.

Step 3.   Sum the individual R-values to determine the overall R-value. Enter the value in both sections of the worksheet.

Step 4.   Determine the U-value of the wall, ceiling, or floor by inverting the value for the overall R-value. Enter the value in section #2 of the worksheet.

The building component U-value will be used in a number of the procedures presented later in this chapter for estimating energy losses and savings.

DETERMINING ABOVE-GROUND WALL HEAT LOSS

The quantity of heating energy lost through above-ground walls depends on the room temperature, the climate, the wall orientation, the wall U-value, and the quantity of the sun's energy that is absorbed by the wall.

Use Figures 21.3 and 21.4 to estimate the annual heat loss for above-ground walls. Figure 21.3 is for facilities located between 25 and 35 degrees north latitude. Figure 21.4 is for facilities located between 35 and 45 degrees north latitude. The figures have been adapted from ones originally developed by the consulting firm Dubin, Mindell, Bloome and Associates as part of a contract with the Federal Energy Administration that developed the publication *Manual of Energy Saving in Existing Buildings and Plants.* Calculate the heat loss as follows:

Step 1.   From Figure 20.1, determine the annual number of heating degree days for the facility's location.

Step 2.   From Figure 20.10, determine the annual average daily solar radiation.

Step 3.   From Worksheet 21.4, determine the wall U-value.

Step 4.   Using Figure 21.3 or 21.4 based on the location of the facility, enter the figure at the number of annual heating degree days.

Step 5.   Move horizontally to the right to the intersection of the diagonal line for the annual average daily solar radiation.

Step 6.   From the intersection point, move vertically to the intersection point with the diagonal wall orientation line.

Step 7.   From that intersection point, move horizontally to the left to the intersection point with the diagonal wall U-value line.

Step 8.   From the intersection point, drop vertically to the axis. Read the annual heat loss rate in thousands of Btu per square foot.

Step 9.   Enter the annual heat loss rate at the bottom of the figure.

Step 10.   Enter the above-ground wall area in square feet at the bottom of the figure.

Step 11.   Multiply the heat loss rate by the area and the conversion factor of 0.001 to determine the annual heat loss through the walls.

This value represents the estimated annual heating energy loss through the above-ground walls.

DETERMINING ABOVE-GROUND WALL SUMMER HEAT GAIN

While heat is lost to the outside through above-ground walls during the heating season, heat is gained through those walls during the air conditioning season. The quantity of heat gained is determined mostly by the room temperature, the climate, the wall orientation, the wall U-value, and how much of the sun's energy is absorbed by the wall.

Use Figures 21.5 and 21.6 to estimate the annual heat gain for above-ground walls. Figure 21.5 is for facilities located between 25 and 35 degrees north latitude. Figure 21.6 is for facilities located between 35 and 45 degrees north latitude. The figures have been adapted from ones originally developed by the firm Dubin, Mindell, Bloome and Associates as part of a contract with the Federal Energy Administration that developed the publication *Manual of Energy Saving in Existing Buildings and Plants*. Calculate the heat gain as follows:

Step 1.   From Figure 20.9, determine the annual number of degree hours above 78°F for the facility's location.

Step 2.   From Figure 20.10, determine the annual average daily solar radiation.

Step 3.   From Worksheet 21.4, determine the wall U-value.

Step 4.   Using Figure 21.5 or 21.6 based on the location of the facility, enter the figure at the annual number of degree hours greater than 78°F.

Step 5.   Move horizontally to the right to the intersection of the diagonal line for the annual average daily solar radiation.

Step 6.   From the intersection point, move vertically to the intersection point with the diagonal wall orientation line.

Step 7.   From that intersection point, move horizontally to the left to the intersection point with the diagonal wall U-value line.

Step 8.   From the intersection point, drop vertically to the axis. Read the annual heat gain rate in thousands of Btu per square foot.

Step 9.   Enter the annual heat gain rate at the bottom of the figure.

Step 10.   Enter the above-ground wall area in square feet at the bottom of the figure.

Step 11.   Multiply the heat gain rate by the area and the conversion factor of 0.001 to determine the annual heat gain through the wall.

This value represents the estimated annual cooling load imposed on the air conditioning system through above-ground walls.

DETERMINING BELOW-GROUND WALL AND FLOOR HEAT LOSS

The quantity of heating energy lost through below-ground walls and floors depends on three factors: the inside temperature, the ground temperature, and the U-value of the floor or wall.

Use Worksheet 21.5 to estimate the annual heat loss for below-ground walls and floors. The figure estimates the annual average ground temperature based on its correlation with the annual number of heating degree days. If the actual average ground temperature is available, use that value instead of the value calculated by the worksheet. Calculate the heat loss as follows:

Step 1.   From Figure 20.1, determine the annual number of heating degree days for the facility's location. Enter the value in sections #1 and #2 of the worksheet.

Step 2.   Multiply the annual number of heating degree days by the factor 0.0038. Subtract this value from 75, and enter the estimated average ground temperature in section #1.

Step 3.   Multiply the annual number of heating degree days by the factor 0.16. Add 500 to this value and enter the coefficient in section #2.

Step 4.   Enter the coefficient calculated in section #2 into section #3.

Step 5.   Determine the wall or floor U-value using Worksheet 21.4. Enter the value in section #3.

Step 6.   Enter the average inside temperature for the facility during the heating season in section #3.

Step 7.   Subtract the ground temperature from the inside temperature, and multiply the result by the wall or floor U-value and the coefficient. Enter the value as the heat loss rate. If the calculated value is less than one, enter zero for both the heat loss rate in section #3 and for the annual heat loss in section #4.

Step 8.   Enter the heat loss rate from section #3 into section #4. Multiply this value by the wall or floor square footage and the conversion factor of 0.000001 to determine the annual heat loss for the below-ground wall or floor. Enter the value in section #4.

This value represents the estimated annual heating energy loss through floors and below-ground walls.

DETERMINING THE WINDOW COMPONENT

Windows represent a significant energy load on a facility throughout the year. During the heating season, conduction and infiltration losses increase the quantity of heating energy that must be supplied to the conditioned space. Part of the winter losses are offset, particularly in more southern climates, by the heating effect of the sun. During the cooling season, conduction, infiltration, and the heating effect of the sun all contribute to the cooling load.

Shading Coefficient

Standard, clear window glass transmits approximately 80 percent of the sunlight that strikes its surface. Different types of window glass, multiple layers of glass, and shading devices designed to limit the amount of sunshine reaching the glass all cause the glass to transmit differing percentages of sunlight.

The quantity of sunlight that a particular window glazing or shading device passes relative to a standard piece of clear glass is measured by its shading coefficient. Shading device values range from 1.0 for standard window glass to as low as 0.25 for externally mounted window louvers. Figure 21.7 lists shading coefficients for commonly used glazing materials and shading devices. The shading coefficient will be used in a number of the estimation procedures presented in this chapter.

Estimating Window Conduction Loss

There are two types of heat loss from windows: conduction and infiltration. While conduction losses take place through both the window glazing and the window frame, for estimation purposes calculation procedures typically consider only the conduction losses through the glazing. They further assume that the glazing area is equal to the total window opening.

Conduction heat losses are determined by the window U-Value, the climate, and the orientation of the window. They are largest for north-facing windows, and least for south-facing ones due to the offsetting effect of the sun. Figure 21.8 lists R-Values and U-Values for common window types.

Use Figure 21.9 or 21.10 to estimate the annual conduction heat loss for windows. Figure 21.9 is for facilities located between latitudes 25 and 35 degrees north latitude. Figure 21.10 is for facilities located between 35 and 45 degrees north latitude. The figures have been adapted from ones originally developed by the firm Dubin, Mindell, Bloome and Associates as part of a contract with the Federal Energy Administration that developed the publication *Manual of Energy Saving in Existing Buildings and Plants.* Calculate the conduction heat loss as follows:

Step 1.	From Figure 20.1, determine the annual number of heating degree days for the facility's location.
Step 2.	From Figure 20.10, determine the annual average daily solar radiation. If shading devices are used, or if the glazing material is not $1/8''$ clear glass, the annual average daily solar radiation must be modified. From Worksheet 21.7 determine the shading coefficient. Multiply the shading coefficient by the value from Figure 20.10 to determine the corrected average daily solar radiation value. Use this value in Figures 21.9 and 21.10.
Step 3.	Using Figure 21.9 or 21.10 based on the location of the facility, enter the figure at the annual number of heating degree days.
Step 4.	Move horizontally to the right to the intersection of the diagonal line for the annual average daily solar radiation.
Step 5.	From the intersection point, move vertically to the intersection point with the line that represents the type of window and its orientation.
Step 6.	From that intersection point, move horizontally to the left axis. Read the annual heat loss rate in thousands of Btu per square foot of window.
Step 7.	Enter the annual heat loss rate at the bottom of the figure.
Step 8.	Enter the window area for that orientation in square feet at the bottom of the figure.
Step 9.	Multiply the heat loss rate by the area and the conversion factor of 0.001 to determine the annual heat loss through the windows.

The annual heat loss calculated by using the figure represents the conduction heat loss through a facility's windows for a particular orientation. To estimate the conduction heat loss for all windows in a facility, the procedure will have to be repeated for each wall orientation that has windows.

Estimating Window Infiltration Loss

Infiltration losses are the result of air leaking between different sections of the window. They are determined by the fit of the window, the wind speed, and the climate. Estimating losses due to infiltration through windows is a two-step process that first determines the rate at which air is infiltrating. Based on this value, the heating energy requirement to offset the cold air introduced into the facility is then calculated.

Use Worksheet 21.6 to estimate the air infiltration rate for windows. The worksheet estimates infiltration rates based on their correlation with wind speed. Calculate the infiltration rate as follows:

Step 1.   Using section #1 of the worksheet, determine the fit factor for the window. A window is considered loose fitting if it is not weather-stripped or if the sash can be moved even slightly when the window is fully closed. Enter the window fit factor in section #2 of the worksheet.

Step 2.   From Figure 20.5 determine the average wind speed for the facility. Enter the value in section #2 of the worksheet.

Step 3.   Multiply the average wind speed by the factor 0.0263. Subtract 0.083. Multiply the remainder by the window fit factor to determine the infiltration rate for the windows. Enter the value in sections #2 and #3 of the worksheet.

Step 4.   The crack length for a window is the total length of openings that exist between movable and fixed portions of the window. For casement and hinged windows, the crack length is the perimeter of the window opening. For double-hung windows, it is the perimeter of the opening plus the opening width. Enter the crack length in feet per window in section #3.

Step 5.   Enter the number of windows in the facility in section #3 of the worksheet.

Step 6.   Multiply the infiltration rate by the crack length, the number of windows, and the conversion factor of 0.001 to determine the infiltration rate for the windows in thousands of cubic feet per minute. Enter the value in section #3.

This value represents the total rate of air infiltration into the facility through the windows.

The building heating system must use energy to heat this air to room temperatures. Use Worksheet 21.7 to estimate the annual heating energy requirements for window infiltration. The worksheet estimates heating energy use based on the correlation between energy use and the number of heating degree days. Calculate the annual heating energy use as follows:

Step 1.   From Figure 20.1 determine the annual heating degree days for the facility. Enter the value in section #1 of the worksheet.

Step 2.   Multiply the annual number of heating degree days by the factor 0.026. Add the value of 3.06 to the product to determine the heating energy use rate. Enter the value in sections #1 and #2 of the worksheet.

Step 3.   From Worksheet 21.6 determine the infiltration rate. Enter the value in section #2 of the worksheet.

Step 4.   Multiply the heating energy use rate by the infiltration rate to determine the annual heat use. Enter the value in section #2 of the worksheet.

This value represents the annual heating energy requirement for the facility's windows due to infiltration. The total heating energy requirements for the windows is the sum of the infiltration and conduction requirements. To determine the annual heating energy and cost savings that would result from upgrading the windows, repeat the calculations for the new windows and enter the calculated energy savings in Worksheets 21.1 and 21.3.

Summer Window Heat Gain

There are three types of summer heat gain through windows: solar, conduction, and infiltration. While all three components are significant, determining the infiltration heat gain is a difficult procedure due to the moisture component of the air that is infiltrating into the facility. The facility air conditioning system must use energy to dehumidify this air. Estimating this energy requirement is best handled by hourly computer calculations using weather data for your location. For that reason, the estimation procedures discussed here for window heat gain will address only solar and conduction heat gains.

WINDOW SOLAR HEAT GAIN. Solar heat gain is determined by a number of factors including the climate, the amount of sunshine the window is exposed to, the window's orientation, and the type of glass used in the window. Solar heat gains are smallest for north-facing, dual-glazed windows, and are largest for east- and west-facing windows.

Use Figure 21.11 or 21.12 to estimate the annual solar heat gain for windows. Figure 21.11 is for facilities located between latitudes 25 and 35 degrees north. Figure 21.12 is for facilities located between 35 and 45 degrees north latitude. The figures have been adapted from ones originally developed by the firm Dubin, Mindell, Bloome and Associates as part of a contract with the Federal Energy Administration that developed the publication *Manual of Energy Saving in Existing Buildings and Plants*. Calculate the solar heat gain as follows:

Step 1.   From Figure 20.1, determine the annual number of degree hours above 78°F for the facility's location.

Step 2.   From Figure 20.10, determine the annual average daily solar radiation. If shading devices are used, or if the glazing material is not $^1/_8$" clear glass, the annual average daily solar radiation must be modified. From Worksheet 21.7 determine the shading coefficient. Multiply the shading coefficient by the value from Figure 20.10 to determine the corrected average daily solar radiation value.

Step 3.   Using Figure 21.11 or 21.12 based on the location of the facility, enter the figure at the annual number of degree hours above 78°F.

Step 4.   Move horizontally to the right to the intersection of the diagonal line for the annual average daily solar radiation.

Step 5.   From the intersection point, move vertically to the intersection point with the line that represents the type of window and its orientation.

Step 6.   From that intersection point, move horizontally to the left axis. Read the annual solar heat gain rate in thousands of Btu per square foot of window.

Step 7.   Enter the annual solar heat gain rate at the bottom of the figure.

Step 8.   Enter the window area for that orientation in square feet at the bottom of the figure.

Step 9.   Multiply the solar heat gain rate by the area and the conversion factor of 0.001 to determine the annual solar heat gain through the windows.

This value represents the annual heat gain during the cooling season that takes place through windows as a result of the sun.

ESTIMATING WINDOW CONDUCTION HEAT GAIN. Window conduction heat gain is determined by the window U-value, the climate, and the orientation of the window. Unlike solar heat gain, conduction heat gain is independent of the window orientation.

Use Worksheet 21.8 to estimate the conduction heat gain through windows. The worksheet estimates conduction heat gain based on its correlation with the number of degree hours greater than 78°F. Calculate the conduction heat gain as follows:

Step 1.   Determine the window U-value from Figure 21.8. Enter the value in section #1 of the figure.

Step 2.   From Figure 20.1, determine the annual number of degree hours above 78°F for the facility's location. Enter the value in section #1 of the figure.

Step 3.   Multiply the window U-value by the degree hours and the multiplication factor of 0.0014. Add 0.678 to this value to determine the heat gain rate. Enter the value in section #1 of the worksheet.

Step 4.   Enter the heat gain rate in section #2 of the worksheet.

Step 5.   Enter the total square footage of all windows in the facility in section #2 of the worksheet.

Step 6.   Multiply the heat gain rate by the window area and the conversion factor of 0.001 to determine the annual heat gain by conduction through the windows. Enter the value in section #2 of the worksheet.

This value represents the annual conduction heat gain through the windows. It is independent of window orientation.

THE ROOF HEATING AND COOLING LOAD COMPONENT

The roof represents a large building envelope energy load throughout the year. During the heating season, conduction losses account for the majority of the roof-related heat losses. Part of these heating season losses are offset, particularly in more southern climates, by the heating effect of the sun. During the cooling season, conduction and the heating effect of the sun contribute to the cooling load.

Estimating Roof Heat Loss

Heating energy is lost through a roof primarily through conduction. The amount of heat lost depends on the inside temperature, the climate, the roof U-value, and the color of the roof. Roof color is a factor because it determines how much of the sun's energy is absorbed by the roof, thus offsetting some of the conduction losses.

The roof U-value is determined following the same procedures used to determine wall U-values. Figure 21.2 lists thermal resistances for roof and ceiling materials. The total thermal resistance for a roof can be determined by simply summing the individual component thermal resistances. The overall U-value can then be found by inverting the value for the calculated thermal resistance. Enter the thermal resistance values for your roof components in Worksheet 21.4 to determine the overall roof U-value.

Use Figure 21.13 or 21.14 to estimate the annual heat loss for roofs. Figure 21.13 is for facilities with dark color roofs. Figure 21.14 is for facilities with light color roofs. The figures have been adapted from ones originally developed by the firm Dubin, Mindell, Bloome and Associates as part of a contract with the Federal Energy Administration that developed the publication *Manual of Energy Saving in Existing Buildings and Plants*. Calculate the heat loss as follows:

Step 1. From Figure 20.1, determine the annual number of heating degree days for the facility's location.

Step 2. From Figure 20.10, determine the annual average daily solar radiation.

Step 3. From Worksheet 21.4, determine the roof U-value.

Step 4. Using Figure 21.13 or 21.14 based on the color of the roof, enter the figure at the number of annual heating degree days.

Step 5. Move horizontally to the right to the intersection of the diagonal line for the annual average daily solar radiation.

Step 6. From the intersection point, move vertically to the intersection point with the diagonal roof U-value line for that roof.

Step 7. From that intersection point, move horizontally to the left to the axis. Read the annual heat loss rate in thousands of Btu per square foot.

Step 8.   Enter the annual heat loss rate at the bottom of the figure.

Step 9.   Enter the roof area in square feet at the bottom of the figure.

Step 10.   Multiply the heat loss rate by the area and the conversion factor of 0.001 to determine the annual heat loss through the roof.

This value represents the estimated annual heating energy loss through the roof. It takes into consideration any solar heat gain through the roof that helps to offset the roofing heat losses.

Roof Solar Heat Gain

During the air conditioning season, the roof contributes a significant load to the building air conditioning system. The quantity of heat gained from the sun is determined mostly by the inside temperature, the climate, the roof U-value, and the color of the roof.

Use Figures 21.15 and 21.16 to estimate the annual solar heat gain for roofs. Figure 21.15 is for facilities with dark color roofs. Figure 21.16 is for facilities with light color roofs. The figures have been adapted from ones originally developed by the firm Dubin, Mindell, Bloome and Associates as part of a contract with the Federal Energy Administration that developed the publication *Manual of Energy Saving in Existing Buildings and Plants*. Calculate the solar heat gain as follows:

Step 1.   From Figure 20.9, determine the annual number of degree hours above 78°F for the facility's location.

Step 2.   From Figure 20.10, determine the annual average daily solar radiation.

Step 3.   From Worksheet 21.4, determine the roof U-value.

Step 4.   Using Figure 21.15 or 21.16 based on the color of the roof, enter the figure at the number of annual degree hours above 78°F.

Step 5.   Move horizontally to the right to the intersection of the diagonal line for the annual average daily solar radiation.

Step 6.   From the intersection point, move vertically to the intersection point with the diagonal roof U-value line for that roof.

Step 7.   From that intersection point, move horizontally to the left to the axis. Read the annual solar heat gain rate in thousands of Btu per square foot.

Step 8.   Enter the annual solar heat gain rate at the bottom of the figure.

Step 9.   Enter the roof area in square feet at the bottom of the figure.

Step 10.   Multiply the heat gain rate by the area and the conversion factor of 0.001 to determine the annual solar heat gain through the roof.

This value represents the estimated annual solar energy gain through the roof.

Estimating Roof Conduction Heat Gain

During the air conditioning season, heat is conducted through the roof to the conditioned space. The quantity of heat gained is mostly determined by the inside temperature, the climate, and the roof U-value. Unlike solar heat gain, conduction heat gain is independent of the color of the roof.

Use Worksheet 21.9 to estimate the conduction heat gain through roofs. Calculate as follows:

Step 1.   Determine the roof U-value from Worksheet 21.4. Enter the value in section #1 of the worksheet.

Step 2.   From Figure 20.1, determine the annual number of degree hours above 78°F for the facility's location. Enter the value in section #1 of the figure.

Step 3.   Multiply the roof U-value by the degree hours and the multiplication factor of 0.0015. Subtract 0.015 from this value to determine the heat gain rate. Enter the value in section #1 of the worksheet.

Step 4.   Enter the heat gain rate in section #2 of the worksheet.

Step 5.   Enter the total square footage of the roof in section #2 of the worksheet.

Step 6.   Multiply the heat gain rate by the roof area and the conversion factor of 0.001 to determine the annual heat gain by conduction through the roof. Enter the value in section #2 of the worksheet.

This value represents the annual conduction heat gain through the roof that must be eliminated by the facility's air conditioning system. It does not include the solar load component.

FIGURE 21.1 Wall Material R-Values

Wall Component	Material	R-Value
Exterior Surface	Aluminum Siding	0.00
	Clay Tile, 4"	1.10
	Concrete Block, 8"	1.72
	Concrete Block, 12"	1.89
	Face Brick, 4"	0.44
	Stucco, 1"	0.21
	Wood Shingles	0.87
	Wood Siding	0.90
Sheathing	Plywood. 1/2"	0.63
	Plywood. 3/4"	0.94
	Rigid Insulation Board, 1/2"	1.72
	Rigid Insulation Board, 1"	3.45
	Rigid Insulation Board, 2"	6.90
	Wood Fiberboard, 1/2"	1.19
Insulation	Air Space	0.90
	Glass Fiber, 3 1/2"	11.00
	Glass Fiber, 5 1/2"	19.00
Interior Finish	Plaster, 3/4"	0.40
	Wallboard, 1/2"	0.10
	Wallboard, 3/4"	0.15

FIGURE 21.2 Floor and Ceiling Material R-Values

Component	Material	R-Value
Flooring	Carpet & Padding	2.00
	Ceramic Tile	0.10
	Concrete, 4"	3.33
	Concrete, 6"	5.00
	Concrete, 8"	6.66
	Hardwood Flooring	0.68
	Plywood, 5/8"	0.78
	Plywood, 3/4"	0.94
	Tile	0.04
	Wood Subflooring	1.00
Ceiling	Acoustic Tile	1.80
	Air Space	1.00
	Asphalt Shingles	0.21
	Built-up Roofing	0.33
	Glass Fiber, 6"	19.0
	Glass Fiber, 10"	30.0
	Glass Fiber, 12"	38.0
	Lightweight Concrete, 3"	3.60
	Lightweight Concrete, 4"	4.80
	Plywood, 1/2"	0.63
	Plywood, 3/4"	0.94
	Preformed Deck Insulation, 1"	2.78
	Preformed Deck Insulation, 2"	5.56
	Preformed Deck Insulation, 3"	8.34
	Roll Roofing	0.15
	Slate	0.05
	Wallboard, 1/2"	0.10
	Wallboard, 3/4"	0.15
	Wood Shingles	0.95

FIGURE 21.3 Annual Heat Loss - Above-Ground Walls
25° N to 35° N Latitude

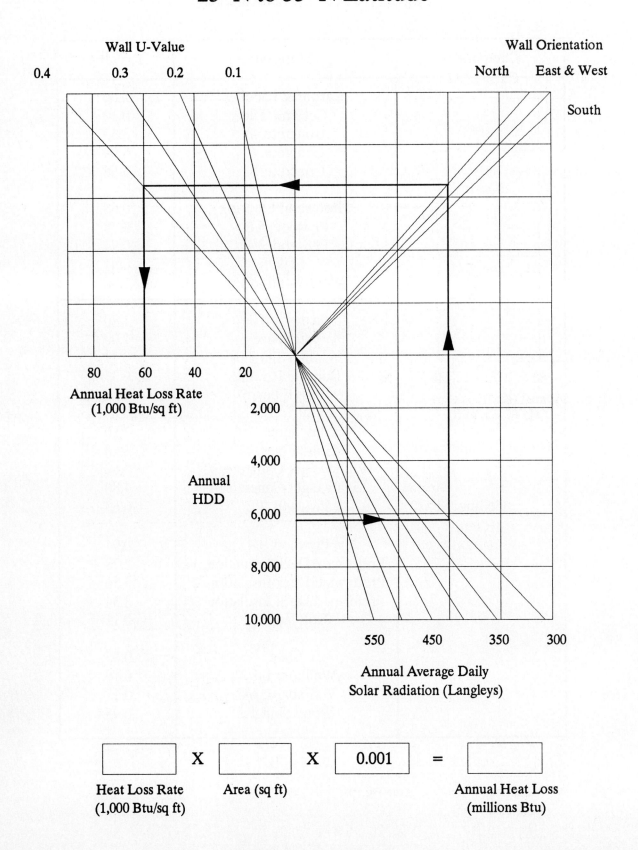

FIGURE 21.4 Annual Heat Loss - Above-Ground Walls
35° N to 45° N Latitude

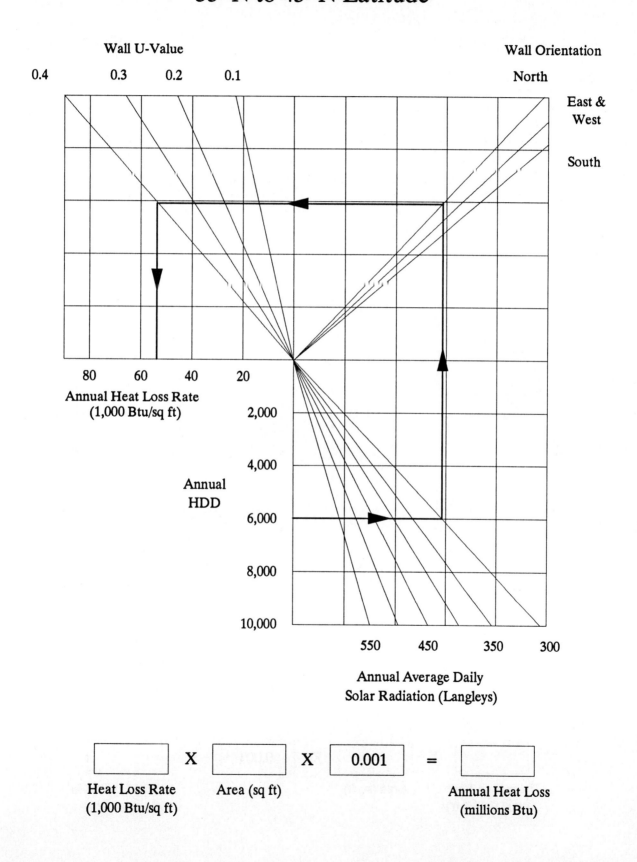

FIGURE 21.5 Annual Heat Gain - Above-Ground Walls
25° N to 35° N Latitude

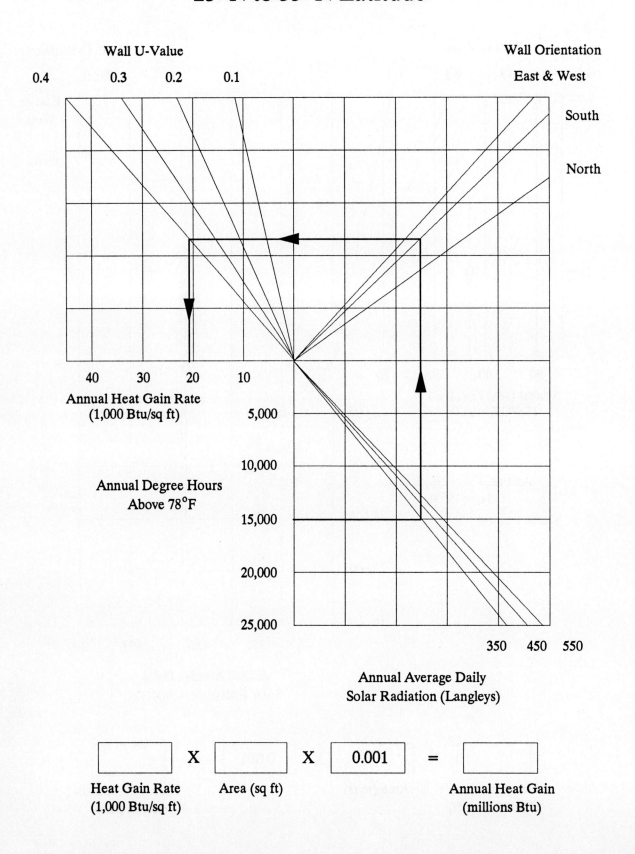

FIGURE 21.6 Annual Heat Gain - Above-Ground Walls
35°N to 45°N Latitude

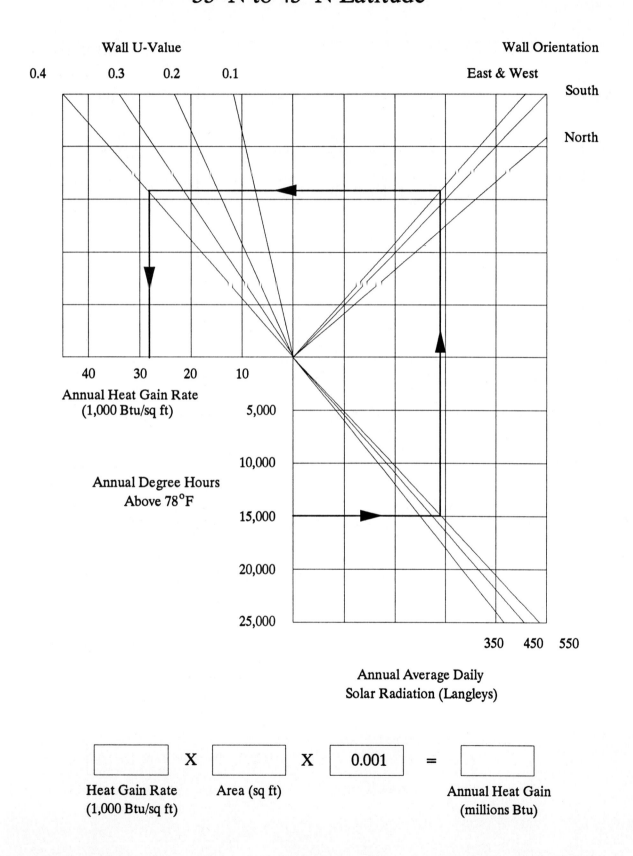

FIGURE 21.7 Shading Coefficients for Window Materials

Material	Description	Shading Coefficient
Glass	1/8" Clear, Single Layer 1/8" Clear, Double Layer 1/4" Clear, Single Layer 1/4" Clear, Double Layer 3/8" Clear, Single Layer 1/8" Heat Absorbing 1/4" Heat Absorbing 1/4" Reflective	1.00 0.88 0.94 0.80 0.90 0.84 0.68 0.30
External Devices	Louvers Screens	0.25 0.50
Internal Devices	Venetian Blinds, Light Color Roller Shades, Light Color Drapes, Light Color	0.55 0.39 .055

FIGURE 21.8 Window R-Values and U-Values

Type	R-Value	U-Value
Single Glazed	0.88	1.13
Dual Glazed, 1/4" air gap	1.64	0.61
Dual Glazed, 1/2" air gap	1.82	0.55
Dual Glazed, Evacuated	4.00	0.25
Dual Glazed, Low-E	2.94	0.41
Triple Glazed	3.00	0.33

FIGURE 21.9 Annual Heat Loss - Windows
25°N - 35°N Latitude

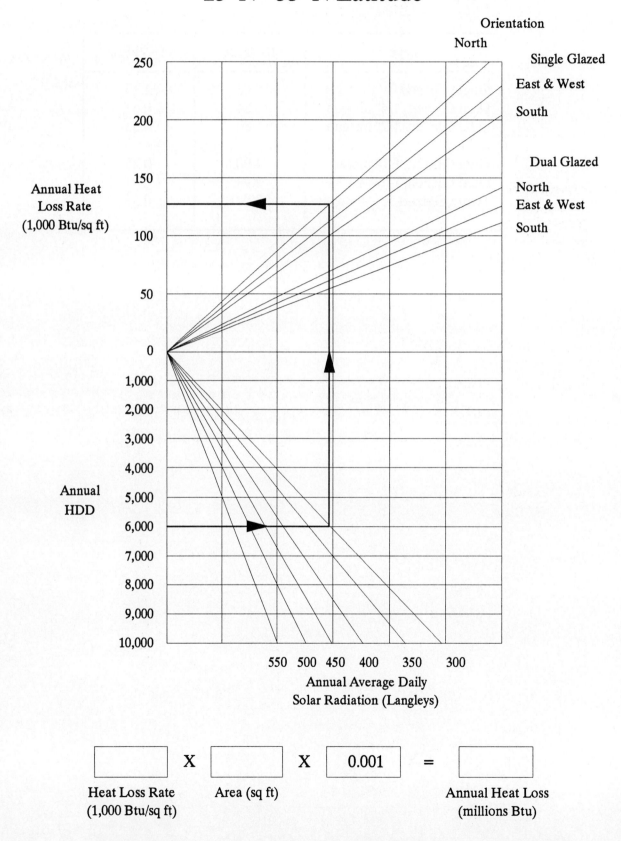

FIGURE 21.10 Annual Heat Loss - Windows
35°N - 45°N Latitude

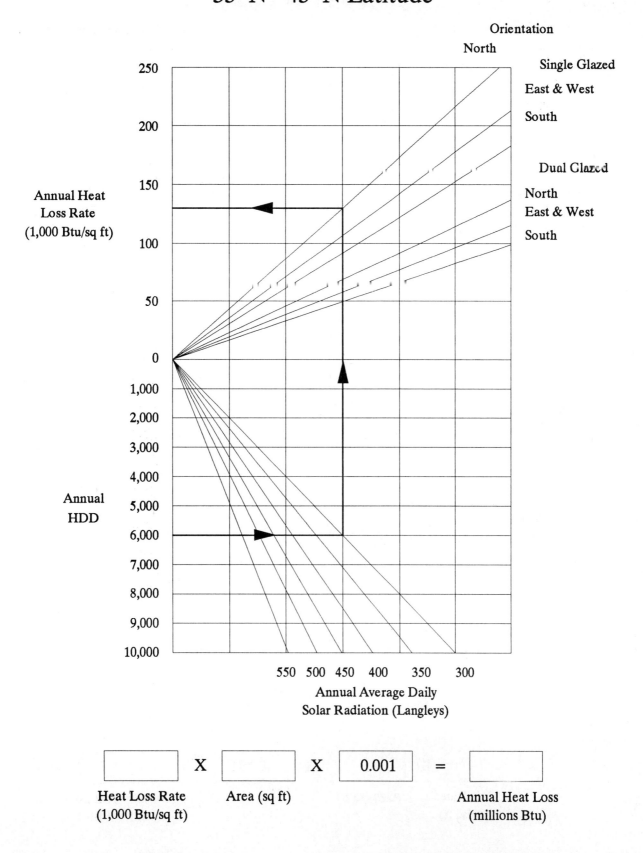

Orientation
North
Single Glazed
East & West
South

Dual Glazed
North
East & West
South

Annual Heat
Loss Rate
(1,000 Btu/sq ft)

Annual
HDD

Annual Average Daily
Solar Radiation (Langleys)

| Heat Loss Rate (1,000 Btu/sq ft) | X | Area (sq ft) | X | 0.001 | = | Annual Heat Loss (millions Btu) |

FIGURE 21.11 Annual Solar Heat Gain - Windows
25°N - 35°N Latitude

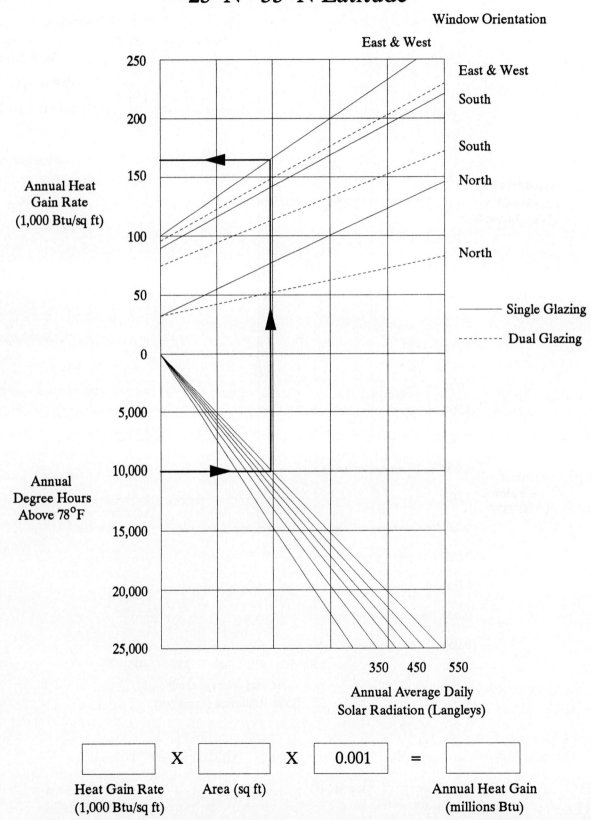

FIGURE 21.12 Annual Solar Heat Gain - Windows 35°N - 45°N Latitude

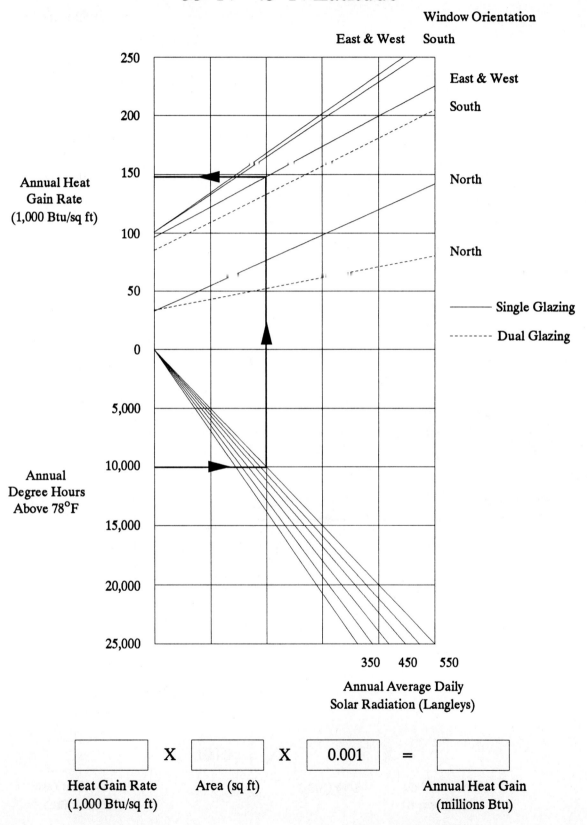

	X		X	0.001	=	
Heat Gain Rate (1,000 Btu/sq ft)		Area (sq ft)				Annual Heat Gain (millions Btu)

FIGURE 21.13 Annual Heat Loss - Roofs
Dark Color Roofs

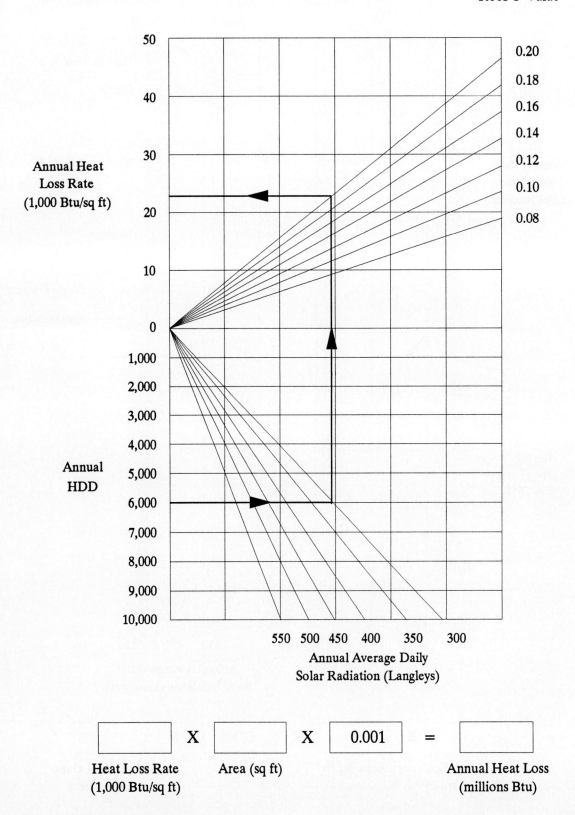

Roof U-Value

Annual Heat Loss Rate (1,000 Btu/sq ft)

Annual HDD

Annual Average Daily
Solar Radiation (Langleys)

	X		X	0.001	=	
Heat Loss Rate (1,000 Btu/sq ft)		Area (sq ft)				Annual Heat Loss (millions Btu)

FIGURE 21.14 Annual Heat Loss - Roofs
Light Color Roofs

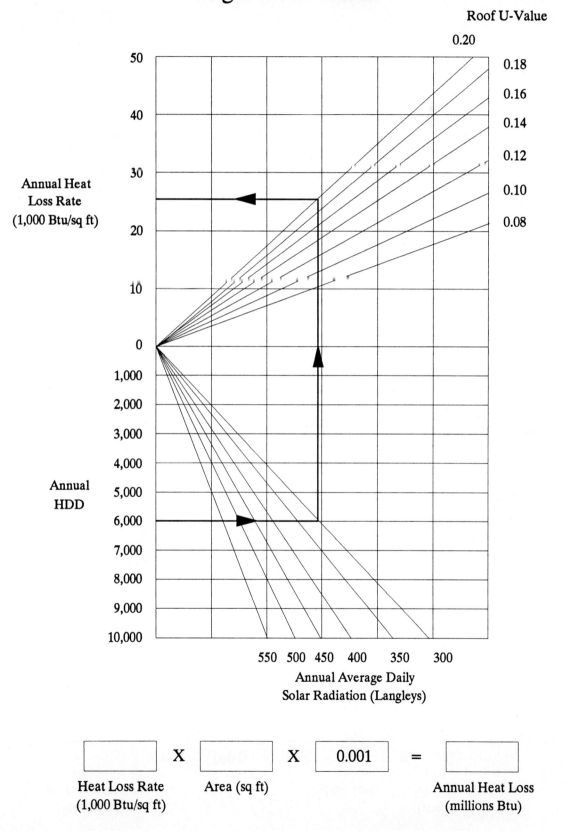

Roof U-Value

0.20

0.18

0.16

0.14

0.12

0.10

0.08

Annual Heat
Loss Rate
(1,000 Btu/sq ft)

Annual
HDD

Annual Average Daily
Solar Radiation (Langleys)

	X		X	0.001	=	
Heat Loss Rate (1,000 Btu/sq ft)		Area (sq ft)				Annual Heat Loss (millions Btu)

FIGURE 21.15 Annual Solar Heat Gain - Roofs
Dark Color Roofs

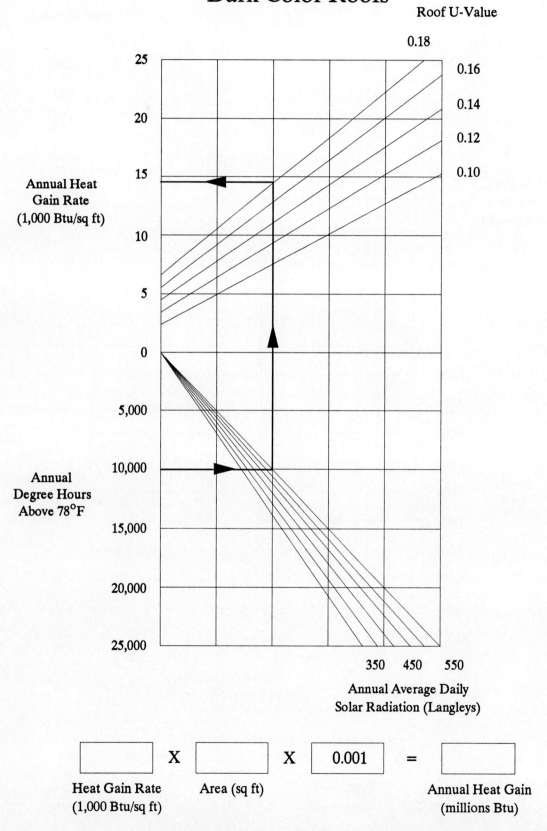

FIGURE 21.16 Annual Solar Heat Gain - Roofs
Light Color Roofs

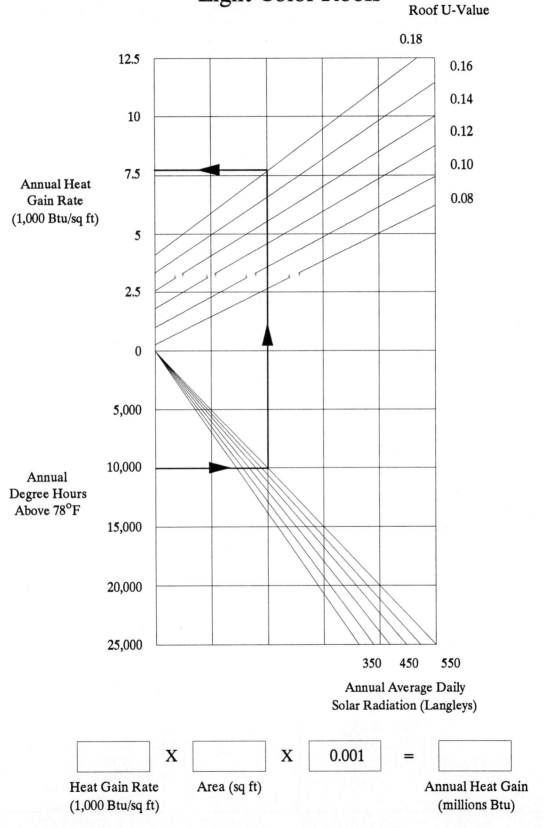

Roof U-Value

Annual Heat Gain Rate (1,000 Btu/sq ft)

Annual Degree Hours Above 78°F

Annual Average Daily Solar Radiation (Langleys)

	X		X	0.001	=	
Heat Gain Rate (1,000 Btu/sq ft)		Area (sq ft)				Annual Heat Gain (millions Btu)

WORKSHEET 21.1 Estimating Heating Energy Costs

1. Electricity

$$\boxed{} \times \boxed{293} \times \boxed{} = \boxed{}$$

| Average Rate ($/kWh) | Conversion Factor | Efficiency Factor | Unit Cost ($/million Btu) |

2. Natural Gas

$$\boxed{} \times \boxed{10} \times \boxed{} = \boxed{}$$

| Average Rate ($/therm) | Conversion Factor | Efficiency Factor | Unit Cost ($/million Btu) |

3. Oil

$$\boxed{} \times \boxed{} \times \boxed{} = \boxed{}$$

| Average Rate ($/gal) | Conversion Factor | Efficiency Factor | Unit Cost ($/million Btu) |

Efficiency Factors

Electric Baseboard:	1.00
Electric, Central:	0.90
Natural Gas:	0.85
# 2 Oil:	0.82
# 5 and # 6 Oil:	0.80

Oil Conversion Factors (gal/million Btu)

# 1 Oil:	7.35
# 2 Oil:	7.22
# 3 Oil:	7.09
# 4 Oil:	6.90
# 5 Oil:	6.73
# 6 Oil:	6.58

WORKSHEET 21.2 Estimating Cooling Energy Costs

1. Electricity

☐	X	293	X	☐	=	☐
Average Rate ($/kWh)		Conversion Factor		Efficiency Factor		Unit Cost ($/million Btu)

2. Natural Gas

☐	X	10	X	☐	=	☐
Average Rate ($/therm)		Conversion Factor		Efficiency Factor		Unit Cost ($/million Btu)

Efficiency Factors

Centrifugal Chiller:	0.11
Gas Absorption:	0.59
Heat Pump:	0.17
Split System:	0.17
Window Unit:	0.20

WORKSHEET 21.3 Estimating Energy Cost Savings

Building Modification: _____

1. Existing Construction

[☐] × [☐] + [☐] × [☐] = ☐

Annual Heating Energy Use (million Btu)   Heating Energy Unit Cost ($/million Btu)   Annual Cooling Energy Use (million Btu)   Cooling Energy Unit Cost ($/million Btu)   Annual Cost ($)

2. Modified Construction

[☐] × [☐] + [☐] × [☐] = ☐

Annual Heating Energy Use (million Btu)   Heating Energy Unit Cost ($/million Btu)   Annual Cooling Energy Use (million Btu)   Cooling Energy Unit Cost ($/million Btu)   Annual Cost ($)

3. Cost Savings

☐ − ☐ = ☐

Existing Annual Cost ($)   Modified Annual Cost ($)   Annual Cost Savings ($)

WORKSHEET 21.4 Determining U-Values

1.

Overall R-Value

▭	+	▭	+	▭	+	▭
Air Film R-Value		Material # 1 R-Value		Material # 2 R-Value		Material # 3 R-Value

+ ▭ = ▭

Material # 4 R-Value   Overall R-Value

2.

U-Value

$$\frac{1}{\boxed{}} = \boxed{}$$

Overall R-Value   U-Value

WORKSHEET 21.5 Annual Heat Loss - Below-Ground Walls and Floors

1. Estimate Average Ground Temperature

$$\boxed{75} \ - \ \left[\boxed{0.0038} \ \text{X} \ \boxed{}\right] \ = \ \boxed{}$$

Annual Heating Degree Days   Average Ground Temp. (^{o}F)

2. Coefficient

$$\boxed{0.16} \ \text{X} \ \boxed{} \ + \ \boxed{500} \ = \ \boxed{}$$

Annual Heating Degree Days   Coefficient

3. Heat Loss Rate

$$\boxed{} \ \text{X} \ \boxed{} \ \text{X} \ \left[\boxed{} \ - \ \boxed{}\right] \ = \ \boxed{}$$

Coefficient   Wall U-Value   Inside Temp. (^{o}F)   Ground Temp. (^{o}F)   Heat Loss Rate (Btu/sq ft)

4. Annual Heat Loss

$$\boxed{} \ \text{X} \ \boxed{} \ \text{X} \ \boxed{0.000001} \ = \ \boxed{}$$

Heat Loss Rate (Btu/sq ft)   Area (sq ft)   Annual Heat Loss (millions Btu)

WORKSHEET 21.6 Estimating Window Infiltration Rates

1. Window Fit Factor

Window Type	Fit	Factor
Casement	Average	3.6
Double Hung	Average Loose	2 2 2.5
Hinged	Average Loose	1.0 5.4

2. Rate of Infiltration (cfm/ft of crack)

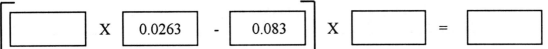

$$\left[\ \boxed{}\ \text{X}\ \boxed{0.0263}\ -\ \boxed{0.083}\ \right]\ \text{X}\ \boxed{}\ =\ \boxed{}$$

Average Wind   Window Fit   Infiltration Rate
Speed (mph)   Factor   (cfm/ft of crack)

3. Total Infiltration Rate (cfm)

$$\boxed{}\ \text{X}\ \boxed{}\ \text{X}\ \boxed{}\ \text{X}\ \boxed{0.001}\ =\ \boxed{}$$

Infiltration Rate Crack Length   Number of   Infiltration Rate
(cfm/ft of crack) (ft/window)   Windows   (1,000 cfm)

WORKSHEET 21.7 Window Infiltration Heat Requirements

1. Window Infiltration Heat Loss Rate

3.06	+	0.026	X		=	

Annual Heating
Degree Days

Heating Energy
Use Rate
(1,000 Btu/cfm)

2. Heating Energy Use

	X		=	

Heating Energy
Use Rate
(1,000 Btu/cfm)

Infiltration Rate
(1,000 cfm)

Annual Heat Use
(million Btu)

WORKSHEET 21.8 Window Conduction Heat Gain

1. Window Heat Loss Rate

$$\boxed{0.678} \; + \; \boxed{0.0014} \;\; X \;\; \boxed{} \;\; X \;\; \boxed{} \;\; = \;\; \boxed{}$$

| | | Window
U-Value | Degree Hrs.
Above 78°F | Heat Gain Rate
(1,000 Btu/sq ft) |

2. Total Window Heat Loss

$$\boxed{} \;\; X \;\; \boxed{} \;\; X \;\; \boxed{0.001} \;\; = \;\; \boxed{}$$

| Heat Gain Rate
(1,000 Btu/sq ft) | Window Area
(sq ft) | | Annual Heat Gain
(million Btu) |

WORKSHEET 21.9 Roof Conduction Heat Gain

1. Roof Heat Gain Rate

0.0015	X		X		-	0.015	=	
		Roof U-Value		Degree Hr Above 78°F				Heat Gain Rate (1,000 Btu/sq ft)

$$0.0015 \times \boxed{} \times \boxed{} - 0.015 = \boxed{}$$

Roof U-Value   Degree Hr Above 78°F   Heat Gain Rate (1,000 Btu/sq ft)

2. Total Roof Heat Gain

$$\boxed{} \times \boxed{} \times 0.001 = \boxed{}$$

Heat Gain Rate (1,000 Btu/sq ft)   Roof Area (sq ft)   Annual Heat Gain (million Btu)

## Chapter 22

MECHANICAL SYSTEM MODIFICATIONS THAT SAVE MONEY AND ENERGY

This chapter presents procedures for estimating energy and cost savings that would result from the implementation of energy conservation measures for mechanical systems. Use the procedures to estimate the order of magnitude of savings. They are sufficiently accurate to determine whether or not additional investigation is warranted. They are not intended to give the exact values needed in order to make funding decisions. If more accurate estimates are required, complete a detailed computer-based analysis, one that makes use of hour-by-hour calculations for an entire year's weather.

The procedures presented in this chapter make use of several of the worksheets from chapter 21, including Worksheet 21.1 for heating energy unit costs, Worksheet 21.2 for cooling energy unit costs, and Worksheet 21.3 for cost savings.

THERMOSTAT SETBACK AND ENERGY USE

Turning down the thermostats in a facility is one of the easiest and most cost-effective energy conservation measures that can be implemented. A quick survey of the thermostat settings in your facility during the heating season will probably show that they range from a low of 68°F to as high as 78° or 80°F. While much has been written about where thermostats should be set, it remains that the lower the setting, the greater the energy that will be saved. The key is finding the balance point where comfort levels are met while heating energy use is kept to a minimum.

The savings that can be achieved by thermostat setback are determined by three factors: the facility's climate; how many degrees the thermostat is set back; and how many hours per week it is set back. The greater the setback and the longer the setback, the greater the energy savings. While the savings percentage for facilities located in colder climates will be lower than that for those located in warmer climates, the total savings will be larger.

Estimating Occupied Hours Savings

Use Worksheet 22.1 to estimate the savings from setting back the thermostat while the facility is occupied. The worksheet was developed using data from computer modeling by correlating the temperature setback and the number of annual heating degree days with the savings produced. The worksheet is valid for temperature setbacks of up to 10°F. Use the worksheet as follows:

Step 1. Determine the number of degrees that the thermostats will be reduced on degrees Fahrenheit. Enter the value as the temperature setback in section #1 of the worksheet.

Step 2. From Figure 20.1 determine the annual number of heating degree days for the facility. Enter the value in section #1 of the worksheet.

Step 3. Multiply the temperature setback by the factor of 1.58. Add 19.4 to this value and subtract the product of the number of annual heating degree days and the factor of 0.0022. Enter the value in sections #1 and #2 of the worksheet.

Step 4. Enter the total heating energy use in millions of Btu for the facility in section #2 of the worksheet.

Step 5. Multiply the savings setback by the total heating energy use to determine the heating energy savings. Enter the value in section #2 of the worksheet.

This value represents the annual heating energy savings that would result from setting back all of the thermostats within the facility on a 24-hour-per-day basis.

Estimating Unoccupied Hours Savings

Energy can also be saved by setting the thermostat back only during the hours when the facility is unoccupied. Lower space temperatures during unoccupied hours can effectively reduce energy use without increasing occupant discomfort. The amount of energy saved is determined by the climate, the number of degrees that the thermostat is turned back, and the number of hours that it is turned back.

Use Worksheet 22.2 to estimate the energy savings that would result from setting back the thermostats during unoccupied hours. The worksheet was developed using data from computer modeling that correlated the temperature setback and the number of annual heating degree days with the savings produced. The modeling established a base setback for a period of eight hours per night, seven days per week. This base figure was then modified for both longer and shorter setback periods.

The worksheet is valid for temperature setbacks of up to 15°F and setback periods of up to 120 hours per week. Use the worksheet as follows:

Step 1. Determine the number of degrees that the thermostats will be reduced in degrees Fahrenheit. Enter the value as the temperature setback in section #1 of the worksheet.

Step 2. From Figure 20.1 determine the annual number of heating degree days for the facility. Enter the value in section #1 of the worksheet.

Step 3. Multiply the temperature setback by the factor of 0.792. Add 9.69 to this value and subtract the product of the number of annual heating degree days and the factor of 0.0011. Enter the value in sections #1 and #2 of the worksheet.

Step 4. Determine the number of hours that the thermostat will be set back each week. Enter the value in section #2 of the worksheet.

Step 5. Multiply the setback time by the setback savings factor and the factor of 0.018 to determine the setback savings factor in percent. Enter the value in sections #2 and #3 of the worksheet.

Step 6. Enter the total heating energy use in millions of Btu for the facility in section #3 of the worksheet.

Step 7. Multiply setback savings factor by the annual heating energy use to determine the annual heating energy savings in millions of Btu. Enter the value in section #3 of the worksheet.

This value represents the estimated annual heating energy savings that would result from setting back the thermostat during unoccupied hours.

ESTIMATING HEATING ENERGY SAVINGS FROM REDUCED VENTILATION RATES

One of the largest heating loads in a facility is due to the use of outside air for ventilation. While building codes and indoor air quality standards dictate minimum ventilation levels for different use areas, most areas remain overventilated, particularly during periods of low occupancy.

Reducing the rate at which outside air is brought into the facility can produce significant energy savings, particularly in cold climates. However, the facility manager must use caution when implementing this energy conservation measure. Too great a reduction may result in indoor air quality problems.

The savings from reduced ventilation rates are determined primarily by four factors: the facility's climate; the inside temperature; the size of the reduction in ventilation rate; and the number of hours per week that the ventilation rate is reduced. Savings increase with colder climates, higher inside temperature, larger reductions in ventilation rates, and increased hours of reduced operation.

Ventilation rates can be reduced during both occupied and unoccupied hours. Two worksheets, one for each appropriate situation, are provided for estimating the heating energy savings that result from reducing the ventilation rate.

Estimating Occupied Hours Savings

Use Worksheet 22.3 to estimate the annual heating energy savings that can be achieved by reducing the occupied hours ventilation rate. The worksheet was developed using data from computer modeling of facility energy use. The savings produced were correlated with the number of heating degree days, the inside temperature, the reduction in ventilation rate, and the number of hours per week that the reduction was in effect.

The worksheet is valid for ventilation rate reductions of up to 50%. Use the worksheet as follows:

Step 1.	Determine the number of occupied hours per week that the ventilation rate is to be reduced. Enter this value as the time in section #1 of the worksheet.
Step 2.	Determine the average temperature set point in degrees Fahrenheit for the facility. Enter the value in section #1 of the worksheet.
Step 3.	From Figure 20.1 determine the annual number of heating degree days for the facility. Enter the value in section #1 of the worksheet.
Step 4.	Carry out the multiplications as indicated on the worksheet. Add the values together and subtract the factor of 17.56 to determine the savings rate in thousands of Btu per cfm of outside air ventilation. Enter the value in sections #1 and #2 of the worksheet.
Step 5.	Determine the outside air ventilation rate reduction in cfm. Enter the value in section #2 of the worksheet.
Step 6.	Multiply the savings rate by the ventilation rate reduction and the conversion factor of 0.001 to determine the annual heating energy savings in millions of Btu. Enter the value in section #2 of the worksheet.

This value represents the annual savings in heating energy use that would result from reducing the outside air ventilation rate during occupied hours.

Estimating Unoccupied Hours Savings

Use Worksheet 22.4 to estimate the annual heating energy savings that can be achieved by minimizing the ventilation rate during unoccupied hours. The worksheet was developed using data from computer modeling of facility energy use. The savings produced were correlated with the number of heating degree days, the inside temperature, the ventilation rate, and the number of hours per week that the ventilation was minimized. The worksheet assumes that during unoccupied hours, the outside air dampers are fully closed. It further assumes that even though the dampers are closed, the leakage rate through the dampers is ten percent of the normal ventilation rate.

Use the worksheet as follows:

Step 1. Determine the number of unoccupied hours per week that the outside ventilation rate is to be minimized. Enter this value as the time in section #1 of the worksheet.

Step 2. Determine the average temperature set point in degrees Fahrenheit for the facility. Enter the value in section #1 of the worksheet.

Step 3. From Figure 20.1 determine the annual number of heating degree days for the facility. Enter the value in section #1 of the worksheet.

Step 4. Carry out the multiplications as indicated on the worksheet. Add the values together and subtract the factor of 17.56 to determine the savings rate in thousands of Btu per cfm of outside air ventilation. Enter the value in sections #1 and #2 of the worksheet.

Step 5. Determine the outside air ventilation rate in cfm. Enter the value in section #2 of the worksheet.

Step 6. Multiply the savings rate by the ventilation rate and the conversion factor of 0.0009 to determine the annual heating energy savings in millions of Btu. Enter the value in section #2 of the worksheet.

This value represents the annual heating energy savings that would be achieved if the outside air dampers were fully closed during unoccupied hours.

FAN CONTROL TECHNIQUES

Variable air volume systems control air flow to the occupied spaces by a number of different techniques. Most of these involve the use of outlet dampers or inlet vanes to restrict air flow. While vanes and dampers provide control over air flow, they are not the most energy-efficient means. As the vanes or dampers close to reduce the air flow, the horsepower draw of the fan motor also falls, but not very rapidly.

Over the past few years, a number of manufacturers have developed variable frequency drives (VFD) that, when connected to the air handling system fan motors, reduce air flow by slowing down the fan. As the system's need for air decreases, the VFD controller senses a load change and adjusts both the voltage and the frequency of the power being supplied to the fan motor. This adjustment results in a significantly lower power requirement for the fan motor in comparison to other control strategies.

For example, when the air flow is reduced to 60% of rated full flow in a system controlled by outlet dampers, the motor energy requirements of the fan typically decrease to about 85% of full flow. In a system controlled by variable inlet vanes, the motor power requirements typically decrease to 65% of full load. In contrast, a system controlled by a variable frequency drive typically draws only 20% of full load at 60% of rated flow.

Estimating the Savings from VFD Controls

The savings that VFD-operated fan systems produce depend on the horsepower of the fan being controlled, the number of hours per year that the fan system is in use, and the load profile on the fan system. Use Worksheet 22.5 to estimate the fan motor energy savings that a VFD-operated fan system would produce in comparison to a conventional control system.

The worksheet was developed using data from computer modeling of variable air volume system fan energy use. The savings produced were correlated with the horsepower of the fan and the number of hours per year that the system was operated. The load profile for the fan was assumed to follow a normal distribution ranging from a high of 100 percent to a low of 40 percent of full load rating. The load profile was assumed to be distributed as follows:

FLOW	TIME (%)
100	5
90	10
80	15
70	40
60	15
50	10
40	5

Use the worksheet as follows:

Step 1.   Determine the fan motor-rated horsepower. Enter the value in section #1 of the worksheet.

Step 2.   Multiply the fan horsepower by the factor of 1,498. Subtract 4.96 from this value to determine the base savings rate. Enter the value in sections #1 and #2.

Step 3.   Determine the annual number of hours that the fan system operates. Enter the value as the use in section #2.

Step 4.   Multiply the base savings rate by the use and divide by the factor 4,500 to determine the annual energy savings in kWh. Enter the value in sections #2 and #3.

Step 5.   Determine the annual average rate for electricity for the facility. Enter this value in section #3.

Step 6.   Multiply the annual energy savings by the average rate to determine the annual cost savings. Enter the value in section #3.

This value represents the savings that would be achieved by replacing a conventional damper or inlet vane-based variable air volume control system with a variable frequency drive system on the fan motor.

Methods of Pump Control

Hot and chilled water systems typically control capacity through the use of throttling valves. As the heating and cooling loads decrease, the valves partially close, restricting the flow of water. As the flow decreases, the horsepower requirement of the pump decreases, but only slightly.

Variable frequency drives offer an alternative to the throttling valve. In a system where flow is controlled by a pump connected to a variable frequency drive, the power requirements of the pump fall off rapidly with decreasing water flow.

Estimating VFD Pump Savings

The savings that VFD-controlled pumps produce depend on the horsepower of the pump, the number of hours per year that the pump is in use, and the load profile on the pump system. Use Worksheet 22.6 to estimate the pump motor energy savings that a VFD-operated pump system would produce in comparison to a system that uses throttling valves.

The worksheet was developed using data from computer modeling of pump energy use. The savings produced were correlated with the horsepower of the pump and the number of hours per year that the system was operated. The load profile for the system was assumed to follow a normal distribution ranging from 100% to 40% of full load flow as follows:

Flow	Time (%)
100	5
90	10
80	15
70	40
60	15
50	10
40	5

Use the worksheet as follows:

Step 1.   Determine the pump motor-rated horsepower. Enter the value in section #1 of the worksheet.

Step 2.   Multiply the pump horsepower by the factor of 1,498. Subtract 5.06 from this value to determine the base savings rate. Enter the value in sections #1 and #2.

Step 3.   Determine the annual number of hours that the pump system operates. Enter the value as the use in section #2.

Step 4.   Multiply the base savings rate by the use and divide by the factor 4,500 to determine the annual energy savings in kWh. Enter the value in sections #2 and #3.

Step 5.   Determine the annual average rate for electricity for the facility. Enter this value in section #3.

Step 6.   Multiply the annual energy savings by the average rate to determine the annual cost savings. Enter the value in section #3.

This value represents an estimate of the savings that would be produced by using a variable frequency drive to control the operation of a heating or chilled water pump.

ESTIMATING THE SAVINGS FROM INSULATING HOT WATER PIPING

Piping that is used for either domestic hot water or building heating loses heat to the surrounding environment. Therefore, additional energy must be spent by the water heating system. The rate at which heat is lost depends on the diameter of the pipe, the temperature of the water being circulated in the pipe, the temperature of the space surrounding the pipe, and the thickness of the insulation on the pipe.

Adding insulation to a domestic hot water or building heating water pipe can significantly reduce the rate at which heat is lost. The greatest savings are achieved for pipes that have no existing insulation, lower savings for those already insulated.

Rule of thumb: If a building's domestic hot water pipe or building heating water pipe is covered with at least one inch of insulation and it is in good condition, it will not be cost-effective to add more.

Use Worksheet 22.7 to estimate the savings that would result from the addition of insulation to bare domestic hot water and building heating water pipe. The worksheet was developed using data from computer modeling of heat loss from pipes of various diameters with differing thicknesses of insulation. It is valid for water temperatures ranging between 100° and 200°F.

Use the worksheet as follows:

Step 1.   Determine the outside diameter of the bare pipe in inches. Enter the value in section #1 of the worksheet.

Step 2.   Determine the average water temperature in degrees Fahrenheit. Enter the value in section #1.

Step 3.   Determine the average space temperature in degrees Fahrenheit where the pipe is located. Enter the value in section #1.

Step 4.   Determine the difference in water and space temperatures by subtracting the space temperature from the water temperature. Multiply this value by the pipe diameter and the factor 0.66. Add 18.4 to the result to determine the bare pipe heat loss. Enter the value in section #1.

Step 5.   Determine the U-value of the insulation being installed. Enter the value in section #2 of the worksheet.

Step 6.   Enter the outside diameter of the bare pipe in section #2.

Step 7.   Enter the thickness of the insulation in inches in section #2 of the worksheet.

Step 8.   Multiply the insulation thickness by the factor of 2, and add this value to the pipe diameter to determine the diameter of the pipe with insulation installed. Multiply this value by the insulation U-value to determine the heat loss factor for the insulated pipe. Enter this value in sections #2 and #3.

Step 9.   From section #1 determine the water and space temperatures. Enter these values in section #3.

Step 10.   Subtract the space temperature from the water temperature to determine the temperature difference between the two. Multiply this value by the heat loss factor and the factor 0.179. Subtract 3.01 from this value to determine the insulated pipe heat loss in Btu per foot. Enter this value in section #3.

Step 11.   From section #1, enter the bare pipe heat loss in section #4.

Step 12.   From section #3, enter the insulated pipe heat loss in section #4.

Step 13.   Determine the total pipe length in feet that is to be insulated. Enter the value in section #4 of the worksheet.

Step 14.   Subtract the insulated pipe heat loss from the bare pipe heat loss. Multiply the difference by the pipe length and the conversion factor of 0.000001 to determine the energy savings in millions of Btu. Enter the value in sections #4 and #5.

Step 15.   Determine the cost of the energy used to generate the domestic hot water or heating water in dollars per million Btu. Enter the value in section #5 of the worksheet.

Step 16.   Multiply the energy savings by the energy cost to determine the cost savings. Enter the value in section #5 of the worksheet.

This value represents the estimated savings that would result from the addition of insulation to bare domestic hot water or building heating water pipe.

ESTIMATING THE SAVINGS FROM PREHEATING BOILER COMBUSTION AIR

When combustion air is at room or outside air temperatures, it effectively cools the boiler, reducing the overall combustion efficiency. If waste heat from the boiler exhaust stack is used to preheat the combustion air, efficiency can be increased.

Rule of thumb: For every 100°F increase in combustion air temperature, overall boiler efficiency will increase by two percent. There are upper limits as to the amount of combustion air preheat that can be added to a boiler. Most limits are set by the manufacturer for that particular design.

Rule of thumb: The upper limit for oil and gas-fired boilers is approximately 350°F.

Use Worksheet 22.8 to estimate the annual savings that can be achieved through the use of boiler combustion air preheating. Use the worksheet as follows:

Step 1.   Determine the amount of combustion air preheating that will take place. Enter the value in section #1 of the worksheet.

Step 2.   Multiply the preheat temperature by the factor of 0.02 to determine the efficiency improvement that will be achieved. Enter the value in sections #1 and #2.

Step 3.   Determine the annual energy use for the boiler in millions of Btu per year. Enter the value in section #2.

Step 4.   Multiply annual energy use by the efficiency improvement and the conversion factor of 0.01 to determine the annual energy savings. Enter the value in sections #2 and #3 of the worksheet.

Step 5.   Multiply the energy savings by the unit cost for heating energy in dollars per million Btu to determine the annual cost savings. Enter the value in section #3.

This value represents the annual heating energy cost savings that would result from preheating boiler combustion air.

WORKSHEET 22.1 Savings From Thermostat Set Back - Heating

1. Thermostat Setback Savings

$$\boxed{19.4} + \left[\boxed{1.58} \times \boxed{}\right] - \left[\boxed{0.0022} \times \boxed{}\right] = \boxed{}$$

Temperature Setback (°F)   Annual Heating Degree Days   Setback Savings (%)

2. Heating Energy Savings

$$\boxed{} \times \boxed{} = \boxed{}$$

Setback Savings (%)   Heating Energy Use (million Btu)   Heating Energy Savings (million Btu)

WORKSHEET 22.2 Savings From Unoccupied Hours Thermostat Set Back - Heating

1. Thermostat Setback Savings Factor

$$\boxed{9.69} \ + \ \Bigg[\ \boxed{0.792} \ \times \ \boxed{} \ \Bigg] \ - \ \Bigg[\ \boxed{0.0011} \ \times \ \boxed{} \ \Bigg] \ = \ \boxed{}$$

| | Temperature Setback ($^{\circ}$F) | Annual Heating Degree Days | Setback Savings Factor |

2. Thermostat Setback Savings

$$\boxed{0.018} \ \times \ \boxed{} \ \times \ \boxed{} \ = \ \boxed{}$$

Setback Savings Factor   Time (hr/week)   Setback Savings (%)

3. Heating Energy Savings

$$\boxed{} \ \times \ \boxed{} \ = \ \boxed{}$$

Setback Savings (%)   Heating Energy Use (million Btu)   Heating Energy Savings (million Btu)

WORKSHEET 22.3 Savings From Reducing Ventilation Rate During Occupied Hours - Heating

1. Savings Rate

$$\left[\; 0.828 \;\right] \times \left[\; \begin{array}{c} \\ \text{Time} \\ \text{(hr/week)} \end{array} \right] + \left[\; 1.546 \;\times\; \begin{array}{c} \\ \text{Inside Temp} \\ (^{o}\text{F}) \end{array} \right] + \left[\; 0.0131 \;\times\; \begin{array}{c} \\ \text{Heating} \\ \text{Degree Days} \end{array} \right] - \boxed{17.56} = \begin{array}{c} \\ \text{Savings Rate} \\ \text{(1,000 Btu/cfm)} \end{array}$$

2. Heating Energy Savings

$$\begin{array}{c} \\ \text{Savings Rate} \\ \text{(1,000 Btu/cfm)} \end{array} \times \begin{array}{c} \\ \text{Ventilation} \\ \text{Rate Reduction} \\ \text{(cfm)} \end{array} \times \boxed{0.001} = \begin{array}{c} \\ \text{Heating Energy} \\ \text{Savings} \\ \text{(million Btu)} \end{array}$$

WORKSHEET 22.4 Savings From Closing Dampers During Unoccupied Hours - Heating

1. Savings Rate

$$0.828 \times \boxed{} \times \left[1.546 \times \boxed{} + 0.0131 \times \boxed{} \right] - 17.56 = \boxed{}$$

| | Time (hr/week) | | Inside Temp (°F) | | Heating Degree Days | | | Savings Rate (1,000 Btu/cfm) |

2. Heating Energy Savings

$$\boxed{} \times \boxed{} \times 0.0009 = \boxed{}$$

| Savings Rate (1,000 Btu/cfm) | | Ventilation Rate (cfm) | | | Heating Energy Savings (million Btu) |

WORKSHEET 22.5 Estimated Energy Savings
VFD Fan Applications

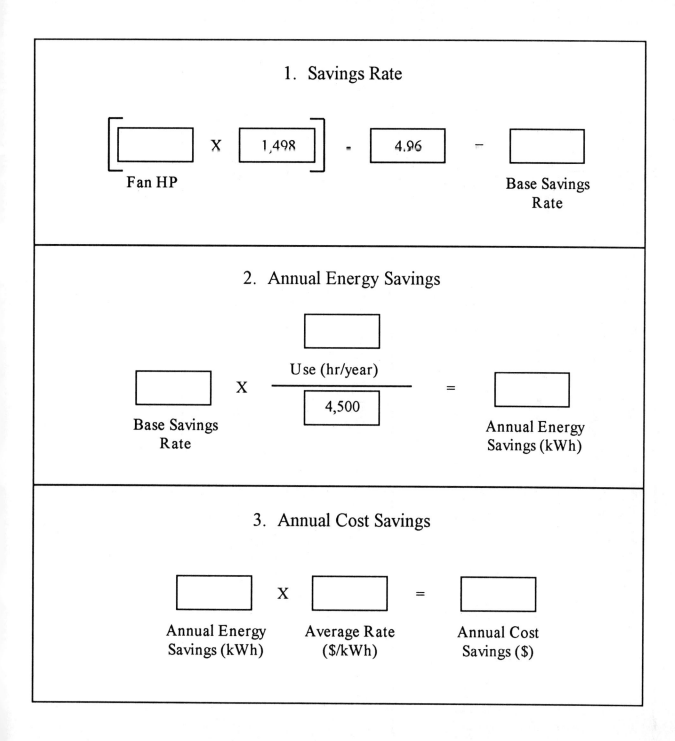

1. Savings Rate

$$\left[\boxed{} \times \boxed{1{,}498} \right] - \boxed{4.96} = \boxed{}$$

Fan HP   Base Savings
                                                                Rate

2. Annual Energy Savings

$$\boxed{} \times \frac{\boxed{}\ \text{Use (hr/year)}}{\boxed{4{,}500}} = \boxed{}$$

Base Savings   Annual Energy
     Rate   Savings (kWh)

3. Annual Cost Savings

$$\boxed{} \times \boxed{} = \boxed{}$$

Annual Energy   Average Rate   Annual Cost
Savings (kWh)   ($/kWh)   Savings ($)

WORKSHEET 22.6 Estimated Energy Savings
VFD Pump Applications

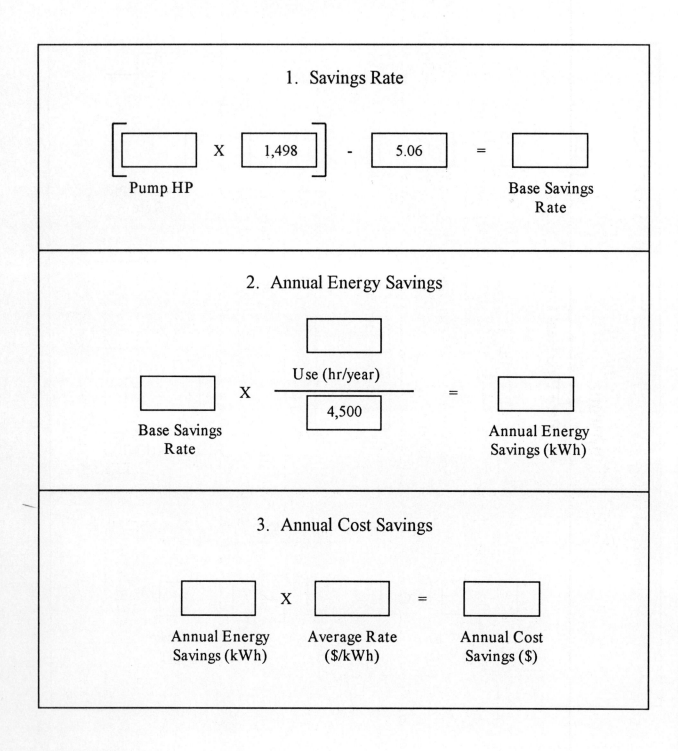

1. Savings Rate

$\left[\boxed{} \times \boxed{1,498} \right] - \boxed{5.06} = \boxed{}$

Pump HP   Base Savings Rate

2. Annual Energy Savings

$\boxed{} \times \dfrac{\text{Use (hr/year)} \quad \boxed{}}{\boxed{4,500}} = \boxed{}$

Base Savings Rate   Annual Energy Savings (kWh)

3. Annual Cost Savings

$\boxed{} \times \boxed{} = \boxed{}$

Annual Energy Savings (kWh)   Average Rate ($/kWh)   Annual Cost Savings ($)

WORKSHEET 22.7 Hot Water Piping Heat Loss
Water Temperatures of 200 °F or Less

1. Bare Pipe Heat Loss

$$\boxed{18.4} \; + \; \boxed{0.66} \; \times \; \boxed{} \; \times \; \left[\boxed{} \; - \; \boxed{} \right] \; = \; \boxed{}$$

| | | Pipe Diameter (inches) | | Water Temp. (°F) | | Space Temp. (°F) | | Bare Pipe Heat Loss (Btu/ft) |

2. Heat Loss Factor

$$\boxed{} \; \times \; \left[\boxed{} \; + \; \boxed{2} \; \times \; \boxed{} \right] \; = \; \boxed{}$$

Insulation U-Value   Pipe Diameter (inches)   Insulation Thickness (in.)   Heat Loss Factor

3. Insulated Pipe Heat Loss

$$\boxed{} \; \times \; \boxed{0.179} \; \times \; \left[\boxed{} \; - \; \boxed{} \right] \; = \; \boxed{3.01}$$

Heat Loss Factor   Water Temp. (°F)   Space Temp. (°F)   Insulated Pipe Heat Loss (Btu/ft)

Worksheet 22.7 (continued)

4. Energy Savings

$$\left[\boxed{} \; - \; \boxed{}\right] \; \times \; \boxed{} \; \times \; \boxed{0.000001} \; = \; \boxed{}$$

Bare Pipe   Insulated   Pipe Length   Energy Savings
Heat Loss   Pipe Heat   (ft)   (Millions of Btu)
(Btu/ft)   Loss (Btu/ft)

5. Cost Savings

$$\boxed{} \; \times \; \boxed{} \; = \; \boxed{}$$

Energy Savings   Energy Cost   Cost Savings ($)
(Millions of Btu)   ($/million Btu)

WORKSHEET 22.8 Savings From Preheating Boiler Combustion Air

1. Efficiency Improvement

$$\boxed{} \quad \text{X} \quad \boxed{0.02} \quad = \quad \boxed{}$$

Preheat
Temperature (°F)

Efficiency
Improvement
(%)

2. Annual Energy Savings

$$\boxed{} \quad \text{X} \quad \boxed{} \quad \text{X} \quad \boxed{0.01} \quad = \quad \boxed{}$$

Boiler Energy
Use
(million Btu/yr)

Efficiency
Improvement
(%)

Energy Savings
(million Btu/yr)

3. Annual Cost Savings

$$\boxed{} \quad \text{X} \quad \boxed{} \quad = \quad \boxed{}$$

Energy Savings
(million Btu/yr)

Unit Heating
Cost ($/million
Btu)

Cost Savings
($)

Chapter 23

HOW TO DETERMINE THE EFFECTIVENESS OF YOUR ENERGY USE PROGRAM

This chapter presents information that can be used to estimate the overall effectiveness of an energy management program. Material presented in this chapter can be used to determine a facility's annual energy use index, the energy use of the facility normalized on a square footage basis. Procedures are given to compare annual energy use to the use in the same facility in previous years. Information on energy use in other buildings is also presented to provide a basis for comparing use in your facility with the national average for that type of facility.

To assist you in determining the most cost-effective fuel to use, methods are included to compare overall costs of alternative fuels.

Since economics is one of the major driving forces behind energy conservation, procedures are given for estimating the simple and compound payback for energy conservation projects. Finally, there is a discussion of ways to determine the life cycle cost of equipment and system installations.

HOW TO MAINTAIN ENERGY USE RECORDS

One of the most important tasks in establishing an energy management program is the development of an historical database of energy use which will help you in several ways. First, by developing a history of energy use, you will have a means of evaluating the effectiveness of the program. As energy conservation measures are implemented, the energy use for the facility would be expected to decrease, particularly if other factors such as weather and occupancy remain fairly constant.

628

Second, the historical energy use data base also provides you with a measure of the energy efficiency of your facility. By comparing the energy use index of your facility with that of other facilities of the same type, you can determine not only where you stand relative to other facilities, but also how much room there is for improvement.

Figure 23.1 lists average building energy use in Btu per square foot for eleven major types of commercial buildings. The energy use in Btu per square foot per year is the sum of all energy use for the facility, including heating, air conditioning, lighting, cooking, equipment, transportation, and miscellaneous use.

The data presented in the figure was compiled by the U.S. Department of Energy and represents the national average energy use for that type of building. Use this value only as a reference value since actual energy use will vary with the local climate, the type and condition of energy-using systems installed in the building, how the building is operated, the number of hours per week that the building is in use, the age of the facility and its energy-using systems, etc.

Finally, as the data is collected over a period of several years, it can serve as a means of evaluating the long-term energy use trends. As energy-using systems age, a slight but steady decrease in operating efficiency can be expected. The historical data will show this. If there are sudden increases in use that cannot be explained by such factors as weather or change in the operation of the facility, then the data would suggest that something might be wrong with the energy-using systems.

Use Worksheets 23.1 through 23.4 to record building energy use and cost by source on an annual basis. Each figure also presents calculation procedures for determining the average annual rate for the energy source and the annual use per square foot. Use the worksheets as follows:

Worksheet 23.1: Electricity

Step 1. Enter the building name and the gross square footage at the top of the worksheet.

Step 2. Get the monthly electrical bills for the building for a one-year period.

Step 3. For each month, record the use in kWh, the peak demand in kW, the demand charges in dollars, and the total charges for the month. Enter the value on the worksheet.

Step 4. For each month, divide the total charges by the use to determine the monthly rate for the electricity in dollars per kWh. Enter the value on the worksheet.

Step 5. Sum the use, demand charges, and total charges to determine the annual totals. Enter the values at the column bottoms of the worksheet.

Step 6. To calculate the annual average rate, enter the total charges and the annual use at the bottom left side of the worksheet.

Step 7. Divide the total charges by the annual use to determine the average rate. Enter the value at the bottom of the worksheet.

Step 8.	Enter the total annual use in the box at the bottom right side of the worksheet.
Step 9.	Enter the building's area at the bottom of the worksheet.
Step 10.	Divide the annual use by the area to determine the annual use index in kWh per square foot.

Worksheet 23.2: Natural Gas

Step 1.	Enter the building name and the gross square footage at the top of the worksheet.
Step 2.	Get the monthly natural gas bills for the building for a one-year period.
Step 3.	For each month, record the use in therms and the total charges for the month. Enter the value on the worksheet.
Step 4.	For each month, divide the total charges by the use to determine the monthly rate for the natural gas in dollars per therm. Enter the value on the worksheet.
Step 5.	Sum the use and total cost to determine the annual totals. Enter the values at the column bottoms of the worksheet.
Step 6.	To calculate the annual average rate, enter the total charges and the annual total use at the bottom left side of the worksheet.
Step 7.	Divide the total charges by the annual use to determine the average rate in dollars per therm. Enter the value at the bottom of the worksheet.
Step 8.	Enter the total annual use in the box at the bottom right side of the worksheet.
Step 9.	Enter the building's area at the bottom of the worksheet.
Step 10.	Divide the annual use by the area to determine the annual use index in therms per square foot.

Worksheet 23.3: Oil

Step 1.	Enter the building name and the gross square footage at the top of the worksheet.
Step 2.	Get the oil bills for the building for a one-year period.
Step 3.	For each bill, record the use in gallons and the total charges for each billing period. Enter the value on the worksheet.
Step 4.	For each billing period, divide the total charges by the use to determine the rate for the oil in dollars per gallon. Enter the value on the worksheet.
Step 5.	Sum the use and total cost to determine the annual totals. Enter the values at the column bottoms of the worksheet.

Step 6.   To calculate the annual average rate, enter the total charges and the annual total use at the bottom left side of the worksheet.

Step 7.   Divide the total charges by the annual use to determine the average rate in dollars per gallon. Enter the value at the bottom of the worksheet.

Step 8.   Enter the total annual use in the box at the bottom right side of the worksheet.

Step 9.   Enter the building's area at the bottom of the worksheet.

Step 10.   Divide the annual use by the area to determine the annual use index in gallons per square foot.

Worksheet 23.4: Propane

Step 1.   Enter the building name and the gross square footage at the top of the worksheet

Step 2.   Get the propane bills for the building for a one-year period.

Step 3.   For each billing period, record the use in pounds and the total charges for the month. Enter the value on the worksheet.

Step 4.   For each month, divide the total charges by the use to determine the billing period rate for the propane in dollars per pound. Enter the value on the worksheet.

Step 5.   Sum the use and total cost to determine the annual totals. Enter the values at the column bottoms of the worksheet.

Step 6.   To calculate the annual average rate, enter the total charges and the annual total use at the bottom left side of the worksheet.

Step 7.   Divide the total charges by the annual use to determine the average rate in dollars per pound. Enter the value at the bottom of the worksheet.

Step 8.   Enter the total annual use in the box at the bottom right side of the worksheet.

Step 9.   Enter the building's area at the bottom of the worksheet.

Step 10.   Divide the annual use by the area to determine the annual use index in pounds per square foot.

THE BUILDING ENERGY USE INDEX

Once the annual totals have been determined for each fuel used within the facility, you can calculate the facility's energy use index. Expressed in Btu per square foot per year, it is the measure used to gauge the energy efficiency of the facility. Use Worksheet 23.5 to calculate the energy use index for a building. You must convert the use for each type of energy used within your facility to Btu. Use the worksheet as follows:

Step 1.   Enter the building name and the gross square footage at the top of the worksheet.

Step 2.   From Worksheet 23.1, determine the electricity use for each month. Enter the values in the worksheet.

Step 3.   Convert each month's use in kWh to Btu by multiplying by the conversion factor of 3,413 Btu/kWh. Enter the monthly values in the worksheet.

Step 4.   For each type of fuel used in the facility other than electricity, complete steps 5 through 6 below.

Step 5.   Enter the monthly use (gallons, pounds, or cubic feet) in the worksheet.

Step 6.   Convert each month's use to Btu by multiplying by the appropriate conversion factor listed at the bottom of the worksheet. Enter the value for each month on the worksheet.

Step 7.   After entering the monthly use and Btu values for all fuels used in the facility, sum the total use in Btu for each month. Enter the values on the worksheet.

Step 8.   Sum the Btu values for each fuel to determine the annual use in Btu for that fuel. Enter the totals in the worksheet.

Step 9.   Sum the monthly total energy use in Btu to determine the annual energy use for the facility. Enter the value on the worksheet.

Step 10.   Enter the total annual energy use in Btu in the lower portion of the worksheet.

Step 11.   Enter the building's gross square footage in the lower portion of the worksheet.

Step 12.   Divide the annual energy use by the area to determine the annual use index in Btu per square foot. Enter the value in the bottom portion of the worksheet.

This value represents the total energy use of the facility normalized for the area of the building. It is the value that you can use to compare energy use in your facility to that in other similar facilities (see Figure 23.1).

FUEL COST COMPARISON

Facility managers frequently have the option of selecting the primary fuel that their facility is to use to generate heat. Although considered most often for new facilities, those same options are available for existing facilities, particularly if the primary heating equipment is in need of major overhaul or replacement.

Pricing is the most frequently cited reason for switching to an alternative fuel. Favorable rate structures can make one fuel source less expensive than other options. And since rate structures vary with location, the lowest cost fuel for one facility may not be the lowest in another. Supply, delivery, and regulatory factors often combine to make a particular fuel more competitive in a specific location.

In order to compare the costs of different fuel types, it is necessary to normalize the costs to standard units; dollars per million Btu. It is also necessary to factor in the conversion efficiency of the primary heating equipment because there are significant variations between differently fueled units. Finally, in the case of central steam systems, it is necessary to factor in distribution losses between the central steam plant and the facility if the central system is to be replaced with a local unit for that building.

Use Worksheet 23.5 to estimate the unit costs for different fuels. Separate sections are provided for each fuel being considered. Use the worksheet as follows:

Step 1.   Determine the average rate for the fuel in dollars per unit (gallon, pound, cubic foot, etc.). The average rate should be for a one-year period to account for seasonal variations. The average rate can be determined by using Worksheets 23.1 through 23.4. Enter the average rate on the worksheet.

Step 2.   Figure 23.2 lists the average heating values for common fuels. These values represent national averages because the actual heating value varies with the source of the fuel. If the actual value can be obtained from the supplier, use that value. If it is not known, use the value from Figure 23.2 for the heat content in units per million Btu. Enter the value in the worksheet.

Step 3.   The conversion efficiency is the seasonal average efficiency at which the primary heating equipment converts the fuel to heating energy. In the case of centralized heating plants, such as those that generate steam or high-temperature hot water for a group of buildings, the conversion efficiency must also take into consideration distribution losses. Typical conversion efficiencies are listed at the bottom of the worksheet. For the type of fuel being evaluated, select the conversion efficiency and enter the value in the worksheet.

Step 4.   Multiply the average rate by the fuel units per million Btu and the conversion efficiency to determine the fuel's unit cost.

Step 5.   Repeat steps 1 - 4 for the other fuels being considered.

While fuel costs are an important consideration when examining fuel alternatives, there are other factors that also must be examined.

1. Availability. There are three parts to availability considerations. First, not all fuels are available in all locations. Check with the local supplier to determine if a particular fuel is available. Second, consider its long-term availability. Use of certain fuels, such as #6 oil, is declining. As a result of the excess production capacity, suppliers are offering attractive rates. However, as demand continues to decline, and production facilities are converted to other fuels, those attractive rates may disappear. Even worse, what may be attractive today could completely disappear tomorrow.

The third factor is the year-round availability. As demand varies during the year, some suppliers find themselves in the situation where the demand exceeds the supply, thus forcing curtailments. Before switching to a different fuel source for economic reasons, consider the historical ability of the supplier to meet the demand. If supply is a problem, then a backup alternative fuel system or on-site storage will be required.

2. Code and Environmental Regulations. The conversion from one fuel source to another can have a major impact on the way in which the facility is operated. For example, conversion from a central steam plant to individual building boilers may require that the boilers be staffed by licensed boiler operators.

   Environmental regulations also may restrict the ability to convert from one fuel source to another. In nearly all cases, a permit will have to be obtained for the conversion. If the emissions produced by the alternative fuel source are different and conflict with the local environmental regulations, it will be difficult or impossible to obtain the required conversion permits.

3. Convenience. Finally, the level of convenience must be considered. Convenience varies greatly with type of fuel. Contract negotiations, on-site storage facilities, backup systems, and safety are some of the convenience-related factors that must be evaluated.

ENERGY CONSERVATION ECONOMICS

Energy conservation in facilities is driven by a number of different factors. Over time, the relative importance of each of these factors varies. For example, when energy conservation first became a concern, the need to reduce use was driven by a shortage in energy supply. Some facility managers were forced to implement conservation measures simply because their supply had been curtailed. The cost savings produced by the measures were secondary or nonexistent, particularly in cases where users of one fuel source were forced to switch to an alternative fuel.

Economics soon came to be a strong driving force. Energy conservation was recognized as an effective way of reducing costs without causing major disruptions to operations. Some facility managers even found that effective energy conservation practices, such as properly maintaining building chillers, increased system reliability, decreased downtime, and prolonged equipment life while reducing energy use.

Recently, a new factor has been contributing to the efforts of reducing energy use: concern for the environment. The production, distribution, and use of energy in facilities contribute greatly to the pollution of the environment. If the demand for energy can be reduced through the implementation of energy conservation measures, then the negative environmental impact of producing and distributing that energy can also be reduced.

While these and other factors help to increase the importance of energy conservation within facilities, the primary driving force for conservation is still economics. Business today will invest in energy conservation only if it can be demonstrated that it makes economic sense. It is your responsibility to demonstrate the value of energy conservation to the organization.

Evaluating Energy Conservation Measures

There are three basic questions that must be answered when evaluating energy conservation measures. How much will it cost? How much energy will it save? Will the investment be worthwhile? Preliminary cost savings estimates can be prepared using standard estimating techniques. Energy savings estimates can be developed using the techniques identified in this book, or through computer simulations. The value of the investment can also be measured using a wide range of economic analysis tools.

Three commonly used tools for analyzing the value of a particular energy conservation measure are presented here: simple payback, modified simple payback, and life cycle costing. Selection of a particular tool depends on the requirements of the organization.

Completing the calculations for a number of different energy conservation measures also gives you the relative impact for each. Since few facilities have the financial capability to invest in all identified measures, you can evaluate several and set their implementation order based on their relative worth.

SIMPLE PAYBACK PERIOD. One of the most frequently used methods for evaluating the effectiveness of a particular energy conservation measure is the simple payback period. Expressed in months or years, the simple payback period is the time required to recover the implementation costs for the energy conservation measures through energy savings.

The simple payback period for a given energy conservation project is calculated as follows:

$$\text{Simple payback} = \frac{\text{Cost}}{\text{Estimated annual savings}}$$

where: Simple payback = the time to recover the cost to implement in years
Cost = the first time costs in dollars
Estimated annual savings = the first year energy savings in dollars

The simple payback period provides an easy-to-calculate measure of the relative effectiveness of a particular energy conservation measure. While simple payback calculations may be applied to any energy conserving measure, they are best suited for those that are relatively low in first costs or provide a fairly rapid return on the investment. Measures that require substantial investment or a long time to recover the investment generally require an economic analysis that takes into consideration factors such as inflation, rising energy costs, and the cost of borrowing the money.

In spite of these limitations, the simple payback period is the most widely used tool for analyzing energy conservation measures today. It may even be more accurate than some of the other more complex tools because it uses known values for such factors as energy costs and rates. The other analysis techniques must make assumptions about where those rates are headed in the future, typically based on past performance.

MODIFIED SIMPLE PAYBACK. One of the strongest criticisms of the simple payback period procedure is that it does not consider the rising cost of energy. As energy rates rise with time, the annual savings produced by implementation of the energy conservation measure increase. The increased savings serve to decrease the amount of time required to recover the initial investment. Simple payback analysis, by using an assumed flat rate for the cost of energy over the entire payback period, produces an overly long estimate of the payback period.

The modified simple payback analysis procedure attempts to correct this by including a factor for energy rate inflation. Energy rates are assumed to increase at a constant rate over the entire payback period. Estimates of the rate of increase can be developed by looking at historical data as well as by working with local utility representatives. The key is to select a realistic value that will serve as the average annual rate increase during the payback period.

Use Figure 23.3 to estimate the modified simple payback period. Use the figure as follows:

Step 1.   Determine the simple payback period in years for the measure by dividing the estimated cost of the measure by the estimated first-year energy cost savings.

Step 2.   Determine the annual inflation rate for energy in percent.

Step 3.   Using Figure 23.3, enter the figure on the horizontal axis at the simple payback period. Move vertically until you intersect the diagonal line for the estimated annual rate of inflation for energy costs. From that intersection point, move horizontally to the left until you reach the vertical axis. Read the modified simple payback period in years.

The modified simple payback calculation procedure retains the ease of use of the simple payback procedure, but offers the benefit of a more realistic payback period calculation based on escalating energy rates. Other procedures can be used that take into account additional factors, but at the cost of increasing complexity.

LIFE CYCLE COSTING. While both the simple payback and the modified simple payback procedures were concerned only with the cost to implement the measure and the energy savings that would result, life cycle costing procedures consider all relevant costs and savings associated with implementation of the measure. The major categories of costs and savings associated with a life cycle cost calculation for an energy project are implementation, recurring routine maintenance, major scheduled maintenance, replacement, and energy savings.

Life cycle costs for an energy conservation measure can be considered to be the total cost and benefits of ownership of that measure over its life span. While simple and modified simple payback procedures are most effective in identifying and ranking energy conservation measures, life cycle costing procedures are most effective in selecting between alternative ways of implementing the same measure. For example, a simple payback calculation might show that it is cost effective to replace a building chiller with a newer, more efficient unit; the life cycle costing procedure would show what model and chiller size would be best.

There are a number of required steps in completing a life cycle cost calculation. All costs and savings associated with implementation of the measure must first be identified and then quantified over the life of the measure. To provide a basis for comparison, those costs and savings must be converted to a common time base and then factored together to determine the life cycle cost of the measure.

There are a number of different manual or computerized calculation procedures that can be followed to determine the life cycle costs for measures. Unfortunately, they are beyond the scope of this book. One source for additional information on the specific steps required to be carried out in calculating life cycle costs is the National Bureau of Standards publication, *Life-Cycle Costing: A Guide for Selecting Energy Conservation Projects for Public Buildings,* NBS Building Science Series 113.

FIGURE 23.1 Commercial Building Average Energy Use

Type of Building	Energy Use (Btu/sq ft -yr)
Assembly	64,000
Educational	87,000
Food Sales	175,000
Food Service	218,000
Health Care	219,000
Lodging	122,000
Mercantile & Service	86,000
Office	104,000
Parking Garage	43,000
Public Order & Safety	127,000
Warehouse	58,000

Source: Commercial Buildings Energy Consumption and Expenditures 1989, U.S. Department of Energy, DOE/EIA - 0319(89)

FIGURE 23.2 Fuel Btu Heating Values

Fuel	Unit	Btu/unit	Units/million Btu
Alcohol, ethyl	Gallon	12,800	78
methyl	Gallon	9,600	104
Coal, anthracite	Pound	13,000	79
bituminous	Pound	12,000	71
lignite	Pound	7,000	145
Electricity	kWh	3,413	293
Natural Gas	Cubic foot	1,000	1,000
Oil, # 1	Gallon	136,000	7.35
# 2	Gallon	139,000	7.22
# 3	Gallon	141,000	7.09
Oil, # 4	Gallon	144,000	6.9
# 5	Gallon	146,000	6.73
# 6	Gallon	151,000	6.58
Propane	Pound	21,500	47
Steam	Pound	1,000	1,000
Trash	Pound	7,500	133
Wood	Pound	6,000	200

Note: The conversion factors listed above are based on nationwide averages for heat content of the fuel. As this heat content varies with location, the conversion factor will also vary. If location-specific values are required, contact your local fuel supplier.

FIGURE 23.3 Estimating Modified Simple Payback for Energy Conservation

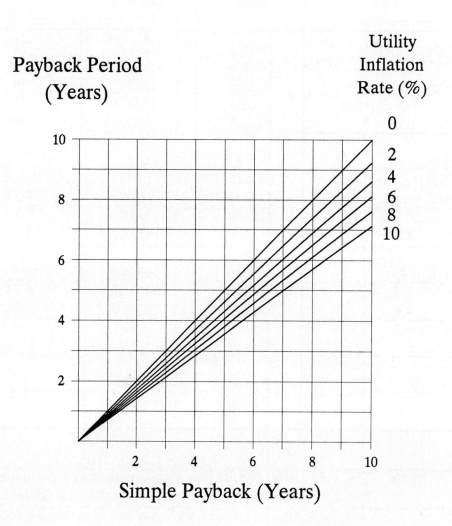

WORKSHEET 23.1 Electricity Use and Cost Data

Building: _____   Area (sq ft): _____

Billing Period	Use (kWh)	Peak Demand (kW)	Demand Charges ($)	Total Charges ($)	Monthly Rate ($/kWh)
Annual Total					

Annual Average Rate ($/kWh)

$$\frac{\text{Total Charges (\$)} \quad \boxed{}}{\text{Annual Use (kWh)} \quad \boxed{}} = \boxed{} \quad \text{Average Rate (\$/kWh)}$$

Annual Use (kWh/sq ft)

$$\frac{\text{Annual Use (kWh)} \quad \boxed{}}{\text{Area (sq ft)} \quad \boxed{}} = \boxed{} \quad \text{Annual Use (kWh/sq ft)}$$

WORKSHEET 23.2 Natural Gas Use and Cost Data

Building: _____   Area (sq ft): _____

Billing Period	Use (therms)	Total Cost ($)	Monthly Rate ($/therm)
Annual Total			

Annual Average Rate ($/therm)

$$\frac{\text{Total Cost (\$)} \quad \boxed{}}{\text{Total therms} \quad \boxed{}} = \boxed{} \quad \text{Average Rate (\$/therm)}$$

Annual Use (therms/sq ft)

$$\frac{\text{Total therms} \quad \boxed{}}{\text{Area (sq ft)} \quad \boxed{}} = \boxed{} \quad \text{Annual Use (therms/sq ft)}$$

WORKSHEET 23.3 Oil Use and Cost Data

Building: _____   Area (sq ft): _____

Billing Period	Stock on Hand at Start (gal)	Deliveries (gal)	Stock on Hand at End (gal)	Use (gal)	Cost ($)	Rate ($/gal)
Annual Total						

Annual Average Rate ($/gal)

[ ] Total Charges ($)
—————————————— = [ ] Average Rate ($/gal)
[ ] Annual Use (gal)

Annual Use (gal/sq ft)

[ ] Annual Use (gal)
—————————————— = [ ] Annual Use (gal/sq ft)
[ ] Area (sq ft)

WORKSHEET 23.4 Propane Use and Cost Data

Building: _____   Area (sq ft): _____

Billing Period	Use (lbs)	Total Cost ($)	Monthly Rate ($/lb)
Annual Total			

Annual Average Rate ($/lb)	**Annual Use (lbs/sq ft)**
$\dfrac{\text{Total Cost (\$)}}{\text{Total lbs}}$ = ☐ Average Rate ($/lb)	$\dfrac{\text{Total lbs}}{\text{Area (sq ft)}}$ = ☐ Annual Use (lbs/sq ft)

WORKSHEET 23.5 Building Annual Energy Use Index

Building: _____   Area (sq ft): _____

Month	Electricity		Fuel #2		Fuel #3		Total Use Btu
	kWh	Btu	Use	Btu	Use	Btu	
January							
February							
March							
April							
May							
June							
July							
August							
September							
October							
November							
December							
Total							

Conversion Factors

Electricity	3,413 Btu/kWh
Natural Gas	1,000 Btu/cu ft
#2 Oil	138,000 Btu/gal
# 6 Oil	146,000 Btu/gal
Propane	21,500 Btu/lb
Steam	900 Btu/lb

Annual Use (Btu/sq ft)

$$\frac{\text{Annual Use (Btu)} \quad \boxed{}}{\text{Area (sq ft)} \quad \boxed{}} = \boxed{}$$

Annual Use Index (Btu/sq ft)

WORKSHEET 23.6 Fuel Cost Comparison

Fuel #1: _____

☐	X	☐	X	☐	=	☐	
Average Rate ($/unit)		Fuel units per million Btu		Conversion Efficiency		Unit Cost ($/million Btu)	

Fuel #2: _____

☐	X	☐	X	☐	=	☐	
Average Rate ($/unit)		Fuel units per million Btu		Conversion Efficiency		Unit Cost ($/million Btu)	

Fuel #3: _____

☐	X	☐	X	☐	=	☐	
Average Rate ($/unit)		Fuel units per million Btu		Conversion Efficiency		Unit Cost ($/million Btu)	

Conversion Efficiencies

Coal	0.75	Propane	0.85
Electricity	1.00	Steam	0.95
Natural Gas	0.85	Wood	0.70
Oil	0.82		

Note: Fuel conversion efficiencies vary widely with the condition of the boiler/converter and the moisture content of the fuel. The efficiencies listed are for dry fuel and a properly tuned boiler.

APPENDICES

APPENDIX A.1 U.S. Conversion Units

Multiply	By	To Convert To
Acres	4,840	Square yards
Acres	43,560	Square feet
Atmospheres	33.9	Feet of water
Atmospheres	29.92	Inches of mercury
Atmospheres	14.7	Pounds per sq in
Barrels	31.5	Gallons
Barrels	4	Pecks
Btu	777.5	Foot-pounds
Btu	0.000293	Kilowatt hours
Btu per hour	0.0000298	Horsepower (boiler)
Btu per hour	0.000393	Horsepower
Btu per hour	0.2928	Watts
Btu per minute	12.96	Foot-pounds per sec
Btu per minute	0.02356	Horsepower
Btu per minute	17.57	Watts
Btu per minute	0.01757	Kilowatts
Btu/sq ft per minute	0.122	Watts per sq inch
Bushels	1.244	Cubic feet
Bushels	2,150	Cubic inches
Bushels	4	Pecks
Bushels	64	Pints (dry)
Bushels	32	Quarts (dry)
Cords	128	Cubic feet
Cubic feet	0.8039	Bushels
Cubic feet	62.43	Pounds of water
Cubic feet	59.84	Pints (liq)
Cubic feet	29.92	Quarts (liq)
Cubic feet	0.00781	Cords
Cubic feet	1,728	Cubic inches
Cubic feet	0.03704	Cubic yards
Cubic feet	7.481	Gallons
Cubic feet per min	0.1247	Gallons per second
Cubic feet per sec	0.1247	Gallons per minute
Cubic inches	0.000465	Bushels
Cubic inches	0.03463	Pints (liq)

Appendix A.1 (continued)

Multiply	By	To Convert To
Cubic inches	0.01732	Quarts (liq)
Cubic inches	0.03463	Pints (dry)
Cubic inches	0.0149	Quarts (dry)
Cubic inches	0.000579	Cubic feet
Cubic inches	0.0000214	Cubic yards
Cubic yards	27	Cubic feet
Cubic yards	46,656	Cubic inches
Degrees (angle)	60	Minutes
Degrees (angle)	0.01745	Radians
Degrees (angle)	3,600	Seconds
Dozen	0.0833	Gross
Feet	0.0606	Rods
Feet	12	Inches
Feet	0.000164	Miles (nautical)
Feet	0.000189	Miles (statute)
Feet	0.333	Yards
Feet of water	0.0295	Atmospheres
Feet of water	62.43	Pounds per sq ft
Feet of water	0.4335	Pounds per sq in
Feet of water	0.8826	Inches of mercury
Feet per hour	0.01667	Feet per minute
Feet per minute	60	Feet per hour
Feet per minute	60	Feet per second
Feet per minute	0.01136	Miles per hour
Feet per second	0.01667	Feet per minute
Fluid ounces	0.03125	Quarts
Foot-pounds	0.001286	Btu
Foot-pounds	0.000000505	Horsepower hours
Foot-pounds per min	0.0000226	Kilowatts
Foot-pounds per min	0.0000303	Horsepower
Foot-pounds per sec	0.001356	Kilowatts
Foot-pounds per sec	0.07717	Btu per minute
Gallons	8.345	Pounds of water
Gallons	8	Pints (liq)
Gallons	4	Quarts (liq)

Appendix A.1 (continued)

Multiply	By	To Convert To
Gallons	0.0318	Barrels
Gallons	0.1337	Cubic feet
Gallons per minute	0.00223	Cubic feet per sec
Gallons per second	8.022	Cubic feet per min
Grains	0.00229	Ounces
Gross	0.0833	Dozen
Horsepower	42.44	Btu per minute
Horsepower	33,000	Foot-pounds/minute
Horsepower	2.546	Btu per hour
Horsepower	746	Watts
Horsepower (boiler)	33,520	Btu per hour
Horsepower hours	1,980,000	Foot-pounds
Horsepower hours	0.7457	Kilowatt hours
Inches	0.0833	Feet
Inches	1,000	Mils
Inches	0.0278	Yards
Inches of mercury	70.73	Pounds per sq ft
Inches of mercury	0.4912	Pounds per sq inch
Inches of mercury	13.5	Inches of water
Inches of mercury	0.0334	Atmospheres
Inches of mercury	1.133	Feet of water
Inches of water	0.07355	Inches of mercury
Inches of water	5.204	Pounds per sq ft
Inches of water	0.03613	Pounds per sq in
Kilowatt hours	3,415	Btu
Kilowatt hours	1.341	Horsepower hours
Kilowatts	56.92	Btu per minute
Kilowatts	44,250	Foot-pounds per min
Kilowatts	737.5	Foot-pounds per sec
Miles (nautical)	6,080	Feet
Miles (nautical)	1.1515	Miles (statute)
Miles (statute)	1,760	Yards
Miles (statute)	5,280	Feet
Miles (statute)	0.8684	Miles (nautical)
Miles per hour	88	Feet per minute

Appendix A.1 (continued)

Multiply	By	To Convert To
Mils	0.001	Inches
Minutes (angle)	0.01667	Degrees
Ounces	437.5	Grains
Ounces	0.0625	Pounds
Pecks	8	Quart
Pecks	0.25	Bushels
Pecks	0.25	Barrels
Pint (liq)	33.6	Quart
Pints (dry)	0.01563	Bushels
Pints (dry)	0.5	Cubic inches
Pints (liq)	0.2	Cubic feet
Pints (liq)	28.87	Cubic inches
Pints (liq)	0.125	Gallons
Pounds	16	Ounces
Pounds	0.00045	Tons (long)
Pounds	0.0005	Tons (short)
Pounds of water	0.01602	Cubic feet
Pounds of water	0.1198	Gallons
Pounds per sq ft	0.01602	Feet of water
Pounds per sq ft	293	Inches of mercury
Pounds per sq ft	0.1922	Inches of water
Pounds per sq ft	144	Pounds per sq in
Pounds per sq in	2.307	Feet of water
Pounds per sq in	2.036	Inches of mercury
Pounds per sq in	0.1923	Inches of water
Pounds per sq in	144	Pounds per sq ft
Pounds per sq in	0.06804	Atmospheres
Quarts (dry)	0.125	Peck
Quarts	0.25	Gallons
Quarts (dry)	0.0313	Bushels
Quarts (dry)	67.2	Cubic inches
Quarts (liq)	0.401	Cubic feet
Quarts (liq)	57.75	Cubic inches
Quarts (liq)	32	Fluid ounces
Quarts (liq)	2	Pint

Multiply	By	To Convert To
Radians	57.3	Degrees
Rods	16.5	Feet
Seconds (angle)	0.000278	Degrees
Square feet	0.1111	Square yards
Square feet	0.00002296	Acres
Square feet	144	Square inches
Square inches	0.00694	Square feet
Square inches	0.1111	Square yards
Square yards	0.000207	Acres
Square yards	9	Square feet
Square yards	1,296	Square inches
Tons (long)	2,240	Pounds
Tons (short)	2,000	Pounds
Watts	204.8	Btu per minute
Watts	3.413	Btu per hour
Watts	0.001341	Horsepower
Watts per sq inch	8.197	Btu/sq ft per min
Yards	0.000568	Miles
Yards	3	Feet
Yards	36	Inches

APPENDIX A.2 Metric Units of Measure

Basic Units	
Measure	**Unit**
Area	Square meter (m^2)
Capacity	Liter (l)
Current	Ampere (A)
Density	Kilogram/cubic meter (kg/m^3)
Energy	Joule (J)
Length	Meter (m)
Luminance	Candela\square meter (cd/m^2)
Luminous Intensity	Candela (cd)
Power	Watt (W)
Pressure	Pascal (Pa)
Temperature	Kelvin (K)
Volume	Cubic meter (m^3)
Volumetric flow rate	Cubic meter/second (m^3/s)
Weight/mass	Gram (g)

Prefixes	
Prefix	**Multiplier**
Pico (p)	10^{-12}
Nano (n)	10^{-9}
Micro (μ)	10^{-6}
Mili (m)	10^{-3}
Kilo (k)	10^3
Mega (M)	10^6
Giga (G)	10^9
Tera (T)	10^{12}

APPENDIX A.3 U.S. and Metric Conversion Factors

Multiply	By	To Convert To
Acres	4,047	Square meters
Atmospheres	75.99	Centimeters of mercury
Atmospheres	10.333	Kg per square meter
Btu	1,054	Joules
Btu	0.252	Kilogram-calories
Btu	107.5	Kilogram-meters
Bushels	0.0352	Cubic meters
Centimeter-grams	0.0000723	Foot-pounds
Centimeters	0.3937	Inches
Centimeters	393.7	Mils
Centimeters of mercury	0.01316	Atmospheres
Centimeters of mercury	0.4461	Feet of water
Centimeters of mercury	0.446	Pounds per square inch
Centimeters per second	1.969	Feet per minute
Centimeters per second	0.03281	Feet per second
Centimeters per second	0.02237	Miles per hour
Centimeters per second	0.000373	Miles per minute
Cubic centimeters	0.0000353	Cubic feet
Cubic centimeters	0.0000353	Cubic feet
Cubic centimeters	0.061	Cubic inches
Cubic centimeters	0.00000131	Cubic yards
Cubic centimeters	0.0002642	Gallons
Cubic centimeters	0.002113	Pints (liq)
Cubic centimeters	0.001057	Quarts (liq)
Cubic cm per second	0.00211	Cubic feet per minute
Cubic feet	28,320	Cubic centimeters
Cubic feet	0.02832	Cubic meters
Cubic feet	28.32	Liters
Cubic feet per minute	472	Cubic cm per second
Cubic feet per minute	0.472	Liters per second
Cubic inches	16.39	Cubic centimeters
Cubic inches	16.39	Cubic centimeters
Cubic inches	0.00001639	Cubic meters
Cubic inches	0.01639	Liters
Cubic meters	28.41	Bushels

Appendix A.3 (continued)

Multiply	By	To Convert To
Cubic meters	35.31	Cubic feet
Cubic meters	61,013	Cubic inches
Cubic meters	1.308	Cubic yards
Cubic meters	264.2	Gallons
Cubic yards	764,526	Cubic centimeters
Cubic yards	764,600	Cubic centimeters
Cubic yards	0.7646	Cubic meters
Cubic yards	764.6	Liters
Cubic yards per minute	12.74	Liters per second
Feet	0.3048	Meters
Feet of water	2.242	Centimeters of mercury
Feet of water	304.8	Kg per square meter
Feet per minute	0.5079	Centimeters per second
Feet per second	30.48	Centimeters per second
Foot-pounds	13,831	Centimeter-grams
Foot-pounds	1.356	Joules
Foot-pounds	0.0003241	Kilogram-calories
Foot-pounds	0.1383	Kilogram-meters
Foot-pounds per minute	0.0003241	Kg-calories per minute
Foot-pounds per second	0.01945	Kg-calories per minute
Gallons	3,785	Cubic centimeters
Gallons	0.003785	Cubic meters
Gallons	3.785	Liters
Gallons per minute	0.06308	Liters per second
Grams	0.03527	Ounces
Grams	0.002205	Pounds
Horsepower	10.694	Kilogram-calories per minute
Horsepower (U.S.)	1.014	Horsepower (metric)
Horsepower (metric)	0.9862	Horsepower (U.S.)
Horsepower-hours	2,684,000	Joules
Horsepower-hours	641.7	Kilogram-calories
Horsepower-hours	273,700	Kilogram-meters
Inches	2.54	Centimeters
Inches	0.0254	Meters

Appendix A.3 (continued)

Multiply	By	To Convert To
Inches of mercury	345.3	Kg per square meter
Inches of water	25.4	Kg per square meter
Joules	0.000949	Btu
Joules	0.7375	Foot-pounds
Joules	0.00000037	Horsepower-hours
Kg per square meter	0.0968	Atmospheres
Kg per square meter	0.00328	Feet of water
Kg per square meter	0.002896	Inches of mercury
Kg per square meter	0.03937	Inches of water
Kg per square meter	0.2048	Pounds per square foot
Kg per square meter	0.001422	Pounds per square inch
Kg-calories per minute	3,085	Foot-pounds per minute
Kg-calories per minute	51.41	Foot-pounds per second
Kg-calories per minute	0.06974	Kilowatts
Kilogram-calories	3.97	Btu
Kilogram-calories	3.968	Btu
Kilogram-calories	3,085	Foot-pounds
Kilogram-calories	0.001558	Horsepower-hours
Kilogram-calories	0.001162	Kilowatt-hours
Kilogram-calories per minute	0.09351	Horsepower
Kilogram-calories per minute	0.06972	Kilowatts
Kilogram-meters	0.0093	Btu
Kilogram-meters	7.231	Foot-pounds
Kilogram-meters	0.00000365	Horsepower-hours
Kilograms	2.2046	Pounds
Kilograms	0.001102	Tons (short)
Kilometers	0.6214	Miles (statute)
Kilometers	1,093.6	Yards
Kilowatt-hours	860.6	Kilogram-calories
Kilowatts	14.34	Kilogram-calories per minute
Liters	0.03531	Cubic feet
Liters	61.01	Cubic inches
Liters	0.001308	Cubic yards
Liters	0.2642	Gallons
Liters per second	2.119	Cubic feet per minute

Multiply	By	To Convert To
Liters per second	0.0785	Cubic yards per minute
Liters per second	15.852	Gallons per minute
Meters	3.281	Feet
Meters	39.37	Inches
Meters	1.0936	Yards
Miles (statute)	1.6093	Kilometers
Miles per hour	44.7	Centimeters per second
Miles per minute	2,681	Centimeters per second
Mils	0.00254	Centimeters
Ounces	31.1	Grams
Pints (liq)	473	Cubic centimeters
Pounds	453.5	Grams
Pounds	0.4536	Kilograms
Pounds per square foot	4.882	Kg per square meter
Pounds per square inch	2.146	Centimeter of mercury
Pounds per square inch	703.1	Kg per square meter
Square centimeters	0.001076	Square feet
Square centimeters	0.1550	Square inches
Square feet	929.4	Square centimeters
Square feet	0.0929	Square meters
Square inches	6.452	Square centimeters
Square inches	645.2	Square millimeters
Square kilometers	0.3861	Square miles
Square meters	0.000247	Acres
Square meters	10.76	Square feet
Square meters	1.196	Square yards
Square miles	2.59	Square kilometers
Square millimeters	0.00155	Square inches
Square yards	0.8361	Square meters
Tons (short)	907.4	Kilograms
Yards	0.0009144	Kilometers
Yards	0.9144	Meters

APPENDIX A.4 Metric Conversions for Fractions of an Inch

Fractions of an Inch	Decimal Equivalents	Millimeters	Fractions of an Inch	Decimal Equivalents	Millimeters
1/64	0.0156	0.397	33/64	0.5156	13.096
1/32	0.0313	0.794	17/32	0.5313	13.495
3/64	0.0469	1.191	35/64	0.5469	13.891
1/16	0.0625	1.588	9/16	0.5625	14.288
5/64	0.0781	1.984	37/64	0.5781	14.684
3/32	0.0938	2.381	19/32	0.5938	15.083
7/64	0.1094	2.778	39/64	0.6094	15.479
1/8	0.125	3.175	5/8	0.625	15.875
9/64	0.1406	3.572	41/64	0.6406	16.271
5/32	0.1563	3.969	21/32	0.6563	16.67
11/64	0.1719	4.366	43/64	0.6719	17.066
3/16	0.1875	4.763	11/16	0.6875	17.463
13/64	0.2031	5.159	45/64	0.7031	17.859
7/32	0.2188	5.556	23/32	0.7188	18.258
15/64	0.2344	5.953	47/64	0.7344	18.654
1/4	0.25	6.350	3/4	0.75	19.05
17/64	0.2656	6.747	49/64	0.7656	19.446
9/32	0.2813	7.144	25/32	0.7813	19.845
19/64	0.2969	7.541	51/64	0.7969	20.241
5/16	0.3125	7.938	13/16	0.8125	20.638
21/64	0.3281	8.334	53/64	0.8281	21.034
11/32	0.3438	8.731	27/32	0.8438	21.433
23/64	0.3594	9.128	55/64	0.8594	21.829
3/8	0.375	9.525	7/8	0.875	22.225
25/64	0.3906	9.922	57/64	0.8906	22.621
13/32	0.4063	10.319	29/32	0.9063	23.02
27/64	0.4219	10.716	59/64	0.9219	23.416
7/16	0.4375	11.113	15/16	0.9375	23.813
29/64	0.4531	11.509	61/64	0.9531	24.209
15/32	0.4688	12.29	31/32	0.9688	24.608
31/64	0.4844	12.303	63/64	0.9844	25.004
1/2	0.5	12.7	1.0	1.0	2.54

APPENDIX A.5 Decimal and Metric Equivalents of a Foot

Inches	Feet	Centimeters	Inches	Feet	Centimeters
1/8	0.0104	0.3170	4 1/8	0.3438	10.479
1/4	0.0208	0.6340	1/4	0.3542	10.796
3/8	0.0313	0.9540	3/8	0.3646	11.113
1/2	0.0417	1.2710	1/2	0.3750	11.430
5/8	0.0521	1.5880	5/8	0.3854	11.747
3/4	0.0625	1.9050	3/4	0.3958	12.064
7/8	0.0729	2.2220	7/8	0.4063	12.384
1	0.0833	2.5400	5	0.4167	12.701
1 1/8	0.0938	2.8590	5 1/8	0.4271	13.018
1/4	0.1042	3.1760	1/4	0.4375	13.335
3/8	0.1146	3.4930	3/8	0.4479	13.652
1/2	0.1250	3.8100	1/2	0.4583	13.969
5/8	0.1354	4.1270	5/8	0.4688	14.289
3/4	0.1458	4.4440	3/4	0.4792	14.606
7/8	0.1563	4.7640	7/8	0.4896	14.923
2	0.1667	5.0800	6	0.5000	15.240
2 1/8	0.1771	5.3980	6 1/8	0.5104	15.557
1/4	0.1875	5.7150	1/4	0.5208	15.874
3/8	0.1979	6.0320	3/8	0.5313	16.194
1/2	0.2083	6.3490	1/2	0.5417	16.511
5/8	0.2188	6.6690	5/8	0.5521	16.828
3/4	0.2292	6.9860	3/4	0.5625	17.145
7/8	0.2396	7.3030	7/8	0.5729	17.462
3	0.2500	7.6200	7	0.5833	17.779
3 1/8	0.2604	7.9370	7 1/8	0.5938	18.099
1/4	0.2708	8.2540	1/4	0.6042	18.416
3/8	0.2813	8.5740	3/8	0.6146	18.733
1/2	0.2917	8.8910	1/2	0.6250	19.050
5/8	0.3021	9.2080	5/8	0.6354	19.367
3/4	0.3125	9.5250	3/4	0.6458	19.684
7/8	0.3229	9.8410	7/8	0.6563	20.004
4	0.3333	10.159	8	0.6667	20.321

Appendix A.5 (continued)

Inches	Feet	Centimeters
8 1/8	0.6671	20.638
1/4	0.6875	20.955
3/8	0.6979	21.273
1/2	0.7083	21.590
5/8	0.7188	21.908
3/4	0.7292	22.225
7/8	0.7396	22.543
9	0.7500	22.860
9 1/8	0.7604	23.178
1/4	0.7708	23.495
3/8	0.7813	23.813
1/2	0.7917	24.130
5/8	0.8021	24.448
3/4	0.8125	24.765
7/8	0.8229	24.836
10	0.8333	25.400
10 1/8	0.8438	25.718
1/4	0.8542	26.035
3/8	0.8646	26.353
1/2	0.8750	26.670
5/8	0.8854	26.988
3/4	0.8958	27.305
7/8	0.9063	27.623
11	0.9167	27.940
11 1/8	0.9271	28.258
1/4	0.9375	28.575
3/8	0.9479	28.893
1/2	0.9583	29.210
5/8	0.9688	29.523
3/4	0.9792	29.845
7/8	0.9896	30.163
12	1.0000	30.480

APPENDIX B.1 Standard Dimensions for Common Structural Wood

Nominal Size (Inches)	Surfaced Size (Inches)	Cross Sectional Area (inches^2)	Board Feet per Lineal Foot
2 x 2	1.5 x 1.5	2.25	0.33
2 x 3	1.5 x 2.5	3.75	0.50
2 x 4	1.5 x 3.5	5.25	0.67
2 x 6	1.5 x 5.5	8.35	1.00
2 x 8	1.5 x 7.25	10.88	1.33
2 x 10	1.5 x 9.25	13.88	1.67
2 x 12	1.5 x 11.25	16.88	2.00
3 x 3	2.5 x 2.5	6.25	0.75
3 x 4	2.5 x 3.5	8.75	1.00
3 x 6	2.5 x 5.5	13.75	1.50
3 x 8	2.5 x 7.25	18.13	2.00
3 x 10	2.5 x 9.25	23.13	2.50
3 x 12	2.5 x 11.25	28.13	3.00
4 x 4	3.5 x 3.5	12.25	1.33
4 x 6	3.5 x 5.5	19.25	2.00
4 x 8	3.5 x 7.25	25.38	2.67
4 x 10	3.5 x 9.25	32.38	3.33
4 x 12	3.5 x 11.25	39.38	4.00
4 x 14	3.5 x 13.25	46.38	4.67
6 x 6	5.5 x 5.5	30.25	3.00
6 x 8	5.5 x 7.5	41.25	4.00
6 x 10	5.5 x 9.5	52.25	5.00
6 x 12	5.5 x 11.5	63.25	6.00
6 x 14	5.5 x 13.5	74.25	7.00
6 x 16	5.5 x 15.5	85.25	8.00
8 x 8	7.5 x 7.5	56.25	5.33
8 x 10	7.5 x 9.5	71.25	6.67
8 x 12	7.5 x 11.5	86.25	8.00
8 x 14	7.5 x 13.5	101.25	9.33
8 x 16	7.5 x 15.5	116.25	10.67
8 x 18	7.5 x 17.5	131.25	12.00

APPENDIX B.2 Plywood Grades

A	Smooth, paintable. Not more than 18 neatly made repairs, boat, sled, or router type, and parallel to grain permitted. Wood or synthetic repairs permitted. May be used for natural finish in less demanding applications.
B	Solid Surface. Shims, sled or router repairs, and tight knots to one inch across grain permitted. Wood or synthetic repairs permitted. Some minor splits permitted.
C **Plugged**	Improved C veneer with splits limited to 1/8 inch width and knotholes or other open defects limited to 1/4 by 1/2 inch. Admits some broken grains. Wood or synthetic repairs permitted.
C	Tight knots to 1-1/2 inch. Knotholes to 1 inch across grain and some to 1 1/12 inch if total width of knots and knotholes is within specified limits. Synthetic or wood repairs. Discoloration and sanding defects that do not impair strength permitted. Limited splits allowed. Stitching permitted.
D	Knots and knotholes to 2 - 1/2 inch width across grain and 1/2 inch larger within specified limits. Limited splits allowed. Stitching permitted. Limited to Interior Exposure 1 and Exposure 2 panels.

Courtesy of APA - The Engineered Wood Association

APPENDIX B.3 Plywood Application Chart

Grade (Face - Back)	Exterior Applications
A-A	Applications where the appearance of both sides is important.
A-B	Applications where the appearance of one side is not as important as the other.
A-C	Fences, siding, soffits and other applications requiring one good side.
B-B	Concrete forms.
B-C	General utility.
C-C, repaired	Base material for wall coverings and floor tile.
C-C	Rough construction, backing material.
C-D	Sheathing.

Grade (Face - Back)	Interior Applications
A-A	Furniture, cabinet doors, and other applications where both sides show.
A-B	Same as for A-A grade, but where the appearance of one side is less important.
A-D	Underlayment, backing, or for uses where only one side is visible.
B-B	Concrete forms.
B-D	General utility, backing material, cabinet sides.
C-C, repaired	Underlayment.
C-D	Sheathing and structural uses.

Courtesy of APA - The Engineered Wood Association

APPENDIX C.1 Estimating Masonry Requirements

1. Concrete Footers

To determine the concrete required for footers in cubic yards, multiply the length of the footer by the appropriate multiplication factor from the table below:

Footer Size	Multiplication Factor
18" x 8"	0.0370
20" x 10"	0.0514
24" x 10"	0.0617
24" x 12"	0.0741

2. Concrete Walls

To determine the concrete required for poured concrete walls in cubic yards, multiply the length of the wall in feet by the height of the wall in feet and by the appropriate multiplication factor from the table below:

Wall Thickness	Multiplication Factor
8"	0.0247
10"	0.0309
12"	0.0370
16"	0.0494

3. Concrete Block

To determine the number of block required for walls, multiply the length of the wall in feet by its height in feet and by the appropriate multiplication factor from the table below:

Block Size	Multiplication Factor
8"	2.250
16"	1.125

4. Brick Walls

To determine the number of common bricks required for walls, multiply the length of the wall by the height of the wall and by the appropriate multiplication factor from the table below:

Wall Thickness	Multiplication Factor
4"	6.75
8"	13.50
12"	20.25

5. Mortar

To determine the quantity of mortar required for masonry walls, determine the number of common bricks and block required. Multiply the number of brick or block by the appropriate multiplication factor from the table below to determine the mortar required in cubic feet:

	Multiplication Factor
8" Block	0.0259
12" Block	0.0272
Brick	0.0117

APPENDIX C.2 Common Brickwork Patterns

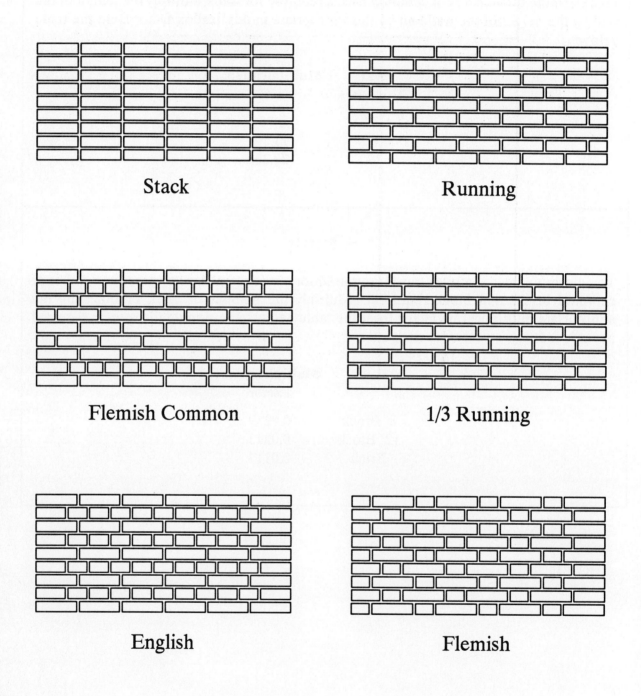

Stack

Running

Flemish Common

1/3 Running

English

Flemish

APPENDIX D.1 Drill Bit Sizes for Wood Screws

Screw Size No.	Pilot Hole	Starter Hole
1	5/64	-
2	3/32	1/16
3	7/64	1/16
4	7/64	5/64
5	1/8	5/64
6	9/64	3/32
7	5/32	7/64
8	11/64	7/64
9	3/16	1/8
10	3/16	1/8
12	7/32	9/64
14	1/4	5/32
16	17/64	3/16
18	19/64	13/64

APPENDIX D.2 Common Nail Sizes

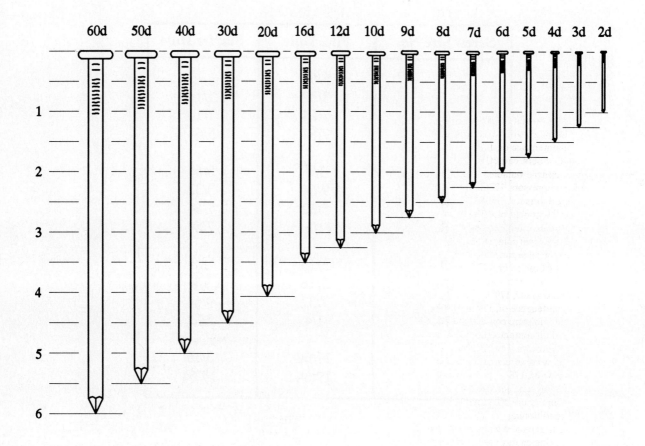

INDEX

$\overline{\text{R}}$